THE OTHER SIDE OF MIDNIGHT

THE OTHER SIDE
OF MIDNIGHT

The National Library of Poetry

Cynthia A. Stevens, Editor

The Other Side of Midnight

Library of Congress
Cataloging in Publication Data

ISBN 1-57553-408-8

Manufactured in The United States of America by
Watermark Press
One Poetry Plaza
Owings Mills, MD 21117

FOREWORD

Throughout life, we store information collected from experiences and try in some way to make sense of it. When we are not able to fully understand the things which occur in our lives, we often externalize the information. By doing this, we are afforded a different perspective, thus allowing us to think more clearly about difficult or perplexing events and emotions. Art is one of the ways in which people choose to externalize their thoughts.

Within the arts, modes of expression differ, but poetry is a very powerful tool by which people can share sometimes confusing, sometimes perfectly clear concepts and feelings with others. Intentions can run the gamut as well: the artists may simply want to share something that has touched their lives in some way, or they may want to get help to allay anxiety or uncertainty. The poetry within *The Other Side of Midnight* is from every point on the spectrum: every topic, every intention, every event or emotion imaginable. Some poems will speak to certain readers more than others, but it is always important to keep in mind that each verse is the voice of a poet, of a mind which needs to make sense of this world, of a heart which feels the effects of every moment in this life, and perhaps of a memory which is striving to surface. Nonetheless, recalling our yesterdays gives birth to our many forms of expression.

Melisa S. Mitchell
Editor

EDITOR'S NOTE

I'll call for pen and ink, and write my mind.
—William Shakespeare, *Henry VI*

The above line succinctly names one of writing's most enduring features—its cathartic capacity. Writing can bring immediate relief to a troubled mind, partly because as complicated as one's thoughts may be, the tools of the writing trade are easily obtained. Of course, "pen and ink" (although some prefer a computer in this day and age) are required; otherwise, all that is needed is a desire to write. The wish to unleash one's mind is the other half of the writing equation, as thoughts that are too difficult to voice often express themselves easily when put on paper. Emotions that might be stifled can find an outlet. So whether penning lines for an audience or for oneself, the author who may not be able to speak his mind can "write [his] mind."

Writing to express the mind can take virtually any format—journal entries, letters, fictional or autobiographical stories, essays, or poetry. Of these types, poetry remains an oft-used genre. Why? Perhaps poetry's lack of restrictions—as one can employ a strict format or no form at all—makes the writing process easier to begin. In addition, while essays, for example, often have scholarly or "practical" contents, poems can be used to discuss almost any subject. Finally, poetry may bring closure more quickly, as its compact style allows the author to pack more meaning into fewer words.

The many poems in this anthology attest to the fact that poetry remains a popular means of expression. While each of the poems on the following pages invites the reader to delve into the author's mind, certain poems shine as examples of their authors' "writing their minds."

One such poem is Roy Rischar's "The Philosopher and W. Shakespeare" (p. 1). In this piece, the persona rails against academia's tendency to scrutinize literary works, Shakespeare's in particular. While undoubtedly Shakespeare intended some deeper meaning in his works, the persona declares that some academics have too much time to dissect the details of literature: "Pastime of aristocratic leisure / sidetracked fools in vain search / of the highest realm. . . ." Here, the phrase "in vain" implies disdain for such seekers. Looking for meaning in each component of a play is done "in vain" because the playwright may not have meant for every detail to signify something else. In addition, attempting to find the ultimate meaning of someone else's work is futile. To try to do so is

> *court[ing] madness in the paradoxical*
> *certainty of why and what*
> *pristine, eternal revolutions of*

> *every aspect, the mind mills of*
> *your will.*

No one but the author can ever truly ascertain exactly what was intended. Therefore, the authority with which some analyzers speak is ludicrous, or "paradoxical certainty." Furthermore, an academic's attempt to find the key to Shakespeare's work also speaks to wanting to "know it all"—if necessary, he will manufacture meaning in "the mind mills of / [his] will." Hence, this comment points to a play on the phrase "in vain"; such overanalyzing is vanity.

Certain aspects of "The Philosopher and W. Shakespeare" hint that the speaker has a particular Shakespearean work in mind: *The Tragedy of Hamlet, Prince of Denmark.* The opening line of Rischar's poem mentions "aristocratic leisure," which easily applies to the character of Hamlet. Hamlet is a prince, and therefore aristocratic; his position gives him time to mull over his situation. This "aristocratic leisure" contributes to the popular literary discussion of Hamlet's inability to take action throughout the play. In addition, the mention of literati "in vain search . . . court madness" alludes to the theme of madness in *Hamlet*, seen in the characters of Hamlet and Ophelia.

Later in the poem, the persona commands, "Go east to no mind / travel south to pleasure of simplicity / north to austerity. . . ." This assertion imitates the various directional references Hamlet makes in the play as indications of his mental state. The fact that Hamlet's sanity could be blown by the wind resounds with the idea that the philosophers can be moved in any direction in trying to fix deeper meaning on the play. Of course, the analyzers staunchly support their theories, "stoic to the end."

This poem's connection to *Hamlet* is most evident with the following concluding lines:

> *there is less*
> *in this world*
> *than is dreamt of in*
> *your philosophy.*

These words echo those of Hamlet to Horatio, after the ghost of Hamlet's father is seen. In *Hamlet* (I. v. 166-167), the prince cautions Horatio against discussing this sighting because Horatio does not know the deeper meaning behind the specter's visit: "There are more things in heaven and earth, Horatio, / Than are dreamt of in your philosophy." By altering these lines for his poem, Rischar presents a reverse meaning: literary philosophers wish to unearth deeper, non-existent levels of meaning from "this world," meaning the imaginary landscape created by the play.

The poet's decision to present his message by echoing *Hamlet* is clever, as *Hamlet* is a widely scrutinized literary work. Rischar's poetic skill is demonstrated further by the adept use of irony in writing what is on his mind: when the reader intricately assesses the poem, an admonition against overanalyzing literature is discovered. Choice words and allusions make a strong case for the poet's message, but this ironic twist directly affects the audience. Therefore, this theme resounds in the reader's mind after the poem is read. Roy Rischar's achievement in "The Philosopher and W. Shakespeare" resulted in his being awarded the Grand Prize for this poetry contest.

Kathleen Guidry's "An Evening's Flirtation" (p. 4) expresses the thought process of a character caught in a difficult position. The piece begins by describing the illicit meeting of two people bored with their lives: "We swallowed dinner, drank our mediocrity dry. . . ." As the poem moves on, the speaker expresses that this relationship, however exciting, is defined by its pressure on her sense of right and wrong:

You enraptured my stale dissatisfaction
Embarrassing my faith, tickling gratified loyalty
Tormenting a shame-colored cloak of celebration
You stoked expensive breaths without subtlety. . . .

In the above passage, the guilt-laden phrases outnumber the only romantic one ("you enraptured my stale dissatisfaction"). Not only does the persona possess a "shame-colored cloak," but her conscience also is "tickled" by remembrance of her family's "gratified loyalty." Furthermore, the persona's mention of "expensive breaths" relays the concept that each breath she takes in her lover's presence is a risk.

The speaker knows she must make a choice about the future of this relationship. She says, "I question the extent of life's gifts; the task / Wrenches my choices of faith, weighing the difference. . . ." Yet the poem's conclusion signifies the speaker's lack of resolution: "My vagabond heart sings to an empty house / Smelling its fade and knowing its doubt. . . ." The description of her "vagabond heart" suggests that she may never decide; the woman cannot be happy with either option because of the guilt she already carries. She does not even appear to know how to decide, as the piece ends with the word "doubt."

"Cyclic" (p. 10), by Deirdre J. Kamber, also addresses doubt, although in a less evident construction. The persona is soothed by the "rhythmic dance" of riding on a train, and she describes herself as "unremarkable, complacent." Yet her laid-back facade conflicts with the uncertainty of her mind. As she remembers an encounter, she ponders its meaning: "Drowsily rewinding the evening's fantasy, a rising miasma of / Umber, butterscotch and rose, the restaurant's haze / Does he, doesn't he, does he, doesn't he. . . ."

The repetition of the question "does he, doesn't he," mimicking the train's pleasing movement, does not seem particularly upsetting. This environment almost allows "miasma" to slip by unnoticed. However, the use of that word, meaning a noxious or dangerous atmosphere, indicates that the character feels something unsettling about the evening. Even her environment, lulling as the train's motion is, gives her crazily mixed messages; she's surrounded by "ads for Rogaine and God, personal injury and salvation." The piece ends not unlike "An Evening's Flirtation" because the speaker makes a decision, whether conscious or unconscious, to not think about her situation. This idea is illustrated by the poem's concluding description: ". . . my mind floats on / Koans on reality darting past, escaping from my thoughtless vision."

Other excellent poems, in which the authors "write their minds," are "Elegy" (p. 4) by Christina Arnold, "The Arietta" (p. 3) by Janet Irene Buck, "Of Culture" (p. 4) by Yeshaswini Desaigoudar, "My Memory is Fragrant" (p. 11) by Debra Monthei, "Eve" (p. 5) by Anna Nordberg, "Poetic Process" (p. 5) by Patrick Phair, "For Lorna" (p. 6) by Gretchen Primack, and "Dachau 2045" (p. 5) by Marci Stillerman. Please be sure to continue your reading, so that you may experience the many other notable poems in this anthology.

The production of this book was made possible by the contributions of many individuals. Thank you to the editors, assistant editors, and office personnel, as well as cover artist Steve Kimball, who all helped create this anthology.

Chris Tyler
Editor

Winners of the North American Open Poetry Contest

Grand Prize Winner

Roy Rischar / Cleveland, OH

Second Prize Winners

Christina Arnold / Fairborn, OH
Janet Irene Buck / Phoenix, OR
Yeshaswini Desaigoudar / Providence, RI
Kathleen Guidry / Heritage, TN
Deirdre J. Kamber / Point Lookout, NY

Debra Monthei / Cudahy, WI
Anna Nordberg / New York, NY
Patrick Phair / Waupaca, WI
Gretchen Primack / Milwaukee, WI
Marci Stillerman / Los Angeles, CA

Third Prize Winners

Elise Anderson / Naples, FL
Tressa Berman / Phoenix, AZ
T. Victor Berry / Oakland, ME
Carissa Bess / Sacramento, CA
Carmel Finnerty Brown / Berkeley, CA
Sister Barbara Bruns, PHJC / Breese, IL
Edward Buatois / Cleveland, OH
Ruth A. Burton / Windermere, FL
Ann Marie Butler / Barstow, CA
Corrie Carreno / Clifton, NJ
Marie Combs / Crofton, KY
Kelly Michelle Crough / Darnestown, MD
Amylyn Dickman Allred / Smithfield, UT
Ayelet Even-Nur / Cincinnati, OH
Widchard Faustin / Philadelphia, PA
Francesca D. Fleming / Billerica, MA
Kathy Fluger / Muskegon, MI
Jerry Gaskins / Tallahassee, FL
Valerie Gaynor / Ozone Park, NY
Randy D. Geiger / Cibolo, TX
Jeremy Bruce Gratton / Mesa, AZ
Bonita Gregory / Canton, OH
Helen F. Gunn / Granite Falls, WA
Jennifer Harrison / Miami, FL
Charity Henderson / Bath, NC
Theresa D. Hrin / Feasterville, PA
Misty K. Hughes / Bay Village, OH
Audre G. Hutchins / Long Beach, CA
Wendy Idzi / Towson, MD
Charles A. Jackson / DuQuoin, IL

Lenore Kielhofer / Monroe, LA
Patricia Kline / Williamsburg, VA
Eugene Jay Lampkin / Beacon, NY
Quenten London / Los Angeles, CA
Samuel Lovold / Kent, WA
Joan E. Matteson / Holyoke, MA
Brenda McCoy / Monticello, GA
Will Moody / Columbia, SC
Sam Moses / West Pittsburg, PA
Barbara Munich-Deger / Manitou, KY
Chas Noble / Durham, NH
Amy Palatnick / Eugene, OR
Cristina Paparella / Sunrise, FL
Sarah Rees / Santa Cruz, CA
Betty J. Rhodes / Columbia, TN
Wendy Rondette / Saint Louis, MO
Matthew Rundle / Ramsey, NJ
Jeneane Schmidt / New York, NY
James Cobb Scott / Middletown, CT
Robyn Lori Shifrin / Pepper Pike, OH
Sandy Smith-Nonini / Durham, NC
Natalie Stroud / New Orleans, LA
Zachariah Stutman / Washington, DC
Lorie Thomas / Charlotte, NC
Thomas J. Tobin / Homestead, PA
Gail Walborn / Grand Rapids, MI
Martin Weinstein / Boca Raton, FL
Cary Young / Aurora, CO
Mordecai Young / Phoenix, AZ

Congratulations also to all semi-finalists.

Grand Prize Winner

The Philosopher and W. Shakespeare
Pastime of aristocratic leisure
sidetracked fools in vain search
of the highest realm—alone to
court madness in the paradoxical
certainty of why and what
pristine, eternal revolutions of
every aspect, the mind mills of
your will.
Think, laugh, lament to your
wit's end.
Go east to no mind
travel south to pleasure of simplicity
north to austerity
on a note of resolution
to wonder why
stoic to the end
there is less
in this world
than is dreamt of in
your philosophy.
Roy Rischar

The Personality Game

I played that game and played it well,
till it brought me here today.
As a child exposed and vulnerable
for protection the blanket would stay.
I wrapped it around me tightly,
and clung through years untold,
manipulating and controlling
behind this shield of gold.
I chose to see no further
and exploited every stitch,
till it lay in threads around me
yet still, I rewove and knit.
As time went on, half-clad I bared
the dark side of my soul,
but burned my head and stooped so low
to make that blanket whole.
I wore it thin, nine lives it lived
till that fabric was no more
and the threads I used for cover,
bore a festering open sore.

Carmel Finnerty Brown

The Arietta

Weeds of plastic words were overgrown.
Parched by flames of ruptured dreams
and bundled up to die a decomposing death.
Ego peacocks strutting sugared wings of need
and screaming for the center stage.

One day she listened to the still.
The silence warm in puddles that
she did not have to step around.
Caution's breeze she didn't hear
in winds that knew the velvet path
to seas of arrant love.

The hummingbird stopped long enough
to draw the whipping cream of him
from hallowed beaks and longing straws.
They tore the splintered fences down
and put up mending walls.
She set a place for two
and let the open air of mingled breaths
softly pencil in the rest.

Janet Irene Buck

On New York

O city of lights, of dark underground caverns,
O city of masses, of nightclubs and taverns,
How tempting you were when first we met.
Your bright lights, your gaiety . . . a stage well set.

You lured me and coaxed me, O city of stone,
To join with your millions and be all alone.
I was young, full of hope and not worldly wise.
I knew not that your lights were but a disguise

To cover the turmoil that lie underneath;
The unfriendly people, the beggar, the thief.
But lo, I was captured, too late to retreat!
The sounds of the engines that roared 'neath your streets

Took hold of my senses, cried out to my heart,
"Stay on, young man, for now you're a part
A part of a world so unlike others.
A place without trees, or grasses, or brothers."

O city of lights, of sounds unrelenting
I'm tired of your speed, this race never ending.
Disillusion brings tears, all I'll leave as I part.
But let me take back what remains of my heart.

Joan E. Matteson

City Day

All the ground is silenced, the air brittle.
Crackling with dew, greenery rises for the turning up of the darkened nova.
Peeking above the shield, augmenting rays search out to fondle inanimate places.
Edges and corners glimmer, building a right angled sky connected by cable webs of busy spiders.
Orange and red crown the sky, igniting a wick to a fast burning world.
Uplifting perched sounds broadcast over intersections of hour-set longevity.
A once hardened wax weakens, flowing through canals that escort puddles of intense sprightliness.
Oozing through the jungle, sounds of havoc tie vines in knots, entangling society's zoo.
Soon the arc completes.
Cages open to wane unleashed paraffin back into a potential fuse.
Slowly the cliff swallows, belching back a crimson blanket, solidifying the reservoir.
Bowing, activity honors the stimulating catalyst, preparing for taciturnity.

Cary Young

Boot Camp

I can tell you about the cold dampness of a tiled bathroom floor
The olive blue skullkisses it so selflessly imparts, after hours
And years of contemplating its depth, deathless
You tell me about my bootstraps and leverage

I can show you the blackest black in my claustrophobic closet
Entangled in the arms of a tattered salty sweater
And the sweet smell of mildew from last year's tears
You yank the steel-toed boots from underneath my head

I can give you a heavenly taste of a sinful Woolite shake
Mixed with just a jigger of hair bleach for that extra punch
And come next week, I'll whip up another one
You might use it to polish my unsightly scuffs

I can play for you an unforgettable song of shattered glass
The two-part chaotic harmony of armies upstairs
Off-key to the untrained ear, never listened
You pull the bloody shards from my scarred bootless feet

I can douse you with the decaying scent of living breathless death
A potency mercilessly smothering, stimuli
Recalling yesterday, and the time before
You still can't see the bootstraps wound around my neck

Natalie Stroud

The Gathering

A beach
Almost deserted
Whitecaps shimmering in late afternoon sun
A cottage
Unassuming beside neighboring condos
Rocking chairs swaying on the porch empty for the first time today
A dining room
Overhead fan humming
Extra-long table, unmatched chairs
A table
Homemade lasagne, assorted dishes, plastic cups
Red and white checkered tablecloth
A family
Father, mother, four daughters, two husbands, eight grandchildren
Heads bowed—a father's prayer
A little boy
Blonde, round-faced, front tooth missing
Happiness twinkling in his eyes
Sneaking a peek at his cousin
A feeling of belonging to something bigger than oneself.

Patricia Kline

Of Culture

1.

before clay lamps of Dipawali
young girls coat their faces
turmeric as mad rivers trailing into buried snow

family's adoration of
pale ambiguity subdues   preserves
sallow verses whispering
"your ancestors were either monkeys or rakshas"

remember the echo of warrior queens
hooked sword   streaming hair   skin
masked in blood

2.

bone caverns encapsulate native stalactites   dripping
amorous gods
rhythmic carnality

nakedness accumulates richly

stricken with organic fear of death and Westerners
young girls parcel
flesh into cotton   muslin
figured stuff

Yeshaswini Desaigoudar

Hiroshimaiamsorry

through streets of rage, ash, light, nothing.
flash in silence, nothing loves and laughs, only
    fire lives, my soul is raw.
fire, i shake in my womb, i am alive in silence, crash
    i cannot listen or live, only tears.
blue morning clear, dew sparkle in corner of sky,
    silence. crash, there is fire and ash, nothing.
flash white, light in blue, which is warm and loves but
    kills and now flesh is raw.
silence, i live in my womb, i am alive in the flame
    that ignites.
crash, i am infinite and everywhere, my soul is shards
    on fire and ash.
silence, the world is nothing and asleep half a million
    souls are raw in light while crash the world is
    silent and laughs.
iamsorryiamsorryiamsorryiamsorry sorry sorry

Ayelet Even-Nur

An Evening's Flirtation

We swallowed dinner, drank our mediocrity dry
Their juices slid down our throats, the splash
Of martini took our consciousness, our innocent lie
Brushing me, leaving me restless, craving a bath

You enraptured my stale dissatisfaction
Embarrassing my faith, tickling gratified loyalty
Tormenting a shame-colored cloak of celebration
You stoked expensive breaths without subtlety

Mirages of naked sapphires and winter's vast
Landscape crack my ordinary existence
I question the extent of life's gifts; the task
Wrenches my choices of faith, weighing the difference

Walls of imagined security
Crumble ancient temples of surety
My vagabond heart sings to an empty house
Smelling its fade and knowing its doubt

Kathleen Guidry

Elegy

If our only impulses
are eros and thanatos,
we can never be rational.

All week I have listened
to the cicadas rising,
to the mating call they have held
for seven dark years like the secrets
we keep, then forget.

The nights have grown too humid for sleep,
and I am limping the shadows of the bare floor,
mumbling, longing, the way that we do
when we are trying to make sense of our lovers
or ourselves.

The words I could not speak
linger in the darkness
like half-finished paintings, like the one
knitted mitten, like the unmailed letters
I have carried in my pocket for weeks.

They may as well be love poems.

Christina Arnold

You Must Have Thought It Strange

You must have thought it strange the way I
sort-of-ran-away
Friday morning
when you materialized from the crowd
to say hello
(in your predictable what-the-hell way)
after these months. I was caught

by surprise, not expecting to you see you,
and, in spite of frank discussions with my mirror nights,
I knew in an instant
the icy reply would sound petty,
casual pleasantries . . . insincere. Trapped

in that peculiar void
with no honest remark to do us justice,
so clean, somehow, to flee.
Amuses me now that I began this thinking
I owed you some . . . explanation. So like me

to seek after cool rationale
when I catch myself
being woman.

Sandy Smith-Nonini

Grandma

It's a dance you do
A horrid jig you've mastered
Smiling in his face
and crying in your pillow
Closing your eyes to his ugly sneer
as he sleeps alone in the bed you made
Ignoring his feet twitching to the TV while you cook his dinner
He plays the music
calls the steps
and chooses the rhythm
He says the bruises on your body are too expensive to take to a doctor
says the coal stove makes your eyes water
and that you stay home because you forgot how to drive.
I see you wince, Grandma, see
the limp in your dance and the crack in your smile.
Your eyes are too bright for his house
Your mind too sharp
Your tired skin too beautiful for his touch.

Take your battered suitcase and my hand.
I will run with you.

Lorie Thomas

Veins Of A Different Breath

I have followed you through the swamps of your mind
     tracked you and your innocence like an untamed beast
        the hunger eating you
           an empty, pitted, cavernous stomach yells
             (only in the background)
               a child, an ape, slouched on the ground
                 eating ants and ignoring the biting flies
               (a horse's tail would lash)
dry and cracked earth reaches like a dehydrated vein
     to tiny finger tips wrapped around steamy toes sweating in heat
        a pool mosquito water, a puddle,
           looks largely warped in sunlight
              almost to look as pure as well water in a bowl
               (yet the bowl is forever parched)

I bathe in a misty sauna, my skin satiating in oil
     the trip is behind me and relaxation tempts my limbless mind.

Then dawn to dusk is breath of a memory
     where childhood lies lost in poverty, (uneducated and starving).
        I palatably draw a grape from its stem lying in a bowl,
          and sigh, as I am full.

       Wendy Idzi

Dachau 2045

Bubbling from the hairline cracks in the glossy pavement
of the new Einkaufszentrum in the town of Dachau
oozes a mysterious thick red substance. Not blood,
the mayor insists despite chemical analyses. And keep it quiet.
Just the suggestion will be bad for business.

The vast grassy surface of the Kinderspielplatz
with its new steel swings and brightly-painted
jungle-gym heaves with deep sighs, toppling toddlers
off their feet and astonishing their mothers with its ever-
changing slopes and hills.

The perfume of flowers planted in the clearings of the forest,
carnations, roses, lilies of the valley, jasmine, chosen for their scent,
and flowering trees and bushes, pouring sweet perfume of apple
blossom, lilac, gardenia, and camellia into sparkling air of Summer,
strive in vain to hide the ancient stink of burning flesh, sickness,
and death that pervades the atmosphere like an incurable disease.

On the mudbanks of the Amper River, the children of Dachau
with cast-off spoons and wooden spades dig tidewater holes
and capture little fishes, tadpoles, and clean white human bones.

     Marci Stillerman

Eve

She hated the garden
The cloying scent of perfection
The symmetry of those eternal boughs wound with fragrant flowers
frozen in perpetual bloom, untouched by the damp stain of death.

The Immutable Paradise
Time's dark hand did not pass over
Where silken waters fed the black soil.
She gazed on it all with eyes dulled by beauty, dried by sunlight,
red with the tears she longed to shed.

The gates were closed behind her, barred, and a large barren earth
stretched and lingered on a haze of horizon
which she had never seen over those earthen walls of Eden,
grown over with strong scented vines
covered with budding flowers of gold and blue.
Never was there so beautiful a prison wall.

She covered her hands in the dirt soaked by a cold rain.
She bled her tears into the soil and watched the grey sky
with eyes jaded by blue.
And the mist-hung moon glowed through dusky clouds.
She smiled and did not look back at those as those gates faded forever.

     Anna Nordberg

Poetic Process

My father picked green tomatoes
Before the frost;
Under the reptilian vines brown and brittle,
He plundered the smooth shiny orbs
Mired close to the black earth.
Wrapped in newsprint
Like glass ornaments of Christmas
He busheled them
In the cellar safe from pierce of cold.

In January he would emerge,
From the basement darkness,
Pull back the wadded paper
Of old news and smudged words,
Ta Da!

Dripping juicy red he sliced
Treasure into wedges;
We were millionaires
In winter kitchen warmth.

     Patrick Phair

In Nessun Luogo

Silence between us—
neither of us has spoken for a while.
I guess you're concentrating on the road;
it winds like a long, grey snake,
narrowing to nothing on the horizon.
I watch the cornfields pass us,
long tantamount rows stretching up
to meet the dull grey sky of a stormy afternoon.
A glance in the rear view,
your eyes back and steady on the road.
I reach over and switch on the radio.
Soft classical.
Tapping my fingers on the dash,
I watch the angry clouds roll by.
And momentarily, a little ray of sun,
like the first light of desire,
slices the sky and breaks over our faces.
You turn with a smile and catch the affinity in my gaze.
Our road to nowhere is long,
but we travel it together.

     Gail Walborn

The Emptiness

In the middle of the night
There is an emptiness.
Call it existential, call it abyss,
But it is just an emptiness
Scratching at the back door again
Wanting in.
It is the universe godless.
The blueprints of the cosmos
Crumpled on Mexican tiles in the kitchen
And jumped upon by muddy boots.
It is where the black lipstick
Smudged across your face is not connected
To your lover's death,
To the field of rice
You walked through young,
To the barking of a dog,
To the edges of the moon.
In the middle of the night
There is an emptiness.

     Cristina Paparella

For Lorna

My grandmother spent
her last days in California

Voiceless, she sat
with a needle of food
and feet anchored to earth

Finally, it ended:
Five hollow years
on the crumbling edge
of the continent

When I bend down
to touch the earth by her stone
my hand fills with dust
that was once hands
tying scarves, cutting bread

This is soil that lies only slightly above
the angry core of the earth:
Scalding, compressed, red as paint

This is soil that lies only slightly below
coils of spent seed pods darkening the hills
imagining the possibilities of their fruit

    Gretchen Primack

I'm So Sorry Little Billy

I never knew that
15 minutes away from me lived a nine-year-old boy who had never
Been to a movie theater
This same boy had never
Seen doors open automatically or
Sat in a booth or
Seen a battery-operated doggy wiggle its tail

I never knew that
His shoes and socks were once cut off of his moldy feet

I never knew that
This boy had only two pieces of notebook paper left and
Did not own a single children's book

I never knew that
The school uniform and shoes I bought were
His only decent clothes

I never knew that
Last year all he wanted for Christmas was
For his mother to stop drinking

I am so sorry
I never knew that

    Ruth A. Burton

Looking

We went through your things today.
All of us.
Together.
We rifled through the pages of your books,
and we peered with reddened eyes
onto the dusty top shelves of your closet.
We put away stacks of fine china plates,
their faded patterns of roses worn dim
from forty years of good meals.
We emptied desk drawers onto your
Belgian rugs and rummaged through
stacks of bent playing cards
and sticky, old fountain pens.
And though we went through all
the yellowed table linens and washed
all of the crystal,
we never found what it was
that we were looking for.

    Will Moody

Refusing The Marriage Of A Friend

This morning,
They wrapped you.
In determined lace,
And polished satin.
Tying bleach white ribbon,
Around blush red skin.

This morning,
I woke myself.
Tattered teddy bear stares.
Tying ragged blue tennis shoes,
below road-rash red knees.

You walked,
Far off ahead.
Firmly pointed,
Charging in white.

I dawdled,
lagging behind,
and looking intently,
backward.

    Elise Anderson

Ann

Her face, gentle as a doe
Though rough, Kentucky worn
Eroded by the hurt of generations
Your sister lives in Paraguay and Uganda
Your soothing face is mimicked
Again and again around the globe
Though you travel only to the county line
We are sisters and mothers and hags
Stirring the life soup
Knowing that we will become only soil again
Having suckled babies around the world
Clucking and rocking their mouths
Our own mouths whispering lullabies
That only a goodness can compose
And that our daughters,
When necessary,
Will remember

    Barbara Munich-Deger

Born Unto You

Pardon me,
as I come into life, as I learn of love,
while my shoulders that you'll someday find rest upon
dislocate in this birthing.

Be with me, though you may need to look away,
while my head where I'll think of you is bloody and
distorted, crowned—almost a miracle.

Wait for me, for the breath that will eventually speak
your name is still silenced. You'll know it first
by the sound of my wailing cry.

Dream for me, for the heart that will long for you
only knows the deafening sound of my own existence.

Reach for me, though my hands that will
someday hold you are as yet still thumb
over palmed fingers.

Hope for me, I'll emerge from my own chamber,
cleansed in grace and mercy, wrapped in the
blanket of sanctification to be received.

Rejoice with me, as I am allowed my first wish—
that my trauma be your joy forever.

    Misty K. Hughes

Snapshots From Norway

Blackbirds clack like castinets
Trailing red ribbon fan tails
Across cobblestone sky
The perfume of yellow curry
mingles with brown bread
In Oslo's morning air
Crisp as flags, red saris billow
Like cloud cover canopies
Over frosted forest of city

Tressa Berman

Sequel

it's time to cache in memory
all my dreams that were
too gossamer-winged to ever soar
and thoughts of
all the things I could have tried
but never did
and all the words I should have spoken
but left unsaid
mute reminders of what might have been
had I with more perception
of life's ways and brevity
not trod its paths so carelessly
that time with measured pace
passed by
trailing in its wake
all those unused things
destined
now that it's too late
to forever lie in wasted state

Lenore Kielhofer

Turtle Cove

Satin leaves, woolen bees
days aglow, boats arow
jasmine breeze, minted teas
misty dew, morning anew.

Mirrored sky, silky sigh
ducks in tow, branches low
gentle wake across the lake
sunfilled clouds, teasing shrouds.

Shoreline walks, beckoned talks
water lapping, kitten napping
wren's sweet song, day prolong
heart in flight, spirit bright.

Brenda McCoy

The Commandoes

Young commandoes, tough and steady,
Wooden rifles at the ready,
Stealthily coming past bush and car,
Plan to raid the cookie jar.
Grandma working in the kitchen
Rules out any thought of snitchin'.
The boys had ventures out of doors
Bored with toys they'd got from stores,
Studied a treasured dried bird beak,
Caught crawdads in the pasture creek,
Scavenged through the gravel pile,
Searching for fossils all the while.
Came home dirty as could be,
Knowing there's be a penalty.
But as they of adventures tell
Can anyone but wish them well?

Marie Combs

Impressions

In the chaos of gleaming blues, whites, and reds
I approached Liberty, leading the laymen, Delacroix's revolution,
but I only saw shadows among oils and age.
I walked across the wooden floors to see Notre Dame,
crowded with Napoleon's aristocracy, yet silent.
Ceiling light filtered onto his hands,
flesh blended with gold:
His outstretched arms, her cushioning hair, the triumphant crown
together within the boar bristles' strokes. Curious angels
and the awed papacy both knew this would be tragedy.
Bonaparte worshipped a woman barren of love,
while history called for him.
A lady, bifocals in hand, brushed my coat,
then a tour came through to capture on film
the rose window, the gold frame.
I turned to see looking on all different
races, traditions, caught in a wonderment of romanticism:
This portrait of a man, idolized as Caesar, centered on canvass,
straining to give order to a problematic age.

Matthew Rundle

Almost A Cappella

Weak the soul, it strains from words plundered down;
Adam a giant, Eve his mate in gilded gown.
Posterns slowly shrink capping Bible dream's woe.
Almost a capella, life regressed to embryo.

Petrified existence one trillion equinox.
Fossilize the beacon, framed in gilded orthodox.
Stumbling prayers fixed on daily goods to gain.
Almost a capella, altar boy to be ordained.

Promise is the cactus; gentile to the infant touch.
Mother Nature cries. Hinduism breeds a clutch.
Fermentation time, gilded cross born the craft.
Almost a capella, cheated wisdom photographed.

Breath of fire, fire of light of angel halo blinds.
Evil melts in his sight, Judaism reminds.
Fear not tempered beast, slumber in your gilded cage.
Almost a capella; invitation . . . disengage.

Quenten London

Wild Side

   She does not sing opera
In her bathrobe and bunny slippers,
Or eat Chinese food under her black
   umbrella in the rain.
She never stays up late to listen to the
   sounds of midnight,
Or does a pirouette in the street all alone.
She never whistles out her window
   to passerby below,
Or fervently discusses evil and world wars
   with a deaf man on the park bench,
   who watches birds eat bread crumbs.
She refuses to let her dreams gaze into the eyes
   of tall strangers embracing glasses of champagne.
She will not walk barefoot in the grass, so please don't ask her.
She'll just wait for the days to diminish, and the passerby to pass by.
They will be forever deaf to a
   song or a whisper,
that will stayed trapped
behind her lips . . . clasped . . . shut.

Kelly Michelle Crough

Westchester

Toast and jelly on the abandoned side porch
dead pine needles between the bricks
the sun is somewhere
behind a scrim of butter and
day camp sounds seep through the trees.

Maybe tonight we'll eat pizza
While the sun sets
and then feed the crust
to the lonely stone lions
at the end of the drive.

Corrie Carreno

Memories

Death is at my doorstep, come for me
betrayal of a saint lost of the way
blind eyes stare out at the world they don't see
monotonous mental day after day
sick puppet in the play we write
the main star, our hero, now look and stare
died yesterday too young without a fight
but all are morbid and just cannot care
my sweet love lost, blessed virgin besmeared
insanity gone mad, now others reign
simpleton's forest, dark, dreaded, and feared
blood, rain twisted, falling from leaves of pain
    but yet one day luminescence we fill
    and hopelessness will find abandoned will

Jennifer Harrison

Firelight Memories

Five people gathered around a fire sat.
Cloaks drawn about each warm and tight,
Conversation muted into the star-filled night,
And watched the fire play.

Each with their own thoughts
of friends, of family, of battles lost.
The passing of strangers that became friends,
The passing of time that never ends.

They gather with them upon this eve,
And chatter, and ramble, and sometimes aggrieve.
Round the wine, the coffee, and the ale,
While another goes on with their tale.

When the night is done and becomes the morn,
With light comes the fire in ashes forlorn.
For hearth fire it is rekindled, the Phoenix reborn,
Memories flow softly into the day's bright scorn.

Yet when once again the night does fall,
And tree and tent become hallowed halls,
The firelight dances, and all gather round,
Memories return without sight or sound.

Ann Marie Butler

Reminiscence

Portents of change does ev'ning bring,
Silence into a night of soft whispers.
The clouds spread forth, orange and azure,
wisping into gossamer threads caressing the joyful moon.
The water on the lake dances a waltz, moved by breath unseen,
accompanying itself in a chiming light.

I could sit here forever and watch the dance,
being nurtured by the night air, and comforted by its sounds,
but when friendly dawn comes as sunset released,
I am reminded of the missing of it,
and its warmth against my face is welcome.

Edward Buatois

Catherine

Red sky at night on an open two lane
the past like a song haunts me again
your name on the wind your voice in my ears
wheels rolling beneath me like so many years
the one place on earth I can clear my mind
the demons that plague me are left far behind
all that I own in these two bags of leather
no needless possessions a life unfettered
smell of wildflowers in the warm evening air
soothes my hard face and streams through my hair
the rumble beneath me a beating heart
destiny's hand tore us apart
but the road before me brings adventures untold
still plenty of living before I get old
and your face in the clouds says I'll see you again
where the horizon starts and this highway ends

Eugene Jay Lampkin

XL

There were never any roses
yet, in the tapestry of time, copious tears
and they with their upswept noses
arrogant narcissists applauding their own fears
there were never tranquil accolades
tempestuous fools dancing in their own light
on empty stages that reminiscence jades
into the cliched daylit ashes of night.
There was forever the doubting child
treading the perilous depths of stereotyped time
fate's chasm has strengthened the blossom, wild
yesterday's bitter fruit has reaped its sweet prime.

Valerie Gaynor

Dakota Boy

I am born of the prairie.
I am son of the plow and the rake.
The north wind that bends the grasses
moans in my ears.
My mind burns like the dry August sun
when demons possess me.
When I am betrayed;
my soul cries like the
coyotes on the section line, and my heart
is as cold as the northern lights.
I am a Dakota Boy.
I hunger for the space between cities.

Samuel Lovold

Untitled

I have seen the blade of grass bow before the
majesty of the wind and the raindrop longing
for the deathless sea, struggle to free itself
from the bonds of captivity.

I have heard a chord of your heart's symphony and
the roar of the sea became a murmur.

I have watched the ray of the sun become
a shadow as it kissed your face.

I have touched your hand and felt the pulse
of poetry.

I have gazed into your eyes and caught
a glimpse of eternity.

I embrace you and all dualities vanish, for
the emergence of love leads to the reconciliation
of contrasts.

Sam Moses

Vanity

I stared and so did she
She looks much older than I thought she'd be
Graying hair and a wrinkled brow
Has that much time gone by 'til now?

Seems like only yesterday
I recall our time at play
Then make-believe and fantasy
Evolve into reality

For each of us the years fly by
We can't stop time, but how we try
The days march on much like a dream
From young to old overnight it seems

I saw her face, the tired eyes
It was hard to hide surprise
Recalling how she used to be
Etched plainly in my memory

Her appearance caught me unaware
I couldn't help but stand and stare
But she was staring back at me
From the mirror on my vanity

Betty J. Rhodes

In The Presence Of Light

I've turned about too quickly
    caught my shadow crying in the corner
He's found another memory of you
    pinned upon his heart

Sensing that I'm watching
    A second glance finds posture more expected
Unable to console himself in a
    life that's torn apart

He values time in darkness
    no guiding light or form to follow
Too proud to let the world see
    The pain he hides away

For when the light is present
    No faltering, just effortless perfection
Proceed with the charade just to
    make it through the day

Jerry Gaskins

Generosity

Lavishly,
The saffron yellow aspen
Spills its coins of gold
Upon the ground.

Impoverished and stark it stands,
But not without firm-rooted hope;
Though mocking winter winds
Taunt it
For its squandering.

Deep within its pithy heart,
The trusting aspen knows
That Spring, with warmth and rain,
Makes new deposits
That will grow abundantly
Through summer days.

Then—
As Autumn waves its Midas wand,
The spend-thrift aspen once again
Will toss its treasures to the wind.

Sister Barbara Bruns, PHJC

Lighthouse

Cloaked in shadows, I look out upon the silent, empty street.
An early morning fog has begun to settle in.
All is dark save for the few street lights not broken,
and our porch light nicknamed "the Beacon."

Beacon is a guide as much as any lighthouse ever was.
only this light would bring someone known, someone feared.
I turn from the window and silently leave my room.
Quickly I descend the stairs and stand to the side of our front door.

From this vantage point I can now see both Beacon and the Lightkeeper.
Curled up in her chair dozing quietly,
soon she will awaken and guide husband and father safely to port.
Perhaps tonight the Beacon will fade. Perhaps . . .

How tired and fragile the Lightkeeper looks!
For two long years she has worked these weekend shifts.
Why does she keep on doing this? I do not understand!
What about our safety—Lightkeeper—yours and mine?

A fire comes to my eyes as the clock chimes and she begins to stir.
Tonight I hate her as much as I hate him!
Softly I turn the switch and watch Beacon die amidst heavy fog.
Daylight came while the Lightkeeper slept. This is as it should be.

T. Victor Berry

Blur Berry

The midget girl wants to walk barefoot!

Fantasies of purple slave stains kiss her tiny toes. Red sandals
choke and constrict. Her father, brown rage and frustration. Her
father's magic tricks, but not today; she was misbehaving. A crystal
chandelier. They are angry. She watched them upside-down. She
watched from inside the rain window and she thought calling the cops.
She was crying and the tears resembled mashed berries.

She wants to walk barefoot!

Anthills and thorns, prickly pears do not scare her. Sister is
picking blueberries, she wants to be with her, barefoot and dirty. She
was crying, thinking of sister and the perfect sweet purple balls.
Ahh, the agony!

Ankles in giant hands. Her father's punishing blow. Not the things
she will remember. These things are not important compared to the
berries and the buckets and the sandals and the heat.

Blueberry spankings, chandelier tears. The blueberry stains on my
hands today make me remember.

Sarah Rees

Amelia

Amelia, what were you thinking when you dared to fly?

Were you tired of bumping along on the hard ground,
with the drone of endless details and chatter in your ears?
Was the silence almost worse—
the blackness and mist of anonymity and not being spotted?
Still, it's difficult to plot a course when there are no smiles
to light a way.
Was the cabin cold and lonely?
Did your father grip the bottle, try to maneuver through life,
only to let you down, down, down . . .
Were the loops and dives and twirls you performed
never enough for your poor, unsatisfied mommy?
Was her glance like the sun,
burning and blinding,
so that you could not navigate like other people?
Were you forced to take to the skies,
to live and die like a star?

Did you find what you were looking for
in the waves,
in the devouring waves that finally embraced you?

Jeneane Schmidt

Afternoon Bath

I played in the sewer as a kid.
I climbed under the chain link fence
my suntanned belly scraping the gravel of the smoothed slide into
my paradise my jungle my rainforest my Congo

I flopped through a sticky batter of mud
cool and wet on my bare feet sour in my mouth
and dipped my toes into a giant tub of smudge and murky water

I trolled for treasure: slimy and frayed ropes (unwanted—last summer's tow line)
a blue rubber long lost in the flood of '84 (it had belonged to my best friend's dad
before the swirling gutter stole it as he swam in the street)
gold trimmed Sanka coffee with edges chewed by a can opener in my atheist neighbor's kitchen
(the best treasures because they were forbidden at my house)
finders keepers

I plucked them from mud like the fudge pudding I smeared on my smiling
teeth when mom looked away in my jungle, the stuff was camouflage
smeared on my arms and painted on my cheeks

Rich and happily tired I'd squint my eyes in the after-school sun
and taste the mud caked on my lips

When the sun reddened, the silhouette of the chain links threw
patterns on the glistening slime of my pond

Amylyn Dickman Allred

Cyclic

Patient repetition, the wheels lull, rhythmic dance
Along track 12, fluorescent lights, clanging wheels, metal rails
Unremarkable, complacent, I lay wearily against the hard grain seat
Lazily staring at ads for Rogaine and God, personal injury and salvation
smelling the soft, stale odor of recurrent festering humanity
Drowsily rewinding the evening's fantasy, a rising miasma of
Umber, butterscotch and rose, the restaurant's haze
Does he, doesn't he, does he, doesn't he
Echoes in the plodding cogs, as my mind floats on
Koans on reality darting past, escaping from my thoughtless vision

Deirdre J. Kamber

You Lent Me Something Once . . .

And you laughed outrageously, uproariously, that night in the other
bedroom—across the kitchen and oceans of thought—sharing your
room so I could have my own. I stayed up listening to you. I
felt so heavy. Very, very heavy. Then sad.
Why don't we ever laugh together like that,
I asked you the following morning on our way to work.

We have a different kind of relationship, you explained, but just as good.
Nicer in different ways. Then I laughed that night at the party.
Out of control—doubled over. I laughed at everything she said.
Old friends will do that, I guess. You sat in the corner
and watched, but everyone else laughed with us—at least smiled.

I glanced over at you sometimes . . . met your gaze. Looked sharply away.
The pain cut deep and I wanted it buried—at least for one night.
You didn't smile. Later you asked me why we don't laugh together
like that. You stared hard into my eyes and asked me if you made me sad.
Yes, I thought. You make me sad.

But I didn't tell you that.
Instead, I returned to you the borrowed explanation.

Robyn Lori Shifrin

Laughing Madder

A chill on the film of my skin
  longs in lonely open solitude
for a touch the brush of your
  thoughtless hand
    —a passing gesture—
sends chills so warm through
  my core, to my sex.

Ancient rumblings of
  chimps in spring bring me back
to the ponds and the forests
  where once we swung, making
    maddened love under a full moon
  with no reserve, our shrieks
echoing through monkey towns
  for all to hear
    when ears of steel
  shrieked back
    with laughter.

Amy Palatnick

The Wailing Wall

Multitudes
blinded by tears,
mourn the young warriors
exiled from life.
With braille-like precision,
fingertips caress
the black,
granite roll call.
Flags, flowers, other mementos
are awarded posthumously,
ceremonial offerings
for sacrifice.
Tears, prayers, hugs,
remnants
of squandered youth
parade the Mall.
Their seance spiritless,
survivors petition for
"remembrance and deliverance . . .
Vietnam."

Randy D. Geiger

Prayers

Words toss here, there
wing around each limb and ear
drift whispers to another
high flying and near

Circle within circles
dancing plays of humanity
seen by the keen eye

Land-bound take aerially flight
marking two-legged grass dancings
stringing words to glide upon
each ripples, gaining height

Circle upon circle soaring
through the blue sky lake
our whispers trailing from red wings
our prayers wake . . .

Francesca D. Fleming

Possessed Or Two Faces For Eve

A sensualist poet, reincarnate, dwells within my brain;
Unfamous then, infamous now, this spirit bard, and vain
Who burst through my subconscious, Mephistophlean, irrepressible,
Hiding, he, behind my woman's skirts, he prods and picks,
And possesses then my tongue with his unchaste limericks,
Plays on words, puns, doggerel, liberally bawdy,
He directs them through my pen; not I, the sybarite that's naughty!
No! My mind's grown round and pure and lustrous as a pearl,
And strongly I'd suppressed this lusty scandalous churl;
But he'd discovered I've a lover, am beguiled and often smile,
He stole inches from my secret and stretched them into miles,
Fanned the flames with fevered words, then cinched up the fetter;
He's found release without surcease in my spicy scarlet letter.

Audre G. Hutchins

Autumn Elegy

Broken appendages of bare forest trees,
slumped in defeat, lie cool on nature's floor
twisted and torn in desolate degrees,
harshly deported by autumn winds' roar.
Harbinger leaves stalking sentinel oak
shelter death in their rigor-mortis veins
while creatures forage a vestige of hope
before succumbing to wintertime pains.

The hoarfrost hour weighing heavy and bold,
shadowing air with a scent of decay,
sequesters life to be dormant and cold
as sand sifting time quietly away.
While late autumn breath sighs shallow and deep,
gentle snow blankets its season of sleep.

Charles A. Jackson

Muffled Voices

We joggle along aimless and lost
through musty, murky, shadowy past,
soldiers of fortune, nomadic, lone,
sheathed in history, dreams overcast,
enshrouding cold drizzle about us.

Turned from our sunlit journey of hope
where conscience captains our work and duty,
when vermin sloughing our trail, assailed
our cache, crushing joy, shredding beauty—
and draped in their ruins you doubt us.

Slyly they sapped our trek in the sun,
those creatures of greed, ambition and blame,
spreading malignance, barring our way,
forcing retreat, surrender and shame—
and they squandered the land to rout us.

Wendy Rondette

"Charles Dickens' Stenographer's Notebook: A Sonnet"

And now, without delay, from here in my
Stenographer's wood chair, stuffed not, cushioned
Un-comfort-giving, yet not by me shunned;
From here, ne'er doubt I scan with eagle eye
The justice sure in this bleak courtroom; why,
Just yesterday the fatal race was run
Here in this room—this very room! To die
Or live: the choice that this reporter won

When in this chair, this hard wood chair, was sitting
A day ago . . . but I digress. And now, without
Delay, from here in my stenographer's
Wood chair, stuffed not, cushioned un-comfort-giving
Yet not (still!) by me shunned; from here, ne'er doubt
I scan with eagle eye the justice . . . sure?

Thomas J. Tobin

Untitled

I'm running out of time
07/08/1996

7434
Days

And it seems as if the
Battalion is upset
Over the new order
The circus act is close
To the grand performance

I can feel it

In my stomach
The flies are buzzing
Around the depths of my insides

And I can tell
When they land
Rub their wings together
And inspect my inner organs

For the sweat from their
Little feet contains salt
And it burns me

Jeremy Bruce Gratton

Origin

No period no comma
no colon or exclamation
no mark nothing at all to reveal
this flood of breath and dust
the greatest mystery
stories to philosophers
theories to scientists
but anthropologists made no discovery
this master key is sealed
instinct and feelings had been revealed
they keep the lies rolling
hoping to make believers
out of everyone
it was either a "boom"
or "evolution" or maybe
a "supreme" that caused
this super flood
but I have yet to believe
for I know otherwise

Widchard Faustin

My Memory is Fragrant

My memory of you is fragrant with
the tiny scent of wildflowers
and a soggy Spring wood
filled with stage coach history and
fruit bearing giants.
The ladders you used to reach
the high branches' sweetest berries
still lean on my mind.
When I look down at my work
I am startled to see your hands.
Hands with blue veins
rising to their duties.
A crooked pinkie shows
I am from you.
Hot oatmeal and raisins bring
you back to me so sweetly
that I nearly touch your face
before you vaporize into the
violet's perfume.

Debra Monthei

Mid-January

Winter mornings
are cold and dark.
Rising is cheerless.

The night's warm blanket-nest
imposed,
and turned my bones to rock.

Listen as the newscaster belabors life . . .
turn on no lights . . .
they sting the eyes and
cast large shadows.

Fumble in the darkness, awkwardly . . .
and be rewarded by the smell of rising heat.

Shuffle along the dim corridor to the kitchen
and peer through the black window.

A distant glow unfurls,
and spreads a bunting of security
filling my view,
entering through the panes of glass
unannounced,
to mingle with the aroma of coffee.

Theresa D. Hrin

Wish

(to Allen Ginsberg z"l)
Dew dropping
from a child's lollipop cheek after
rolling through—hugging and laughing
the grass his
bed to carefully create STRONGroots.

Rain falling on the last
peach in the brown
wicker basket steal it take a
bite and cringe at the
sweetness of sticky juice rolling down
your tongue, jumping to your chin and
dropping on your chest
piercing your heart

Sweat travelling from
brow into your eye am
crying for it
drip
drop
but do stay.

Zachariah Stutman

Response To Atwood

Why would you want such a thing,
"to watch me sleep."

As you enter my sleep
My warmth will envelop you.
You may lose yourself in the electricity
You spark in me.

What makes you think of calm pleasantries.

Our souls may rise "toward your worst fear."
I will then become one of those objects that consoles you

I would take all of those
You wish me to be
because
it is necessary.

Charity Henderson

Flatbread Side

Bitterly sourful sauce fennels down the vaporize
as molasses ponders through tarragon in a curry of powder
dashes the pepper to celery stalks turmeric seed
to sweeten the salt in spiteful cider
and mustard up hot fruit depealed with a single root
from tears cilantroly bubbling to caraway the hours
of raison cumin when carrots produce the garden
seeds roll along a pod splashing a tide of basking spices
in an oregano arousal of a supermarkets dreamful suprizal.

Kathy Fluger

Sunset

The old man sits dozing in the sun
Still as leaves on a brackish pond
His eyelids flutter
What incarnation is playing out
Behind the hooded lids?

The hands that grip the chair
Brown-spotted, blue-veined
Eagle talons
Mourn the strength that ebbs with time.

A fiery ball ravages the horizon
Searing everything it touches
Making motes dance in the air
Like angels on the head of a pin.

The distant landscape seeks revenge
On the cruel sun
Rending the monster with its keen edge
Causing it to fall from sight.

The earth writhes on its diurnal axis
Feathery mist descends on the somnolent land
A day has ended.

Martin Weinstein

Untitled

And now we come to parting at long last
we two, the loving and the strong in heart
dulled by the hunger of the days apart
I work to forget, and so deny the past.
This was my past—a time of hope and laughter
being together—loving, gay and proud
wrapped in your arms, blanketed in cloud
bright when we met, and grey the hours after
This is my present—spring that tastes of dust,
tears and silence take the place of joy
smothered in sorrow that I must employ
To quiet the heart I do not trust.
Now, I am angry that my love is strong,
it starves so slowly, and it hurts so long.

Helen F. Gunn

Security

When we're forty and bound
In the security of daily marches
And multiple separations,
We will be the only ones
Who refuse nostalgia's easy bait;

We will be the only ones
Who never knew those times
We could lie in bed for no reason
Except that we felt so secure and warm
Knowing we wouldn't have to put
Our bare feet on the cold, hard floor.

James Cobb Scott

Highways

Pavement flows like the mighty rivers
of my somewhat checkered past.
And like a Finn or Sawyer, I ride them.

If there were chances for change,
I probably missed them, again. Sad?
I suppose there are those who have no regrets,
and therefore no memories.

Maybe they have the secret to bliss.

I choose a different road.
I choose the road of Frost and friends.
F. Scott and Zelda and Ernest.

I'd rather fight the wars and drink the wine.
Let others sit, not I.

Chas Noble

Dear Pele

I have come to know you so well
It seems I haven't slept for years
My body has thinned and
My eyes have turned old
Your wings, sharp as raven's claws,
Have sunk into my thighs
Keeping hold
I watched you once from far away
Now you are my own
I have given you my sons
Made them lie down in fire
Sat with them between the walls of envy
When I'm empty, kill me with
Your insensitiveness
And young are my thighs
To which you hold on
With blood of apathy
And slight anger
A shade of sadness
From the over leaning tree of insanity

Carissa Bess

Telephone

So we talked
a conversation full of apology
without either saying "sorry."
Voices conveying the regret
the hurt and loneliness
of days gone by . . .
The anger of changed plans, wrong timing,
important "things" destroying
beautiful moments together.
So we said some words through
an instrument this morning.
Words meant to hurt and heal
to reaffirm our belief in each
other and in our "feeling."
Yes, we talked . . .
We had a conversation that would
never have happened
if I had not called you.

Bonita Gregory

Fading of an Icon

You see them everywhere at a pastoral distance
dying, alone.
Majestic hulks of desiccated bone,
Their listing frames become their gravestone.

Such beauty they display in their demise,
Their giant remains depicting their size.
They were raised with pride and served with distinction.
Now they die stubborn, prolonging extinction.

They gave shelter to horses, cattle, and crop,
A haven to critters, a farmer's workshop.
Like the outhouse, the lighthouse, and the red caboose,
This icon has out lived its financial use.

Edward J. O'Brien

The Philosopher and W. Shakespeare

Pastime of aristocratic leisure
sidetracked fools in vain search
of the highest realm—alone to
court madness in the paradoxical
certainty of why and what
pristine, eternal revolutions of
every aspect, the mind mills of
your will.
Think, laugh, lament to your
wit's end.
Go east to no mind
travel south to pleasure of simplicity
north to austerity
on a note of resolution
to wonder why
stoic to the end
there is less
in this world
than is dreamt of in
your philosophy.

Roy Rischar

Their Legacy

Promethean progeny, still shackled to scythian stone;
Inheritors of Hephaestus' flames, stolen from thunderdome;

Who blacked out boroughs to blind eagles in the night;
Who burrowed from the blitz then joined the firefight;

Whose frenzied firestorms rained bright from clever craft;
Whose thunder blockbuster fists smashed their genius past.

They groped crazily into heaven with blind sagacity;
Their nuclear neon torches burnt psychotically;

They stole not heaven's reign, nor its deepest mysteries;
Their golden fireballs glimmered not majestically;

They devised for beneficiaries a prodigious legacy;
Their gifts to be squandered madly in perpetuity;

Prostrate progeny, still lying on rubble pyres;
Inheritors of flame, burning in genius fires.

James Cooksey

Proper Birds

Water spotted all about
the tile counter,
She pours Brazilian,
and rests her stair
in the aromic steam -
fogging windows who
look upon the cottage garden
see small brutal birds,
in proper suits, of garden colors,
squabbling over seed and perch.

Chris Uhler

Bleb

Scaling fjords of green in peat moss dreams
Plankton eyes stare surface high below
Alabaster skies mirror atmosphere rays
Canyons too tall to tickle peaks
Elude views virulently raise
Man picks his name in stone
As bleating mountains sing shrilly
Naked nerves bond man and cliff

Mordecai Young

Sonnet XVI

Not one thing, no one, noticed that summer came
and disappeared. A splash, a flash of light dashed by
unseen. Autumn fell, a spell burst earth to flame;
while life itself prepared itself to die.
Not one thing, no one, saw the cloud that brushed
perhaps an inch of white upon the ground;
Unheeded went whatever force that rushed
in and crushed to silence every hint of sound.
Not one thing, no one, recorded that today
had blended into something less, had fled
to yesterday. Nothing, neither prayer nor praise
can resurrect this moment once it is dead.
Not one thing, no one, saw what had been missed;
so many songs unsung, so many lips unkissed.

Marie E. Colaneri

Sunset Celebration

I blindly clutched his hand as we raced
through stagnant mobs on DuVall Street,
dogs in a herd of sheep. Humid winds
splayed the edge of my white skirt and
tousled his black hair. On my wrist,
a beaded bracelet danced circles.
Blended melodies and laughter
spilled out from open bar doors.

At the dock, a yellow-haired girl leaned
against the rail, luring melancholy from a violin.
Her case unfolded black velvet, begging. Rumors
of a cat leaping through a flaming hoop found their way
to the back of a cluster we paused at, on our tip-toes.
He must starve them, whispered a woman
to her balding husband. A wilted man with tattered
cuffs hunched over next to a rusty bicycle, palm fronds
flooding its basket. Head lowered, his knowing hands
braided the greens, shaping a top hat.

Jeana C. Watters

Waiting for Daybreak

We go to a park to listen to a poet,
And we begin writing poetry for Him.
He seems there for the others, but...
I keep writing on napkins with whatever I can find.

I stare at a lamp burning,
The poet's voice coming through
As if from the lamp's flame.
I am strong when I know it is my turn.

Listless...lost...
Covered in honey that drips off the ends of my fingers
Falls in the dusty dark dirt...in the darkness.
My arms and face stretch to heaven waiting...

Waiting...for someone to taste.
Waiting...for the sun.

It comes...a warm glowing from within.
Leaving behind the tears,
Leaving behind the pain,
I feel the light.

I fill with Amazing Grace.

Nancy Riffe

August

The heat
burns the land
kills the weak and helpless
to make the survivors strong to start
A new

Richard A. Shaut

The Portrait

A lifetime ago when our years were new
We scanned the future, planned what to do.
Life was a canvas for the artist's creation,
we created a portrait of our aspirations.

What a montage evolved tinted with laughter,
shadowed with tears,
it was a masterpiece that covered our years.

The painting is finished. I am alone.
It will never be diminished, though you are gone.
My heart is the easel that holds our picture,
a glorious mixture of bitters and sweets,
of giving, of living of triumphs and defeats.

Ever in my heart, its colors won't fade,
our painting......
bright as the sunshine, soft as the shade.

Georgie Brooke

Portable Life

Hunger comes faster than nightfall
The cold is a persistent enemy
Space in a doorway, on the sidewalk
Is a race never ending
When you're living a portable life

Memories of better times fade with each passing day
Dreams are all you really own - except for your name
When you're living a portable life

But whether by choice or by chance
I am here
Don't ignore me or forsake me
Unless, by choice, I choose to stay

Phyllis D. Jeff

Be A Friend To Others

To all the friends we cherish,
to those we see each day,
To special friends who live nearby,
to others living far away.
With love to share
and friends who care
And life's finest things are there
for you to bare.
It is nice to go away, to be with others,
but home it is to be for mothers.
Never be too busy if someone calls
Think a while and give a smile
so you won't be bored at all.
If someone needs help
for a lonely heart, lend an ear
and offer a cheer,
Before we go apart and be
a volunteer.
Nettie Katz

His Art

I looked through the window into the sky,
And saw a flock of geese flying by.

In the valley, I saw trees colored in hues of green;
A picture more beautiful, I have never seen.

The Lord Art is done in such a perfect way,
That it gives one happiness to live day by day.

God gave us the birds, their beauty to see.
God created the world for you and me.
Janis B. Drinnon

A Wanting

Misunderstood because of the tears,
The world wanted so much, too much,
The perfect face, body, and mind.

Distraught by the screams of expectation,
The people demand more than could be given,
The impeccable age of innocence.

Aghast over the bleakness of the requirements,
The flocks of unknown pillage the dreams of a child,
The flawless way to just exist, a modest part of the vast world.

Estranged by those who scrutinize the every move 'with love',
The entirety of the universe give passion to a damaged fantasy,
The immaculate path to fame in the heart.

So with that, a wanting awaited,
The wanting of the way not to live, never to be,
The pills, the knives, they were a way.

A wanting for a disappearance of the soul,
The sickness developing into a contagious disease,
The disease of hatred, wrath, and rage.

A wanting for the fury that burns deeply within.

The flame blown out with a single, slight, unknown assassin.
Jean Sung

This Demon Of Night

It's night time he comes, when we are but only
Out of long shadows mocking, 'tis us, He is stalking
Candle light dances, on walls as they flicker
And sounds of the night, are starting to bicker
There's no heavy feet walking, no help from doors locking
He greets thee and me, when we are but only
He to has a Sir-Name and we know him, as Lonely!
John C. Martin

Our Flag

The early significance of the flag can be seen
In the hope and joy so long ago
Experienced by Francis Scott Key,
While in the thick and battle, glancing toward the sky
He could see Old Glory still flying high.

Throughout history, vivid memories of the Flag come to mind
For example, the world conflicts in another space and time
Showing scenes of survivors, victorious in battle
Erecting the Flag, just to say, Look, World,
We've conquered another battleground, today.

So much more could be said, but this must end somewhere
But before it does, let's re-live again beyond the sky of blue
The triumphant astronauts accomplishing what they planned to do
And how we shared their victory, when the Flag was placed in space.
It seems it brought Earth and Moon together, as History took place.

As we reminisce over the Flag and victorious deeds of God and man
Forget not, the realm of shattered dreams and the price paid
That over this great land, the Flag still may wave
May we take the dishonor to the Flag, sometimes seen of late
Replace it with Love, rather than Hate.
Virginia Greening

I Think Of You

In that final hour just before the dawn
There is a quiet place to which I'm drawn
High on a hill, with Boston as my view
I take a few moments and I think of you.

Another hour passes by
The sun ascends into the sky,
Its light reflects upon the morning dew
And once again I think of you.

Time continues and all too soon
I find myself in afternoon
I see the sun of gold against the sky of blue,
So I stop once more and think of you

By now you know what I want to say
That I think of you throughout the day
And even when my day is through
I still continue to think of you.

For when I'm done crossing a day of life's streams
Conscious thoughts turn into dreams
And dreams—I have more than just a few
And in my dreams I think of you.
Thomas Newman

Finals

Silence is Golden as Concentration Takes Place.
Moving eyes upon the paper in each case;
Speechless lips upon each case;
Speechless lips upon each students face.

Noise is at a bushing doubt;
Loudest is the rustling of papers that shout.

Hands to foreheads to keep them still;
And pens glide upon each sheet of paper as drafts are made of
Each ones last and final "Will."

Chewing of pens and knuckles take place
As the end of true false take stake.

Sighs are heard and tapping of toes
As foreheads come down to the tables in woes.

Pens of blue and black and pencils of gray
Hurry to finish the test and the day.
Colleen Harmon

Abiding In The Vine

Just keep trusting in the Lord,
Remember your armor and your sword.
Your life can be so mighty and fine
If only you are abiding in the vine.

There is so much power in the blood,
If you use His words like a flood.
They'll know we're Christians by our love,
When abiding in the vine from the Lord above.

Isn't the love of Jesus something wonderful.
Open our eyes Lord, ah Lord God, 'tis so joyful.
What a mighty God we serve, angels bow before him.
Shout joyfully when abiding in the vine and the limb.

Seek Ye first with just a closer walk with Thee.
I will enter His gates with Thanksgiving, on bended knee.
You alone God are my heart's desire, you the joy giver.
Abiding in the vine, I will arise and go forth,
To cross the Jordan river.

Eleanor Pinnell Reid

A Young Man's Dream, An Older Man's Reality

Many many years ago, I had my life all planned
I'd make a fortune, retire, a young and wealthy man
But dreams are not reality, life is full of turns
Living life is nothing more than lessons to be learned.

Childhood was easy, all the things I had
Everything I wanted came from mom and dad.
From mini bikes to snowmobiles, go-carts and new bikes
jet-skis motorboats and B.B. guns, all the things I liked

Vacations to new places many miles from home
Freedom for this little lad, to let his spirit roam
A cottage on the flamage, a cabin in the woods
All these things I'd give my kids, only, if I could.

Mom and Dad you spoiled me, thank you very much
I thank the good Lord daily for all my early luck
Thanks for all the many things, you gave this little kid
Thanks for all the memories, of all the things we did

Now I'm much much older things have not gone right
Someday soon I'll work it out and make our futures bright
But for now I'll sit and write, of stuff I used to know
I'll write of things I like to do, and let my spirit grow.

Douglas C. Schnitzler

Thanksgiving

Let's be thankful our way for Thanksgiving Day
Plus each one when rising up to go in our way.
The Lord was gratifying when He loaned us out
To mom and dad so why rush around with doubt?
He knows our feelings among existence of things
So be thankful for life among troubles or bangs.
Be polite not rude as you proceed in the universe
For earth's last rides is unknown but in a hearse.
From this time the soul moves forward in progress
To where one has chosen eternity perhaps with rest.
If all is righteous on arrival at the Pearlie Gates
A reincarnation awaits survivals not one second late
To partake his quantity of the on-going jubilation
For the soul's redemption the Father granted salvation.
But if procrastination has been a victim of the soul
The Hereafter that lies in store will remain untold.

J. C. Flowers

Christmas Morn

Happy are we, this Christmas morn!
For to us, a Savior was born;
His coming brought us salvation,
He saved mankind from eternal perdition.

Shepherd on the hillside came down hurrying,
To pay homage to the new born King;
As prophesied long ago by the prophet Isaiah,
In Bethlehem, will be born the Messiah

Tarry not therefore to Bethlehem,
Let us all go and worship Him,
Come on, everybody, all of you,
And sin, "Gloria in excelces Deo."

As there was no room for them at the Inn,
And the comfort of home is nowhere to be seen,
There was no choice for shelter but the stable,
Where they rested after a long and tiresome travel.

Let us therefore celebrate the Savior's nativity,
And proclaim God's infinite love and mercy,
And sing with joy to Jesus "Happy Birthday."
Sing with joy to Jesus "Happy Birthday."

Andy L. Bunuan

Embrace Me, My Love

Embrace me, my tender lover,
Enfold me within your arms,
Let my spirits gently drift,
Caress my body, within your charms.

So many nights I dream of you,
And long, for your sweet scent,
I dream I'm walking the shore again,
Irresistibly drawn to you, serenely content.

The glow of the moon, upon your face,
Can never be told by voice, nor pen,
The delightful ripple of your smile,
The soft wave of your hair, when blown by the wind,

The sultry sweet whisper, of your voice,
Yet, when angry, can loudly roar,
But when tender, can lull you to sleep,
Into dreamland, to dream of you once more.

Embrace me, my masterful lover,
I am enslaved by Neptune, I shall never be free,
I shall drift with the tide, in your bosom,
You, my wonderful love, The Beautiful Sea.

Bonnie Durham

Mayfield

I lift my eyes toward the sky
awakened by the morning mist.
Dew drops collect in green cupped leaves.
Grass below unfolds as the water falls.
Violet flowers grace the fields
in the May mornings
as I walk along a trodden pathway
leading to the still waters
that flow from the winter's spring.
The flowers are in full bloom
by the afternoon warmth.
As the wind sweeps through,
tree leaves flutter as the birds sing.
Butterflies float by.
Moon days appear unexpectedly.
Restless in the evening,
the moon outshines the sun
as the sun retires out of sight
into the good night.

Janice M. Chang, J.D., Ph.D.

It Is Time

It is time to consider and
    Think what you should do
From now and when is
    Jesus coming through.

A home in Heaven is
    Prepared for me and you,
He is waiting for your heart's door
    To open so He could come through.

Check now the love letter
    The Bible it is called so,
And study the lives of his employees
    (The prophets) and learn to know.

Come now, come all, He is
    A wonderful Saviour!
It is time to consider
    And think what you should do.

It is not the time to be fuzzy and angry,
    For he is patiently waiting
For your heart's door to open
    So he can come through.
    Cornelia B. Domondon

June Is Here

Adorned and elegant, a bride we'll see,
For soon to be wed, this June, for thee.
Her maidens, and cadets are all in a row,
And for thee, he is wearing a trim Jabot.

Admired in lace, and a heart sincere,
Being refined, and radiant, for her time is here.
Gracious raiment, and ribbons will glide, and flow,
While a sprinkling of petals, will guide below.

Chiming bells doth toll, once more,
For a bride is thus given, here at the door.
Presented with something-old, and again new,
Bringing something borrowed, and also blue.

Embellished a flower-girl, whom all will adore,
Wearing a floral halo, and lilies galore.
Ensemble are companions, and partisans too,
Sharing the moment, when they say 'I do'!
    Lani D. Dunham

Kay Sa Rah, Sa Rah (Que Sera, Sera)

He loved her with all his heart,
To please her was his longing desire.
Whatever she asked, he'd try to comply,
There was no end to his attentiveness,
Each one tried to please the other,
doing things they thought would be appreciated.
Something they were doing just wasn't working.
They'd try living together, that might work,
except doing that brought forth other problems.
Separately they were able to function well.
Together their differences got in the way.
What happened to their love and understanding?
Explaining about their relationship, that was difficult.
Was it true love from the beginning?
Or was it physical with love overtones!
How does one ever really know that?
Maybe they weren't mean for each other.
If that's true what will happen now?
"Mothers say: "Kay Sa Rah, Sa Rah"
Which means: "Whatever will be will be."
    Eve Westaby

Life Is A Sea Of Many Ships

Our life is a sea of many ships
Cruising to destinations unknown
A battleship to protect us in our journey as we roam.
Courtship becomes a relationship when we are born.
From companionship and love our life takes form.
Hardship come along and make the sea quite rough.
Leadership guides us through is things get too tough...
Citizenship to live in a country we prefer
And ownership to have a home we adore
Worship calms the sea, bringing peace to
The soul, to help weather the storm...
Partnership with our maker when we are lost and forlorn
Scholarship to help with financial goal
Fellowship to let the good times roll
Penmanship to write of all these ships in life
...the good times, the bad, the toil and strife
Waiting for our ship to come in
Don't suppose mine ever will, I'm running out of time.
So I just enjoy each day and give thanks for all that is mine....
    LaVon Prahl

Better Never Late?

In truth I tend to procrastinate
Putting off things that I should do.
I dillie-dallie at the starting gate
Regretting it when the day is through.
The problem is, that the things wait
All the ones that I leave undone.
So when later comes, albeit my fate,
The time to tackle the task, is gone.
Would I could be like the doers,
Who promptly use their time
Doing their duties, these eager movers
Don't let things pile up, like mine.
I'll really get at it I promise myself
Tomorrow, just wait and see . . .
I'll empty the boxes, put things on the shelf;
Later, finally, later, alas . . . that's me.
    Eunice Abby Reding

Some Visuals For Peace

Huddled together with those who clutch back
all those innocent, ageless faces cry
While enemy, gunner soldiers, each with
fire, confident justice is done, kill on.
Raw war, life's rotten rhythm radiates.

Resounding distortions surge horror through
blameless bodies, their futures, with spasms of
solicitude that explode inside their
souls, like mortar guts a shack; a home no
longer known, the homeless and the vacant.

Longing for serenity with all their
boundaries assaulted, the harmless live
with weeping wounds, dirty waters, shadows.

Those whose families and friends, the creatures
too, who are blown into scraps, rain down on
the barren land like blood drops of the saints.

Life roars on, many times out of control. It
regurgitates itself. Repression and
depression and the battles fought, don't halt
to sounds and thrills of the newborn babies.
    Betti Edmonds

Country Living

The morning sun cast a golden glow
As it sends its warmth to help young plants grow
To grow and to bloom in glorious hues
Of reds and yellows, pinks and blues.
The fragrance in the air is sweet and mild
And off in the distance the call of the wild
Gives music to all of the beauty around
What a peaceful, soothing and wonderful sound
The fish in the stream swim lazily by
While I sit quietly gazing up at the sky.
Amid all this beauty I feel such bliss
Big cities are places I'll never miss.
A house in the country, a place to roam.
A family to love, this is what I call home.

Carole A. Adamitis

The Wind That Blows

I sit listening to the wind that blows
And your image comes to me.
Of a woman in moments of reflections
setting under the old pine tree.

I listen to her feelings.
I hear her inner cry.
Of a loss of her loved ones.
Who choose this time to die.

I watch the white clouds floating.
Toward the eastern sky.
I hear the cry of loneliness
in the whisper of the wind as it dances by.

I miss my beloved family
Why did you have to go?
You were so young and lovely,
That day you choose to go.

Dean Nielson

The Delegation Of The Crows

The delegation of the crows came with
an almost distinctive amount of amusement
Their wide and boundless manifold
published an orderly and systematic worthiness

They had no pride or vanity of heart
they were high-souled, lofty and noble
unlike the outer birds who had become to
unreasonable sitting on their exorbitant perches

The delegation of the crows were
unintoxicated cool and self possessed
with unbroken divine conviviality
their community did not stifle love nor conceal malice.

The delegation of the crows
had come home not as conquering heroes
but simply as masters of exalted purpose
who could subdue any proprietor.

Eugene F. Wiesner

Troubled

Troubled times are mine
No help can I seem to find
I smile with tears in my eyes
And pray no ones sees through my disguise.
I will I were wise and smart
I wish I had a lighter heart
But troubled times are mine
And no help can I seem to find.

Jackie C. Deemer

Off To School

Happy days will soon be back,
We'll shed our heavy winter clothes.
Hang them over the rack.
Where can they be - our light weight garments?
It's so toasty warm, this light outfit will be just the one.
To keep us from sweltering under the sun.
"A coat? Mother!! Summers time is here!"

"But it looks like rain, dear."

The girl didn't see the sneaky cloud
Over the next door's roof.
All she saw was the bright sun
As she ran off to school, then poof!

The cloud let loose and she got wet
So back to Mother, you can bet
Who helped her into dry things.

The all can learn, but how long does it take us
Without our Mothers?

Lillian M. Cavil

That Boy Of Mine

We could be playing 42,
and having lot's of fun.
Pop would say we called the kid's,
they sure stay on the run.

We have a lot in common,
makes for easy conversation.
Invariably the topic turned to the Kid's,
they were conquering the nation.

The casual way
Alvin would say
"That boy of mine"
was never meant to brag.

The pride he felt was in his voice,
and his eyes.
Just as if he had raised the flag.

Clara B. Bailey

Cloud Magic

Clouds entwine across the mountain peaks in ghostly fog-like mist,
Writhing and swirling the dancing phantoms move in lissome mime.
Taking spectral form they frisk beneath an azure vaulted sky,
Creating fantasies which live but a single breath of time.

Donning dragon tails wing selves to dark and secret caves,
Then disappear in the magic of eventide's shadowed maze.
Castles with spheroid turrets rise above cloud filled forests,
As knights of the round table ride through Camelot's dusky haze.

Tall masted pirate ships cast anchor across the seven seas.
But disappear as sightless winds fill the white and muted sails.
Puppy dogs and kitty cats frolic in cloud's illusive play,
And phantom faces briefly hitchhike on springtide's flurried gales.

Always moving and ever changing the clouds soar high in space,
Bringing new worlds to those who fear not nature's passing scenes.
Years pass as illusive veils float in life's immense parade,
'Till age forbids the visions which ruled youth's intrepid dreams.

Ah! To ever be the lad who wanders fancy's brief sojourn,
To board illusion's timeless cloud ships which sail the windswept
     waves.
But the tower bell will toll its age old and reclusive call,
And passing time will hide the phantoms of childhood's magic days.

Elizabeth MacDonald Burrows

The Winter Fest

Every year of our life we have a Winter Fest
The ones in October to the start of May are usually the best.
The place we have them is at the closest hospital
Where they still cook with a good iron kettle.

Some people get a cold and some get the flu
I don't want either one but I don't know about you.
Some people get a cold and their face will turn red
They have got sinusitis and they have to go to a hospital bed.

At that time of the year our hospitals will be busy
'cause some people will get sick and their heads will get dizzy.
But some people like winter 'cause they like the snow
But if you would ask me I would say "no."

The doctors are real busy that time of the year
And the nurses are on the run if they really do care.
Some people get housebound and that gives them the blues
And some get pneumonia and that's not good news.

When we eat at the hospital we have a good meal
But hospitals are not free so we always get a bill.
That's why I want to stay out of them as the winter goes by
Because if I got one of their bills I'm sure I would cry.

Joe Dunkin

Untitled

The bomb was lit beneath the bridge just beyond two crystal rivers
In the midst of the evil deed its wick had waves and flickered
The cunning man had slid behind the rusted, lonely shed
He laughed and watched his "work of art" in hues of gold and red

Silhouettes screamed and hissed, shriveling in defense
Clawing at the fertile earth to escape a flaming fence
Again He laughed and licked his lips; sweet as honey is revenge
The torment they had passed along has come around again

The cloudy night had given way to ray of salmon sunshine
The old oak tree did its duty, shading where He resigned
Stubble ridden, He awakened, starving from his fun
To satisfy his lonely hunger, He decided to eat his gun

Elizabeth Jesson

My Wonderful Daughter, Jeannie

When you were just a baby, cradled in my arms,
Your delicate beauty revealed all your baby charms.
As a little girl, you were a joy, adorable and sweet
With golden ringlets, like a crown, set upon your head,
Also, you had a lovely, melodious voice,
And sang entertaining family and friends,
As you grew up, you became even more endeared,
You were my baby, the little girl I had reared.
When you became a teacher, you made me very proud,
I wanted to shout it, from the roof-tops, clear and loud.
Then, what a beautiful picture you made as a bride,
As you walked down the aisle with your Dad at your side
And on that blessed day, when you gave birth,
You gave me the most precious gift on earth.
Josh, a splendid grandson, caring and loving just like you,
You taught him very well, now a college student who does excel.
You've always been a wonderful daughter, one beyond compare,
The dearest daughter anywhere.
For your Happiness, Good Luck and Good Health, I forever pray
May your dreams and wishes all come true, each day in every way.

Irene Kanter

The Boy Next Door

His devotion and love for my wife
Is deep, and honest, and sincere.
Such emotion is seldom seen in life,
Only a son or other kin shows such care.
In so many ways he shows his devotion;
The surprise notes and greetings at our door,
The gifts of cakes and sweets she dotes on,
Thoughtfully sharing with her things she will adore.
The look in his eyes, a parting embrace with emotion,
Not even a real mother could expect anything more.
His name, Matthew, lends itself well to a feeling I devise.
I sometimes imagine him as an older man of the clergy,
His posture gentle, strong sentiment in disguise.
But with unfailing, plodding, persistent energy,
For my wife, he creates many happy memories, and more;
This marvelous young boy that lives next door.

Robert Unger

Viewing Nature

I found a place I really enjoy,
To watch so many birds, what a ploy.
It's on a small lake on the Root River,
Where you can watch the scenery quiver.

It where the ducks come for a swim,
Along the wooded islands with light so dim.
Overhanging trees and bushes galore,
Among wild flowers, grasses, shrubs and more.

We can hear birds chirping and the Ravens "caw",
The geese talking as they fly through the draw.
Woodpeckers rapid rat-a-tat-tat hollow tree pecks,
Squirrels jumping from trees to the decks.

More geese talking as in a V they fly,
They fly off into the sky.
Some will circle and start to descend,
And make a stop in their flight which will soon end.

Some stop to eat and maintain their energy,
What a sight it is for us to see.
It foretells winter's cold and blowing snow,
As we see the leaves which off the trees blow.

John A. Strommen

A Valley Where I Walked

'Twas so peaceful 'n quiet, almost as if
Someone had stopped the world from
Twirling to let me get off to smell the
Roses 'n other flowers in a valley where
I walked...

My life to then had been filled with a
Medley of strife 'n worry 'n despair, and
Never expressing concern for another, yet
Expecting something in return, but I was
Relieved of all those things in a valley
Where I walked...

Instead, life became one of caring, and
Compassion, but in a different light;
There was no darkness, whereas before
'Twas night forever; but not in a valley
Where I walked.....

Serenity prevailed o'er all mankind and
As greetings were voiced, the words were
Sweet, almost syrupy, when spoken in a
Valley where I hoped to walk forever...!

Robert H. Wyatt Sr.

Metamorphosis

How mad and angry I am with you—
knowing the answer, and not telling me . . .
later—
How mad and angry I am with you—
for not knowing the answer, and telling me so . . .
later—
How mad and angry I am with me—
I should have known it's up to me, why didn't I see it?
later still—
How I've learned to forgive myself—
first by forgiving others; not blaming—
then accepting myself—my uniqueness . . .
Choosing to learn—grow—
change again toward my dreams . . .
No anger or hate—to fuel the fire of my desires . . .
No pain to react off—or set direction . . .
Becoming the person I've always been.
Sensing heartfelt direction from within—
Finding peace of body, mind and spirit . . .
Being me—and feeling fully alive . . .

Lynne Adele Riedy

We Are A Family

He asked, "who am I?"
We smiled and said with no regret, "my son, you
are brown, a beautiful tan, you'll grow up to be a
very strong man. The life you lead, may sometimes
be mean, but son, remember our little creed:
The colors of our family,
White, brown and black.
We love each other, respect, there's no lack.
A family is a family, no matter what color,
Two wonderful boys, a father and a mother".
He asked, "where am I from?" We smiled and said,
"the blue sky, white clouds, and a bright sun of red.
In a world full of colors, God sent you with glee,
we longed for a child, and you were he".
And then our boy asked, "my brother and I will never go away?"
We smiled with a tear and said, "you're here to stay.
We'll teach you the colors of life, the shades of
difference in a world full of strife.
But one thing will always remain, our family is one,
with love, we are the same".

Barbara P. B. Catanzaro

Feline Antics

What a stealthy one, this furtive feline
so gracefully poised there at the window
While undetected he swivels his spine
aligning himself to start stalking low

Some quarry that moved, catching focus
has become the claim of this prowling one
Unaware of his aim so curious
my attention's on a stirring rerun

But intently fixed on his own instincts
this skulking dweller maintains sly pursuit
Nearing its victims, the cat's physique sinks
between set shoulders for the final scoot

Although well aware of feline antics
I'm nonetheless snugged enjoying my show
when, with a lunge, fulfilling his tactics
he pounces his prey . . . my big wiggling toe!

As I jerk it back, there ten feet away
he gapes naively as if to allude
Then, as the trained, I obediently weigh
my cat's instructions to prepare his food.

Bob G. Martinez

Nature

Nature! Nature! Born from mother earth's womb
from earth's watery sweet fetus nature evolved and emerged
first the sea and then the land
nature gave life a loving hand
God breathe His sun's spirit from the far reaches
the great mountain's majestic features
the plants and then the creatures
that is what the Bible teaches
the fish shed their gills according to Will
from hence came life lusting for God's sun
then the birds were born to nature's word and call
the earth and nature were becoming one
God decided to give it His all
giving life to this blue ball
He breathe His soul into a man
nature was taking its final stand
the orb of life continues to evolve
as the earth does spin and revolve
what next after man
but to become God's hand

Allan H. Lambert

Santa Claus

*In memory of my Great Grandfather,
the legendary Orvil Thornburg, Jr.*
Santa Claus is full of joy,
He always brings kids a toy.

He will be coming at midnight in a few days,
Won't it be great if he stays.

He is a jolly old man,
He always has a special plan.

He has all sorts of names,
He never plays games.

He works all night,
He has to go on a long flight.

Yes, - Santa Claus is busy
But he never gets tired.

Nichole Albert

The Smallest Star

Once there was a teeny tiny star
So small he couldn't be seen from far
He yearned to be big, but he was not
He was really just a small, little dot

Up there in the sky so black and vast
He wanted to get bigger very fast
So he began to eat things in the sky
He ate every single cosmic passer-by

Gobbling up novas and the Big Black Hole
Enlargement now was his only goal
He ate a whole constellation just for play
Washing it down with the Milky Way

The growing star took a great big bite
Out of every kind of galactic light
Not a single astral thing was too big
As he spun through the sky on his gig

Munching up all the fiery comets
He then consumed the orbiting planets
He said, "My heavens, this is really fun
For dessert I'm going to eat the sun!"

Diane Elizabeth Arnold

Healing Hands

Dear Lord, I stand with you with heavy heart,
Before me is a land of darkness.
A land that I must pass through.
With your healing hands I will be able
to pass through the darkness.
Your grace and healing powers flow from your
hands to me.
Allow your grace to flow to those who pray for me.
With their prayers and your healing hands
I will be able to accept the outcome
and your will.
I give my soul and life to
your healing hands.
Amen

George A. Bradley

living the life i got

i'm gonna keep on livin' the life i got.
once i thought i had the world by its tail.
once i thought i had my oyster, pearl and all.
then the giants started coming—coming they did.
some as friends with lies and deceit
falsely droppin' out of their mouths.
some as a wind shift in the night.
some in bodily delight stealin' my energy.
they took what i had,
didn't leave me much with which to fight.
but, He gave me my life back
and
i'm gonna keep on livin' the life i got.

Audrey Kathryn Bullett

Number Three Tub

Mom heated the water, then filled it full,
That old number three tub.

It was Saturday night and time for a bath,
In that old number three tub.

In front of the stove so I wouldn't get cold,
She would place that number three tub.

I would climb in, my knees 'neath my chin,
When I sat in that number three tub.

Then taking the soap, I would scrub me so clean,
While I soaked in the number three tub.

A ridge digging my back, and my toes curled up tight,
Squeezed in that number three tub.

The kids today with their showers and such,
Don't know what it's like on Saturday night.
To bathe in a number three tub.

Joyce A. Daniels

The Sky

The sky is blue with clouds of white
That roam around each day and night,
The stars make up a dipper so clear,
They shine and sparkle throughout the year.
The moon lights up a heavenly glow,
Shining at night for us to show
How much we enjoy all these things
The comfort and joy they all bring.
The heavens above will open their gates
And bring homeward bound all the greats,
I wish I could be there when they arrive
Up in the heavenly blue sky.

Mamie Medrano

My Heart

My heart is like a rolling stone
it never knows when to leave well enough alone.
I saw you what a sight I said
ole those blue eyes an hair of red
honey will you be mine?
The way you walk the way you talk
Makes my heart feel like a rolling stone.
It needs a place to call home
Honey will you be mine?
Take a change in me
an you will see
we can work it all out fine
my heart is like a rolling stone

It never knows when to leave well
enough alone.
I am in love with you so bad
Do not make me sad
we can make it just fine
an my heart will be yours alone
honey will you be mine?

Mary Elizabeth Tucker

There Really Are Angels

One by one I counted as snowflakes fell
Mom said Angels were shaking feather beds
But these were wet and pretty shapes,
They weren't feathers, I could tell.

She laughed and said to really see,
to look beyond what could be there.
The Angels were cleaning house she said
Enjoy the show, it's something free.

Then when the Angels were finally done,
and the pile was all around,
I walked along a crystal path
rays of light danced from the sun.

Mom was right, bells rang on high
for Angels touched the earth with glee.
They made a magic world in white
from feather beds in the sky.

So when it snows see what Angels bring
A beauty beyond compare.
It really isn't cold at all
when your heart and soul can sing.

Carol Pfankuchen

Earth

Mother so stable, unwind without haste. Moving
Slowly in elements that trace, silently the
Course of mankind. Whence and whither form the mysteries
Of life as His course guides His mission, exploring.

God's theater is His enjoyment. He creates every
Form, yet each soul has its place. Earth's movement perfect,
Effortlessly in harmony, within the cosmic space. Timelessly
You twirl. Moving without encumbrance, permitting

Life to unfold as season's form, whirl. Earth's stability
Permits life's experiences. Quietly, patiently, Life's stage
Encourages growth, change within. Prayers, heard in the wings,

Continue as we sin. Mortal's years swiftly play upon life's
Stage, voicing it monologue, questioning its place.
May I become as earth's dust, experience grace?
Love spins this sphere. Awaken within love's skill.

Only a pure heart moves subtly, becomes the Divine's Will.
To become, Wage War Within. Challenge thoughts, words, deeds
Impure, the cause of sin. Manage your being. Someday, laboriously
Heart will experience earth's balance, its aim, His game.

Tom Caudle

This Little Girl

This little girl with golden hair,
With bouncing curls and a happy air,
Doesn't talk, for she's not yet two,
But her mind is quick and her feet are, too.
She worked so hard when I watched her play
Out in her yard in the sun one day.
She climbed up high on the ladder tall
While I stood below so she would not fall.
Down the ladder and then to the swing,
She kept on trying everything.
Next to the rungs near the rope with the knots,
She planned to slide down all by herself;
But I held her and helped her as she slid down—
She made me think of a little clown.
The slide came next; she could even climb up;
I marvelled again at this little elf.
She has great courage, no fear of the height,
And always a smile and boundless delight.
I think of her now, dear Jaclyn by name;
She'll capture your heart and you'll not be the same.

Miriam Bellville

Unjust Justice

The Judicial System needs a permanent fix
to replace the constant bandages.
Unfortunately that starts with politics
to create laws with proper appendages.

There's something inherently wrong
with a system rewarding the criminal
that ignores the plight of the victim,
and makes what's right appear sinful.

The law may allow, for instance,
a criminal to have a plea bargain,
making the punishment less than deserved
and the victim at the mercy of legal jargon.

The law may ignore a criminal threat
and can't act until something's done wrong,
while the victim continues to endure the fear
and wait without knowing how long.

What's just is often extremely unjust;
what's fair is often unfair.
Many laws should be strengthened with the victim in mind
and the criminals taught to beware.

Charles E. Stickle

Antonio And Hera

To remain coupled to change
As if under the signs of passing clouds
The granite mountain had embraced
Its dark shadow of shame
To cover its sons in a grave cadence
For a cavalcade unswerving passages inward
When freedom was the prophet at a crossed path
On the shores of wavering lust for lips
Of the embrace still bruised
And shoulders of the snivel fretted
Eternity was a plate
In its circle entrenched
Where grief tore its own hair in disdain
And where the sound of a newborn man
Found the tremor of aging hips
Yet untouched by the passage of men
By the rain upon field fecund
Of seeds and vast spaces
For March hail had broken the burgeon off
Ancestral twigs

Vahe A. Kazandjian

The Preacher's Wife

The preacher's wife is her husband's best friend.
She sits near the front pew and says her Amens.
If the congregation seems to be a little cold,
She gives her support with her heart and her soul.

The preacher's wife has an attentive ear to lend,
Always finds the time and a hand to extend.
She responds to all, whether young or old,
And does so out of love with a heart of gold.

Her intention is to be on one accord,
With her spirit toward others as unto the Lord.
Her presence is greater than the eye can see,
Faith shows her the way God wants her to be.

Her service to the Lord she has vowed to dedicate,
To help create an atmosphere where all can relate.
What a glorious church family in which to be,
With such a preacher's wife for the world to see.

Ruby L. Boston

Tea Party

A festive table set for tea;
Little girls in mother's dresses.
High heel shoes and parasols,
With braids, and golden tresses.

Fancy hats and dainty tea cups,
A dolly in a wicker carriage.
Tea cakes and conversation
As they pretend to talk of marriage.

Shiny bracelets, and ear rings glitter;
They talk their grown up talk.
And when their tea is finished
They push the buggies down the walk.

Strolling in the sunshine bright,
They play out the days charade.
Mothers watching from the porch,
Wish the years could be delayed.

Remembering when they were young,
In the days of let's pretend,
Mothers, seeing into the future, wish these days would never end.

But, we must grow up...

Ed Manning

Farewell, My Love?

Eternity is here. It took so long to arrive;
Yet it is was only a light-year away. We had our eons of joy,
Among the universes of stars. There is no real sorrow;
Just bittersweet reveries of what was not to be.
Our sacred moments now lie dormant,
Never, again, to be awakened,
By the chirping of love's sweet melodies.
Pictures of thy smiling face, a forever symbol,
Of former happiness, flicker fleetingly,
Across a sunset-speckled, scarlet sky,
To embellish my thoughts of a longingness for thee;
Only to disappear, anon, despairingly,
Into a gray galaxy of grief.
After eternity, what then? Will the soul of friendship,
Still find its way through a wake of falling stars,
To nourish our hungry hearts, with a re-kindling of the lost sparks?

Frank L. Wilhelm

The Melting Pot

Whatever became of "the melting pot"?
Which nation or race didn't matter a lot!
To many churches, we walked side by side
And we all held "Old Glory" high with pride.

We didn't forget our mother land
But this was our country! You understand?
Learning the language helped make us one
And we joined our neighbor in work or fun.

If one had a problem we all helped out.
'Twas "a melting pot" without a doubt!
So what has happened? How can this be?
We've built massive walls. We're no longer free.

We must guard our tongues; watch what we say.
"Grass" is no longer grass and "gay" no longer gay.
We must bolt our doors, and lock our cars.
We trust no one; we're behind prison bars.

We speak to our neighbors but know them not.
Can it be that we have just forgot
What made us strong was "The Melting Pot?"

Ruby Burke

I Saw The Rock From Another Planet

And God's Face Was On It

I've seen the rock from another planet on TV
Jesus face is on that rock.
Letting me know that he is every where even far away.
God control earth, planets and everything each and every day.
No one knows from day to day.
What they will see on earth or far away.
He's every where to protect us, night and day.
We all have a debt pay.
Whether on earth or far away.
I can see him on the tree next door.
I see him every where I go.
On the rug on the floor or paneling on the wall.
or on the wooden door.
I see him no matter where I go.
I know he loves me each and every day.
I know I'll meet him someday and speak to him and say.
I did my best for others day after day.
I received a thank you which was OK
Because love is the right way to live day by day.
And take time to thank God and pray.

Mildred Tolbert

Untitled

Time seems to linger for a time,
as we wander through our day

We remember ongoing hours of,
our former childhood play

The endless twilight of our dreams,
as we're tucked in bed at night

With fleeting thoughts of far off places,
ending with the morning light.

Now it seems as memory goes,
Time passes far too soon.

It's almost summertime,
with its never-ending moons.

Eileen R. Volpe

Spring

Spring is supposed to be the time
When you start out fresh and new
When the sun shines down on all the earth
To melt away the dew.

When flowers begin to blossom
And gardens begin to grow
When old things start out when again
Before the next winter snow.

Spring is the new to many things
It brightens your life and makes you sing
It cultivates all your winter dreams
You feel the sun's warmth and know it's Spring.

Spring is such a special time
To see what nature has done with pride
Colors for all the world to see
It says to all "enjoy me."

Spring warms the land and brightens the spirit
It says to all, "Come on—get with it."
I'm here for all the world to see
And that is why that they call me—Spring.

Evelyn Ricketts

Hannah

A friend of yours for many a year
    You mean so much to me, my dear
We played together when very small
    Swam at the lake and had a ball.

School time together came along,
    Now all those time are past and gone
We still are like two peas in a pod
    We are still together, I do thank God.

We worked together when quite small
    Our deeds of yore, were always a ball.
Cruises in later years were so much fun
    So many memories but they are not done.

Some friends do come and they may go
    Seventy four years together, as you well know.
Our friendship will continue thru lifes end.
    You will always be my dearest friend.

Kathryn Heinke

We Can Make A Difference (Absolute Values)

We, the unsatisfied, yet uplifted
By our passions to cultivate a future for a
Generation, trying to preserve the
Absolute values of our integrity
In order that our unity advance.

The same that do impugn these passive,
Apathetic times, that surely have impeded
Our mutation of genius to our species,
Imparting diversity of spirit, hope, and
Courage in a world sublime.

Shall articulate with one great shout!
For all the earth to feel that humans
Gain the rich reward of peace, and limitless
Rebuilding, innate philosophies,
And wisdom, immortalizing Love.

Dismiss the tragedy and forms of chaos,
Replace with kindness, tears of joy and
Brightness, renew our universe, and forfeit uninvited
Forces, at doors of cribs and masses, replenish
Golden goblets with our flame of fire.

Charlotte M. Liebel

Temper Tantrum

The Mall at peak of patronage
   would be the stage of rage,
When mom and dad with tots in hand
   let Junior take command.

His screams shocked some to silence,
   those close by would wince.
While Junior on a roll increased the pitch
   without a hitch.

Strangers thought the source of torture,
   a serious cut of torture
The parents look without excuse,
   and some suspect abuse.

Arched back and flailing limbs define
   the tantrum of a kind
That Junior has where crowds abound
   and exits can't be found.

Some with eyes averted seek escape
   and pay with haste,
Prodding kids to action
   and away from this distraction.

The Tyco Terminator in transition
   makes a quick decision,
And just before they reach the exit,
   with a "sorry" tries to fix it.

As mom and dad with sister crying
   leave, with Junior sighing.
The crowd alert will soon disburse
   making Junior feel much worse.

Rambo on a rampage in the Mall,
   went berserk in front of all.
And from one word the rage would grow,
   when his dad said 'No!'

    Marylin Matthews Reed

What Beauty Means To Me

The colors of the Rainbow after a warm summer rain,
The chirping of birds, when it's spring again.
The various hues of the Autumn leaves,
As they gently float from neighboring trees.

A clear blue sky, not a cloud is in sight,
The twinkling of stars, "A full moon at night".
A walk thru the park will reveal to you,
The song of a Lark, grass sprinkled with dew.
A long winding pathway that stretches for miles,
You wish you could stay, you face is all smiles.

As evening approaches and the sun sets in the west,
I prepare myself for a good nite's rest.
I pray to the good Lord in heaven above,
To protect and take care of "Those Whom I Love".

    Edward J. Hotujec

The Waterfalls

You see the waterfalls constantly falling.
And wonder where is their beginning.
Their beauty is enchanting and as
you watch them, they appear
more intriguing.
You just want to keep on watching
without any interfering.
The beautiful waterfalls will continue.
You wonder if they will ever stop.
But who can tell since
we cannot see their
beginning at the very top.

    Rachele Becker

My One And Only Love

You are everything that I hold dear to me
You are my world, my one and only love,
My life, my soul, you are the sweetest thing
I know that I hold dear to me
For you are my only love, for me

For as I go singing through life
You will always be by my side
As the world goes by.

Farewell to my secret love
Who knows what could of been,
And yet you came into my life
When you did.

I have loved you in my mind,
The image of you, will always
Be with me the rest of my life.

It is strange how
You can find love
In the strangest places.

    Peter G. Frangia

Shadow

I am a shadow, full of suspense and mystery
I lurk behind doors and chambers
I run past mirrors and walls of a desolate mansion
Abandoned
Isolated

I follow the winged movements of a raven
I feel the deathly still wind, echoing calls from the spirits
Shrieks
Screams
I hang near a picture, a portrait of a ghost

As doors swing open and closed
I flicker near the candle
And see a claw pass over a clock
I swing back and forth on a rocking chair
Hearing faint mumbles from a closet door

I stay on a rocking chair
As the sunlight appears
Commands
I will now stay here until sunset
When the darkness closes in

    Chris R. Houk

Untitled

In this winter storm, the wind blows strongly
The sand in my eyes alerts all my senses.
The tide is high.
Tasting the salty drops of water on my lips
Inhaling the ocean air, that feeds my soul
I search for my path,
In the depth of the sea, reaching for the bottom
I hear the crashing of the waves
The flapping of the seagulls wings,
Along the water edge, like an agonizing cry
Calling for me, as if I belonged there
Silently screaming no, in a turmoil
Finally I sat down, finding a resilience that amazed me
Time passed, the storm is gone for now
The serenity of the sea is immense,
Until the next one.

    Sonia Guarda

My Shedding Black Kitty

Spring has come to the land, and how do I know?
My long haired, black kitty is telling me so.
Wherever I look, there are clumps of black hair.
They go out with me on whatever I wear.

A fine lady called in a white woolen dress.
She left quite upset in a black furry mess.
Huge black fur clumps are dropped all night and all day.
It is useless to put the vacuum away.

In preparing a meal, one must be aware
That strange foreign object is just a black hair!
In bed and asleep in the dark of the night,
That flying black fuzz was the cause of my fright.

When I plan to brush you, just what do I see?
Huge knots that hurt you, and then you hate me.
And so, my dear kitty, how glad I shall be
To greet next fall and the first snowflake I see.

Sherm Connolly

The Flower

Flowers are a beautiful token of love,
    given for all occasions.
Peeping up at us with smiling faces;
for special events, affairs, and
    business celebrations.
Easter flowers are crucified by the
cold weather, beauty fads fast.
We the people have seasons of life
    just like a flower, we age.
Artificial flowers are an art,
they give seasons of beauty.
Seeing them every day they become
    something that collect dust.
For every thing there is a season.
The life of a flower is a good example
    for us the people.
God gave us beauty, love and joy
to share with our fellow man.
Let us not collect dust before our season is past.
Our eternal life depends on us the people as a flower.

Doris Lambert

My Lady

Blue Ridge Mountains are covered with green foliage
Clouds rest on top of the mountains
Mountain trails writhe like life's road
Valley waters fall into rivers like passing days

Flowers blossom and birds sing
Everywhere beauty is alive
But my lady wants to leave
Oh my lady

When the sun has not set
Let us love awhile
Love and anger linked like chains
As far as the Blue Ridge Mountains

Our faces age showing wrinkles
Now, only a few mountain trails to travel
Always in our hearts
Love stayed constant like the blossoming mountains

Michael I. Byun

Intuition

If intuition is very strong for you,
It might be difficult to share,
Your intuitive powers, with a few.

Patience and time,
Will prove your intuitive true,
When you keep following thru.

Choices in life can be made clear,
by a quick insight without fear.

If you are sure of this intuitive power,
be sure to act upon it, wherever you are.

Stop and count the times, it has
worked perfect for you,
Then go ahead, see what next to do.

Somewhere some trouble might be lurking,
So be sure that your mind keeps perking.

Margaret R. Fields

Expectations

What is it. . . .that you expect?
Daffodils and Zinnias high on a hill.
Cotton clouds changing pictures across the sky
perhaps. . . .just perhaps you'll find them
bye and bye.

What is it. . . .that you expect?
Thoughtful courtesies that speed your day
rude — belligerent — arrogant — bores
perhaps. . .just perhaps. . .the choice is yours

What is. . .that you expect?
A. . .love so precious that it must be shared
A lonely — empty existence that Self destructs
Perhaps — just perhaps. . .from the last you'll be spared

What is it. . .that you expect
A dream pursued — till fulfilled
shattered hope bent as a willow wet with rain
perhaps — just perhaps you will re-think
your choices again.

What is it that you expect?

Geraldine Bullock

Why Poetry?

Why do we write poetry you ask?
Now you've given me an enjoyable task
Telling a story and making it rhyme
Words fill my thoughts all the time
Without poems there'd be no songs
We'd really miss those sing-a-longs
Expression emotions - messages from the heart
Putting it together is fun once you start
To tell about the babbling brooks
Or expressing how the scenery looks
To bring back memories we hold dear
Or just some foolishness pleasing to the ear
Some poems can sooth the mind
While others a happy spot may find
Praising God for all we've been given
To let him know we're thankful to be livin'
The beauty that surrounds our life
Or the help words can be in times of strife
Happy or fun - religious or nostalgic
Having poetry is really fantastic

Peggy A. Wolford

Hope And Prayer

I hope and pray for many things
That never come to light,
But hoping helps me focus on
What matters most in life.

I hope for peace in the Middle East,
Though that may never be,
So I pray for health and loved ones,
Plus goals I'd like for me.

There's hope in all that's spiritual,
But my religion says to pray
Is a much more powerful influence
When I need to find the way.

Some prayers have been unanswered,
But it always seems in time
That there was a hidden reason
I later found sublime.

When I wish and dream for things to groove,
And no-one seems to care,
I'll never, ever abandon hope
Because I still might have a prayer.

Derek Fell

Mikes First County Fair

A thing of beauty I did see
The other day beneath a tree.
A lovely girl was sitting there
I could not help but turn and stare.

And then her head did turn my way
I stuttered, stammered and walked away.
Her eyes I felt upon my back,
I thought myself the biggest sap.

How would I ever know the one
Who Make me stutter, turn and run.
And then a smile spread 'cross her face
As I returned to my standing place.

I asked her if she's care to share
My cotton candy from the fair.
She nodded yes, I must confess,
We both became a sticky mess.

Then from afar I heard a cry,
A father's yell - A mothers sigh.
Where could he be, our little boy,
He's only three, our pride and joy.

Edward L. Brown

Life's Gems

Friends are like precious gems.
People without them know such a void.
They come in all sizes and colors, and can be rich or poor.
All are truly valuable assets.

Today we celebrate the birthday of one special friend.
She has a pretty smile and laughs freely.
I kid her about her weekend "therapy sessions."
Observe her merrily riding along on her Craftsman.

This special friend is closest to her sister Jean
And her delightful children — Thos, Jennifer and Alison.
She cherishes her many friends and friendships.
My special friend is Shirley Brown Merritt.

Happy Birthday!

Dot Hutchinson Kelly

Things That Go Bump In The Light

I shan't tell you of monsters and goblins, or
creatures that spring from beneath your bed at night,
but of things that make frightful sounds in the daytime . . .
those things that go bump in the light.

There's a strange creaking you hear that says something approaches,
but is presently not in sight.
Then with a thump it seems to draw tauntingly closer,
and at once finds a new place to hide.

Surely present as you passed through your doorway last evening,
why did it not make use of the night?
For creatures come out only in darkness,
ashamed to be viewed in the light.

But this intruder lives in the creases of your conscience,
born of dirty little secrets, and those shameful things you do.
Perhaps in time you shall see, attempts to escape it are useless,
when the one you seek to escape is you.

Consiwella R. Ray

Ducks 'N The Ol Pond

There's an 'ol pond I often stroll about "peaceful harmoniously
Siren" I always go by myself to seek a higher peace above my
means sadly and lonely I meditate and think countless
ducks appear their quacking love for attention
cohesively natural and oh so dear they swim from

Out of the water with an eagerness that engulfs a flame
that begin to start to surround me with a natural duty
to claim "vociferously louder and louder the rave" with
a thunderous of quacks "suddenly my reason for being there
undoubtedly has great purpose in fact these ducks don't care
about what's on my mind "they only want me to see" their

Natural need that movement give 'em crumbs and let them be
I swiftly reach in my bag and give 'em all I've got my bag is
now empty turned inside out with no more to give then
not rapidly back to the water a sea of wings and feathers
they rush flightfully they gracefully take a loft with a

Tenderness and touch "they've all gotten from me what
they truly wanted "love and affection and reason to be
now I've learned it was I whom received far more than
much from a inquiring community of unity of ducks

Cerdan Smith

Live For Today

To dwell on yesterday takes away from the person
we are today.

To blame others for our mistakes in the past
will not allow us to live for today.

To dream of tomorrow makes us forget who we
are today.

It's too late for yesterday and we don't know
about tomorrow, but we do know about today and
the loved ones who share our lives now.

We can't be happy living in the past, nor can
we be happy living for the future, but we
can be happy living for today.

Shirley Hall Milkoff

Look To Him

If you need strength for the burdens you bear
Look to Him. He is there. He is there.
If you trip on the way, stumble and fall,
Look to Him. He hears your call.
If you feel unloved, lonely and blue,
Look to Him. He's been there too.

Marge Williams

The Haunting Of Hampton Court

Could there have been, perhaps, another way?
You wander down the halls of Hampton Court
Remembering that dreaded, fateful day
When Henry first announced you game for sport.
If, flattered like the others, you agreed
He'd ruin you then hold you in disdain.
The more you answered "no" the more he'd plead
(A cornered rabbit earmarked now for pain.)
A smarter move than giving all for naught:
You bartered for the marriage bed instead.
And is that not what all good girls were taught?
Who'd think a queen could ever lose her head?
The unfair gamble was on x or y,
A chromosome that only males supply.

Margo Koller

President Clinton

I pray, God be with you, President Clinton.
We have asked you to lead us, in your strong, peaceful way.
This is our Country, our great Land of Liberty.
In your second term, the last years of this century,
God be with you, our President, grant you to give your best.
Many nations look to you, North, South, East and West.
You are the people's choice and we pledge our trust to you.
Lead us across "The Bridge," onward to the light!
Where we will never start wars, but for peace, always fight.
God be with you, guide and give you wisdom too.
With strength and courage, take command!
We will be proud to follow you.
Give us brave men and women too,
whose lives are dedicated to serve with dignity,
in this great land of "Right and Liberty."
President Clinton, God Bless You!

Grace Rosen Baldwin

Reggie And Me, And A Dogwood Tree

Memories of good times serve me very well.
A hill and a garden, in my mind I can see.
All this means that I have a story to tell,
About Reggie and me, and a dogwood tree.

I remember the Hill; the maple sturdy and strong.
And the rope swing, where Reggie swung free.
All these memories are much like a happy song.
This is about Reggie and me and a dogwood tree.

"I remember when Reggie was but a Wee lad."
As I held Him, I wondered what He would grow up to be.
And on the rope swing, He said push me higher dad.
And this story is about Reggie and me and a dogwood tree.

The little tree was eight inches high, and seemed timid and shy,
It was moved to our country home, where it would always be,
The little tree grew and reached for the blue sky,
and this story is about Reggie and me and the dogwood tree.

The years rolled by, and my son is strong, handsome and tall,
In six years, the dogwood was eight feet tall, as all could see.
It blossomed in the spring, and dropped leaves in the fall.
And I finish my story, of Reggie and me and the dogwood tree.

Curtis D. Watkins

Rain

Gray clouds release heaven's tears,
into golden sands and golden years.

Spring flowers suckle morning's rainy dew,
while fall leaves envy what they once knew.

Children run outside to play in cascading mist,
as elders search rainbow's end for youth's bliss.

Moisture replenishes earth's scorched clay,
yet its wealth cannot renew old age's way.

C. Kay Bassett

Dreams Never Die . . .

So many dreams washed onto the shore line.
Waiting for someone to carry them home.
So many lives taken by surprised.
How could someone be so uncivilized?
So many waves bonding each heroic name.
They will always be remembered
Especially for their fame.
So many people searching night and day.
They too need a hug to help them along their way.
So many tears shower the Earth.
We ask why knowing it hurts inside.
So many dreams remain e'er be seen.
They will last in our hearts.
So many dreams give someone a fresh start.
They will carry on those left behind.
Dreams will never die,
But it's hard to say, "Goodbye."

Judith Tiller

Kay Dee

She stands the oldest, first one in place;
golden blonde hair pulled back in lace.
Lightly touch of blue lay soft in her eyes,
personal charm with deep family ties.

Whispers in the night, three sisters in one room.
Sweet smell of powder, lightly perfumed.
Secrets in the dark forbidden to say,
memories close to heart; in the home and away.

Although our lives took different roads,
and the years ran rapidly by;
her familiar face will never change,
and her inter-soul will never die.

Pondered thoughts forever touched my life.
A gentle being, loving mother, a kindly wife.
In my heart she will always stay;
my oldest sister with love, paved my way.

Lori P. Evans

Don't Spoil Our Sunset

There may be a cloud of polluted air
That hovers over New York City.
And if you're out on the Island somewhere
There's a sight both curious and pretty.

Colors are splashed on the western sky
As the late day sun descends.
Ever changing as the clouds drift by
Because refracting light bends.

Don't ramble on, my scientific friend
On the characteristics of light,
Or you may cause the magic to end
And spoil this miraculous sight.

There's a Master Painter that causes a hush.
(As I would prefer to view it.)
The beauty of His celestial brush
Overwhelms me. That's all there is to it!

Let the breezes fade, note the placid seas,
The sky and the silence both golden.
Let twilight bring out our fantasies
Please sir, don't try to control them.

William H. Bloom

My Casso

In the realm of love and acronym
  Make room and add for she and him
    An endearment to call one another
      Committed as spouse significant other

Then filling out forms such as a census
  Would not invade privacy or give away status
    It does not demand contract, ceremony, or lasso
      To think of one's life mate as truly "My Casso"

My casso is a fiance or fiancee, a husband or wife,
  Or any two people planning and sharing their life
    Then Hallmark and card shops can honor the times
      In considering sentiment or writing out rhymes

Each mention and remembrance of mate and co-mate
  Remains personal expression and way to celebrate
    What binds together the union of love in a duo
      With a special reference as simply "My Casso"

Sherill D. Rose

An Angel Unaware

Brother can you spare a dime?
For this poor wretched soul of mine.

I may be an angel unaware
In disguise to see if you really do care.

If you give me something to eat
An angel of light you may greet.

If you turn me away then some day God may say
"Remember that poor soul on the street you met
the other day?

That was an angel unaware
I know you had a dime to spare.

You said to him 'you were out of time',
And that you 'did not have a dime'.

A blessing you missed on the street that day.
That was a heavenly angel being sent from
Heaven's ray".

So the next time you see a beggar on the street
He may be a messenger from God for you to greet.

Brenda Faye Larimore

Needing You

On this day, my sweet dear Sis,
I want to say I love you with no regrets.
Oh, dear Sis of mine,
I always want you by my side.
I need your love at all times.
The times I'm mad and times I'm sad,
You can always understand
'Cause you're my sister and 'cause you care.
The love you have for me —
It's like a cure that gets me back on my feet.
Please, I say to you,
Don't ever leave my side
Cause without you I'll be sad.
You are part of my life,
And without you, I won't survive.
You are like water to a plant,
And so for me dear Sis,
You are my angel that always sets me free.
I love you, so I repeat myself but for you dear Sis,
Those words will never change.

Lucia Preda

Untitled

Morning brings those gentle rings,
Alarm clocks, hate those doggone things.

Rush make breakfast - rush eat breakfast,
Rush wash dishes of said breakfast.

Dress to look best look like all the rest.

Run to the subway train just pulls away.

Wait for the next one
Isn't this just fun.

It comes roaring in
Dirt, dust, lots of wind.

Look around me
And what have we!

Sleepy faces, haughty faces,
Showing trouble and its traces.

Faces leering, faces staring,
Faces that are tired of bearing.

Painted faces, dirty faces,
Coming, going, endless places.

Children's faces - like those best,
Theirs are filled with happiness.

Alice Chase

Re-Do

Go to any graveyard and take a look around,
and notice all the people that are planted in the ground.
The good and bad the rich and poor,
the fat and thin and many more.
The happy, sad and in-between,
some cherished souls and some just mean.

They played the game their time they spent,
not knowing they were heaven sent.
To pass the test of Karmic law,
they came, they lived, they died, they saw.
They know the answers, themselves they meet,
till final judgment is complete.

The "Maker" views their life content,
explaining what it all had meant.
And some of them the chosen few,
to those the Lord will grant "Re-Do".

Steve Fappas

Young Love

When we both were, oh, so young
You were my hero, oh, so strong

Trips to the local swimming pool
Were such a great way to keep cool

In grade three, we sent notes of love
Across the aisle and to heaven above

Our friendship and love grew through the years
Even after we were separated, oh, the tears

Our paths rarely crossed beyond our youth
Soft written words, our love expressed in truth

Wherever and whenever time brought us together
It was as if time stood still, whate'er the weather

We would hold each other, such grand embrace
Neither of us willing to look reality in the face

We seized the joy of the present moment, never
Never wanting to let go of each other, never, ever!

So many, many things happened to keep us apart
There was to be no consummation of the love in our hearts

Lila G. Kuehnert

Treasures Of The Heart

As children still, in His sight, we offer loving gifts to
　our Heavenly Father for His good pleasure;
Come, bring to Him to-day, your heart heaped high with its
treasure,
　That He may bless and multiply its own measure.

Loving-kindness shall fill the largest cup;
　Then faithful trust in Him another will fill up.

Patience perfects a pliable mold, for it must adjust to fit the
　needs of the hour.
Hope and desire fill twin pitchers to be poured o'er the burning
　coals of the will, to make the steam of its power.

Earnest intents form and shape tall vials that for truth and
　wisdom's fair judgement are meant;
Obedience to the Father's will with willing heart, opens heavenly
　windows for Love's pure sunshine to you to be sent.

Joy arising out of your love for Him shall be as a precious vapor
　filling all with the sweetness of His Spirit's Guiding Light.
Thus, your heart becomes a special place, where He will share with
　you, the treasures of His measureless Love for you,
　In pure and endless delight.
Doris E. McClure

The Glorious Gate

I saw a gate that had no lock
But looked somewhat exciting.
To my sad and sudden shock,
I found the inside not inviting.

There was another gate - so beautiful and great,
Made of iron and brick, with lots of wire above.
Was it to protect a magnificent estate?
Or was it made from fear without a sign of love?

Another gate stood stately poised and tall,
As proud as one could hope to see.
The ambiance seemed to beckon one and all
As many quickly entered - but not me!

So special was my urgent quest
At a time of need so great,
I couldn't put my mind to rest
Until I knew my fate.

With continued effort toward my goal
I searched to find the glorious gate for me.
The one that was open to receive my soul
As I go from here to everlasting eternity.
Virginia L. Bass

Dear Little One

I hope this quilt is special
I stitched it just for you
And I bought this tiny teddy
to keep you warm and cuddly too.

Lay down your precious little head
and close those sleepy eyes
your Guardian Angel will watch over you
until it's time to rise.

And when you wake up from your nap
you'll be all full of pep!
Then there will be plenty of time
to do "some of this" and "a little of that".
Carole French

My Secret Garden

I have a secret garden, where I often go
To rest and dream of things that never can be so.

There is a swing in my secret garden
Where I can sit and ponder
What my life is, has been, and will be
I wonder?

The coolness of the shade
And the flowers bright and tall
Help me find the inner strength to deal with
What's beyond the wall.

The trickle of a tiny stream
A butterfly so small
A cardinal upon a branch
I hear his happy call.

The sky above an azure blue
With lazy clouds drifting slow
Trees all cool and green
And shadows still with dew
All this makes my secret garden
A place I love to go.
C. Higginbotham

Azurest

While we continue in retreat on this planet,
Grant us grace in supplication
As we pause to recollect
Our entity's human relations
Thou who art the Defender of Life,
The Creator of mind in man
In whom intuition is rife
With good-will to spiral the Plan.

When we know not what to do,
Thou guide our every way,
Come to our rescue,
Keep us from going astray.

My our spiritual inheritance
Earn for us among the "braves"
A retreat of noble permanence
Advanced souls transcend the graves.

When burdens are a multitude,
Tribulations no more to test,
Give us peace and quietude,
A brave, fallen warrior home at rest
Thurman Wardell Lyles

The Winter And Me

Dear Mother and Dad
No doubt you are a little sad
But when this reaches you,
You won't feel so blue;
Although am almost blue with cold
I force a smile and try to be bold.

Indeed, I shall have to bear
Another white X-Mas like last year;
After this you may be certain
No more white X-Mas in this austere Britain,
For soon you will see my dear face
Among the people of my own race.

Britain's winter will be withstood
Despite the rations being not so good;
With you uppermost in my thoughts,
I shall fight the battle that must be fought;
If I should not survive the wintry weather
Please think of me always - yours forever.
Hugh D. Wright

Those Words That Burn

With words that burn we did part that

afternoon.

A most bitter hour it shall always be

I shudder still and grow sick at heart

when the words you spoke come to me. . .

too memory ——

With spiteful song you echoed your harsh

good-bye

Your voice with a chant of deathless music

With eyes so cold; and an empty soul

you spoke those words; those words. . .

Oh! Those words that tore my heart in two

with many tears I shall always recall

that afternoon — when ——

You spoke those words so harsh to me

those words; those words. . .
  "Those Words That Burn."
    Leah Simmons

Go Toward The Mountain

Go toward the mountain,
Keep your eyes, your heart, your soul on God,
Don't stop searching for the rainbow,
Don't stop reaching for that dream.
Don't stop believing for the impossible.
The path that leads to glory,
That belonging to God alone is long as it is narrow,
But it's a path that'll do you no harm,
Do not look back to what was,
There is nothing behind you,
That can change the path you lead.
Go toward the mountain,
It's where eagle soar high, there you will find the answer,
That keeps you wondering why,
There are no coverings to your lookings,
Only the truth you've kept inside.
Wondering for the meaning,
To the path you took in stride,
Just go toward the mountain,
And God will be at your side.
    Carrol Belcher

Children

I am Myself!
I am Happiness with cheering smiles beaming from my porcelain face.
I am Happiness speaking hopeful words of wisdom to others.
I am Happiness living with joy all around me.
I am Happiness looking at one day at a time.
I am Happiness bursting at the seams, laughing whenever I feel like it.
I am Happiness experiencing everything with my tender heart.
I am Happiness holding wonder like a baby holds a cuddly teddy bear.
I am Happiness knowing what is inside people is what counts.
I am Happiness loving the warm streaming sunshine.
I am Happiness not minding rain, for I just play in it.
I am Happiness experiencing all of the little things in life

I am Myself and will always be myself!
I am Happiness finding it everywhere!
I am a Child!
    Amanda Nave

Those Passed Away

A locket, a picture, a withered bouquet
Conjure mem'ries of old love of those cast away.

The old porch, a-creaking
The rockers did sway,
With laughter and stories
From those passed away.

Sunset, on the blue ridge,
Reflecting on rust—
Fading, dying old mem'ries
Decrepit dead lust.

Thund'ring railroad, below us
Old tracks we knew then,
When the old love was the new love,
When we never asked when.

Long walks, through the pine woods, the creeks and the glen,
Picking berries, wild roses and original sin.

Red clay dirt roads now paved roads the soured scent musk—
Morning is evening upcoming mud dusk.

A locket, a picture, a withered bouquet
Darken mem'ries of old love—of those passed away.
    Andy Martin

Frosty

Summer was almost ending,
A new season was beginning.
We thought of it like all others.
A time in life for two brothers.

Autumn is a time of dying
the wind sounds as if it's sighing.
A loneliness it seems to bring,
with such a change in everything.

It came as my son was leaving.
To touch my heart already grieving.
Death came and took "Frosty" away.
With me he had spent his last day.

He left on the 14th of September.
We have precious times to remember.
We loved his body so healthy and strong.
God called him quickly before he lived long.

He left behind his Mom and Dad.
And a son with a heart so sad.
A sorrowing sister and brother.
A whole family who loved one another.
    Gerrie Harman

Silent No More

Tho, I lay silent for several years
  now I speak again.
My freedom of conversations
  I enjoy with family and friends.

When the doctors thought of letting me go
  God heard someone's prayers.
Now I can speak and thank Him
  for my every wakened hour.

As my family stood there rejoicing
  I spoke to everyone.
I'll never forget my miracle
  from the Father and His Son.
    Ruth Stuart

Give Me A Rose

If I could have a rose today,
Happiness would come my way.

If I could have a rose tomorrow,
It would give joy, and bring less sorrow.

If I could have a rose this week,
I'd feel all the love, I'd seek.

If I could have a rose this month,
I'd feel more closeness, and less confront.

If I could have a rose this year,
I'd feel more strength, and have less fear.

If I could have a rose and it may have a thorn.
I'd thank you Lord, for the day I was born.

If I could have a rose this day,
And not just when I pass away.

Just one rose from a flower bed,
I will take it now, not just when I'm dead.

So give me one rose, it will lighten my strife,
For one little rose, will add to my life.

Matt J. Chlebanowski Sr.

My World

Take a trip in my world.
Imagination is your guide.
Climb my tallest mountain
where you will lose your breath.
Explore my wildest jungle
where the animals are untamed.
Pick the succulent grapes from
my most plentiful vineyard.
Taste the finest wine from the cups of my hands.
Sweat in my hottest desert,
Then cool off in my icy-wet Arctic.
Dine on my creamy pastries which
your mouth can't resist.
Dive into the depths of my deepest valley
And lose yourself with me.
Reserve your one way ticket now.

Kristen Vanek

Headstones

Observe weather worn civil war headstones.
Below lie remnants of brave soldiers bones.
Sherman, Stonewall Jackson, Pickett, all heroes,
Lie in those long, rutted rows.

Both sides proclaimed God was on their side,
And into that ill-fated battle they would ride.
While others marched in blinding wind and snow.
Each bent on striking the other a fatal blow.

Confederate, General Lee, West Pointer was he,
Binoculars in hand, observing gray coats as far as he could see,
Men and young boys with guns as toys,
On hillsides, in a corn field, and in trenches concealed.

Those old headstones above and old bodies below
Evoke images of how much blood did flow.
We now weep as united countrymen,
And reflect on what might have been.

An American flag flutters aside each grave on Memorial Day.
Here young and old, northern and southern come to pray.
Iconoclasts will ask why was the war fought?
Patriots will proudly say, why weren't you taught?

James L. Mack

Brother's Love

My brother came to visit me in a dream.
In this dream we were children, and it was the most wonderful dream.

He made me laugh with stories about silly things.
He held me close to him.
He made me remember things from days gone by.
It truly was a wonderful dream.
His spirit must have known that I needed him for
this brief period of time.

When I had awaken, all I could think of for days
was this wonderful dream of my brother.
He will always live on in my mind and in my heart.
It made me sad to know that I'll never see him, talk with him
or share in any future experiences while I'm alive,
However, I am very hopeful that I will see him in another place and
    time.

My brother has been gone for many years,
I barely knew him as a child or otherwise,
I am really glad he came to see me in my dream.

Sharon M. Jipson

Summer Nights (Night Scents And Sounds)

Fireflies like shooting stars
shoot through the night air.
The silence of an early summer night,
a falling leaf can be heard.

Evening falls, leaving in our memories,
the fragrance of honeysuckle, jasmine and gardenia.
Being carried by a breeze, as delicate as wedding lace.

Warmth from the setting sun, has left upon the earth
lingering fragrance, the goodnight embrace of a lover,
the sound of strong footprints, all of these
.........................fading into a memory.

Sounds of Summer Nights.
The calling of whippoorwills,
the croak of bull frogs, calling their mates.

Stars glistening so high above,
gives light into the night like twinkling stars
on blades of soft summer grass.

Summer night scents and sound, sweet words,
remembered dreams, a song within the heart.
Summer nights.

Betty Lee

Abiding In The Vine

Just keep trusting in the Lord,
Remember your armor and your sword.
Your life can be so mighty and fine
If only you are abiding in the vine.

There is so much power in the blood,
If you use His words like a flood.
They'll know we're Christians by our love,
When abiding in the vine from the Lord above.

Isn't the love of Jesus something wonderful.
Open our eyes Lord, ah Lord God, 'tis so joyful.
What a mighty God we serve, angels bow before him.
Shout joyfully when abiding in the vine and the limb.

Seek Ye first with just a closer walk with Thee.
I will enter his gates with Thanksgiving, on bended knee.
You alone God are my heart's desire, you the joy giver.
Abiding in the vine, I will arise and go forth,
To cross the Jordan river.

Eleanor Pinnell Reid

Darkness to Darkness

Dedicated In Memory of Jonathan Richardson 1-12-97

On a Sunday morning you came from darkness to light
It was the beginning of your short plight

Years of learning and yearning
With a desire and willful burning

You gave love without end
And the hearts of all you'd win

Your soul warm and kind
The best son one could find

God was your guide
And he stayed by your side

Then darkness claimed you back one Sunday night
But through the darkness you found eternal sight

For God's hand you took hold
And found rest and peace for your sweet soul

Nadine Tiller

Reminiscence

Laughter from your open arms
Smiles full of moonbeams
Your voice dancing with such pleasure
Our enchanted life you have in store
Teasing, touching, blue pools holding me
Holding me into you, embracing a dream . . .
Gentle breezes kiss my cheek
Searching, longing to see
Is that you, your loving hand
'Tis only the wind
With tender reminders of yesterday
Lingering memories
Tears, one last dance
Caressing hands stroking
Fingertips, drifting away
Never again to soothe, to embrace
Once, just one time again . . .

Jayle Ess

Fathers

There were seven then. I counted carefully.
The one who left, still mourned, his burdens
Placed on other's shoulders.

The one who played dark, evil games, the torment
Of his soul met me at sixteen.

There was the moustache, arrogant lear, I've
Castrated him forever. Almost.

There was the good one. Still alive, but unavailable.
He's valued much too late.

There was the other. Fat, impotent flesh, guiding my
Reluctant mouth. Again.

There was the slow-warming one. Twenty years to decide he
Liked me. Then he died.

There is my friend. He tries to father, sometimes.

I forgot to count the priest urging my shamed confession,
Breathing hard. One more stroke for Hell.

God, are You my Father? Your child waits.

Pat Pabst

My Song To Mary

How can I say I love you?
How can I tell its depth?
'Tis not like the blustery, lithesome
    Winds of springtime,
Nor the warm breeze of summer's
    Soothing touch,
But like the golden leaves of
    Autumn's changing
When memories of years gone by
Float through the mind and
    Warm the heart
With images of years of blissful peace,
Of unspoken words which only hearts can know.
How do I love you? Words say not enough—
—Only the song within my heart
Can tell its wondrous joy.

Ronald Linford

Grace

She runs gracefully towards the sunshine
Life beckoning with all its powers
Suddenly in its grip
She uplifts her arm
And proclaims His overwhelming love
To fall at His feet weeping with joy.
Now that her troubles were over
He her weary soul comforted.
Her pain slipped away
As she besought Him
Rejoicing that she found Him
She felt warm and safe in His embrace
In the knowledge that His love would endure
When no mortal man could sustain her
With the false love they offer her.

Verna L. Teter

Country Boy

You loved tractors, you loved trucks,
Hunting is where you ran into ruts.
Your smile brightened your whole face,
Your laughter lifted everyone on the place.
You were loyal, you were proud;
You never let anyone down.
You did all that was asked without a complaint,
Happy or feeling bad, you went ahead, just like a saint.
The cards were stacked against you, it seemed,
But we pulled for you, cause in your eyes, we saw a gleam.
Your fighting spirit touched lots of lives,
And it gave us strength in the trying times.
You were the glue that held us together,
We will love you, forever.
When you left us the tears did stream,
It took a while for the memories to beam.
We thought we had lost everything,
Then our memories started to sing.
Our memories of you will pull us through,
And seeing you again is what we have to look forward too.

Belinda Riddle

The Potato Couch

Just about everyone has one. . .a couch that is,
but the question is, is yours a Potato Couch?

It offers you comfort and safety from the world outside
and in many cases hours of solitude.

It could be your best friend in disguise...never
offering any harmful criticisms or opinions,
but where is the praise from your silent friend?

Donna Heyen

Old Letters In A Shoe Box

Those old letters in a shoe box.
The memories that it unlocks.

Here's one from my mother.
She said that she's fine and everything's OK
She said she regrets the day I moved away.
She said grandma's heart failed and grandpa died.
She said your sis loves you and today she cried.
"You left so long ago.
You should come home, you know."

Here's one from my best friend.
He said that all is well and nothing is new.
He said we had so much fun and "I miss you."
He got married, I don't even get a call.
He said he promises to, at least by fall.
Until then, time goes by.
Old letters make me cry.

And as the time goes by in ticks and tocks,
I read those old letters in a shoe box.

David Rogenski

Day After Day, Night After Night

Day after day,
sheep run astray.
Day after day,
horses neigh.

Day becomes night,
the sun is not up but the moon is so bright.
The owl takes off in flight,
night after night.

The fish still swim,
Birds sit on a limb.
The lights are now dim,
Now I lie down and sing a hymn.

Day after day, night after night.

Emily Shellenberger

Before

Before you came into my life
I was so lonesome and blue,
I thank God everyday when I found you,
When I reached out and touched your
hand, I found the strength to face
anything that life may bring.

You taught me what real love is.
I love you more than life itself.
Your smile was warm as the summer rain.

No other person can make me feel the
way you do.
You're the only one for me.
You make my life complete.
You're the only one I always dream about.
You're always on my mind,
And in my heart.

I don't want us to ever drift apart.
I want us to be together until the end
of time, and if God is with us this will
come true because he knows how much I love you.

Lynn Jones

Lift Up Your Heart

Life has a way of sending things,
    That sometimes seem unfair.
But maybe that's the time for us
    To bow our hearts in prayer.

If we can only use our faith
    And send our will His way,
He may be leading us, you see,
    For yet a better day.

If we can only look ahead
    Beyond our heart and grief,
I know there are some better times
    To help provide relief.

When shattered dreams and plans go wrong,
    And things look dark and bleak,
If we can keep our senses sharp,
    I'm sure we'll hear Him speak.

Life has a way of healing hurt,
    A way of opening doors.
There comes a strength from deep inside,
    As life and man endures.

Jerry Copeland

The Foundation Of Our Country

Our country needs a firm foundation.
Righteousness and justice for every nation.
Why can't we live in peace?
With righteousness wars would cease!
With justice for the weak as well as the strong!
We could change the things in this world that are wrong!
People of every race have a right to be here.
Each of us have feelings of love and fear.
Let's all work together, we need a new start.
Look for the good in each other, open your heart!
Ask our heavenly father to show you the way.
The way, to get our country together today!

Prudence Meily

This Love

There is a love that's yet today;
'Twas dormant through the years.
A strong and deep and pure love,
Despite the doubts and fears.

A Love that's grown to heights unknown.
What will this Love arrange?
Shall blossom, plus: More love for us.
Shall last through any change.

What is this love that is so true
That does not fade away?
Why, it's the love I have for you
That fills my heart each day.

And it's the love you have for me
That only you can weigh.
And it's the love that now exists
between us everyday.

This love's the answer to all my dreams,
And you're my dream come true.
This love will permeate our lives
And keep me close to you.

Laura Tesoro Liccketto

Abandoned

The bars swing wide and he's shoved inside, on a cold damp floor
made of stone. He whimpers and cries to anyone who can hear,
please don't cast me out and put me in this place all alone.

He longs for a home and someone to care, and to lie upon a warm
soft rug by the fire, a few crumbs from their table is all he
would ask, just a pat on his head would warm his heart, and help
him to forget his troubled past.

In dreams he chases butterflies in soft green grass, with
sunlight dancing across his happy face, then the loud barks and
the soft meows down the way, brings him back to reality and this
sad lonely place.

Down the corridor he hears all the cries from his fellow
creatures you see, will this be the day the visitors will come,
and a little boy or girl, will take me home with them and adopt me.

Rosalie Adams

Mother

My Mother is the one you see, she gave me life
and taught me what it means. She brings
laughter to my face, when my world seems gloom
she helps me place, what's right or wrong,
she makes me strong.
She's been around since I was born, she is the
star I do adore.
As a child, I remember the days, she held
my hand and helped me stand. Many a days
that came and went, she was there
my faithful friend,
She wasn't always at her best, some times
she needed more than rest.
I'll never fill those shoes of gold, but in my
heart her ways I'll hold. Now a mother,
the years have past, but through my memories
my mom was grand.

Francesca D'Angelo

New Life

Don't curse your fate,
and don't curse "God" for
what was sent your way.

All though you are in pain,
"God" is with you all the way,
"He" is guiding you day by day.

You think it's the end,
but really only the beginning
of "New Life" without pain.

You won't pass-a-way and life end
it's the day you'll be reborn to
begin again.

Your body is a shell for everyone to see,
but your spirit continues for "eternity."

Do not despair because of some
injustice done to you!

"His" light will come shining through,
and there will be "new life" for you!

Wilma Richardson

Searching

Banish the poison from your heart
Let the sunshine kiss your soul
The darkness in your heart will vanish
Fervent lips of life and love will find you
And love shall triumph.

Heinz Lietz

The Man Unknown

Transcend the foe of the man unknown,
For victory shant be his.
Friends disowned, parents were said dead,
And a stranger in the night be his only friend.
Believing in the everlasting,
Dying by a grave.
His footprints lay in the newly fallen snow,
Soon to be lost forever by the wintry wind.
The man no more had dignity, self-respect, and pride.
What made the man lose all he had was,
He was the foe, of The Man Unknown.

Andrea Moravec

My Roller Skating Coach

He knows some students can be witches
He keeps you in and out of stitches
Handling people with gentleness
Always displaying his humbleness

During your lesson he is attuned
Sometimes inquiring about your wound
His patients/patience he sometimes has to rejuvenate
The outcome is never second rate
His wit...no one could duplicate!

His sense of humor is like no other
And when he decides to torment you...Oh brother!
From work to sport there is always a smooth transition
For you see, he is also a physician

Carol Lynn Hutchinson

Heart Finds A New Home

The nights are long laying awake
How much longer is it going to take
To find me a heart, so I may live
To do some good with all the love I can give

I need the time to show my family I care
The thought of leaving them I cannot bear
They mean so much and deserve all my love
For they stand with me and pray to God above

The doctors and nurses know my pain
But with my family I see the sunshine through the rain
My family gives me strength, especially my wife
She guides me through all the trouble and strife

God has blessed me in many ways
But, I sat and waited for many days
To receive from God a new start
And now he has blessed me with a new heart

Thomas F. Nairn

I'm Still The Same

Take my heart, take my life,
Please remove the twisting knife.
Every word you have said, turns the knife,
I'm almost dead.
Your cruel unkind words,
Echo in my brain,
Making me go completely insane.

Take my soul, take my pain,
Leave me normal, keep me sane.
Take the words of disrespect and shame,
Be proud of who I am,
I'm Still The Same

Jason Tiller

Combat

The blood is red upon the sand
As soldiers fight and take a stand.
A stand for what someone might say.
Perhaps it's just to get their way.

Belief in what their leader said,
Will lead them to what lies ahead.
With guns raised up in fear and pain,
They charge the beach as one insane.

And on the other side they too
Are poised, gun ready, to pursue.
They, too, take aim and fire away.
Many young men will die today.

The scene repeats throughout the world
As others with no flag unfurled.
Kill because of their Ethnic hate
Victims die in this needless fate.

Whether for good or wrongful cause,
The pain's still felt and one gives pause
Wondering in this earthly din,
For why this mankind's carnage sin?

Wilma Spaur Wood

You Are

You are the alpha and the omega,
The beginning and the end.
You are the great I am.
You are the Lily in the valley.
You are the rose of Sharon.
You are the true and living God.
You are the prince of peace.
You are the mighty counselor.
You are the bright and morning star.
You are the Lord of Lords.
You are the King of Kings
You are a shelter in a time of storms.
You are a bridge over troubled waters.
You are a solid rock.
You are the lover of my soul.
You are worthy of the highest praise.
You are God and besides you there is no other,
Nor is there none like you,
For you are!!!

Nedra Mohammed

Aging

We all recall times as a tot,
    when asked our age, we lied a lot!
If queried when we were barely seven,
    we'd like to say, "almost eleven!"
Or. . .use of fractions brings a laugh,
    remember saying, "Twelve and a half?"
As years spun on, we became quite sage,
    awaiting our long-sought "driving age!"
Then when marriage became a fixture,
    older age crept in the picture.
Weddings were the things to do,
    and raising kids, a facet too!
Time really seemed to go quite wild,
    when asked the age of your eldest child!
Its age had reached a figure high,
    so now again, we're forced to lie!
Your offspring true, had reached a stage,
    that is referred to, as "middle aged!"
So-oh, "Golden Years" should not be shunned,
    but please enjoy them While You're Young!

Walter F. Bandelow

To Thomas — My Love

As love takes flight on winged things,
my soul rejoices as my heart sings.

With happiness over something so right
how could love like this help but not take flight?

On wings of honesty, truth and admiration
with gentle consistent, tender cultivation.

As trust builds hope...Faith in believing
as only time will continue revealing...

Un-dying respect and open communication
all built on a friendship firm foundation.

Strong enough to stand, yet un-afraid to fall.
Not always eye to eye, but together through it all.

Leaning on each other. Caring for each others hearts.
Mental emotional support when together or apart.

With mind, heart and soul, giving credit where it's due,
by thanking the Lord above...for blessing you with me...with you.

So as we build each other up, we ask the Lord above
to strengthen us in faith and perfect us in love.

As life stacks the deck we draw yet another card.
Precious words on a page in a Bible my love...Lean Hard!

T. J. Thompson

Unknown Soldiers

We are the unnamed; we died in wars supposedly civil;
Wars with the World, In Asia, and on Native Soil;
We mourn the loss of our names and identities,
yet we know who we are!
We understand the honors our bodies portray;
Entombed in this marble sepulcher, our Souls
feel the steps of our Guardians, the keepers of the Spirit;
We have wondered among ourselves, why behavior never changes;
We all agree that what is wrong, is war itself;
It takes not care of the World's woes;
All in all Death Doth Win, and societies youth he doth mow;
We've tried so hard to tell you, the answer we have found;
When you open up the Sepulcher, to add another of the war torn;
Yet, we are the Unknown, the Dead, the Lost, the Unwanted;
No more the Enemy, the Deserter, the Unrecognizable;
Now we are the Unknown Soldiers of Arlington, never forgotten;
You may mourn our loss, but We Cry For You!!!

Michael Walter Sunday

Oh Father

"Oh father, oh father what new for me"
"My son, sit down and let me see"
"I just turned ten father, play with me"
"I am very busy my son, can't you see"
"This ball given from you to me, please my father,
    please play with me"
"I need no more comments, I am busy, can't you see".

"Oh father, oh father I am home once again
    cheering and smiling for the time to spend"
"I am old and I am weak, there is no way I can speak"
"I just earned my fame father, please speak to me"
"I need no words, there is no way I can speak"
"Then I leave you father once again, maybe next time
    you'll have time to spend".

"Oh son, oh son lend me your ear, I haven't spoken or
    expressed for sixty-five years"
"My dear father, I have kids of my own, I have no
    time for you know"
"But my son please, just for a little while"
"I'm sorry father, but I must go, go for a while".

Chad Lyman

Hope Of Peace...

Oh peace you live in every one of us, like a cherished dream
An aspiration, a thirst for well being, peaceful surrounding
We hope for you, we pray for you
May the sunrise of your glory
Melt our anger, appease our fears, dried our tears
Warm and charm our hearts
Like a brilliant gem
That our eyes will never regal of his ravishing beauty
Made peace your loving little children
Give us toy of brotherhood, games of parenthood
Let us rest our head on your shoulder, our arms around your neck
Like a expression of tenderness
We love to hear you say.
Children I was always near you
Hoping you could see me too
Look at my face, there is not a single wrinkle
Of treachery or trickery
Take us Mother for a lasting trip
By sea of offering hands to a virgin land...

Gilberte Brown

Keeper Of Stone Park

Take me up
Where your thoughts are high
To a point of land beyond reach,
So I may build you a house amongst the stars
With a kettle drummer in your back yard.

You know the house, the fireplace is you,
Kitchen, and yes, bedroom,
Even the woodshed, if you like.
The carpets are made of flowers,
Zinnias to give away.

Our neighbors have constellation names,
And only visit every hundred thousand years or so.
The light from our porch can be seen
By any young boy with a telescope, riding the moon
Down the dawn's horizon, before we turn out the light.

Hurry, come along, let's go there now
Before the sun comes up, before the toads
Cease their marching song, before we
Discover we're not her all alone
Amongst the stars.

Jarrett Buys

For The Love Of Me

He conquered sin and death for us
To give us lasting life,
In heaven sharing bliss with Him
Instead of eternal strife.

But how many people are really touched
By His suffrage on the way,
Or feel the blood of sweat run down
His brow that fateful day.

Who can say they cry for Him
And want to share His pain,
Or love their fellow neighbors
Showing He didn't die in vain.

He's never hurt a living soul
For He was peaceful as a dove,
But He's damned and cursed from day to day.
This gentle man of love.

So let's amend our ways and show Him
We're not a total loss,
For suffering pain no man could bear —
For us upon the cross.

Louise E. Fogell

Mother

A tribute to my mother. Doris Ada Talbot

Those caring hands and loving eyes,
Stay in my heart from year to year;
Her cheery days hid weary nights
And helped ,me grow up without fear.

The endless hours of toil and care;
Loves details found in little things
Like, "Brush your teeth," and "Comb your hair;"
-What comfort every memory brings.

And as the years have quickly passed,
Rememb'ring her with blessed thought,
Her spirit lingers with still;
The legacy her life has brought.

A mother now of forty years,
My children's children growing strong -
In life and character and gifts
The glories all to her belong.

Ada Church

Rain

Pitter patter as the rain it falls
Fond memories it usually recalls
From the wind in the night a song that is blurred
From the trees and the birds these words unheard
Mother Nature is crying, is crying a tear
Drawing you closer to enfold you near
She kisses the ground with a sparkle of gleam
It's prettier than your wildest dream
The grass given chance to quench its thirst
After the flowers have been nourished first
She cleans all the dirt and soot off the streets
These tears Mother Nature repeats and repeats
After all the good that she does do
In a round about way it is for you
So what right do either you or I
Have all these things outside to deny
The pleasing thoughts of the coming rain
Just to please ourselves and be so vain
Let it rain, Let it rain, Let it rain.

Arlene Zecca

Mommie

How wonderful it is
To be blessed with you
A mother, a friend
So dear and so true.

No matter what life decisions I make
Or which of life's roads I choose to take
Whether my choices are good or bad
You only shrug your shoulders, and never get mad.

You are my foundation
The pillars of my being
You've taught me responsibility
And how to keep believing.

So I salute you today
This very special one
My beautiful mother
The day you were born.

Kimberly S. Brown

God's Ways

How great is God on any day
True and strong come what may
What is man but crumb and clay
Must he rage and roar
Without praise and honor to Him
In whom all ownership resides
All his strength will reduce to cries
Yet mercy and forgiveness always
stand ready
Each moment for the asking
But many leave it behind
Never knowing hell and horror beckon them
All because they could not
reckon with His ways.

Beth Turner

Water Fall

I love those summer thunderstorms,
which just materialize.
And transform lazy afternoons,
with dark and threatening skies.

And then the clouds, as if an cue,
begin to swirl and race.
As distant claps of thunder,
seem to meter out the pace.

Once gentle breeze, now bends the trees,
as though they were but cane,
While bringing forth to all they touch,
the cool, sweet scent of rain.

With brilliant, blinding flashes,
an awe-inspiring sight.
The lightning spreads its fingers,
through the heavens dark as night.

And as the tempo quickens,
and the rains begin to fall,
One cannot help but contemplate,
the beauty of it all!

Robert A. Logrie Jr.

If I Opened Up My Heart to You

If I opened up my heart to you
let you see the side I hide away
would you always be there for me will
you still want to stay
When I wake with tear stained eyes in
the middle of the night would you hold me
gently and tell me everything's all right
If I told you all my dreams and secrets that
I keep in a place of their own will you
understand me more or would you leave me
all alone
Now that I've let you know all the things I fear
will you laugh out loud or whisper "It's okay"
softly in my ear
There are so many things I'd like to share with you
this is how I really feel
These words I say are
true

Anthony O. Giovannelli

Time To Make It Right

My beautiful black children; put down your fears.
Your fathers have heard them for many years.
We know it's sad, because many of us are out of sight.
But a million of us have marched in Washington to make it right.
You see my beautiful black children we never ran away.
But some of us were young and scared, and afraid to stay.
Now is the time for all fathers to no longer roam,
But to find your loved ones and come on home.
My beautiful black children,
Hold your heads up high.
Be proud, stand straight.
Together we fly.
For having a good father, you'll see love
That is strong and will never die.

Jeffery P. Jones

Close To My Heart

You're always in my heart.
You're always on my mind.
If we were to part,
truer friends I could not find.

Your friendships are dear to me.
As friends we'll never part.
I now see,
you're close to my heart.

Each of us will go
her own separate way.
I'll always know
some words we don't have to say.

A friendship is an art
that must be perfected over time,
and ours will remain close to my heart,
for it is a friendship that is truly sublime.

Nicole Roskov

Shall A Nation Survive While Such Prevail?

Pork barrel out of empty coffers
Stolen from homeless, hungry eyes
Justice fraught with human flaws
Black robes flaunting Godly laws
Ripping thunderous wails from mothers' wombs.
Shall a nation survive while such prevail?

Misdeeds blamed on personal "devils,"
Entertainment at gutter levels
Sitting presidential scandals masked
By liberal and adoring media.
Noble stance for national good gone
Shall a nation survive while such prevail?

Compassionate giving through private sector
Purse strings guarded by deficit hawks
Each one reaching out to others
Wise, honest, scandal-free government
Human life once more cherished, protected
Through such a nation shall prevail!

Jay McRoberts

Artist

The gifted ones seem to be wounded angles
Never fitting the charade this world offers,
full of stigmas and people living in raw sewage.
Brush and paint never journey across the canvas of their lives.
Some are sad songs, lonely teardrops hanging on a beam of sunshine.
So many they touch, chanting their spirituality,
Their art is a doorway to see, feel and taste love.
It's lonely having a gift from God,
having to tuck one's ample soul through the eye of a needle,
surviving in a world where they feel they don't belong.

Anthony J. Williams

A Certain Stillness

A certain stillness surrounds this scene
(A homicidal void as yet unfilled),
Which seems to favor demonic deeds:
The murderer lifts the knife to strike —
The dying choke on their blood to plead.
All of Heaven dare not look to see
When a lost soul cannot wait to flee.
But Stillness cannot cloak the rage
Against the light of now fallen prey —
Their roles, shortened by the silent blade.
The murderer's fate — a private shame
When Death takes him from this earth-bound stage.

Lawrence Darrell

The Muse of Dance

Such beauty, gracefulness and talent.
Can she be a mere woman or is
she something more?

Does she sense my amorous, admiring gaze?
What ethereal pleasure to see her
swaying like a Leegarya in a
gentle breeze.

Lissome one, will you be the center
of my solar system?
Can I orbit around you absorbing
your life giving warmth and light?

Panos Kokkoros

Remembering You

The pictures of you that I hang from my wall
Create the tears of heartbreak as they start to fall
I never knew a love could end so fast
But now our relationship is a memory of the past
We had our good times and also the bad
But our relationship was the best I ever had.

At night I look up in the sky and always end up asking why
I look up at the moon and out way far
And I'll write your name on every star
You cheated me and I cheated you
But we both knew that's not what we wanted to do
Then something happened and I don't know why
And I still don't know the reason you died
You took your life and that meant to me
You were very unhappy and wanted to be free
I still always remember the day you came to me
And asked me if I wanted to be your bride-to-be
That day never came but another thing did
And you would've loved him if you only had lived
He'll never get to meet you but he knows it's true
That no other daddy is more special than you
But even now that we'll be forever apart
Just always remember that you're the one in my heart.

Ronda Hawes

Winter Window

Fields of white lay under night,
like clouds across the sky.
Silence screams from within,
its echo's fill the air.
Tender doilies lace the trees,
heavy on the boughs.
A soft still descends over the land
to dream a different dream.
Shadows can not cast their light,
upon the brightness of this winter's night.

J. D. Harper

Special Friend

I spread my wings and hope to find.
Someone friendly always caring always kind.
A special friend to share my life.

I looked so far and couldn't see that she
was standing next to me. Work brought us
together it must be true, because I found
a special friend in you.

They say friends are forever I don't know
if it's all true but I will take my chance
with you. And only time will tell if a true
friendship is there.

I don't know when the friendship began.
But I hope and pray it will never end.
And if in time we drift away, I'll look back
and remember and cherish all the
moments that we've shared.

And one more thing to my
special friend, that I'll always
care and love you until the end.

Ruth O. Garza

Wedding Presents

(They Received Seven Double Boilers)

I wracked my brain and beat my head
To think of a gift when you were wed,
Then I decided to use my nerve
And visit your home, where I could observe.
If I had not found that you did not possess
A cross cut saw, cotton gin or lard press,
A turning lathe or a hog oiler,
I'd doubtless have sent a double boiler.
So off I went with money to invest
In things I thought you both could use best,
And because I love you like brother and sister
Here's to Jane and John, Missus and Mister.

Lucille Crawford

Why Do You Do This

How can you hurt the ones that care the most about you,
Why must so many others pay for what you believe you must do,
Are drugs the only things that make you feel good?
Have you not learned anything from the past, many had hoped that
   you would,
When you're out running the street,
Does the thought occur to you, that your children have nothing to
   eat,
Those that care about you so much, can only try,
To help when they are able, while your children can only cry,
Nothing is sacred that you wouldn't sell,
Everyone knows that when you do drugs, things aren't going well,
You became a different person, it's plain to see,
What are you children learning, what are you doing to me,
Have you not seen enough, of how drugs will end
Haven't you found out yet, who to call friend,
Does the expression on your children's face mean anything to you,
How can you possibly expect them to keep loving you,
There are many that care, why don't you know,
Apparently it's not mutual, for you treat them like so,
Perhaps one day you'll wake up, maybe too late,
And realize that those who love you, just couldn't wait.

Louis Graziaplena

The Storm

The sky was cloudy, the clouds were black,
With streaks of white mixed in the back.
There was going to be a storm, no doubt of that.
Then came a sudden vivid flash,
Followed by a tremendous crash,
It shook the ground with an unearthly power,
Till everything moved from tree to flower.
The children all ran to get out of the rain.
A young boy slipped and shrieked with pain.
As the darkening clouds towered overhead,
This is storm, they all would dread.
Finally the storm was moving away,
The children all thought it time to play.
Spreading across the sky so bright,
The biggest rainbow, a beautiful sight.
The children would never forget the birth of
The bright of the terrible storm that
Shook the earth.

Jean Montgomery

Her Majesty, The Marbled Cat

With east of mind I languish here
among the bubbles of bath,
breathing the heavy air
and petting the marbled cat.

The steam makes hazy the everything
as it floats in the cubicle room
and the marbled cat begins to sing
in a gurgling purr of a tune.

She lay on her back to stretch and reach
but nary a yawn she'll speak.
She rolls and turns and bids me scratch
her belly, and give it a tweak.

As the bath water cools about me
I tell the kitty to scat!!!
but she keeps on purring with glee,
that self-absorbed marbled cat.

I towel myself dry as I stand in the tub
looking down at kitty on the mat.
Another cold bath for the sake of a rub
for her majesty the marbled cat.

William C. Hardwick

My Dad

Dad, you were a "Giant of a man"
You were farmer, Blacksmith, and builder
Not very tall, physically, but tall to me!
If God would grant one wish you again, I'd see!

Together you and mother raised a family,
And taught us to earn our way
when your work was done You'd find time to take me on your knee
You gave me love for books.
Dear Dad - your above all to me!

God gave you a long long life
Tho old age without mother
Wasn't what you'd of ask for - it wasn't fair!
I think so often of my youth
Of your beautiful eyes and curly hair!

Dear Dad I see you in my children
And in our grand children
The same large eyes and curly hair
I think you're looking down
You and my long lost mother
I just can't wait to see you there!

Muriel McIntire Jr.

The Night Calls

The night calls to me beckoning with its promise of rest
And I am so tired now from all the day's tests.
My weary body will lie upon the soft bed
While the down pillow will cradle my head.
It has been so many hours since I arose from my place
Joyful and eager of the day ahead to face.
The morning was fresh with the scent of new life
And my tasks, although hard, seemed incredibly light.
By noon I was ready to taste of life's fruit
To nourish myself through the long afternoon.
My tasks though seemed more difficult somehow;
What was easy in the morning weighed hard on me now.
I met the challenge of those long hours I faced
And I'm sorry to say not always with grace
But I feel I did accomplish everything I could
And not just merely what I should.
The shadows grow longer now and the children are long asleep,
I hear the night calling me, beckoning me to its keep
To where I can finally lie upon my soft bed
And have the down pillow cradle my head.

Nancy L. Strander

Libbie Bacon-Custer

Libbie Bacon-Custer, and her husband George,
Left their home in Michigan,
Heading for western shores.

Settling the West, opening land for all,
Libbie Bacon-Custer, army wife, did not stall,
Leaving home and comforts,
Following the call, to aid her husband George.

Furnishing log cabins, adding cheer,
Buffalo hunting, Indian fighting would be near,
Hardships in Winter, she did not fear,
For dear husband George, was there.

Libbie Bacon-Custer, only daughter of a judge,
Left her home and family,
Living in army tents and then,
She would be first to see,
What splendid sights would be,
In the settling, of the great Western Plains!

Julie Ann LaHood

The Gentle Touch

Your skin is like silk
Your eyes are like diamonds
Your face is like the sun which sets in my heart
Your heart is as deep as the ocean ever flowing gently across my
    fingertips
Reaching, grabbing, but maybe it is all a fantasy

Yet I know it feels so real

One day your heart will flow from my tips
and land softly across my gentle lips.

Timothy J. Fitzwilliams

Soft Snowfall

Some trees are wearing chain mail,
And some, warm caps and mittens!
A few are covered and round as kittens!
Others have armor of silv'ry lame,
And one, just a powdery, lacy beret!
Is it all in tree-shape and texture of bark?
When the snow comes down in gentle sail...
Only the breeze can say for sure
It blows where it will, as it feels the lure!

Virginia Pease Ewersen

Winter Evening

The wind goes whistling down the cold and lonely valley,
Playing with the pines and the birches that it sways,
Dark clouds are gathering silently, swiftly,
One with the clamoring rough stormy days.

Out o'er the tree tops crows call to another,
Far over the sea a gull cries out to its mate,
In the warm room behind me a boy laughs with his father,
A fire of rich pinewood burns low in the grate.

Those high stars that circle the steep mountain crest
Are one with the clouds and the light of the sky,
The fish that slip gleaming like opal and silver
Are one with the streams that flow silently by.

In my little back room tall shadows are leaping,
To play with the firelight that flickers and gleams,
Hid in dim corners great words lie a sleeping,
Awaiting the touch to give life to my dreams.

Andy Marshall

Inner Beauty, True Beauty

To me, what makes a person beautiful
is how they are inside
To me, what makes a person ugly
is how they are inside
But we are so caught up with
what's on the outside
We are so caught up with perfecting
what's on the outside

We are obsessed with looking pretty
pretty people don't make a difference in the world
smart people make a difference in the world
kind people make a difference in the world
caring people
humble people
thoughtful people
compassionate people
These are the people who make a difference in the world

If we don't work to perfect what's on the inside
we will become men and women with the faces of angels
and hearts of stone.

Laurentz D. Beckford

In Memory Of My Brother Robert

I don't have much he ever gave
Material things - for me to save
Except a rose from off his grave.
But I have other things to see
In memory of him and me.

Of childhood days - the musty smell
Of cave - and pigeons - old deep well;
Of puppies - secrets not to tell;
Of tadpoles, snakes, an old tin cup;
Of Christmas - playthings - growing up.

Parks and picnics - flying kites;
Springs and Summers - wintry nights;
Sleigh rides, prayers, pillow fights,
Haircuts, new teeth, storms and toads;
Back to school down dusty roads.

Quarreling, tramping new - mown hay;
Grown-up talk - too old for play questions, answers, what to say;
Bow ties, girls - books to read; autumns - lilacs gone to seed.

These gifts are treasures none can see
Or touch or feel or know but me.

Rose Ann Dunlap

The Fuzz

Pigs
Oink, Oink
Love to arrest Punks
I wish they were gone!
Can't be Fair
Eternally cruel

Beat on innocent people.
Refuse to be fair
Unfair Judgment
Take drugs from people.
And then attempt to sell them back to people.
Love to inhale doughnut
I hate most of them
Tough on kids like us
You can't trust them at all!!!

Michael Schwart

Winter's Journey

Winter she comes...
and brings home all the lies springtime
promised.
Her crystalline lights dancing off the
snow no longer bring the sparkle to my eyes
they once did
Reflecting,
Life,
Love,
Laughter.
Instead she now diminishes them.
Blinds me with her brilliance, her
radiance.
As she freezes so do my feelings.
Her long, icy, fingers wrapped around
me much too tightly;
I find no matter what I do, I
can not generate enough warmth to melt them
To escape...

K. A. Barber

From Where I Sit

The cold wind ruffles through the trees
Just as it touches your nose you sneeze
The seagulls squawk in the air
As the young ones in their nest play

The wind ruffles the water in to waves
As they rushes to shore
you can see small fish in the bay

As I look up in the clear blue sky
I can see the planes
As they go swiftly by

Over the pier with the boats at quay
I can see the fishermen
As they take their catch to bay

Oh how lovely it has been this February day
If only people took sometime to pray

Anthony S. Benjamin

Faces

Two faces in one
Staring back at me
An expression of love
Made flesh my eyes
His nose, my lips, his
toes, my hair, his ears
our love so real, so
dear.

Carla L. West

Untitled

Puppy broke the dish but they didn't see.
Now I'm sittin' in the corner feelin' sorry for me.

Big brown eyes saw the frown on my face.
Long floppy ears heard my fall from grace.

Puppy barked once, puppy growled twice.
He chomped on my finger and he wasn't very nice.

He peeked under my arm and he tugged on my pants.
He jumped up and down doin' his puppy dance.

Puppy gave up. Called it a day.
He finally understood that we couldn't play.

Closed my eyes, leaned back in the chair,
and my foot got warm while I was sittin' there.

I'll get blamed like I always do,
but it was puppy that peed on my left shoe.
Joe W. Allen

Dad

You are so very dear to me, able to comfort me when
times seemed too unbearable.
You held me not only physically but emotionally.
You were always truthful and faithful.
You were my dad . . .
I will always remember you . . .
Your sense of humor, of always being there.
The knowing that we all belonged together.
Your love for life was enchanting.
You moved me, supplied me with inner strength.
I witnessed the understanding and love you shared with mom.
Two people so very much in love.
A love so warm you both would glow.
You were my dad . . .
You are gone . . .
I hope you see through my eyes, to my soul,
to the soul of your daughter,
who loved you deeply and misses you.
You were my dad.
Debra Hoffman

The Poor Fish

Your performance was magnificent, your acting divine.
You sure know how to master your proven line.
I was the poor fish who swallowed and found out too late.
You stood on the shore of life and threw out the bait.
I took what you offered — hook, line and sinker.
I learned my lesson too late, and you proved quite the stinker.
You looked me over, gave my heart a big whirl,
And led me to believe, I was the only girl.
And after you saw how you convinced my loving heart,
You threw me back into the water; seems we're oceans apart.
I go on swimming in the sea of memories so blue.
The fisherman's long gone, and the fisherman was you.
My heart is so tired, for I have longed much too long.
If you were to throw out your line once more, would I be strong?
Fisherman, fisherman, you fish no more.
I'm in the sea; you're somewhere on the shore!
Dorothy Husar Krosky

In My Mind

A life time of sleep. Content in the world I'd like to keep.
  Travelling to distant lands, feeling so deep.
A place of great importance, embrace the slow entrance.
  It wades in my spine, working all the time.
    I'm all alone; only in my mind.
Ian Carr

Child Of Abuse

In the silence I stand screaming
  Though I never make a sound.
I can't stand this constant pressure
  Though no causes can be found.
The heart is beating wildly,
  Blood pumping through my veins,
Nothing now is hurting me,
  So why the tremendous pain?
I can't seem to think too clearly,
  Confused, distorted, is the mind.
So many endless feelings
  Jumbled up inside, entwined.
How can this all be sorted through
  So life makes some kind of sense?
Can't bear this state for too much longer
  Because the feelings are too intense.
So in silence I stand screaming
  Never making any sound.
Just can't stand the constant pressure
  For no causes can be found!
Katherine E. McGaughey

Moon Pictures

Have you seen a picture of the moon
  as it shines on the meadow
  and dancers swing to and fro?

Have you seen a picture of the moon
  as it outlines the skiers
  and they fly through the snow?

Have you seen a picture of the moon
  as it gleams on the apple blossoms
  and casts a fluorescent glow?

Have you seen a picture of the moon
  as it highlights the lovers
  and they sing, "I love you so"?

Yes, I have seen all these pictures of the moon
  as it rises slowly in the sky
  and shines down on us in sublime splendor.
Dorothy Nandresy

The Lesson

Tonight as I retire I think of the past,
the lessons I learned I know that will last.
The deeper I dig a better me I see,
forever is lost—the old one called me.
A new flower has blossomed, a radiant glow seen,
I'll grow and I'll flourish and come to full bloom,
with more knowledge and learning, my memories will zoom.

As they lay sleeping my mind it still goes,
from out of this thorn bush a bountiful rose.
So no one can tell me that I am not smart,
for once in my life I looked in my heart,
and found there is treasure more precious than gold...
Because as long as I have memory by lessons I've learned.

So stand by my side and wish me good will,
for by writing my feelings, my dreams become real,
and will out power the bad that roams the earth,
and I know the meaning, the meaning of worth.
Sandra Bauer

Be You My Brethren?

The time is nigh.
Can't thou not feel it?
E'en now the trumpets sound o'er the mountains and across the
plains. Can't thou not hear it?
What shalt thou do?
Wouldn't thou but run inside and lock thy doors?
I for one shall gather my family.
And upon the soil that we have tilled for over a century
will I wait for the coming of the host.
For I know it is the host of the Lord our High God.
And I would gladly greet him upon that field.
But lo! Hurry away I must,
for I wish to gather as many of my brethren
as is humanly possible.
But ere I go, I would ask of this of thee.
Be you one?

> *Y. L. Henry*

Crayons In The Sky

We are crayons in the sky
Pictorial transformations passing by
Pushed by mother nature's hand
Circling the world, allegiance to no land
Floating on air of billowing softness
A front-row seat designed for incredible loftiness
Meandering the sky's highways as we go
Touched by wonder in our tow
Lingering moments to hang around
Playing leapfrog with rainbows far above the ground
How long the journey, we do not know
The perception of it all, mysterious as we blow
Calm winds the smoothest to ride
Fleece to cover the tempest we cannot hide
Memories of yesterdays gone by
A glimpse of tomorrow, expectations flying high
Carved from a bigger picture drawn by fate
Tributaries in clusters, binding life for generations in wait.

> *Carolyn Bruns*

Mother

M is for the many ways you show your love for me!
O is for the overwhelmingly loving mother that you turned out to be!
T is for the tenderness only a mother could give.
H is for the happy home you've made for me to live!
E is everything you've done for me, how will I ever repay?
R is for the rareness that is in your loving way!

   As years pass on, and I grow older, I become more fully
aware, how much I love my mother, and how no one could ever
compare!!!!

> *Domanick Angelaca Barthlein*

Waiting Bairn's Periscope

Here I lay in heavenly bliss
When on my cheek, an angel plants a kiss.
My periscope open to such a glorious glare,
As the face of my carrier looked back and stare.
She feels nervous as she thinks about my life
But she needs not to worry, I will live by her advice.

Her face appears to be tired but yet calm
A look that is ready to take on my paths harm.
I can tell that trust and love will be there for me
Because of the warmth in her eyes I can see.
The happiness and joy in her smile
Lets me know my birth is worth my while.

> *Daniel A. Bell*

Good-Bye

I wanted to see him but was afraid.
Tasting the salty tears for two days had made me thirsty.
More tears. Tissue boxes strategically located on tables.
The air conditioning was dry. Rooms were hazily lit.

As more people arrived I drifted from him.
My tears gave way to laughter, smiles.
People I didn't know knew me.
Family I'd never met. A friend I hadn't seen in years.
Outside was hot with Jacob, Matt, and Mary.
Thank God for Mary, we were alone.

Cold dry air again.
Final good-byes. I waited for my turn.
Sue knelt, I heard sobs, Ann hugged her, tissues in hand.
Lips trembling I kissed him.
The shock sent me into hysterics.
He was cold for the first time.
The fabric of suit lapel sopped up my tears
as gentle arms encompassed me.

> *Ann Elizabeth Tillman*

Fallen Stars

As darkness comes near
My vision becomes unclear
There is nothing more to follow
No more hopes or dreams to swallow
All the goals and ambitions wiped out
As I stand confused and full of doubt

I will need to stand tall and not fear this
Event though those dreams I will miss
I must start to burn a new light
That will lead me away from the darkness of night
With this I can stand proud again
Instead of wondering "what could have been"

If I ever begin to doubt this new light
Then the darkness will have won the fight
With this doubt there will be no hope for me as a man
If all I say I "I wish can"
Each day I believe and grow strong
This belief will steer me away from thoughts that are wrong

This struggle I must face alone
And the obstacles I will face are yet unknown

> *Edward Estes*

Afterthoughts

You twist beneath me,
Rustles the sheet
Into which our form sank so deeply,
Lifts the cover, of darkness,
Morning sun, first rays,
Golden fingertips that caress
A shadow from engulfing me
As your eyes pierced the darkness
Just hours before.

Pillow peeks from beneath locks
Strewn into exotic patterns
That shimmer with the new morning.

This, the pay off for a night raised on dreams
To gaze upon your slumb'ring form
Gained in beauty each passing moment
Turns longer as a leg, arm shifts in silence
That fills my head as the loudest music
Revels about my admiring ears.

A stir. Don't wake, not yet.
This moment deserves to flourish.

> *Doug Drowley*

The Trembling Time

The lightning sounded like it cracked the earth in two.
That splitting sound shook the room.
I knew that my life was about to change.
My life about to meet Doom.

And since that time of the trembling,
My lover left me crying.
For now my lover lives in Russia;
And now my heart is dying.

Erin Elizabeth Moyer

The Touch

There's hell to pay for the touch
one which grasps children by their unsuspecting fates
one that chokes age-old truths into current, modern lies
one which tries to understand your pleas,
yet ignores them out of pure ignorance.
The touch molests your mind and soul as well as body
making you feel alone and distraught
in a world of pure hatred
in a world of too much grief.
The touch makes you afraid,
it makes you cringe for your life.

Huddled in a corner of a dark, dreary alley
is a boy who is scared, afraid of a black death
that may not agree with his born-to-be wild trait
but with the touch, who cares?
The boy looks out at a pure, unsuspecting girl
running down the sidewalk
soon to feel the touch.

Jason Cantone

Shields

When light of truth seemed forbidden.
I built a shield, to keep it hidden.
My shield I covered with knotted lies.
To hide this shield, from my own eyes.
With passing time the lies felt true.
The shields they covered, forgotten too.
Until one day while searching self.
I found in mind, on a dusty shelf.
Useless tangles of knotted lies.
Cutting those knots, now seemed wise.
As I cut and cleansed there it stood.
The shield I built, when sure of good.
Without the lies to give it place.
My shield and I, face to face.
Truths locked inside now brought pain.
Lies and shields, the real bain.
Truth about lies is good and bad.
Truths behind shields, are great and sad.
Behind my shield truth continued to grow.
Nearly surpassing, my ability to know!

Donald Southards

To Duffy - Only A Dog!

But where else do I find a friend,
Who can match what I desire!
Whose demands are very, very few,
And without his love - what would I do?
Whose head will snuggle under your hand,
And the wage of his tail, will beat any band!
There is no reproach - he will lick with his tongue,
He sooths with the sick, he sure does belong!
Our moments together - it sets me thinkin'
Being without him - has my eyes blinkin'!

Oliver L. Morgan

To My Grieving Wife

For whom do you grieve, my love
For she who has gained eternal peace
Or do you grieve for those who must make do
With her memories, till they too find release.
For whom do you grieve, my love
For she who lived a good full life
Whose hours were filled with the busy pace
Of being physician, friend, mother and wife.
Her days on this earth were truly well-spent
Many lives touched by her gentle grace
Many patients comforted by her healing touch
Their spirits revived by her smiling face.
So why do you grieve, my love
We are players on the Milky Way stage
And some of us leave but hardly a ripple
Some sorrow, some anger, some rage.
Your mother, my love, was the gentle rain
who nourished the earth, trees great and small
She has found her rest in the ocean of time
So grieve not my love, celebrate.

Sabi Singh

The Apple Tree

I left him asleep under an apple tree, eyes closed tightly.
His soft hair was blown by the wind.
No sound except the sounds of wind chimes,
little clinking objects of tin.
The paled face turned towards the sky,
shaded by the beautiful tree.
Eyes closed so tightly against fate,
so desperate to be free.
I left him asleep under the tree,
until the bearers came.
No longer safe under the apple tree.
All in all, it was for the same.
Asleep he was laid to rest.
Held in the Gentle Mother's hold.
Objects of wonder no longer pondered,
the mind was already old.
I left him asleep, forever lost.
The dreams of life long spent.
Folded closed with the future,
just as he had been sent.

Brandy Marie Seiler

Abstract Soul

   Deluded fears of betrayal,
the spirit expires within. The misery so
abstract, the suffering soul cries out.
   The shattered semblance of reality
quietly retreats. The delusions of deception
conquer the absent oblique core.
   The twisted matter churns and groans,
the abscess within emerges. The ultimate
vengeance now composed, impede the
blood from flowing.
   One last cry for help unnoticed, one
last cry for mercy heard. One last breath
then darkness nears, the life is
barren forever.
   The anguish soul set free, plague
no more by affliction. Those who are left
behind, crushed and bewildered, wonder
why?
   If only someone had listened.

Mary Fisher

Convertible, With Rumble Seat

Convertibles today, are modern and sleek,
While some of their predecessors, had a rumble seat.
How many girls can imagine the joy,
Of sharing an old-time rumble seat with a boy;
Enjoying the wind and the rain, as well as the sun,
The world flies by, and everything's fun.
Snuggled together for warmth, and for love,
Twinkling lights, and at night, stars above.
People so friendly, they'd wave at you;
Every corner and street, held something new.
Recalling such happy-fun times, brings a smile,
And tingles of joy, at re-living the past for a while.
We've aged a bit since then, that's true,
But partner, I'd take another rumble seat ride with you.

Eve Turkheimer

Untitled

I'm a watchman on the wall,
watching the world heading for a fall.
Morals are lost, people corrupt
our enemies plan to blow us up.
No discipline at home or prayer in school,
children suing parents, murder is in, too.
No honor in marriage until death do us part
no longer about love, or feeling from the heart.
No praise for the creator will bring judgement one day
unless the world repents for its sin, it will pay.
Watchman on the wall is there no hope?
Ours is in nothing less than Jesus Christ
and His blessedness.

Raymond S. Tracey

Lost In Love

Enter my kingdom, come to my land.
For it is dark and lonely here.
The only soul spirit is left...mine alone.
My life missing so much, the need for a touch of another soul.
The sweet sound of the voice that whispers into my ears,
I long await thee.
The want of a body next to mine, skin to skin.
How I wish to feel you breath, so close to me.
I would never let go, for the sun is too precious.
My skin instinctively needing the warmth onto it.
I am addicted.
How unique and lovely this sunlight is.
For now night arrives and you shall leave me again...
Behind alone in the world of misery.
It was only a dream, as I awaken I realize nothing has changed.
I am still alone.

Yasser Hussain

Just A Pillow

As the clock ticks, the night sky gets darker.
The seconds seem endless. The hours are forever...

I think of Him, my Love, my Life.
I think of the miles that separate us...

I wish to see Him, to hold Him, to love Him.

I caress my pillow...

With my eyes shut real tight, it becomes Him.
I hug it and squeeze it, I hold it, I love it.

Then my eyes open and I realize...
It's just a pillow...

Annette Clark-Brown, MD

Bled

A shattered heart bleeds darkly beating,
with skin shallow pale and pulse that's fleeting.

Alone and still through cold and dismal,
the haunting chill of silence fizzled.

As mirth and quirk quells haunt and hallow,
and slipping wits hit gravest shallow.

Cackling groans that were dusty dry,
echo wildly into gray into sky.

Cauldron's bubbling of brewing breath,
beckoning nearer eloquent death.

Between one beat and near to numb,
an eternity passes and finality succumbs.

Tim Kirschbaum

A Prayer For A Little Boy

Dear Lord...
I'm praying for a little boy tonight that I have yet to meet.
But I'm sure that when he arrives, like his father, he shall
be just as sweet.
I pray that he will have a loving home and a life that's
full of joy.
That he will be provided for and all will love such a
solemn little boy.
May he look just as his father with gentle deep brown eyes.
And a cleft that indents in his chin to show his family ties.
A wish that places dark curly strands atop his little head,
And perfect little fingers to count the numbers that are said.
Please, dear Lord, bless him from his head down to his toes,
That when this little boy is born he will flourish as he grows.
And when he comes into this world please let him know what's true,
Because for this little boy, dear Lord, any less will never do.
  Amen....

Stefani Atchison

Lapiz (The Pencil)

The Lapiz dissipates tranquility across the papel
Preserving all thoughts - an unbreakable citadel.
The hand which lolls her makers her style unique
Be it romantic, harsh, soft or oblique.
Swishing, stroking, saving serenity
Beautiful, beautiful infinite legacy.

The vindictive lapiz is an insatiable tool
Distends her evil into a blood-filled pool
Ripping, crushing, affronting the lambs
The lion-like lapiz cringes not at those that it damns
Dissent not, those who claim the sword is weak
The lapiz transforms royalty into the meek.

The variegated lapiz has power like none
She gives an answer or inquires for one.
Paralyzing, criticizing, complimenting, recommending,
With this gorgeous lapiz, I proclaim all which is good!
With this horrendous beast, death, seize me if you would!

Rachel Nicholson

Criticism

Really without a reason,
Not a cause to create influence,
Unfortunate are the ones to be given such hatred and anger,
Nothing to completely mend the broken pieces of yesterday's
destruction,
Still searching for the ones that were lost on this painful journey,
Tomorrow's outcome will determine the souls final status,
If you hear the cry of death
Be careful how you choose to deliver it into your chosen words of
criticism.

Rhonda J. Aurand

Drifting

Drifting off to space,
to an unknown world.
Wondering what is out there,
what's to come?
When I will return,
No one will know.
How far I go
is clearly up to me.
Who and what I meet,
is surely to me a puzzlement.
It will definitely change,
each time I go.
I guess you will just have to find out for yourself,
what it is like to drift off into space.

Amanda Dawn Wills

Touched By An Angel

As I sit in darkened gloom
No light shining in
Sullen, saddened solitude
My only mortal sin
And as two score of years have passed
It's just grown all the more
'cept for the night
when I saw the light
of heaven's angel at my door
In golden gown a dream come true
an answer to my prayers
and though she's gone for many years
In my heart she is still there
So as you listen
Please remember when you find your true love
It's a rare and treasured thing
God's gift sent from above
And when you find her, hold her tightly
Don't let her come un-clutched
Open your heart and let her in
When by an angel you've been touched.

Michael R. Berdeguez

Optimism

Every day there's a new beginning
In every challenge a chance of winning
Making life worthwhile by love contained
Is the essence of God's creation maintained
Finding opportunities in other places
Deriving pleasure from seeing new faces
Having left our home for a bright new land
We pray to fulfill our dreams as planned
Life is a challenge of right and wrong
The choices we make can be set in song
Whatever our choices, having done our best
God will smile when we go to our rest
When we are shaken by life's events
Whether of good fortune or accidents
How we perceive the future, will be
Our true image, for the world to see
Seeing the future with saddened eyes
Can offer only a life full of sighs
Having someone who really cares
Allows for joy, in a love that shares

Harry Newman

Speechless

There aren't enough words to express
    what your love has allowed me to see,

The pain and suffering you endured
    and you did it all for me.

All I can think to say is "Thank you",
    but, I know that won't suffice.

You gave your only Son,
    no words could ever match that sacrifice.

I give to you my life to do with as you will,
    and yet in my heart I know that my devotion is little still.

So Thank you! Great and mighty Father,
    from the bottom of my heart,

For loving me so much,
    and giving me a fresh new start.

    In Jesus Name
    Amen

Child Of God

A Diary Of A Lost Planet

The beaches are overwhelmed with the lost souls
Of the surface dwellers of our world
As the shore scores with its pretentious waves
And brittle enchanting kingdoms

The inland's streets are lighted with
The Urgency of Reality
Radiating a true brilliance of its own
Yet no one can be seen

Lorel Don Zaide

Ego

Such a short little word, with explanations many.
Your ego is your self, sometimes uncanny.
Your ID, a part of you that is yours alone, unique.
It exists, when you are awake, it is there in your sleep
It is a persona of feelings, and how with life you deal.
It is emotions of your self esteem, your self regard you feel.
It is your psyche, your personality, your mind.
Sometimes without reasoning, sometimes becoming unkind.
An individuality, a greater part of pride.
Sometimes obscure, sometimes it cannot hide.
A part of dignity, enclosed in self respect, unrelenting.
A part instilled from birth, but heaven sent.
    Your soul.

Fern Barlow

Eternal

If you love me, please tell me so
I love you more than you'll ever know
Touch me and tell me it's true
Say that you need me like I need you
Eternity washes over my skin
This love that stings me from within
Every night, I still yearn
This hunger inside me, it still burns
Kiss me with that sweet divine
Hold me close
Whisper that you're forever mine
I will always love you, need you, feel you
I want you for all eternity
Please, I can't live without you
Will you ever love me?
Say it, save me from this cold, dark earth
Squeeze me, you're worth more than the single breath that I'm worth.

Laurie Schackart

My Many Angels On Earth

I'm sitting here,
At a window at the start,
Of a new morning,
And my head and my heart,
Are feeling a little bit stronger inside,
Because I no longer have to hide,
Because of my many angels on Earth.

A long time ago.
I thought friends were a realm,
Untouchable to me,
Unable to see,
Because I wasn't beautiful enough to be,
Part of this great mystery,
But now I am,
And it's no longer a mystery,
Because of my many angels on Earth.

Now I feel good again,
And ready to begin,
Thanking them,
My many angels on Earth.

Jackie Dillon

Who Or What Am I?

I look long into the mirror,
    Not sure of who or what I see.

Is this the reflection of a stranger
    Or is this the untold reality of me?

I look deeper into the eyes,
    Touching the bottom of the soul.

I can see the never-ending darkness,
    I can feel the everlasting cold.

As I reach out to touch the emptiness in the mirror,
    A blood filled tear slowly trickles down our face.

A piercing shiver runs quickly down my spine,
    Frozen and unable to move, I cowardly look away.

I slowly start to turn back to the mirror,
    Terrified of who or what I will find.

Realizing it's time to fulfill a lifetime of longing,
    Destined to face the answer, "Who or What Am I?"

Christa Puckett

Keeping My Neighbour Awake

I get up in the morning at a quarter to five.
I turn on my stereo. It really comes alive.
It makes lots of noise. The speakers don't sound right
And my next door neighbor doesn't sleep well at night.
The telephone starts ringing. It rings loud and clear.
My next door neighbor is complaining, because my stereo he can hear.
He gets out of bed. He comes to my door.
And as soon as he leaves, I just turn it up more.
The louder it gets, the more he complains.
Until my next door neighbor is going insane.
He puts ears plugs in his ears and a pillow over his head.
He's tossing and turning all over the bed.
The noise only gets louder. It just never stops.
Until my next door neighbor is calling the cops.
He leaves the station and he's coming code three.
The door bell rings loudly. "Oh, I'm getting company."
But, he confiscated my stereo. He just took it away.
Now I'm writing poems for poetry contests, since my stereo
    I can't play.

Rita Henry

Secret Pain

Was I the only one who saw the pain in his eyes
The pain it seemed was so easy to hide

Hidden shame
Hidden fears
Hidden rage
Hidden tears

Through his eyes, deep into his soul
I could only see what he had not told

Through the walls, past the fears
Came what had been those hidden tears

Only for a moment he let me step inside
Just long enough to see the pain he tried to hide

So secret, yet so vain
came what will always be a hidden pain

Christina Dougherty

Precious Dreams

Precious dreams - they drive me,
precious deeds survive me.
My heart it's inside me,
you can't see it!
Inside it is an inner heart.
It is the heart of everything.

I am all alone.
I am on my own,
but I have seen the throne
on which my heart sits.
All along the way right up to today
I have seen the way it won't quiet,
it won't submit,
it won't forget.
Its root is in the infinite heart of everything.

John Williams

The Beach

I feel the breeze as I walk along the path
The rumbling of the waves as they crash along the sand
My feet sink into the moist damp earth
My hair blows with the wind, whipping my face with the wild breeze
as it moves along the pleasant sky.
The sun so warm and bright makes my body tingle with warmth
and delight
I run along the shore running with the wind, I hear my name being
called I try to listen but it is a faint whisper, I run until
my head is dizzy and confused
I fall on the sand and daydream into emptiness, then I rise and
escape back to life..........

Teri L. Schmoe

Rainbow Dreams

I was standing alone on the mountain,
cold arctic air all about.
As I knelt down, I wondered if I'd survive.

The snow started to fall, and my toes went numb.
I huddled by my fire, slowly flickering out,
praying for life's warm heat.

Just when I was about to freeze,
an angel was at my side.
She wiped the frost from my face and chest and held me.

When I awoke, she was gone.
But I feel her, she is with me always.
No matter how cold it is outside, my heart is warm within.

Jay Michaal Bookout

Scarlett

There was a day; when my heart did not sway
It was that day; when she looked this way
  I could not resist; as my heart stood still
Such beauty really exists; and try again, I will
  But pains still remembered; unsure and unknown
My walls soon crumbled; which were once solid as stone
  It's been a short while; but to me seems so much more
I so love her smile; the sound of waves on the sea shore
  How I feel; it should not be said
Mind of glee; heart so sad
  In love I fell; the first in years
And now holding back; all of my tears
  God speak to me; and let me know
If I should pursue; Or if I should go
  A kiss for all time; with a twinkle in her eye
The answer I heard; oh in love am I
  There was a day; my heart so warm
It was that day; held arm in arm

Kevin Hirahara

Past The Moon, Targeting Star

It stole the magic from the land,
Draining all of life and light.
Magic seeks its unknown maker,
Prowling unheard deep below sight.
The castle was buried,
A strong, enduring keep.
Deep in the earth it groaned.
A stealthy dagger, movements unseen,
Turns to find its beacon home.
Past the moon, targeting star,
The castle grows bright, alive once more.
Shadows drop away unseen
Pulling away, crying in fright,
The sky rips open as colors swirl,
Dancing sky fire ablaze the night.
The castle arises, piercing the clouds,
It shimmers and gleams,
Turns a translucent sheen,
And fades away...
Past the moon, targeting star...

Parima Pathipvanich

Valentine's Day Ditty

2 hearts beating as one;
in time to the rhythm of love.

Can you hear the melody and the notes
carrying you to a place that can and should be eternity?

The sound is like ice cream on a warm Summer day
it soothes as well as satisfies the hunger that yearns.

I felt it and I wish it was a city that I could live in forever.
Get to know the neighborhood and definitely live on every breath
of my Lover.

I knew every tear that you cried
and wanted to mend your heart
so that you might be my bride.

I would, if I could, make the sun in your image
so people could witness the beauty I see every day.

Chad Walrod

I'm Fine...

I'm fine...
There's nothing whatever the matter with me,
I'm just as healthy as I can be.
I have arthritis in both of my knees,
And when I talk, it's with a wheeze.
My pulse is weak and my blood is thin,
But I'm awfully well, for the shape I'm in.

My teeth, will eventually have to come out,
And my diet, I hate to think about.
I'm overweight and I can't get thin,
But I'm awfully well, for the shape I'm in.

I get up each morning and dust off my wits,
Pick up the paper and read the obits.
If my name is missing, I know I'm not dead,
So I eat a good breakfast and go back to bed.

The moral is, as this tale we unfold,
That for you and me who are getting old.
It's better to say "I'm fine" with a grin,
Than to let others know the shape we're in.

Rosa del Rio

Even Dead He Is My Life

When I met the man I knew, he was a child
and though his heart was true, he was not mild
he flew through life like an angel
all who knew him, loved him if able
he was my friend, my brother, my love
I hope that he is flying with doves
his love was immortality
it is now for eternity
when the angels sing
I know Brock's coming
he is in my heart, and is a part
of my life, he can't be set apart
I will not cry too long
he wants me to be strong
he had a quote that gets me through life's chores
it's "In the immortal words of the Doors,
The time to hesitate is through."
Thank you, Brock, I love you too!

Aaron Reitmeier

As I Sit Here And Wonder

I often sit and wonder, "Who is there for me?"
I sit and think of the times and how it used to be;
I wonder if it will ever be again,
Sometimes I have to ask myself, "Who truly is my friend?"

Often it seems nobody cares,
A listening ear never hears.

I sit and think of how this world is full of hatred and war,
I want to cry out and tell them not to be that way anymore.

Everyone has problems and heartaches,
Mine is the toll that the heart takes;
As I sit and think of the broken hearts and promises.

Does anyone ever think of what they are doing?
Do they realize what they are choosing?

These are the things I think of and ponder,
As I sit here and wonder.

Jennifer Beckler

Somewhere, Their Exist A Friend

When you're feeling alone,
When you're feeling scared,
When you feel like darkness is surrounding you,
Look out your window,
Take a moment to listen
To the cold breeze passing you by,
Take a moment and look above,
At the dark blue sky,
You'll feel the comfort of a friend
Lurking out there,
You'll here the sounds of sweetness
Comforting your ears,
Warming the heart,
and you'll know,
Somewhere out there in the darkness
With the cold breeze,
With the dark blue sky,
Exist a friend who cares.

Maya Bhakta

Untitled

I am blank
I have been this way for a long time now
Motionless
Empty
I sit without thought
No deed is done
No revelations are had
I rock back and forth in my chair
I do what I need to kill time
It will come at a destined point
I try to rush the clocks to get there
The impossible proves impossible
Through all the commotion there is no motion
In all of my noise there is no voice
I will come to myself when time allows it
I sit and wait

Kristin Cattrano

Being Human

The God within has begun to Stir.
Slowly, feel the surge,
As it pulsates through your being,
Growing,
Expanding
To Omnipresence.
A holy-healing light flows through you,
As you embrace and amplify this Love that is God,
Know that you are protected.
Like a magic wand of the universe,
You are an initiator,
A presenter of the infinite,
With all the love and joy that God can bring.
Rejoice and live your life with peace of mind,
And total freedom of your soul,
On every level of the physical and astral plane.
You are the power known as love;
Forever blessed,
You are a spirit being human.

Tom Justin

Hairdo

I comb back my silver hair in smooth wings
Straight from a middle part.
Dignity for a Quaker widow,
Looking the part.
And at the end of the wings,
At the nape of the neck,
Telling on the little girl inside,
The little duck curl.

Lois McLeod

Christina's Star

I stare through the windows at the warm spring night,
The stars overhead seem to burn so bright,
I choose the brightest that's within my sight,
And visions of you, in my mind, take flight.
How soft was your skin, we held hands that day,
I'd forgotten how love could begin that way,
And each little squeeze, as I knew to say,
The love's like the sun, it starts with one ray.
Your name is the song from the birds in the trees,
And each time I hear it, I'm weak in the knees,
If whispered so softly, it puts me to ease,
Our love's like the warmth of a soft summer's breeze.
They're the blackest of black when in love, I'm told,
Yes, mystery's what your dark eyes behold,
But your overall beauty, you know I am sold,
This love's like clay, we as sculptors can mold.
Your words through my mind as I try not to weep,
Your picture I clutch as I fall fast asleep,
I miss you already, my heart starts to leap,
Your love is the one thing that I'll always keep.

Daniel Park

Momma's Hands

You held our hands when we were small,
And we were not afraid at all.
You worked so hard for many years,
Cleaning or cooking or drying our tears,
Skillfully preparing holiday meals.

Crossing the street or climbing stairs,
You never let go, you always cared.
You held our babies and they knew,
A warm and caring love from you.

Now I hold your hand again, for me and ones not here.
Only this time it's the last time, and my eyes are full of tears.
My heart is so heavy it's breaking in half, never more on this
earth will I hear your laugh.
He waits to take your hand now, and I must let go, crying I do so.
With a smile you say good-bye, and I let go and cry,
Good-bye momma, good-bye

Deborah Hurtado

Dream

I dream of the day our eyes meet again
Reminiscent of that one autumn day,
When the warmth of your smile first touched my heart
If only for a brief moment.
How I long to feel that warmth again
To gaze into your eyes, to hear the whispers of your voice
And feel your soul touch mine.
I dream of the day you take my hand
Walking side by side with you,
To a world of dreams and anticipation
Where time stands still for us.
Then return once again to our special place
To chase a beautiful sunset, hear ocean waves against the ruins
As stars appear at twilight.
So dream of us and days gone by
Where memories linger still,
Dream the dreams of love we share,
Of happiness and laughter.
Then once again I dream of when I hold you in my arms,
For darling sweet, you'll always be forever in my heart.

Cathleah V. Entena

Love

Love is something so deep and strong,
something no one can deny.
Love is something that fools no one,
not even the fools that love.
Love is a feeling that one cannot describe
for it holds so much.
Love can be something that comes and goes,
love can be something that hurts.
Love is something so wonderful,
something that everyone longs to have.
Love is the word I use to describe the feelings
I have for you.
Love is a wonderful word.

Katy Luttig

Yesterday's Path

A child? Well, I don't know.
   I suppose I could of been.
Run wild? Oh yes indeed,
   time and time again.

To old, to fast.
   This world just keeps me running.
No time, I hast
   for movies, sports and sunning.

Each day the same. I'm thrown no curve.
   I wake, I work, I weary.
I have no name, to those I serve.
   They all just call me "Deary".

No rest for me. It's my own fault.
   My life was my creation.
The moral here is, "Don't leave home
   or quit your education".

Deborah M. Vacanti

To Donna's Mother

Her youth exhilarated me,
Her joy inspired me,
Her love of life blessed all who met her.
Her loss brought me sorrow that cuts to the soul,
Your loss hurts me deeper than you may ever know.

I pray to God that she will be well cared,
That Jesus and the Angels have a special place prepared.
Because I know you regard her as a very special person,
Don't feel alone in that emotion,
For any who have love in their heart can feel it yet.

Jeffery Geer

Yesterday

After all that I've been through over the years,
I have lost the will to trust so easily.
It doesn't sound fair for all those that may come to follow,
not to even be given a chance.
Could they see the scars behind these eyes of mist,
will they understand the pain that I have felt?
Would they stay to fill this emptiness forever,
or will they leave me here alone again?
I've spent so much time building walls,
to shelter me from another broken heart.
I've pushed everyone so far away,
denying anyone the right to get close to me.
I've tried so many times to forget the past,
Every time I let my guard down I get smacked in the face by reality.
It is lonely here in this box that I've constructed,
but is safe and free of tears.
Yesterday is closer than tomorrow, it seems,
I know it won't feel like this forever,
Maybe when the right man comes along,
all the yesterdays will disappear.

Kelley E. Petersen

What Will You Do?

What will you do boy if I told you I loved you?
Will you say you don't love me,
Like all the others did?
What will you do boy if I told you my heart
Beats faster whenever you pass by me?
Will you stop passing by me, like so many
Have frequently done in the past?
What will you do boy, if I told you that every night
I dream sweet dreams of you and me together?
Will you dream of me staying away?
Boy what will you do, if I told you all these things?
Will you stay or will you just walk away and ignore them?
I wish I knew the answer, so when I finally tell you
You can say to me that you've been feeling the same about me
But I guess until then I'll just sit and dream
Of that moment when I will be yours and you will be mine forever.

Marycelis Natal

Silent Thoughts

The night falls silent, a breeze brushing gently against my face.
The night grows cold and still with every second that passes.
The deceitful, hateful congressman runs through the night hiding
   his past.
A tight grip grasped on a gun, wondering who is lurking in the
   darkness.
Seeking shelter out of the cold a child walks to the door.
Hard working men surpassing death to keep the ends met.
Working hard to pay the collar that the tax man says he needs. And
   has to get.
The landlords at the door, when the night falls upon us.
The love in the night, the bills at the door. Taxes are due,
brace yourself fees at the back shall bleed,
The night falls silent, a breeze brushing gently against my face.

Tracy Hurst

Untitled

Once again I had loved, only to be hurt
By you and your deceitful lies
In spite of the love I'd given you, you left me
Inside me jealously drowned out my pitiful cries.

Inside of me my heart was slowly wilting
Like your roses on top of my dresser
Within the hidden corners of my sorry soul
I remembered your deceit when you kissed Her.

After endless nights and many moons,
Like a lazy fog my love dissipated.
Between us there now is a brick barrier
For your pathetic sorries are already belated.

By betraying me you lost my love,
Up and away in a red balloon it sailed
Towards the outstretched arms of the glistening sun
Since I came to the realization that you had failed.

In spite of my memories
Of our love that had once been my backbone and inspiration
Because of your excuses that were stuttering symphonies, was I ever
To love again on occasion?

Barbara Palomino

For A Lost Love

You may not have always been there
Though, some how you showed you cared.
How often you're thought of you'll never know
So, this little poem is coming to show,
You're remembered more often than you'd
ever guess.
And, wished lots of joy and happiness.
May our new found love continue to grow,
Through every high; through every low.

Stephanie Studler

To Christine

As wind through the trees makes a forest sing,
  So your love through me rustles a song,
A song of my branches and twigs and leaves,
  A joyful song from a loving breeze.
A singing tree in the wind am I,
  Green-leaved and growing toward the sky,
A sapling of love stretching outflung limbs
  Toward the sun and the stars and a thousand things.
Your skyborne zephyr of warm sweet love
  Flows down from my leaves to my deepening roots,
To nurture the darkness deep within,
  The darkness of underground and beneath,
To bring your love to my taproot of life
  And breathe spirit into the dark.
Thus the breezes of heaven uphold the earth,
  And the roots of the tree gain breath.

  Tom Howe

The Girl Left Behind

I was made to be a good girl
To be seen, but never heard
To never let a man see me with no make-up
To dream white picket-fence dreams...

And I held them—long after his words,
not his fist, took me down

I was made to be a good girl
To make peace at any price
To always set a pretty table

But how does a girl learn to speak when
It's time to be a woman when
She was made to be seen, but never heard?

I lost my own voice, only heard myself through others
I was even grateful for the role, but it took me down
Not fast, but far and low

'Til I came to my crossroads
And was made to sing my own song
Martyrdom will never find a home in me again

  Jane Butkin Roth

The Creators

At one point in time
God created a masterpiece. It grew from the ground;
towered Heavenward. Then branched out profusely
to provide shelter for birds that fly;
It kept the Earth from crumbling
It bore fruit to feed the hungry.

At another point in time
Man created a masterpiece. It grew from the ground;
towered Heavenward. Then mushroomed out profusely
It offered no shelter,
for the birds were dead
It caused the Earth to crumble
It bore no fruit,
for there was no hunger.

  Kay Moore

Heaven

Heaven is a special place.
It's where you see a beautiful face.
A face of God, Joseph, Jesus, and Mary.
Up there life is a bowl of cherries.
Everyone gets along and sing songs.
Together it's merry and gay and every day is a special day.
Flowers in bloom, the sun shining bright
there is never a sad face or a look of fright.
Yes heaven is a special place
full of happiness, laughter, and grace!

  Savannah Jean Storms

My Living Ghost

We are close, yet far apart.
I see him, but he is not really there.
He is in my life and out.
He is the ghost that haunts my dreams.
He is the one I can talk to and fear.
He is my best friend and enemy.
He is everything and I...
I am the leftover.
He is the icy fingers that run down my back but,
  he is the warm sunshine that brightens my day.
He is my brother Peter.

  Candice Serrano

Ode To The Ocean

There sits the ocean
like a magic potion,
so calm and quiet what a beautiful site,
and yet raging and deafening a monster of fright.
I wish I could just sit and lie on the beach,
with the waves and the ocean just within reach.
It is cold and forbidding covered in ice,
but warm and inviting oh so nice.
Sometime you can't see because it's deep and dark,
but when it's clear and shallow you can see a scary shark.
I love the ocean,
and all its commotion.
It has other names like the drink and the sea,
but whatever you call it, it's still the ocean to me.

  Winston Bibee

The Nighttime Of My Soul

It was the nighttime of my soul, scattered among the memories
Of broken dreams and promises, where no one ever sees
the painful longing in my eyes
As I stand alone and search the ever changing skies . . .
Looking for the one who can,
Gather together this drifting man.

And if I find it not, I will pull from within my soul,
The pieces of the puzzle that, again will make me whole.
And though my life is darkened still, it is only just twilight,
My eyes adjust to the loss of you, as my soul begins its fight.

To step into the future where, the world I again can face,
But beside me there will always be
A small and lonely space . . .

  Sharon De Vries

Angelic Heart

As her wings surround me,
I feel an infinite sadness.

Thousands of angels come to me,
Yet only one I desire.

She is flying high above,
Helping others.
I am a demon to her,
Forever damned.

She is my savior,
And she knows not my desire for heaven with her.

Forever burning pain of longing for.
The death of a man is complete.

The pain shall last no longer.

  Brandon Marlowe

Poison

You say you like the hurt I give,
your head falls back as you shriek
at the reflection of your foolishness,
mocking you with laughter in the mirror.
Deserting vows of love unkept, I turn and walk away.
Stretching the reality known best, my job is completed.

My perversion offers eternal bliss.
Ignorance hides the deceit I inflict.
The potency of emotion will draw you nigh,
the familiar ecstasy of infinite pain.
As poison, I work slowly,
slowly killing you with excruciating pain.

Destroying delicately with dissuasion, I am undiscovered.
You slip into my arms, betrayal is unveiled in my caress.
Your contaminated soul obsesses with
the decay of untold dreams.
Addicted like a drug to my tainted love,
worshipping the mirage that is Poison.

Sarah Engelhardt

Forever Bound

"With this ... I thee wed." Ring of promise?
Only an arena to some,
Defined by ropes and mats
For bruises and wounds
Cruel blows exchanged
Forging links scars of iron
Infinite cost the broken trust
Borne of these chains
There are pains beyond this veiled flesh
I never knew could render me
So powerless.
I have grown one with my bonds,
Blood into rust, no longer seeing
Where flesh stops and chains begin.

And you dare ask?
What strange power is granted unto you
This broken life to circumscribe?
How is it you see me in my difficulty?
Forever bound is a long time indeed.

AgN2Au (Mark A. Sippel)

Loneliness

Out of the night it creeps,
slithering and snapping
clawing its way into your soul
eating away at your flesh
gripping bitter bile engulfing you,
threatening your every thought
it starts with your heart
moves to your brain, quietly eating away at your inner thoughts
about to explode into a million tiny pieces
can you feel the teeth? Eyes watching your every move?
You cry, you shout, you vomit...
but it won't go away
he put the noose around your neck
and pulls as he shout his name...Loneliness!!!

Pamela Woolford

July 16, 1945

   You are there!
Red-Orange-Yellow-Green-Blue
   Indigo and violet.
The atmosphere rent asunder,
billowing vaporous clouds
and the sound shock waves like rolling thunder.
The atoms releasing their pent-up energy.
The basic elements turned to glassy obsidian
or jelly-like and spongy.
   All humanity was there!

Nile B. Norton

Despair

Long ago I had a feeling
the feeling of despair

I do not feel it anymore,
I shut it out behind a door

A door I have within my head
Despair is gone; with the dead

It will not come back; there is no key
It's one more thing, I can not see

I've learned to thrive off other emotions.
Love, to me, is an incredible potion.

I live contentedly for the time
For that I hope is not a crime.

Seth Boynton

Sadaam Hussein

He lived in Iraq,
Invaded Kuwait.
He troubles our country,
Uncertain is our fate.

The war has begun,
We've fallen apart.
Sadaam has broken,
The Patriots heart.

He used chemical warfare,
We used missile attack.
He killed many people,
And that's quite a fact.

He kills, He threatens,
Things roll through our heads.
And all we can think about is
bloodshed, bloodshed....

Still life goes on, we pray in sorrow,
Hoping that peac will come tomorrow

President Bush has done quite a job working on the war,
So many have died, will there be more?

Lindsay Campbell

Spider

Fine clear threads of friendship, sweetness and sincerity
And the strongest thread of all
Respect
The invisible web
I could not see to avoid

Nightcap with a twist
And the first thread has been woven
With each display of tenderness, each long conversation
The weaving became more intricate
And the web got sticky

Cool, damp grass
Soft August breeze
Your moon passes over my sun
An awesome summer eclipse
Your interlacing almost complete

The final touch
A shared adventure
Animal instincts only
All inhibitions dissolved
And I am ensnared.

Stephanie Wargo

Evil Delight

Burning with water as she ran
the cold sting, a longed-for sensation
holding her arms out,
they morph into wings
her feet no longer touching the ground
the white sky turned a wonderful gray
with pain still pressing deep inside
she lets herself go . . . . . her mind is gone!
It's raining now it's flowing now
then she smiles,
drowning her foes
pain! pain! pain! feel it!
thunder loud and hard
clasping them between her claws
she squeezes so painfully
their cries make her laugh, such evil delight
she is evil now against her will
malevolence pouring,
she throws the limp bodies
sweet sweet satisfaction soft bones breaking on stones

Anica Solis

Sonnet On Systematic Theology

A child, free, in youth's full flower
    Barefoot, careless, full of life,
Is imprisoned by the Spirit of the hour
Subjected to the surgeon's knife.

Happily he once played by the shore
of a creek in summer, catching frogs.
Now he toils beneath the bore
of pale, pedantic pedagogues.

His friends, the angels, played along
Swam and fished, and skinned their knees.
Today a seraph's saddened song
Chimes in horror as he sees

Science gone the wrong direction
And God submits to vivisection.

Jacob R. Weber

You Bring Out My Best

You bring out every hidden desire within myself.
It's like hot pop-corn, while popping.
It starts off as corn kernels with so much to offer.
But it is still not at its potential,
Until the fire ignites it.
Which sets off spontaneous energy.
Releasing hot, fluffy kernels of success.
That's how you bring out my best.

Stephanie C. Guidry

Storm

I hear the wind
hitting my window pane

It whistles through the trees
blows the driving rain

The storm is out there raging
the clouds are black as night

The thunder rolls and crashes
the lightning flashes bright

We're snuggled deep in bed
on sleepy waves we ride

As the storm keeps on coming
raging hard outside.

Katy Hall

My Prayer

I want to go home on high
To be with my God when I die
Sometimes I wonder why
There is thunder in the sky
I want to grow to see
my adult years and face all
my fears every place
that I have been
God has been there to
guide me along the way
In all my hard times and
grief God has always help
me find my peace even
If I grow to have my own land I will always
need a hand in what I
have to do God has been
there for me and he can be
there for you too.

Jennifer McDonald

The Greatest Miracle

"Have you seen a miracle?" asked he.
"A million miracles," said I,
"Each bud that blooms, each rolling sea,
Each majestic mountain that frames the sky.

"A newborn babe cradled in mother's arms,
A summer breeze to cool our brow,
A cracklin' fire that lights and warms,
And living love both here and now.

"But the greatest miracle is yet to be,
When from these earthly binds I fly
With angel guides to set me free,
My soul will soar where my heart does lie.

In love and light, my destiny fulfill,
I'll soar on wings of eagles
So full of joy, my heart will not be still,
To serve the Author of Miracles!"

Erin Anne McMahon Oneisom

the beast

If I died today many would understand,
why?
the reason itself is very simply,
the beast
the beast that I live with.
the beast that is in my head
my head is full of thoughts of this beast of my mind
these thoughts are eaten by this beast in my head,
with each of these thoughts the beast eats, it becomes bigger,
until it consumes me
and I become what I have always dreaded,
the beast
I am the beast, in my head
please remember me as before not the beast that I have become
I have become the beast

Stephanie M. Hiscox

A Man Without God

What happens to a man without God?
Does he search to find a way
like a man lost at sea?
Or deject the man who tries —
And say "Let me be"?
Does he go all his life like a man oblivious,
always thinking he's in the right?
Or does he ignore the voice —
Like a man who likes to walk in night?
Maybe he just wanders around aimlessly,
Or does he lie down helplessly?

Fiel Amiga

Winter In Maine

Entering the town of Rangley Lake
Early in the morning, is a vision.
Ice cracked along the path
Reaching the sky,
Feeling one with its illusion of solitude.
The roar of the articat
skimming the lake.
I step out of the car, though it's below 30,
and for a moment
I feel weightless on air.
As smoke, fills the frame of my face, from my breath
a mixture of winter, wood and motor oil
fill my being with excitement.
Something about going seventy miles an hour,
With the fingers of winter licking your face,
The redness burning on your cheeks.
What a thrill!
Your own heartbeat drowning out the motor of your sled.
The winters of Maine,
touch your soul.

Alisa Dawn Boyko

How Do I Know

How can one tell if love is in the air
Does it awaken new senses
Does it bring sweet memories
How do I know if it's love

How can I tell if my heart is true
How does it feel to love
I desire to be with you always
But is it the same

I never want to lose you
Always must be near you
Am I just a fool
How can I tell if love is in the air

How do I know if you feel the same
Will you tell me or must I take a chance
Is love a special bondage
How do I know if it's love

Can you help me to find out the truth
Will I always be this confused
All I want to know is
How can one tell if love is in the air

Louis O. McKiney

Nursing Homes

Old and feeble
with no one to care
Put in a home
forgotten they're there.

No one comes to visit
No one makes a call
It's almost as if
they've no family at all.

A kind word, a smile
or a gentle touch
Does not seem to me
to be asking too much.

Lord, Bless the people
who enter these places
And help us each day
put a smile on their faces.

Pamela Daniels

Tears

Tears that fall because of pride
Tears streaming down because someone lied
That flow without relief
Tears that strip away all disbelief
Tears filled with emotion
Raw and torn
Tears that say "good-bye" as we stop and mourn
Tears of regret in the restless morning hours
Tears of self-pity, like wet, misty showers
Tears that well up in frightened eyes
Tears of pain
That burst out from darkened skies
Tears of realization
That your life will not last
Tears of joy from a forgiven past
Tears that come because of blame
Tears that come because of shame
Tears that follow in forbidden places
Tears gently running down bruised, beaten faces.

Stacey Short

The Closet

I stand alone in the closet, unknown objects around me.
A terror deep inside. Which way to turn?
Dare I?
To feel the intensity of societies demons
Tearing, ripping shredding.
Pride...dignity
To face the rejection and pity heaped upon-
A weeping soul?
I stand still to avoid bumping these terrors.
Praying that I will not become
A victim of this terrible disease.
A light. A faint light at the end of the closet.
A door that leads to acceptance and light.
Oh, how I want to reach the understanding light.
The light all of us reach for.
Only a matter of time before we all stand proud.
Making a light of our own.
I hold the handle, knowing that I too will one day be
A ray in the burst of light.

Sarah Spieth

That's Life

This unique body of mine
Created by God at just the right time
to do certain duties, no more and no less.
Just expects you to do your best.
Time is the one thing we all have.
To spend as best we can.
To fit into God's plan.
Each moment is here and
Then it is gone.
Do all you can with it, then carry on.
Just go with him hand in hand,
And you will surely fulfill his plan.
He'll keep you in his sight,
Both day and night.
To make sure you have a successful plight.
Then when it is your time to rest.
You can truly say
Good night and God bless.

Imelda Frey

I Have This Other Jimmy

I have this other Jimmy.
He creeps up like no other
when he shows he knocks me off my feet,
sending chills thru me.
He causes me so much misery
I try to ignore this evil demon
I'm going insane, hoping my Jimmy will
hurry back and undo this pain
He will hear my cries and try to protect me
from that beast that hides within.
But in reality both of them are him
His love for me can be oh so strong
He can treat me like a lover should
He promises that will be it, this time will be
different.
Standing by his side, I have to believe
cause he's everything to me
I hope and I pray that this day will come
because I love my Jimmy so very much.

Rita Charboneau

What is The World Coming To

What is the world coming to
There's so much trouble and pain.
When are we going to wake up
To face the world, which we have so much to gain

There's so many diseases, gangs and war.
I ask again
What is the world coming to?
It has gone too far.

We live in a world of fantasy
Which is just a dream.
It's time to wake up
And come together as a team.

We live in a world of plenty
Which we cannot see.
Things are not the same
Or the way it should be.

I ask again
What is the World Coming To?

Jacqueline Jones

A Gift From God

Every day is a gift from God,
The gift of a road our feet to trod.
As we journey on toward beckoning days
Let us follow God's word along the way.

Shadows are there we do not see,
And a rugged hill for you and me.
But let us carry a book that makes it clear
The way will be safe with God so near.

And if He's helped thee so far.
He will not fail you now!
How it must wound His Loving Heart
To see your anxious brow.

Oh, doubt not any longer,
To God commit thy way.
For in whom in the past we trusted
Is the same God of today.

For the God who built the road for our feet,
He will be our guide down the street.
And the road we go will be bright to the end
If we have God, our gracious friend

Frances E. Snow

Sonia

As she embraces me,
I never want the moment to end.
The world around us goes silent
As I utter the only words my heart can say.
I turn to her with joy in my eyes.
Knowing that I've captured the queen of all
butterflies.
She breaks away.
Leaving with me,
a sense of completeness,
In her beauty and joy.
Darkness needs the light.
As I need her to survive!

William Wiseman

Idea

Notice Life because you should
Remember what you see
Notice Death because you should
Remember what you see
Omit Repetition
Trust knowledge
Increase Awareness
Cross out denial
Except Repetition
Examples of things to you
Mean I've had those same examples
Experiences never change
Memories seem the same
Brothers and sisters
Enchanting aren't we all
Regret. Register? Relax!
Rehabilitate! Reinforce!

Rebecca Ann Martin Twymar

Ten

Ten men standing at the sea shore,
Ten men standing at the sea.
Ten men live, and
ten men die.
Which ten live, and
which ten die.
You tell me since you're the sky.

Jessi Blank

Fireflies, Butterflies

All the colors swirling 'round
without the slightest thought of crown
Fireflies, Butterflies
Twice the same, yet
different for the others sake

Unruly worlds beyond the light
Set the stage, the time is right
demons from the cosmic riff
parade their howls of pain, the gift
Fireflies, Butterflies
twice the same
can it be the only way

Confidence is nil to death
lovers' stifle halting breaths
portend to vice, yet never rhyme
forever in our earthly time
Fireflies, butterflies
twice the same, yet
different for their own sake

David D. Zielke

Among the Shadows

The warmth I never thought possible comes to me now,
For life was so cold and desolate,
The sweet embrace of an unexpecting
victim comes as a chilling pleasure,
To know at anytime I can take them and as them as my own,
As my mouth touches the cool flesh I feel their heart rate quicken
. . . I hear it,
The fair white skin of a kindred spirit livens occasion,
I don't want to flaw such a perfect piece of work,
but what choice do I have?
I pierce the tender piece of meat with my gorgeous fangs
quenching my thirsty veins till they hunger no more,
In a way I feel sorry for my donor but how else to survive,
Who will be my next young meal?
Who gets to stare the evil in the eye?

Tonya Sennett

Empathy

A soft descendent breeze
Flitters grace among
The weeds—melancholy—
Not seen or felt by another
Except the weeping heart
Yet who's still unknown.

Feel blue lap upon the
Loneliest of blue.

Compassionate whispers
Ripple soothingly
A puddle—desolate—
Where unuttered hopes have fallen
Amidst still shallows of
All untouched waters.

Feel blue lap upon the
Loneliest of blue.

Candy Krebbs

Untitled

Oh women, women
Drink from the cup of blood
That was left on the altar of waste
Reject defeat
And you will not be defeated

Disavow prejudice
And you will not be enslaved
For ours is the period of enlightenment
We benefit from all the ones of us
that have gone before
like sacrificial lambs
for our deliverance

Ellen Larson Bedard

Untitled

The sun rises over the horizon,
spreading millions of glistening peaks
on the water.
As the tide comes in, it seems
as if the radiance rolls in with each calm wave,
spreading warmth across the sand.
Soon we forget the chilled wind
whipping across our cheeks.
Staring into the endless glimmering ripples,
time and space soon become irrelevant.

Tara C. Bailey

Invisible Child

Your cries went unheard every word every word
Never seen never heard ignored by all each and all
Never noticed invisible child lest you fall lest you fall.

One day you went away far away far away
No one noticed no one cared you went away invisible child
Went and stayed went and stayed.

Then you prayed and prayed with all your heart you prayed
You were finally heard! Every word every word
Ignored no more invisible no more! Finally heard finally heard.

Your dreams came true love came too, love so true
A love like you never knew lest you fall lest you fall
Your heart calls. . .

Lou Nied

Untitled

Procrastinate
If we could rid
This world of its pestilence
If we could rid
This earth of its racial hatred
Oh, what a joy it would be,
Forever youthful.
I believe I would procrastinate
Remember, putting off until tomorrow
What you could do today,
Puts you in a world of your own,
Not necessarily the best.

Robert Cronin

Who Am I

I am who I am,
Clay of the earth and breath of God,
Destined to live for a time in this world
and forever in eternity,
Invited to walk in truth and in peace,
Called to touch with love all whom I meet,
Challenged to lift burdens and mend
what is broken,

Summoned to sing of the beauties of the
universe,
Led to discover hidden riches in outcasts,

A dreamer of dreams,
A singer of songs,
A climber of mountains,
A pilgrim who loves and is
Beloved of God.

Alice M Doyle

Ole! Ole!

There's a cozy hideaway on a tiny patch of land
down there by the Rio Grande where Rosita entertains
while all the patrons exclaim Ole! Ole!

They come from miles around to hear that clacking sound
and to watch flamenco with its passion and gusto.

She's the big attraction there wears a flower in her hair
clack, click, clacking castanets in a lavish Spanish dress
while the patrons all exclaim Ole! Ole!

Her kisses are as festive
as the dances that she gives
with an existing tempo
that makes you wanna dance too
on a tiny patch of land
down there by the Rio Grande.

Margaret Rose Venturin

Our September

I watched a gull soar high above,
As I walked near a September sea.
I saw your face in a thousand waves,
And it seemed you were still there with me.

I think of you when Autumn's brush
has touched the leaves with gold,
And etched a masterpiece on Mountains high,
Colors so beautiful to behold.

When snowflakes weave their magic spells
And Winter shrouds the land,
I still can see your sunny smile,
And feel the warmth of your gentle hands.

As nature turns her carousel,
And displays her works of art,
You will always walk with me
Through the seasons of my heart.

These placid places, where we dreamed our dreams
And talked of things to be ———
But, I will remember you most of all,
When it's September by the sea.

Margie Worrix St. Laurent

Life Gone Away

Seldom comes the time
When we find true happiness,
for all the freedom I have known,
there's something I certainly Miss,
A few caring words from her,
A simple loving touch...
Yet when it was more important,
I hardly took time to care,
When she asked me what was wrong,
My feelings I couldn't share,
day by day I distanced myself
from her soft embrace,
And now I painful remember
the tears rolling down her face,
Baby" I love you" she said to me,
But I couldn't hardly hear.
Being that within my mind I
was gone to that distant place,
life gone away...

Benjamin Riley

Innocent Politics

Papi, are we eating today?
The meal on Friday was really good!
Why do we have to skip some days?
Leaving the stomach empty is kind of rude.

Papi, are we playing today?
When you're not here I think of you.
My friends are fun; and they're okay.
But you're the best, and that is true.

Papi, are the soldiers coming again?
I heard you talking about a boat.
Who's that person called "Fidel"?
Can I go with you? Should I get my coat?

Papi, I saw Mami crying last night.
She was looking at the picture of Titi Erica.
You know, the one that died in a fight.
A fight in a place called "America".

Papi, I'm tired, can you tell me a story?
Is tomorrow going to be better?
I know, I don't have to worry.
I know we will always be together.

Luis A. Lopez, Jr.

My Son

They matched them for the others wed
A reluctant choice for her, they said

But what could happen they would say
For each of them live so far away

Of course passions flared as passions do
And seized the feelings of these two

So innocent, so fresh, their love so soon
That they would wed that month of June

Now, both so young, so full of life
He the husband, she the wife.

And they would rest in each other's arms
And come to know the other's charms

And he would hold her close to him.
And they would dream of cherubim

And in that summer and on that site
She conceived their child that night

And at his precious birth they knew
That they would always and forever . . . love you.

Dennis L. Nelson

Try to Understand

To the wife of every trucker
This is written just for you,
For the times that you are left alone
And for all the worrying too.

Every week you watch him leave
As that truck rolls out of sight,
And you never know where he'll be
As the day turns into night

Remember the day you were married
When he promised to always love you,
No matter how far away he is
Be assured he's thinking of you.

He doesn't like leaving you alone
But he has to be out on the road,
'Cause once he gets started, it's in his blood
And he has to deliver that load.

You sometimes feel there's more to life
And that God has cheated you,
But, He guides your trucker home safe every week
What more do you want Him to do?

Nancy Freeman

Horses In The Trees

Life could be exciting if things were turned around.
The nights would be so noisy if the silence were the sounds.
If the sunshine could be sipped and the moonbeams could be chewed,
And the hollyhocks were totem poles, and midnight was at noon. .

If colors were all black and fire trucks couldn't be seen,
And bananas were all white, could the school bus all green?
And if the squirrels were horses, and every bush a tree,
This world would be a forest, hoofed creatures climbing free.

How wonderful, the fun and song,
If vacations were all year long!
If the rain fell upward and the fish could sing,
Horns would jingle and bells won't ring.

Would you go to school and would dad go to work
If teachers were just clowns and the boss a soda jerk?
If we had rocks for dinner and the grass was feather mats,
And dogs could meow, what about the cats?

Gail M. Bunch

Propriety versus Permissibility

How like a fool I rushed in heatedly
When usually I'd keep more of a distance.
More often, I'd just long repeatedly
And hide behind my usual reticence.
It's the eternal no-win situation—
A woman who moves first is far too brash;
And women's lib can't help with this frustration—
What's "proper" and "permissible" still clash!
Too often, gentlemen themselves hold back
And even say we should be more aggressive!
Most likely then the pushy oafs attack—
Their way is not to hang back acting passive!
Are there some unknown, complicated rules?
If so, why don't we teach them in our schools?

Rebecca Howard Augustine

Do We

Do we know how someone else can feel?
Is their pain no less real?

Cries all inside
Yet they abide

Courage have they fault not their own?
Eyes project fear, are they alone

Imprisoned in a body they no longer control
Tragedy has taken its toll

Do we know of their strife?
Heartache companion for life

Dependent on strangers for every care
Shame impossible to bare

For without you, they are lost
Human dignity bought for monetary cost

Dealt a mortal blow
Basic defense has ceased to flow

No future, barely remembers the past
A fortress of solitude, till death at last

So do we know you ask
Only God accepts that enormous task

Nola Kinziger

Cultures of Texas

Spain began the magnificent story,
By venturing forth for God, gold, and glory.

Lots of fun from Mexico,
Ranches, rodeos, fiestas and tacos.

Belgians built the land-saving irrigation,
To help create a beautiful nation.

Next came French vivid imagination,
Lieutenant Fuolois began the U.S. Military Aviation.

Dutch brought forth beautiful dinnerware,
Baron de Bastrop, with Stephen F. Austin, had his Texas affair.

The Irish and Chinese drove the silver spike,
To help Texas see the intercontinental light.

Japanese rice fed the pioneer,
Along with watermelons, potatoes, and corn by the ear.

Scottish stonemasons built the capitol and dome,
So the government could have a home.

Germans were givers not takers,
Carpenters, educators, musicians, and peace makers.

Czech's native newspaper and beautiful dancing,
Keeps them steadily advancing.

Lawrence W. Duerson

Blind Acceptance

Invaded by a lack of recognition, the pure oblivion.
Wanting nothing by feeling nothing — value they do not know.
Dissuaded by dissonance, crazy beside approval,
They believe it's accepted — so prevalent it becomes so.
Until we're all crazy, until we all do not know.

Messages sent throughout, we accept them
And believe them to be our own
Without a clear ability for our own reconnection
We follow through and follow behind.
Crazed with need, desire for value — lacking
Lacking beyond any form known, that we don't even know.

So filled by their ideas, bombarded by nothingness
I feel disgusted, I feel ill. I am letting this be
Through too crazed to see
That everything is me and I just don't know.

I can not listen, of something I cannot hear.
Limitation grasped by pure hatred and fear.
I am reluctant, I am taken
The pure love in life, forsaken.
And I don't even know.

Jennifer C. Smith

A heart lies

Dreams are shattered in the night.
A heart lies broken on the floor.
A lone teardrop races down my cheek.
Inside it is all the love
I've ever had for you.
All the joy.
All the laughter.
The pain and the sorrow.
Catch this tear in your hand.
Please, before it falls.
Save it before all the love is lost.
Love me like I love you.
Take this tear and kiss it away.
I beg you.
She turns, she runs, she hides.
She's gone forever.
Dreams are shattered in the night.
A heart lies...

Freddie J. Fuller, Jr.

Awaiting Outside Fates Door

A hollow heart for an extended span.
Wishing the void to fade, but it still stands.
Comfortless,
Someone to love, I long for
the hallways of chance ends with closed doors.

Is it my destiny to expire with hollow heart?
I desire my wounds be attended, before
I part.

A thorny existence without endearment,
the answer the rose.
A woman to accompany me, would drive this burden,
to a close.

So I await the day fate opens
that door,
And out walks the woman,
I've been longing for.

An embrace I've abided for what seems to me
an eternity.
Ever will I cherish her presence,
With tear-stained eyes, open doors, I'll see

Michael Moses Peterson

Loss of Faith

Because you did not pray to me each and every night.
Because you never could see me in your sight.
Because you never could see that good overruled bad.
Reasons such as these make me feel sad.
The angel in the cloud, you mistook as a bat.
Your favorite you chose over a dove, you said appeared a rat
You misused other souls to get what it was you would want.
What good you could do for others you'd shunt.
Your children had to suffer the life you chose for them.
Until they grew up realizing that there was a hymn.
Reasons such as these, I have great despair, for one day,
I will not see you in the air.
When life comes to an end, and souls descend, the way they
were in life will determine the end.
My arms will not reach out to you because you would not believe.
So remember the immaculate glare of light at the end,
Will not be me.

Deann Allen

To And From Here I Belong

As we drown ourselves in the
nakedness of our dreams, headed down
onto Indian woven sheets we sleep.
Sacredness lies
in the red blood stain of our past
Ancestors. Old men around campfires
passing around the forbidden pipe singing
enchanting prayers. Falling I walk among
children imitating their great past
Heroes in a land untouched by man.

Madness walks on all fours and on
my hands and knees I fall.
Crawling like some unmolded pieces of clay
of creation. From the dirt I once belonged.
To the same dirt I will become again.

Jason Young

Dandelions

Somewhere there is a field of dandelions
growing wild, growing tall
maybe it's heaven, maybe I'll never see it at all
there must be a place of beauty though
on this earth, cuz all I see is death
we slash at the forest and rip at the sky
and then we wonder where are the dandelions
children play in graveyards, we walk on stone
we continue to hinder the grass from growing
a man is killed just down the way
it wasn't my brother so I don't care
I think about it close
and I want to know why everyone isn't crying
and then we wonder where are the dandelions

Black Swan

Angel

The angel of love, the angel of night
The angel that falls within your sight
The angel that walks alone in life
But does that angel do alright?

When the angel calls, does he call for you?
When the angel walks, does he walk with you?
But if that angel left your sight,
where would you be tonight?

So walk with the angel and call his name
And live the dream that you once made
To be with that angel all night and day
And fly far, far away.

Fiona Stone

Come My Way

I'm all alone once more. Trying
to keep my head up high, while
my heart is dragging on the floor.
Another love has left me again today,
Why does it always end up this way.
I'm sick of falling in and out of love,
I'm sick of seeing what I have seen.
I'm sick of this all too familiar routine
I need to find that special love that will
take my heart to the moon, stars and
heavens above, I need to find that
special one that will never let me down.
Cause it really sucks being on the ground.
So as the sun rises and falls every day,
I sit here waiting for another love to come
my way.

Frank Hogarth

Call me

We were lying naked on top of the covers.
She touched me. She asked me for my
phone number. I tell her I will call her instead.

But I'll never call her. She doesn't love me.
She didn't cry when I left.

I was lying on my back, wondering
what I should do. She asked me what
I was thinking.

"Nothing," I said, "Just looking at the ceiling."
I told her I would miss her
And I will.

Chad Vandergriff

Together

When we met it was fate from the start
you came to me and took my heart
now I spend every waking hour thinking of you

Your love fills up my soul with smiles
I'm close to you even over the miles
that keep us apart

I pray someday we'll narrow the span
and walk with each other hand in hand
into eternal bliss

For it is you my dear who has made me alive
and I'll not rest until we arrive
on the threshold of happiness

Together

Brian Fink

Untitled

The voice rasps—delay.
Sighs, cries, murmurings.
They sit, they pace—
Restless feet, restless hands—

A match sparks, a cigarette glows.
Newspapers crackle,
baby cries, Mother soothes.
The soldier whispers softly
A maiden's eyes speak love.

Nods, Concentration
Faces hear anxious looks—
How long? Much? little?
now? at last—wait ends.
Happiness comes again.

Louise H. McQuistom

Myself

My windows to the world
are the same color as leaves.
My lips are the same
color as a cherry.
My hair is the same color
as a tree trunk.
My feet are longer
than my hair.
My hair is as curly
as the waves on the sea.
My cheeks are like
roses.

Shandra Lassley

Screams For Help

Stifled by my thoughts,
Shaken by my fear,
My inner screams that
no one can hear!
Tortured by my loved ones,
Ignored by all the others,
My outer screams unheard,
even by my mother!
The tremble that takes
over my body,
the tears that pour out
of my eyes.
The loud scream that begins,
The quiet scream that never
ends!!

Lisa Loving

Lonely Moments

Some days I feel so lonely
As lifes problems all creep in
It's as if no one cares or understands
I'm all alone, the world is dim.

I fight to find the right path
But there's always a stumbling stone
What do I do, where do I go
How do I call this place a home.

A home is full of laughter
Great talks and games and such
If we could just pray together
Oh, that would mean so much.

This home is very lonely
The walls are closing in
Please God, reach out and help me
My lonely soul is very grim.

Beverly W. Kochanski

Eclipse

secretive longings
desires only known
to friend moon
and myself
the stars winked
and thought perhaps...
and whispered
to the clouds
who were sure they knew...
but my heart
eclipsed
and covered
my ambition
until I
was no longer
me.

Darla Jill Ealy

Shrouded In Darkness

If my cold eyes
were not shrouded in pitch darkness
perhaps, I could personally see
a little clearer into thy soul.
The downcast sight
narrows my already impaired vision,
tunnel vision views the hectic world
as ants crawling at my naked feet.
My temper at careless times
unrestrained and unleashed upon you
causes you to run far and fast away,
promising to return another day
I would sorrowfully comprehend
if you turned your face,
never glancing solemnly back
but my fading eyes
are shrouded in eternal darkness
my sigh is dimmer, so...now gone.

Christine Alison Bennett

I Quietly Watch The Sunset

I quietly watch the sunset
over the hill. As I looked
down in an open field.

I notice the grass was
green as it changes colors
of the leaves on a tree.

The skies are blue and
the wind softly blew down
the stream, nearby a
waterfall.

Shades of color like a
rainbow to enjoy
a beauty will last forever.

Robert K. Byers

A Little Red Wagon

A little red wagon,
Was the transportation,
As a little girl and boy—
Pretended—they were on vacation!

When you are five,
And seven years old,
It doesn't take much—
For an adventure to unfold!

Growing up together
These two had lots of fun,
As the years rolled by—
Until school days were done!

They were inseparable,
As loved seemed to grow,
Like in a "Fairy Tale"
There was only one way to go!

In a red station wagon,
To make a dream come true,
That was planned in childhood—
Their "Honeymoon" —was in view!

Adeline Fleischer

Home

The breeze so light and gentle
Comes wafting through the door,
The golden sun is sinking
Leaving shadows on the floor.

Birds are warbling happily,
Crickets begin to chirp,
And children run to daddies,
Who just came home from work.

As peaceful night descends then,
And windows start to glow,
Much warmth and love shines outward,
On lawns and flowers below.

Mother's cooking in the kitchen,
Sister's studying at her desk,
While Daddy reads the paper.
On his lap the baby rests.

A warm and cozy feeling
Creeps over me to see
A true and loving family.
Why can't this always be?

Loyce Craig Vickery

Poe's Ode

How it welled up in his mind?
Perched there always just behind
and chilling to the bone was that
dammed crow.
The feeling just beyond
the vail, one gets reading in his tales;
The spector perched there, was in the
mind of Edgar Poe.
The Bells for him tolled endlessly,
when he lost his true love, Annabel Lee.
His melancholy phrases penned on lines.
But as time passes through the years,
that persistent Raven reappears, and
dwells within the mind of Edgar Poe.

G. Milton Luttrell

Progress

Psalms sing of times
such as ours
cycles of growth
rounding as always

Upward spiral
broadening life's potential
the great paradox
seeming the everlasting riddle.

Tunes of timelessness
that is now
Highs that are low
the eek! That is wow!

Older and wiser
awaiting evolution
auto designs hurrying
towards anti-gravity chairs

lightening the uncomfortable
effect's of technology
true perfection being
no doubts, light years away.

John F. Roberts

Untitled

Big firms, with power and resources,
Must see hand writing on the wall.
Debt interest, and defense expresses,
Must diminish, lest we fall.

We need marketing corporations,
To enlist masses for the fray.
As war bond drives hyped and our nation,
Tax free bonds bought, tax shelter way.

Collateral yearly we pledge to buy.
2 percent bonds from treasury flows.
No danger to our money supply,
As banks to treasury money goes.

And we pledge half trillion flow;
Defense and interest paid. Amen!
In time we might pay all we owe,
Or else consolidate again.

Foreign investors might interfere,
Yet who needs safety more than they?
Masses may seem quite unaware.
Portfolio mavens should praise the day.

John Adams

You Are So Wonderful

You keep me happy
You keep me warm
Just to believe
I'm all yours

You created me
With great powers
Which no man
Can ever erase

You make me strong
When I'm weak
Just to remember
It's okay to teach

Every one around me
How to speak
Great things about one another
To keep the peace

You are truly so wonderful
Because you're one of a kind
You stay on my mind
All the time

Judy A. Hayes

Grief

I feel you waiting for me,
quietly, silently.
Already reaching out
to enfold, to overtake me.

Today, I sense
the heartache, the sorrow.
Waiting with forbiddance,
for the mourning of the 'morrow.

I hear your quiet whispering,
"Soon, soon enough,
You will face the presence
of grief's company".

Dolores Harvell

Los Angeles

From fingers moist with ocean mist
To chain of mountains on Her whist
We live within Her friendly palm
Where lives are long, breezes calm
Her daily sun does smile and pose
Except when rain must quench a rose
Her trembling hand I do forgive
Here in its grasp I'll always live!

Leland Embert Andrews

Thank You, Father God

I could not close my eyes this night
   Without a word of prayer
To thank You for the things You've done
   Your tender, loving care.
For all the joy You brought to me,
   The song that's in my heart,
The sureness of abiding love
   That never will depart.

Though shadows press on every hand,
   I have no thought of fear.
The sunshine of eternal love
   Will dry each falling tear.
Oh, Father God, be Thou my strength,
   My joy and comfort be;
And thank You, Lord, for one more day
   That You have shared with me.

Doris Wirtz Dixon

The Poetry Contest

The National Library of Poetry
Has been publishing books for
   many a year.
Every month they have a contest
To see what poems are going to endure.

There are prizes awarded for any entry
That has qualities of art,
Worthwhile to read,
And that is worth publishing in
   anthologies,
For people who have an artistic need.

It is very rewarding for anyone
To see their own poem in print,
Whether it wins or not, it's fun
   to read it,
After the book has been sent.

Jack A. Feldman

Over The Fields

Where are the church bells
Are they rusting in the tower
For I can hear them ring no more
When I was small and very poor
My dress so old and soiled
I would not go to church
But when I heard those church bells
I thought they rang for me
My heart felt good right then and there
I sing a song so quiet
That only God could hear.

Ruth Culver

Haiku

Amid the glooming
Woodland objects take
   strange shapes
Eerie sensation!

With melting snows
Violets emerging are
Announcing springtime.

At evening crossroads
A terrapin stops midway
Time of decision.

On a leafing bough
A robin burst forth with
   song
Gladdening the heart.

Early morning light
Squirrels among the branches
The sound of gunshots.

Beautiful butterflies
Flitting over the flowers
Blessings of summer.

Beatrice M. Gartee

The Heart's Never-Ending Dance

Being in love is like being blest
   with a never-ending Valentine's Day
It's giving the gift of your heart
   forever and a day
Yes, love is a feeling that
   we should not waste
Unlike many material things
   that can be replaced
Once in the heart
   love can never be erased
You see, true love is enchanting
   and everlasting
It's all the ecstasy
   without even asking
And once a heart falls into
   love's soul-stirring trance
It'll feel like it's forever
   been bewitched by romance
For being in love always will be
   The heart's never-ending dance!

Carl Schmidt

Why Do They Insist

Why do they insist
That I forget
The best of me
I feel...

I know they're only
memories
But a part of
My life still...

I cherish the moments
When I remember
And yes, I
Shed a tear...

But please don't
Ask me
To forget
Those memories I hold dear...

Thelma V. Hoover

The Parting Tide

Overhead the cry of a seagull
reverberates.
The sweet fragrance of time wafts
softly in the wind as
cold
translucent waves
collapse
over moistened sand.
/Cloud shadows obscure the
light.
Footprints dissipate as the tide
withdraws.
A storm approaches.

Kimberly Joyce Heaton

A New Day

For waking me up this morning
For letting me see a bright new day
You have been mighty good to me
You fed me when I was hungry
You gave life to my body when I was sick
You even choose to heal my soul
You have been better to me
than I've been to myself
I've got to say thank-you, Lord
for letting me see a bright new day
you just keep on making away
when I didn't have nothing
you gave me something
Thank-You Lord.

Charlotte Simpkins

Tulips Divine

Love and Tulips
Go together.
Not like daisies
Without good weather.
Tulips sprout at
Easter time to
Let us know it's
Almost time.
Now they're ready
And here they come.
Not love and tulips,
But dandelions.

Walter Bundschuh

Walk With Me

When it seems I'm all alone
And no one's near to help me stand
I feel Him gently take my hand
And say He'll walk with me.

And when the sky is dark and low
And demons come from every side
I know deep down fear can't abide
Because He walks with me.

With joy I sing and my heart's full
Of Jesus' love and God's grace
I look up to the Lamb's fair face
As He walks with me.

I know inside it matters not
How hard the path or steep the trail
I'm not alone, I will prevail
For Jesus walks with me.

Hollie McCullough

Trust And Try (My Hymn)

A golden rule, He gave us,
The Lord our God who made us,
But how we stray
from that Noble Way:
From that Rule Divine
in this, our time.

We must reline
while there's still the time,
And with God's Grace
Regain again our place.

So, when our days are done
and the course of life has run,
then to dust we'll return
Until we see God's light:
Trusting in Him
To make all things right. Amen.

Thomas W. Clarke

Pray Only To Sleep

A lightly downed thought awaiting,
The curtains of night-time smiles,
To soothe a sleep, of dreams restful.
Tiny fingers dancing in tenderness,
Through a halo blanketed warmly,
In a scapegoat hidden peaceful.

A placebo for erasing fear,
In bundled security created,
By the mind . . .
Amid dormant abandon of reality.
Allowing the brain to sleepwalk,
On a journey of veiled serenity.

Gentle voices rendering inanimate,
The visions of sunlit conformity.
Turn away your premonitions tainted,
And color the soul softly.

JohnWall Duddy

A Parents Love

A parent's love is pure no matter
what you do in life. They are
always there to pick you up and dust
you off when the bike you're riding
on through life tips over and you fall.
They are always there to say "Things
will be okay" when the monsters come
out. And they are the ones who wipe
the tears away when the bullies in
life push you around. There is no
purer love than that of your parents.
Even after they are gone you carry
their precious love deep in your heart.

Alberta Lynn Bartlett

Young Love

Gentle as the breeze,
soft as a pillow,
a kiss.

A kiss so tender,
so sweet.
Love at first sight,
that is how they meet.

Holding of hands,
fun times together.
They were first friends,
now they are
lovers.

Jenny Teachout

Night Of Pleasure, Lifetime Of Pain

My sister,
What did you do?
Did you not learn?
All of our female family have married,
before seventeen.
They were all abandoned by their loves.
Because they became pregnant.
Your one night of pleasure,
will become a lifetime of pain.

Midnight feedings,
dirty diapers,
screaming children.
Your disappointed dreams.
Hope you can live your life like that,
In a rut,
Stuck from your trying to be
Free.

Stephanie Beck

A Dream

I gently take your hand
Gaze into your eyes
Lift your precious face
I long for your embrace

Starlight in your hair
Sweet laughter in the air
Want to fold myself inside you
To lay my head beside you

Let time go by without us
The world can turn without us
Wistful beauty, my heart aches
As from this dream I awake...

Michael Svetecz

Reflections Of His Love

When you're feeling rather low,
And find you have no place to go,
Just come to Jesus in your distress,
And He will give you peace and rest.

Though the storms and tempest blow,
And the fear will grip you so,
Just put your hand in Jesus' hand,
And He will guide you through the land.

Reflections of His love show through,
In every thing you say and do,
Storm clouds cease and you can rest,
For with Jesus, He's the Best!

Alice Lyman

If Hearts Could Speak

What tales we'd have
if hearts could speak,
the war-torn sagas
of the paths they seek.
With narratives of
all the tortures of hell;
with legends of courage
and sufferings befell.
The heights of desire
their novels would relate;
compassion and daring
their myths celebrate.

But mine beats out
a tired refrain,
too pooped for eloquence:
"There-is-pain."

Robin Parker

Untitled

A lot of happy occasions
And also a lot of hurt
That's what I used to have
before I came to the Lord.
And in darkness between shadows
I was walking without hope

And those who would walk beside me
would offer their affection
But they couldn't show me the way
Because they were lost themselves
But now I can see the light
The darkness is all behind me
For Jesus has set me free
And he also walks beside me

Astrology used to guide me
when I read the Horoscope.
I use to think they had power
The stars the moon and the sun
For now the truth is me
Now the one I praise and honor
is the one who made them all

Yolanda Martinez

Ship Of Fortune

To these men a fortune fell, the
teacher, the servant, the man of will.
These merchants running ships with
ease, carrying gold, silver, and jewels
thru the keys.
One ship sinks beneath a wave, one
taken by pirates to another place,
one makes it home proud and brave.
Hey! Hey! We lost no goods this
trip, the luxury for millions is
on my ship.
Gold, silver, and jewels to please,
silks, china, spices, and tobacco
brought across the seas.
To some misfortune fell; each one
served with a mighty zeal. For their
families we pray a boundless wealth,
for each survivor, love and good health.

Martha Couch

Two Lives

It's forty years and a little bit too
since I lay eyes on you
It's sixty five since I arrived
But that doesn't make me blue

It's a son like you to pass my name
and that's a thing of pride
a thought to carry in one's heart
of this you qualify

We both have climbed the famous hill
and down the other side
and somehow through the years, it seems
enjoyed the bumpy ride

I am so very proud of you
the goals you aim for too.
Your life, your wife, your sons,
reflect that special light from you.

Harland L. Stephens

We Were Meant To Be

Certain chance occurrences
Have caused our paths to meet.
Destiny has joined our hearts
and made our lives complete.

Not all lives that cross
Produce a union that is strong.
Fate can sometimes tempt
and then remind us we were wrong.

Fortune has confirmed
our love is not a false disguise.
Love is something we in time -
we'll truly maximize.

Something rare has happened -
Life has given us a chance.
There is something natural
and true in our romance.

Days are so delicious -
Time is special, minds are free
I believe our love is real
and we were meant to be.

Barbara J. Lowell

Pinion Pine

Your arms reach
higher and wider
than the mountain range
and the grasses
kneel at your feet.

You have
taken the time
to stay through
the entangling
storms of time.

Your inner self
stands straight:
the full
symbol of life,

Home
for the pinion jay.

Irene Schultz

Wondering

I lay here dreaming
Of what could be.
Putting myself Elsewhere,
to where I can't see.

I know I must go
to quench my mental jest.
My life has a purpose,
a continuous, righteous quest.

The sun might rise again
and warm my chest and blood
Or night will fall forever
My soul's flower, a dying bud

Spread my arms and sail away,
searching for my need
Up above on moonlit clouds,
to plant my passing seed.

The dream rushes back to me
and I'm forced to quickly stand,
as I descend from the heavens
with my full grown flower in hand.

Stephen Piotrowski

The Mount Wherein

I'll go to walk
A while it seems
Along still earth
And easy streams

I'll stay to seek
The marble stage
Within warm crease
Of nature's age

I'll rise to speak
For worthy plans
Cross pristine dreams
Cross distant spans

I'll fall to climb
Rich time in peace
Through fertile springs
Whene'er I reach

The mount wherein
I trust to pass
The last day's birth
To deathless ash

Steve Cherico

Silenced

We watched you slip
fought to help you stand
(silence showed itself to you)
We watch you fall
reached to hold your hand
(silence slipped into the room)
We looked into your eyes
saw darkness hidden there
(silence filled a hollow you)
We listened for your words
searched for hope beyond despair
(silence stole your soul from you)
Silenced
There was nothing we could say
Silenced
Our tears are lost to you
Silenced
You are forever silenced.

Melissa Willis

O Love, 'Tis Sad

O love, 'tis sad
few know thy depth
though many profess
such knowledge to posses

As they bring forth
in verse, in song
and through other arts
images of bonding hearts

O love, 'tis sad
few know thy depth
could they but see
thy boundaries
as clear as me

They might discover
as they explore
that souls also bond
for a lifetime
and beyond

Thomas Wisnowski

A Dream

Between sleep
                and awake
Between destiny
                and fate
Between peace
                and strife
Between death
                and life
Between you
                and me
Between us
                and them
A dream. Our dream
Holds us by a thread.

Cynthia Mullaly

Eric's Gifts

"I have a present for you"
He called, as I approached his door,
He held up a small package,
As he had done, so many times before,
The little gifts, he gave to me,
Could be almost anything
A letter he had written, a picture,
Once it was a small key ring.
Today it was a little fan,
Crayoned in red and blue
"Because", he said "I was warm"
"And thought you might be too."
But the most precious gift of all,
Was the one you could not see.
For wrapped in each small package,
Was the love he gave to me.

Evelyn Becker

The Watch

Who am I
standing tall on the rocky shore,
Keeping watch
Hour after hour...
Season after season...
Year after year...
Watching, watching, warning, warning...
Who am I
silently viewing the scenic sights,
and spending sleepless nights.
Red eyed and bleary
I am forever weary...
Watching, watching, warning, warning...
However lonely,
I stand proudly
here on the rocky shore
as ships pass by in Bass Harbor Bay
Forever more...
Watching, watching, warning, warning...

Jacquie Wesson

Take Me

In the dark of the night
With the depths of my soul
I whisper take me
As I am
You cannot separate me
From what I want to be.

Lisa Decker

Dreams

When I was small,
  I used to dream
Of possible things
  Like peaches and cream.

But then I grew
  Into my "teens"
And fantasy came
  To ruin my dreams.

For when I woke,
  With pain I saw,
That that which was mine
  Wasn't mine anymore.

And life goes on
  Just as before,
Bringing those dreams of
  Impossible lore.

Miriam L. Gomez-Bracety

Eternal Love

Dedicated to Fran
It seems like only yesterday
Or was it long ago?
A flame departed from my heart
And left an ember's glow.

The years that pass can never dim
Nor continents divide
My deepest, dearest thoughts of him,
Though he's not by my side.

Those precious moments that we shared
Will ever dwell with me.
A laugh, a kiss, a tear or two
Are just a memory.

The angels hold him gently now
Awaiting my return

Charles J. Kasper

To My Little One,

As I Watch You Grow

Each and every day as
I watch you grow,
All the little things you do,
All the little things you say,
The way you make me laugh,
by the funny things you do.
You make me see things
differently from your point
of view. I like to see your
hopes, your dreams, your
fears...the simplest happenings
traced out in love become
a pattern, for my book
of memories.

Joan Labrie

Grasp The Dream

Grasp now the dream
  ere it pass away—
One fleeting moment
  in the passing day.

Breathe deep within
  the chambers of your heart;
Time's but a hand's breadth
  till you soon depart.

Doris V. Neumann

Never, Never Land

Never worry
Never late
Never cry
Never, never hate
Let's go to never, never land
Where everything is grand,
Wouldn't you like to be in never land?
Where we'll walk hand in hand.
Never jealous
Never rude
Never spiteful
Never cruel
Let's go to never, never land
Where we'll walk hand in hand,
Wouldn't you like to go to never land?
Where everything is grand.

Elizabeth Johnson

A Special Someone

Someone special is always
there for me, always there to
pick me up when I fall,
and at times it was a long haul.

I'd always ask opinions when it
was decisions I had to make
whatever I decided she would
always say—I'm sure it
will be the right step to take.

She has always been there for me and
I'm sure she'll be there for you.
Do you know who this person is?
Do you have a clue?

Just sit down and talk to one
another, after all I do—
because that special someone
is my mother.

Rebecca Wilson

Gift

I have a gift for you,
it's really not a lot.
Please try to understand,
because it's all I've got.

Please take care of this,
My gift is one of a kind,
you'll never find another,
so unique in design.

It grows a little fonder,
each and every day.
It's the thoughts that count,
I guess you could say.

No matter what happens,
you'll always be a part,
of my little gift;
the gift called my heart.

Amy Michelle Yelton

Dawn

Through the cold gray of dawning
Like a bird on the wing,
Speed the bright rays of sunshine
For each living thing.

For each slender grass blade,
For each tiny flower,
The bright gift of sunshine
Fills each brilliant hour.

E. R. Case

A Precious Gift

Our youngest son is Derrik,
A very bright young lad.
He needs lots of attention,
He gets it from his dad.

His dad is understanding,
Derrik learns a lot from him.
Like how to cope with others,
And not act upon a whim.

Derrik's a very caring person,
With a very loving heart.
He tries so hard to fit in,
To please, to be a part.

A precious gift this child of ours,
Derrik is his name.
He'll melt your heart and take it,
You will never be the same.

Carla Lee Ota

Walk Away Home

Walk away home child, walk away
home, it's getting nye onto thunder,
the chill will come and the rain
will fall and the wind will blow
a gale and whistle around the
eaves of the house with maybe
a little hail.
Come sit with me and listen
and hear the weather wail, it's
calling in a new season and
winter will prevail.
Your heart will be warmed
by the hearth tonight instead
of that warm old sun, so
snuggle up close child, snuggle
up close and lets both,
walk away home.

Lila Bingham

Some Need . . .

Some need death,
But they lack the blood.
Some need evil,
But they are a waste of Time.
Some need life,
But they should not live.
Some need substance,
But they do not feed.
Some need being,
But they lack a soul.
Some need punishment,
But they don't value it.
Some need death,
But they lack the blood
To bleed.

Chad Parsley

Expect The Best

For all the hurt I suffered
and all the pain I bore.
It didn't make me love less
It made me love even more.

We shouldn't hide our feelings
or play childish games.
We should give our all and then some
and in faith expect the same.

Gloria E. Sparrow

When I Whisper

Tonight I feel like writing my love,
Not just about you, but about the
Trees that dance in the wind, and
The flowers that laugh when I
Whisper to them about my love for you.
Tonight I feel like dancing, but not
Alone my love, I want you to come and
Dance with me and the trees and
The flowers that laugh when I
Whisper to them about my love for you.
Tonight I feel like sing, not just about
You may love, but about the sunny skies,
The pleasant breeze, and about the
Trees and the flowers that laugh when
I whisper to them about my love for you.

Karmen Marie Curry

It's More Than A Game

Once you've really felt the hit
you never quite get over it.
There is nothing more profound
than the simple solid sound
of bat that turns fast balls around.

It never leaves your conscious mind,
the times your eye and arms combined.
You'll never feel you stand so tall
or know the wonder of it all,
'til you've heard that awesome sound
of bat that turns fast balls around.

When all your swings are a perfect fit
the horse rind leaves in low orbit
and then again the magic sound
of bat that turns fast balls around.

One more time I'd go for broke
before I leave this world as smoke
to hear that haunting, taunting sound
of bat that turned fast balls around.

Robert Torgerson

To Dorothy With Love

Thirty-four years ago.
Can it really be?
That you came to share your love,
With your Dad and me.

We held you in our arms,
And gazed at you with love.
"May our little girl be blessed"
We prayed to God above.

We saw you grow through childhood.
Through school and college years.
We saw you marry William,
As we shed our happy tears.

And so again, the time has come
To send our wishes true,
That life from now and evermore,
Will hold the best for you.

Now looking back through the years,
On this your Special Day,
We both agree — We are the ones
Who were blessed along the way.

Beatrice Shepherd Gallagher

You Pretty Little Thing

You look like an angel
From the heavens above
You are so pretty
And so full of love

I can look into your eyes
And tell that your home is not here
You are nothing but an angel
From heaven somewhere.

If I could hold you in my arms
I know my hope is in vain
I could love you forever
You pretty little thing.

Sam Mattix

Deep Shadows

At night, when shadows are deep,
And I cannot sleep.
I think of things I hold dear,
Many thoughts of yesteryear.
How rapidly the years have gone by.
As I reflect, I almost cry.
For wasted years, days and hours.
How unused time devours,
Precious are years, days and time.
Well used time, sublime.
Devoted we may well be
But all too late, we see.
How better we could have used our days,
To better our lives, in so many ways
These are my thoughts, at night.
With shadows deep,
When I cannot sleep.

Mattie M. Stewart

More Than Love

Through darkness I had walked
without your hand as guide
now that your love is in my life
I walk into the light

With you there is a whole new world
which just in dreams I knew before
your tender loving ways each day
have touched my inner core

Irina Creaser

In Time Of Bereavement

Thoughts Forever

You are not here
  but we feel your presence.
You are not here
  but we have visions.
You are not here
  but we have memories.
You are not here
  but you are loved.
God gave of strength
  that's why we are strong.
God gave us courage
  we have no fear.
God gave us faith
  we have no doubt!
God gave us Grace
  that's why we are able to carry on.
Thoughts of You, Thoughts of Thee,
  Thoughts
I'll hold forever
  Forever in my heart!

Deborah Ruffin

Untitled

They come like rain, these tears I cry.
Trying to endure the pain, to
  understand why.
They took this man made only of love,
Placed nails through his soul and
  hung Him high above.
My heart cries out to those who are
  too blind to see,
What could have been saved for
  eternity.
More children are born to this
  world everyday.
Will they stay wrapped in his
  arms or be carried away.
In His name we all must pray.

Terry Straub

On Mecklenburg Avenue

I sit quietly on this busy street
looking how life goes on.
Infantile voices pierce the air
here and there.

Noisy cars rumble passing by
while I sit silently, observantly.
Eternity is being lived here
but it could be lived anywhere.

It's only time that's spent
the only currency we all have abound
Were it not, but for space and matter
who would know I'm here and now . . .

But, I am!
The whys and becauses long foregone.
Just a breath away from death,
just a beat away from there!

Ketty Molina Vargas

My Child

Dedicated to My Son, Alex Jacob Garvin
You're growing so much my child
every minute of every day
wonderful things are taking place
in a very special way

Each day I wonder what you're like
but never a clear picture can I see
I imagine little hands and feet
and bright eyes that gaze at me

Time has gone by oh, so fast
I can't believe you're almost here
I long to hold you in my arms
and cherish you so dear

Soon you'll come into this world
you'll have so much to see
and I will be so proud to say
that you are a part of me

Kerry Lowery

Continuum

Do not mourn the fallen leaves
But do rejoice for the little green
bough
For in the spring it may nest a
dove
And the fallen leaves shall hear
words of love
Such as "forevermore."

John F. Tullis

Take Care Of Me Lord

Take care of me Lord,
I am your child,
for I am the head,
and not the tail,
I am above,
and not beneath,
for you are the one,
that I really love,
and without further a do,
you said, I'll take care of you.

Take care of me Lord,
I am your child,
for you are the one,
who gave me this poem,
and I know that you are never wrong,
if I look around,
then I will see,
that you are the one,
who takes care of me.
Take Care Of Me Lord

Kenneth Harris

Awake!

As the splintered wings
  of nocturnal solitude
  end their starry flight
    and fold upon the withered dreams
    they captured in the night
While the tattered minds
  of forgotten images
  flee the screaming dawn
    and cease to rend devoured eyes
    they beckoned death upon
Vague memories
  of our whispered labile thoughts
  seek the pulse they lost
    and rise against the wanting sun
    they hid with sleeping frost
So the pounding skies
  of corporeal caress
  again the moonless find
    and cry beneath the reigning dark
    they orbit 'round the mind.

Jeffrey N. Froning

Seasons Of Life

Fall appears by chance
  taking a downward
    direction.

Winter appears suddenly
  taking a troubled
    connection.

Spring appears calm
  taking a spirited
    protection.

Summer appears eager
  taking a passionate
    affection.

There are reasons
People must come and go
This is the:
Seasons of Life.

Frances Kelley Capie

Thank You

The work you do
  To pull things through.
The help that you
  Have given to me.
I am not too blind
  to see,
You know,
  Care
Understand
And do more than hear
  You listen.
You play a role
Somehow in my very
  important life
"I love you"
  Wish you the best
and most of all
  I Thank You!

Shana Graves

Highway

Our eyes did not meet by design
Yet both of us were seen
Fifty five mile-per-hour air
And two windowpanes between

Her look was unexpected
I had made no invite
Who knows what made us cast our gaze
The timing just was right

Communication impossible
You know it's always so
Nothing was known of the other
Each had separate ways to go

Passengers we both were
With no power to alter course
So we paralleled awhile
And soon our eyes divorced

David Nurenberg

Elegy Of The Oklahoma Bombing

April 19 of ninety-five
Began in a normal, routine way;
But who would have ever thought
A twist of fate would be that day.

Terror In The Heartland!
That day in ninety-five,
A blast was heard miles around:
Balls of fire shrouded the sky.

At Murrah Federal Building,
People hustled to and fro;
Many lie dead and wounded;
Others mesmerized by woe.

The voice of Oklahoma
Was heard weeping far and near:
Funeral after funeral,
Sad, bitter tears.

The Alfred P. Murrah Building
Is of daily life no longer a part:
But sadly, it forever stands
A true memorial in the heart.

Walterrean Salley

My Darling Valentine

I'd give you a kiss,
If I could be sure,
That you would not miss,
The thought to endure,

For if our lips meet,
I sense that my heat,
Will reject retreat,
Know not how to part,

My kiss is a seal,
Of soft tenderness,
To show what I feel,
My love to confess,

My kiss is a gift,
To last forever,
Emotion to lift,
Our hearts together.

Larry A. Fable

Gone On Home

It's been a year since you
went away
But in my heart it seems like today.

Seventy long years you were here
to teach and guide
But oh how it seems such a
short while

You left behind so much
beauty and grace
I saw your smile in my
Sister's face.

"Amazing Grace," "It's Gonna Rain"
I know you are singing those
gospel songs
Blending your voice around God's
great throne

We have calmed our fears
and dried our tears
because now we realize you have
simply gone on home.

Dorothy Butler

Second Glance

I really though I knew you
Until the day I entered silently,
Catching you alone, unguarded,
With your thoughts displayed openly,
Briefly I saw everything you are
Fascinated, I wanted to get closer,
But suddenly you closed the passage
Reproachful excuses,
Self-Conscious apologies
As your thoughts dispersed
Like sunbeams in a cloud burst.
Composed again,
Nothing conversation,
Hiding the discomfort
With the familiar plastic facade.
Can I never hope for
A second glance?

Debbie Edwards

Herman

Father-in-law
pees on feet
Alzheimers.

Joanna Todd

Sugar Crystal Love

Sweet tea,
and blood from the heart.
Pure sugar,
that runs through my veins.
Sweet tea won't ever run dry,
I fill the cup when I cry.

Everything we own,
we can't keep forever.
Though every day I live,
I won't tick forever.
But everything you love,
you'll try to keep together,
you won't lose it ever,
you can love forever.

Jeff Weitz

Society Slave

Sins committed in the past
Lodge memories forever last
Greed and lust be the fall
Make and break of us all
Guide through depths of turmoil
Heavy-set endless toil
Mirror image of the day
Fall apart, here to stay
Sense driving rhythms of the band
Burning through
Feel backhand motions of my hand
Stabbing you
Friends whose lies seep through sand
Something new
Guide the restless, turn in their graves
Ending abrupt, subject to change
Smell the burning
Nothing to gain
Forever yearning
Forever vain

Aida Sakkal

Melancholy

Oh, long ago
and far away,
skies were glowing bright.
Breezes blowing soft and free,
whispering in the night.

And then one morn
the skies grew dark,
with shadowed hues of gray.
The wind threw rain upon the lands,
and chased the sun away.

DeAnna Bingham

Life

Life is a long, dark corridor,
covered with spiny needles,
its poisonous tips sharp
and pointed.

Winds blow you down it and
all you can do is follow
the path.

Yet, somehow, it takes you back,
in the darkness and silence,
waiting, hoping, for daylight.

Tina Fisher

Midnight Oil

In my metallic black Olds,
putting miles on the counter,
I notice the night sky and its
midnight darkness, most
mortals silent as ever.
I smell the engine, the
black, burning oil. I drive
with only the moon
as my guide. Stomach
growling, I pull out melting
chocolate to satisfy the
hunger. There is no need
to go home to a dark
and empty house when I
can be violent and carefree
with the angel of death
beside me, knowing that
my driving alone can put me
in a coffin six feet under.

Amy Decker

Finished

Dreaming dreams with a hopeful heart
Filled my soul when I was young.
Fearful screams and hopeless laughter
Filled my voice when I was done.

Xtian Collins

Where The Dead Reside

The dawn refuses to break
The light will never touch this side
For even the sun's afraid
Where the dead reside

The living are shunned here
The good are despised
Those here are all evil
Where the dead reside

If the light does touch this side
Even the dead will die
Long dead flesh will burn and decay
Where the dead reside

Their souls left them long ago
To go to the other side
Now they live without life
Where the dead reside

Here they'll stay in eternal night
Never to leave this side
Lifeless lives of lifeless light
Where the dead reside

Phil Wallace

First Kiss

There you were.
Without hesitation I pulled you close.
I whisper your name.
Our lips meet in a soft embrace,
nothing between us.
I feel your skin and warm breath,
your heart next to mine.
Souls shared.
Our passion melts the world around us.
Time stops.
For once I am complete,
fully alive,
and for a brief moment heaven is ours.

Krister Larson

Number 1

Broken Barricades, Bleeding Tears.
Malnourished light exposed.
Cacophonous night denied.
Madness metastasizing -
Melancholia.
Vows tomorrows faceless Fears,
end this Blissful solitude.
Light reflects life's long toils
While darkness heals the soul.
Red Raindrops easing righteous pain.
Fire in the grave. Fire in the heart.
Salvation Revoked.
Redeem my Spirit yesterday.
End this Bounty-this
Solitude.

Alice Mayo

Insanity

Woven into cloth
The pictures in my mind
Hanging on my wall
Right before my eyes
Piercing at my heart
Stealing every breath
Horrifying thoughts
   Laughing at my innocence
   Tearing me apart
   Taking my control
   Killing all my loved ones
     Leaving me all alone

Erin Elizabeth O'Donnell

Life

Propelled into the stream,
Traveling at light speed.
With strength and urgent
Desire, I take the lead.

Catching fragrant scent,
Hinting of lilac and rose.
Continuing amid a swarm,
Just following my nose.

Catching sight of you,
I struggle, tired a spell.
Reaching for your essence
Closed in a tight shell.

Suddenly, with open arms,
You engulf me, my soul.
We become one bonding,
Sharing, creating, becoming whole.

Through teeming trials
We exist in endless strife.
We share a thread from
Our creation to death of life.

Scott H. Hendricks

Sands And Tides

Beautiful to him -
As clouds on a summer day
Carefree and light as a feather.

Handsome to her
A quiet lake in a forest
Cool, calm, and soothing to the eye.

The tides pulling-
Sand grabs as they are made into one
Heavenly, together they are.

April Michelle Hart

Bubble Troubles

There I was, stretched out, relaxed,
All warm and wet with bubbles.
And then, of course, the telephone...
It started having troubles.
It rang real loud, just once or twice.
Just long enough for me
To jump right out and slip, and slide,
And fall and hurt my knee.
And so I thought it would be neat
to train my doggie, Rover
To run and fetch the telephone
And bring it right on over.
It worked out fine until one day
Dear Rover I did spy
Waiting by the door to get
His ordered pizza-pie.

Kat Carter

My Love Is As A Watchman

My love is as a watchman
Standing guard upon thy life
My love is your protection
From every fear and strife
None shall come nigh thee
None shall succeed to destroy
My love is as thy watchman
None shall stand with any plot or ploy
I am your high tower
To me you can always run
I am your rear guard
The battle's already been won
When the battle rages on
There seems no end in sight
My love is ever watching
even though the darkest night
My love is as a watchman
Never ever fear
My provision is your security
My power is ever near.

Kim Mattison

Intimate Contemplation

If snakes had hands
they would be such as these
that I watch dart across the canvas
serious, direct,
demanding control of the brush
and the dripping colors.
Looking past hands to arms,
past arms to paint-splattered shirt,
past shirt to face
frozen in intimate contemplation.
I'm silent
as I watch him
standing in a darkened field
under a shower of lost fire-flies.
I speak.
"Are you imitating life?" I ask.
He sighs, "No,"
a long deep pause,
"just painting."

Deanna Williams

Untitled

The beat of my frantic no-show
heart moves in grooves at each of
the steps you take from beneath the
wish list in this jealous void I call
an enduring vision.

David Bonarigo

As The Beginning Ends, And The End Begins

He rises up,
Above his end.
He looks down,
Peering at those he loved.
He sees his children,
Crying, overwhelmed with sadness.
His wife, his mother,
Grief stricken forever.
A stabbing light ray,
Turns him to the beginning.
Slowly he walks,
Traveling towards the unknown.
A great being embraces him,
Leading him away.
Its arms provide comfort,
Warmth and peace.
Its peace in relaxing,
Allowing him to let go.
Finally, he walks into paradise,
And begins again.

Abbie House

Together

Together we work,
Together we stand,
Together we are, hand in hand,
Together we build,
   Together we lay,
Together we know we'll always stay
   Together we hold
   Together we'll cry,
Together we'll be until we die
Together we live
Together we love
Together we are, forever

A.C. Conrad

Native Man

Native man. I dreamed you.
Dancing in the forest.
A beautiful naked man.
Twirling between the trees.
Hands stretched to the sky.
Hair in a wild swirl across your cheek.
Heels pounding the moss.
Native man. I dreamed you.
Moving with the wind.
Streams running in your veins.
Skin lanced with sun and hemlock.
Eyes shut to feel your ecstasy.
Heart pounding to the music of earth.
And drums of ancient fathers.
Native man. I dreamed you.
But you were real.
And I lay hiding in the leaves.
Just to watch.

Debbie O'Neill

Grace

Of all the Grace that I receive
None proves more the Master,
Then when I ask Him for His Will
And He gives me the answer.

In Jesus' Name He gives His Power
To do just what He asks us
Such Grace as this we need to tell
To others all around us.

Elmo Mathias Pinard

The Moment

I introduce myself
I'm calm
reassuring
in control
I lead my new friend
somewhere quiet
and peaceful
and then
I drop behind so slightly
then grasp
they freeze
I bite
I take my fill, then kiss them
in thanks
then join
the night

David A. Nichols

Belonging

Where do I belong...
 For I fear
  to dance with the prosperous
  beg with the poor
  or hate with the murderous.
I love what I believe,
 I believe in what I love;
For all I want are thy
 smiles,
 laughter,
 and
 happiness.
My hopes and dreams
 are a mixture of
 thine compounds of values;
May all be equal
 when thou art perished
 for then I shalt know
 where I
  belong...

Karen Porter

Witch Hunt

We've flown far and high;
You and I.
We've kissed the moon
Caressed the sky.
We've danced on sunlight
And swum through tears
But now the end is finally here.
Those who are shackled to the ground
Have learned our secrets.
They hunt us down.
"Witch," they say as they draw near.
Their ears are dead they cannot hear.
One last chance to say goodbye
Before...
Again...
It's time to fly!
Our souls entwined in one last flight,
We reach the heavens of endless night
And sit by the side of our Master,
The Lord of Light, Life, and After.

Sarah Howard

Sad Autumn Roses

Sad autumn roses
crane toward the Indian sun
too soon forgotten

Scott Dellabella

Vampire

There is no heaven
There is no hell
There is nothing I know not well.
My black heart from pure desire
In the end I shall not expire.
Skin as white as winters snow
perching eyes deep and low.
In the shadow where I lay
Like a hunter waiting for prey.
Darkness is my light,
hidden in the night.
My hunger has gone unfed
thoughts of blood run in my head
I am your darkest fear
but I am standing right here.
Close your eyes and say good night,
Now I take my deadly bite.

Christina Lawson

An Angel As My Guardian

An angel as my guardian,
An angel like a Tower.
An angel stands beside me,
It poses as my power.
An angel loves and guides me,
And helps me through hard times.
An angel sent by God alone,
It helps me through life's rhymes.
An angel sent to tell me,
My mission here on earth.
An angel that has been here
Ever since my birth.
This angel, I admire.
This angel is my life.
Lord, I remember you always,
Through my strength in strife.
An angel as my guardian,
An angel like a Tower.
An angel stands beside me,
It poses as my power.

Roxann Havener

I Thank God For My Grandma

For her quiet peaceful home,
Where God's love is undeniably known,
For saying what's on her mind,
But in a way that's so kind.
Though since childhood the
miles kept us apart,
Her smiles always been on my heart.
I thank God for her soft touch,
Her warm hugs and loving smiles.
Even through some hard trials.
And even now, when I take my boys,
I know they feel the same joys,
As they play with the same old toys.
In my grandmas home where
God's love is undeniably known.
I thank God for my grandma.

Tami Hall

Possession

Any and everything a man
owns, he will either keep,
sell, or give away. Yet there
is one thing a man has that
he will neither sell nor give
away, but will ever keep, and
that's his word.

Jon S. Scott

Cry

The echo of the ocean
In a bright pastel seashell
The cry of a soul
Yearning for release
Barred from escape
Trapped in a tiny prison
The shell wasting away
Alone in a sea of infinity
Stranded on a beach
The briefest touch of the tide
Marks an endless passage of time
The cry of a soul
Breaks the depths of an eternal night
Echoing in an ocean of silence
Until the day
The shell erodes completely away
And the cry of a soul
Vanishes forever. . .

Jason D. Peek

Rivers Of The Night

The rivers of the
Night move slowly,
Deep inside your
Mind, feel it take
Its grasp on you,
Its silky waters
Feel divine.
Drowning oh so steadily,
Deep into that stream,
Now feel the darkness
Of that water, steal
Away your dreams.

Derek Bailey

For K

I feel a presence
That defies description
A connection so strong
It transcends space and time . . .
A voice that calls
In the midst of a dream . . .
A vision that appears
As I trudge through the day . . .
A glance . . .
A touch . . .
A feeling so deep inside my heart
I know this presence
From some other place . . .
Some other time
It is the Soul
That matches mine.

Tracy L. Simmons

A Whispering Wind?

O' magnificent wind from whence you came
 Was everything the same
Were you a whisper on someone's lips
 A breath that grew to blow
To devastate, lay all low
 That before had grandly stood?

Or were you a whisper on someone's lips
 That gently touched a cheek
That grew a bit to a delicate peak
 Then, lightly drifted by
Leaving with the softest sigh
 A balmy, docile whispering wind?

Mary Burford

Walk Along A Beach At Night

White sands
Black night
Both muted
By pale moonlight.

Cool breeze blowing
The ocean roars
As two lovers walk
Along the shore.

Footprints follow
In the sand
Behind the lovers
Hand in hand.

Sea oats whisper
Among the dunes
As the lovers pass
In the night,
Along a beach
In June.

William J. Worlds

"Somewhere Out There"

It's great to know somewhere out there
I have a Dad.
He's my best friend and pal
I never had.

Just thinking of the possible things
He could have done with me.
Tells me he's the finest Daddy
in the world "to me."
Yes, there are other fine Dads,
I agree,
But they will never compare
to my daddy and me.
When I have trouble
I think of my Dad,
for he could be the best pal for me.
When I grow to manhood
"What a man I'll be"
If only I could see
my Dad with me!

Andy Aitken

Ode To Sweety

She was a fuzzy ball of grey
when first brought to me—
Abandoned by her Mother, and
could barely see.

I held her close and loved her,
and talked like a Mother should.
She stayed so still and purred
as if she understood.

She grew and learned to love me,
with all of her kitty heart.
I was her only Mother—
We must never part!

Time went by for nineteen years,
and our friendship grew,
She thought I was her Mother
and that was surely true!
Now, there is a lonesome place
since my Sweety's gone,
But, the memory of my little friend
will forever linger on.

Lois L. Zirk

Untitled

Though but four weeks are we apart,
and the distance not so far,
still, I yearn to hear your voice
and touch your hand
and feel the beat of your heart.

True, it's only but a little while,
and time passes more swiftly now,
yet, I burn to kiss your lips
and hold you close
and see your lovely smile.

The days pass fast enough,
but the nights - interminably long!
Oh! My love, I miss you so
and the things we both know
beside you, where I belong.

Lester Segarnick

Till Paradise Was Lost

In the garden made
When foundation laid
Stirred and created earth

A peace it ruled the air
It was sweet and rare
'Till paradise was lost

Flowering plants there be
Next to young sapling
Of white tressed cherry trees

The blooms of peach and red
Guard where feet will tread
'Till paradise is lost

Then would twig give way
For someone to say
The way to lose it all

Life polluted by sin
Letting darkness in
And paradise is lost

Elizabeth Richardson

To My Son

He was born in a strident cry
no doubt about it he won't be shy.
Doctor, family and friends
not much physical expectation
What a surprise! What an explosion!
As time went by, he had grown strong,
all presupposition reveal wrong
Then he became a man on his own
ready to conquer the throne.
He became very athletic
and reminded me of those athletes
participating in the Olympics,
pompous appearance on a pamphlet
What an experience when you're young
to be lucky as you're growing
day after day playing
games after games, winning
with no defect
so goals reaching are no secret.

Julie Montfort

Please

Though I've not seen you in thirty years
And we're miles and miles apart
That one kiss we shared makes me beg
Please! Let go my heart!

Esther L. Alvarado

In Love With You

I see you as
A female complete,
And you've knocked me
Off my feet.

When you greet me
With a hello sweet,
Increased is
My heart's beat.

When your
Eyes meet mine.
I'm sent to a cloud
Higher than nine.

You fill me with
Thoughts of desire,
And have sparked
Within me love's fire.

Night and day
It for you burns;
Night and day
I for you yearn.

Mark Johnson

Lust

Lust is a greedy one,
It roams the earth alone
In need of none
Other than itself.

It grabs - it takes

With no thought of errors or mistakes.
What matters is the now.
How the void is filled

With whom - and how.

It has no accountability
And least of all respectability
That is the nature of lust.

And if you must partake
Well, then you must.

But keep in mind
The pleasure's brief
And there lacks the trust
With the rogue and rascal
We call lust.

Sylvia Savala

Looking Back

Dark and snowy - cold winds blowing
Deep in the dark and silent hush
Only a quiet breath is heard
Everyone is off in dreams
Not I - no peaceful rest I earn
Thoughts that come from long ago
Memories I watch unfold
Jump around inside my head
I toss and turn and curse my bed

They say, life flashes before the eyes
When a drowning person dies
Not I - when images appear
Looking back down thru the years
And I can't sleep; I do know why.
If I could back up and start anew
There are things that I would do
To change these thoughts - and
Give me peaceful sleep

Rose A. Dombrowski

Cronus Too, Weeps!

I have lived a million lives,
not once have I tasted Death;
Though countless times I have tried,
I failed to end Nature's breath.

Wisdom be my companion,
always he is at my side;
Experience is my scion;
Oh, if only I had died!

Civilizations I saw...
their lives, their glory, their fall;
Bloody wars, too well I know,
where triumphant Death stood tall!

Is life to be unbroken?
Have I not earned my repose?
I alone am forsaken;
Why must I witness chaos?

In this life, I've known the joys,
still the grave I long to see;
loud and clear shall I rejoice,
when Death claims and conquers me!

Noel San Pablo

Life

Life's a little imp,
Who slaps you in the face;
Then he vows he's sorry,
And helps you win the race.
He laughs when you are down,
And chuckles when you're blue,
He claims to love you early,
Then makes a face at you.
Today he's sweet and loving,
With a heart of solid gold;
Tomorrow wears a cynic's smile
That makes your blood run cold.
Each of us has met him,
In person or disguise,
But to know him you must love him
If you are truly wise.

Shirley Duffy

No Greater Love

I gaze upon the wind-tossed sea
And ask myself how can this be
That God should love me so.

His son he sent to calvary
A ransom there to die for me
O that He loves me so.

Then in the stillness of the morn
Upon the wings of angels borne
He answered me,
"My child someday you'll see."

Georgia Poe

The Color Of His Love

The color of his love is red,
The blood that flowed; for me it bled,
Upon the cross He died for sin,
All my burdens He took within.

Just before my savior died,
He looked to heaven, and this He cried,
My God, my God, how can this be?
Have I not died to set men free?

Nicholas Jameson

Growing

Why is it nothing hurts more
Than the truth
Another day despairing what?
Why what I'm not, I suppose
As even though you're here
With me, the distance
Is growing sacrificed
To have you, watching
You grow - as I
Despairingly fall further
And further behind
If I can't face you
I can't face the world
Your reflection is
Blinding to the deadened light that
Still remains within me.

Seeing the flower wilt,
Hoping it won't die.

Elaine Courtier

The Quest

Under the skies of a hot summer sun
In the year of our Lord
Nineteen hundred and ninety one
Between a celestial gathering
And a lunar eclipse
A legend that once was
Became a legend that is
Stonehenge gives its secrets
Under a hot summer sun
But only after a millennium
And only to one
The circles were left for all to see
But only true believers may find
The keeper of the key

Chet Tyrakowski Sr.

To My Dad

I see the shutters bang!
I see the curtains sway!
I see the view from inside.
Father, is that you?
I see the man who lifted me to the sky.
I see the looming figure,
Invincible to the world.
Father, is that you?
I see the grass, green as
Emeralds on a wet, dewy morning.
I see my future, I see my past.
I see the man whose name is
Courage.
I see the man whose life is
Pride.
I see the man who name is
Father.

Blake A. Sandford

October Nights

October nights what
a fright ghostly sights
Starry nights
Rustling leaves
Give me the frights on October
Nights!

Jenny Decker and Katie Donnelly

Sunrise, Sunset

A sunrise,
The start of a new day.
No surprise,
This golden light display.

Endless source of energy,
Giving life.
Around about we see
Daily Strife.

Like the sun
Our boundless powers race
From beyond,
Awaiting our embrace.

Oh, understanding
Let us face
Loving, sharing, caring,
Endless grace.

Then fading light will for
Us to get,
No more chances before
The sunset.

Bruce Robert Johns

Jingo

Shiny red apples
    in a clear crystal bowl
Long burgundy tapers
    candlelight glow.
Round table cloth
    of Battenburg lace
when my Valentine comes
    There's a smile on my face
His whiskers stand out
    his tail has a curl
it's all for Jingo
    my little pet squirrel.

Hazel Gray Miller

Window Undraped

In that quiet time
Of fading light
As giant shadows
Stir across the land
And birdsong hangs
Suspended on golden threads,
The heart reaches out
For the yesterdays
Gone in the eyes of time,
And memory
Heals not the heart -
The ache clutches boldly,
Persistently -
Your absence questions the need
For my tomorrows -

Mary F. Sharp

Why

You said our lives
should be together
In this lonely world
two would be better
girl it is plain to see
You are leaving me
your wandering eyes
Can not hide the lies
was it something
I said to you
or was it something
you had to do.

Ray Acosta

Between Lust And Love

The sweetness of the mango juice teases my tongue, yet
it is not the warmth of the sun which has, my body, won.

Passion seems to be more than just sexual attraction,
for as I do cry; my tears are the balance of what may, in
another world, happen.

Time almost suspended forces not a sound of protest
from within. I watch the light move into patterns, raising
one word which possesses all of eternity's sin.

My disposition has yet to be reclaimed, while thoughts
of a never ending kiss endure a wild abandonment, never
to be tamed.

Sometimes while allowing the snow to clasp my naked
body, I sense the very presence of pure love and raw
hatred clashing inside the vines, which sprung the glory
of a non-tragic death endowing all but the sweetness of
a rare mango juice.

Lori Comis

Listen to the sounds that times makes!

Listen to the sounds that time makes!
A spider spinning cobwebs on a sunny hill,
A caterpillar crossing over a windowsill.

Listen to the sounds that time makes!
A turtle turning on a blade of grass,
A schoolroom where a century there's been no class.

Listen to the sounds that time makes!
The soft snow falling on a prickly pine,
An icicle melting in spring sunshine.

Listen to the sounds that time makes!
The rubbing together of the bee's knees,
The deafening roar of a fleas sneeze.

Listen to the sound that time makes!
A golden leaf falling on the frosty ground
and a thousand other crashing, grinding sounds.

Listen! Listen!
Listen to the sounds!
Were you a ladybug like me...
You'd hear them all very Loudly!

E. Laurence

Iowa-Easter 1978

Inside, my chest is heavy
Outside though, the hot sun glistens on the bright snow,

I hear birds,
It is still day

Have my lengthy beliefs been in vain?
What is the truth of the future?
How can I know? What should I do?
I love you so deeply.

So many times I am alone.
Interests tho many, cannot satisfy like warm companionship
My tears have dried, tho welled-up.
Tiredness of solitude fills me.

Soon I'll know, I pray.
The urgency of needing your response calls -
I'm filled with heavy heart
Stay close to me, dear God. Please let me hear from you.

M. Jane Keil

When Grandpa Died

Friday
Mom is home from the hospital.
Surprise, we're glad to see her.
"Grandpa's died," she says to us.
Quiet. Pain. Grief-stricken.

Saturday
Back from bowling.
Happy to be with family.
"How ya doing, Honey," Godfather says to me.
Joyless. Crying. Downhearted.

Sunday
The wake.
Lively and beautiful is how the flowers smell.
"Come here, Buddy," I say to Brandon with open arms.
Mournful. Distress. Memories.

Monday
The funeral.
Pleased to look so good in a new outfit.
"Come here my big goon," I say to Dusty.
Breathless. Extreme sadness. Accepting.

Jennifer Morse

A Home

A white picket fence.
With grass on the lawn.

A big bay window, where the sun shines thru
It looks real good, it's a nice place to live.

It's a house
But is it a home?

Early that morning they leave out the door
They return at the end of the day
The lights are all lit and it's bright inside.

It's a house, but is it a home?

There's a mother, a father, and two little kids
There's laughter and plenty of play
It's not in the money, or the things that they have
It's all in the love they display.

It's a house; and yes, it's a home.

Jerry Pendleton

Israel God's Apple

Israel God's apple bestowing blessing or curses
Hebrews irrigation delta irrevocable benefits
Turmoil enemies versus Operatives

Tragically Jesuits put the casket
They say, "Did the Israelis defer Jesus?
Let's condemn them"
How much more the wrath of God be on?

The Meeks were the priest
We are just wild branches
Ingrafted into Israel vine
The Natural Branches will turn in obedience

Jesus will go to the City of David
Calling it the New Jerusalem
Hundred forty-four chambers God

This will be ironic to some
Don't let it be you
The apple of God's eye is Israel

Donald Taylor

Wrestling For Control

I looked above where Christ is said to be
I needed his power to stabilize me
I called out in faith
Remembering his word said a twinkle is all it takes
I confess with my mouth my faults
I need that redemption his blood bought.

When I believed in my heart
I felt the power surge of my life jump start
I knew I had connected
And my lifestyle would be corrected.

After this powerful experience in life
I begin to see the whole world in a different light
I begin to do things I never had the nerve
I begin to face life instead of trying to swerve.

I check my words and actions with the book
I realize my inheritance was waiting
Faith, surrender and obedience was all it took.
The wrestling continued, but the control
Was fully dominating
Now life is so fascinating.

Walter Davis

One Life, Eternal Sacrifices

A problem arouses instead of you
Your naked legs, tangled in with mine, now
remind me of lonely death.
I cry, I pray, I watch the time
My heart
Nothing but a tiny figurine that you summon
from a parental staff.
The goodness of your magic, your possession,
protects me from the outside world, yet
nothing else.
Look into my eyes
Are you illiterate? Do you not read what my
heart feels?
Your interest are dead; yet I live
I'll not let you preserve my life for yourself
I redefine selfish - lonely one
Even though tomorrow comes,
Tomorrow comes another end.

Debra A. Woods

Untitled

I never grew tired of saying I love...
Although in return, just silence responded.
Bittersweet was the air, in moments of peace.
Tears of heartache, and dreams that grew scarce.
But time does go on.
Years bring wisdom.
One learns to replenish
Through planning and gibberish.
The words many long for, can come unexpectedly.
The smallest of miracles, can speak without words.
To an open heart, though, they should be easy to hear.
So far, many episodes
Have shaped my performance
In the scenes of life.
Nevertheless, I have discovered,
Silent words, loving looks, and an honest heart...
In the smallest, yet most significant loophole in life.
Innocence, in the eyes of a child.

Liesl Duntley

Life Is Like A Forest

Life is like a forest
And we live among the trees
the love I've found within you,
Flows like the gentle breeze,
Being so lonely in this forest
Kept my eyes wet with dew
One day the sun shined through the trees
And that's how I found you
Heaven must be here on earth
The moonbeams are your prize
The sunshine is all around you
And the stars are in your eyes.
We're like two birds in this spacious forest
And each must play its role
We'll be forever young, in our secret place
but in the forest, we must grow old
Darling, should I ever lose you
or someone should clip your wing
I'll become secluded in my part of the forest
For I will have lost my everything.

Luciel McCord

And She Chose Me!

Feminine beyond belief; beauty such as sirens know.
Tenderness to soothe all grief; sympathetic nature's glow.

Dainty, breathless poise and grace; needs protection now and then.
Blest, divine, sweet, trusting face, that which nurtures virile men.

Strong of spirit, never quits, faith in God surpasses all.
Wins her battles by her wits, always there whenever I call.

Love of music and the arts; leaps to help her fellow-man.
Captures male and female hearts in a way no other can.

Makes her man feel like a king, so instinctive are her ways.
Nothing has a hollow ring, honor's bright as sunlit rays.

Breeding spotless as a queen, bearing, manners, just as fine;
Principles, the best I've seen, can't believe that she is mine!

When she loves, she gives her all, totally, as one can be.
Makes me feel I'm ten feet tall. Can't Believe That She Chose Me!

H. Alexander Baldauf

Ode to Ula Mae

Ula Mae was a woman, a lady, a child.
She grew up poor, tattered and alone.
She longed, longed for something of which
no one knew. She hurt, she sighed, she moaned and groaned.
We thought it was her heart, but dear God, it was her soul.

She said Lord, help me, give me a chance, give me a house.
She said, let me live, Lord let me live, live, live,
live to see my children grow up.
Then she said, Lord, let me see my grandchildren grow up,
Yes, Lord, my great grands, too. Oh God, just let me live on.

Now God, I want to see Mama and Papa who died when I was a
babe. I want to see Annie Bell and Lewis,
Yes Lord, life has not been the same since Andrew went on,
and Lord, I want to see Jesus. . .face to face.

For God gives life and God gives love
God gave us a mother who was filled with love.
She's gone home now to be with Jesus, mama, Papa and them all
but she left us with the love and the life
that she'd prayed would live on.

Dr. Joyce Bowie Guillory

Dreaming Diamonds

The moon is high,
The skies are blackened.
Night has won over the day,
But not for long.
Her song will not be sung forever.
Dawn creeps up and pushes her away.
The sun takes his rightful place.
The birds begin their song of praise
At the arrival of the new day.
The stars are gone forever,
Waiting for their mistress to appear,
Waiting for a chance to dream
The dreams that only they can understand.
The sun blazes on
With no thought about
The sister who will rise again
With her dreaming diamonds.

Melissa Keyser

Impaired

As I sit here in the night,
Looking at the sky so bright,
I can't help wondering what it's like,
to live in silence or have no sight?

Never seeing beautiful things, like birds,
or trees or even Spring, Never hearing music
or a baby's cry or even airplanes in the sky.

No one knows or even cares, about the ones we
call Impaired!

The blind can't see, the deaf can't hear,
So this is for you because I Care!

Mona Mathis

The Chesapeake

Chesapeake, O Chesapeake, once your wondrous shores did show
The print of moccasined feet that silently trod the snow.
Men cherished verdant forests and the feast felled by the bow,
The silent nights with only sounds of waves upon the shore,
Clouds of geese against a sky, white-ribboned by the wind.
This was nature's peace and treasures from your grassy floor.
But now that bounty is no more;
Those footsteps silenced on your saddened shore.
The forest now lies low, fallen to the blow of adze and axe,
No longer harbors all the life that was.
The swans renew, their spirits whistling through the winds of time,
Mourn once pristine shores that no longer rest sublime.
But calls of geese transcend the path to death.
The eagle soars on winds that give it breath.
Your mighty heart still flows 'mid hills that gave it birth.
The osprey now takes up the cry; its fledglings now deny
Man's hand to sever all the life upon the earth.
And so in time your waters will not grieve,
The bounties of your bosom we'll receive,
As your many rivers flow through you to the sea.

Laura Neitz

Never Have I Felt This Way

Never before has it been true
Never have I been able to say—
I love you.

You have made a difference
It is true
Here finally said—
are the words
"I love you."

Dorothy Hrynyk

Family

The gentle smiles on their faces,
The proud looks in their eyes,
The way they talk about me,
The way they live for me,
Tells me how much they love me,
No matter how bad I've been.
But I grew up and changed a lot,
I was no longer a sweet teen.
My rude and harsh behavior
Surprised and injured them a lot.
The cozy nights and cheerful weekends
Were now spent in fights of rage,
And we were driven two separate ways
Our friendship, love forgotten long ago.
But if they'd give me one more chance
Maybe I'd try to work it out,
But now there's no time,
I had three strikes and now I'm out.

Yana Dubrovsky

I Am Walking In Your Grace

I feel a sense of disparity today in my life,
Actually, it has been creeping up on me, causing me strife.
Disparity a quiet stranger, happiness he is trying to erase,
My Lord, —— I am walking in Your grace.

My heart feels far away, drowned in loneliness,
Who will understand my feeling of such hopelessness?
Why has Your presence left without even a trace?
My Lord, —— I am walking in Your grace

I have been strong, maybe, too much in control,
And now my emotional limits have taken their toll.
I call upon You, Lord, let me see a glimpse of Your face,
My Lord, —— I am walking in Your grace

I have allowed stress to be in charge of my yesterdays,
Slowly choking out the Light of the One to whom I pray.
My heart does not like the feeling of this emotional place,
My Lord, —— I am walking in Your grace.

Help me to see those things that I can let go,
Allowing the Light of my heart to return and glow.
Let me filter reality as light filters through lace,
My Lord, —— I am walking in Your grace.

Candy A. Estes

Snow

Ever so gently
And softly you fall.
Being partial to no one,
But falling on all.

Your whiteness shows purity
And beauty so fair,
As you seem to slowly
Fall with such care.

You cover mother nature's
Children with white.
And make the lonely world
Seem oh such a Sight!

Of grandeur and splendor
And beauty untold,
For after you've come
She's a sight to Behold!

Ruth Elizabeth Jones Stone

Elements

I felt a draft and heard the laugh
Of the wind coming through the pane
Then came a sigh as clouds rolled by
Too sad to stop the rain

Soon came the banter to set the canter
Of the drops that fall in tune
To this music sweet nought can compete
Except the rainbow that crosses the moon

Through the colors bright, there comes a light
From the heavens in all its glory
Burning across the sky, the shooting beams they fly
To let the stars tell their own story

Then comes a calm, to embrace the dawn
With the fragrance of nature so sweet
A soft morning song, the earth sings so strong
To the drum of life's padded feet

David M. Vacca

Mama

If I should stumble, if I should fall
If I don't come when you call
When it's time for you to leave
Mama, wait for me

If you should leave, if you should go
If you don't already know
I will chase you down the street
Mama, wait for me

Don't leave me here one hour, don't leave me here one day
Don't leave me at all, Mama, please just stay
'Cause I can't be here without you, these toys just won't do
Mama, pick me up and take me with you

If I should miss you, if I should cry
Will you wave at me good-bye
I'll see you through my tears
Mama, I'll wait right here.

Leland Strebeck

Untitled

You left me standing there
Acting like you didn't care
And now there's not a day
That I don't say
That I don't love you anymore.

And I don't love you anymore.
I've never felt this way before
Cause I don't love you anymore.

My mind has been at war
Since you walked out the door
And now there's not a day
That I don't say
That I don't love you anymore.

And I don't love you anymore
I've never felt this way before
Cause I don't love you anymore.

Words spoken are very few
And I don't know what to do
Cause I don't love you anymore.

Candice Beth Anderson

Oh, To Be Free

On the day of my birth the Lord said to me,
"Free as a bird you will be, you will be."

Into my childhood, dancing with glee,
Free as a bird I will be, I will be.

As a young woman with a whole world to see,
Free as a bird I will be, I will be.

Off to the chapel; the wedding's at three,
Free as a bird we will be, we will be.

Living and loving, we age gracefully,
Free as a bird we will be, we will be.

A retirement party planned just for me?
Free as a bird I will be, I will be.

Reading and sewing and watching TV,
Free as a bird I will be, I will be.

No longer to hear, no longer to see,
Free as a bird I will be, I will be.

So when I am gone don't cry for me,
Free as a bird I will be, I will be.

Chantele B. McDermott

Dreams Vs. Reality

Never shall I see the sun's true rays,
Nor the clouds draw back to the star's brilliant shades.
I walk with a smile untrue to my name,
As if my heart stopped beating
When the wind was sustained.
I only pray that the rain that pours down my face,
Shall wash away my tears, sorrow & disgrace.
My life is but a dream,
Still lingering when I wake,
When my eyes truly open,
My soul refuses to negotiate.
I think about the days I simply wasted away.
Wondering where my mind went,
as I sit here today,
Just close my tainted eyes,
I'll fall into distant sleep,
My dreams are always better,
Than my true reality

Spring S. Palser

To Live Is Not To Die

To see is to be,
To be is to see,

If you say hi you say good-bye
If you say good-bye you say hi,

To walk in is to walk out,
To walk out is to walk in,

If yes means i will,
No means i won't,

To live is to die,

We all die,
Except for the one who does not:

See to be,
Say hi and never say good-bye
Walks out but does not walk in,
Does not believe in yes,
To live is not to die!

Ashley L. Simons

A Love Letter To My Life

A heart once wounded was I, left wandering lost in the snow;
I searched for warmth and safety where love just could not grow.
My eyes grew tired, my limbs were ice; my heart had little strength.
I starved for a tiny sip of nourishment to drink.

Over mountains I had climbed, trodding valleys in-between,
Chasing rainbows above and sunsets so serene;
I set foot in many deserts some colder than the ice;
I lost my way, I lost myself what I did sacrifice.

I screamed and yelled across the land crying out in fear
For anyone to rescue me and take away the tears.
I prayed that I'd find shelter before it was too late;
Before I gave up searching before I grew to hate.

No one called, no one answered not one sign of hope appeared,
Wearily I wiped my eyes and my vision slowly cleared;
And behold what lie ahead but you within my sight;
A fire within the chilling air a peace brought to my nights.
Now a kindling flame burns within my heart
And scary things inside get lost within the dark;
And soon they'll disappear as I become your Wife,-
Because you have my love and have become My Life.

Laura M. Enloe

Confession

No one knows my dirty little secret except
my sister and the one who took me there.
The place had a feeling of sorority,
but we kept our repentant eyes down.

Cross-legged in summer dresses on the cool tile,
we listened to the matron.
She gave her sermon on what to expect
by way of pain and convalescence.

Summoned, one by one, we marched
along the dim corridor to a pre-designated chamber.
Still warm from the last sinner, the table was covered
with paper and awaited me.
I climbed up and put my feet in position -
the faint swell of my belly exposed.

I was vacuumed clean before I knew it.
All I remember is the nurse's face,
her antiseptic smile, and my fingernails
making crescent moons in her kindly offered arm.

Susan H. Ilich

My Love to You

Love is falling......
yet getting up over and over again.

Love is learning.....
that my way isn't always right.

Love is letting go.....
even though I want so badly to hold on.

Love is holding hands.....
through good times and bad times.

Love is accepting.....
both accomplishments and failures.

Love is leaning on God.....
so I can be there for you.

Love is.....
forgiving the past, not worrying about the future, and

Mandy L. Lafevor

Ballet of the Leaves

It was a cold crisp November day as a I stepped outside for
my usual daily stroll.
The sky a clear blue broken only by big white fleecy clouds.
The trees were now almost barren of leaves.
As I stepped onto the street a slight breeze tousled my hair.
Everywhere were crisp brown leaves tumbling and swirling
in all directions.
Walking down the street the leaves circled my feet as if
asking me to come and dance with them.
Almost, as if by cue, a stronger breeze began to blow.
Watching in awe, I realized I was seeing a ballet created
by Mother Nature.
Yes — here it was, in all its natural beauty—The
Ballet of the Leaves.

Kathryn Shivers

Canadeilgeld

Decaying death dances numb, dumb and in
Different on the devil strip.
Waiting, wading
Below the sizably slim shadows of
Children's slender shapes, as they slip
Into the unmethodical methods
Of human; apprentice to non
Compes mentis.

Incubus incubates cool corruption
Inside the wide wind and air thin,
Feting, fading,
The incandescence of adolescence.
As it lessens, time's tale begins again.
weak wonders ponder its presence within,
Without-it is-continuous
Never finis...

Noah Pollock

Together We Pray

The day is long, the night is longer,
The morning comes to fast,
and the dawn keeps getting colder.

Always wanting more and more
no money,no time for a life anymore.
What do we do to keep ourselves sane?
We pray to Jesus Christ and
In God's name...

Things will get better, you'll see
Never give up, especially on your dreams,
The days will shorten,
The nights will too.
The mornings will come slower
and the dawn will have a special warm
glow just for you.

Life can be good, just wait and see
There is a lot out there
for you and me.

Cambri Freeman

Halloween

There was a vampire on Halloween.
There was a little pumpkin queen.
There was a monster that gave me a fright.
There was a ghost that came out at night.
There was a goblin that was very scary.
There was a little kid that dressed up as a fairy.
There was a skeleton that was really bony.
There was a mummy that was a phony.
Halloween is great time of year.
Halloween is a great time for fear!

Ashley Altman

The Flower of Love

There's a magical garden in a faraway place.
Filled with blooms of amazing grace.

Each flower unfolds with mystical wonder,
From whence they come is something to ponder.

Each petal is a masterpiece designed by God above
My favorite flower is the flower of love
Which grows more beautiful in every way.
Nurtured by caring, laughter and even tears someday.

Blessed is he who finds the key that opens the gate.
Look very hard, for it is Never too Late!
    Alice I. Muus

The Crossroads

Going to the crossroads they said
a meeting place for all
to share a dream
or just make plans
for the work and its demands

Tomorrow tomorrow they said
tomorrow at the crossroads

A hiding place for many
to cleanse their soul and minds
a place to comfort those that are left behind

Tomorrow they said
tomorrow at the crossroads

Let us rise with patience
let us run with pride

Tomorrow tomorrow
they said tomorrow at the crossroads
    Marie Davenport

Rose

He always brought her roses
Though I never knew just why.
This time he placed them so lovingly -
Then he began to cry.

He didn't notice me standing there
So I made not a sound.
I could see this man really cared
As he knelt there on the ground.

Slowly, he gets up to go
Brushing away his tears.
He said, "You know, roses mean I love you
And I have all these years!"

As I stood there, wondering the reasons "Why"
Of this visit of a man from long ago,
He noticed me and asked my name -
"Rosalyn," I said, "but everyone calls me Rose."

A smile crossed his face
Taking place of all his tears.
As we stood there, all alone, together
The reason for the roses became perfectly clear.
    Doris A. Bowen

In Dealing with Stoicism

Life is a tremendous abode,
Forever laughing at our stead.
Reality is blatant,
An aggressive improvisation
    Holly Jaquint

On Remembering My Best Friend

I dreamed I followed thee in death
Our spirits float in friendship's love remembered
Of beauty's faith unquestioned in its prime.
All mind and music wrapped in sounding parchments
Creating joy in blissful admiration.

No doubting stones to block the fire-
Works of thoughts rekindled from the Marvel
Of love unknown to me before her life
Set freedom to my soul, the singing gifts
Reborn from deafening condemnations.

Perhaps awakening I might find
A better soul that still is mine
And not confined
By suffocation of the spirit's mind
But taking flight beyond the grave
I might love again my life to save.
    Corinne C. Delafield

Searching

What light is reflected from the soul?
What thoughts are seen so ever bold,
Why must there always seem to be,
Something forever calling me.

When will I ever stop to see?
That which is greater than you and me.
What should I do, what must I say?
In the twilight of each passing day.

Who is there . . . who's calling me?
To come back and get off this troubled sea.
I've traveled the world but couldn't find,
That certain something, that true peace of mind.

Now giving thanks that I have seen,
All the splendor created from a dream.
Oh, that life may never cease.
To let me live in perfect peace.
    Hermann J. Humble

Dancing In The Flames

Dancing in and round the flames is forever man's connection to man:
To earth, to air, to the water of life.
Thoughts and feelings flitter in the flames of imagination.

Wind whispers in the trees. Birds glide on currents of air.
Aromas of rain, flowers, and death intermingle eternal moments.
It is hard to be bear and raven in one.
We shape shift through the ages in a communal dance of joy,
Or fall, sobbing our anguish and loss, to the Gods of our fathers.

Then our superior brothers come to take it all away.
To leave us empty words of better, wiser, faster, easier, more.
We forget how to dance in the flames of our lives.

The raccoon, the possum, the deer, the elk, become road kill.
Our lives become a frenetic dance of external energy,
Beating against the walls encircling our inner awareness.

The fire is extinguished.
We are lulled from mourning its loss by instant communication.
The instant gratification of canned laughter, canned music,
Canned art, and canned love.

Let the Phoenix rise again from the ashes of existence
Beating massive wings in a growing spiral,
Then diving straight into the embracing flames of life.
    Margie Hill

Letter To A Friend

When I was 20, my best friend died.
He died in hell, a place called Nam.
I joined the corps, to even the score.
After 2 1/2 years in hell, I hadn't done that.
Now my life is hell . . .
Nightmares come a lot;
I can't forget what happened then.
January through March I used to stay drunk.
We lost many brothers and never gave up.
Out of the Corps in '69 . . .
I drank and fought like I'd been taught.
Hard I tried to make some sense of it all.
24 years since I came home, I went to the wall;
I found your name, I shook like a tree leaf.
My hand upon your name, I found the release;
Finally I could say, "good-bye ole friend."
For the first time, since the Corps,
I cried tears down my cheeks, I'll see you soon,
Ole friend . . . who knows, maybe you're better off.

Gordon H. Volkmann

God's Wondrous Works

Dedicated to God

I will praise God all of my days for God is Awesome.
His beauty is all around me.

For his glistening sun soothes my soul
and his pillaring clouds comfort my heart.

For his strong winds stir my sensuous
and the heavenly lights take me beyond.

For I can not ignore God's wondrous work.
Yes he is my God, he is my fortress.
And I will praise God all of my days,
yes I will praise God. . .all of my days.

Cheryl P. Tyink

Sanctity

If there's one thing people crave
It's the thing I've failed to attain
My outstretched palm could not reach the object
Happiness, a myth to me, is exhibited by others
My failure again is crystalline
But you always understood my pain; relieved my anguish
While the world snickered at helplessness
The happy figurines all wrapped in subjectivity
Questing for something to set them apart; make them different
While I sit outside the arena; scorned for it
But you knew and still loved me; worshipped me
Let them all search for individualism for they all search and
that makes them all the same
True individuals...just are
You could understand this without me dissecting it for you, couldn't you?
You, my peace of subconscious; my sanctity; my soul
I wish you lived; but you know that
Maybe you'll come later and I'll live inside your imagination
as a symbol of all your failures.

Nicole Blair

Fear Of The Real World

As we torture the God pan, into delivering angels and demons into our hands oblivious to oblivion addicted to bliss, wasting and ignoring the gifts. We feel only pain and smiles, hiding the rest and hoping for the best, we wash our hands in pain, grief and regret. And try to make the spirits speak looking for answers of where we go, we look with our minds and not our souls.

Paul Whiteside

The Perfect Little Christmas Tree

I saw the awesome Christmas Tree outside the city gates.
It stood there tall and elegant for all men to partake.

As the Tree stood on the hill in all its glory and its might
I couldn't help but notice the brilliance of its Light.

It shone across the sky and land for all God's men to see
in hopes it would draw all men to this perfect Christmas Tree.

And hanging on the branches were ornaments of fruit.
I saw patience and faith. I saw kindness and truth.

The most important fruit of all, of all the decorations:
The fruit of love hung on this Tree and next to love...
Salvation.

And underneath the Christmas tree I saw the gift: the Lamb.
He came to free the world from death, to save all in the land.

Who is this perfect Christmas tree whose word cuts like a knife?
This perfect little Christmas tree is the
Tree of Life!

Diana L. Whitehead

Untitled

I wake to you each morning;
my eyes instinctively look for you.
I long for your embrace;
to feel your gaze upon my face
Every day I wait for you;
to envelope me in your arms;
to shower me with warmth;
and your glowing charms.
Sometimes you must leave me;
behind your companions, hide.
But you know I'll always be waiting;
for you to come back to my side.
Your brilliance astounds me;
your blazing ray's surround me.
You have the ability to make me smile;
run, play and beguiled.
So, as you float up there;
among the billowy clouds;
beckoning me to play; I will be down here;
waiting for you every single day.

Terrie Neave

How We Love This Rose

That tender young bud now is a blossom
That bathes in the light of the sun as it grows
Always looking up as if it were smiling
This flower of life the beautiful Rose

   Handle with care this beautiful flower
   How long do they stay Heaven only knows
   We would if we could keep them forever
   For God only knows how we love this Rose

My mother dear is such a beautiful flower
Her kindness and love will warm any day
Now carefully carry this beautiful flower
A most precious Rose for the masters bouquet

   Handle with care the most beautiful flower
   I wish she with could stay for Heaveb only knows
   We would if we could just keep them forever
   For God only know how we love this Rose

Eddie L. Trammell

Untitled

Crippled and whimpering
  stripped of pride
worthless and weak
  he should be cast aside

Angry thrashing around in my head
  telling me they don't understand
don't understand my crying
  that the world should be taken under an angry hand

Make a list
of all the weak and worthless
stand them in a line in front of a firing squad
I am the judge, jury, executioner and I am God

I decide who dies and when
smashing he who has no defense
I inherited this world to live and die again
before Hate took over I'm sure life had meant something then

But no, I won't cry and I won't laugh
leaving fear in my path
a path that leads to a dying world abyss
I am the son of the catalyst!

Santiago De Jesus Reynoso

The Rural Ruler

When in the fields, love is the ruler, and all the problems in
  life, all its inhabitants, all its conceptions, bow before this
  majestic king.
We two, being one, run freely through the knee-high grass,
  gliding, as not to awaken its shapely form.
Not a wrong is stirred from our soul, and not a horrible thought
  of the world today shall penetrate our minds.
When the air is relinquished from her lungs, she gently hangs
  around my shoulder.
At that moment a fresh Northern wind blows the sweet aroma of her
  hair upon my face.
I help to support her, just as I always wanted to do.
When our legs have withered, we fall unto the ground as the
  yellow and orange leaves of Autumn have done before us.
When lying beside her I commence to caress her soft flesh and
  feel the curvatures of her figure.
Slowly I ascend above her like a stormcloud over a grassy plain
  and rain upon her kisses so soft we both fail to remember if
  they actually existed
How can the world and all its realities compete with us?

Jeffrey A. Sunn

The Guide

I thought I heard her crying.
I thought I heard her plea.
I thought I saw the image very,
Very clear.
I didn't know what to say,
What to say?
What to do?
It was my turn to step in.
I couldn't budge
I couldn't move.
I tried to speak-but only a squeak.
Oh, help me!
What do I do?
Somebody, help me
Let it all end.
I tried to step in, but...
Silence and yet a soft whimper was all that remained.
Her body was harmed; her emotions, too.
I tried to let her know I was there and comfort her.
The healing shines through after the time has passed.

Janice Goetzinger

My Prize

Many times you find only one prize for a good accomplishment
Your chances of having first place run slim.
Bright thoughts of a prize worth winning
On a day that you started a new beginning.
Beauty is what made you stunning for such an accomplishment
Bravery was what made you strong to fight for first place.
Yearning to see this prize presented with love and affection
Smiling at a prize that has been created with perfection.
Pleased to one day say, "I got my prize through hard work."
I've done my best at making this dream come true,
Reaching deep into my soul searching for love that I knew
Everyone telling me, this prize may one day make you blue.
Sadly to say, my heart has been broken, my prize stolen
I lost the one accomplishment that gave me strength.
Lost the prize I came as close to winning
Only You know what this really meant to me.
Virtually hard to let go when you want it so bad
Especially when the prize captured days you were happy and sad.
Only now has the time come to say how I feel
Understanding the reality call - my prize was to gain your love,
the sweetest of them all; I love you.

Adrienne Steward

Finding Myself

My family, the pain, burnings of regrets;
of past and lost in present.

Hoping for answers and
Living in dreams; of pain, loss; of youth and heart.

Learning, still dreaming good, bad, sweet and evil
Still lost and unwanted in my heart.
I look for my way to understand and feel again.
This time...not as a youth, but as a lost soul.
Wanting to find my heart, and the lost
love of my family.

Yet, I wonder on I feel myself grow
A heart, a sound, a love
Yes, I've found my soul

I believed, I needed to hurt
and please everyone.
Still no one came to be with me
I know now that;
I am love and happiness.
All on my own.

Lisa C. Brock

Faceless Lover

In the middle of the night, I feel you gently reach over to me
Pulling me closer to you, as close as is possible to be
I smell your sweet breath as you whisper words of love
My mind soars, thanking all that is holy and sacred above
I feel your strength and your power, as I succumb to only to you
Not out of duty or respect, but of the desire to do . . .
The loving, the caring, the experience that only we can share
I can feel your hands caressing my body, your fingers in my hair
I taste your lips as you gently place them on mine
The world ceases to exist as does time
I reach out for you and I can't touch you
I sit up calling your name, wondering what next to do
I turn on the life of the lamp, my heart slowly dies
Realizing that it was only a dream of repeated nights
Disappearing entirely with the morning's first lights
I lie back down, tears streaking my face
While my heart beats at a dangerous pace
Here, alone in the dark, I can't help but wonder why . . .
You only come to me in my dreams . . . leaving me alone to cry.

Leigh Anne Williams

Wingin' It

Adventures of life best taken on the wing

Wings of flights of fancy...
glimpse of what may be, could
be, would be

No limits of time...space...
self...belief

Wings of sight...light...sound
nudge toward a higher place

Rested...tested...challenged
let the adventure begin again
but only upon the wing

Up above the fray is clearer
the path. . .on and on ever onward wingin'
it all the way

Lynne Small

The Good Shepherd Weeps

Sand brown carpet of plush hair,
lost in the silent movement of amber stems.
Golden eyes glitter with fire, the prey chosen.
Tempted by tall grasses,
white clouds of wool
venture toward savory pastures,
and the slinking king.
Others stumble up a narrow rocky path,
clacking hooves and trembling wails,
sense of danger pressing at their backs.
A wild visage smirks,
spiked mane spears the sky.
Pounce of the attacker,
immediate surrender to evil power,
soul lost to tears of the claw.
Tongue laps sweet, steaming crimson,
echoes smacking lips and crunching teeth.
He celebrates the victory
while above mourns the loss of one
who strayed.

Ashley Townsend

Take A Little Time

Make some one happy today,
Sprinkle a little sunshine along the way.
Through the road of life we make haste,
When much of that time is just a waste.
You will be happier when you remember to pray.
At night, morning and all through the day.
Pray for leaders family and dear friends too.
Offer a helping hand in the work they will do.
Working together great goals can be achieved,
With the Lord by our side and our "Faith to Believe."

Charlene Patterson

Ideality

So finally it's you I see, there's just one word "Ideality,"
It is our word . . . to describe the finest thing . . . you, and me;
"Ideality." See we are above and beyond all fantasies in a realm
too high for reality; on a stage where stars long to be . . . caught
in a state of "Ideality." You simply are what I am to me, a
symbol of life granted unto me, a blessing only God could bring
from his highest heaven on eternity. See communication is our
currency in this our world of "Ideality." Our constitution is
honesty, which love surrounds for security. We have a legacy of
devotion to improve our boundaries of forgiveness, and with this
we are the envy of every witness, having all there can be . . .
having what we have . . . having "Ideality."

Emerson Johnson

Rosewood

As I sit and watch the days go by, and
eat the fruit that fills my thighs, I dream.
I dream of a life full of happiness, a
heart full of love and a mind full of knowledge.
I dream of climbing the highest mountains
and swimming the deepest waters. I dream
of dancing with the one I love under the
moon filled sky. Why do most dreams vanish
into the thick midnight air? Why do people let
dreams fly away with the wingless birds?
Don't let reality swallow up the dreams. For
when the dreams are gone, they will
never again surface. So run from reality
and hold on to the dreams. For dreams
are the only keys to open the doors to
happiness. I shall never let go.

Paula Marie Wood

Peace (Be Still)

I fear, in the wee hours of the night...the stillness when
everyone is asleep, the unknown of what is to come,
what is, what may come, and why our existence. Does
it matter, or make sense, do we really know. Is it just
an allowance of pleasure, suffering, fun, sadness...it doesn't
last...not for us..passed on to offspring, maybe. But why,
what is it all about? Worlds decay and no longer exist...
better ones are built...even better ones are developed. Is it
a conquest for the greatest whatever, that may never be..
is there ever the best...when we don't know when it will end
or if it will end. It's supposed to end. Why are we, why is it,
why, do we really know? Is it a dream or is it real? I can't
remember what happened last year on this day. Is it a dream
that is being dreamt by a higher being? Was I really here
last year at this time or is it all part of that dream? There
may be some documentation of this time, a letter that I
signed, maybe, or a picture that I took. I was here, it does
exist, it is, but why, do we know, do we really know?

Deloris W. Ellis

Tea Ell Sea

When I met you,
    Inside I was angry. Bitter. Cold.
My life going on,
    In a wrong direction.
You have now come into my life
    and your love has me seeing
A seemingly indeterminate road of happiness, truth, love.
As we talk, I hear what you say.
    Even though at times, it is with difficulty.
I look so deeply. I want to be inside.
My loneliness to hold you can not be explained.
There are no words.
I wish to be joined. Physically. Silly.
The time I spend,
    Looking at you, thinking of you, wanting you,
Are wonderful and precious times.
I truly thank you my darling...
...For your inspiration, for your love,
    for all of the desires
    we share.

Tami Burnett

My Friend, The Wind

I feel the wind,
Blowing itself, upon me,
Around me, thru me, engulfing me,
Ever changing, unpredictable, never constant,
Just there, to feel its presence,
My friend, the wind.

Mark Abe

Untitled

Between friends with alone
life in still strange for me
itself beautiful world am I here?

I swing away for this moment from it all
as the sky
shaped in my form
I don't see any limits anymore
although trapped in my own web of emotions
suffocating under balast of my living
I feel like I am unattached dreamy
restless unlimited independent self directed
liberated unrestrained untied open free

Aga Kalinowska

In The Corner

In the corner is where am I,
To watch the shadows drifting by,
To hear the winds go howling past,
To know when thoughts and dreams are cast,
To see the seasons change with time,
To make you hear my senseless rhyme

In the corner is where am I,
To watch the shadows drifting by
None know I'm here, or, none save me
I'm the one who nobody sees
Yet I see them when they don't know,
I feel the feelings they won't show

In the corner is where am I,
To watch the shadows drifting by
In the corner do I dwell alone?
Am I the only with senses honed?
Out of all things both fair and fell,
You, too, are one who should know well

In the corner is where we dwell...
Though you don't know us, we know you well

Heather Bragg

What Do I Want From You

What do I want from you,
But to treat me as I would treat you.

What do I want from you,
Only respect, as I respect you.

What do I want from you,
Understanding, patience, and a kiss or two.

What do I want from you,
Laughter, sharing, caring, and let's communicate, too.

What do I want from you,
Love me deeply, as I would love you.
What do I want from you,
But to spend the rest of my life with only you.

Gail Hester

London From A Tour Bus

Bridges and buildings, churches and homes,
Places like cathedrals with huge domes.
Towers of London that reach the sky
So many souvenir shops - everything you want to buy,
Look here!
Look here!
They are museums everywhere!
Hear the golden trumpets blow,
'Cause here is the queen - this can't be so!
As you look as far as your eye can see
Where the ground meets the sky
Yes, this is London!
Me, Oh, My!!

Ashley Butler

A Housewife

Not enough time;
So busy is life,
Sometimes I get dizzy;
Being a housewife!...

There's dishes, lunches and laundry,
Bathrooms, dust and mop,
The homework, vacuum, and phone calls,
Some days I want to drop!!

The shopping, appointments, and dinner,
Windows, stove, and paying those bills,
Organizing, sorting and directing;
Some days I've had my fill!

There's breakfast, fridge and fire to tend,
Clutter, baking, more errands to do,
Coupons, nursing, and bathing the kids,
Some days there are my needs, too!

Being a housewife:
Some days I get dizzy;

So busy;
Is life...

Laurie Talley

Loving Too Much....

When times are tough
And everything seems lost
Where can one get help?
And how much does it cost?

Cost is not the answer
No matter what the pain
Cause no matter the loss
Someone will always take the gain.

Now that things are straight
And moving a head is what we need to do,
Forget about the past, hold me tight
Cause honey...I love you!

Sometimes I don't understand
Why you get so mad
I wish I could always keep you happy
And never make you sad

But as we go through life... Together, you will see
When that day comes how happy you and I will be.

Causing you pain is one thing I never wanted to do
But controlling my love and emotions is one thing I will do for you.

Ronnie Harrell

The Master Weaver

Our lives are but fine weavings that God and we prepare,
Each life becomes a fabric planned and fashioned in his care;
We may not always see just how the weavings intertwine,
But we must trust the masters hand and follow his design.
For he can view the patter upon the upper side,
While we must look from underneath and trust in him to guide.
Not till the loom in silent and the shuttles cease to fly,
Shall God unroll the canvass and explain the reason why;
The dark threads are as needed in the weavers skillful hand,
As the threads of gold and silver in the pattern he has planned;
Sometimes a strand of sorrow is added to his plan,
And though it's difficult for us we still must understand;
That it's he who fills the shuttle, it's he who knows what's best,
So, we must weave in patience and leave to him the rest.

Ralph Fister

A Bad Case Of Oniomania

What does it mean?
What do you do?
You can hear the
Constant ringing
And rattling.
The honking!
The buzz!

Then you try to come down
With a hum of a lullaby.
But then you feel
The rustling,
The squishing,
The sweat beads,
The swirling!

You can't
stop it!

You lunge!
You thump whack-slap!

You then walk out of the store with no money
But walk out instead with bags of junk!

(P.S. At home, don't blame me, you can only moan and groan.)

Jessie Owens

Wondering Thoughts

I watched it snow last night.
I watched the ground turn white, amidst the flakes.
I saw my yesteryears, their happiness and tears.
I recalled being just a little girl,
When simple things brought great joy.
I thought of the years after that, and the fun I had,
   getting where I'm at,
Then I wondered where all the years have gone.
And how far it is from here and Heaven's dawn.
But as I stood there in the autumn of my years,
I realized I could face my winter without fear.
  For it is true;
No one walks the path alone,
For God's light sees us all, safely home.

Alys Nicholson

Friend Also A Lover

It's strange how you can know someone
for such a long period of time
Be friends with this person
hang out and drink wine
While you're constantly searching
for a lover so true
And all this time
he was right in front of you.

So much senseless and
wasted time I've spent
When my senses weren't looking
often times I've dreamt
Searching, hoping and praying one day
that God would have mercy
and send love my way
Tears, despair, closed my eyes for I was blue
Felt a warm embrace,
looked around
and it was you.

Carline Diana Hamilton

Distraught Female

A manic hyper person I am with serious phobias I possess.
Safely sheltered in isolation from the world my life is such a mess!
The fear of germs and diseases keeps me in a panic state of mind
Depression has already sized me and I worry
All the time.

My destination concludes from one room to the next.
The yard outside has pollen particles to which
I am allergic.
I exercise with precaution not to excite the
Blood flow to my heart.
Medication is taken hourly after all the vitamins
Have digested apart.

Some say I am psychotic though others may disagree.
Although I am destitute, distraught, female
I am quite organized
  Categorically!!

Cheree Renee Lopez

Spring

After the winter, dark and deep,
Spring has risen, as from a dream.
Gone the snow that longed to keep
A frozen world in lasting sleep.

From a windy gust, soft and sweet,
Come the raindrops, promising life.
Bursting forth the rain to meet
Tiny leaves beneath my feet.

From the flower's bloom, full and white,
Grown from seed, stored underground.
Spread the meadow with flowers bright
A floating scent that brings delight.

In a tiny shell, spotted and round,
Waits a life, feathered for flight.
It shatters the egg and peers around
For a loving mother waits to be found.

Gwen Elwood

Me

Look inside me then you'll see
What is real is not free
Truth inside me is not shown
My true spirits have never flown
What is locked within shall never be found
For inside, thy soul is deep, almost underground.
To understand,
Is to know thy great demand
Within the body is the soul and the heart
My heart has been crushed; my soul, torn apart
I knew since the start that this was to happen
Because now they are strong, and I have weakened.
But I will try to fight until my end
If I have at least one good friend.
Just look long and hard, then you'll understand
That all I need is one helping hand
To guide me away from darkness and fear
To enrich me and save me, like sun upon a tear
Inside me you'll see that when I am free
You will see the real me.

Ammy Xiong

Season Changes

I look at leaves along the way,
  each day they show me a more beautiful display;

The yellows, crimsons, oranges and greens all mingled together,
  always remind me of our ever-changing weather;

Soon they'll be gone — all crumpled dead on the ground,
  making a bed soft to the eye,
  and then only a few weeks 'til they bid us a fond good-bye;

As soon the dark ground will hide away,
  under many frosts and snows,
  blanketing our way and biting our nose;

Long will it be 'til the early morn air,
  brings us a message of sunshine and fair;

But soon then joy will once more be restored,
  when the spring songbirds warble their tune,
  we through the winter many times implored,

Now the sun shines a bright, shiny day,
  and our hopes and our smiles soar with
  each footstep along the way!

Carol L. Ruddle

One Night In Heaven

  Baby if I could, I would spend every
last dollar I had to buy you a ship. Not the
kind of ship that would sail us across the
seven sea's, but the kind of ship that could
take us closer to the stars that we see.
We could use the cloud as our pillow, while
the universe would be our bed, and the
sun would shine like a candle above our
lonely heads, and when we have reached
our peak, to scream out in passion we need
not be afraid, and the juices that we would
let go, would float gently into the milky way.
Then as tears of joy ran down my face, I
would look into your star field eyes and say
these words to you before heading back to
earth, those words would be that I love you,
and to ever lose you would really hurt. See
baby we spent one night in Heaven for what
it was worth, but why not spend the rest
of our lives like this back here on Earth?

Anthony E. Perkins

The Chosen Path

I can not take your troubles.
I can not take your pain.
And even though I struggle to,
my efforts are in vain.

For you have picked your pathway
and I have chosen mine.
But, I can always love you
and that shall be a sign

Of the way we've walked upon this earth,
the paths that we've both taken,
until, my friend, we meet with God
and from this dream awaken.

So know that though it seems so,
you never are alone.
For there are those that love you
while you dwell so far from home.

Cheryl Partyka

His Very Burden

Softly as the sunlight spills
across my slumping shoulders,
I look to you and beg you please
do not treat me as your others.

I think of you so far away
hiding off into your corner,
no sunlight strikes upon your face
though I feel your heart begin to race.

But only God now knows
the exact plan for this:
His very burden.

Frightened, we must help ourselves;
me, here by the light - you, there
in His darkness. Both of us...in silence.

Eugene Marks

Together Again

A year has passed, since he told her good-bye
  Oh! Since then how he has cried.

For the year, his life incomplete
  Her soul it was, he chose to meet.

He was the life of all the family occasions
  His laughter will linger in a peaceful rest haven.

Thank you for teaching us the Cajun way to love and live
  Now to you our hearts and prayers we give.

As old glory was folded into hands it was laid
  He was awaiting heaven, a place so safe.

Then end was near as the bugle played clear
  His spirit was drifting to meet Granny so near.

Their souls met again as the rifle fired loud
  Together again, afloat in the clouds.

Now PawPaw and Granny are together above
  Both without pain and can feel our love.

They will watch over us with love and care
  Two spirits joined, and once again a pair.

As I look up above to the clouds where he lay
  I can just hear him saying "laissez les bon temps rouler".

Kayla D. Little

Untitled

Where is my smile? Has it run away?
Like my ex with our children, has it gone to stay?
And a special friend, who had helped me pull through.
I spoke too open and honest, now she is gone too!
I need my friends, now more than most,
for our father won't turn me into a spiritual ghost.
If he would rid this body, so a spirit I'd be,
there'd be no hurt feelings and my children I'd see.
My spirit would rest, right about their home,
I would see them always and never be alone.
Tho I could not hug or hold their hand,
these rights were stolen away from this man.
There's nothing left in this life for me,
except two children I love, yet cannot see
I've asked our father, on many a night,
to stop me from seeing the next day's light.
If suicide were right through the eyes we see,
my life would be gone and my spirit set free.
But, the father above, left clearly a no,
so like it or not, through life I shall go.

Jim Stewart Jr.

Summer Evening

A warm summer day is a perfect time to
lay on the freshly-mowed grass
and gaze upward toward the heavens.
A sense of smallness results as you realize how huge the sky is.

The puffy clouds, like white fluffy cotton candy,
slowly move, creating pictures of past memories
and future dreams- "that cloud looks
like a farm, and that one resembles a futuristic car"

The sun slowly settles on the horizon,
causing a very colorful stratification
of clouds; the sun is on center stage
and the clouds are its audience.

The first star appears as a
pin of light in an inverted bowl;
soon the bowl is filled with hundreds of tiny pins.
In the background,
the crickets create a
natural stereo of sound.

Thanks God for creating this
beautiful world!!
Daniel E. Eberly

The Waltzing Stars

Oh, my! Look in the sky you can see the stars dancing,
such a beautiful dance indeed it is.
To my eyes it looks like the waterfall waltz,
shooting and falling all different ways.
As I watch I see one shoot underneath the sea
swimming about its way, up the waterfall
like a fish finely making its way into
a little sound in the sky near the moonlight heaven.
My mind cannot believe in what it sees
This might be a dream and not real
but it is very real indeed
it is more real than a dream.
Mary Ann Miller

Paranoia

He's peeking through my window, I know he's watching me;
The darkness brings his image, despite reality.

Everywhere I go, people look at me;
I wonder what they're thinking, what vision do they see.

A multitude of strangers, encountered every day;
Our eyes meet for a moment, then quickly glance away.

Just once I'd like to reach out, and touch a stranger's hand;
And ask what he is feeling... I know I never can.

Too many lonely people, are traveling through space;
Staring straight ahead, a blank look on their face.

And I am just another, afraid to really see;
It's easier than way, besides...people frighten me.
Karen Simkin

Future

What's new in the years to come,
High and mighty now lay low
Rich and poor have felt the blow,
Wealth nor riches can save us from
the confines of the grave;
Prisoners' chains are bursting asunder,
Liberty they cry in voices of thunder,
Loudly their mouths proclaim it all around,
and freedom smiles on every brow, your
life before you unfurls as it floats o'er
half the world.
Martha E. Johnson

I Am Your Fortress

In time love becomes a scary thing,
confusion is the mystery in everything.
Together you and I will always stand tall,
and without caution even the strongest can fall.
Nothing can beat a failure but a good hard try,
but failure without effort we will surely die.
So when you've lonely and you need someone
around to care,
just listen to the wind and I'll be there.
There is strength in our love but it takes two,
I would travel around the world just to comfort you.
Forever for you my love I will always express,
with me you're on solid ground for I am your fortress.
William A. Robles

Garden Gate

There I was standing by the gate
Knowing full well my friend would be late

Late as always I wonder why.
Should I wait or go on by?

Inside I simmer and grind my teeth
I stomp my feet in unbelief.

What is her problem I want to know.
She keeps everyone waiting. Why is she so slow?

Out she comes smiling all the while.
She's my best friend by a country mile.

She grins and tells me all the news
Never once stopping to ask my views.

She chatters and never notices how angry I am
Not even when I give the car door a slam.
Opal Gilbert

Love

Some time I say to my self I wonder
if I am going to find the right man to love!.
Love is some thing that will come
but it takes time to find someone like that.
I wonder if the man I love
will be good to me or do things for me, or
be there for me through the good times and
bad times.
Love is some thing people look for
all the time and are always looking
for some one who will love them.
I know I loved this one person,
and he loved me but he moved away and then
I moved and our love just came to end.
He did everything for me;
Someday's you just don't know
were to find love and God will
give you love you just have to have
the time and when God knows your ready for it
he will give it to you.
Melinda Thompson

Just A Soldier

Just a soldier, searching for his soul
wondering what he's doing here out on patrol.
At one time his eyes soft, was full of innocence
now dark and cold, see's only man's greedy ignorance.
Just a soldier, trying to save a country's life
but also losing his soul and possibly his wife.
He dreams of home and his family
and of all the places he would rather be.
Just a soldier, is all he'll ever be
'cuz his memories, he can never flee.
Cathy A. Bliss

Sunset Sunrise

As I am watching the sunset
on my given day
    I think of events that happened
all along the way.
    The words I've said,
the people I've met
    as I watch the sunset
I reflect

    As I am watching the sunrise
at the beginning of my day.
    I look above for guidance,
to help me on my way.
    Jumbled thoughts and memories
come to my mind
    In life I've found there's nothing nicer
than being kind.

Freda Bledsoe

Untitled

You have gone but not forgotten.
From this world you've left behind,
You wanted to go home to be with Jesus.
From the pain and woes you have gone.

I can't believe I won't see you again on this old earth.
And it's hard not to hear your voice.
But someday we will meet in glory
Where there will be no more parting.
You were a wonderful friend to me,
you will never cry from loneliness, or
suffer with any more pain.

You are with the one who loves you
Where peace and happiness dwell
So goodbye, my dearest friend, from this earth you have gone.
We'll see you over yonder when the battle here
Has been won; you are gone but I'll miss
you, nevermore to talk awhile.
Rest in peace with our heavenly Father,
rest in peace 'til we meet again.
Goodbye for now.

Mildred J. Bennett

To You, Dad, On Your 80th Birthday

Just another day you say, maybe so,
but just the same, today it is your birthday.
Eighty years and did time fly, I doubt you'd say it did.
It stole the color from your hair and lined your face with age.
But I still see your blue eyes twinkle when you make us laugh,
with tales from so long ago; could this have been my dad!

You've seen so much as years have passed, both the good and bad.
The war, depression and the loss of family and friends.
You took a wife, she's at your side for fifty plus some years,
add three children, all grown up; Grandchildren number five.
I know you're proud of all of us although we rarely share,
the things we feel or wish we could express along the way.

Life's a struggle, this I know and try to understand,
how hard it is for you to now get through every day.
And could we move the hands of time many things we'd change.
But never would I change the man I honor here today,
For I feel blessed and very proud that I can call you "Dad".

Happy Birthday with Love,

Julia Bishop

Your Job Is

Those with degrees are barely landing jobs
Militaries are cutting back
Everyone's a bargain shopper
Wal-Mart is putting malls out of business
Thinking about not going to school and getting a job
Doing what
Pumping gas is no longer in demand
Vets have most the janitorial and warehouse jobs filled
The mistakes I made cost too much now
Besides you have a job and your job is
Staying in school
Going to church
Cutting the grass for your father
Babysitting your niece
Learning to cut your nephew's hair
Helping out in the kitchen
Watching your mouth
Minding your manners
Kissing your girlfriend on the forehead
And asking God to help us all

Margaret Gardner

Reflections

Sitting alone, I gaze through the frosty window pane
At the new fallen snow gently covering God's majestic land,
Children playing, their laughter floating through the air
My thoughts wander to days past, to days of yesteryear.

Oh, it seems only yesterday my little one romped in the snow
Leaving icy puddles on the floor as she frolicked to and fro,
Her messy boots and wet mittens to be cleaned and dried
There was no keeping up with her no matter how I tried.

Oh, it seems only yesterday she found the little puppy
His coat matted and dirty, his ears long and floppy,
Wagging his tail, he licked her face as she giggled with delight
Her eyes shining, she begged to keep him knowing I could not fight.

Oh, it seems only yesterday she whispered and giggled on the phone
Sharing little girl secrets meant for her friends ears alone,
Quickly she was growing up, soon a young woman she would be
A simple prayer was offered, "Lord, always keep her close to Thee"

Hours pass and the world outside darkens as I sit alone
Why, she's all grown up and married now with children of her own,
As I arise from the chair, tears of gratitude roll down my cheeks
"Lord, thank you for your grace, for always keeping her close to Thee."

Opal J. Queen

For Deborah Anne

I offer you my heart.
I offer it to you as it was given to me,
freely, without conditions.
What once was mine now belongs to you,
to do with as you will.
All that makes me who I am
rests in your gentle hands.
With each beat, my solemn vow
conveys a message of love to your soul.
I belong to you; I belong with you.
I will see forevers dawn
touch your face with soft and golden light.
Together, with you, all things are possible,
Finding you was but God's first miracle.
I must never forget...the feeling that washes over me this day.
I must never forget...that you bring to me this gift that words
cannot define.
I live my life this day...as always...in the light of your love.
I remain this day...as always...yours.

Angelo Louis Nicosia II

Untitled

Upon my breast her fair facade doth press
I feel her heart with mine the meter keep
I bid her close her eyes and welcome sleep...
"Forget the bad and calm all your duress
for I shall stay awake without digress
in word, or thought, or deed; I vow from deep
within my soul to thee, my dear, so sleep."
May God with all his might protect and bless.
"Our love," says she "will guard and keep this night
as we succumb to sleep and drift to dreams.
Now close your eyes with me my dear and rest;
Tomorrow soon will come and bring its light
To shine upon some key of what life means.
To build our strength anew and aid our quest."

Charles J. Korecki

Realm Of Intuition

Is this journey called life, just a game?
Are we all mere players in our destiny?
Oh what a shame.
Though each century brings with it various progressions,
Leaving still so very far to go, so many indiscretions.
During our trek, there are winners and losers,
But when dawn turns to dusk, there are no choosers.
Why would this be the finality of our being?
Surely there is much more we should be seeing.
There has to be a reason this will repeat.
To accept this journey as only a game, would ultimately
mean defeat.
Certainly this wasn't the overall intention.
There has to be more, much more distinction.

Marilyn D. Patton

Music

Music is something special,
it doesn't fade away no matter what.
You hear so much that it has its part.

Music is more than a "5" letter word,
it consists of so much that it's hard to ignore.

Don't stop playing that...
someone said, it might change your life
listen for yourself cause it could be tonight by...

Listen so you do, listen carefully
so you take heed to the...
Don't stop cause you could be set free.

Randy Morales

Fair-Weather Friend

As I walk along the shore
sandy pebbles of emotion prick my toes.
I welcome your inbound current,
wavecrests gleaming with sunlight.
I walk from shallow to deep waters without fear.
I feel your pulling.
I continue to swim, the water is so warm.
I stay...floating...
Suddenly, whitecaps come crashing down.
I've lost control.
The tide rolls me forward, then,
wrenches me back.
The indecisive waters render me weak...
My energy is slipping away.
A storm front abounds, I feel cold.
Where did your warm waters go?
I am drowning.
You do not see.
You cannot save me.

Linda L. Riffle

Choice

I'm afraid the tests have shown, my dear,
You'll have a baby's love...
Unless, of course, you pay the price
To have the child removed.

It stunned the girl to hear the word,
But, soon, recovering,
I suppose...the thing you said.
Must be the better thing.

Later, back behind the clinic
There was such an awful scene.
Two alley cats were poised to fight
For a thing they held between.

There, stretched between the cats, there was
A piece of human flesh.
The reminder of the unborn
Had become some alley trash.

No thought of wasted life reprised
T'ward the annals of living time.
It silently joined the millions
Who were victims of the crime.

Doug Wright

Apprentice

In the back door came a gray bearded man through the sun's arches
of gold.
I ran to help as he rolled an
ivory music box into the house.
I saw that
he only had four fingers to each callused hand.
He watched me stare, but it didn't seem to bother him...
I wanted to know what had happened, but
my respect for him was so thick that
I had no chance of squeezing a question through.
He had asked me to open the amber piano cover and wipe
the dust of the surface of the faded white keys.
Without rival challenge I did so and noticed
two thumbs stuck between the ebony.
"Are those yours!?" I cried.
"No", he calmly replied,
"They're yours".
I
looked down
and was very happy.

Matthew A. Donnelly

Free Free Free

When I was a child of three
The world was a big place to me.
I tried to dance on my toes
My mama told me I was to bold.
When I was a child of five
I had a garden that grew wild
oh! What a pretty sight to see
my garden meant every thing to me.
When I was a child of six
I went to school and was
made sick. A cruel place they sent me.
There - I learned that I was
not a pretty child, my eyes were
To big, my lips to wide
My hair to short, there I was taught
That I would never be
what the Lord said I could be.
I must admit it hurt so bad, as I get older I got mad.
Now I know I am free and I will be what I will
be

M. C. Watkins

My Prayer

Oh, Lord take me back to Tennessee
Where the waves on the hills are as soft as the sea,
And the air caresses both plant and me.

The field of green stretches beyond sight
While dogwood blossoms move in flight.
The church finger points upward toward God
While elbowed oil wells move all night.

Here-horses gallop in play
And man's whispering soul rises high
To meet the promise of the sky.

Barbara Dill Myers

I Love America

I love America, the greatest place on earth,
I love America, the nation of my birth,
My home, America, the land of liberty,
I love America, it's the land for you and me.

From Atlantic to Pacific where the mighty rivers flow,
From the long Canadian border to the Gulf of Mexico;
There are hills, and plains and valleys, mountains rise in majesty,
Forests, deserts, and vast farmland, rivers running to the sea;
All across this mighty nation, people working to be free,
That is why I love America, the land of liberty.

As I travel o'er the highway and I view the majesty
I'm reminded of God's blessings and our country's history;
For wherever I may journey, God's creative hand is shown,
And I have a special privilege that this land is mine to own;
Oh, this land I call America, our fathers gave to me,
And I pray unto Almighty God, He'll keep the U.S. free.

I love America, God gave this land to me,
I love America, from sea to shining sea.
My home, America, the land of liberty,
I love America, it's the land for you and me.

Carol E. Troutman

Destin

When destiny brought us together and fate tore us apart,
There you left me standing you took along my heart.

When you came to me that winter day,
Promises over promises you would never drift away:

Having laid in your arms your caress so strong,
Makes me wonder just what was done wrong:

When you took my heart that day,
Gone were the words I wanted to say:

But if you're ever in doubt of one that loves,
Try to remember the memories above:

Always keep in mind if our love was destined to end,
Love yourself because no body else can!

Stacey Bowles

The Prairie

The great tranquility and smoothness,
of this forever stretching land-
Standing in the vast grasses,
I realize how meek I am to nature.
The never ending frontier,
upon which I pass my years away.
A universe of space and freedom,
my peace and joy of life.
Barren of trees,
The earth feels the total warmth of the sun
Life is open here,
there is no hiding.

Jeriann Kelley

Remember

Remember when the days were so long,
We thought Christmas would never arrive.
The school days seemed ever so long
We wondered if we would really survive.
Our birthdays came but once a year
Oh! What a long, long wait!
The minutes in church were hours, I fear.
And we never, ever dared be late.
The hours were sixty minutes, always.
The weeks were seven days without end.
The months were many unending days,
While a year was an eternity to spend.

Now the dates just scurry by,
As the hours so swiftly fly.
While the weeks race by so fast
And the years all hurry past.
Old man time really speeds along.
Life has become too short a song.

Mary Hamann

Children

Touched by an Angel, laughter and surprise,
children playing happily under bright and clear blue skies.

Parents looking Heavenly thanking God from up above,
for such a precious gift they have, these children that they love.

Listen to them carefully, cradle in loving arms,
tend to all their hurts and pains, and keep them from life's harms.

Children grow so quickly, one by beginning families of their own,
so hold onto all those memories and you'll never be alone.

Touched by an Angel, laughter and surprise,
children playing happily under bright and clear blue skies.

Lorrie Ann Norris

Words On Paper

Did you say what I said when I told you when to say it?
What did you say? I believe that I forgot it.
Why did you do that when I said it couldn't be done?
Why would you say that? Some times you're just no fun.
Why did you cry when I asked you not to cry?
For the same reason you lie when I ask you why we die.

I ask myself and I always see,
that this world holds no place for me.
I try my best to understand,
why it was I was made a man.
I might have been better as a bird or a tree,
instead I'm left with what you see.
With all the problems of my kind,
can you understand why I've lost my mind?

Christopher Michael Brown

Essence of Emaciation

Anticipation

Not knowing when....
Indifference,

Not caring.....
Emaciation,

Not eating.....
Essence,

The point of.....
The essence of my Emaciation

is my Anticipation and Indifference

Carlotta C. Ray

Judgement Day

One little girl born to her womb
Could it be its just to soon
To judge this infant so small and new
the words "judgement day" ring true.

She grew up quick and against her will
very big shoes she had to fill
She was loved and cared for in a strange way
and judged on everything she would do or say.

Doing what she thought was right turned out wrong
she kept on fighting because she was strong
grown up and married and out of that home
now happily raising a girl of her own.

Never understanding why they couldn't get along
she kept her distance even if it was wrong
remembering the good and the bad she will do
the words "judgement day" still ring true.

She has accepted the fact that it will never be
the bonding and closeness that she promised me
everything that happened still happens today
She prays for an end to judgement day.

E. T.

Touched By A Demon

Drowning in a black sea of deep depression,
Contemplating my impending separation,
Wanting out, wanting to be lifted,
Hoping in some way that I am gifted,
It is dark down here.
Can you feel my fear?
Meditation, medication, sedation,
So many ways to hide my desperation.
I look up and see you there,
Wondering if you really care.
I want this demon out of me.
That is when I'll be free.
Ever searching for a solution,
Should I be in an institution?
The name of my demon is depression.
Now I have finished my confession.

Jacquelyn H. Bailey

My Life

My life began in the deep woods of Maine,
A place named Brassua with six families.
We had a lot of animals to tame,
It wasn't a site like the large cities.

We had porcupines and some big black bears
Who would all of a sudden come from nowhere.
I never was caught by one. I was lucky
To be able to run around and play.

My mother at twenty-nine, she passed away.
This was for us a painful tragedy.
My father always missed her through his life.
Since then, for him living was just a strife.

He had to bury his wife on this day
And was separated from all his kids.
No room for us, orphans were too many.
This is what this bad influenza did.

My brother and sister went with my aunt.
I was lucky to be with grandfather
Who took care of me like a little ant,
Treated me well, you cannot find better.

Don Duquet

Mommies Little Girl

Another night without a wink,
As I lie I often think,
Tears run down my rosy cheek,
Thoughts of comfort I try to seek,
But every time I think of you,
Leaving me in a world so blue,
I can't help but wonder why, even though I often try,
My feelings for you remain my own,
And so to you they are not known,
Thoughts of love surround my heart,
But expressing them I cannot start.

You've dedicated your life to me,
Someday I'll have to set you free,
But I will not until you know, I love you more than words can show.

So when that day has arrived and gone,
Come to me before the dawn, in my dreams while I sleep,
Tell me you know my love is deep,
And you can see how I feel, that my love for you is real.

Tina Allen

The Reflecting God

The hold of truth beyond the strength of me
I face the things I fail to see
I hate the hypocrite that in turn hates me
At least I have my dignity
People strip away the things that make them be
    And idolize what they feel is free
They neglect things that can be gained honestly
What they have become is beyond the understanding of me

    Living on your knees-conformity
Or dying on your feet for honesty
People who refuse to be part of one of these
Are the only people I would not refuse to pity

    In reality I suppose I am a fraud
    But in my mind I am still the reflecting God.

Bryan Ogden

Faith

In our chaotic and unpredictable world
We are held hostage by violence and hate.

We have tossed aside our faith
Like the garbage tossed outside.
We must search to reclaim it
As we would search for a lost child.

And when we find our faith
We find what we can truly
Trust and believe.

Now held together by peace and love
In a joyous and united world.

Matthew Lane Alexander

My Love For You

I love you more and more each day;
I don't know why I have nothing to say,
My love for you burns as hot as fire;
I know my love will never tire.
You hold my hand.
I start to cry.
Because I don't know if your love is a lie.
Do you love me?
Or do you not?
Please tell me so,
But please don't let me go.

Jennifer Martin

Life Without The High

Life without the high is very fine indeed
A life without the high I must soon succeed
Because when worse comes to worse
It's enough to make me curse
And of course it's all the worse
A quite funny thing that will make one's glee disperse
An' them beasts in that joint, all stupid and hairy
Those smoke suckin' gorillas who think they're so scary
The high is filled with dastardly deeds
Fascist slogans and campy creeds
To most it is fine or just horrible one
But after a while it's a joke of a battle to be won
And after the smoke is cleared and things look back up to par
One can make sure they go on, preferably very far
And keep from the high and its atavistic deeds
Because it seems a lot that it's something nobody needs

Maurice Carter

Newness Of Victory

How be this? For they were dead by my hand;
Surrounded by thorny vines and dry land!
They were driven by heat, roaming the earth.
Out there, amongst the dust nothing gives birth!

Ravens scoured about to douse royal remains;
No man quite possibly could have made any gains.
Dust storms and stirring winds both dominate there —
Even the greatest of travelers must beware!

The waters alone would have left them ashore
All of these burdens they just could not have bore.
Explain to me now and explain to me quick,
For even now I have become very sick!

Well, Si're, the one conclusion that I can see
Brings me to the way only this mishap can be.
The heat was caused by a light-giving sun,
Which lit up their path, wait! I am not done.

Ravens are live beings, and we all must eat.
Leading them to food was the raven's defeat!
Dust-made clouds blinded what enemies could gaze;
Their High Supreme must be the Ancient of Days!

Marvin Eric Moore

Inspired By A Friend

The beauty of youth may look pretty from afar,
But what comes from the heart really shows who you are.

We go through life day by day,
Meeting new people along the way.

Like the radiance of dew on petals of spring,
A special warmth inside, a new friend brings.

Euphoria from the feelings inside
Gives an inner peace that will never die.

They give you the courage
To not get discouraged.

Once in your heart you know its began
An everlasting friendship without any end.

Kathleen Ann Breaux

Love

Love is pure,
love is sweet,
love is the feeling that goes straight to the feet,
love is a blessing,
love is treat,
love is something, nothing can beat,
so why guard your heart so near, with fear!

Matipa Charley

Survival

Cancer!
It's back, it's back, it's back.
Second time. What now? More surgery.
No radiation, this time Chemo.
Mental well being - 90% survival rate.
Positive attitude.
Yes, I will live.
Eighteen months, five surgeries, I'm fine.
Mental well being, positive attitude.
Bills and cards, cards and bills.
I will survive.
100,000 miles on the car,
shortened grocery list
circled want ads, second job.
God please I couldn't "survive" a third time.

Betty Rebeck

The Ice Princess

I sit alone this night in my palace of ice, high upon my throne.
My heart is empty, bitter, cold like a blackened stone.

My tears freeze hard as they stream down my face.
My heart cries out for someone, someone to melt this place.

The walls that surround me were built by my soul,
To tear them down now becomes my only goal.

But alas, I am a prisoner - my heart has not known love.
To set my sad heart free requires a gentle love.

Can you be the one with the touch like warm, soft air?
Do I allow your love to melt me?
Do I love you? Do I dare?

Oh, to replace this palace of cold,
With dancing colors, bright and bold,
To let go the pain that drains my heart,
To feel happiness, to make a new start.

To you, my Prince, I hand the key,
Open my heart and look inside of me.

In isolation, I have lived so long.
But I have found you now,
And I am set free, like a song.

Erika V. Queen

Trick Or Treat? — Autopsy On Halloween

Black bags pulled from a van,
hiding charred reminders of yesterday's fire.

My evening spent with the dead,
Like Quasimodo hunched over a family of four,
sifting endlessly through internal organs with names:
Ricki, Lori and the kids.

Ricki and his tattoos — STONED, a cross with wings —
epithets to a life.
Cops insisting on fingerprints
only Old Spice clung to their skins.

Lori — her body exorcised of flames,
but not of men's comments.
Even in death women cannot escape
the scrutiny of men's eyes.

Black and Decker arrives, hungry for access.
My hand knocks at the door,
my fingers sign silently, "Trick or treat,"
ribcages open and I grope through a marriage
of blood and urine,
eagerly searching for an elusive organ.

C. M. Hipp

Jane

Let me tell you homeboy about a
girl name Jane, I puffed her lips
and she went to my brain
I needed this woman three times a day,
a man on the corner said son you have to pay,
so I paid my dime and bought me some
time and Mary Jane, kept me flying.
She would pick me up, and let me down
turn my whole world upside down.
I puffed Mary Jane on a Friday night, when
I woke up I thought I was in a fight.
I woke up on the floor, I thought someone
was knocked on my door
I open it and to my surprise, there she was in my eyes
I tasted her on my lips, and my mind took another flip.
There she was in some steam, you know how it felt in a dream
She told me I was a dope, all my money going up in smoke.
I didn't know what to do, everything she said was coming true
So I'll tell you before you go, when it comes to Jane just say No!!!

Rodney Minion

Hustler's Philosophy

Many people want to be hustlers, they think
it's heck of a game.
It may bring you good luck and fortune, and may
bring you misfortune or shame.
While I've been a hustler all my life
striving to get ahead.
There were days I sported like a king
and days I went unfed.
See there's always something to distract your mind.
To cause you to flounder and fall behind.
But always strive to save the day,
let nothing negative stand in your way.
Daily do what must be done,
positively to see that success is won.
Cause whomever you are and where and
whatever you play.
Remember it's the dues we all have to pay.

John Brown

Escape

Come with me
Embark on a journey of no return
Let our minds meet
Let not our souls yearn,
Nor starve for comfort, compassion or care
Let's freely give of each other
Honestly touching, feeling, uninhibitedly releasing. . .
The stress, toil, fears. . .tears
Join with me as one - entwined
Divinely blessed by God
Sharing, yet wearing our individuality
To eternity. . .we shall love.

Sharon A. M. Usher-Grant

Peace Beneath The Mountain

As I stand beneath the clouds
at the foot of the mountain
my face lifted up to the sun.
I see rainbow in the rain
lilacs in the snow. Lily of the valley
in the field.
And the scent of roses that fills the air.
Purple - white - crimson red against
the pale blue sky.
He is here - yes He is here.
God in all his glory.
And I'm at peace.

Daphne M. Aderman

Shiver

Father?
The shivering is coming!
I have crossed the creek before my feet
and climbed the wall that held my fall.
Coming to grief, running.
I have crossed the pillage,
wrinkling the tall brown grass on playgrounds I pass
and topped the hill above the shabby field.
It is coming!
I am just in front of the shivering.
The shadow is before my path.
Mother's oak, I have passed.
I crossed its laughter while taking the pasture, playing.
Father?
You must clear the cellar before it takes wrath.
The shivering has crossed our path.
The shivering is here, father.
The sheltering is here.

Thomas Hayes

Angelic Vengeance

You thirst to fathom the mystery of your
actions
you thirst for reasons in feeling the way
you do
you want the jewels in the web, but won't get
that intimate with the spider
you ignore the motives you, yourself can't
comprehend
you let the black winter soothe you, while
all along looking for the blue sky's smile
can't remember the dusty good bye that happened
when you were away
but vividly recall the dreams that thunder through
your perfect world
the demons are your monstrous angels, who
contradict you on everything you choose
a wild fern grows in the isolated bed of the woods
but when company can't reach it, it dies there on the spot
once you learn your name and can remember your own face
is when the Demons leave and Angels take their place

Shelley Burke

Sweet Baby Brianna

From the first time I saw your face
I knew that it was love.
You are such a grace,
a blessing from above.
I knew then, from the very first day,
my life would change forever.
Each new day that I see your smile
I know that the change was for the better.
I never dreamt that I could love so much
or be loved so much by you.
Nothing could ever compare
to the day I gave birth to you.

Diane Marie

Untitled

I see the sunshine rich and golden
I see the ocean wide and blue
I see the trees tall and green
I see the flowers beautiful and bright
I see the land so full of peace
I feel the power of God so strong
I feel his love upon my shoulder
As I shiver from the beauty of his everlasting love
I look around me, and all is well
With God beside me, all that I will is mine

Pearl Bernard

They Robbed Banks And They Robbed Trains

They robbed banks and they robbed trains.
They were Frank and Jessie James,

Cole Younger and his brothers,
Did the same,

They robbed banks and they robbed trains
Along the Kansas Missouri plains

But they didn't stay alive to enjoy their gains.

It was the Dalton boys who rode,
Lookin' all over Kansas for gold,

That's in a bank or on a train,
Stealing another man's gold, they were the bandits of old,

But they didn't stay alive to enjoy their gains.

So take heed young man, honor your fellow man,
Don't try to steal his gold, you've got to walk Johnny Cash's line,

Be honest truthful and kind, or you may find you'll never grow old.

Bryan L. Jury

I Love You

I love you with all my heart
And deep down that feeling will never part
To me you are perfect in every way
In my heart that feeling will always stay
From the first time that I saw you
I knew that this was true
Together we will always be
Forever just you and me
Though others may go away
With you is where I'll always stay
Your eyes make my heart dance, and your
smile drives me insane
My heart jumps at the mention of your name
No matter where you go
I just wanted you to know
I love with all my heart
And from you I'll never part.

Kimberly Daniel

First Kiss

Nothing is sweeter than the first kiss
One that tells me something new,
That you are mine at that moment
Cherish, I do cherish that bliss,
Of every year of this date, to have this kiss anew
And always, its memory brings enjoyment
Nothing is sweeter than the first kiss
After this one come many more
And none resembles the one,
Which is on the top of my list
With all the countless kisses, I am in need of more
They too have my heart won

Pierre-Marie Gustave

Unheard Voice

Selfishly giving life, only thinking of your own
Forgetting a precious child, in which you would disown
Creating a soul to never hear its voice
Making up for your ways by saying it's your choice
Not able to describe such sadness that I feel
For those you give a heart to think it's yours to steal
Given a chance, but only for you to take
Just living long enough to pay for your mistake
To see one glimpse of my first smile
Would it, then, have been worthwhile?

Holly Sutphin

A Wyoming Impression

Wild horses and lazy cows.
Cigarettes dropping from lined cornered mouths.

Wind frizzed stiff sprayed hair.
Wyoming negligee called long-johns underwear.

Wide horizons with colorful skies.
Married cowboys whispering yesterday lies.

Shy Volkswagens and intimidating trucks.
Long dusty roads, leather and mucks.

Clanky railroad cars that go here and there.
Calvary soldiers who vanish into thin air.

Sun parched soil where grazing antelope eat.
Western boots for many feet.

Kick up! Drink beer! Watch the Rodeo ride!
And, just let all the rest slide.

Diane K. Luster

In The Warmth Of The Sun

First held you in the warmth of the sun. Not knowing
what had begun. Heart shaking, hands tremble.
Made love, first time, comedy? Probably. But still,
love made with feelings not felt with any other, New feelings?
Yes, every time, not just the first.
Once told your eyes, prettiest ever seen. I look at them
day and night when I close my own.
Time continues, a bond should too, so I am told. But to
keep pushing away? Only the one getting pushed hurts. Poor,
struggling, Yeh, I guess I am. Just trying to fit in, for love.
But to hold your hand made me a king, rich, standing tall.
Now, rich memories, just a man where a king once stood.
Is there a place where loved ones gather and hug? Where
no one is ashamed of one?
If there is such a place, I can wait. I can wait to hold
you once again, in the warmth of the sun.

John J. Hazelwood III

Memories

Love has passed, time it seems stands still for me.
Each passing day brings thoughts of what has been
The memories of love I clearly see.
Remembering your touch with tears unseen
I hide my hurt and showing no despair
Trudge through each day reminiscence of you.
But I find no solace without you then.
Days of laughter and joy have been to few.
Feelings of defeat empower my soul
Since our togetherness has forever gone.
I pray for hope to soothe this angry toll
And ease my burden with a morning song.
Knowing you wait in your heavenly place
With an angelic smile upon your face.

Joan Fox

Old Fool

Someone's in my house, someone I don't know.
He's just an old fool who can't hurt
anyone.
Still his eyes are what worry me most.
They seem to look at me with blame and hate.
Seeing everything no matter where I go.
Even in my mirror looking back.
They made me stop shaving weeks ago.
On that morning the old fools eyes
tried to make me believe he was me.

Gary W. King

O Canada

O Canada, O Canada,
How gracefully you lie
With your snow capped mountain ranges
And ice laced rivers and lakes.

You awe me with your splendor
And humble me with your beauty
You leave me wondering at how
Niagara came to pass.

I ask of you, O Canada,
What is it like to be envied
By nations great and small
So powerful, so wise?

I watch you swell with pride
While I feel quite depleted
My soul cries out to yours
With questions and longings.

For how can you, O Canada, be so whole,
Yet so diverse
With all your many cultures and tongues
And yet still be thriving and united as one?

Emily Elisabeth Edgeman

Rolling Along

Big ole semi-truck rolling along,
Blowing black smoke from the stack.
Polluting the trail we'll take back.

Heavy foot is pressed to the floor,
Trying to make that engine turn more.

I can't see anything in the night,
I'm just following the glow of the headlights.

For all I know it is a desert out there,
But in the middle of the night, who cares.

Semi keeps roaring along. . .
Radio keeps blaring out songs.

Cigar smoke is all around,
That stogie is about burnt down.

City lights shine up ahead,
And remind me of the world in which I live.

Won't be long now and I'll be home,
But I'll just spend the night then drive to another zone.

Damned this life that I'm living!
Is it even worth the effort that I'm giving?

Ray Merenda

First Glance

the day you walked through that door,
I knew my life would soon mean
more, than just a mere co-workers'
attraction. For just a glance is
all it took, for me to see your
appealing look.

I knew then I had affection
growing in my heart, that caused
rhythmic contractions.
As time passes on, we began
to talk about little things, Big things
But still in my subconscious I wanted more
I wanted to hold you, kiss you,
Each time you walk through
that door.

Joann P. Witten

The Gypsy Joker

A misty memory, both vague and clear,
Arrives unsolicited, at times unpredictable,
Playing its unique rhythms on my soul,
Awakening moments of concrescence,
Faded in time,
Hidden within the substance of my being.

This visitation separates me,
Sanctifying my unconformed soul,
Making me unlike the clamorous crowd,
Who go about unturned by all but the most,
Mundane of mysteries and never asking,
Why does this happen to me?

Hurried and pressed by another's agenda,
A Gypsy Joker is hidden by life's particulars,
Rarely seen by anyone, known only to himself.
A glimpse betrays his secret at moments,
When magic rescinds science,
And the existential sting quickens the soul's eyes.

This misty memory is life.
It brings together the parts,
And gives meaning to the whole,
Unveiling the Joker's self,
To similar gypsy-souls,
Declaring, "you are not alone."

Rocky Miller

A Secret Once Told

You once told me a secret, you told me you loved me
that was the secret you said.
To hear I love you from your mouth, the tone in your voice
I didn't need anyone else but you.

Now I sit here with tears in my eyes, the pain inside.
When you told me that secret I could of swore it was for real.
But now I'm not so sure, because I think you found
someone new.

Is the secret you once told me the same for her.
Do you say it as true to her as you did to me
or was I just a fool for believing in thee.

I said I love you, I meant it, I thought you did to
But obviously not!
Because you don't see the pain, that's in my way of
breaking away from you my love.

Natasha Malmstrom

Granny's House

As the morning sun reflects its rays off the
    window of my past.
I glanced in, and there she stood, over an ole
    white stove in a gazing trance.
Her hands, cracked from years of family care
    and her hair gray from time gone by.
With eyes that where soft, and gentle, and a
    heart twice her size.
Her happiness was the sight of your face, and
    a simple hi.
As I watched, she cooked with a peaceful gaze
    as though she were visiting days gone by.
You always take for granted, these days you
    think will never pass.
But then one day you realize, that these days will never last.
No the house was not a mansion, and the car was old not new.
But those who were lucky enough to have visited
    Granny's house are wealthier it's true.
Now the house is empty, with only voices of the past.
And often I think of stopping there just to take a glance.

Larry Thompson

Ooh! Those Peach Roses

I'll never forget the moment when I opened my duplex door.
I felt like I was on a ocean, and
before me a bottle of peach, live, long-stemmed
roses had been washed ashore.
I immediately picked them up and hoped to
find my name on a card.
And surely enough I had been chosen...To be admired.
..."Giver," you are the more special
person of that precious moment...
I couldn't see another color for a mile.
And if you should ever read this poem.
"Please realize," you've caused this woman to smile!

I have to say I wished we could have
shared that moment from the sky.
It was special to me.
The roses made me blush, I even felt shy.
I didn't once have a moment of fear,
or of a harasser in my life, nothing of that sort.
I just felt a touch of the Master's hand
and placed thanksgiving in my heart.
Even today I thank you...

Carolyn Y. Palmer

Beloved

Not dead just gone. Not gone just dead.
All for one. None for all.
The acrid harmony of this beloved song
Rumbling through my head.

Nothing ever dies;
Rather it thrives.
Feasting on the mortals immortal soul,
Making a nest, building a home
In the translucent eyes.

As simple as a rose.
As painful as a kiss;
A kiss of ignorant bliss
As it intoxicates virgin lips
Filling the ears
With the enchanting melody of bellowing crows.

The passion of red.
The passion of the vengent
The vengent dead.
The painful touch of a red petal.
The red essence - lethal and yet essential.

Amanda Moressi

The Doctor

Going to the doctor is such a chore.
Takes all you got just to get out the door.

The trip there always seems to take all day.
Dreading the ride every inch of the way.

Once you're there, sign in, sit and wait awhile
Until the receptionist pulls your file.

When your name is called, you go to the back
With all the enthusiasm you lack.

When you think you can't wait one more minute,
The door opens and the doctor in it.

He gives a short talk, a shot or a pill
Then you leave the office still feeling ill.

Follow doctors orders to the letter
Then, very soon, you will feel much better.

Kay Sturgeon Clark

Captive

Lost in a world of confusion
A sea of darkness
Drifting through the night
    without the light of day in sight

A world of damnation
A world of ridicule
A world surrounded by love
Love unable to shine without the light of day
Ambling through life
Yet not moving anywhere
No past; no present; no future
Less than existing

One recognizable forward motion...
Searching;
    for perspective
A body filled with possibilities
wrapped up in its own hate
searching for its own punishment
    for lack of forward motion
Trapped in a cage in which it built

Mary-beth K. Huthmacher

Headlights

The last thing I saw was the headlights.
It was dark when I came to.
I was standing in a hall way.
I could hear a man's voice yelling something.

I was intrigued by it.
I walked to it.

I entered a room with hundreds of people.
A man was yelling "so, you deny Christ.
In your life you say Anti-Christ, there's no God.
You'll change your mind quick enough!"

Then I was in my bathroom and I hear my sister scream.
I smell burning flesh.
I can feel the heat.
I look down at my legs, I'm engulfed in flames.
I hit my door, but it won't open.

I can see the man laughing at me.
"So you don't believe in God"
I try to scream, but it's stuck in my chest.
I wake up screaming.
The last thing I saw was the headlights.

Andrew Riggs

You Shall Return No More To Me

My thoughts are whirling as you pack
Will you ever go and not come back?
You have a habit of walking out
Every time I yell or shout.
But this time, deep inside I feel
You shall return no more to me.

Two weeks have turned to three, then four
Dear God! I plead, don't make it more.
I sit and listen for your call
I hang your picture on each wall
I listen for your footsteps, but silence tells
You shall return no more to me.

Forget the past, the future lies ahead to see
This is what they say to me.
Lift your chin, sing a song, be not wan.
Oh no! I can't—I have a plan
That will surely prove all wrong for thinking
You shall return no more to me.

Lanna Allison

To My Lover - A Lesson In Drink

Love is consumed in haste as with one's
first taste of ale,
Rushed to completeness then belched away.

Time passes and soon love is no longer
swilled but enjoyed,
Like the nectar of the vine—
bittersweet in tanginess.

At last when all has matured, love is
caressed as an aged cognac—
bedded in fine crystal as the body
in silk and satin.

The scent as stirring as nature's own musk—
the taste seducing the tongue with a liquid
kiss, all hot and fiery.

Copper lights swirl as bodies,
cast in candlelight,
sway in motion and with a whispered sigh—

Love is swallowed in quiet reflection.

Christina Felter

The Great Regret

A man is lying down looking at the ceiling fan.
Bursting of depression because he's a diseases man.
Starting to regret all the times heroin was injected.
"Addiction" made him share needles, therefore he is now infected.
Sadness fills his heart, because his immune system is no longer
  protected.
Thinking not only he will suffer, but his whole family is affected.
Different types of feelings roam throughout the house, and more will
  be built.
A successful architect with a lot of guilt.
Waiting patiently for the day his judgment allows his peace.
Waiting, for his life to expire his lease.
The final days and he's writing his experiences, so others will not
  follow.
He learned that in this world your pride you must swallow.
Blames it on temptation and mostly on pressure.
His children will grow up without a father, because of his selfish
  pleasures
Time is his enemy, he must fight to the end.
That evening he fell asleep and never woke again.

Glen Puicon

Wake Up Everyone

You wake in the morning, and feel so sad,
  And wonder why the world is so bad;
Then your thoughts shift to better days
  And know God will help along the way.

Faith, love and patience is needed here
  So you can face life without any fear;
So perk up my friend, with hope you should
  Amidst all this chaos, life is still good.

Rita Vaillancourt

I Don't Want To Fight

Help me, Help me, I'm in a fight
Help me, Help me, it's not alright
It's not cool, it's not fun.
I'll get in trouble like anyone
I'd rather have a chocolate chip than
get a big fat bloody lip.

Besides getting hurt and getting dirty
I don't want my mother or father to worry.
So if you listen to what I say fighting isn't
right anyway.

Kristin Ann Dunnells

In My Thoughts

While reflecting upon this cold lonely night,
  All I can dream of is holding you tight;

I feel the need to hear you say words with meaning,
  And words with truth,

Three simple words being,
  I love you;

In my mind with deep thoughts,
  I know the fear and anguish you fought;

Each day only lingers when you're not there,
  Our lives are too short, too foolish, and unfair;

Execute me for lying and convict me for trust,
  But I'm only human,
  And in my life, your caring and tenderness is a complete must;

Now I reflect on the early morning light,
  And my cold feelings,
  Of the lonely night are gone,
  But I dream about what it's like,
  To be with you at dawn.

Connie Hein

The Flower

A nine year old girl dressed in hand-me-downs,
barefooted, stands to attention on a hot asphalt parade
ground in a small Australian country town, head bowed,
tears flowing, painful ache in the heart with the knowledge
that JFK had died some hours before. The seed was planted.
She shuffled her feet, the heat rose and time went by.

A few years later the seed had grown into a flower,
She grew her hair, put the flower in it and ached for
San Francisco. Small minds in small towns gossiped over
her free love and such.
She shuffled her feet, the heat rose and time went by.

In the institution where mostly white middle class kids go,
she sat on the floor grasping Marx, Ghandi, MFDP notes,
Walt Witman and a free Vietnam leaflet.
She shuffled her feet, the heat rose and time went by.

In her apartment in Pacific Grove she looks over jewelled
hands to the sea. Her copy of Food First makes up land
fill near a toxic creek on the other side of the Pacific.
And somewhere the petals of a flower have decayed.
She shuffled her feet and put ice in her glass.

Dianne Butler

School's Out

I see the snow falling gently, covering the
  school grounds.
The kids are having a good time throwing
  each other around.
I see the kids pulling on each other, and I can't
  tell one from the other.
I see some of the cars streaking by, while other
  ones are slowly creeping by.
I see the teachers leaving fast, putting their feet
  to the gas.
I see the school buses all lined up in a row, but
  the parents' cars won't let them go.
I hear the car horns honking and the motors
  running and making a lot of noise.
You see, it's hard nowadays to tell the girls from
  the boys.

Benjamin F. Jackson

Poet's Prose

Epic poetry is my quest, to write a tale of writer's unrest;
He thinks and ponders, dreams mighty dreams, yet the pen is quite
   still;
He pains and racks his soul for the song that never unfolds;
He yearns for burning passion to quicken his soul;
To write as poets write;
Glib and clever, beauty and praise, rhythm and time are on his mind;
He stares at empty paper and sees not the beauty of his soul;
His pen is still as death, he is blind as blind men are;
Seeing with eyes not his own, knowing not the beauty;
The beauty of a poet's soul;
Pen in hand, his heart quickens, he writes a measure of line;
He smiles for he knows his writer's unrest is a thing of prose;
The pen, not still, flies and soars about the paper;
Measure and rhyme is what his soul finds;
He laughs and smiles, he writes as his soul crosses the miles;
The poet within smiles, remembering his poet's prose,
for it is his license to write only as a poet knows.

Scott M. Mallory

David

Why is the sky blue
Why does it rain
Why is my heart aching, and so full of pain.

Why did you love me, and make me come alive.
Giving my heart the will to survive.

Why can't I understand why you took
your love away.
Why can't I stop praying you will
come back some day.

Why can't I stop crying and hurting myself.
I do not want to put my heart back on a shelf.

Why is grass green.
Why is my heart breaking in two
Why can't I stop thinking about you.

Kimberly A. Bedford

The Journey

And the journey begins...
Spiraling down into confusion and chaos,
Groping in the darkness for comfort,
Reaching for solutions and finding no answers,

And the journey begins.....
Seeking knowledge, religion, and love,
Grasping in all the wrong places,
Turning to God in desperation,

And the journey begins...
Finding the mysterious, yet familiar wonders,
Leading to joy and unexplainable serenity,
Amazing at His Awesome Presence,

And the journey begins....

Shelley Smith

Ode To The Master Plan

Have you ever been thrilled by the sight of a deer
Captured the beauty of a majestic tree
Listened to the songs of the birds upon your ear
Admired the wondrous beauty without a tear?
Without God's plan for nature and beauty the world
   will have lost the master plan
And we will be blinded for an eternity.
I plead with you—leave God's plan intact
Assure posterity the same joys we've had.

William B. Holman

A Dream

I dreamed that I looked into your eyes
And they said "I love you and want you by my side"

My heart responded, beating profoundly
My love for you I give very proudly

You wanted to share your dreams with me
And to love each other eternally

We wanted to see the world together
Each new place would bring us closer than ever
We fell in love more than before
Clinging to each other forever more

But alas, we could see the world
Only through each others' eyes
For I woke up to realize
It was just a dream of being in paradise

Myrna M. Salgado

The Chair

It came from her mother who bought it so long ago,
and many a babe did she rock so lovingly to and fro.
Many a meal they were given with care and love,
many a fear chased away with the warmth of a hug.
And when the time came she passed it on to my wife,
so another young babe would have it in their life.
The warmth and the music that fill the air,
with the gentle, loving rocking, of that old chair.

O. L. Norcutt Jr.

Send Me An Angel

Send me an angel, straight from the heavens above,
   someone to be my best friend, one pure as a dove.
To watch my every step, stand by my side as I learn,
   which roads to traverse, which to evade and turn.
To show me to love, trust, and mostly to care,
   to learn when I am wrong, and bring joy when I share.
To know when I am strong, and when I am weak,
   to trust in the knowledge I dispense when I speak.
See the good in my heart, for it is often not shown,
   to notice steps of maturity, for I have surely grown.
I trust in my angel, to bring the best out in me,
   my loving, intelligent and jovial side for all to see.
I have met such an angel, with the qualities above,
   with the power, reason, honor, and love.
This angel has seen with her very own two eyes,
   The good times and bad, sunshine and the cloudiest of skies.
Her heart is of gold, and often seen to be true,
   will find the good, the best in all of you too.

Alex Greene

The World

The words escape my lips, as this cold wind dries my eyes,
The smell is sweet, while the wine is bitter,
Each step I take grows filled with pain,
Nights are filled with light, and days grow darker each minute,
The salt stings my tongue with my words of indiscretion.
My thoughts are mindless, my speeches are empty.
The world is a cold place, and as strange as
it seems, the colder it grows, the better I feel.
Shadows of truth hide in slipstreams of lies,
as my night comes to an end, I feel as if
so does my life,
But still I awake to face a new day in
this cold world, where right is
unacceptable, and wrong is the
inevitable way of the world in which
we live, and so it is a reversal
of the world.

David Vail

Friendship

What is this thing called friendship
that we all so deeply need?
At times down on knees at night
this is for what we plead.

Sometimes we have a problem
that seems alone too much to bear
if only we had a friend to lean on
someone we knew who cared.

Someone we could turn to
no matter the time, day or night
someone who would drop everything
and let you know it's going to be alright.

Sometimes that friend may be close at hand,
closer than you realize.
But you may have to take the time to look
deeper than you can see with your eyes.

So if you ever need a friend
remember I'm not far
and one of the greatest rewards of friendship?
True friends accept you for who you really are.

Laralee Seidel

Soulmates!

To every flower that dies
That gets cut or pulled from the earth
The soul that was once powerful
Now weaker than if stabbed
When trees split down the center
From the tumbling earth
And blood, not sap, seeps from its cracks
For every God that decides to take the flower
May laugh
Because they feel no sorrow
And for every branch that hangs
A secret that no one bares
That takes my heart and shoots the arrow
That shares the soul mates
That once were.

Erica Davis

Memories Of War

Forced from our homes because of religion
While others in the world paid no attention.
Some getting permission to depart
Those who have died remain in our hearts.
Husbands and wives and children no longer together
We are forced to work in all types of weather.
Sent to camps where we know we will die
We soon discover there is no need to cry.
God's test for us to keep our faith
Yet more people are dying everyday.
People line up to face their graves
Their own lives they bravely gave.
Shot with one bullet in the head
Would cause millions to fall dead.
Those who were lucky to survive
Were covered with soil and buried alive.
Ropes around the necks of people whose chairs fell
Their bodies would soon burn in the pits of hell.
Nazis of Germany do not regret
But something in history no one will forget.

Jodi R. Hunt

The Aging Day

"The creation is the beginning as dawn introduces day,
    all darkness disappears, sun brings forth its ray."

The sun warms the earth as day grows a little older,
    awakening the morning flowers, life seems much bolder."

"Day is slowly aging and a mild summer breeze...
    sways the colorful flowers, caressing the trees."

"This aging day has grown old when dusk is near,
    night slowly takes over and sparkling stars appear."

"Full moon in all its splendor slowly taking its place,
    looking at the world with such a happy smiling face."

"Night is gradually ending, day has almost died,
    day will soon start over again, with dignity and pride."

William T. Joynes

Moonlight Madness, Sunlight Sadness

He runs crazy throughout the night,
Hardly a silhouette in a sliver of moonlight.
    One solitary tear slides down the cheek,
Of a scared little boy too frightened to speak.
    Where has he gone, where has he run to,
Why did he run, why did he have to?
    The day is dawning, arising too soon,
Great streaks of sunlight conceal the moon.
    Two people are worried, too tearless to cry,
Their little boy ran, they want to know why.
    Where did he go, where did he run to.
Why did he run, why did he want to?
    Darkness is coming, coming again,
The boy he just sits there, too scared to go in.
    What will his parents say, he fears so much,
He has no idea they worried such.
    To face his mother and father, he gathers the courage,
To tell them the story of his midnight scourge.
    He wants only to tell them, to tell them with gladness.
That in moonlight was madness, yet with sunlight came sadness.

Jennie Cunningham

To Sarah With Love

Loving birthday wishes to a daughter so dear,
May God bless you as you ring in another year,
Turning three is a special milestone in life's endless journey,
We'll see boundless curiosity, dreams and a charming personality
so worthy,
Of all the unconditional love a faithful mom can impart,
Upon her darling daughter who will always occupy a special place
in mom's heart.

Patty Carolan

True Treasures

Have you ever taken the time to think what goes on in our minds?
The lovely thoughts, the purest thoughts, bring inner peace and
    never binds.
Life's not meant to pursue selfish pleasures.
Family, friends and neighbors are the true treasures,
Not limitless possessions we do not need,
Nor senseless effects that bring foolish greed.
Oh times gone by when a wrong deed or careless word
Could be taken back and had never been heard.
Such a short time we're on this earth.
What a privilege for us to prove our worth.
The world we're in is up to us
To make it for all an infinite plus.

Dorothee Long

The Overflow

I had an awesome dream one night
Wait just a moment, let me get this right
I ran outside and to my amazement
I saw a pool of water on the pavement
A pool standing upright with water all around
I just stood there looking down on the ground
It was crystal clear, so quiet, so peaceful
I'm telling you it was unbelievable
The next day I told my dream to my friend
She sat there a minute, she didn't pretend
She said, "Oh, honey, don't you know
God has given you an overflow."

Deborah Kaye Adamo

Mind of Mine

Wonder in the wind,
Stars in the mind.
Blow by swiftly like a day in time.
Look to the heavens and see what you got.
A day in the sky, is it all for not.

Randal R. Minehart

Depression

The brokenness of her Heart left her soul as though
   the Apocalypse had occurred, leaving the carnage of
   destruction behind.
Pain that is incomparable to any other.
Devastated and detached from those around her,
Dilatory she sank into an oblivion that seized tenaciously
   against her mind and soul.
Lacking in her compassion she aphorism only her vacuousness.

The years transcended while her mind and soul devolved into
   someone unknown, unliked, unloved and unwanted.
Traveling in her loneliness, feigning the existence of
   contentedness, sliding deeper into the black abyss of
   depression.
Though she knew not what to call it, knowing not how to help
   herself, nor who to turn to, the abyss lightened, giving
   her the opportunity to see beyond the darkened tunnel.

Still more years passed before she began emerging from the
   cocoon that she had tightly shrouded about her.
Evermore careful not to slip back into the cloakness of
   depression, she looks now at her children and smiles.

Anne M. Search

The Golden Spoon

High upon a little shelf, there lies a Golden Spoon.
And when I asked to touch it the reply was very soon.
In moments I would tarry, and dream about the Spoon.
In hopes that day would come and chase away the gloom.
My eyes do meet the spoon you see, for I have grown so tall.
And I could easily touch the shelf that hangs upon the wall.
The Golden Spoon seems smaller and tarnished all too soon.
And now I look upon the shelf and hate that dreadful room.
Don't put your dreams upon a shelf or in a Golden Spoon.
Don't sacrifice your inner shelf for time does pass too soon.

Gloria Fobert

My Dearest Mother

My dearest mother means very much to me,
you mean more to me than honey does to bees,
as long as I'm alive, I will succeed and survive,
two things my mother taught me, since the young age of five,
try hard at things I do,
even if I don't have a clue,
I come to you if I'm feeling blue,
cause all words out of your mouth eventually are true.

Stephen Camacho

Thorns Of A Rose

I see oceans of flowers I dared to run through
Roses without thorns, then there was you
Thorns filled your stem the deadliest of all
But magnificent beauty was all I saw
I heard the wind whisper, "touch if you dare
That's a flower of pain, no beauty is there!"
I would not listen, I did not heed
I laughed through my tears as you made me bleed
As I held you closely it cut like a knife
My love for you was taking my life
Yet I held on tighter and awaited the day
When all your thorns would be taken away
Your petals wilted, I held you still
Until the pain of your thorns was all I could feel
As the first snow began to fall
and there was nothing left at all

Elizabeth H. Breedon

Awakened

I stood upon a wooden bridge, worn and tattered.
Willow tendrils gently kissing.
Reflection of sturdier braces and strategical
beams of a hundred years.
A million shoes, heavy upon trusted boards.
Sweat, blood, and tears.
Forgotten dreams.
Fear not foul weather, oh rusted iron.
Once bright, mighty rails, forever standing.
Waiting, waiting, all weather.

John M. Hughes

The Life Of A Foot

The life of a foot has its ups and downs
I have taken a king to receive a crown.

I have taken a poor man to scrounge for food
I have taken a leper to exiled seclude.

But my favorite time that I can remember
Is a small but still glowing memory ember

When I took a blind man to see a Jew
Who cleansed his eyes and his spirit anew.

Chris J. Marley

Patients Are People, Too

When I was in my young teens,
I used to dream of becoming a nurse,
not just to wear the white uniform,
but to aid and help people working in the hospital.
I visited the hospital with my mother.
Watching and observing the nurses as they helped people,
I wanted it to be me helping the sick patients.
They looked so helpless:
Some with nosebleeds, others from automobile accidents.
After I finished high school, I got my first job
working in New Falls Hospital in the housekeeping department.
This was not for me so I went to Washington D.C.
and enrolled in Nursing school.
I felt different and was proud of myself for being qualified
to work with the sick patients and not be afraid.
After some years had passed,
I returned to my hometown, which was in Louisiana.
I communicate with patients throughout my duties,
their concern of their Medical History.
So I am overjoyed to be a part of the health care team.

Estella Sanders

Martin Luther King, Jr.

I have a dream said Martin Luther King.
I have a dream. I say that
There'll come a day
When my children will play
And dance and sing with children of all colors.

I have a dream, whispered Martin L. King,
That All children will grow strong.
They'll know right from wrong
And sing Freedom's Song
Till harmony rings throughout this country of ours.

I have a dream...So died M. L. King
Showing the world his spirit.
In those hearts who hear it
His message's so clear it
Echoes as it rings, "I have a dream...,
　　Have a dream...,
　　　A dream...,
　　　　Dream."

Barbara E. Courtney

Poem Of The Islanders—From Sappho

1st Islander. (1st Islander steps forward, chants.)

I have one eye in my forehead.
It glows at night, a ruby red.
It lights my way where'er I go.
I thank you, God, for its warm glow.

2nd Islander. (2nd Islander steps forward, chants.)

I thank you God, God of the sun
For the three legs that make me run
In circles, I know not where.
But I'm still happy, both here and there.
And all around me.

3rd Islander. (3rd Islander steps forward, chants.)

Don't pity me that I am blind.
I thank the gods that I can find
The path in dark of night and fly
Above the peaks into the starry sky.

Glenn L. Blubaugh

Snake Eyes

King snake! King snake! Where have you been?
　"Been 'round the world," he said with a grin.
"Saw a lot of pretty people and a lot of pretty places,
　but the strangest exhibition was the human races."

Kevin Snyder

Breathe

The last one slowly fades
with flesh melting and dripping from brittle bones.
The weight of emptiness pinning the weak to the earth.

I called for you, waited for an answer,
Only to feel the sting of each echo slowly gnaw away hope.

Your skin, so cold, unresponsive to my touch.
Cramped and drowned in your world
With limp remains kissing the ground.

How does it feel not to breathe? Not to feel the tapping of your heart?
I asked you, waited for an answer,
but couldn't hear through the molded soils of our past.

There's nothing left for me now.
But to wait.
For my turn.

Janet Cappadona

Grandma

I'm glad I have a grandma like you.
The love you share shows me you really care.
Through your work you give us gifts, never forgetting the
day we were born.
I see in your eyes the hope you carry for each and every
one of your children and grand-children.
What you give me can't be measured or weighed, nor can it
be taken.

Thank you, Grandma, for everything you do. I thank God
for giving me someone like you.
I can see with my own eyes that things around me are
falling apart; but you're a part of a Deeper Love. I
love you no matter what.

Kraig Wilson

Angel In The Crowd

Reverberations bring an image back to me,
Hauntings of a dream almost realized,
How many times can one be touched by grace,
Only to watch its splendor lose grip,
And plummet into a world of forfeited anticipation,

I strive to exact a new dawn upon myself,
Hoping morning's ascension will cleanse what was,
Yet the thought cuts into me,
Grating thorns ever sharpened by loss,
Leaving my soul to bleed loneliness,

How many times can I be touched by grace,
See an Angel in the crowd,
Blessed by a beauty rarely revealed,
Cursed by a lore of what could have been.

George Chumo Jr.

A Dream

As the night falls over us all
And we wait for the dream weavers call,
Our minds drift to a much better place;
Where together we stand face to face
With our enemies and know inner peace.
Where harmony helps us to release
The hatred we seem to hold dear,
And a past that we never can clear.

As we drift on a cloud in our dream
We see life that is torn to extreme
Like a card game that's lost from the start,
And a friendship that's torn all apart.
Then at last we see dawn disembark
Like a soft green mystical park,
That beckons to all who can hear
Of a life and a world without fear.

Jane E. VanDeest

A Walk In The Rain

divine branches pointed tight
they shimmer in the dark light.
arms stretched out farewell the sun
against a pink sky-the new day is done.
my companions and i (two others and me)
with rock in my hand, move on steadily..
though the crunch of the stones is loud
as we trod,
i seldom look back,
the night is so black.
a soft rain falls from my head to my feet.
the trickle of the stream,
the sprinkle on the leaves,
is enough to put me to sleep.

Kitty Bergert

Engagement Day

Sixteen years have come and gone
And I hope you love me still,
Cause when you asked that question of me
My answer was I will.

I hope you have no regrets
Cause we've been together so long,
I know I don't, but how about you?
Are your feelings still as strong?

Sixteen years later if you asked me again
Maureen - will you marry me?
I wouldn't hesitate I'd answer right away
I pledge my love to thee.

How about the future, what do you think?
Will we have sixteen more?
Just in case you have a doubt
From me to you - I'm sure.

Maureen A. Babec

Mississippi

You have the ability to draw near to You
    Those things that are precious.
With Diamond eyes and Onyx skin, there are many
    Tales that rest inside your boarders.
Your boundary stretches far on either side
    And only the very brave may cross You.
I wonder what treasure lay beneath Your surface
    Will you open up and show me.
The night brings forth Your wisdom
    And the day carries Your essence to waiting hearts.
Like many others, I too have wished for Your gentle
    Breeze to whisper deep within me.
I will cross over if only
    You wait for me Mississippi.

Goldine Benjamin

The Ocean Weather Inside Me

My ocean is choppy from a storm that past
When the sun comes out, the seaweed is
twirling like little children dancing

When a hurricane hits the seals are
screaming in search of their mothers

When rain is pouring the sand is as
wild as a horse

When the sky is blue the ships are ready
for anything

But when everything is calm there's nothing
to do except just swim around

When a twister is swirling
The mother seals are holding their babies tight

And how I don't know what it's going
to be like tomorrow.

Jamie Zawislak

Our Night Together

I walked along the beach one night,
and saw you standing in the moon light.
You reached out your hand for me to touch,
And whispered in my ear "I love you so much"
upon the sand we laid that night,
in each others arms in the
warmth of the light.
I'll never forget our night together,
I just wish it could have lasted forever.

Jennie Barnes

The Majestic Buck

The forest glistens with morning dew
As sun shafts filter through the trees
Revealing foliage in multi shades of green
Enhancing the wooded serene
The forest green blends with brownish hues
Under a brush in the clearing
Betraying slanted eyes asleep in dream
Enhancing the wooded serene
Upon his head like King with crown
Wearing his antlers with wisdom profound
Hidden and safe from earthly harm
He sleeps and dreams

Ann Whelan

Kathy's Goodbye

Remember me, in the morning sun
For what has happened, can't be undone.
    Remember me, when the stars shine bright
    For I no longer, have need of sight.
Remember me, when you see that shining moon
I can't explain why, life ended so soon.
    Remember me, in the mist of rain
    Rejoice no longer, do I feel pain.
Remember me, in the darkness of night
My eyes are closed, they see no light.
    Remember me, during times of great cheer
    No longer, shall I hold you near.
Remember me, in the good times and bad
I gave to you, all that I had.
    Remember me, when you go to sleep
    My eyes are dry, no reason to weep.
Remember me, at the start of each morn
For I have loved you so, since the moment
    you were born.

Betty Ann Watters

Child's Plea

My name it does not matter, my age is only two,
I have no say in where I go,
strangers plan what I will do.

If I could only speak my mind,
and have it change the law,
this would make the ones in charge,
hear us when we call.

I've known such pain, and also fear
I've been pushed, shoved and battered.
I am asking all who's reading this
do you care or does it matter.

Perhaps in the future, that is if I survive,
with God's help I will change these laws,
and help others stay alive!

Bonnie M. Sears

Reflections Upon Gazing At An Empty Bottle Of Snapple

There you sit, empty and dusty upon the shelf,
Drained of vitality,
Drained of purpose,
Useless, but for decoration.
Do you understand me?
Drained of motivation,
Drained of energy,
Exhausted, barely functioning.
Mechanical life.
Will I end up like you,
Old, empty, and useless?

Christine Gillingham

Nameless Beauty

I sit here in the mist of your beauty, wondering
  what it would be like to hold your slender body.

I sit here gazing upon your beauty hoping, to one day
  know the feeling of your heart beating upon my own.

You are nameless to me, but still I ponder the idea
  of your delicate lips touching the surface of mine.

We have spoken twice before, but still you are
  nameless.

The words we have spoken were short, so
  I make excuses for why you are nameless.

Excuses for why I am nameless.
You walk upon my direction, and I prey that
  you walk to me.

I prey that you approach me, and become
  a name, but you do not.

So every time you walk upon my direction, I prey
  that one day you loose namelessness.

Christopher Allen Ver Strate

Conversations

My pet cat and your pet cat,
Sitting by the fire.
My pet cat said to your pet cat,
I've got a dog at home.

Talk about cats now, cats now, cats now, cats now,
It never happened one day.
The reason I don't know what they say,
Is that they can't speak my language.

One fine day there were two chairs
Sitting by the table.
One chair said to the other chair,
"Nothing," they can't talk!

Talk about chairs now, chairs now, chairs now, chairs now,
My cat sat on it one day.
If you don't believe this story, well
Ask the floor, it saw it too!

Aaron Reiter

Oklahoma Blues

Was sittin' on the balcony one lonely fall
Watchin' cars go speeding by
When I heard the sound of blues playin'
Made me wanna hang my head and cry

  I started thinkin' of the times
  When I first started seein' you
  Drivin' in Oklahoma at night
  Listenin' to the blues

Laughter came easy back then
Stars were always bright in the sky
Tears were no where near us
Now they fill my eyes

  Wanna be by you outside
  In one of the cars speeding by
  But the sad Blues Voice is telling me
  Oklahoma Blues is gonna make me cry

Wishin' I had the power baby
To be sleepin' close to you
In Oklahoma on this cold fall night
Listenin' to the blues

Della Chippewa-Sapulpa

Baby's First

It is Lauren's Birthday,
Today is her Special Day,
We have all come to visit,
With her toys, she will play.

She'll sit up in her chair,
The candle she'll blow out,
She smiles at everyone,
As she crawls about.

She hugs her little bunny,
As she sits there and coo's,
and throws a kiss to us,
from across the room.

I see her little teeth,
As she laughs at me,
She is so happy today,
It's as plain as one can see.

She's Grandma Betty's Pride and Joy,
Uncle Larry's too,
She's Bob and Karen's Daughter, but she belongs to all of you.

"Happy Birthday, Lauren"

Norma M. Dubinsky

Your Face

When I see your face I compare it to how the world should be.
How beautiful each mountain, each sea would be.
The waves of the ocean, how the eagles fly free.
I compare your face to how the world should be.

Your eyes so blue as the world up high.
They sparkle like stars up in the sky.
With your skin so smooth, like the setting sun,
behind some mountains the beauties won.

When I see your face I compare it to how the world should be..
No sorrow, no pain,
Without the crying rain.
Without guilt and lies,
And no last goodbyes.

Your smile as perfect in each and every way.
The worlds one sigh,
Like the white clouds that roll by and by.

Shalina Delp

Seasons

To everything there is a season
There are many floods we must endure
But, comes the rainbow after
There's the sunrise
Then the sun sets
Darkness comes
Then the stars come out
There's the cold of winter
The mountains covered with snow
Then there is spring
Filled with flowers that give us those sweet fragrances
Birds fly by and sing
The trees gives us shade even though many are old and bare
Autumn always brings the crisp colorful falling leaves
And last comes summer
When everything living enjoys what God has given
I'm so thankful for the beauty of the seasons
They give us such a lift!
Isn't it great that God has shared this with us day by day
In the beauty of the seasons

Shirlene Polk

Three, Little Words

Sittin' here, in my lonely room, thinkin' of you, all through the night.
How do I let you know, or get you to understand, just exactly what
  you mean to me.
You know I am not good with words, when feelings are involved,
And yet, I have to find some way to say those three, little words,
Maybe, I can sing them in a song, with a melody as sweet as you,
Or play like that guy with the really long nose, what's his name.
Or act like Romeo and pledge my undying love, to you, my Juliet,
Maybe, I can write them in the sand, so you can see them as you
  walk by,
Maybe, I ought to just swallow the lump in my throat and tell you,
But, can I dare take that ever so important risk, just come right
  out and say it?
One thing I'm absolutely sure of, of which I have no doubt,
If I don't let you know, I will have lost you for sure,
Which I truly don't want, for you are worth holding onto,
So believe in what I'm saying, and don't you ever doubt,
With every breath I take and every beat of my heart, I love you.

J. Neal Nitsche

From A Child To A Man

When we are young things are beautiful and our feelings are free.
There is no hate it's just you and it's just me.

We grow seeing things as they are supposed to be.
Like little angels enjoying life, loving you and loving thee.

We care about people, places and of course things.
All so precious with our giggles and our heavenly wings.

As we get older things start to change and we learn the world, we
start to figure out the difference between a boy and a girl.

The love that we had and the beauty that we've seen,
it's all gone now so we grow selfish and we grow mean.

You taught me how not to understand and with this lesson I've
grown and become an angry man!

Please don't hate me because I'm different from you,
because that's the way it's supposed to be.

Haven't you got the clue? God made us different and without sin,
so that we could grow strong and become well rounded men.

So growing from a child to an adult really shouldn't be that hard.
If you can remember the beauty and always remember
There Is A God!!

D. C. Krazy

168 Treasures Of The Heart

It was an April morn, when sadness came our way.
  A moment in time, changing our lives forever.
  Tears followed with waiting, a feeling of helplessness,
pain and grief.
  Such a tragedy, breaking our hearts in two. Our angels
passed away.
  Reminiscing their photo's and last moments that we shared.
  Clinging to our memories, that happened along the way.
  These precious being's are truly a gift from God. They
shall live on through us, each and every day.
  Causing me to realize that each day we live, we make
memories with those we love so dear.
  168 bright and shinning gems, truly are the treasures
of our hearts.

Saundra J. Bauer

Angel Of Darkness

As I sit in my room in the middle of
the night and stare up at the ceiling,
the darkness fills my mind.
My body begins to shake with fear
for I know this evil that consumes my mind.
I have been here before.

It is the Dark Angel come to strike me down,
tearing at my tortured soul piece by piece
till I can no longer feel a thing.
I can not stop this vile thing
for it is a part of me,
a part of my devilish past that can never be removed.

This monster that hides in the shadows waiting,
haunting and trying to destroy me
for the rest of my life
I do not know if it will overcome
or if I will continue to,
Only Time Will Tell.

Kathryn Sanchez

Show Me How To Live, My Friend...

I see friendship in your eyes...
Look at me Love!
You can hardly see me, can you?
Squint your eyes my love...
I am always here.
Breathe in the night air, my friend.
The cold wind tingles my soul.
Your touch is soft, and the stars shine bright.
This setting is perfect.
I desire to remain here forever.
Can we stay here forever?

How is it that we can sit and dream together?
Is this the true taste of friendship?
I have never had a friend like you.

I will not forget you when the summer is past.
How can one forget one with such life?
You live my friend.
You teach me to live.
We shall never be apart.

Shawna Pierson

So Thankful For...

So thankful for each and every thing:
The flowers, trees and birds that sing,
Friends and family who are loved so dear
Mean so very much every day of the year.

Smiling faces and helping hands,
A faithful friend who always understands,
The pilgrims who travelled the oceans and seas
To come to America to worship as they pleased.

Indians who taught them how to farm the land,
Fish, hunt, and use their hands.
All the blessings of each shining down,
The little dewdrops on a summer lawn.

Flowers that provide such a sweet perfume,
Oh! So beautiful when they reach full bloom.
Colorful birds that congregate among the trees,
Their cheerful songs are sure to please.

A warm cozy house in which to live,
All the trees for the restful shade they give.
God for His Glory which I truly give praise,
Provides shower of blessings in various ways.

Annabelle Cochran

Disenchantment

You're in my daydreams
You're what I like to call security.
My reality is enchanting
and the blood I bleed is only for myself
but sometimes I kind of want to bleed for everyone who hurt me.
And I'd love for you to watch me cry —
to feel my melancholy
to kiss the tears off this baby-like face.
love is suicide
but suicide will not come to this Angel of great beauty.
My dream is to love someone for eternity
until I can guard him after I perish.
It's inevitable
we're gonna live forever
whomever this may concern.

Kristina Rae

Where Are You Tonight, Jean?

I saw your picture on the front page.
    That beautiful smile made me feel great,
Until I read about the black bow on the door.

Lloyd came around the corner of the Union
    To check his mail.
All I could do was to sound empathetic.

Not the one with the "Cincinnati Zoo."
    She promised to take me there someday.
But it's too late.

I'm glad that she is no longer suffering, though.
    Why should the best among us suffer anyway?
Only God knows.

I'm going to miss you, Jean.
    Just like the Chancellor said.
It's so hard to accept your leaving.

You always wanted the best for everyone.
    Now we can only wish you final peace and rest,
Because you've been such a true friend to many Rebels in crises.

Ken Daugherty

The Rangoon Saloon

fly china skies
    skip hong kongs
        land in mandalay
            the golden dragon play!
            stand in line
                for the clear balloon
                    split then search
                        for the silver moon
                            time is tight!
                                take a rocket
                                    to the rangoon moon!

an r. paul production

Our Only Ocean

Even on a calm day, the ocean never rests;
From sunrise in the east to sunset in the west.
Far below the surface many creatures lie;
But acid rain and outfalls may soon cause them to die.
We have a chance to save it, if we do our very best;
To stop polluting our seas, that is our biggest test.
I worry for my friends who live beneath the sea;
Who will help their cause, if not you and me?

Lisa Califano

Solacing Anguish

Buried deep in denial, from myself, from all,
lies a place in my soul only I know exists, and yet
even I do not comprehend.
I lay powerless to change it, for it is a memory,
or is it a possibility?
I can't tell.
Only one holds they key, but where is the lock?
Where is the safe?
Sealed inside, wanting release, no less,
love,
crying to the darkness, darkness like the sky -
a thousand points burning brightness like a gift upon the eye.
Only concealed, covered by clouds
leaving only the brightest of the bright shining through,
letting me know they're there.
A beacon of light in the unfathomable black...
Do I imagine a break in the clouds? Do I dare not?
A sky without stars or a love without her, there is no difference.
And I will wait here, watching my stars,
waiting for the wind to push the clouds out of sight.

Austin Dagen

The Velvet Stone

There is a place of irrefutable emptiness, a place where the damned
and unwanted are forever
A boy stands here alone and empty, his story is written in stone
from his own blood
The demons gather to feed on his pain
Shadows of his life are opened
His opened wrists secreting his escape
No one was there to pick up the pieces
His sanity and the desperation to keep a grip on reality gone
The shadow who told him to take the blade
His life and mind screaming for the end
Warmth that he felt as death took hold
Blood that he played in as if a child
Seeing death come for him with smiles
The demons that gnawed on his flesh
Crying to stop the pain they caused
Hearing the laughs as they drank his soul
Seeing everything slip away
Never reaching the age of understanding
Feeling his life being ripped apart
Knowing that all is lost because of insecurities
There is nothing left except the screams and the velvet stone

Kenneth Riess

Austin

Austin is my little grandson
and he is almost two years old.
He talks in this own language mostly,
so I've been told.
He spent a night with me,
so next morning when I opened the shade,
he says in his own
sweet little voice ah, day!
He calls his toy cars and trucks la bye bye,
he loves to play with his la bye bye's.
When we go some place and he sees cars on the road,
he gets all excited and says la bye bye, la bye bye.
He is such a special child.
He's precious, adorable and so divine.
Even though he is Nick and Ray's son,
he really seems like mine.

Gladys J. Jump

Night Of Sorrow

The world has become a giant serpent.
My heart, soul, cries out for wings to take flight from high above.
I'd spy to find my gentle child.
Wings and wind will find the right direction.

I will find where hides the evil serpent.
Where hides that evil serpent there be my gentle child.

Power of God be with me to slay the evil serpent.

Kneeling in darkness mocking silence of this room.
Where once upon a time happy dream, joy, laughter prayers were said.
In the torture chambers of my mind, grasp my hand.
Walk with me, I am afraid.

In wandering of mind, soul, in the deafness of sorrow,
almost didn't hear a voice so softly speak to me.
Rise above your tears of sorrows, hear this, my gentle child.

Woe to those who bring harm to the innocent ones.
Let them fear Jehovah God's wrath of anger.
His justice is great and swift.

Woe earthly man of your debauchery.
"I come as a thief in the night" I TH.5:5
O, wings of justice O, Jehovah God slay the evil serpent.

Sophie Padilla

At Least One Good Friend

Can you hear my silent cry,
It's my destiny to die!
I live day after day,
With nothing to eat, and no place to stay!
Can you see the real me, can you hear my heart rendering plea!
I can not read, nor can I spell
There was no doctor when I fell!
I do not attend any schools
I have no weapons, I have no tolls!
My life is a daily struggle
for me there is nothing but trouble!
I have only one wish, only one hope,
With my life to be able to cope!
Would you not do a good deed,
for your help is all I need!
For the few precious cents it would cast you.
My life could be brand new!
Just a little time on your part
Could win you my very heart!
World you not a little time on me spend.
Then I could say, I have at least one good friend!

Justin Campbell

Resurrection

Across the land
cold gray clouds blanket the sky
Filling the air with a lethargic state
Pastures with dry brown grass stand like small
tombstones
Announces death across the land
Oak trees reach up to heaven like old men's arthritic
hands
Begging pardon from God for some forgotten sins from
so long ago
A cold dry land longing
Waiting
For the resurrection of life
Spring

Julia Trevino Hernandez

My Hyacinths

During the morning
  I gathered hyacinths.
Life was good.
  I was happy.
The world was beautiful,
  So was my world.
Now it is mid-day and I have no hyacinths.
What became of them?
  Did I lose them?
Oh! Now I remember.
  They were taken from me,
"They" said the loved me,
  Yet, they snatched them from me,
"They" say they love me,
  And still no hyacinths.
My life is now lonely, empty,
  Depressing... Unbearable.
If I had only one, one hyacinth,
I could tolerate my lonely life.
I must find a hyacinth, please, just one, for my sunset.

Helen Mendez

Beautiful Flower

In the grass beside the road where many a foot has trod,
  where the weeds and vines grow thick in the earth's fertile sod.

Blooms a single lovely flower
  its beauty is wondrous to see,
  ''tis the flower of nature's love -
  it grows there for you and me.

Many a man's walked by
  on the lonely rocky road,
  and many a man has stumbled
  under his heavy, wearisome load.

Many a man has seen it -
  the flower that is growing there,
  and many a heart's been lightened
  for the flower is so fair.

That no man can look upon it
  and not new strength attain,
  for its beauty fills the soul
  and overcomes the pain.

If you are sad and lonely, weighted down with care,
  search for the beautiful flower - you'll find it growing there.

Cpl. Edward F. Wilson

His

  His words are like sweet cherries,
His whispers are like gentle breezes,
His touch is like that of a silk rose,
His lips are soft like cotton,
His laugh is that of a young child,
His notes were like getting valentines
everyday of the year,
His kindness and caring is like
God's sensitivity,
His creativity shows adventure,
His eyes are like that of a sapphire,
His muscles are strong and solid, but yet
they're always kind,
And his love is pure and strong,
He's everything I want in a man
So I know he's the one.

Laura Voytek

Fay

Fay means faith the faithful one.
Fay once said, "you may not see it nor feel it,
but you got to have faith".
Fay said, "things get worse before they get better,
but you got to have faith".
Fay always said, "speak those things that are not as
though they were,
that is how you have faith".
And if you were to ask Fay "where are you in life",
she will answer, "in the prime years of my life".
Why? She never doubted in God who named her
Fay The Faithful One!

Barbara Walker

Stern Sculpture

Stern sculpture do by the word
Hand that mocks thee.
Stand alone in mystifying wonder
Who are you without me?

Formed from packed earth
Your truth is one to be unknown.
Blank is your stare, speech is your snare
Penetrating is your visage of stone.

Keep from the world the turmoil you brew.
An image is better than lies.
Do unto others as done unto you
In the end you are the one who dies.

James M. Lorengo

Happy Face

Sorry for the things I may have said and done.
It must have been all but fun.

When I see the sun shine in your face
makes this a happy place.

Now that the sun has gone down
I wear nothing but this frown.

Soon I will leave this place.
But only with a happy face.

Robin L. Noennich Sr.

The Winter Magician

The wind howls with a wail of bone chilling sound.
it twists, blows soft silent snow into abstract forms.
Mounds of sculptured soft powder snow lie in wait
of acceptance or rejection of its creator.

The wind howls while it plays the frantic magician
with seemly unrehearsed program of sheer madness.
The wind twists the forms again and again with vengeance
through out the night.

All is covered with a blanket of white ermine.
Some forms are tall, some are bowed, as if in honor,
to the power of the wind, offer no resistance.
Great illusions of power, and might, are formed

The wind explodes into sheer fatigue, which gives
eerie silence to the aftermath of madness.
The Sun gives warmth, with shadows, creates jewels
of reds, greens, blues as a fitting crown to abstract
forms in the Kingdom of Winter Wonder Land.

Margaret M. Wolfer

One Too Many

You've taken my wife away from me
You've taken her chance to be happy or free
You had a few too many to drink
You thought you were fine, now what do you think
A life you took, it's so damn unfair
I often wonder, do you really care
When my kids ask, "When's Mom coming home?"
I tell them she's not, we're now on our own
So next time you feel like just one more drink
I want you to sit there, just sit there and think
What if this happened to your very own wife
Is that one more drink worth taking her life?

J. Edward Murrell

No Clouds And One Sun

My angel that flies at sundown, the one who provides for me and
the day that is to follow.
No one can see you but I can feel your spirit possessing my
every move....
I walk at night, no one holding my hand, no one but you to
protect me, no one to hold me when I am down and no one to
pick me up when I fall to the ground, except you my angel that
fly's at sundown....
When I am walking I think of only you and my life that lies
ahead praying for guidance and sincerity to walk another mile
to go on with a smile, not thinking of death or looking back
on the past....
I need only one follower the one shadow and only one thought
in my mind, you the one who helps me through it all my angel
at sundown, my heart my sparkle in the sun my angel....
Let there be no clouds and only one sun that I can see and
only hearing your voice, my angel at sundown.......

Michael Wayne Robbins (Freedom)

My Secret

One day sitting in class I realized my dark secret.
Mrs. Gamboa was talking about "incest."
It may seem like such harsh word,
But to some of us it's so normal.
Some people wouldn't even wish that on their worst enemy.
Unfortunately by the time you finish reading this poem,
Somewhere a child has been molested.

God was with me that day, which day?
The day I broke the chain.
I reached deep into my soul and told my deep, dark secret.

My heart cried for days,
And it will cry 'til the day I die.
It hurt to realize the place I called home,
Was where I was hurt the most.
Little by little my heart is taking the pain out.
My family blamed me,
But soon enough they realized "they" brought it on me.
They also realized we weren't alone.

Yaneth Torres

What Happiness Is!

Happiness is a baby smiling,
Happiness is a dream not dying.
Happiness is a husband and wife,
Loving each other the rest of their lives.
Happiness is a Sunday show,
And all of the family wanting to go.
Happiness is a dinner for two,
With candles, and flowers and sweet perfume.
To me this is what happiness is,
But true happiness is learning to live.
Without worries, anger, and pain,
Loving each other exactly the same...

Melissa Renee Dunseith

Kela's Song

A faint voice drifted through from the other side
From the Source of light
Sweet melody whispering softly of Love
Gentle seduction calling me Home
Reminded me of your love.

I was afraid I would lose you
But the voice reassured
If you follow the Light
Your path will find mine.

Follow the light
Until the sun sets on your journey
And I will see you again in the morning.

Steve Roberts

Lord Please Build Me A Grandson

Give him a happy face and a giggle for looking at clowns and
teddy bears.
Let him believe in tooth fairies, leprechauns, and Santa Claus.
Make him fingers that fit around granny's little finger, hands
to patty cake and catch a football and to create like his daddy.
A heart full of happiness and love and as big as a football field.
Make him kind and gentle and sensitive like his mom.
Give him arms big enough for hugs.
Make him small enough to cuddle but big enough to protect his
little sister.
Because he is being born into a very special family know he
will be perfect in every way.
Last of all let him stand tall and proud and leave his mark on
the world.

Jan Bates

The Life Of A Soul

The sun will rise and the sun will set,
  but my soul, however, knows no rest,
The light does come and then it goes,
  but it is the darkness that takes its toll.
For it is the darkness that comes at the end of each day,
  that I can feel within me in fearsome ways.
And though I may seem to shine bright with light,
  only God knows I am filled with fright.

It is the ways of this world within me, I cannot deny,
  that overcome my mind and weigh me down in every stride.

My soul has been at constant battle everyday,
  and my life is forever left astray.
And with everyday that does now past,
  I cannot help but wonder how much longer I can last.

Benjamin Berg

Grandma

It didn't take much to please Grandma—
family and trinkets were her favorite things.
Grandma lived a simple life.
She never wasted words or entertained strife.
Her smile was as bright as Jesus himself.
Her laughter was present even by herself.
She had the energy of a lion hunting her prey.
A quiet spirit like the sunset on a warm summer day.

Even though grandma is not here today,
Grandma lives on in us anyway.
So take heart, we are her dreams fulfilled,
her smile, her laughter, warmth and wisdom.
We are grandma.

Kim Poellnitz

Tomorrow's Man

Forgiving the day I had used for
myself, selfish and mean and ignoring the
help.

Believing a man who's sins run deep, is
healing my soul and my heart when I sleep.

Holding today so precious and true, to
remember the things that I have to do.

Lifting myself and rebuilding a man is
completing a guy who hadn't a plan.

Coming on strong each and everyday,
the willingness to forgive unforgiving
ways.

Living my life with direction in mind,
will give me a strength and power inside.

Lord, grant me the time, and the
patience I need, to walk in your garden
and plant all my seeds.

Bernard T. Latzy Jr.

Myself An Inspirational Prayer

I, myself have an illness but I will not let this fear me.
It is a disease that many of us can not explain
Yes it is, and Lupus is it's name.

There are so many people who are sicker than I
But I still, sometimes sit and cry.
I try my best not to let this get to me
But to pray that God will cure me.

But one thing I know this will not always be,
Because there are so many people
who are praying for me.

Instead, a lot of us feel sorry for ourselves,
Just thank God, that we are here and he cares.
So, I'm not going to worry about what I have
Just to thank God, that I'm alive and well.

Now, they say that I'm a diabetic,
But God can correct it.
If I pray, I'll be okay
Because God will show me the way.

So, I'm not going to let this get me down
Because God can turn... All diseases around!

Bonita A. Reeder

To Zarathustra

Did the Wise Lord request an offering of fire?
Or did we simply want to share our deepest fascination,
Watching the fire split the night
As an echo to the distant stars?

Our hearts danced as our hands trembled
Before the carefully contained flames
As fire without called to fire within.
We made for ourselves lights in the night
As we began to find our way.

Today the fire is surging.
It trembles beneath the surface
And it flashes out into the open.
Day is cast forth into the night
As the energy lines our streets,
Flickers in our cinemas,
Flashes upon our billboards
And flutters in our homes.

Did anyone request an offering of fire?
Or did we simply want to share our deepest fascination?

Charles L. Kinnaird

A Prayer

Thank you Lord for all have givin'
You have brought peace in this life that I am livin'
When I was down you reached out your mighty hand
You picked me up and my new life began.

You gave me hope and brought harmony into my life
You showed me a new way to look at my wife
You taught me how to read your word
And to see the beauty in every creature and bird

I want to thank you Lord for finding me when I was lost
For forgiving me of my sins, and for showing me the cost
I want to thank you for givin' me a church home where I go
Where your Heavenly love does flow

I want to thank you Lord for giving me these words that I wright
I want to thank you for givin' me strength and courage to do what
is right
I offer my life to you
Please let me learn to live, love, and to serve as you want me to
Amen

Billy Hughes

Men

Keep it clean
except when he screws up
and now the carpet is mud- and tomato sauce-stained.
Hair in the sink, on the floor and across the toilet,
as an unrinsed toothbrush and razor
decorate the vanity.
Soda cans are now ashtrays
and drinking glasses become trash cans
as I am left to correct it.
Food left uncovered
and dishes from yesteryear
finally come in from his truck,
while I hold Lysol in my hands.
I could say that men are swine
but somewhere a woman is this way too.
So what if my books and clothes
are strewn across my bedroom floor,
At least they're clean!!

Veronica M. Villareal

Tell Him Now

Whatever work your man is doing, thank him
for it, don't delay. . . Tell him that you think
it's worthy, tell him now, right, now, today. . .
if he buys you something nice, thank him
once — no, thank him twice. . . Tell him now,
and don't delay, for that can cost an awful
price. . . Give him all the praise that's due
him, now's the time to tell it to him. . . After
work, ask how his day went, tell him how
your day was, too. . . Don't delay, because
someday, the fates may take him far from you
. . .if you truly love a person, tell before it gets
too late. . . You never know when he'll be
called to travel through that Pearly Gate. . .
give him all the praise that's due him, now's
the time to tell it to him.

Felicia Gallus

While You're Sleeping

While your laying beside me sleeping I wonder,
Do you dream about me like you say you do?
Sometimes during the day my gaze drifts toward the sky and I wonder,
Do you think of me like you say you do?
I would never questions your love for me.
I would however question the degree of your love for me.

Nicole Tafoya

Dreamers

The evening's daunting glow smiles down,
Onto the faces of dreamers.
A dark rider on its dawn, parades through the night sky,
Lead by a brilliant footpath of virginal stars.
A gallant thunder shakes the sky,
Tumbling down upon the world a murderous silence.
The air is plagued by the scent of flowers, and
Sweetened by the scent of mystical darkness.
Dreamers lay helpless, alluded by the mystery.
Bound in their beds,
By the chains of an unseen puppet master.
This is an enchanted delight,
Thriving in a world, submerged in apathy.
Dreamers look on,
Closing their eyes to this world of mediocrity.

Megan E. Morrissey

The Promise

Good Noah built an Ark to hold the animals and men.
Two by two they came as the Lord commanded them.
All the people laughed, and said, "Noah's lost his mind!"
Because they did not listen, they would all be left behind.
The heavens opened wide and the rains came falling down!
And when the storm had ended there was a sea upon the ground.
An olive branch was found by a single white dove.
And Noah fell to his knees and gave praise to God above.
Two by two they left as the Lord commanded them.
And a rainbow-painted sky was God's promise to all men.

Linda Edge

Shadowed Hopes

Beyond this place across the ocean
I am young... lost in the shadows
My hopes screaming for freedom
My memory stolen from the evils of my past
Someone please help me... please talk to me
Help me escape the hell from within
I feel like I am drowning in the ocean
My feeling is weak now
I can't speak!... I can't move!
I wonder where I go from here...
It doesn't have to be like this
All I need is someone to talk to me
My head is thinking but I cannot feel
No feelings!... no hopes!
I cannot breathe now
I am going nowhere...
I am going nowhere...

Onam Kansaki

Remembering

Where has your body gone, to ashes, my son.
The look on your face is that of heaven, my son.
You went with the light this time.
No more pain, no more suffering, my son.
Because now you are with God and at peace, my son.
Now you can walk, play, jump and do
everything you couldn't here on earth.
I will always remember you, my son.
For now your spirit will live on for everyone, my son.
Someday we will all be together again, my son.
Good-by for now, I love you, my son.
So now the pain is gone, you are at
peace with God, my son.

Janet Duke Graves

Music's Last Dancer

Upon a canvas of illusions
I painted a dancer.
Music's last dancer.
My brush strokes became her moves
and she pirouetted over the blank slate of my life.
Within a rainbow of colors
she transformed my world
leading me into a dimension
where no boundaries lie
except those of the imagination.
I gazed into her soul,
inspired by her passions;
she carried me into a realm undiscovered,
and broke the seal that held in my soul's cravings.
Then, as I turned to seek her, she had vanished.
And with her went
the magic,
the life,
the love,
and the music.

Rosalyn Antoinette Richberg

Friendship

Friendship is good for me to have around,
    It lifts my spirits off the ground.
Whenever I'm in the depths of despair,
    Friendship will lift me back into the air.
Although I try in my mind's own eye,
    Friendship can't really make me fly.
Friendship is like a treasure,
    My friends are priceless trinkets.
If someone robs my friendship, which is my pleasure,
    I'll cry into little blinkets.
Friendship is like an ocean,
    That reaches deep inside,
My heart swells up with emotion,
    And I can't stem the tide.
Whenever I'm in a fright,
    A friend and I walk by the White Way of Delight.
If I didn't have friendship, because it's very rare,
    I would always be in the depths of despair.

Julia DeLuca

The Longing For Spring

Oh, how I long for spring, the time for melting of the snow.
I watch the snow geese turn home from their southern retreat.
Farmers plowing fields to plant new crops, for it is time to sow.
Bulbs breaking through the ground to burst into bloom in all colors
for our eyes to entreat.
Oh, how I long for spring, after the refreshing cold of winter, the
warmth spring will bring.
The trees with their new green leaves and the blossoming dogwood.
The robin digs for worms, and in her nest, new birds will sing.
A new year, a new Spring, like a new beginning and it is refreshing
and good.

Margaret L. W. Culler

en route

Leaning over the rail,
night allowed us to see ahead
the lights of the island.
Waves fanned out rippling the flat,
blue-black water. My anger scraped
scales off dead fish resting on shore.
I made light of your lack of affection
You talked about how you must look her up
in Paris. I thought how I must erase
this place from my map or how I must embrace
you for having so little use for me.

Lynn Fitzgerald

Nature's Own Caress

My needs are simple,
as simple as a country cottage
with a cute, quaint, little garden,
and to take a cup of tea there,
with an itty bitty biscuit
in that little paradise of my own,
and have a good old Victorian romance book
cupped in my hands,
and a cuddly cat in my lap,
and to feel a cool breeze on my face
and a warm sun's embrace,
and to smell the fragrance of roses
wafting with the wind,
and hear the birds
chirping sweetly on their perch overhead
and experience the whole of that day
as nature's own caress,
and to know that the morrow
brings more of the same.

Violet Guajardo

The Clown Man

He is a creature of the night
A man of much might.
You see him now, and then you see him naught
Is he his own being or is he bought?
Does he follow a script,
Or has he risen from a crypt?
Does he represent the good of all
Or does death spring forth from him in all its sallow pallor?
Is it a smile he wears or is it a frown?
He is certainly not a man, but he surely is not a clown.
Look-out Life! Look-out Death!
The Clown Man breathes a deadly breath!

Michael S. Vincent

I Walk Alone

I cross this river alone, it is my chosen path.
I walk with confidence across this barrier I break.
A long road that has been much awaited.
It speaks of comfort to ease my doubt, it speaks of faith of
my journey intended.
Ahead, I see the light. It is the glow of my dreams, the rays
of my foreseen vision.
Behind, is all that I have seen, all that has been said.
And it is left with all that has been done.
I walk alone as I cross this river.
The river of all that is the future.
I step forward and beyond the light.
This warm, welcoming presence.
I cry out as I touch my fate, and whisper, "I am here."
I cry out into the light and shout, "Now, I can begin!"

Claudine M. Hansen

Halloween

Come night fall, scary goblins, ghosts and all
Windy night, witches in flight, black cats, brooms in a fright
Make believe, all in fun, Pirates, Cowboys on the run
Door to door, trick or treat, lots of surprises on our street
Costume party, apple bobbing, candy, popcorn, food a plenty
Decorate with a scarecrow, bats, hats and a shadow
Pumpkin carving, eyes, nose and grin, put a candle in my
skin, now I am a Jack-O-Lantern
Haunted House, frightful fun, scary masks, want to run,
touch the slime, want to climb, must go on, to the end, and
so I do, with a friend
Halloween, what a night, so much fun, so much fright

Sharon Veeh

Existence

The capability of resistance is present
in the wolf's eyes and it is
deteriorating my mind.
Unable to scream myself back into
the world of mortal sanity.
Unable to resist the temptations
that are scattered around this hell.
The creature of my soul guides me
along the path of black and white
and assists my being into its perception.
Giving in to the tenacious torments
of devotion.
My beast sits on my simpering face; taking
a likeness to the warmth
of my faint breath, the dullness
of my doleful eyes.
The wolf conjures my life
into existence; sends it away
with the heart of a demonic angel.

Rachel Dana

On Painted Wings

On painted wings you'll fly someday
Into the sunset's warm and shining ray.
On painted wings you'll fly someday,
And heaven won't be very far away.

On crystal shoes you'll dance someday
You'll pirouette into eternity.
On crystal shoes you'll dance someday,
And heaven won't be very far away.

On golden clouds you'll sing your song.
You'll reach the notes that they all said
Could not be sung.
On golden clouds you'll sing someday,
And heaven won't be very far away.

On silver seas you'll sail someday,
And feel the windswept waves refreshing spray.
On silver seas you'll sail someday,
And heaven won't be very far away.

Jeff Brewer

Ailing Children

Dear Lord, Please hear my words
It's for the children that I pray
Watch over them while they sleep
And comfort them through the day

Help them heal so they may go home
To be held in loving arms
Return the innocence of their years
And protect them from any harm

Dear Lord, Please help their parents
ease the pain that they feel
Strengthen their hearts in this adversity
So they can help their children heal

Bless this family with your grace
So they may heal with God's speed
Surround them all with your love
In their desperate time of need

Gregory Bell

The Lie

"I tell the truth," most people say,
For they've been taught no other way.
But what if all you did was lie?
Would not the truth forever die?
If one lies to make friends,
He will lose them in the end.
If one lies to get his way,
It will eventually go the other way.
If one lies to run from pain,
He runs and runs in vain.
If one lies about how he feels inside,
His feelings from him will forever hide.
If one lies about his identity.
Then forever no-one he will be.
If the man who lies wishes to change his ways,
Will he be condemned to pay for all his days?
The answer to this I do not know
But down the road to this answer I must go.

Keith Burgoyne

Ode To A Sanctuary Light

O honored Lamp!
Which stands on constant guard
Throughout a sleepless night,
Reminding Him that now, at last,
He has found a friend
Who would proudly watch,
But slumber not
Until the spark of life has burned
Itself into nothingness.
And having given all -
Submits to death and darkness.

I envy you!
For you enjoy the role
Which I would gladly play,
To consume myself for Him
Unceasing, night and day.
To spare Him loneliness
Whate'er the cost.
To herald Him before all men, myself to be unseen.
If I could live like this, I'd know what life should mean.

Mary H. deBarros

Patiently Awaiting Baby

Our prayers daily' of each ticking minute, as every moment flows
slowly, and precariously through the hour glass, on the sands of
times. Where patiently awaiting baby. Rain or shine.
It does not matter, what's your gender male or female.
Big or small, short or tall.
We don't care what's the color of your eyes, we know you shall
Always see clearly, because your looking at life, through God's
All seeing eyes, and because you're our special child.
It will not matter what's the color of your skin. We will
Love you baby because you're our sweet and precious kin.

Now little one' all that we are asking of your anticipated arrival
That you come healthy, wise and fine, at your own pace and time.
Now whether you're rude or sweet, you can always depend on
your family. Helping you to develop, stage by stage
gearing you morally, patiently guiding you, by our hands,
and our hearts lovingly.
Our adoring baby, the last and final wishes, is that you
Arrive safely on earth, to receive our warm love, hugs, and kisses

Patricia Ann Jones

I Wonder Who Died Last Night

I wonder who died last night —
Everyone is too upset to say.
It must have been someone we all knew well
I hate seeing my loved ones grieve this way

I wonder who died last night —
I've never seen my father cry,
He's always been so tough and strong
My mother asking, "why, oh why?"
Selfishly wondering what she did wrong

They all surrounded a hospital bed,
And since no one there would let me know;
I would see for myself who lay there dead
And prepare to let my feelings show

I wonder who died last night —
Peeking over my mother's shoulder,
To see who it could be,
Realizing then, as my body turned colder;
The tears that fell. . .were for me.

Lisa Boswell

Synonymous

They are... empty gargoyles hovering above wooden poles
   wearing hungry eyes, leering from reddened holes.

From crooked grins billows death's pallid smoke
   atop spines long ago broken by master's yoke.

Yellow scars lie hidden by lightless friend,
   while miniature demons linger on matchstick's end.

Quenching inner fire with liquid poison cure,
   while splintered teeth gnaw flesh of pure.

Riding watchposts on revolving doors
   viewing amber world from all fours.

They are... swollen dragons rocking on ashen planks.
   Resting on crimson jewels, they give thanks.

While head bows still fevered mind contemplates.
   Belching righteous fire that foretells truer fates.

Empty arms outstretch to fondle starving fold,
   While rotten bones snap under scales of gold.

Narrow reptilian eyes dine in upward air,
   While clawed hands seek young flesh to tear.

Rising on paper wings to grasp heaven's view.
   Excluding all others where seats are few.

Bill Martin

Memories

When I walk along this path
I remember when I was little

I remember the grass, too high for me to see over
I remember the dirt, blowing in my face

I remember it going on forever
With my never knowing when it would end

I remember the waves rolling in on the beach
I remember the horizon being right there to meet it

But now when I walk along this path, all I can do is
remember
Remember the good times I had

Agell O'Shaughnessy

One More Time...

Please touch me one more time,
   So that I can feel you deep inside.
      Please hold me once again,
         I never want this feeling to end.
            Please look at me like you did before,
               I wanna read you just once more.
                  To be engulfed in your being,
                     To know exactly what you're seeing.
               I loved to love you.
            I knew you knew.
         It gave me pleasure.
      It eased the pain.
It gave me hope.
Would you do it again?
   Would you love me, like you did before?
      Could you love me just once more?

Shelley Havrilesko

The Road To Dreams

Let's travel down the road to dreams
Where nothing is what it really seems

They will take us to lands far away
Where all children do is dance and play

Where the river flows of chocolate milk
And the grass is but an ivory silk

A place that rains gum drops
With frosted covered mountain tops

Children riding on Cherub's wings
While through the land you hear them sing

Children running bare foot in the sun
Everyone having so much fun

Now we must say goodbye
A tear child don't you cry

For we will be back some day
Where all the children dance and play

Again we will travel the road to dreams
Where nothing is what it really seems

Lillian R. Pemberton

Soldiers

Left behind I see myself standing
Bewildered by what I called love
Traces of you are all around me
Little treasures of time past by
I hold them close and I do not cry.

Though not so hard for me
Because tears never come too easily
Guarded by my soldiers
For them there is no rest
They keep all of my pain
And tell me it is best.

Even then some pain slips past their doors
Little memories of people I once adored
They are all gone from me
And all that is left to remain:
Are little broken pieces of fantasy,
My soldiers and my pain.

Sharon Fisher

All Alone

All alone a man sits in an antique coffee stained chair
All alone a man dreams of grandchildren hugging
  and telling childlike stories to him
All alone a man stares at a picture of his beloved Gwen
  who passed away four years ago
All alone a man turns and looks at a kitchen knife deciding what
  to do
All alone a boy walks up to an old Victorian house
All alone a boy asks for some sugar
All alone a boy talks with an old man
All alone a boy plays cards with an old man
All alone a boy feels warm inside
All alone a man feels loved

All alone a boy and a man fall asleep
All alone a boy wakes up
All alone a boy calls the old man's name
All alone a boy cries over a man
All alone salty tears fall to the ground

James Garlock

Thoughts Of Home

When the troubles of life seem exceedingly grave
And things haven't gone as I'd planned
Then my thoughts wonder home, where I once felt so safe
To that peaceful and mystical land.

For there I found comfort when some childhood care
Enveloped my worked with its pain
I was ever aware that my loved ones were there
That thought made me happy again.

I can still smell the blossoms of spring's budding trees
And feel the warm grass at my feet
And hear the rich songs of wise nature's elite
Oh, the nectar of life was so sweet.

As I now look back on those days long ago
With their simple but genuine schemes
Thoughts of home make me sad, but I truthfully know
I will always return in my dreams.

Catherine Georgy

God's Greatest Of Gifts

I carried you in me for nine plus long months,
We thought that you'd never come out.
But then at the end of a long and late night,
Pain started and I gave a shout.

"It's time, I believe, to get going right now
Before she is born on this floor."
We rushed to the labor room fast as we could
To find we'd wait six hours more.

I groaned and I grunted, I screamed and I cried,
And just when I couldn't go on,
The sweetest of sounds that I ever did hear
Filled the room and I knew it was done.

Weeks pass and I try to remember the pain
And the sickness that I grew to hate.
The long sleepless nights and the wadding walk
And the tiring overdue wait.

But I look at you lying there precious and sweet
And those memories all seem to fade.
Instead I kneel down and I thank God above
For His help in the life and that we made.

Lori Murray

Let My Voice Ring Out

My heart yearns to cry out.
Praises and worship it craves to shout.
Though my tongue is never silent.
To my Lord it craves to be defiant.

So evil can be the tongue.
Full of words, harsh and strong.
Yet in composed times,
words of love and comfort does it chime.

Who controls this tongue of the things it does?
I am helpless in all the evil it does
Jesus cleanse and purify this mess,
So my heart can have a rest.

For if praises I do not shout,
Worship of my Lord will the rocks cry out.
Let this not be,
for my heart does cry out to thee.

Cheri Ann Hubbs

Wishing Star

I am so small, yet so very large.
Shining in an ever stretching pool of darkness.
There are others like me, I know.
But who or where they are, I know not.

Every night I shine here, faithful in my heavenly post,
A silent listener for those who would care enough
To share with me their wishes and dreams.
And though I cannot answer, I hear you.

I know your most intimate dreams;
Who you love and what you hate.
And those of you who wish upon me true...
You, some night your dreams will come true.

Erika Vance

Souls

As the soul feels the wind;
and the eyes see the clouds,
and the body feels the sun;
One can not be complete till all is done.
Yet we let days go by,
without ever glimpsing the soul through our eyes.
For rejoice, dear souls!
as there will never be
another soul for you, nor me.
Feel each pleasure, as much as each pain,
so that each soul may see the gain.

Jodi Kelley-Leathers

Nature's Rhythm

Clouds softly floating above
form shapely silhouettes.
Caressing the warm air which
freely gives life.

Lofty shapes floating continuously along
flirting incessantly with each other,
revealing their beauty while
gracefully approaching a remote destiny.

Delicate bodies amusing our perceptions.
Reflecting shapes of familiar sights
that flood our memories,
as we recognize their brilliant presences.

Enchanting phenomenon's swirling around,
entertaining in mesmerizing ways,
as we admire their rhythm.

Dennise S. Cardona

September Night

I recall that breezy September night,
As sweet, sincere thoughts of you fill my mind.
You whispered, "I love you," and held me tight.

You carried me away, as would a knight,
In your masculine arms, I was confined.
I recall that breezy September night,

As we walked and talked in the soft moonlight.
Hand in hand, turned to me with eyes so kind,
You whispered, "I love you," and held me tight.

The love we share is pure as snow is white,
Just thinking of our love makes me blind.
I recall that breezy September night,

You made the fire in my heart ignite.
I loved it when your arms around me twined,
You whispered, "I love you," and held me tight.

For I love you, too, with all of my might,
I am glad it was you that I did find.
I recall that breezy September night,
You whispered, "I love you," and held me tight.

Peggy Hernandez

This Angel Of Mine

In the eyes of God few are divine
an angel of mercy will always stand by
please let me know give me a sign
send me an angel or just let me die

In my eyes an angel stands near
a bit of color in a world gone gray
look away and she's gone I fear
heaven sent or hell will pay

In my eyes an angel divine
she's all I can see has God struck me blind
in my eyes this angel of mine
an angel on earth is so hard to find

For one precious moment all time is lost
as close to heaven as this sinner will get
our time together no matter the cost
send me to hell the devil I've met

I know she's no angel and I know she can't stay
a joke God plays from to time
he sends me a lover then takes her away
she's still in my eyes this angel of mine

Kent Hunter

Cast To The Wind

Cast me to the wind to the wind of Your Spirit, Lord!
Enfold me in your gentleness when there is stillness . . . .
Hold fast to me when you've got me going to and fro . . .
It matters not how I fly, quickly or slowly or not at all;
For I know I am in the folds of Your Spirit, Lord, guiding
me in a firm but gentle way, leading and directing me
on the path you have mapped out for me.
As I fly in my journey to my Father, I go with
confidence, confidence that only He can give!
Father, you've given me the faith to know I
can trust in You completely!
I've been told not to cast myself to the wind . . .
Oh!!! But this I have done!
But!!! It's the Wind of Your Spirit, Lord!
So cast me to the wind, to the wind of Your Spirit . . . .
And let me fly swiftly into the arms of my Father . . . .
Where I will nevermore . . . be . . .
"Cast to the Wind!"

Anna M. Wambaugh

The Flame In My Heart

A flicker of light with a golden flame
Will she hear my voice when I call her name?
My mind tells me no, but my heart answers yes
My heart knows the answer, as the light I caress.

So I speak all the words that my heart will allow
The flame seems so bright — she hears me now.
But time can't stand still, dawn starts a new day
As I watch the lights flame start to flicker away.

As I speak my last words, my tears now I fight
My words have all faded and so has the light.
The flame has since gone, from this world did depart
But will live on forever down deep in my heart.

Frances Burke

The Charge Of The Fairy

I sound at once this vibrant conch to point all human ears,
And for a flash you'll be like me; I'll give you all my fears.
Now I shall speak with words that ye may lend a mindful ear.
My pillows, called your clouds above, made softer bed last year.
These nights I lie with misty mind, thinking of the trees,
For on the nights I fall right through, they catch me with their leaves.
And then I drift inside their wood as human form may not,
Their language whispered shivers me and shall not be forgot.
They speak of fire and blankets thick of grayish cloud-like smoke,
How millions of their ancient reds did vanish in one stroke,
How nights were filled with fire and flame when noble siblings fell
And Sherman's curses casting them into your land of Hell.
This Eden once was lush with green where flowered fountains splashed
In waterfalls pink orchids swung; these since have all been slashed.
Demeter's breath once blew to me petals for a boat
These remnants left from chainsaw dust do not provide such float.
For Eves of now the air she blows is whispers in the wood.
Secrets for unlocking spells, those only humans could.
So heed this warn, a fairy's charge: with Mother Earth make peace.
Your human hands hold now the keys to Persephone's final release.

Angela Mitchell

Midwest Dying

They say our sunsets are the best around,
Our lives filled with the color of rain,
Flashing blues and grays—unseen on the primary color wheel.
The mix of damp heat and ghostly light
dripping incautiously over honey golden corn fields—
it was the color of his hair in November.
The white clapboard house, blind to the late Indian Summer,
opened itself to the silver moon and caressing breeze,
finally beautiful, bathed in the disguised repression.
Black thorns shadowed the deep purple backdrop—
Pricking my finger to force the bloody stains
    across this Olympia of stars.
He froze to death in pinstripe pajamas, as thin as a spider's web
    against his dilapidated door.
Inhaling the suddenly cold air, departingly rich,
    a breath of red wines and anniversary parties—
Those who heard, laughed: farmers, truckers, hardened lawyers
me—the tears touched my face with the grace of a mother,
    for I couldn't paint his evanescent soul.
Angels melted his gray hairs and calloused feet
with their heavenly oil lamps,
Pouring him from China goblets—white, like his bare room .
    in the rays of death's dawn—
Into the thick deafening wax of our beautiful Midwestern lives.

Anna Scott

When The Days Go By

When the days go by
  I watch the sunset far, far away
When the days go by
  I watch the people change
When the days go by
  I watch the children grow up and leave
  memories with the family
When the days go by
  I watch the rain drizzle
When the days go by
  I watch myself grow old and it seems sad
  that all I ever did was watch
    Melanie Dahl

Regenerate

I played hookey today
  where the hills run wild to the sea,
the waves play tag with my toes,
  and the mountains are misty and green:
To watch the otters play,
  to hear the lark sing,
and to watch the ocean sparkle and gleam.

Today, I ran to the sea
  to heal my body of the sores and woes
that the world will bring,
  to let the wind remove from my soul
the dust and the hurts that will
  accumulate there,
to renew, refresh, and become me once again.
    Dennis A. Glover

At Rainbows End

The wonder of the rainbow,
God's promise, from ages of old.
Its beauty and glorious splendor,
At its end, a pot of gold.

Believe that pot of gold exists,
For every man to see.
Not in form of golden coin
Or material fantasy!

The rainbow is each ones own life,
A miracle to behold.
At birth you start your destined climb
To seek that pot of gold.

It teaches joy, is sorrows gift;
Laughter learns from tears.
From compassion and understanding,
Man conquers his own fears.

When we reach the rainbows arch,
God plans we all descend.
Gathering each piece of life's precious gold,
Our pots filled, "at rainbows end."
    Janet D. Hoover

A Child's Journey

Most of us remember images as a child,
Sometimes when we'd cry and
Sometimes when we'd smile.

From infancy it appeared that we were
destined to do the right things.

And as we grew to achieve our
problem - solving life,
We realized the need of our Mother's wings.
    Sally Phillips

Season To Season

Just sitting on the veranda sipping my tea,
And the afternoon sun is still warming me.
The fall breeze runs its hand through my hair,
Is the season changing as I sit in my chair?
The leaves on the trees turn bright orange and red,
As you age, time slips away faster they said.
Just last week it was so sunny and warm,
We were grilling hot dogs and having sweet corn.
As people cut the grass for the last time this year,
I feel that cool weather is drawing quite near.
The ducks bid goodbye as they fly overhead,
They need no convincing, by instinct they're led.
The smell of leaves burning means it's harvest time,
When the fruits of our labors are in their prime.
I rise from my chair and stroll across the porch,
It seems season to season is the passing of a torch,
Which is meant to keep things fresh and anew,
And more often than not, will renew me too.
    Jeannie R. Holtz

Theft Of A Heart

You didn't have to steal my heart
It was already yours, it beats for you
Please nourish and protect it
When you are near it beats proud and strong
Unlike being apart, leaving me lost
  and alone.

Still, it's mysterious how you stole it
I never saw it coming
Nor did I realize it was gone
Did you hypnotize my eyes
Or just take my love by surprise?

I'll never report this theft either,
I want you to own me and my heart
In your hands we feel safe and secure
You make me complete,
And without you in my life
  my heart simply wouldn't beat!
    William Fuller

Our Bishop

I know a great Bishop from west;
The saints all agree he's the best,
When he preaches his goal:
Is to have the anointing unfold,
And the power of God fills our soul!

He started very early in his youth;
His desire was to win souls for truth,
He stepped out in faith:
He gave lots of hand shakes,
And baptisms were done for Christ's sake!

One thing that we love him for most;
'Tis how in the Lord he can boast,
When he comes to the church:
It's worshipping first,
Then all offerings and tithes will disburse!

We call him the Prophet of today;
His preachings and teachings we obey,
For when the trump shall sound:
And the saints gather around,
With our Bishop and Lord heaven bound!
    Arlene D. Dopwell

Remembering Mother

It has been stated and no doubt fated
that one never sang for one's father.

I never sang for my father nor did I
    write a poem for my mother.
This fact gives me wonder, why I laid
    this asunder.

It is a sad thought that upon her leaving,
I should find the need to write this reading.

'Tis strange that in my voice and inflection,
I hear my mother's voice with affection.

So many statements came from her lips
that I now use the same quips.

Even the sound of her voice resounds from me.
Involuntarily and not by choice.

So as they say, "This one's for you, Mom."
No bells or grand forte—straight from my
    heart to you.

Edith M. Watson

Freedom

Freedom is a mighty thing,
Of which few have had a taste!
Most men have lived their lives in fear,
And have not known the waste.

To be a person bound by another;
Going with the flow to get by.
This person has not known freedom
Or how high he could really fly!

The man who has not freed himself
Has no one else to blame.
The thoughts that bind you are inside your head.
To this you should lay claim.

Oh, to be free from the thoughts of others,
Who judge you by what they see.
To fly and soar, and conquer the world
In freedom, to whatever degree!

Your faith in God gives you freedom.
He doesn't hold you back with distrust.
You're free to be whom He's made you to be.
Go ahead! He insists! It's a must!

Joyce James

Rose versus Love

as the winter begins to demise,
alas! there is the Rose waiting for the warm summer skies.
so intriguing, yet, so small
the aroma is mystifying- to your heart it does call.
i would compare a Rose to true Love,
full of happiness and pain blessed by God above.
heed caution to the Rose's long sharp thorns,
for they can pierce the skin, just as the heart can be torn.
the Rose is eccentric from its color to its scent,
Love is confusing, words are spoken —
often wondering what is meant.
but both Rose and Love are tranquil in my mind —
only the life of the Rose — not Love nor beauty are lost in time.

Natalie L. Bloss

Paradise

    What is this paradise I seek?
Where can it be found?
Is it in a new car,
Or is it near or far?
Is paradise in a book,
Should I even bother to look?
Is paradise hidden in the arms
Of that voluptuous young lady
I just seen?
Or is thinking that obscene
Can it be found in a oblation.
Or is it just fascination?
"Oh!" Paradise where are you?
Who or what are you?
I need your serenity because
So many things perplex my tranquility.
On this issue I have
Much perpended but that
Feeling of exuberance has
Constantly eluded me...I will never stop seeking my paradise.

Orville Goodliegh

The Treasure Chest

Standing on the hillside,
I secretly placed another treasure into it.
No pirate of the highest seas, with the largest ships,
Mightiest swords, or the grandest of cannons
Can ever find it, but I know you can,
For these treasures are not only mine,
They are also yours.
You asked for a map,
But it has already been etched upon your heart,
Which we made a long time ago.

Sitting at the head of the bow,
I removed all of the paces: the treasures in my life.
I saw the gold glistening in your eyes
As I shared medallions and memories, pearls and pictures,
Sapphires and souvenirs, coins of wisdom, thoughts, and praise.

Laying upon the seashore,
I saw the "X" approaching.
I placed the treasure chest beside me and smiled,
For I noticed that it was beside you, as well.
It was just before you showered me upon the waters.

Erwin Estrada

The Stranger

He looked as if he hadn't eaten in awhile
Had that innocent look, like a child,
He said he was down on his luck
Left a family behind, and a broken down truck.

We didn't have too much ourselves
But when you have nothing, anything helps,
He ate the bread and gobbled down the meat
While he sat on the step to rest his feet.

Soon he was crossing the railroad track
His coat over his shoulder, turning to look back,
It would be dark very soon
And the only light would be from the moon.

My brothers followed him in the car
And took him to the next farm, not too far,
Where he worked and saved his fare
So he could go back home to Delaware.

I wonder if he's doing good
Lord knows we helped him all we could,
Times were hard and money short
But we didn't give that a second thought.

Mary Lou Moore

The Priestess

Born on the Nile, her beauty glows
Slowly, innocently, as the great river flows

She learns her chores, dress, culture of an Egyptian girl
She is becoming a polished pearl

A new sunrise, the years have past
She has received her life's calling, at last

To serve a God, and pass his beliefs along
Both in lecture and in song

This Priestess, beauty prevalent at mid-age
while others, unhappy with fate, hide their rage

An idol to the old, a teacher to the young
The love for her grows, in songs still to be sung

Time brings the Priestess to her golden years
Her day in this life gradually nears

She prepares with dignity and grace
Anticipating her new life, one to embrace

The day has come, she's mourned by all
Even in death, portrays a toy doll

The Nile still flows
Her beauty still glows
Ronald A. Mosley

Seed Of Life

Nurture the seed, until it grows
Protect the baby from earthly woes
Feed the child from the breast of wisdom
Give the child guidance of the holy kingdom
Provide virtue, from the ways of old, you learned
Educate them that respect isn't given, respect is earned
Cuddle with love, while instructing about life
Let them know that life has chance and strife
We must beacon the children to have focus,
for what's to appear
building strength for the burdens they will bear
Teach them to reach for the sky, even if it only leads
to the top of a hill
Teach them to have patience, which cultivates strong will
From the seed, came a life to mold
A loving blend of a character to hold
Alesia Young

Untitled

Seconds are minutes and minutes are hours
Days are so long when we don't get along
Nights are cold, scary, and so alone
Baby I wish I just could go home
I get so sad thinking of what we had
It wasn't a fad
You were my baby and I was your man
To buchcum bay said the sailer man
I tried so hard to do my best
I loved you more then the rest
I miss you I miss you so much I can't deny
The distance between us seems as big as the sky
Why oh why has this happened to me
Please God tell me because this is misery
Baby I know I'm not perfect not even close
Everyone has their hang ups even a ghost
Jesus is perfect in every way
And He is the only one able to say
So maybe if I smile and I pray
Jesus will come and save the day
Shawn D. Barnwell

A Lover's Prayer

Lord, please help me find that special man
Whom I can share my life with hand in hand

Filled with compassion and body built strong
And not afraid to tell me when I'm wrong

When I hear his name, it makes me smile
Knowing that, for me, he'll go the extra mile

And in return I'll fill him with love and joy
By giving him the greatest gift, a girl or boy

I know as long as I put my trust in Thee
This prayer will be answered for Me
Pamela R. Brown

Enshrined

The love that I feel, how not can you feel
rejoice in my deep heartfelt passion.
The goodness of we, how not can you see
take stand in this wonderful bastion.

The music I hear, how not can you cheer
all around the strings, drum, reeds and brass.
The fragrance of bloom, how not can you swoon
and run barefoot in warm summer grass.

Sip honey dew trace, how not can you taste
the succulence, crown jewel of the vine.
Down aisle we'd go, how not can you know
that our life dear, our love, is enshrined.
Michael R. Lee

Our Love

My dearest love, as the days continue I am reminded of the day I left. As I pressed my lips to your silky white skin, a single tear trickled down the delicate curve of your cheek as if I were never to return again. As I embraced you I whispered the same sweet words I spoke to you on the day of our wedding. "To you I pledge my love till death do us part, and even in death our love shall thrive until we meet again in the heavens above." Our love will go on because it is pure and true like a first kiss in a flower spotted meadow on a breezy summer's day. "As I bid you farewell think only of the love we share. Whisper my name and let the wind carry it from your lips to mine.
Robert Allen Milbourne Jr.

Untitled

The universal master plan is without fault.
  It's perfect.
No oversight or errors are found
  within its plan.
Each living thing was given a job to do.
Mistakes that we might think are there
  most certainly are man's.
So give us all a chance
  to be what we're meant to be,
that each in spite of travesty,
  can live with dignity
Maxine A. Putney

The Shoes Of Christopher

Oh, what a story shoes could tell, of little boys that weave a spell
upon those that love this lass, adventures dear our hearts do grasp.
What encounters scan the earth, these little shoes that trudge the turf,
How many times they jump with glee, or spatter mud that hits the knee.

Tread thee softly upon the stair or scruff the fabric of some chair
Trip among the pebbles small or climb the rocks adventures tall.
Sink so softly in the sand covering trails upon the land,
Once so clean and oh so new, are grubby scenes with treasures true.

How we love you little boy, shoes tell a story like a toy
Favorite use like everyday, proves the pleasures of the play.
Just like good buddies, tried and true, these little shoes say of you,
Places taken in secret ways are the glory of younger days.

Someday soon the time will pass, these little shoes will fall from class
New shoes shall suddenly appear, a little larger but so dear,
new adventures they shall hold for little boys with love so bold.
Enjoy, enjoy these pleasures new, let your greatest dreams come true.

Helen Fraga

Continuum

Subtle whirlpool eddies churn...a frame to the froth...
The leaping torrents whose myriad sources...are not known
For I want only of their common purpose...to the sea is peace.
To the deep and freedom's doors...
A headlong dash to rocky shores...
Or depths which see...the endless scuttle of mute claws.

And in this churning labyrinth I stand...and peer to the lower edge.
Hiding under lazy willow boughs...a hatch drops noiselessly.
It swirls and dances to tempt;...a pearlescent shape moves.
An opaque shadow flash...
A leap! ... A splash!
The dance ends in a twinkling...lending itself to the whole.

Amidst the hatched group, a counterfeit....with spine of steel
Strikes the water in anonymity;...the gentle wake is torn asunder!
A luminous spray of tinted pain...which changes but alters not the flow.
The willow waves adieu...
The eddies swirl anew...
Continuing the metamorphosis...lending of self to the whole.

Frank L. McGeary

Sweet Acceptance

In every sunrise of the dawn, I'll see your smile bright.
In all the cheerful birds that sing, I'll hear your joy take flight.
In mountains regal majesty, I'll sense you...awed and meek.
With breezes' gentle caressing, your whispers brush my cheek.

In Autumn's blazing artistry, you thrilled in Nature's forum.
In every placid lake and stream, I'll feel your comfort warm.
In every snowflake delicate, I'll see your spirit dance.
In all the flowers budding forth, I'll smell your sweet fragrance.

In rainbow's grand triumphant hail, I'll hear your precious laughter.
In starlit nights, through cloudless skies, you'll touch my brow hereafter.
Of all the treasured memories, the things I cherish most,
Are those which joy in this, God's earth...To you they draw me close.

You've gone now little mother bird - flown beyond the sky,
To trade your tattered feather coat, for robes of purest white.
Sweet Mother, though I grieve I know, you're in Jesus...

Susan Lee Hughes

My Grandmother's Home

My grandmother's home
so peaceful and sweet
So quiet and neat
It is a place I like to be alone resting.
Cozy at night
Warm when it's light
I wish I was there every day,
So when it's warm I can play
But I go there only once a year
My grandmother, so nice and sincere
My grandmother's home

Jeff Schroeder

Don't follow me

Bubba never meant any harm
He just shot some drugs in his arm
All he wanted was some fun
Now he's laying in a cell
Thinking about what he could of done
He could have O.D or just been
permanently off his feet.

Bubba he stopped drugs and started doing right
Making an honest living like everybody can.

He changed I mean really changed
It took lots of time and placements
But if he can and anybody can make
A change in their life.

Please take this from an honest man!

Charles K. Irish

News?

Burning, churning,
Weeping more.
Who am I
In this world so bitter sore?

Twisting, bending,
Say no more.
When will you end
You're scathing lore?

Hiding, spying,
Get the scoop.
Let us know,
Who's flown the coop?

Watching, waiting,
Don't be late.
Why am I addicted
To the things I hate?

Richard A. Brown

Jacqueline

Jacqueline, held her head up high.
A silent prayer to the sky.
Stunned in shock, so deep.
For all the world, she could not weep.

You and Jack, were our very own.
In your grief, you are not alone.
Majestic, with solemn fortitude.

We offer our prayers and solitude.
For you, we pray a brighter tomorrow.
Time to heal your wounds and sorrow.
Peace be with you, in your time of need.
Forgiveness, is asked for this sorrowful deed.

Joann Grove

Silent Cry

Listen and do not speak,
For the world sounds different when we do not speak,
Some fellow might here the sounds of the ancient grasshopper at their feet,
while others here the cry of neighbors dying down their street.
Yet, many more sounds slip from under the door,
with it taking hope, humor, and strength
   and leaving the pain, sorrow, and perhaps death.
Where could it be meaning by these terrifying sounds?
Why do they hunt you, me, friends, and neighbors?
How can it be that the littlest sounds frighten the world.
Many people jump, while others go out and hunt.
Then the gray Timber Wolf Cries,
for it talks to the moon up in the high sky.
Listen and you can hear the wolf cry.
Or maybe, just maybe it was the wind amongst your side.

Steven M. McGuirt

One Million Plus Black Men Are One

The million man march was a complete success. It was needful and
necessary. Not only for the million plus men, but for the women that
love them, the women that hate them, the children that are from them,
the Whites that were against them, the Jewish who think it was about
them, the Christians who didn't understand them, the sisters who felt
slighted by them, and all the rest of us who appreciate them for
going. We love you. We respect you. We admire your courage. We
lift you. We stand with you. You, are our hope for the future, our
light at the end of a dark tunnel. You, my black brother is a
courageous creature. A fine creation. Strong, gentle and proud,
with your Kingly walk, and your Respectful talk. Why? Because you
love yourself. Warm, wonderful you. One Million Plus Black Men Are
One. You know who you are. Original. Authentic. Never can be
repeated exactly the way it was. No one can add or subtract from you.
No one can change what you've experienced. Unmatched, unknown,
unheard of until that great day October 16, 1995. Keep the vision!!!

Ellen K. Gordon

A Touch Of Spring

Come, take my hand and flee with me into the heart of spring,
To watch the sun rise bright and new, to listen to the mourning dove sing.
To walk together by a racing brook, brimful with bountiful rain,
Our hearts keeping pace with the overflow of alternate joy and pain.

Let us sit on a log and watch sunrays, spreading through the trees above,
Whose branches hold promise of bud and leaf, the gift of the nature of love.
And robins, brownthrush and bluebird, joyful to be part of the day,
Wing from tree to tree, and limb to limb - into the sky and away.

Let me see in your eyes a reflection, the communication of love and peace.
The joy of capturing this moment together, apart will never cease.
A glance, a touch, the sharing, the knowing, a binding bond for two,
The wonder, the essence of thought, the feeling and unspoken view.
O, come with me into the heart of spring, where only love can see,
That this spring of springs will forever remain, a part of you and me.

Irene Brown Dahlem

Black Family

Black family, I don't know if you, he, she and I will be together in the end.

At this instant known to us as the beginning lost am I complete
thoughts of you, you have made me think about life, death, love and
hatred and the fact that many times I had to leave the household just
so that my new government may help you.

For they, made positive sure I could not, as a man, but all that is
changing now and I, hoping to stay alive as long as you, knowing that
they have with a humongous bullet shot your heart to pieces, my black family.

Blown apart your dreams now seem, but henceforth into centuries my
ears, my heart, my shoulders, my pocket and my love will yours always
be. Of this I will speak no more, and ever should one or all of these
be your request or angelic demand, it shall be.

Hensworth Hensley Charles

True Loss

Send me away with a steady voice,
Don't cry while I am leaving
I'll walk towards the sunlight straight
and wait my time of grieving

Cheat me not, oh lord my heart
Let stone be solid through
I'll need the strength of diamond hard
survive the loss of you.

But wait dear Mother, not yet, don't go
thy son once more embrace
For God and heaven I swear I see
when I look into your face

Now lay you down in scented fields
A dress that's sterling white
Your world become a summer's day
and mine a winter's night.

Morgan Chappell

Sailing

I drift and float, ever so lightly, like a feather
endless quests I must endeavor.
I sway and rock from side to side,
with each coming of the tide.
A compass rose to guide my way,
from dusk till dawn every day.
I cut my path like a knife
with steadfast speed and relentless strife.
Often times I own a maiden's name,
but I can not speak, thus, I have no shame.
No gas, diesel, or fuel I need,
just the wind and my sheets of speed.

Thomas Sean Parker

My Special Mother

To Mom - Mada Robling
I knew I had to let you go
I didn't know if I could
you suffered long and hard I know
And I knew you understood.

I knew you are in a beautiful place
Streets paved with silver and gold
I wouldn't call you back on earth
because I love you so.

I hope one day to see you there
A place I'm striving to know
So please forgive me if I'm sad
For not wanting you to go!

She loved her children and grandkids too
each one in different ways
Her special touch her loving words
to guide them, while she prayed.

So, How do I say good-bye
To a special lady in my life?
Who loved us more than I could tell,
So, I thank you mom for being there.

Malanna Merriman

Our Leaders

Our leaders spend too much money as
 they must cut down on the taxes and
The expenses or one of these days there
 won't be any money to fund the
expenses of America as remember
 that mother nature has hurt the
tax payers in different ways too
 as too much is spent on education
expenses for schools and sports so
 sports must be cut out from
education expenses and also there
 must be discipline in the home and
the schools as this would save money
that's used in jails and also stop
 more crime in America and also
we all want equal rights so one
 or more races or colors should
not have a celebration day for that race and unless this is stopped as
 all must pay for expenses of America and we all must work
and stand together in America as Americans

 Irene Mary Larson

The Bowen Farm

The Bowen's have a farm under the big blue sky.
There is a creek that runs through it where the minnows go swimming by
and the pheasants in the meadow chirp at the crows up high,
on the Bowen farm under the big blue sky.

In the spring they plant their garden and then the race is on,
the weeds have the advantage, but with their hoes they battle on.

The deer near by are waiting as the corn begins to rise,
they know it will be ready when it gets up to their eyes,
on the Bowen farm under the big blue sky.

For the raccoons in winter there is not much to eat,
So they head for the Bowen barn cause they know it's full of meat.

They quickly kill a turkey and leave before sunrise,
they know if Bowen sees them, he will shoot between their eyes,
on the Bowen farm under the big blue sky.

 Norval Bowen

Romeo And Juliet

The Rose Garden stands alone as if a story is untold.
Its territory is breath-taking from all glimpses of eyesight.
Only those true to a Rose may enter upon reason.
The woman walks so elegantly, yet her beauty is alive and well.
She stares at the rose only to back off...its beauty is left untouched
An admirer is watching from the balcony above,
 noticing this divine scene, and
 picking of the many roses in front of him
 with its single, unscented snap of its stem.
He dashes down and approaches the ross garden as if he were awes truck
She realizes she is not alone, and stands to run from a moments silence,
Yet, the man simply apologizes for his disturbance.
She is caught off guard and smiles in reassurance.
He slowly gives her the rose, and she beckons to its beauty.
She thanks him, as they walked on both admiring the one rose that bonds them together.
And it was all upon this precious garden that Romeo had found his Juliet.
The love is everlasting for the rose shall last a lifetime.

 Teresa Iacovangelo

I'm All By Myself

I'm all by myself.
It's so hard to try,
with no one there by my side.
with no one there,
all I do is cry.
I have so much to tell,
but I fear of all the eyes.
Everything is my blame,
And all I hear is shame.
I would love to tell all my life,
But all it is, is a very sharp knife.
The moment I step outside,
So many reasons for me to run and hide.
I can't do the little things
I hold so dear,
'cause it's all those little things that I fear.
I hate being all by myself.
I want someone there,
Someone right here,
who understands and cares.

 Jennifer Lee Eldridge

Bravery

It is not mentioned much,
Is it a strong will or a gentle touch?
Can you find bravery in everyone?
Or is it inside the heart of only some?
Is this feeling we call "bravery" real?
Is it an action? How does it feel?
Afraid of nothing, is that what it means?
or is it more than all of it seems?
There were many wars and many men,
When the men died was it bravery then?
Standing up for what you believe in,
Meeting someone new,
Is that bravery? Is it in you?
Does anyone know what bravery is?
Does it shine out of you?
Is it hers? Is it his?
We think we know who is brave,
But deep inside, they might be afraid,
If you know bravery's inside of you,
Please let it stay and let it shine through

 Tamara French

Forget Him

Forget his name, forget his face,
Forget his love and sweet embrace,
Forget the times you were together,
Remember now he's gone forever.

Forget the way he played your song,
Forget you cried all night long,
Forget how close you two once were,
Remember now he's close to her.

Forget the emptiness inside,
Forget the way your love has died,
Forget the slow and aching pain,
Remember love will come again.

Protect your aching heart from harm,
Forget his sweetness and his charm,
Forget his cute exciting face,
Someday, someone will take his place!!

 Carol Ann Clem

A Diamond

A warm sunset, glittering like silhouette
As it retires behind the horizon's wall.
Crystal-sparkling beauty, replicating God's glory
Forms an image on the eye . . .
And dazzles as lightning illuminates, the darkest crevice of the sky!

Not a mirage infatuating the mind,
But an antidote replenishing wounded tentacles of my anatomy.
A hope seasoning doubts, refreshing troubled hearts,
Reforming souls; eliciting the values it imparts.

A refined image escorting the dawn of day,
Condescending with character that culminates all virtues.
An infinite love, a disposition divine,
Clad with wisdom of the highest calibre....
Warming all perimeters of my flesh... It is my sweet
diamond Samantha!

Daniel Lazare

Lauren Ashley

Lauren Ashley, like a whisper on my pillow there you were.
Fragile, velvet, a fragment of me.
Laced in pink, etched in delicate silk, like a feather in the wind,
your fingers on my face.
Almost touches like an artist's brush, imprints on my face,
as your fingers memorize with their trace.

Eyes framed with ticklish lashes, always laughing, teasing, slowly time passes.

Crayon smiles on a piece of colored paper now faded in a drawer of memories of you.

Lauren Ashley, my angel who slept under my heart, waiting by heaven's
gate, polishing the stars of fate.
My masterpiece still not complete.
Once just a thought in my mind, only a doll in my imagination.
Like magic you appeared from my dreams.
Nestled in a vision from the past.
Tangible now to my touch, I celebrate my creation of you.

Lori Henderson

Honor Unbestowed

I dug his old uniform out of the box that lay on the back of the shelf;
I dusted the ribbons he'd hid in a drawer (the ones he had kept to himself).
A worn, faded photo completed the touch—a curly-haired boy with a
smile—and into the pocket, youth's image was tucked: the old man would exit with style.
The somber procession inched slowly along to a hillside just outside of town.
My bitter emotions competed with grief as the cortege began to slow down.
The hearse made its way past the autumn-blazed trees to a freshly-dug grave near the road;
respectfully solemn, the birds hushed their trill; six pallbearers shouldered their load.
The service was standard—three songs and a prayer and an eulogy
brimming with praise for the valiant old warrior who'd fought hard in
'Nam, then, forgotten, had lived out his days.
And with a salute and a click of their heels, the color guard right-faced away;
the sad, haunting strains of "Taps" echoed forth, and we wept as the young bugler played.
Too soon, it was over—they gave me the flag: "From a grateful nation", they said.
Then clearly I heard, each soft, whispered word:
"You've waited too late, boys, I'm dead."

Brenda G. Parks

If I Could Catch A Rainbow

If I could catch a rainbow and then put it into a little jar,
I'd then use a little basket to try and capture the brightest star.
And when these jobs I have mentioned above are satisfactorily done,
I'd ride on the back of Icarus on a journey around the sun.
Next I'd gather all the flowers in the world into a huge bouquet,
Then, I'd learn animal language so I could see what they had to say.
Now these things I've talked about would surely be much easier to do,
Than for me to attempt to try and describe how much that I love you.

Frank Reecher

Nigeria

A special thanks to God up above
That I was given the best grandchild to love
From the origin of her name
Life will never be the same
She fills me with pride
My feelings I cannot hide

That from my little boy
There came such a joy
He made me shout with glee
When she became generation three

To the sweetest little girl
In the whole wide world
I want you to know
That I love you so

You carry my future and are a part of my past
My hopes for you will always last

If there were any way that I could order
You would be my choice of a granddaughter

Daisy Cogdell

Halted Possiblities

She could have been the one who found
The cure for a fatal disease,
He might have been the explorer not bound
By the mountains or the seas,

What if she could sing the song
That until her, never seemed right,
What if he were a leader strong
That would lead his people right,

She could have been the mother of
Your grandchildren some day,
He would have been her man in love
That would never go away,

They could have been a million things
And how bright their lights could have shown,
But because of the end abortion brings
What would have been, will never be known.

Allen Womack

I Wonder

As I sit here tonight and wonder where you are.
Why it's three a.m. and your still afar.
I wonder if you're out with some new girl.
I wonder if she makes your heart just twirl.
I wonder if you think she's the one.
I wonder if your having a lot of fun.
I wonder if she's looked at your hand and
noticed you're wearing a wedding band.
I wonder if she's noticed the wedding band,
the band that I put on your hand.
I wonder why I'm sitting here alone again.
I look at my clock it's four a.m.
I wonder where on earth you are,
then I see the headlights of your car!
I wonder if I should just give up,
maybe if I leave you'll give her up.
I wonder if I should just pack my bags
and go back to my mom and dad's.
I wonder if I should walk away,
I wonder if you'd beg me to stay.

Amy Oakes

One Magical Christmas Eve

An inevitable meeting; a friend of a friend.
You entered my life with a laugh and a smile.
We shared a conversation here and there, a football game in bed,
Cuddling on the couch, holding hands,
And a dance alone in a crowded room.
Was it only because I was there and you were alone?
Or was there something more?

Having spent my life seeking someone like you,
You were more than I ever imagined,
I saw our child in your eyes as we kissed;
Someone meant to be, but never will.
I saw future Christmases spent before the tree fading before my eyes.
What separates us, I know not, but that it is more than just distance.

Instead of mourning what will never be, I thank you for this Christmas
Memories of good tidings, cheer, tenderness, and glimpses of love
Passed between us that Christmas morn.
Shunning all that might be, I watch you exit with a sigh and a tear.

Lisa Castner

Soaring From Within

If I could have but one wish—an eagle I would be
I would soar thru the sky—in the direction of love
To the future—I wish that could be
Thru the clouds of great expectations
Thru the rays of sunshine—that spread love—that would never cease
Where thy neighbor loved their neighbor—no locks on the windows or doors
Where friendship and trust were a way of life
And racism existed no more
Tho' the turbulence of life has ruffled our feathers
And the storms are always near
The winds of wisdom—encourage our journey
The our hearts are still in fear
Perhaps there is a rainbow—somewhere beyond the realm
Of a soaring eagle in our hearts—with a love that overwhelms
If we could all just be an eagle—if only for just a day
Soar to the heights to where freedom is free
And understanding is on the way
Where prejudice was a detour—along with hatred and sin
Soar to where peace and love—forever—soars from within

Carolyn Merideth

The Beauty Of Death

Drops of dew fill the petals of a dry and dying rose.
The streaks of moisture give the illusion that life has been reborn.
A creeping sun ascends over the distant horizon, casting shadows around the rose.
The petals tighten as if they could withstand the day.
A silent reminder of the beauty of death,
The dying rose withstands the sun.

A lively ant crawls up the stem and cuts away petal.
The falling beauty lifts its fragrance and the succulence overflows.
A hummingbird hovers above searching for sweet nectar,
Finding none of flies away, leaving tranquility untouched.
A silent reminder of the beauty of death,
The dying rose withstands the pain.

A mother's child is laid upon the garden soil.
Cooing softly to itself it slowly crawls with eyes solely upon the rose.
Reaching out it catches the stem and from its hand a trickle of blood flows.
A crying child continues to hold, for the rose holds the key.
The answer to keeping death at bay is what the child holds,
But time will steal the knowledge away, and death will quickly follow.
A silent reminder of the beauty of death,
The dying rose becomes a child.

Brian Bolin

The last gift

Thank you my mother, O' mother of mine
For your beautiful rose you left behind.
The beautiful color, always one of yours,
Will always be, your final gift to me.

The rose bud opening, with all your love,
The smell of the rose, as sweet as you are.
Will forever remain in my heart of hearts.
All the days that we shared together with love,
All the memories, more happy than sad, I believe,
Will sustain me all the days of my life.

Thank you, my mother, O' mother of mine,
For the beautiful rose, that you left me behind.
May God's love hold you till the end of time.

My mother, O' mother of mine.
I left you a rose behind today.
My final gift to you, from me,
With all my love, God bless you, and
keep you safe.

Janice M. Graulau

The Sound In My Head

In my head there is a sound
That takes me away from the place I'm found
It may be soft or O so loud
No matter how it makes me proud

Sometimes it may bring me down
But if it left I'd surely frown
There's so much beauty, stuck within
It takes me places I've never been.

I may be nuts or on the edge
But if I am, I've found a wedge
A love for something that can't be dead
All because of the sound in my head.

Matthew G. Wendorf

The Questions

The answer to everything is simple and clear
We come and we go like the shedding of tears
Whatever, whatever, oh, so easy to say
You'll find your endeavor if you pick the way
Whatever they tell you it doesn't mean a thing
For it's the things that you do that the future will bring
Fed to the liars; the fools are food
Deep in your heart there are songs that will soothe
Share your dreams with your parents and kids
The more that you say the better you'll live
Don't waste your arrows, you'll need them one day
Your choices seem narrow when misfortune's in play
Questions be answered as the questions are told
The cycle continues as pathways unfold
But you'll never find the answer, not even a clue
For all that we know is just something we knew
And keep the faith for you shall grow
Sadly my friend, this is all that I know.

Mike Alcorn

Sky

listen as she speaks to you
listen, voices flutter through
the barriers arranged by you
though light and raindrops never do

thunder calls through waterfalls,
rising tides and ocean walls
I can hear you when you sigh
through the water in the sky

T. George Marshall

In My Dreams

In my dreams, everyone lives happily ever after.
In my dreams, every kid gets Willy Wonka's golden ticket.
In my dreams, Peter Pan's not the only kid who can fly.
(In fact, all kids can fly, they don't need a license, and they never run out of gas).

In my dreams, I don't need driver's to drive.
In my dreams, there are no "R" rated movies.

In my dreams, I go back in time and tame the dinosaurs.
In my dreams, I go to magical jungles where unicorns take
me on awesome adventures.
In my dreams, I travel in spaceships to faraway galaxies and make friends with the locals.

In my dreams, all people are treated equally no matter how they look.
In my dreams, everyone has a happy home.
In my dreams, everyone's dream comes true.
In my dreams, there's a universal language so I can speak to anyone in the world.
In my dreams, I can E-mail extraterrestrial.

It's funny, but in my dreams, there are no bedtimes.
In my dreams, I never wake up until the exciting conclusion is over.

So whenever someone says: "Oh yeah, in your dreams, Michael!",
I say: "Cool!"

Michael Shoretz

Thunderstorm Named Thundersnake And Its Lightning Violent Rage

I wake from my slumber as I hear the sky roar,
and the lightning lights! Light up my face

The energy I suddenly feel brings to mind a sense of invincibility;
as the thunder rolls on through the clouds;
to some distant, far-away place

Fiercely the thunder rattles my bed,
to make me aware of who rules the night sky;
a thunderstorm I've just named Thundersnake
and its lightning violent rage

As the thunderstorm surges on,
the faces it makes would scare anyone of little faith

I stand to watch the storm through my window,
captivated by its violent winds

I feel its pain; as the thunder clouds bring rain,
and the lightning cripples a tree

Powerlessness overwhelms my soul,
as the raging force unleashes its source, a violent temper in the air

And as quick as it came it leaves again,
an impression flashed upon my memory;
of the thunderstorm I named Thundersnake,
and its lightning violent rage

Jack Masters

Fate's Destiny

Far, far into a distance I see through a shadowed past, dimly;
Visions skewed, twisted and blurred, my mind helplessly stumbles.
Then out of the darkness, through a mist her face appears;
So lovely, rimmed with long dark flowing hair and features of Goddess.
A smile, clear and full eases forth beneath her beautiful, flashing eyes.

Briefly, in the waning light a tear glimmers on a saddened and
troubled face. My heart races and I want to draw her near to my breast and comfort her.
Reaching out my hand, she shakes her head and slowly turns away.
As quickly as a light is off-switched, darkness comes and she is gone.
Peering blindly into ebony space I search in vain for a presence no longer there.

Weary, my eyes slowly close as I realize we are all victims of uncontrolled fate.
Far, far away in a distance I see through a shadowed past, dimly...

Thomas Gideon Smith Sr.

The Miracle Of Change - God Changing Me

I now see a glimpse of God.
Not face to face,
but I feel Him brush by.
I hear Him whisper.
I sense His mood.
I trust His love.

So when I ask God for
a miracle,
I must be prepared for a
paradigm of change.

His changing me,
His miracle.

Erlene Wilson

My Light

I had a dream the other night
And it gave me such a delight.

I was in the a forest
Away from the world,
Not knowing what to do,
I put my mind on you.

Like a fantasy you appeared,
And my heart was filled with tears

You call my name
So sweetly.
I became yours completely

At that moment I realized.
You are the light that
saves me from the dark skies.

M. V. Porter

The Chosen Path

I choose a path
That is rocky,
Narrow, twisting;
Winding, and curvy.

Some question why
I have chosen this way,
I say because my Lord
Will bring a brighter day.

When times are hard,
He lends a hand.
Over foothills and mountains,
I walk, seeking His land.

I fall into a hole,
But my Father rescues me.
He sets me back on the path;
He gets me back on my feet.

Alas, it has come,
To be with the ones I love.
To have pleasures untold,
With the Lord up above.

Crystal Woodyard

Gloucester

Oh, Chesapeake hold me close in your bounteous arms.
Along the shores of the York River with your mystical charms.
Oh, Haynes Mill Pond and the old mill that is no longer there.
The ducks and geese swim the waters with out as much as a care.
So gentle the tributary of the Aberdeen Creek south of the Clay Bank.
History never forgot the Rosewell Manor, but over time its importance shrank.
White Marsh in Gloucester County my grand fathers old home.
Lawson Farm and Abingdon Episcopal Church is where the memory of my ancestry use to roam.
The cry of the Osprey maybe heard along the shore line of the York.
While the White Tail Deer roam the woodlands around the corner from the Gum Fork.
Canoeing the misty waters while passing cypress trees along the winding path of Dragons Run.
Near the banks of the Piankatank River in the sweltering summer sun.
Oh, the bounty of Blue Crab, claims, and Oysters along with the salt water spray.
Watermen along with their catch in the warm month of May.
Blue Heron stalk their prey in the estuaries as they ponder.
After dark, the nocturnal creatures opossums, and raccoons mossy on over yonder.
Hear the old Hoot Owl cry out around midnight.
The Humming Birds hover while seeking sustenance at dawns first light.
Gloucester forget me not as I write of past life's there.
The Lawson Farm was a lot of hard work, but a joy in the country air.

James Lawson

The Mystery Of Cocaine

It's amazing the powers she contains,
She can make the mind react to ease your pain,
controlling with the greatest of excitement.

Never asking much, and always looking to please her victims,
Knowing the source can't remain,
or proclaim the possessions on their way to fame.

Her background is simple,
created to please the mind, soul, and heart, by overwhelming powers,
causing self destruction or even death, if she isn't stopped in time.

She knows the force she puts on the mind.
She can't be tamed, she refuses,
when she can have anyone or anything by giving a taste of
love so sweet and false.

She gains the possessions of your life savings and children.
She replaces your wife or husband,
and always makes false promises without saying a word,
and accomplishes her goals just the same.
Then slipping away like sparkling grains of white sands.
She is later seen in the grasp of another.
As the mystery continues on and on,
soon to end in a painful nightmare of the next helpless victim.

Glendon M. McGee II

Sonnet XXXI...For Anna

Sometimes when the sky is clear
One can see satellites yet under this precarious crescent
I can only hear your voice seductive in the moonlight
You are dark at twilight, although I know the edges of your mouth

I can imagine your kisses - precious and delightful
And your smooth skin touching mine in musing
Say something glorious with your lips speak softly
Soothing against the grey dark expanse look up my love

Feel the embrace of moonlight - perhaps this tiny insect crawling
Is the prince, longing for your kiss over the ages
Or is it the roots reaching out to enfold you with my affectionate arms
We are just a moment together, painted in the shadows of this grizzled tree

Lovers in the unique history of this place on our earth
Ah love, this is your wind of quiet sighs, kissing away the hushed day.

J. E. Dorsey

The All-Nighter

On an all night vigil
darkness accompanies me
As one we seek the maker
it's time he set us free
All of hell waits here beside us
there is a massive debt to pay
Not heaven or earth can save him
Come dawn
it's judgement day

Brandi Adams

Winter In Maine

The spruce speaks in
Chattering whispers
Deep from within
The peat-bogged forest
Covered now with winters snow.

The gathering gulls
Soar upon the wind
Reeling their darkened
Shadows upon the sea.

In this world of winter solitude
The symphony of nature
Continues to carry out its charge.

And like the very stillness itself
Embarks upon a new day.

Ben Richmond

Friends And Lovers

You were my friend
and I was yours
I love you now
and no one know
who would ever think
that I'd love you
but of course you
know I do
I kept it all inside
I felt like I could die
you know our friendship
was all so great
But friendship last
more than hate
so let's be friends
instead of lovers
because I can't stand
to suffered.

Diana Fabian

The Hight

As you walk the paths of life,
Leave a light for me.
I'm tired of stumbling in the dark,
It would be nice to see.
The time we're here is very short,
We have to do our best.
The trials and troubles that we face,
Won't be our only test.
We'll have to face our pain and sorrow,
With hope and joy and trust,
We'll pray to God to lead us on,
And live with things unjust.
And as we walk along life's path,
We'll look ahead to see,
A distant light amid the gloom,
The light you left for me.

Gary Mather

A Windows View

Windows of the world,
that sometimes close and open, like the blink of an eye.
That break, when stones are thrown, heavy and hard.
Glass that shatters, as does the heart in pain,
was it not easier to close all from the truth, than to allow any to enter again.

Windows of my heart,
Thou closed, there is no life within.
Leaving stones unthrown and glass unshattered,
open arms to all that is new and sane.
Yet, endless streaks revealed,
for all and none to see or feel.

Forever rainbows do you bring after the storm, no more tears to fall.
Wipe them clean as I do often, though to find one more storm.
Glare at night for all to see, what's been hidden behind the screens.

Close them well, for it's the night,
when all seems darkest, tomorrow will be light.

Maria Delos Angeles Guzmeli

Precipice

Write delight, concur with one,
Essay to do, convey in few,
Survey the ink, before to think,
Span the Nile, believe the style,
Share a verse, in silent face,
But send it up, with spirit hast,
No man may snare one hidden line,
Yet, knowing deep these things I show,
So, look upon this working vine,
To bear the fruit that symbols sow,
Concealed in me, a flavor see,
Nor do refine, one jotted line,
Stand away, then reaching near,
Feel the shedding of a tear,
Hang on my face, to trickle down, unique all lament be,
To change my countenance, though not to frown,
Will blur all light to see,
Though dark engulf every bound, with word and pen light here is found,
And these are deep things brought from deep, so slow with foot
lest it be steep.

Roy Hibbs

Eve

She hated the garden
The cloying scent of perfection
The symmetry of those eternal boughs wound with fragrant flowers
frozen in perpetual bloom, untouched by the damp stain of death.

The Immutable Paradise
Time's dark hand did not pass over
Where silken waters fed the black soil.
She gazed on it all with eyes dulled by beauty,
dried by sunlight,
red with the tears she longed to shed.

The gates were closed behind her, barred, and a large barren earth
stretched and lingered on a haze of horizon
which she had never seen over those earthen walls of Eden,
grown over with strong scented vines
covered with budding flowers of gold and blue.
Never was there so beautiful a prison wall.

She covered her hands in the dirt soaked by a cold rain.
She bled her tears into the soil and watched the grey sky with eyes jaded by blue.
And the mist-hung moon glowed through dusky clouds.
She smiled and did not look back at those as those gates faded forever.

Anna Nordberg

October

October comes so softly, in
pink and quiet beige.
With azure skies and soft
white clouds, and evening purple haze.

With passing of each perfect day,
She's getting oh so bold!
Brilliant reds and thistle down.
The world is turning gold.

Milk weed pods exploding,
and aspen magic glow,
October as her very best,
before the quiet snow.

The scurry of the small brown mouse,
among the fallen leaves, small
wings against the sky, whirling leaves
on bubbling brook, October bids goodbye

The harvest moon o'er distant hill,
has caught the aspen glow, her
last farewell, but will return
We know! We know!

Dorothy Law

Light Of A Child

When I think of bring a child into
This world I shutter,
So much darkness,
But then I remember,
That darkness needs the light,
Our children are his light,
To shine through the darkness,
To show the world a love,
A love only a child can give,
So count your child a blessing,
A blessing of his love.

Dee Bailey

Devil's Prison

Walking down the Devil's trail
Smoking dope and making sales. . .
Searching where evil lurks,
Hoping that His plan would work.

Then descending from up above,
Was the Angel's hope of love. . .
With this love it was shown,
The other path I hadn't known!

Walking toward the guiding light,
Gave me visions of His sight. . .
With this light I did see,
Where He really wanted me!

Now I know what road to take,
First there's time I have to make,
Here I sit in this cell
For I took the road to hell!

Toni Lemieux

Autumn Guest

Frost-smitten mornings, cobalt skies
Half-dressed trees, dazed sun
Baled hay, orange-red pumpkins
Smoke bellydancing from chimneys
Wood stair-stepped by the door
Black iron kettles straddling open fires
Fresh slaughtered hogs hung to butcher

Welcome, November, pull up a chair!

DeLee Davis

Legion Of Clowns

With pleading cries they broke the silence and begged the light to show
but in my world of tortured clowns the winds change don't blow
with fragile souls and oars of glass sad jesters float in fear
on lakes of fire and bitter strife with waves of blood and tear
the skies are black, but they see blue, and pretend that they are grey
they revel in the dark of night and learn to shun the day
their hearts are black and cold as ice to that I can attest
vile rhythms beat with hate within their sunken chest
they gaze at me with weeping eyes and hope I'll set them free
from the shackles of prayer they wear to which I hold the key
little do my thralls suspect, their hope is felt in vain
for when I hear their wailing cries I tighten up their chain
the clowns did kiss with ruby lips my hand while passing in
this tragic kingdom that I built within the minds of men
as mortal men they made mistakes when their souls were free
now they're bound and tethered clowns for all eternity.

Mike A. Hernandez III

Absorption

If the earth could speak, it would whisper that it knows your secrets.
If the earth could laugh, it would laugh because it has seen your solitude.
If the earth could smile, it would purse its lips together because it has felt your blood strain
through its soil.
The earth would tell you that the snow is not very pure or true,
And that the rain is always cold, even in scorching summer.
It would tell you about the dead man with frozen fingers lying in its heart in the city.
It would whisper of the child drowning in its pools, and you would hear it shriek in agony.
If the earth could speak, you would know what witnessing death for ages can do to a mind.
And if at the center of the earth is its mind, then that mind must be mad,
Crying and ripping its flesh with its own brown fingers.
And as the earth absorbs our madness, our senseless suffering and
annihilation,
It turns inside itself and screams horrifically.
And if the earth could speak, we would lock it up in a windowless,
white-walled room and let it die.

Andrea Latorre

The Dock

As I look through the thick fog that surrounds me like a blanket,
I see the mountains.

I see no details, only their shadows, like some ominous creature,
out there, on the sea, waiting.

I try to hide by turning around and shutting my eyes,
like some scared rodent in a cage.

The mountains still remain, looming high above the horizon,
growing like a cancer, growing slowly,
like they were trying to blot out the sky forever,
throwing the world into an eternal darkness,
from which it cannot escape.

I can feel them staring at my back,
like they were trying to bore
right into my soul, and take it away.

I turn and face the mountains again,
defiantly as prey futilely fights its attacker, to no avail.

I am engulfed in the darkness of the mountains,
like a giant, black monster, they swallow me whole and devour me.

I open my eyes and the darkness flees like a cat startled by a noise.

I am standing on the dock, alone.

Michael D. McBride

Children

Boys and girls
are born everyday
We care for them
in every little way

We teach them to be strong
in body and mind
in hopes that they can handle
in life what they might find

They ask many questions
some large and some small
so we try to answer them
answer them all

We would like to spare them
the pain when they fall
but they must learn
how to bounce their own ball

They all grow so fast
so big and so tall
We try to remember
when they were just so small

Chris Argyros

Happiness

Elusive,
Yet ever sought
As an end
Unto itself.
It skitters
Across our awareness,
Pausing briefly.
It imprints
Our heart
With its fleeting presence
And is gone.

Carol A. Casavant

Who Cares?

A dog and a cow was talking,
and walking slowly along.
The dog was chewing grass,
The cow was chewing a bone.

Up spoke the dog with a southern
drawl and this is what he said.
"Another cow like you ate bones,
and now that cow is dead!"

But they kept chewing 'til
they got sick and wanted so
much to go home.
But on their way, they fell in
a ditch, and grass grew over
that bone.

They can't walk, or even
talk, while time goes on and on.
Poor dog, poor cow? Well that's
What happened and how.

Betty Jean Jones

A Three Wish To Go

I'll stop to think
and wish you were here,
I'll move much faster
and see it coming clear
this is not what you might say;
but I wish you were here today,
this is not what you might say;
but I wish you were here today

Rey Ortega

MSA

I drove tonight, mesmerized by the glinting reflections on concrete.
Mesmerized by thoughts of a conversation.
I sat there last night, listening.
I am unable to love. He was kind enough to notice.
I am incapable of giving myself to anyone.
Letting go. Body and soul.
And so I thought of you...

I was sixteen, you seventeen.
I knew how to love, then.
I knew the weightlessness of jumping—not the weight of measuring.
I knew, then.
I remember, now.

I am almost thirty, you are.
As I stood there, the fool, alone and watching you break your promises,
  break your habit's heart, there was something I didn't see.
Someone you took with you.
I was blinded at the time by my own glinting reflections,
  by the melting scenery around me.
If only you'd left her where you'd found her, that other me.
The one we give away, sometimes too freely.

J. Cipolla

The Other Side of Life

Where is the other side of life?
Is it beyond the deep blue sea, this place no living man can see?
Is it behind the green-grass hills? This life that no-one knows, but feels.
Is it above the highest peak? Is it below the deepest hole?
It's for the strong, or for the weak? It's in your heart, or in your soul?

It's sad that we don't realize, that we can live in paradise,
That we create our own fate, that it can never be too late.
It's all about the choice we make,
The rules and morals that we break...
For every friendship that we fake, for every risk in life we take...
There is a price that must be paid,
A bond, a friendship must be made.
For every single time we cry, for every person we watch die,
For every jewel that we buy, for every truth, and every lie,
For every river we leave dry...
We stand and watch as life goes by.

This life is not beyond the waves,
It's not beyond the hottest fire,
It's not beyond the deepest cold,
...It's in the love we so admire.

Anton Markovski

The Cross

When you look at the cross there's more to see than what lies without.
If you look long enough you'll see what it's about.
The cross bears a lot of suffering and pain,
for Jesus died there so salvation the world would gain.

To some the cross may look simple and plain.
To others it's full of love, suffering, and pain.
There's more to the cross than meets the eye,
for long ago Jesus our Savior was sent there to die.

He paid the price to set us free.
To show the love he has for you and me.
To some it's a symbol of who we worship and praise,
to others, they see hatred and set them to a fiery blaze.

I don't see what good that would do,
because the real cross hides in the hearts of me and you.
If you cross is true there is nothing that can bring it down,
because we all know in our hearts someday,

We want to stand beside the man with the crown.

Nicole Day

But Not To Laugh

Once I hard a story of a Man who fed
Five thousand with a few small loaves
  Of bread:
I thought the story strange so turned
  and laughed.

Last fall I saw men throwing wheat away
On soft black ground. "Why don't they
  make some bread
Instead," I said; then turned away
  and laughed.

Today I saw them bring the harvest in,
And when I thought of all the loaves
  that it
Would make, I turned away, but not
  to laugh.

Madge Haines Nelson

Lord, I Didn't Ask To Be Here

Lord, I didn't ask to be here
But Lord, here I am
Lord, I didn't ask to be here
I'm just a lost little lamb

People always laugh at me
I can't understand why
If only they'd try helping me
Instead of making me cry

Lord, I didn't ask to be here
I can't help being slower than some
Lord, I didn't ask to be here
To be laughed at, labeled "dumb"

Oh Lord, I pray for all these people
Who always make fun of me
For one day in your holy temple
You'll open their eyes; they'll see

That I didn't ask to be here
But oh Lord, please accept me as I am
Lord, I didn't ask to be here
Please help this lost little lamb

Linda Beasley

As I Cry...

As windswept sands teeter
along top the highest dune.
As crickets sing in rhythm
beneath the sullen moon.

As fruit trees stand subtly
with their bounty ripe to share.
As streams flow on southward
shaping new turns here and there.

As raindrops work like magic
to a plant that wouldn't grow.
As the sun burns high upon us
watching waves ebb and flow.

As flowers wilt and wither
leaving colorful memories behind.
As God cries down from heaven
worried about all mankind.

As snow capped mountains glisten
while reaching for the sky.
My pain seems so endless.
Lord hold me as I cry.

George Robert Newcomb

A Soldier's Grave

I walked into a room, a room filled with memories.
The years of a life soon wasted,
in a fight for his life, for his country

I turned and saw the drum and flute
of an early settler fighting for freedom.
The solemn beat of the drum, the independent song of a flute.
Taken away by a man with a rifle, and a blood red jacket,
red from the years of fighting.

As the drum faded I saw a hat swaying in the wind.
A brave soul preparing for battle,
his troops advancing, marching, scattering, at the sound of cannons.
Their one brave fight at Waterloo that ended abruptly,
as that one brave soul died away from sight.

An airplane flew overhead.
I ran when I saw a dropping bomb,
a bomb of war and death.
One man wanting only one race,
one country fighting for all their rights, but still so many deaths.

Close behind the airplane flew helicopters, ready with machine guns and missiles.
Ready to shoot down at the people, the people in the rice fields.
Soldiers called them V.C.'s, North Vietnam's army that fought the south.

As more soldiers got involved, the more they died away.
As I turned to go, after seeing all the pain rush by.
I finally realized where I was, inside the many soldier's graves.

Andrew Goodwin

You

I dipped into the inkwell of my mind and came up with
a sketch of you. You...I haven't thought of you in a hundred
years it seems, yet, there you were, as plain to me as last
nights dream! You...I've forgotten your name, though your
face is as clear as a portrait I passed but a moment ago in the
corridor of time. Each line of you is etched into my deepest
thoughts. You must have been something to still do that
after the rust and dust of these many years. The warmth of
your sudden smile spread my heart with fields of sunflowers
bending to the warm wind. Vividly you came and swiftly you
vanished from the empty shelf of my age. How you touched me!
......You will never know, for now I recall you died that
very same day my eyes took this picture of you. God, how you
were ripped from my eager arms before they held you even once!
How we quaked with youths desire to be free! To fly and find
the highest peak to dance on! God, they took you away! They
bound you in the chains of death and dragged you from the
wakening spring! You...I've forgotten your name. All this
time you've wintered in my snowy head, sleeping quiet like
until just a moment ago. Now you've gone again and I wonder,
...was there ever a spring...a You?

Dieter Wagner

Are You Real?

Thousands upon thousands of immortal stars dusted the huge arc of
heaven, the soft warm breeze came whispering in off the ocean; the
receding waves seemed to gracefully caress the glittering sand, the
bright full moon smiled its approval as fireflies danced with their light-
bulbs loosen. Two silhouettes swaying in the waning moon light, eyes
twinkling with merriment, in a voice barely audible "Are You Real?"
Or just a fragment of my imagination. A thought that took flight in the
deep recesses of my mind; dancing to the capricious dictates of my
emotions long extinct, burried and almost...forgotten. "Are You Real?"
Or a dream that plays with my restless slumber holding your warm
You real? or am I lost in a mental haze that was founded upon
illusion with every throb of my pulse and every breath, I breathe setting
every fiber in my body to trembling, in the very mist of wild intoxicating
passions awakening a need based upon desire, so strong and
unequivocal request "Are You Ready?" Or is my mind filled with erotic
images of what could be?

G. J. Duperry

Teddy Bear's Secret

If you come real close and near,
you can whisper in my ear.
All the troubled words you say,
I will help them go away.
Any tears that you may cry,
on my belly these will dry.
For I don't tell what I am told,
I keep it safe as I grow old.
Then every hug and warm embrace,
I welcome with a smiling face.
For I am yours and yours alone,
I like it here in my new home.
So when you're feeling sad and blue,
you pick me up, I'll pick up you.

Dianna Witkowski

The Crush

He is my patient secret;
An emotion left unfilled,
A field still left untilled.
Oh, true and fertile blanket,
Waiting to hold and protect.
Forever my heart is willed
To his soul, blind and gentle.
Yes, still my patient secret.
As time passes feelings fade,
Still his memory remains.
In my heart deep scars he's made,
Constant, bound with loving chains.
My heart bleeds from Cupid's blade.
My patient secret remains.

Liana Matisziw

It's A Girl

I reach my destination,
fear overwhelms me.
The pain sharpens,
the pressure soars;
is my heart still beating?
Breathe and relax.
I release Niagara,
the awaiting moment quickens.
My desire to be shot increases
with each immortal thought;
will I survive such a curse
before the blessing?
O wretched pain,
leave this carriage of fertility!
The time has come
I deliver with a tremendous force,
and behold - a child is born,
feminine in nature!

Jamie L. Witmer

Alone with my Thoughts

As I travel through my mind
fear grips me,
happiness engulfs me,
and hope teases me
on the outskirts of my consciousness.
The very thought of success
boggles the imagination
and paralyzes the soul.
While failure lingers
ever so present
as to invite its consequence,
and during this bittersweet struggle
Can we become me?

Michele L. Simmons

Follow In Your Footsteps

I want to follow in your footsteps and be the mother you were to me.
Hold one child in my arms, another on my knee. You've done so much — no charge or fee.
Follow in your footsteps and be a Mother just as thee.

You're the one who holds the gentlest heart.
Follow in your footsteps and be wise and smart.
You gave everything, everything it took, neat and clean — a fabulous cook.
You read tall tales from our favorite books.
You were always, always there to love and comfort in a moment of despair.
Yes, for your children it was love and care.

You made no differences — you were just and fair.
And taught us as brothers and sisters we must share.

Right by our side if we were sick,
there to intervene of we passed any licks.
Things that went wrong, you would always fix.

The pain was severe, from the lash of your switches.
But, now, that I look back on it.
We didn't have much, yet children of riches.

You set your rules that we had to stick by,
Like: get along with others, and be honest; don't lie.
I'll follow in your footsteps until the day I die.

Karen R. Banks

Love: Marginalized or Utopian?

Unknown, unseen, but aforementioned and closed
Of Marginalized people, but it was aforementioned.
It approached me decaptivating, remaining unexplained.

Is it rhetorical or neo-rhetorical that my heart
Pounds at the invocations of the doggedly silence
Hovering over my existence?

I want to conceptualize this yearning,
Make sense of this pleasurable image;
But it is rhetorical, not actually real.

My sunken imagination: sullen, bleak.
My obsolete love, lacking terminology and construction.
Reconstruct something not constructed in the metaphysical and rational.

For this is what must be bledgedly done to become captivated
In the explainable theoretic.
Yet, is this just a catastrophe:
Uncontrolled, yet reality; undamageable, but harsh?

Or is this a rhetorical complexity
Passionately occupying my body and soul?
Unknown, unseen, but aforementioned and closed.

Valerie Kinloch

Secret Desires

There was no love so unbalanced,
Swaying with a daily wind of indecision.
Yet a strong persistent thread of dreams holding steady,
Not fully knowing which way to go.
Clinging to the foundation of what is and was and having
A strong the desire for the unknown.
Making no commitments to the first or second.
Drinking in the excitement, adventure, if you will
Of the anticipation of both sides.
Chipping away bits and pieces of what was and is.
How long the white horse and shining armor before the horse
trips and falls and the power is gone.
What will be left behind in the wake of the excitement, power,
control, and glory of the moment.
Hopefully the foundation, someone who understands what
desires lurk among men.

Genny Rose

Misleading

You teach me to love
And I'll teach you to hate
I'll do what you want
Because you're worth the wait

You you're very complex
And very misleading
The verbiage is harsh
Loneliness I'm feeling

My focus on you
Is not a mistake
I dream about you
Then sadly awake

I train you in shadow
I give you my sleep
Don't misjudge the actions
Or read in too deep

I tempt you with kisses
Give you what I make
My actions and motions
Are that of a snake

Snake Blocker

Evaporation

Then —

Love filled my bottle
To the top,
Sealing the cap
So, time improved the bouquet.

Your bottle was filled
Less than halfway,
Leaving off the cap
So, evaporation took place.

Now —

What good is my bottle?
Soured contents are bursting it
And soon it will empty with
Foul smelling remembrance.

Yours is not damaged
It can be reused,
But I will have to buy another
God, they're so costly.

Genie C. Schiegg

Daydream

When I first saw you I knew
Ours would be a love so true
And when changes came we'd grow
And you'd never let me go

So you'd love me till forever
And forsake your love I'd never
For as time goes by we'll know
How we love each other so

Or at least that's what I dreamed
For as real as it had seemed
It was only in my dreams
You were mine by any means

For you only knew my name
To you love was but a game
Of my love you never knew
Thus it went unquenched by you

Emily Britt

The First Time I Ever Saw Ice On The Ground

In Mississippi the climate was usually warm. I woke up one morning and the ground was covered with ice. My brother and I went outside to investigate this new thing. We discovered that we could not stand up or walk on the ice. Our father gave us an old chair that was made of wood. He gave us a push and off we went across the ice. This was my first experience sliding on the ice.

My brother Phil and I enjoyed the ice storm. Adults were not impressed because they were not able to get around without slipping and sliding, to the children this was fun. There was a hill near our farm called Pea Buckle hill. My brother and I decided to go there and slide down with encouragement from an Aunt. Climbing the hill was really hard work but falling down and sliding backwards was fun. We reached the top of the hill. The trip down was very exciting. I had never moved so fast in my life. It took my breath away. It was the first and last time I slid down Pea Buckle Hill.

Louise Ghoston

My Children, My Life

I was young when I was blessed with you,
Girl one and boy two.
Beautiful in pink and handsome in blue.

Growing up together,
I was there for you, and I bet you never knew,
you were there for me too.

Rainy days we'd sing and play.
Sunny days were the times I'd wish we could runaway from the night.
We knew, the man you called Daddy, would be home to fight.

I'd put you to sleep early, hoping you wouldn't hear my fallen tears.
As I waited for the dawn to brake...
Oh! how I longed for my children to awake.
With every new day I promised a better way

That was then, and I will never allow you to live it again.
Through all our pain, Together we gained
A wonderful bound,
Together, forever, through the dark of the night, till the dawn and the light...
You are my children, my life...

Sonja K. Wallace

Untitled

Flaming;
the heart spills long, drooping, tear-like drops of thick, red blood.
Loud screams from deep within the saddened, frustrated,
eager soul are held in bounds.
All in the past, experiences intrude in the future so deserved.
This mangled, poisoned, hopeless malediction must be burned.

Burned;
this curse needs be, past the point of no return.
So no innocent branch upon my tree will ever be contaminated.
This thick, unwanted truth and sickly, jagged path
shall no longer be debated.
Flourishing with true power, my soul is enlightened,
for change is what I yearn.

Yearn;
for what I know, through tedious, extended work can be done.
For, I am the one behind the wheel and in the driver's seat!
Yes, I have the magical, red ruby slippers upon my feet!
My thoughts are clear and smiling now.
Change has begun.
A bright, new sun has risen.
And my ties are none!

Janice M. Stilley

To The Greatest Mother Of All Mine

Mother,
the greatest word that
was ever created.

Mother,
does not love, but is
love at its purest
found on earth.

Mother,
who is always
right to a child.

Mother,
when mistakes are made
they are forgiven
for they are overlooked.

Mother,
there for me
in love and hate,
passion and compromise,
in this world
and the next.

Marion Highsmith Mansfield

The Dying Prayer

I looked around and cried for help
But none could seem to hear me.
Couldn't they see me suffering?
Why didn't they stop and help me?
This wave of torture is something new.
Can't they see what it's done to me?
I didn't ask for it, it just came,
Please help me I beg of thee.
When they were low I picked them up
I helped them on their way home.
Why do they forget all I've done
And treat me like I'm loam?

The sun is almost down,
I will not live the night.
There's no more I can do now,
But pray to reach the light.

Stephanie Tolley

Spring Dawn

Jonquils peeping their bright
Yellow heads
Out from under their
Cold winter beds,
Roses their petals all sparkling
With dew,
The trees, their branches
With fresh leaves anew;
The bird's call of spring
Their mates soon to bring.
Forsythia shining like gold
In the sun
Tell us spring has surely begun.
Nature again her beauty unfolds
Fresh and young from the long
Winter cold.
If I were a dewdrop, I'd dance
And I'd sing.
I'd dance on every beautiful thing,
T's spring.

Ann Livingston Stary

Tiger Woods

A moment in time when greatness is apparent.
Crowds weaving ever closer to the 1st tee.
Elbows shoving, nudging for position. Just a glance.
His eyes. They say it's in the eyes!

He's not a big man in fact, he's just a boy.
Caramel faced and shy, he welcomes us with a smile.
What a smile. A broad grin exploding with confidence like the morning sun.
We feel his aura of destiny. It is real. It is now!

There is also a sense of wonder. Does he feel he belongs?
Will he allow his ultimate meeting with destiny?
Can he cope, after all this was a white man's game?
He is quickly assured however, as the crowd roars, "Tiger - Tiger".

His grin thanks us with each chant and just as suddenly, stops.
He glares soberly down the long fairway, eyes fixed.
Set his tee and once again steps back for one more determined look.
He is about to assault the 1st hole.

A hush umbrellas the crowd, not a sound but a click.
That click made by perfect contact that most golfers rarely hear.
We watch in awe, so far, so near to the green, as it should.
For after all, the young man I am speaking of is the great Tiger Woods.

Richard Girouard

My Mark

When life's last breath escapes me, a sheet shrouded ov'r my head,
What will last to measure my days: What I did, How I lived, what I said?

Scores I have earned and medals won, those radiant tokens of the past.
But yellowed clippings, tarnished plaques were never meant to last.

Few will draw their inspiration and recall my achievements and plan.
They tell but only a portion of me - small measure of the total man.

Any fortune, too, that I leave behind, and apportion to those whom I know.
Begs the questions, "Why wait til now to give gifts needed years ago?"

We enter the world with nothing at all and will depart from it just the same.
Gold has no value if unused in life, death only reveals greed's bane.

The written or spoken words that we leave will eventually wither and fade,
unless our spirit conveys their meaning before our mortal life's paid.

Unsure of how our lives will leave a mark upon this place,
There is but one thing sure in memories to etch your face.

Trophies and titles and trusts matter not, their worth will have dulled or been spent.
But friendly bonds and love will last long after the body has went.

To share your life with ones you love is the greatest bequest of all,
For it gives in life a sacred gift enduring beyond death's pall.

So whatever days the Master has set on earth for you to live.
Make your soul a gentle friend, with love for others to give.

Greg D. Kubiak

I Hear the Cry

When will we realize that through pain and suffering we cannot shut our ears and eyes;
I hear the cry....
We, as humans, must understand that through terror and power we cannot
prosper and gain; don't you see the pain? Don't you hear the cry?
These lives that have perished through no fault of their own, these children, these mothers,
these families who died; Oh yes indeed, I hear the cry!
Broken hearts, broken dreams, broken chances to survive;
I hear the cry; yes, I hear their cry.
These who punished for pleasure and gain, not caring for those who are left with such pain
look to themselves as heroes, they think;
But justice will come like a wind that will shake, and make them
realize their grave mistake. I hear their cry....
For this day in your life don't despair and don't' cry;
let God bring you peace and let God dry your eyes.
Let's remember this day; let's remember their lives;
and above all things, let's remember their cry.

Candida E. Calderon

A Legacy

A lone, bald eagle soars,
    against the cloudless blue sky,
Across majestic mountains
    snow-covered
    with the sparkle of winter.
Powerful wings spread boundlessly
    beating strong
    against the current,
Gracefully above
    the mystical green pine trees,
Minted white with frost.

Hovering above the nest
    a single, pearly white feather
    is blown in the wind,
Leaving an immense legacy
    for others to follow.

Cetaya Register

A Love Letter

My Love!

It's me who wants to tell you:
    "I love you."
You are inside my soul.
I opened myself to you and
    I find understanding.
I give my heart; I give my love.
I will share the joy of living with
    you.
You are the most marvellous
    person in my life.

Your always loving wife.

Monika Hirschenbaum

The Redwood Storm

The storm came early that night.
With deep sounds in the sky.
And tornadoes dropping till June.
The wind was restless when it went
through the valley.
The rain trembled with sadness.
The thunder rolled like a wave.
The lightning crashed like a symbol.
But for all of Redwood,
the storm went by.
Leaving damages like no other.
The sadness grew the happiness
was no longer.
For the storm had died in Redwood.
With no survivors.
It was marked there,
that the storm was just a myth.
But that night it came true.
For now that storm is famous,
just like Redwood.

Kellie Juneau

The Answer

When darkness is all around you and
there is no bright of day, then all
of life's problems surround you and
your friends turn away.
You're searching for an answer in all
of your despair, and the answer that
you are seeking has always been right there.
Jesus is the answer he lives with us
each day, just keep your eye on him,
his light will guide the way.

Stella Moore

Florida

I moved Florida in 1994
Boy I never thought I would go back for more.
All I could do was strive and think success
For when I got a taste of it oh what a mess
I started to drink and party a little to
And boy can I tell you I never felt so blue
It has been sixty days and I am squeaky clean
Now tell me the truth don't I look lean
Enough about me what about God he came to the rescue what a great job
the priest came near me and my heart started to pump before I new it I was lying like a lump.
He touched me not once but even twice I can't explain it there was no ice
My mother told me I would never be the same I hope not that would be a damn shame.
I will soon head back to the state that could of ruined me but that was not my fate my
connections are good and they ate not from the hood I will team up with Mr. Marshall and
Mr. Fox maybe one day we will own the red sox Leonard calls me a little spark plug he
better get ready I'm going to take home the rug this company is so new I was the second
person hired for I hope they have a spot for me and I was not fired

Matthew James Little

Shadows

God created such a beautiful world.
The bright colors and aromatic splendor of flowers
The cheerful singing of the birds and the
fluttering of their wings while in flight
The mountains which stand tall - overlooking the wondrous earth below
The Oceans, Rivers and Streams with the sound
of rippling water and the force of the high majestic waves
The beautiful, clear blue sky with Sunlight that brightens our days
The sound of the rain beating against my window pane
The rains that help our flowers to grow and the
crops which prosper to feed the hungry
The dark sky of the night which is filled with
stars that sparkle like diamonds
The trees with their branches swaying to and fro
and tops reaching up to Heaven above
The churches where people go to congregate and worship the Lord

I see these things clearly in my mind, but I am losing my eyesight
I lift up my heart in prayer to my Lord, and I hear His voice saying:
"Be not afraid" "I will guide you in this plight."
I envision my Lord holding me in His arms - knowing that He will be my Guiding Light.

Shirley Ruth Caron

The Bedtime Battle

To bed we go, but wait, not yet!
Our nightly routine we have not met.
The "bedtime" announcement is always great shock.
It sounds like a bang and is hard as a rock
At least when it's heard, but sometimes it's "muted",
By TV or music but, dear, we're not stupid.
Your ears have been tested, your eyes see the time.
In the minutes you delay, we make up this rhyme.

The snacktime at bedtime is the longest of day.
Perhaps it's because afterwards there will be no fun or play.
Nothing to look forward to but a big, boring bed,
And an occasional school assignment that "forgot to get read".

Finally in bed, but not yet asleep.
Are we crazy to think we won't hear a peep?
Laughing, talking, whispering, sneezes,
Bumping, jumping...the silence she seizes.
"Good night, dear," we say once again,
This time followed by a count from one to ten
We'd rather not ground you—we know it's no fun.
So when you grow tired, you actually have won. . .the bedtime battle.

Debra B. Samblanet

Bed Time

It was a dark
and rainy night,
he begged his mother
to leave the light.
She said no
and darkness came,
for his fear
there was no name.
His brow not move,
his lid not blink,
the unthinkable,
the boy could think.
Then the shadows
began to creep, the young boy
started to weep.
Through the boys
salted tears he could see
his worst fears, but for a minute
he did find, the moving shadows
were in his mind.

Jennifer McGowan

Winter Night

Snowflakes drifting down,
sparkling in the winter moonlight.
I look out my window,
dreaming of you
the man I've grown to love
and trust with each day
we spend together.
So amiable yet powerful,
you fill my heart with happiness.
We may be as different
as each snowflake
that touches the earth.
But as I watch them fall they
unite together as one.
You are my future, my love,
as I am yours.
Together we can build
a life as one.
You are my love,
the only one.

Krista L. Overfield

Mother

When I would cry
mother would be there.
She would be so sincere
and wipe away my tears.

Mother is kind in her own ways
she has a lot of things to say
to steer me the right way.

Mother taught me love
and respect
In a way she knew to accept.

Mothers are tender-hearted
and kind
she will always have a
special place in my mind.

Ann Connolly

128

Father's Love

He will be with you now and forever;
Never again will there be miles between you.
The pain of the recent and the injustice of the past are gone in his life.
But the spirit rejoices at a new beginning.
He will be your strength when you feel weak; draw from him all you need.
His well will never run dry,
He will be there for your joyous times and your triumphs.
And also for your sadness and failures;
To wrap his love around you and hold you till you are strong again.

Of all he could not give of himself here on earth he has
  unlimited to give in heaven.

When you feel lost look no further than in your heart; for his spirit
  is within you to guide you.

Never feel alone; Never be afraid, for you Father is with you "Always"

Kista V. Franklin

Young Love

I'm only trying to follow my heart, yet so many people keep telling me
to be smart.
Do what's right they say. How should I know what to do?
Because I'm presently stuck without a clue.
Half of me is pulling away saying, "no";
Half of me is pushing towards thinking, "so"—
So what if I keep getting hurt, it's only my feelings. There inside
where no one can see. Oh how much not hearing those three words is crushing me.
Smashing me flat to the ground. Until I talk to you I
won't hear a sound. Friends keep telling me to do this, or do that.
But I am not like a cat, for I can't just keep prancing around not
caring what happens. I confront you and ask if you really care, and
of course you say , "yes" and give me that innocent stare. I can't figure out what to believe.
Am I foolish to keep giving your reprieves?
But is it you who is to blame because our opinions aren't the same?
It just seems like we argue all the time, as if all our conversations are
hateful, down to each individual line. I'm told to just wait, that it'll come.
I fear just a little late. I know that there's love here but is it supposed to come with all this fear?
I'll be patient to see what will come of this. But for now, I'll wonder what's in your kiss.

Kimberly N. Bodner

Can I Be Number Thirteen

The Lord Jesus when he began his earthly ministry, asked some men.
If they would follow Him to glory and help in souls to mend.
Most were fishermen and of our Lord they never heard.
But there was something in His voice, they listened to His word.

Now, Jesus asked me the same, to follow him.
I hear it often and will hear it more as my eyes forever dim.
Can I be number thirteen, I ask to enter his fold.
To join the other twelve who now live in houses of gold.

I won't deny you Lord three times before the cock crowed.
And I won't betray you like Judas, whose greediness showed.
I'll be like a rock like your favorite Peter.
So can I be number thirteen Lord, I know my life would be sweeter.

I've followed your word as best as this mortal could.
While here on your father's planet, I ask you Lord if you would.
Can I be number thirteen Lord and join your precious flock.
Because I'm waiting for your return, as I gaze at that ticking clock.

Donald Szobodi

Thoughts About Nature And God

The white clouds above, a white mass of semi-dense moisture
that puffs and rolls and then dissipates — God's masses of soft cotton balls.
The tall ponderosa pines look up to the blue sky and white clouds —
swaying back and forth, talking to each other.
God looked at the Earth, and He was pleased. He covered the Earth
with water, air, plants and trees. He created the animals, fish and birds.
Then He pointed at man and woman and said, "You a soul!"

Moritz E. Pape

If I Could Fly

Fly fly fly like a hawk
I'd give up all means of talk
Fly fly fly above the trees
I'd soar away with the breeze
Fly fly fly to be free
Not to worry just to be
Fly fly fly away
In one place I'd never stay
Fly fly fly through the trees
If I could fly I'd be at ease
Fly fly fly like a hawk
I'd give up all means of talk
Fly fly fly above the trees
I'd soar away with the breeze

George Sherwood

Where?

In the mid of the night
I heard it clear.
That my true love will
soon be here.

Out of the still there
came a light.
But not my love, no
where in sight.

As the wind blows and
the trees whisper.
But my love is still not near.

But oh where could my true
love be?
For he has not come
to see me...

Tina M. Washington

Growing Old

My heart is young...my spirit free,
I live my life with dignity.
I Laugh..I Love.. I dream... I cry,
Rejoice each day as it slips by.

No hair of white could ever take,
Away life's pleasures that I will make.
No lines that cross my weathered face,
Would ever try to slow my pace.

Experience time...precious and sweet,
Confront the challenges that I meet.
I question you, to be so bold,
To think that I am growing old.

Donna Bernatovich

The Edge Of Death

I touched the hand of the dying.
I felt the cold reality of my mortality.
The suffering of the dying swept
Through my fingertips like a
Sharp bolt of lightning.
Wrinkles and folds of flesh
Giving passage to the
Inescapable pull of gravity.
Her mind drifting in and out
Of past realities
Then encountering a world
Known only to her.
Goodbye for now
Sweet mother.

Tricia Peters

James Dean, My Hero, My Friend

All my life, I have dreamt of this day;
To walk where you have walked, and
stay where you have stayed.
My dreams have become a part of yours;
what I feel today, is unlike anything I have ever felt before.

Your soul has been with me each day of my life, but here, in your town;
Your presence surrounds me, and your pain breaks my heart.

What I thought would be tears of joy, are now for sorrow;
For a life that never should have been taken,
For someone whose presence lives on inside me, as each day
turns into a treasured memory.

Your soul was found by many, long before I was born
But the impact you have made on me, has carried me through
everything that I do;
And has made me what I am today.

Thank you for the legacy that you left behind
The courage you have given to many,
The confidence you have given to me.
You are, and always will be
Loved and cherished, in my heart; from now until eternity.

Michelle L. Settle

A Wedding Day Message To Friends

Each couple's love is as different and beautiful as the uniqueness of
   a snowflake the mysteries of it more profound than even reason,
So many things have been written about the cycles of courtship and
   commitment, and yet even 20, 30, 50 years down the road,
   two lovers still ponder the days half in amazement.
Is there not a seed which activates the soul to find another
   perhaps for some, as early as conception?
And do we not wander through matches that might have been
   until the moment when calmness stares back into our souls?
For it is in an instant which everything that has gone on before
   clicks and like a ghost writer merely develops what was indeed
   already so.
The world of today seems so unsure, and yet
   generations before us must surely have felt this same anticipation.
They also took chances, found love, and when lucky entwined the two.
For hundreds of years brides have been nervous;
   grooms have gauged the road ahead,
Both knowing separately that somehow there would always be:
   a hand to fit snugly in their own, a set of eyes to welcome them home,
   a matching heart to beat as one.
If life could always be as happy as your wedding day, the entire
   notion would be auxiliary.
It is because of the seasons that you must cling to each other and
   believe with patience that Spring will somehow always return.

Debi Yergen

Why Do I Come Back?

   Well I just got done ending round two of our relationship. Is
there going to be a round three? I honestly hope not. I was hurt too
many times because of you and I have given up too many things because of you.
If you would just open your eyes long enough to see that I really did care.
I was wounded by you, but yet I came back to you so you could make me all better.
You said you almost cried, but could it be that you lied? Were you telling the truth?
I don't know if your words even faze me anymore, I've heard those same words more then once.
The words that bring me back to you every time. The sad voice and that cold feeling along
with unbearable pain. What are you trying to prove by doing this time and again?
I don't want to waste my time on something I know can never happen.
Honey I'm sorry, but there will not be a round three, or four, round two was one round too many.
Should I feel sorry, for you and your words? Are you going to hurt me more,
or just let me be happy!
Sorry it happened like this, but you know, on my end there will be love always.

Jessica Cumming

Take Two

Though our time is done
There is something that I see
The way that you look
And still long for me

But I have moved on
Why are you still behind
Someone new is controlling
My heart, soul, and mind

I guess it's okay though
Desire is my speciality
Because you got to know someone
Who wasn't really me

I appreciate your longing
Because I want her too
That actress inside me
That you thought had loved you

Liz Smart

Springtime

Clothed beneath a mask of snow,
The world awaits the time
When springtime juts its head forth
And growth is so sublime.

Wrapped within the rays of sun,
The buds upon the trees
Announce that spring is here now.
And then there's that nice breeze!

Nighttime brings a wealth of sound
As birds sing us to sleep.
Leading to another day
When new insects start to creep.

Mary B. Wadzinski

Insanity

I am insane
I hear the rumble of all things
it's like a computer gone wild
spinning its tapes in a motion of
constant movement, turning, turning
I am insane
the voices I hear kept saying that
I am, and I feel they are correct.
My head is like a race horse one
minute I'm at a trot, the next I'm
filled with dangerous thoughts bent
on the destruction of myself.
I'm like a drowning man, purposely
I keep going down, really hoping
someone might be able to rescue me
but knowing it want happen
so insanity is here, a cowards way
out of a world going too fast as
I submit to grief brought on by oneself.

B. Bailey

Eternal Solace

Dark clouds slowly kill the light, a cold wind blows into the night,
As she rides across the sky
A black mist seeps into the ground, a dense fog rolls without a sound,
Silence echoes her dark cry
Seeking those who hear her call, those who want to leave it all,
Behind to join her on her flight
There they will know her peace, find the solace that they seek,
The cost is her eternal plight

Souls of the lost know her pain,
Tears of the damned hers to shed,
Alone, again

Sorrow's washed onto dark shores, as the sea of tears she
wept still roars,
A silent song forever sung
Never will she be as free, as those who call her seem to be,
Forever guiding those who come

As summer's blazing hear can kill, winter's howling fury chills,
Burying under white which once was green
As season, this will end, but not to end, to begin again,
Forever she will be unseen

Stephen V. Allange

My Life In Review

While doing time in T.D.C. I asked myself, What happened to me?
My life on the outside, I thought was good,
But now I know, I wasn't living as I should.
My friend was the bottle, I trusted no man.
My life was miserable, which no one could stand.
But my life was empty, I was lost in sin.
The more I drank, the more trouble I got in.
I've learned a lot in the months I have been here,
Your freedom is everything, cherish it, faithful and dear.
I am still a prisoner here in T.D.C. but glory to God, he set me free
My body belongs to T.D.C., they locked me up for a while,
But my spirit and soul belong to God, even my smile.
I once was blind, but now I truly see.
Jesus Christ, my Lord and Savior, really does love me.
To those I have wronged, I ask for forgiveness and a new start.
Since receiving Jesus Christ in my life, He gave me a new heart.
If any read this poem and are lost as well,
Get your life right with God, or join me here in Hell.
Hell on Earth is called T.D.C.
But always remember my friend, only God can set you free.

Arthur Earl Stearns

We Called Him Geronimo

His home was always here—in Mimbres land.
Here, he, his father and generations of grandfathers lived with gusto.
Here, he was taught his way of life.
Here, he earned the right to leadership.
Here, he learned of the "white-eyes"-and their trickery.
Here, he learned to hate
and to kill
for the protection of his tribe and his land.
Here, he is the greatest or the worst of Indians.

Here, in 1997, I walked where he walked.
Here, I stood under the 2700 year old trees,
the very same trees he stood under,
Here, I saw his mountains resplendent in their beauty.
Here, I learned
and
I understood.

Rhea M. Coleman

The War

Oh, the terror in their eyes,
as the tear fell and fell,
from their sad but frightened eyes.

The terror in their eyes,
as their pale limp bodies fell,
fell to the ground without a sound.

Oh, the terror in their eyes,
as they screamed,
screamed in pain.

The terror in their eyes,
as the guns fell,
fell to the ground.

Oh, the terror in their eyes,
as the guns go off.
But, they hear no sound,
no sound at all.

The terror in their eyes
as they lie there without moving.

Oh, the terror in their eyes,
as they cried and cried.

Devon Sterling

To Jupiter And Mars

They claim soon they will be able
to fly us all to the moon.
Perhaps even farther to Jupiter and
Mars carried by a gigantic missile
with a stupendous boom!
Our childlike wonder continues with
unbounded fascination!
To discover more and more about
our limitless creation.
Will we ever come back from this
Star Wars mentality?
To hear Planet Earth's urgent cries
of facing reality!
While millions and millions of
dollars are spent on never ending
experimentations in space,
Would it not be just and right
better spent solving and alleviating
the multitude of problems facing
our human race

Shirley A. Joel

Heaven Awaits

The oceans waves are beautiful.
The current is so calm.
The sunrise is so peaceful.
It's beautiful at dawn.
As the sun was rising
A noise caught my ear.
It was a very loud trumpet.
It wasn't far from here,
And then I saw Jesus
Floating through the clouds
On a great white stallion.
He's here to take us now.
All my life I'm waiting
Just to see his face.
Now I'm going with him
To the Holy Place.

Brittany Muller

Dare To Be Self

The signs are present
The fingerprint, DNA

We are different
Yet we try so hard to be alike

We spend half our lives trying to fit the mold,
And the other half trying to figure out how to escape.

Some know they are different but don't know how, why or what for

Others go astray, a little haywire
You've read about them, the mad geniuses

Most just dream, they sleep while their wings are clipped
They forget how to fly, how to soar
So they walk, crawl even sink into despair

Your youthful strength should be preserved to evolve into distinction

Safeguard your heart, Free your mind
Treasure thought, Embrace courage

Remember the signs
You are special, one of a kind.

> *Deborah McKnight*

The Paradox

I had been lying face-down in the ditch for quite some time
Being too frustrated and weak to even lift my heavy head
Above the sunken level of the mirky, muddled waters
Or I would have seen the light reflected in its glassy stillness

You see, I got all turned around and lost my way somewhere back there
Following the silly, painted clowns through their maze of mirrored walls
Aimless and blind, in search of my self and my God
I found only the bread crumb trails of scattered and broken lives

When I had finally tripped and fallen into the darkness and stench
Of my own misery - the lonely and silent, huddled mass
I retreated further into the eye of the mind and truly saw
The beauty of the storm that is raging through my restless spirit

It is the perpetual opposition of unceasing flow and under-current
That makes the mighty river so turbulent and wild
It is also that very attribute that gives it direction and purpose
The proverbial Yin and Yang are so expressed in all of Life

Now as I sober in the redeeming warmth of the fiery Eastern sun
My weary and wretched body is dredged up from the filth pit
Inspired to again walk upright with my gaze on a star's salvation
For I see I am a microcosm of the brilliance and mystery of vast creation

> *Rebecca E. Camp*

L.S.D.

And so the birdman flew. Is this what his dreams were all about?
Is this what his absurd high really felt like?
As he flew into colors of red and blue his inner ego grew and grew.
And so the birdman flew, yet no one looked skyward to appreciate.
He'd merely licked the surface he desired - kissing the sky his wings
outstretched like a cry for help - could he have dreamt he could fall so fast?
Did he ever dream at all?
And so the birdman soared into reality, his wings tired, his eyes sore
his mind vivid with the new horizons he'd reached, the new ideas he'd provoked.
And so the birdman flew into colors bold and new - Inventor of a new
race portraits hung: the painted face.
And so the birdman flew and from above he saw
Creations he'd made, lurid, sordid, defiant of the mould
Alas the birdman flew - was this his highest point?
Could he not soar higher?
Could he not touch heaven?
Could he die?
Could the birdman really fly?

> *Paulene Hadden*

Meeting

Our locked eyes charged the air,
a circle of flames ignited around us.
Protected, we left words behind,
followed a silent conversation
cleared by our commitment
to witness each other's presence.
No time hindered our exchange.
Held in this eternity,
we might have stayed forever,
but separation had been
designed from the beginning.
Praying our parting would not
erase the memory of meeting,
we broke our gaze.
Our connection dissolved.
Saddened, I bowed my head,
honored the doe for helping me
return to the covenant
of a forgotten promise.

> *Linda Whitesitt*

Help In A Predicament

Are you in a situation
Wondering "How can it be?"
Are your choices leading you
To trust in one who cannot see?

Do they propose you just give up
Or do they say to just give in?
Or maybe they don't see the place
That your decision left you in.

Do you know someone who cares
Enough to help you every day?
Have you succeeded by finding them
And listening to what they say?

So maybe you have walked the path
Where successful people fall;
But you still stand and follow them
By listening to their call.

So when you make the wrong decisions
And need someone to say
That they are sure you will succeed-
He'll be there every day.

> *Heather Wigboldus*

Untitled

The soft smell of rain
A streak of light so very bright
Extreme break of silence

> *Laura Dedmond*

My Lost Soul

Set back the clocks,
The ship is sailing slow.
The winds have died,
The downpour is heavy.
Brilliantly-lit ship; hovering clouds;
Mine eyes are blurred,
By the rustic rumbling fog.
The seas roar.
The day darkens.
Drifting along, hark-
I thought I saw land!
Time is no element,
The ship bobbles,
The wind has died.

> *Kristen Nolfi*

Holy Ground

They point with piety towards the heavens.
They reach out with expanding determination, challenging a
limitless sky with incessant growth.
Their limbs like lifted hands in silent prayer, silent
except for the wind that moves them.

They sway and dance in celebration, touching the hem of God
in exaltation. Theirs are the gnarled hands of the common workman,
the battered hands of the crucified.

They have leaves which are richly green, dark leaves which hide the
mystery of a cave; so green that all Eden seems to reside there.
Eden when man still walked with God in the cool of the day, before
lies and death, before murder and decay.

They stand proud like canyon walls, worn and twisted by time,
thickly barked and knotted; each fibrous layer a ritual prayer, a
pledge made to God each Spring, a testament to their eternal struggles
to serve His eternal being.

They are what men call trees, clumsily for lack of better words.
In Truth they are the living thoughts of the purest God,
incarnate words rooted in Holy Ground.

William D. Howard

The Seasons

A little red haired boy, the one I passed by when I had the shoes
I was too young to tie

The one I happened to miss when it was cold in New York
He felt the same cold as me, in his own school, doing his own work

When I never knew he owned time, he moved the sun and the moon
My world would revolve around him when time would allow it to

Every corner he skirted around and even from state to state, but
time was true when I met this boy because it showed he was in my fate

This force that brought us together keeps us bonded tight
This boy who moves the universe brings my world warmth and light

I saw him, but I did not know he turned seasons,
and it was in his eyes I could see all the reasons
   He'll make winter warmer with his embrace,
   flowers in spring will look to the sun to grow in every place
   To summer he brings warmer weather,
   and at his whim, the leaves will fall from September through December

Now I look at my angel and I look up above,
to see all the stars that shine for me with his love

Jennifer Proctor

Untitled

As the wind blows, my memories begin to flow, and all I
can remember are the passionate nights lying next to
her. The way we loved each other was right out
of a fairy-tale, but it was real. My love still
grows and the pain still shows and she's there,
but I'm here and whenever we're together the
world just slows to a halt. I will see her again and I
know she'll wait for me. We both believe in love
and we know love has no borders and love will always
find a way. As I remember the loneliness I experience
when she's not with me, I become a victim of love.
And life can be cruel, but we must see each other through
tough times. For I know patience is a virtue, and I
must wait. For the wait makes the meeting more
wondrous and magical. My love is like a painting and
without her it's missing a portion. Like a puzzle,
without her I'm missing the most important piece, Life without
love is like being sick and cold, not even the wisest
man knows what love beholds. When you've got love life can be much sweeter.
We can follow and love can be the leader.

Brandon Staggs

On The Beach

On the beach, on the beach
Lovers here, lovers there,
walking and sitting everywhere.

Out in the open night
Where the stars are shinning bright.
Couples kiss and caress
While I sit on my log relieving stress.

Orion is out ready to fight
With his little dog of might
Tonight the twins were out of sight,
Preparing for another night

Oh! On the beach, on the beach,
The tides are very low
Leaving room for me to bellow.

Now I sit on the sand
Just waving my hand
Saying to myself
Oh! On the beach, on the beach,
What will be next.

Sophia Paul

Heart Quest

From distant shores, and desert sands,
And mountains reaching to the sky,
The world has called to me
And I
Have wondered endlessly,
"What was this urgent voice
That spoke no word,
Yet filled the silence with a cry
Only my listening heart heard?"
It called me to a rendezvous
In a secret place
Only my heart knew.
Then I looked and beheld a vision fair,
Life, enshrined in a dream
Was waiting there!

Phyllis Burchfield Fulton

The Butterfly

I saw a Butterfly
flying swiftly through the air,
Flapping its wings,
without a worry or care.
The wings looked like rainbows,
so beautiful to see,
I wanted to take it home,
to show my family.
But that would be quite selfish,
so I let the Butterfly fly go,
What happened to that Butterfly,
I guess I'll never know.

Dalia Ganz

Truth

Communication or Manipulation
There's always a Choice
One offers Freedom
The other, Remorse
Directness and Honesty
So simple, So clean
Words that we speak
Truly reflecting what we mean.

Sandy Hanson

Our Greatest Gifts

Sometimes we wonder where our greatest gifts are in store.
We think they are in this world's possessions, at least that's what we are searching for.

We realize where life's greatest treasures really are, you see,
they're really right in our heart, we don't have to go far.

We strive for more and more and work around the clock, no matter how hard the fight.
We take for granted our ability to walk and talk, our hearing and our sight.

Our greatest gifts cannot be measured in money or gold,
just knowing we have our health and family, and the moments we feel, these can never be
   bought or sold.

We wake up one day and realize, Why I worked all those hard and long hours,
when the most precious gift is the love we feel toward one another and just a simple
   bouquet of flowers.

So friend, it doesn't matter how much money you make in the world,
the more you have, the more you will want and will only wish for more.

What really matters is what's in our heart, and when our lives are over and we then do part,
Only then will we need to know where our destiny will fall, the good
things we do for other people will surely we worth it all.

We will then see this place was really only a stopping place, for our
Lord, we will then see face to face. Our greatest gifts are within,
not measured in the eyes of men.

Patricia A. Selvage

Smooth Stones In Blue

Smooth stones in blue resting in your sanctuary.
The rhythm of the gentle waves flow quietly across your back.

I am envious of the emotions that so lovingly shape you.

Are you aware of your being?
Your emotions are not unfeeling or you would not be so beautiful.

Your solitude is controlled by a knowledgeable sea as it pushes
you away, almost as if to say goodbye.

You know where you are going, while we wander aimlessly to our
destiny as in an endless search.

Smooth stones gently cradled by the sea.
With open arms she effortlessly offers her precious gifts.

Unknowingly, we pick up the stones and carefully turn them in our hands.
Your smooth cool touch felt soothing to our rough hands.

Your finely defined lines were noticeable from your experiences of life.
We then realized how you were a symbol of strength and support.

There are more smooth stones but none like the two that we had found.
Were you a rough stone at one time like me?

Lynn Rowe

Love

Love is beautiful, Love is endless, Love is hard, and Love is painful
all wrapped into one big bundle of emotions. Love is beautiful for
those special bonds. Love is endless even when the ones you love
pass on without you. Love is hard it is something you must work on
all the time. Night and day and day and night. Day in and day out.
Love is very painful when the ones you love die or say mean or
cruel or bad things to hurt you. Love is all around all of us. We
are all loved in so many different ways. But one thing I know is
when you think that the love is not there at all, it is because no
matter what, we are all loved very much by God. God loves each and
every one of us, big of small, good or bad and happy or sad.
His love for all of us is endless. I know this because I have lost
6 loved ones in less than three years. But God is still blessing me
with his Love, even now as I write these words. God Loves us all,
and I love God and I thank Him everyday for all the love I have,
and have had always.

Deborah Thompson

Just For Glory

At the break of dawn
The castle gate is drawn
The sword raised high for battle

My army moves along
Like Satan's hellspawn
Crushing all who stand before us

All the bodies lying dead
The banners soaked in red
An army that none may conquer

And in that morning light
With steel shining bright
I took my seat upon the throne

And those who dare try
In chains ask me why
As I spit upon their face, I cry

I did it just for glory
I did it just for glory
I did it just for glory

Craig Gerard Hogan

Let Us Prey

Let us read what has been written,
   But see with more than eyes.

May we hear that which is spoken,
   Yet listen to the whys.

Can we note what has been shown us
   And know what it belies?

Let us prey upon our senses,
   Aware of what we do.

May we pray our concentration
   Will hold and see us through.

Can we pry right through our bodies,
   Endow what we eschew?

Willard Allan

My Dark Angel

My dark Angel,
Who hides in the shadows of night.
Who wonders the lonely streets,
Barely guided by the light.

In the peaceful world beyond,
How I want to join her.
To see things through her eyes,
And not just in a blur.

Knowing where I'm going in life,
Knowing my future day after day.
Knowing how I'm going to live,
And if I'm there to stay.

Following all the followers,
And sticking with my friend.
Doing what it does best,
Until the very end.

Listening to all the sounds,
Arguing with the voices in my head.
When I'm with my Dark Angel,
I know I'm already dead.

Amy Williamson

The Song Of Myself

Alone,
he sails,
quietly, alone
into the Mighty Seas, searching and discovering.
As the great barriers and winds of night blow strongly,
tearing the sails of this bleak ship,
alone,
he sails quietly into the night,
lost, sailing into the deep, rough seas,
with no land in sight,
wondering if he should return and live in joy without peace
or search for new land and live in peace without happiness.
Alone, he sails, trying to find new land.
But hoping someday that the dark will turn to light and he can live in
a land where happiness and peace are one.

Darshan Pather

My Angel

To meet the angel of my dreams...
My angel I once knew long ago, has eyes of soft seclusion. The smile
whose breast would hold me close.
The caress to warm my heart, the voice to sooth me to sleep. The
hands to reach out and beckon me to places so sweet. My angel has a
heart so pure and so honest. I feel so vulnerable, so open. My angel
shows me the peace and love I have seeked for so long. Yet to meet
the angel of my dreams might frighten its soul away from me forever.
I might see that it wasn't the heavenly angel I had fallen in love
with, had trusted in and had touched my heart with its profound
perfection. This would rob me of my dreams then how would I live
without my angel? Without my dreams my heart might lose faith.
Though if I met my angel and all was true... I might miss out on a
friend who would warm my heart, sooth me to sleep and reach out to me.
My angel who is so pure and honest.
My profound perfection.

Stephanie Pinnegar

LIFE

As I sit here and ponder the life I've lived,
I remember when I was a kid. I used to play, run, and basically have fun.
When we began to get a little older we experienced what girls
were like and wow what a incredible sight.
We then experienced the book work we used to love and hate.
We then learn to drive and sometimes to make those stupid mistakes.
Soon we go on the first date and, boy, what a wait.
Quick as a light we finish that high school sight.
We then choose that school or work fate and sometimes wonder what was our golden gate.
We then go on and sometimes meet our mate, the one we learn to love or hate.
Sometimes we have kids with our mate or completely alleviate that fate.
Oh yes can't forget midlife and sometimes that crisis that it makes.
We then send our kids to their certain fate at that school of love and hate.
With the kids grown, we soon begin to enjoy our chosen fate.
We then see what we have accomplished in that glowing light of life.
Now we teach the grandchildren we love to tend and mend.
We then sometimes find it hard to hear and only listen to what is near.
 Slowly we begin to lose the ones we love so dear and enjoy the life we have so near.
The end is near and we start to remember the past that flew by so fast.
We died on the day of are last rest and became a memory to most of the rest.
In all of this remember life is great, so embrace its great eternal fate.

Travis Adams

Sweet Spring

What once seemed A Cold lifeless Place; Has left us suddenly without
leaving A trace. The Cold has Past and the rain has fallen; The Birds
in the distance with their mating sounds Are calling. While the
flowers push themselves up threw the earth; It is time for their New
Birth. The grass thickening greener than green; As wildflowers
submerged Coming up in between. The warmth of the Sun's own embrace;
Has left A glow a pond everyone's face. Spring is here it Came at
last; But it too will be leaving us just as soon and as fast.

Mary Ellen Newbery

A Tyrant Called Death

Death walks soft beside me
His touch is gentle upon my brow
He has become familiar to me
Controls so many of my thoughts
 I've no more tears to dry
 No more fight, cry I
 No longer hasty am I
 No longer hasty am I
Death changed my observations
And many actions, He
Has become almost a friend
suppliant am I, ready to go
 A tyrant, you say?
 Perhaps, my friend
 But, heaven's nearer today
 The tyrant guides me.

Patricia J. Compton

My Life

I have lived a long life
full of sorrow joy and pain
Now I give a life
to this cruel world

I promise to protect you
from the evil and hate
I promise to teach you

How to learn and to love
I promise to give you
all the knowledge that I have

I promise to love you
through all the joys and sorrows
I promise to understand
when you have a problem

I promise to listen
when you need to talk

I promise to let go
when you want to grow up

Always know that I love you
my child

Taunya A. Milligan

The Way To Love

As the universe stretches eternally
The love between two people will grow.
Their thoughts are intertwined together;
Happiness is what they will sow.
The feelings ignited between them
Is a love no less than pure.
For one, the other is the cure.
Wherever one of them is
The other will be there too.
They hold each other in their hearts;
They know their love is true.
The world would be a better place
If everyone loved as they.
There would be no confusion or hatred —
There is no better way.

Amanda Creed

Night

The owl in muted knowledge perched
long upon the bough of blackened birch,
then into the pitch of starless cloak
he echoed his unminded, tortured croak.

Diane Swartz

The Eagle That Is I

I see an eagle in the sky; I watch him as he soars
Suddenly it comes to me and my heart within me roars
That eagle above the clouds is I. Why am I bound here below
When my spirit wants to fly? The burdens and cares of this life,
The Lord makes me to know keep me within this body instead of being
The eagle that is I. I want to be free,
To soar above the storm. I want to be me.
To feel my blood warm from the wind against my wings,
I want to fly until my heart sings
With the freedom I know that I can never have here below.
I watch that eagle in the sky with a feeling akin to jealousy.
"Surrender all your cares and woes," a voice whispers from within me.
"Give them to the One who understands and knows
   How much you desire to be free.
Soon I will come, then what a story you will have to tell
Beyond the clouds of glory. Till then, my child, be patient and wait."
Peace fills my soul as I listen to that voice coming from on high.
I know now that I'll soar through Heaven's gate
   On the wings of the eagle that is I.

Elvina E. Stanley

Indian Tales

Tell me the old Indian tales, my father.

Of the lone wolf howling at the moon.

Tell me how our braves went out to hunt the bear, deer and buffalo.

Tell me stories of their brave deeds, and how they slipped through the forest like grey
   ghosts on phantom feet.

Some say their presence still lingers in the mountains and in the early morning mists.

They say you can see what looks like campfires burning.
It is an Indian legend, my son. An echo of our past.

Evelyn Finch

Anchors

Anchors which are cast,
Not in calm seas
Of one's own heart,
Can never hold.
But adrift and lost
Are searchers unloved,
Of whose ships
Have set sail
Upon storm-ravaged lives
Of others.

Donna Huff

Today My Love

In your travels today...
   remember me as I will remember you.
My love will go with you...
   every second, every mile of the way.

Take caution, My Love
   that no earthly creature
   lures you into the darkness
   of a troubled mind.

And when the flames of daylight
   hide behind the rim of the earth
   and we are together again,
   life will have true meaning.

Ruth A. Rutherford

Untitled

Lost, lonely, and confused
Dear God I feel so used

I used to know where I was going
now I don't know where I've been
I have no command with the time passing

I used to have friends
Today all I have are opponents

Once I knew what I was doing
then I was so smart
now I am ever foundering

Lost, lonely and confused
my God I feel so abused.

Gerri Shannon

Bailey To Brock

He is my rock...
My Brock.
Brock makes me smile
Even while
He may be sad
Or feeling bad.
He is my rock.
My Brock.
We run, we play,
We talk, we pray.
There is no other
Like my brother
Brock.

Mary Crouch-Lantz

Resolution

I realize how much you hate me,
so spirits of darkness take me.

As I tread next to death, you cry,
And I wonder why?

I realize that you faked me,
you tricked me to think you hate me.

I try to leave the darkness,
And rid myself of this madness,

I push these thoughts aside,
And swallow my arrogant pride.

I ask you to be my bride,
And you abide.

Dan Drenberg

Free

A cloud,
A leaf,
Bug, bird, sand
Water flowing o'er rocky river beds
Winds billowing, leaves floating
Being
Cleansed in summer rains
As, my soul and my thoughts,
Fresh as the verdant air
Become free.

Edith Hotchkiss Wall

Untitled

When times are quiet and peaceful
I like to think
About things I love:
   Seeing the stars on a clear night
   A light spring rain
   Dew on the grass in early morning
   A golden sunset
   The taste of a snowflake
   The sound of a babies cry
   a child's laughter
   A peaceful walk through the country
   The smell of a rose
   Animals grazing in a meadow
   The roar of a fireplace
   A soft hand in mine
   The sharing of two people
   You
All of these,
   Beautiful
Things I cannot have.

Timothy A. Balz

Empty Heart

When little I thought about presents,
My love for someone grew.
Larger, Larger, Larger.
I just didn't know what to do.
She touched me and said she loved me
Then I knew she didn't care.
She said it with such politeness.
I just had to go somewhere.
I went down the dark, dark street
Trying to find an answer to my problems.
And all I found was an empty heart.
And a memory long, long gone.

Tomas D. Herrera

Deep

I pull the shades down
on top of the sunset.
So bright, so vivid, so sinister.
I stare back at the mirror
and see the same expression.
I long for the moon
and noisy crickets,
and run through the forest
naked.
Naked as a bride
and jump, leap, dive
into the reservoir,
water flowing
so deep.

Loren Trigger

The Penultimate Poet

I am the mirror of Me,
I am the vis-a-vis
   who
having had his habitations
among my several selves, hence
though dead; hence though dying; hence
I live; from thence
(and face to face,
like a moving void along
a hollow lobe of space,
i/ I am), ever plying
pinched prose posing poetic
across the woven waters of
an empty page; i/I am
the interlinear id, i/I am
the penultimate poet whose
latter lines linger longer
than the half-life
of an empty soul...

Truman Patch

A Simple Love Song

"O my Luve's like a red, red rose,"
Burns said, and sounded sure.
But what about the hollyhock
that struggles to endure?
And from the cracks of sidewalks
a brave dandelion appears;
along a windy highway
goldenrods toss yellow spears.
A bird drops seeds—a sunflower starts
and grows and grows and grows
so beautiful and stately
though it's surely not a rose.

Love may appear in any place;
I know that this is true
for I have found it everywhere
and, dear One, so can you.

Mary Jane Richeimer

The Gift

Come step to the line of the facile
Most do-
Some don't know any better
Some are afraid not to
Some just don't care.
Those that don't however
Have the greatest effect
Though they'll never know-
And that is the gift.

Lawrence S. Davin

Dikembe's Old Haiti

Voodoo
in the streets of Port-au-Prince
ancient family amulets around my neck
I make dance
and trance in
forever now
my out of focus eyes
mystify
Western people
like childhood days
when grandfather
the priest,
   Dadaheydra,
twisted the rooster
with rum
in the countryside
before the French arrived
and we rode the horse
She came in on

Daniel T. Buttino

A Wilted Rosebud

My Lady, of word so measured,
Though not of mind or deed,
Whose graceful being I treasure,
Whence sprang my yearning seed.

Our careless moments consecrated
A rosebud for tomorrow
(I was with love intoxicated) ...
And bore less joy than sorrow.

That rosebud never bloomed.
Did I to Reason heed too much?
'Twas not the season to be enwombed;
It wilted for my impetuous touch!

Like the Ganges would thine eyes weep
If thou felt my pain in part.
But, Oh! Whoever grieved as I, so deep?
With that rosebud ceased my heart.

Jacques R. Island

Untitled

Yesterday when the tree was planted
There was no fear of tomorrow
From above and below it was comforted
And even dared the lightning to strike
But tomorrow brought a new wind
One whose name is 'Merciless'
But he was his own worst enemy
In that he did not remember the seed.

Michael Stevens

Being Without Home

I could have paid an architect
To build me a home
Invested in new clothing
For mine, I have outgrown
With transportation limited
My hallway serves my street
Now I must travel
Without shoes upon my feet
A man so poor in riches
Canned food I must consume
All these tender delicacies
I enjoy in a cardboard room!

Thomas L. Lowrance

The Child That Never Was

In my younger years I always
   knew you'd be a part of me.

As life went on, I doubted
   your existence.

By my own decision, I resolved
   myself that you would never be.

But don't despair, sweet one,
   as you live with me through
   other's children, for I am
   your teacher.

Jill Noud

Untitled

Perhaps it's just the timing?
Or,
maybe it's the time I've been away?
Locked in coherency!
Legally binding,
and morally blinding.
Ah,
The reasons we all act this way.

Roger M. Benfield

Familiar Stranger

At 13 you called me "Daddy's Girl"
and always held me tight,
I trusted you not knowing...
your plans for me one night.

A secret lies in my bedroom
if only those walls could talk,
Then maybe they would have warned me
something strange was in your walk.

Many nights you looked in on me
always making me feel safe,
This time your reason was different
so was the expression on your face.

Unaware of your intentions
still trusting...I sensed no danger,
You entered my room Familiar
when you left you were a Stranger.

Chris Gooden

Colors

If you see the color,
and it's often red,
the fixation you feel,
is often dread.

If you feel a color,
and it's often blue,
you can immediately grasp the fact,
I'm deep in something of you.

If you wear a color,
and it happens to be black,
you definitely know,
there's no turning back.

But if you paint a color,
such as white,
your soul is nothing,
it's dreamy and out of sight.

Melisa R. Wiese

My Life

A lot of people say my life is great
and that I am very lucky,
a big house,
lots of friends,
but if you look inside and see,
I am not very lucky,
you tell me:

As my step dad does drugs I can see,
how my life is going to be,
he leaves for 3, 4, even 5 days at
a time,
and we are wondering if he was
dead or alive.

It's hard to think it's him
in there,
it's hard to think he has life
to spare.

Beth Dey

To: Amanda

God sent her from heaven
and she just turned seven
when she cries from her fears
she asks me to kiss her tears
I would never lie
she says mommie please don't ever die
Lord please don't take me just yet you see
'cause I'd like to see her grow up,
be happy and get her degree.

Phyllis Stanley Caldwell

I Could

In the forest of dreams
Searching for sunshine
In the rain
A leaf from each tree
To escape reality
If I could touch a tree
I could see the dreamer in me

John R. Starlin

Jessie's Lulla-By

My precious one; 'tis time for bed.
Close your eyes 'n relax your head.
Dream of honey and gingerbread.
The sky is red but not to dread.
Hush, hush, your pets are all abed.

Lullaby, lullaby, my precious one.
'Tis time to end your daily fun.
The cricket's songs have all begun.
The day is done and gone's the sun.
Hush, hush, my precious little one.

Sleep, sleep; No need to weep.
A loving God, your soul will keep.
Cuddle in your blanky and sleep.
Count the sheep and watch them leap.
Hush, hush, the birds no longer peep.

Lullaby, lullaby, please don't cry.
Your Mommy is here to rockee-by.
She loves you dearly, none will deny.
Close your teary eyes and let them dry.
Hush, hush, 'tis time for bedee-by.

Eldwin Kendall Lane

Death Hurts

As you lay to rest
on this day,
you showed us you loved us
in every possible way.

It seems as if
we're so far apart,
but the love we have for you
will never leave our heart.

I don't understand
how this could be,
why did God
take you away from me.

We just want
you to know,
the thoughts and memories
will never go.

Amber Novak

My First Day

My mother put me on a bus
to send me off to school,
She said the lunch was free
and that is very cool.

I met my teacher at the door
who said, "come in today".
She read the rules to us
and said we couldn't play.

I tried to read a book,
She said I'm wrong,
I say, "I is", and she days, "I am"
this day is getting long.

She gave us blocks
to count by 5's and 2's,
I built a house
She said, "You lose".

I can remember that day
I wanted to play
like I do at home
and say what I want to say.

Sandra Thompson

Song Of War

Engines, mounting tension-
running down the track today,
why God, am I in this place?
With war paint smeared across my face?

Children come to talk to me-
but I am blind, I cannot see
so much blood I saw before-
I don't want to see no more.

Why God, must I shoot these men?
Only to kill more again -
my heart is turning black with rage-
why God am I in this place?

Why God, must I see each face?

Dan Szymczak

Untitled

Julius Caesar
Was a swell old geezer
He washed his feet
In the ice cream freezer

Robert Dahne

Fog

Misty it creeps
'round the foot of the trees;
and slowly begins to rise.
Misty it creeps
'round the foot of the trees;
reaching for cloud-covered skies.
Curling and swirling,
tiny pearls of white—
A never-ending sea
blotting out all shape or form
but that closest to me.
Water-filled droplets
firmly enmeshed;
an army of soft, misty might.
Retreating defeated
with the appearance
of summer sun's
warm rays of light.

Rose Judnick

A Teacher's Leave-Taking

Tell me not 'tis time to go
I'd rather linger still,
Are there not pages, chapters yet
Receptive minds to fill?

But cycles, seasons, nature's laws
To start and then to end,
Let memory its silvered web
Embrace a time, a friend

Frank G. Flores

The Blue Sky

The blue sky
I look at the blue sky
And see a friend
An ice one
Who I can come
to for problems
and help.
I like you for that
the blue sky
is just so beautiful
and pretty I love
that blue sky
and you for being my friend
the blue sky is
pretty isn't it.

Wendee Willis

In His Eyes

My Hispanic eyes are angry
they are burning with rage
they no longer see the beauty
oh, my - they have changed

My Hispanic eyes are angry
they look saddler as days go by
who took the glow of life from his eye?

These Hispanic eyes were smiling
I remember vividly the time...
it was in them that I saw my future
and the rest of my life

My Hispanic eyes are tired
they need to rest and sleep..
and with them they take my visions
and bury them so deep.

Eliya Azoulay

Appropriate Revenge
(For All Who Have Been
Oppressed, Abused Or...)

I know why that caged bird screams...
in shame
facing down
trodden from a
shackling abyss of
control
no freedom
no equality
control
I know why that caged bird screams....

....Will...

I know why this caged bird sings.
Endures oppression
retaliates regression
obtains freedom
desires control
no equality
control
I know why this caged bird sings.
Tonia Minor

Hopeless

My hopeless isn't new.
It's been for quite sometime.
Well hid
　　behind a good facade,
　　my heart will beat
　　for a thing that may never be.

My hopelessness isn't new.
It faded but yet grew
　　in a bottle where it lives.
Packed away
　　I'll take it out another day.

My hopelessness isn't new.
Still I dread the day when it is viewed.
Then everyone will see,
　　the true lonely and hopeless me.
Audrie Doll-Ewertz

A Knight's Lost Love

Come love, be with me.
We need know grief, from love
my love, my lovely dove.
Come when the time is good for you.
You don't have to say, I do
but if you do, don't be blue,
I would always want to be
close to you.
Come love day or night, come
when the moon, sits just right.
Come, you don't have to stay for long.
Come, my love, I've written, you
a song about your sparkling eyes.
Come get your surprise.
Come, my love, let me write,
in your heart how I become
your knight.
Shawn Henley

Confusion

What is this pain I feel?
I try to deny it,
But I know it is real.
My thoughts just go in circles,
Running through my mind
I try to look for answers
But they're so damn hard to find.
No one tries to help me,
No one even cares.
They say it's not their concern,
It's not their pain to bear.
I've got a lot more life before me,
Many more things to learn,
But if things continue this way,
I'm afraid I'll crash and burn.
I need someone to be there,
Before it gets too late.
This pain is overwhelming,
I'm afraid I just can't wait.
Tiffany A. Wendel

Darkroom-Lighthouse

Obvious is the darkness
in this place of yours,
With shadows bending and
Blacks and whites climbing walls
never ending until light.

Obvious the darkness
with time passing,
noted by the hands of the dial,
and you moving carefully thru the
maze of events and the time
to develop what is hoped to be
for then will come the light of future.

Obvious is the darkness, yet there is
clarity in this space rendered dim
A light so clear I notice,
The light from which you see
is yours!
Louis S. Silagy

Untitled

You have made my life so wonderful,
My face they say it glows.
All the love I give you,
Will always, always flow.

So much love to give you,
All for you to take.
A beautiful life together,
Is all I want to make.

You are truly a beautiful person,
Certainly one of a kind.
It is only but a miracle,
For you to share your life with mine.
Gary David Allen

Children

They grow day by day
How cheerful and full of energy
So innocent and talkative.
Their loving words
Please and I love you.
They teach you how simple life is
eat play sleep eat play sleep
They bring so much joy to life
day by day as they grow.
Christina Herriott

Sky's

　I keep an eye on the sky
with a wink in my eye
I think wonderful thoughts as I
Look in the sky
The sky makes me wonder what
it is like to fly wide in the sky
like a bird in the wind flapping
its wings up and down up and down
and when it lands
it looks up at the sky with a
beautiful wink in its eye thinking
thoughts it had never in its life
thought before the wonderful fly in
the wide sky the thoughts
were such wonderful ones no one
could think ones like these.
Malissa Choukas

Us

What happened
can you recollect
The world was once ours
But has now been invaded
We needed no song to dance
Now the musics is on and I dance alone
I had all the answers
Now only questions
You were my dream
Now only when I sleep
To night I hope I never wake.
Derek McAfee

Face In The Mirror

The day had come
But, I'm not ready
I look at the face in the mirror
I hang my head and sigh
When I really want to cry
Can this really be true
I look at the face in the mirror
Can this be
Me
For every wrinkle and tiny line
there is a story
some happy, some sad
I look at the face in the mirror
and smile
Yes
It's Me
Linda Scott

Once Again It's Spring

Once again it's spring
Let everyone shout and sing
What joy this weather doth bring.

Once again it's spring
Let's fly with our wings
And to the world bring
Love with a sting.

Once again it's spring
The feeling of life is astounding
Desiring it to be everlasting.

Oh bliss!
Once again it's spring.
Joy Johnson

Be Mine

I can't say when it started,
maybe the second we parted,
since we've been separated
I've been empty hearted.

Thoughts of you fill my day,
morning, noon and night,
dreaming when you and I will lie,
beneath the stars so bright.

My love for you is so real,
the beat of my heart you can feel,
feelings so deep with desire,
burning with volcanic fire.

Say you'll be mine forever,
promise you'll leave me never,
making each day seem anew,
with a love in my heart that is true.

I love you more now than then,
It will continue this way to the end,
Growing into infinity,
until the end of humanity.

Christopher R. Hunter

Reflections Of My Husband

Eyes of blue
With a twinkle
Mop of hair
Beard of gray

Deep in thought
Very pensive
Can be caring
And sometimes sharing

Gentle nature
With strong will
At times illusive
And non conforming

Future trips
With excitement
Silent times
As he goes

Does he love
Or is he lost

Take a look upon the waters
Can you see him or just reflections
Connie E. Zimmerman

Idolize

How I always think of you
I can never put you out of my mind
Binding to you like glue
My love for you is one of a kind
Your voice is forever embedded
Deep within my heart
Ready to race full speed ahead
But this must a false start
Too young to determine
The realities of love
Knowing that I cannot win
If we are together by jove
To my special friend
Don't make it end

Diem Nguyen

Me

Me,
I am me,
the person who tells me
what to do, where to go, even what
types of p.j.'s to wear,
when I think of me,
I can be whatever I want to be
Jump, run, fly...
But not die
Even though I live in a city,
A corrupt city,
I will never fall down to pity
For I have confidence - you will see,
whatever happens,
let it be
So when me thinks of me,
All I have to say is
Me, myself, and I

Akua Ampadu

Read To Succeed

To read is to learn,
To learn is to know,
To know is to try,
To try is to grow

So try, you might win,
So try, you might lose,
Nothing comes free,
You must pay your dues

If you choose not to try
For fear you might fail,
Then know in advance
You will end near the tail

Try, Try Again
If you want to succeed,
Double the volume
Of the pages you read

Don't act like a Goat,
There's no time to tarry,
Take your head and your butt
To the local library.

Albert Blitstein

Rolling Thunder, Howling Wind

Rolling thunder, howling wind
They were true unto the end.

Battle cries rang in the air.
Sounds of war were everywhere.
Open wounds were dripping blood,
Bodies buried deep in mud.
Warriors' cries resounding true.
None were sure the number slew.
Rolling thunder, howling wind,
They were true into the end.

Many deaths, both good and bad.
Many tales, both great and sad.
Great survivors, young and old,
Very few have ever told
The stories of the cause that led
The war that left so many dead.
Rolling thunder, howling wind,
They were true unto the end.

LaurieAnne Cruea

The Decision

My life is slipping
through my fingers
like tiny grains of sand
Now only a few grains remain

If I reach out to take your
hand, will these few grains
be lost forever?

Or will you help me
hold them there
Paula Kenneman

Shoes Of Hell

Who is this stranger
This man that I love.
In my dreams he is perfect
In reality he is Hell.
He walks in shoes full of ego
Stepping on my soul.
He compliments himself
Before putting me down.
He loves his life
His way.
He walks in control
Of himself and of me.
I am his robot
His servant.
I walk in shoes of Hell
As he walks over me.
Cherie L. Bell

earth song (accountability)

Take me to your heart
and cast me not aside
nor look upon yourself
too proud
that you may not cause me
to lose
feather fish or beast
pebble seed or cloud
and ultimately
decisively
ourselves
Ana W. Caeidhe

Time's Choices

Time has gone by.
Your day is here.

Be wise and enter it...
...with no pain or fear.

Hold your head high.
Stick out your chest.

Be sure of your choices...
...make them the best.

Show all your love.
There's no time for hate.

Be aware of your splendor...
...before it's too late.

Nichole Andrews

From There To Here

From the shadows of a lifetime,
From the then, the distant past,
Come refined and golden nuggets,
Come the things which always last.

From a world of constant hardships,
From a far and distant shore,
Sails a ship that is built for us,
Laden with our earned store.

If we dance, we pay the Captain
For the riches thrown away,
In our ignorance and smallness
We knew not it was the day

To enrich the time and moments
As they come to you, to me,
To accept a heavenly friendship
From the powers that ever be.

From the then into the present,
The inheritance of grace,
Come the wisdom of the ages
Bestowed on the human race.

Mildred L. Cherry

I Thought I Knew

I thought I knew
    when I was young
that happiness
    were songs I sung
that smiles I wore
    made all things right
that life was long
    and always bright

I thought I knew
    when I grew up
the way to fill
    my loving cup
the means to win
    over unjust
the ends to keep
    my faith and trust
I thought I knew.

Sonia L. Russell Harmon

Returnings

As long into the sky we climb,
A life again I've left behind,
A change as silent as the song
Of a bird, its cry is long,
As once again the space is crossed,
A change is made but friends not lost,
Time though shifting, changing seen,
Is always and forever green,
New and founded on the love
All friendships formed from up above,
A child at first and now a man,
Friendships founded, a life began,
I understand and once again,
The worlds change and a past will fade,
An eternal game of love and life,
Trust and friendship always strive,
In these eternal games.

Todd Andrewsen

Angel In The House

A cleaning lady,
    some many say.
Housekeeper,
    might be the official name;
But, maid
She is not,
Nor, slave
    to the dirt
    of a careless shoe.
Woman, cannot be denied
    strong and proud
    through the piping sounds
    of demands and wants;
Always working,
    with a weary hand.
Though toil will tire,
    And sadness comes in waves;
A song forever,
    this beautiful woman,
Mother of all the world.

Stefanie A. Forster

The Nursery Rhyme
Turned Nightmare

Humpty Dumpty was an adopted child.
The fall from the wall wrenched her
From the circle of arms
she trusted would hold her.

Horses and men,
Therapist, and soul-searching . . .
nothing could heal the cruel wound
concealed within her reshaped shell.

Fading images of her forsaken baby's
fall still flicker,
Echoes of her screams still reverberate
in my dreams.

Sally Shlakman

Your Tops

We get a kick out of you
Your singing is in complete harmony
We get a kick at how
You express all the words
We get a kick - when you
Roll your eyes
We get a kick at how
You do the flirty flirty
With the girlies in the crowd
Yes we get a kick out of you
So keep on singing
We all love your songs
We get a kick out of you
You are the best.

Joseph Serino Sr.

Untitled

Life leaves tracks,
Strife makes marks,
Across our backs,
Through our hearts.

But if from scars
We turn in shame,
Then all our pain
Has been in vain.

Kathleen A. Allen

Abandonment

The curtain of black
encloses like a sack
leaving the question of
life or death.

Stale cries of wonderment,
listless tales of woes;
Icicles of loneliness,
hanging from your nose.

Question of pangs of worth,
needy, all alone,
groping for the crest
of the storm.

Janet Zarate

A Friend

When you are lost,
    I will show you the way
When you hunger,
    I will offer sustenance
When you are afraid,
    I will be your light
When you are cold,
    I will furnish warmth
When you are weak,
    I will share my strength
When you are lonely,
    I will be your companion
For I,. . .
    . . . Am your "Friend"

Richard A. Plume

Worry Angel Prayer

Now I lay my worries to sleep,
in Worry Angel's heart for keeps.
I trust she'll take them far away,
where love can work its magic way.
I'll need a peaceful, carefree rest
so love can guide me to my best.
To concentrate on learning love,
I've got some help from up above.
For that's her job and pleasure too.
My mission will be clear and true.
She's placed my worries in love's domain.
Now I'll be focused on this plane.

Margaret R. Bunes

Public Relations

It never hurts to smile
or give a friendly nod hello,
A smile won't break your
ugly face, and you might
be surprised to know
that people are people the
whole world round, and
they have feelings just like you
So limber up your "Ramrod Back"
Relax the muscles in your jaw,
You are no big thing upon
this earth — be nice to
people. They will be nice to you.

E. H. Young

The Sounds Of Passion

Listen and you will hear
the sounds of two lovers.
As they unite
and become one with each other.
The sounds of passion
that come from the soul.
In a shout or a cry
in a whisper or a moan.
The sounds of lust
as they both catch a breath.
Then they again begin
their sins of the flesh.
The sounds of a kiss
bring their bodies closer.
While the sounds of a touch
tell them the night is far from over.
And as the passionate night comes to an end
only one sound can be caught.
A sound that comes from both bodies
the beating of the heart.

Tupuivao Wilson

Sweet

Swing, sweet, sunset wild
Wave goodbye to the flower child
Baby, basking, bonny girl
I opened the door to our grown up world
Cry, crazy, crow came
He figured you would never be the same
Mother, Mary, mourning love
You said goodbye to the turtle dove
Hoping, hurting, hunting found
You weeping to the dusty ground
Anger, angry, ankh lashed
With her spear, a baby slashed
Voluptuous, vampire, violet eyes
How to love one you despise
Hush-a-bye baby, don't you cry
You know that you were made to die.

Eve Granzow

More Than Words

In my arms forever,
That's where I want you to be
To hold you in an endless embrace
Together, you and me
Every day, the farther I fall
With every kiss, the more I know
With every hug, the more I feel
Every minute with you, the more I'll show
You're everything I want
You're everything I need
I'll do anything for you
You know I aim to please
I want to kiss you all over
Careful not to miss a spot
Caress your every curve
And make your body hot
Indulging in the ecstasy
Of making love all night
Then feeling you in my arms
Until long past the morning light

Ryan Bansemer

My Forever Soulmate

The profile of a face with curves of perfection.
Fingertips caress over flawless velvet silk like skin.
Emerald blue eyes hypnotically mystical and inviting.
Lips so enticing, one's thirst is never quenched.
The meshing of bodies connect, like pieces of a puzzle.
Heart beating in rhythm, will explode like a volcano.
Rippling heart beats intensify a rollercoaster ride to ecstasy.
Uncontrollable emotions flow untamable like wild animals.
Bodies penetrate to a cosmic catatonic state.
The volcano ultimately erupts, lava flows bountiful.
The ferocious beasts become weakened and subdued.
One's body retreats to a peaceful serene state.
Gratifying was the moment of climax.
Magical is the seed sparking creation.
A potion of eternal pure love nothing can destroy.
Soil engulfs the root of unconditional love blinding soul to soul.
The growth of fertile harvest, with continue the legacy of the two.
In everlasting time and space it is they who are forever soulmates.

Marijean Majka

Night Angel

Your breath swirls,
soft upon my skin.

Your eyes drown me,
Loving, wanting and yet dim.

Your hands bring fire,
Still now, as they did then.

I blossom like a flower under your care.

Guiding your touch,
Here-now here-yes! There.

I call out your name,
As I explode in the dark .

Then I wake and you are still gone,
But, leaving your mark.

Lanell Cheek

Untitled

Long flowing braids to lock her knowledge
University of the streets is where she went to college
Large, deep, brown eyes know hardly nothing
Or like showing you're fake is like you're really something
Nose spread wide open like some art on display smelling all the
   bullsh*t coming my way
Her lips either smiling or ready to pucker
But she is always ready to spit out the truth, shes one motherf****r
She is sometimes mistaken for a dealer because shes fierce, a
   feller
What you see is what you get
It ain't cheep and it ain't free
It's unmistakably undeniably me.

Ashley Marie Hatker

First Love

Fire brand lips suckle;
Two volcanoes shudder, blow;
Molten lava flows!

Patricia L. Stubbs

The First Time

Softly, gently I gave in. I knew all along that he would win.
His cool hand upon my cheek, sweet scent, so sweet, I'm now so weak.
I feel I'm drifting - a taste so pure I know I'm shaking, I'm still not sure.
The lights are dim yet seem so bright, I need to run yet can't take flight.
I see him move close by my side, "I'm so scared," I softly confide.
His gentle voice so close to my ear, "I won't hurt you. You have nothing to fear."
His voice - he sounds so strong and sure - the inevitable pain I might endure.
With gentle persuasion I hear him say, "You must open up or there's no way."
"That's the way, just a little bit more." A thought flickers by, "will I be sore?"
I feel him in, I feel him pull
A soft ripping sound - then a brief lull.
"Not it's done, was that so bad?"
I know I've lost it, but I'm not sad.
Again his hand upon my cheek
Now I don't feel nearly as weak
My head is slowly beginning to clear
I laugh at myself because I had fear
I'm quickly up - I stumble from the booth
But my dentist stops me to hand me my tooth.

Barbara Joy Gleason

White

My curse is to fill pages,
They look so like me, empty and waiting,
That I've got to do something to fill the void,
I'd pour liquor on them but I know it will only wash them out,
So I pour liquor in me and set my throat on fire
And then open the flood gates and let my beer filtered thoughts
Fall into their opens arms.
My empty spaces becomes cluttered
And memories flow down the edges of the basin and onto the floor.
I trample them.
And then I give them away,
Have to, I can't keep holding onto them anymore.
So the page opens up and takes all the things I have to give,
And in return for a purpose it gives me solace.
A co-dependent relationship that's based on bullsh** words
and empty spaces.
Unhealthy? But solace and purpose can save the world.
Well, if not the world...
Then maybe me

Wayne Francis

A Wanting

Misunderstood because of the tears,
The world wanted so much, too much,
The perfect face, body, and mind.

Distraught by the screams of expectation,
The people demand more than could be given,
The impeccable age of innocence.

Aghast over the bleakness of the requirements,
The flocks of unknown pillage the dreams of a child,
The flawless way to just exist, a modest part of the vast world.

Estranged by those who scrutinize the every move 'with love',
The entirety of the universe give passion to a damaged fantasy,
The immaculate path to fame in the heart.

So with that, a wanting awaited,
The wanting of the way not to live, never to be,
The pills, the knives, they were a way.

A wanting for a disappearance of the soul,
The sickness developing into a contagious disease,
The disease of hatred, wrath, and rage.

A wanting for the fury that burns deeply within.

The flame blown out with a single, slight, unknown assassin.

Jean Sung

Sexual Acts Of The Frogs

Sh*t, sh*t, sh*t,
Hate everyone's bath.
8 candles to which I see.
Glowing endlessly.
In the odyssey,
Of the Cocoon,
Gliteringish toons,
of Baboons,

Sally born, 2 years to her name,
Dead!
Blown out of her brain.
Raped and mangled,
Like some florescent Ragdoll,

The killer walks off 10 deaths.
By his own hands,
All at his own command,
None were over 8.
And all, were raped

Jason Weigand

Untitled

The bomb was lit beneath the bridge just beyond two crystal rivers
In the midst of the evil deed its wick had waves and flickered
The cunning man had slid behind the rusted, lonely shed
He laughed and watched his "work of art" in hues of gold and red

Silhouettes screamed and hissed, shriveling in defense
Clawing at the fertile earth to escape a flaming fence
Again He laughed and licked his lips; sweet as honey is revenge
The torment they had passed along has come around again

The cloudy night had given way to ray of salmon sunshine
The old oak tree did its duty, shading where He resigned
Stubble ridden, He awakened, starving from his fun
To satisfy his lonely hunger, He decided to eat his gun

Elizabeth Jesson

My Wonderful Daughter, Jeannie

When you were just a baby, cradled in my arms,
Your delicate beauty revealed all your baby charms.
As a little girl, you were a joy, adorable and sweet
With golden ringlets, like a crown, set upon your head,
Also, you had a lovely, melodious voice,
And sang entertaining family and friends,
As you grew up, you became even more endeared,
You were my baby, the little girl I had reared.
When you became a teacher, you made me very proud,
I wanted to shout it, from the roof-tops, clear and loud.
Then, what a beautiful picture you made as a bride,
As you walked down the aisle with your Dad at your side
And on that blessed day, when you gave birth,
You gave me the most precious gift on earth.
Josh, a splendid grandson, caring and loving just like you,
You taught him very well, now a college student who does excel.
You've always been a wonderful daughter, one beyond compare,
The dearest daughter anywhere.
For your Happiness, Good Luck and Good Health, I forever pray
May your dreams and wishes all come true, each day in every way.

Irene Kanter

When I Think Of You

When skies are gray,
and the air is cold,
when sad songs play,
and old memories take hold,
I think of you.

When one lone bird sends out her call,
echoing silence in the air,
When tears with snowflakes start to fall,
and I tell myself I do not care,
I think of you.

When nothing seems to matter,
and I feel I can't go on,
When laughter's just a clatter,
and everything seems wrong,
I think of you.

When my life has no meaning,
and the new day holds no prayer,
when I need a friend to lean on,
and someone who really cares,
I think of you.

Judy Wilson

My Child, Whose?

Abandoned, cold, hungry and left alone,
Shivering bodies, eyes etched with pain with no home.
Sometimes left for pick-up trash,
Lord please help us erase the pain from the past.

One little baby girl born with 6 fingers and toes,
Almost perfect to God who knows.
Another born before her time,
Almost starved because mom neglect to feed on time.

One small child virginity ripped and ravaged,
Her body taken and her spirit and mind savaged.
My heart reached out to heal and help,
My anger grew with the blows she had been dealt.

He sent a baby boy afflicted with HIV,
I have loved him and taken care of him you see.
Perhaps I can adopt him some way,
I want my child, who's to be my son one day.

I am a mother of many little ones who,
Hearts were broken and hurt and abused.
It hurts so bad to see them go through,
My child, whom I love no matter whose.

Sharion Taylor

Untitled

Friends are something you get to choose
And best of friends you never lose
Near or far they are always there
To show how much they truly care
Unspoken words they understand
Love is given with each helping hand
Friendship is a love of a different kind
True friends are very hard to find
They pick you up when you're feeling down
Trust and understanding is always found
My love for my friends will never fade
I'm so happy with the friends I've made
So much laughter and fun to be had
Without my friends I'd surely be sad
I just want to tell you how much I care
If you ever need anything I'll always be there
Though no one knows what's around the bend
Friends will be friends until the end

Linda Ziemba

Outlaw

I stole an hour from the county, took a day from the state.
If my hands were gold-plated a finger they'd take.
I have to walk the straight and narrow, can't stumble or fall,
For if I'm ill or tired, I am an outlaw.

Two halves of a family that couldn't make it together
Can't make it apart, the ties can't be severed.
For as long as either half has too-little gold
I'm branded an outlaw by the state hard and cold.

The company, the county, the state, my ex-wife
Tear at my flesh taking parts of my life.
If I were chilled in the wind, or stopped to cry.
The vultures below would see that I die.

When I think I am falling and hope is gone
I see you again and my heart is with song.
I'm working today in wind bitter and raw,
But tomorrow I'll see you and they can call me outlaw.

Ronald L. Judson

Untitled

How is it that people have eyes and yet can not see
the beauty in the things around them?
Everyday people spend billions of dollars to buy things that are
beautiful to look at.
But how can you buy,
morning dew on blades of grass?
How do you buy,
a smile on the face of someone you love?
How is it that people have ears and yet hear so little?
Everyone trying to out talk everyone else.
When was the last time you tried to out listen them?
When was the last time you listened to the birds sing or even the
   sound of the wind?
Why is it that the blind see beauty and the deaf listen to so much,
but we who have all of our senses take them so much for granted?

AKIBA

My Love

We met as teenagers, young and free
We fell in love and became the best of friends
Although our future seemed uncertain
We knew that we would be together until the end.

Some years later my love became the victim of a careless accident
My heart and soul felt his pain and anguish
I prayed to God that an angel from heaven would be sent
to grant my one and only wish.

While sitting in the waiting room, I heard a voice down the hall
I laughed with much joy as I made my discovery
My love was up talking and shouting to us all
He was going to make a fine recovery!

Each day would hold a new challenge for my love
I tried to help him through this traumatic time
Together I knew we could help him rise above
And like a star he would once again shine.

Today our love is stronger than ever
I am so proud and happy to be his wife.
There is no doubt that there is no one better
for me to share this wonderful life.

Christine A. Doran

Mist By Mist

Time through time,
you did a crime.
Day through day,
you were away.
Night through night,
I held on tight.
Hour through hour,
I had no power.
Life through death,
you were untold to be the best.
Come through coming,
you lived your life now it's time to live mine
Mist by mist,
I miss you wishing you were here
or I were there!
I love you Tata (Daddy)

Monica Andazola

The Vietnam Wall

Two walls joined together,
What do they mean?
They speak of life forever.
They revive the dream.

They carry our heroes o'er the Great Divide
That separates them from the other Side.

They clearly form the letter "V"
That always stands for "Victory."

They signify 'Nam as a united land
Seeking better things with our helping hand.

They make one part of David's Star
Shining so bright in heaven afar.
They are the bloody beams of the Holy Cross
Helping us to bear our loss.
They are the arms of the author, Maya Lin,
Beckoning all to rest within.

Kevin J. Harrington

We Were Two

We were in the fast lane of the American Dream,
The Mercedes 300E did 0 to 60 in 8.1 seconds,
Our personas were treated as though they had been
honed at the same factory,
Perform... perform... many businesses... many investments, but...

Where does this path lead? Where did the joy and fun go?
When did we start talking about the weather?

So many months... years... all a blur... Weddings... Funerals...
just sign posts flashing by on the highway of life... grey
hair... wrinkles and $1800 suits that just won't fit.

One day... after years of waiting... we were three... Born 1:58
A.M. after 14 hours of deliberation about this incarnation,
A scaled down version of a human being, was welcomed.

The joy of watching her first sun rise filled the room and
permeated our very souls. We are filled with awe as we
again experience the first sight, touch, smell and taste.

Alissa, our bundle of Joy, cracked open the shell of misery
that had confined us for so long. Now...we long for
tomorrows filled with the adventure of learning experiencing
and seeing hope.... We Are.... joyously.... Three.

Richard F. Renales

A Pity

Within spring grasses green and tall
  is where I happened upon them all.
Small bodies no longer than the palm of my hand.
Colors of white, black and tan.

Each day I'd search the grasses complete
and find another...
    ...so dead so sweet.

Why their mothers left them that way
  is still a mystery—I just can't say.
Perfectly formed, some crying blindly to live
  no mother's devotion...no milk could I give.

By the end of a week sixteen bodies had been found
  guilt-free mothers sat around.
They watched with cold detached hearts
  while their own babies spirits did depart.

Why should I question these irresponsible cats?
  Some human mothers aren't any better than that.

Sharon Figone

Idaho!

The greatest state of all
beautiful are the rivers and streams
where the rivers rise and fall
and makes the eyes of others, beam.

Waters where one can fish and dream
the greatest is our state,
our dams, our lakes, our streams
no other has the likes to compensate.

No other has the likes of it,
makes no difference
if it was yesteryear or today
God put the waters of Idaho here to stay.

Mary Alice Knapp

Angel From The Light

The brightest light that can be seen
Shines from the heavens, beyond reality.
Purest of all forms that can ever be true
Was the angel of the light, who came and took you.

I sometimes stare into the sky at night
In search for the angel, that came from the light.
A dream of Elysian fields, reality for you
Reaching for nirvana, an existence come true.

Soaring through the clouds, aviating through time
Multitudes of angels, paradise in mind.
The starry skies of heaven, forgiving all your sins
Closer to the light, driven by the winds.

My field of dreams, forever to be
My guardian angel, to remain by me.
A faithful desire, being together again
Is a genuine wish, from the beginning to the end.

Terry Ann Shuman

Incubated Dreams

Dreams come in segments, dripping wax as they burn in the mind.
Thoughts are simple water droplets, leaking down the spine.
Ideas are waves of mighty oceans, pressing ever on,
And lying in the stillness is a soul forever gone.

Lost inside a different womb, too large to comprehend.
Finding wealth and happiness in a tunnel with no end.
The old times are behind him now; the new life just ahead.
Swimming in the real world now, the land of all that's dead!

Jeremy B. G. Goldstein

Untitled

I stand by the open window,
Feeling the cool breeze
On my flushed, tear-stained face.

The whistle of the wind
In the leafless trees below
Sings a song of comfort to my broken heart.

I see a red lea flutter,
So hesitantly to the cold, brown grass
Like the drop of blood that has just fallen from my hand.

I look down on the world,
From my high perch,
And find it bearable.

Amy Loiseau

Untitled

There is a time
When night and day are one.
When the deep blue sky
Is lit by a shining star
That even the sun cannot overshadow.
When the moon is a glowing sliver in the sky,
Its light in harmony with the sun's gentle rays.

There is a time
When there is no time.
No pain of the past,
No fear of the future.

There is a time
When everything comes together.
When feelings begin,
And thinking is ended.

There is a time
When there is nothing at all,
And nothing matters,
Except the moment.

Meghan Grady

The Soul

The soul, it is something that some people do not understand.
A soul cannot be sold or given away,
But a soul can be corrupted or contaminated.
Someone with a corrupted soul is like someone that has no soul.
Without a soul, you cannot "live."
The soul is where your hopes and dreams are stored.
Many believe that once a soul is bad, it cannot turn back.
I believe that a soul has the power to do anything.

Patrick Urban

Untitled

The sky is blue, but looks grey today,
For the love of our lives has flown away,
God took him away,
His life too short,
His short young life he had to abort,
He needed an extra angel to help him cope,
One that was filled with much love and hope,
He took you away filled us with grief and sorrow,
Hoping and praying we'll feel better tomorrow,
We know that you're in God's loving arms,
Forever protected from anymore harm,
We'll love you forever and ever you know,
But somehow that just doesn't soften the blow,
We want you home, home here with us,
But God needed you more and in him we shall trust.

Christine Ramirez

Where You Stand

On this day you are joined together in front of friends,
family and the Lord above. May you never forget the
feelings that have brought you together, the meaning of your
rings, and the value of your love.

When things get tough hold on to each other, love each
other, and when it seems to rough, hold out your hand.
Remember to communicate and listen, the love you joined on
this day, and remember to give enough room to let your
love grow and expand. Take the time to hear what your
hearts have to say and genuinely try to understand,
remember to thank God for joining this woman and
this man, and finally, remember the promises you've
made to each other where alone, you no longer stand.

Lisa Marie Ansell

Every Settling Dusk

With every settling dusk, and every waking dawn,
Another year has come and gone.
Oh, how I miss those blue eyes and freckled face,
You left your mark, all over the place,
Especially that smile of yours and your quick-witted charms,
Why can't I hold you just once more in my arms?
You were snatched away from us too fast,
It makes me long every day for the past.
I try so hard not to be blue,
While clinging to the memories I have of you.
Every day the time slips away,
I find myself wishing I'd said what I wanted to say.
Sometimes it saddens me deep,
So much, uncontrollably, I weep.
Realizing that the best and rest of you is gone,
I find it hard to believe that life must go on!
Knowing this is what you expect out of me,
Although I do so much want to disagree.
Each day I hope the next won't be as tough,
For I hurt from missing you so, so much!

Beverly Tischer

A Tribute To Daughters (Sherry)

A daughter just might be,
The most wonderful person in the world,
A man may be proud to have a son,
But a daughter is there for everyone.

A daughter is born to be,
A symbol of love, beauty, and charity.
Wherever she goes, and whatever she does,
Her life is special to friend and family all.

A daughter is kind and soft,
She is pleasing to the touch.
Her hair is sweet,
And her eyes are honest and always loving.

A daughter can be a sister,
A daughter is a friend,
She makes her parents proud,
One day a man will have her for his own?

A daughter is a part of life.
That only a woman will truly know.
So God gave us daughters...
And a daughter is there for life.

Michael G. Southern

Untitled

After a while
you realize that love is never a sure thing
and promises do get broken.

And you realize that pain can grow
and tangle your emotions.
Your heart grieves with every tear you cry.

After a while
you become scared.
The chances you once took are now walls
blocking your every move.
You hurt.

But with each passing second, you begin to heal.
The pain slowly eases its grip on your heart
the tears fade away.

And you realize that it is okay to smile
that things do get better.

You've hurt... you've grieved... you've learned.
But most of all, through, every heartache,
every tear cried, and every good-bye...
you've learned to live.

Mary Eldridge

My Compelling Medusa

Awake.
A lobby.
A hotel lobby in the forest of time.
A time when people breathed the world
but did not share the exhalation.
The body was too feeble with a seething oppression
to see the stains of yesterday's sweat.

Like the uptown hooker
who crosses her legs
not for comfort but view,
your eyes evoke prisms of prayers.

Like the bumble of a bee
who flights to heights
of this and there,
your eyes transcend the altar of my attention.

Like the doors of a church
burdened with the responsibility
of the living
your eyes turn me to stone as I seek salvation in your face.

Bradley Jay Phipps

Intense Fear

My heart races repeatedly, bouncing inside my chest.

Tension consumes me; my muscles flex in defense.

My breath hiccups a short inward gasp.

My arms reach out groping to find support.

My legs thrust forward; kicking for life.

My skin tightens, sealing the terror within me.

My blood flushes my veins in a single fluid movement.

My face whitens, shocked, looking of horror and

My eyes reflect the fear that I feel.

I hate it when I lean back on a chair too far.

Erik Jay Johansen

Forever Yours

One day we'll meet again, my love
Where did you go these last four years?
Your illness consumed our every moment
We had no time for everyday joys
And now you're gone and the mind remembers
The life we had - the ups and downs.
You were my partner, my love, my friend, my helper
You always made the hurts go away
You always made the road less bumpy.
The memories go back to when the children came
They grew and spread their own wings.
And always you were the center of our lives
Always there to guide and counsel
Never taking time for yourself
Your faith during these last dark years
Spread to us and gave us hope.
But now the dark and lonely nights are endless
With constant thoughts of only you
And though they say "she's coping well"
My tear-streamed pillow gives me away.

Frances Carusillo

Untitled

OrGive I am pardoned, an offense forgotten
EcipRoCate a mutual give and take, and I equivocate
NsPire a guide, a source, a breath of life; in me a spark ignites
NdUrE Despite hardship, a chain unlinked, a tolerance borne
OuRiSh I am fed, a desire sustained
EfiNe A meaning determined, I am afforded a greater understanding
HelTEr I am protected, covered from harm, safe within a haven
OnOr Imbued with reverence, I am glorious and noble
Nhabit I reside in and have found a home, an even presence exists
RoSper I thrive and grow, am rendered fortunate and successful
HarE Given with openness, I partake equally

FrIenDshIps...the ones truly lost are seldom found....

Jerry L. Kramer II

Complete

My heart fluttered at a passing thought of you,
I pondered and realized what I was afraid to do.
To Love again; to live life I must have you to be complete.
With you in my life, life will exciting and bittersweet.
Face to face with myself,
My life is like a book on a shelf.
The more I have loving memories of you,
The more I can face the tomorrows anew.

C. M. Nelson

Meet Me Halfway

I need someone who'll understand.
Understand, and hold my hand.

I thought I had but I was wrong.
So, I built a wall and built it strong.

Another love, and another good-bye.
I turned my back and started to cry.

Once again, I loved too much.
All that is real, is this pain I clutch.

You're better off if you'll just go.
You'll never understand this pain that flows.

So go away, and leave me here.
I'll only run, if love comes near.

There must be someone, somewhere, someday.
Who will love me forever and meet me halfway.

Lucilyn Wherritt

Who Are You?

Who are you to say I can't succeed?
Who are you to believe I can't achieve?
Who are you with remarks, my skin's too dark?
Who are you to say I've missed the mark?
Who are you to think I can't be taught?
That this messed up world is all my fault.
Who are you to say I can't walk, I can't talk?
I can't read, I can't write.
That my future doesn't look too bright.
Who are you to say I need Ebonics?
When what I really need is Phonics.
Let go of me!
Turn me loose, I say!
Must I hear these words everyday?
You don't know me or how I feel.
Going through life not knowing what's fake or what's real.
I don't know why life dealt me this card
or why my life has been this hard.
I don't know why life dealt me this hand, but I've come to realize
that I really can. I can. . . I can. . . Who are You?. . .

Angela Vereen

Reach Out To Others

Reach out to others every day,
Yes, reach out to others in every way.

Reach out to others with a loving smile,
It may be just what they need, and it's so worthwhile.

Reach out to others and speak a kind word,
Perhaps they need it if they are disturbed.

Reach out to others with compassion and care,
It might lift them up if they are feeling despair.

Reach out to others with a listening ear,
They may need someone who will be still and hear.

Reach out to others you see in tears,
Encounter with you may release all their fears.

Reach out to others with words that are kind,
Meeting you will be a friend they will find.

Reach out to others and help them to understand,
God's their loving Father and He's holding their hand.

Sister Agnes Curran, PBVM

Nineties Woman

She's a nineties woman I want you to know.
She has no time to be moving slow.
Going to college and raising a child,
-making her way through a world gone wild.
She can't stay home. She has to pay that bill.
If she won't do it, - no one else will.

Hey Nineties Woman, where you rushin' to
Is there room in this life to run beside you?
You're so hard to hold onto.
Guess I'll get by with thoughts of you.

Trying to make a leap and catch up with your star.
Run as fast as you can just to stay where you are.
If you keep on pushin', you'll find your way.
The world's gonna hear from you some day.

Every day at the job they've got demands on you.
How are you gonna find time for that mid term too
The search goes on for a man on the level,
but all you find are in league with the devil.
Hey Nineties Woman would it be wrong
for you to slow down and listen to your song?

Bradford Earle Randolph

Faith

They liken you to an ancient wall
  In the wash of the sea of Time,
Which wears the mortar from your joints
  To weaken you so you'll fall.

They greatly err, mistaking you
  For the rubble of human thought
Piled up by man to withstand Time's sea,
  God's test of redeeming worth.

You are the rock beneath it all,
  Single, Seamless, One.
Against you crashes Time's thundering sea,
  You fling it back as a spray.

David A. Freed

Willing Heart

There's nothing more precious that I can
give than to tell you how you make me feel;

To open and reveal the hurt inside that you can heal;
remove those scars they do reveal.

There were times in love where pain grew
strong; when hate seemed more my fate.

I have never known a love so real; that
pierced my hate and will; I offer you with
all I feel, my willing heart that you may
heal. Into my loneliness you have come
restored my faith a new.

So if you believe as I believe, then never
hurt or still this willing heart that you
have healed.

Wayne M. Wall III

Melissa

Someone who understands your dreams,
and encourages you to reach them,
is a friend.
Someone that listens with an open heart,
when everyone has shut you out,
is a friend.
Someone who will stand behind you when you are right,
but will stand in front of you when you're wrong,
is a friend.
Someone who is there in your time of need,
and knows just what to say,
is a friend.

Someone who is there to lead you through the dark,
even when there seems to be no glimmer of light,
is a friend.
A friend is all of this and more,
she is a gift from God,
like an angel being guided by our father himself.

Amberly J. Lake

Please, Lord

I wuz sittin' in the kitchen aperched upon my stool
Watchin' Grandpa do his work 'cuz he still goes to school,
Thinkin' 'bout the things we do when it's a shiny day,
We go outside and have some fun; he really loves to play.

But it's been rainin' so much, Lord, we never get to go.
It's way too muddy in the yard, but this I'm sure you know.
I miss the fun out in the yard that me and Grandpa had.
Why are we havin' all this rain? Is it 'cuz I been bad?

If I have, forgive me, Lord, but please just let me say
If it don't stop this rainin' soon, he'll be too old to play.

Windell R. Mimms Jr.

Constructive Learning

Is not learning a pleasurable experience? It is also sometimes painful. Often times we receive criticism and it is classified as constructive or destructive. But does this reception not depend on our individual perceptions? Is there anyone who can not learn from a constructive standpoint? Lessons learned should not be forgotten. How can one forget the lesson learned that caused a life to be saved...yes, maybe even your own?

The world is not only populated with the supercritical...As you stop and reminisce...have not some critics used wisdom in their delivery that left a positive effect and lacked an ulterior motive? Can we attempt to re-align our thinking because even through criticism...negative or positive comes into your life invited or uninvited...make a concentrated effort and be determined to receive and channel it as an opportunity for a constructive learning experience...no matter who the messenger may be.

There is Joy and Growth in choosing to learn constructively.

Valerie L. Matthews

My Maple Tree

From my window I can see
Fall colors on my maple tree
Leaves of yellow, red and brown
All will soon come tumbling down
Leaving branches stark and bare
To shiver in the wintry air
The tree will sleep 'till spring time when
Bud and leaf will come again

May R. Francis

Peace - A Walk In A Forest

Peace is like walking through a silent forest.
It's the touch of the while angel's warmness,
     The birds soaring high or a deer walking by.
The flowers that show Mother Nature's pride.
No guns, fights, and wars
Just peace like a bald eagle soaring high.
Just plain old peace or the touch of God's hand.
Loving, sharing, peace or, the smell of
     spring or fall or, the sound of birds chirping
     in the morning.
Like sitting around a camp fire all warm inside
     and that is called peace.

Josh Henningson

A Wish To Leave This Chair

Be damned all for the pain I suffer
helpless as I am behind these closed doors I mutter.
Passing by, my eyes uplift this smile I seem to borrow
Like the mirrors inside each time they break
as do the steps of walking, I'd just love to take

My tears fall sweet yet sour
For this burden I have without my power
I walk still and straight bellow all unto my way
with the hopes to keep on going even after the unpleasant
words they say.
From them not just to glance but a thought for me a chance.
A chance for when I come for none to sit and stare.
But again they stare so I only keep to hoping.
Then again they stand unto my path to turn away
among them none who care.

So then again I damn those who look upon this chair
then I wish as so my life would be as fare
My wish just one to be granted, granted just for me
from the heavens I could just be wanted
and my life could just be free.

Paul Holtgrefe

Pu' Pe' He From Sacred Falls

As I strolled the trails of sacred falls.
Her serene beauty abounds before me.
Entering into her deep valleys of lush greenery.
I am greeted by a small white
fragrant flower, that scent the misty cold air.

Pu' pe' he, a wild flower that blooms
along the trails of sacred falls, in abundance.

Pu' pe' he, a wild flower that once
ornated the head and shoulders,
of kings and queens of the royal
family, that once walked these mighty trails of old.

Bending towards gently retrieving
a blossom from her caressing care.

I whisper in silent words of greetings.
I adore you, pu' pe' he, and gently
caress your ever so sweet soft
petals against my cheeks, with love from my heart.

And, as I depart you, I adorn myself with this beautiful blossom
that has been taken from your bosom, oh! Sacred falls.

For now, I must bid you love and aloha, until my return.

Dennis P. Kealoha

Untitled

Last night you held me in your arms...
You said your love is like the air I breathe,
that'll follow me no matter where, or if I'd ever run away.
Your words, precious notes to a beautiful song
I remember by heart even to this day.
Your angelic smile, like a pearl, a rare treasure
that offers splendor from its beauty and grace,
You and me, the happiest picture adorning
the walls of my heart where I can see the beauty of your face.
Your enthusiasm, tenderness and compassion,
my wings that let me fly so high until they broke and I fell.
You, my angel, that took me to heaven but then
let me back down, leaving a soul left to dwell...
Last night you held ime in your arms and
I saw you smiling at me, telling me we'd be forever
living in a dream.
You didn't lie; when I finally opened my eyes,
you were gone, my love,
just like in a dream.

Imelda Reyes

He Knows

How I really feel
Is feeling like dying
Call it no guts or respect,
Call it anything you want

He knows, he sees
Oh how I could not sleep
It's dark, it's bright
It woke me up for the night

My pain, my tears, and my prayers
Day and day, and night,
Nighttime in my day, and day in the night,
In the night, in the night

I wait, it doesn't change
I listen, it doesn't stop
I look, it's not there
I hope, I pray

How I really think
Isn't any of your business
How I feel, you cannot feel
I ache, I hurt, (and) I'm loved.

Margie S. Chism

As I Fall Asleep

Late at night, unable to sleep
Thoughts of you run through my mind
I feel an emptiness so deep with in

I look out the window
Now gazing upon the moon
I wonder are you looking
Are you thinking of me as I think of you

Wishing you were here with me
A feeling of restlessness fills my heart
I feel so helpless as I stare into the dark

All the world seems to be sleeping
All is so quiet
Even the wind is just a whisper

As I lay my head upon the pillow
I close my eyes
A tear rolls down my face

There I find you in my dreams
You put your arms around me
Love fills my heart, as I fall asleep

Tina Nash

In My Heart My Friends Will Stay

My friend you are, and that you'll Stay.
Even if we separate and go our own way.

We would have rough times with each other,
But whatever happened, one of us would be there for one another.

If we do part, I promise till my dying day,
In my heart you all will stay.

And I hope one fine day,
In the future we will come together and stay
this very same way.

Ashley Olin

The Conversation

"Whither goest thou, yon lice bug
I beseech thee, quit thou my gaze
Lest I crush thee 'neath mine gauntlet!"
The bug stopped and looked up, speaking
"Lo, methinks 'tis the visage of mine God upon me.
Fallest I to mine knee, resolv'd forthwirth to pay homage."
"Villainous bug, hearest thou not
Mine business with thee? Be off;
Quit this place"
"He speaks," says the bug
"And yet I know not his tongue
Nor his design.
Pray, share thine wisdom, speakest thou divine truth?
Tellest me."
Quoth the exterminator, "Stupid bug."

David Sweat

November

Flurries falling here and there,
With the fresh smell of cinnamon in the air,
The baking of turkey makes me feel so good,
just like thanksgiving should,
Drinking hot chocolate is the best,
While the birds fly south to build their nests,
Crisp autumn leaves crunching on the ground,
Hardly make a sound when the wind blows them around,
Family's gather to share pumpkin pie
and add whip cream sky-high,
when it's all over our memories are saved in our hearts,
and we can remember them part by part.

Greg Marchesiello

God's Grace

God Grace is every where
but we need to know that we
need it in our hearts
Because Jesus care
This is the only way
we can receive it.
is ask and we will know it's there
we can't go on ignoring
His love for us
in life so one can receive His
we just have to do our part
God Grace is ever
near. We will not have to fear
Just keep our trusting Him and He will take care of everything
Him have don't get weary
Our journey is just begun
Grace and mercy is what it take
The read is ever winding rough and steep.
but step by step, His Grace leads
me with miles to go before I sleep

Alma Bailey

An Ode To Aunt Linda

Once upon an evening dreary
Looking in the fridge quite weary
So I could find a slab of meat
Meat, ah meat, oh what a treat

A slab of meat loaf would really thrill me
These 'Veggie Burgers' are going to kill me
The meat meals in my house are very few
When it comes to meat my mom says P.U.!

Filet Mignon with sauteed onions
T-Bone steak with broiled scallions
Chicken soup riddled with pasta
Roasted beef and smoked kielbasa

The dishes above just hit my fancy
They're good enough for the Pharaoh Ramses
My good Aunt Linda always pulls through
With the best food in Pennsylvania and New Jersey too!!

Thomas DeZolt Hanrahan

Children

You carry on day to day
While someone cries far away
You think the biggest problem is not having a new car
You never once stop to think of those starving afar
Children walk around with no clothes, no shoes
Yes, it's true they're paying, but do you know who's dues?
How can we see what's happening, yet look the other way?
The promise of tomorrow, our prices they do pay
Money is what we want, it's all we think we need
While in another land there are mouths we should feed
I know that we all see it
But do any of us care
Just stop and ask yourself
Is it really fair?

Jessica Meck

Little Girl

Little girl little girl, say your prayer,
Tell it all to Jehovah for he will care,

Little girl, little girl give the poor a dime
Please Jehovah! Get rid of crime!

Love Jehovah with your heart, strength and mind!
Love Jehovah for he is kind.

Amanda Cummins

Untitled

During summer days, we would become toasted fish, and sun-colored
fences would become tight-ropes.
And our jeans would become constipated of cocoa-roasted puddles.
And our mammas would be sitti'n on the porches holding lemonade
In one hand and band-aids in the other.

They would sit and chat of two-week old beauty parlor gossip
As we would
Launch to attain the choke-cherry fruits, and
Throw rocks at the honeycombs.

The summer-licious aroma of the stands' sweaty apricots and
raisons and nature-scared apples, and the cotton-puff-filled
fields made us forget about home until our bellies bawled

....then we would outrun the chimerical grass sharks.

Chimere Lynch

Dad

Dad, when I was very young,
I didn't quite understand;
The things you wanted instilled in me,
Were part of the Grown-up Plan.

You tried to teach me right from wrong,
I know it must have been hard;
The more you tried, the louder I cried,
Leave me alone, I want no part.

Yet you never gave up on me,
You knew something I didn't knew;
That one day the lessons taught,
In me, would begin to show.

Now that I've become a man,
I know exactly where you were coming from;
Had it not been for you sticking with me,
The battle never would've been won.

I hope that I will never let you down,
And you won't mind telling anyone;
Hey! See that man?
I am proud, that He is My Son.

Bobbydyne McMillan

Sonnet To Dad

A quiet man lies here within this tomb.
Is there no sense of justice? No fair play?
He was taken from me, aye, a bit too soon;
Who would but give this man another day?
If only I could see him just once more,
And stroke his brow, and comfort him somewhat;
There'd be nothing in this world left to explore,
I'd stay awhile, and leave all else to luck.
When last I saw him on those stairs, so proud,
I knew within my breast the end was near;
Whisp'ring gently, for I could not speak too loud,
I cautioned him, tread light; he did not hear.
Oh, Dad, I loved you so, albeit too late!
Ne'er fear, dear heart, I'll see you at the gate.

Shirley M. Rovezzi

A New Beginning

I sit in my room where it is pink and pretty,
So far away from the hectic city.
I am so happy to be here away from it all,
I was so glad when I answered the call.
It came at a moment when I was so tired,
To make a decision before I retired.
Why not escape to a great new beginning,
It would be just like the great final inning.

Merle Monteforte

To The One I Love , A Barrenness Cry

To all my love
You were there
For nine monthly cycles, I was hid
You were there
When I saw my first peek at dawn
You were there
In my first stumbling attempts
You were there
I'm now near wrinkles, and empty
I long for the innocent I've yet to hold
To smell the fresh new dew of milk
No fruit, has my tree prepared
Which leaves me barren, desolate — in despair
My life is incomplete, hidden in shame
Only you can answer my cry
Somewhere, when time was void
Was there a plan for me?
For my eternal days
Do I have myself to blame?
Are you there, still?

Easter Moore

Untitled

You were everything to me
I cried over you, I would have died for you
I would have done anything just so you would come be mine
why can't you understand how much I ache just to have you by my side
you were everything to me
but now at least I can't say I didn't try
and I can move on without a regret ever passing by
now I can see your face, look up into your eyes
and not feel anything inside
because you were someone I would've done anything for
but now I realize I never was or ever will be anything to you
so it's easier now for me to say goodbye
and let you go with only a few tears falling from my eyes
instead of my whole world crashing down right before me

Becky Carlson

Cruel World

A cruel world we live in, the only world I was given
From smallest to tallest there is struggle
The white and the black have color tuggles,
This is a cruel world we live in, the only world I was given
Twelve years of school, a job is expected after graduation
"Sorry we can't hire you because you don't have enough education"
Middle class to lower class due to inflation,
A cruel world we live in, the only world I was given

They say no advice is good advice
I guess that's why when elders speak, generation X scatter like mice
Sex, drugs, and money in my neighborhood surely entice
Will I be forgiven for my sins or will I pay the ultimate price,
Yes indeed, a cruel world we live in, the only world I was given
Those that read this should understand what I'm feeling
Today's life is unstable like cracks in the ceiling
The world turns so fast there is not enough time for healing
While most solve their problems with robbing and stealing,
I choose to coop with my raw dealing,
The cruel world I live in, the only world I was given

Steven D. Johnson

Tribute

Through a shadow of doubt; you are my light....
When my path seems uncertain; it's your hand I choose to take...
A trace of bitter-sweet sentiment touches my crimson soul...
Our authentic bond remains an enigma to those which heed its tale..
My defender; thou art my being; you are indeed my sanity in this
world of craziness..

Kiersten Clements

The Last Unicorn

When the mists have cloaked the trees,
And the hunters have called it a day;
When the butterflies folded their wings,
And upon the grassy fields they lay;
As the flowers droop their heads in deference,
You may catch a glimpse of the last unicorn.

In the still depths of the forest,
As the moonbeams gleam upon the lake;
When all of the cheerful, chirping birds
Have ceased their noise to make;
If you move slowly and look carefully,
You might be able to see the last unicorn.

If your heart is devoid of evil intentions,
And your soul is pure and good,
And the reflections of your mind
Lead you to do all that you should,
Only if you believe with all of your might
Will you be blessed to behold the last unicorn

For it will reveal its splendor only where truth abounds,
Where faith resides, and where innocence dwells.

Miranda R. Rabatin

The African Soul

Sing your glory, sing oh Africa
Cling to your past, cling oh land of mighty kings
Your past has been buried in the ashes of violence
Your children have been scattered around the world
Yet your shape is still intact

Sing your glory, sing oh Africa
Bring back your memories, bring oh land of brave warriors
Your territory was forced to drink your children's blood
Your fertile brains were deported overseas
Yet your face is still exuberant

Sing your glory, sing of Africa
Ring your royal bells, ring oh root of human race
Your mountains have been drenched with your hot tears
Your eyes are fed up with the cruelty of your oppressors
Yet your shriek of horror is still misunderstood

Sing your glory, sing oh Africa
Wing your message, wing oh root of sagacity
Your children's heart cannot vibrate without your blood
Your soul cannot breath without your past
Yes! Your hope is always high

Diasonama J. Mafuta

God's Power And Plan

Sure you are special, you are by far,
God's heavenly plan earthlings shouldn't mar.
The Master created us superior for a reason,
To rule and represent Him in all seasons.

You're not the only one puzzled by life,
The uncertainty does cause some strife.
Why look for peace in the wrong place,
It's easily found through God's grace.

The void and search for the unknown,
Yet ignore the simple remedy the Father has sown.
He always gives you and me a choice,
Trust Him, repent, and show remorse.

Money, power, and worldly goods,
Don't yield contentment and never could.
Faith, joy, and happiness yours can be,
Allow God's love to set you free.

Laurine Simons

For Leroy....

I watched him,
the barbs of their derisions
clinging to his flesh,
beneath fossiled brows
eyes of liquid steel
carved in a face of molten determination,
mirrored their circled journey of ignorance.
Gaze fixed on El Tucuche.
Fragments of a dream clings
to a disembodied dream catcher,
rendered useless by their duendom,
yet he toils on.
Flayed fingers worked the canvas with an urgency,
time held no promises.
Shameless reds encircled warped yellows,
while cool blues invite earthy browns
to witness the demise of a people
a people
trapped between midnight and dawn.

Lennox Alleyne

Illusions

They say they hate you
by the way you act
but do they really know you?
Or just the mask you wear?
You are wrapped up in a little package
yet one that means a lot
I swore to you I'd never leave
it wasn't you I promised
but your lame little act
I see through it like a window
My fears are overbearing
due to the sea-saw like relationship
that is us
you left me only after I left you.
But I never knew you
I only knew your permanent Halloween costume
that you wear 24/7
but my love, all you are is
a clown.

Cristin A. Napolitano

Mother

A year ago you closed your eyes
We gathered together to say our good-byes
As you drifted into a heavenly sleep
Our hearts and minds began to weep
After months of feeling lost with grief
Came a day that brought some relief
While standing in Church this Christmas Eve
I saw you with Dad, this I believe
As I looked to the altar, I began to view
The Lord Jesus Christ embracing you

As I awakened from this heavenly grace
I saw your smile on a child's face
She stood there holding her mother's hand
Just as I remember doing in another land

I soon began to realize
As I wiped the tears from my eyes
I once again can hold your hand
When we walk through the Promised Land

William J. Farly

Ode To The Computer

My boy and I were playing games as we are won't to do,
News flash says that, to keep up, we need computers too.
I barely manage it myself, I thought, as he yelled "boo!"
After all, the child isn't that much more than two.
The alphabet's a piece of cake with videos to view,
And numbers, because we milk cows and we count every "moo."
But computers to a preschooler, now that was something new.
Why, I've just cleaned the VCR and pondered who to sue
For sculpting it so sandwiches go in and turn to goo.
He colors and he cuts out shapes but he still eats the glue;
He can't stay in the lines as yet and chooses any hue.
Computers require disciple and I began to rue
All the times we chose to play and did not listen to
Dr. Spock (or was it Emily Post?) who said that you
Should take your child to museums and the opera in lew
Of opting for McDonald's then to ToyLand or the zoo.

Leianne Wright

Oh Cherished Mother

Oh cherished mother,
How you faced death,
Like a bold, armored warrior
Striving to soar about its potency,
Focusing - not on the enrapturing power of self-pity
But on nourishing the beloved,
On the pathway to answers,
Rarely centering on the tears that
could not be washed away,
On the stars that could not
Pierce through the blackness of the sky,
So that with time and mankind's guiding hand
You found the key
That bestowed you the will
To lock the steal doors of despair,
Transforming heartache to an elongated passage
With roads so windy and far reaching
That to journey would be to rekindle that
Which may best remain only of memories creation

Susan Loeb

The Angelic Man

Facts, worthy to repeat,
Concern a trip in summer's heat.
Two ladies to protect their feet
Used horse and buggy for relief.

For many miles, all went well.
Then galloping horses created a story to tell.
Into grass one lady fell
While stones and rocks quelled the other's yell.

From the field, the angelic man came—
Somber, sad, James by name.
A moving toe! Would his be fame or blame?
Yes, his home and her home became the same.

Summer passed! Then winter's snow!
Prayers sounded from high and low!
Love ignited, for heaven and earth reflected a glow,
And the lady's health knew no foe.

Mother's rose bush fresh with morning's dew
Speaks peace anew.
In statue the angelic man grew,
Symbolic of a select few.

Ann B. Kissam

Stick In My Eye

Some days are like crabby monsters all grimy and green, I
Guess you can tell my moods exceptionally mean, some
People like shingles really get under my skin, I think
"Why am I like that" it seems almost a sin, then I cross
The path of a mirror and what do I see, why it looks like
A stick, in my eye, the size of a tree! In shock I think,
"Ouch, oh my God!" please help, now what do I do? Now I
See with new eyes, "Oh Lord, I am such a fool." I look
Again, I'm relieved, that tree is no longer there, but my
Soul clearly ponders the message this vision shares, for
In my mind I judged this man, not understanding his heart,
I'm glad to have found the ugly in me, for now I know where
To start, through new eyes I looked at my mood and found
Where my heart has been, I realized my frame of mind could
Lead me into many sins, I have to nurture that tree and
Plant it in fresh new soil, I'll prune and pull weeds,
With laborious heart I'll toil, "Dear Lord I pray, I have
To start somewhere, I promise to try," and "oh, I almost
Forgot, thank you dear Lord for that stick in my eye . . ."

Jan Lubecke

One Wish

If given one wish, that you knew would come true, to spend with the
　　coming of night
For what would you wish when you saw that one star, shining so
　　clear and so very bright
If poverty you know would your one wish not go for money and gold
　　and such things for wealth?
If sickness you know would your one wish not go toward curing your
　　body and a lifetime of health?
Only one wish to spend on all you may need and all you may want
With all the things I want and need in confusion my thoughts would
　　be caught.
Would you wish for the power to control the world if given this
　　chance?
Fame may be your only wish; actor, singer, great knight on steed
　　with a sword and lance.
Would you spend your one wish thinking only of you?
Would the world be forgotten and the hardship we've been through?
Our history tells its tale and much of what we hear is wrong.
But would any of this cross our minds until after our one wish
　　was gone?
If given one wish, that you knew would come true....

Jason W. Putney

Circus Parade

The parade is gone now.
Still faintly sounding, the flippant calliope.
Finally the Avenue falls quiet.
Vanished, gone, the buoyant, boisterous crowd.
Like autumn leaves, reluctant to join the wind.

Only the empty thoroughfare remains,
Littered in the horses wake the
Green-brown steaming heaps,
With nostril-stinging odors floating.
Inflict an acrid, sour stench.
Nasty end to a frolicking day. But listen!
A little tempest! Hear the curious rushing around?
There! It is the water wagon,
Flushing down the Boulevard,
Hurrying all the refuse into gutters.
See it tumbling, fleeing along downhill,
As though to catch the horses.
Perhaps to teach them better manners.

Howard R. Dentz

For You

A soft synchronicity of mechanical
complexity, where souls boil in the friction
of the unison heartbeat. Exciting into vapors,
dancing upon restless lips, condensing as one breath.
Swallowing passion's fire laced in a kisses flavor.
Purity surrendered to gaze into the eyes of
eternity. Melting into one flesh by a heat
unmatched by a thousand summers, and leaves
the sun jealous of such temperature and
radiance. This night was not meant for a
mortal world, yet it slaves to the electric
touch of oscillating rapture. Intoxicating
perfection of symbiotic intention. Golden
ring of promise cast in the union of a
dream, drifting forever as an endless
embrace. I am the last to seek the
capability of an ordained completeness.
I stand alone in belief of you; my vision.
I live only for the possibility of fantasy,
only for the myth of happiness, only for you.

Cory P. McClellan

Change

Smile within your soul
this change is stormy, it thrusts you from side to side
loving and hating you all at once
propelling you into a kaleidoscope of emotion;
but you must celebrate the wonder of the change; relinquish to the
change

   The change will lead you to a pleasure unfulfilled
   the change will soar with your spirit
   the change will rock you, love and challenge your psyche to
   unknown pleasures

Become this change; feel its sinuous warmth envelope you - the
tartness of its taste, while it rolls over you

The hardness of its penetration into your being, the delight of its
madness the wonder of the change.

Pamela Marlowe

Clear Thoughts

As I walk, the breeze ruffles my hair
The clear blue waters lap at my feet
The sand oozes between my toes.

I rest to ponder the water's beauty
To let the sand envelop my feet
To watch the wind clear things from its path.

I recommence my walk - slowly, pensively,
Basking in the calmness, the serenity, the peace.

Heather Batchelor

For Daemon

I am alive in this reality
what is my life? What is my dream?
I long to bust out from this womb-
To breathe sick air until my tomb-

When do I begin to have a choice?
Before I birth? When I grow hair?
I make sounds now - is this my voice?
I want to know love.

Whatever happens, however, long I live -
I am a part of you, eternally -
When I am not seen, I am so near -
My voice is loud, strong and clear!!

David Stashko

Malfeasance No Reason

The order of the day is how to deal with everyday life.
Contemplating where ones soul the essence of their being.
You need only look in the mirror.
Some are imprisoned by their deeds.
What they've done.
But others are caged without their knowledge.
Lost inside themselves.
If only we had personal x-ray machines.
So we could follow our veins follow them like road maps.
That lead to the brain.
There lies the key to freedom.
Freedom from ourselves.
Which is the mist the world tries to grasp.
Keep reaching searching because at the end of this mighty journey.
Lies the rainbow of humanity.
Malfeasance no reason the invisible handcuffs.
That can only be broken by love and understanding.

Charles Caldevell

He Said He Loves Me

Time seems to have frozen
but the mind just can't be fooled
as the days pass I discover
I may never trust another

You give me pleasure spiked with pain
but to me the both feel the same
living in this house of pain
will I ever have a name

All I ever do is hide the wounds
where the blood just won't congeal
couldn't ever take my soul
cause it isn't there to steal

Voices calling from inside my head
I can hear them. . . .I can hear them
vanishing memories of things that were said

It's the voice of your laughter that echoes in vain
In the vessel of sorrow and pain

America Soliz

The House

Dreary walls and curtains, cold and wooden floors
Cobwebs on the ceiling, spiders on the doors
Creaky rotten stairway, a dusty handrail, too
Broken pictures of the kids, myself, and you.
Walking to the bedroom where we would always be
No love was made, just fighting or watching the TV
Memories of all the days we spent in total silence
The kids, they grew and all they knew was to live in this sad quiet.
The drawings they drew with their very own hands are now thrown
   on the floor
Everything was left behind when we all walked out the door
Daddy and the two kids go one way down the street
Mommy goes another where we never again will meet.
Dreary walls and curtains, cold and wooden floors
Cobwebs on the ceiling, spiders on the doors
Creaky rotten stairway, a dusty handrail, too
Broken pictures of the kids, myself, and you.

Krista Burgess

Snow

The snow slipped in
Softly like a kitten
Then it grew more fierce
And quickly covered the ground
Reaching for the horizon
It spread itself like a sleek white tiger
And purred with the winter wind

Ningjun Qi

You Are My Sunshine

You are my sunshine,
  My ray of light.
I look to you for love and guidance,
  You are everything in sight.
I need not see you to know
  That you are there,
I need only to think of you
  To know that I care.
With every thought of you
  I can reach out and touch you.
And even if you travel far,
  Though you may not be before me,
Your light is brighter than any star.
  The strength that carries me through
This world of fast pace
  Can be found only in the presence
Of your grace.
  How brightly you make the candles burn.
Oh, how my heart pines
  For your return.

Shirley Lee Finney

Alone

Here I sit all alone
No one to talk to because you are gone
My mind just keeps thinking about you
The good times we had together
The cuddles we shared
The long passionate kisses
The wonderful hugs
The tears I saw you shed when I left to go home
The tears you saw me shed as I waved goodbye
No one can understand our love but us.

Elissa

Ants

Ants,
Just ants,
Little black ants.
Sightless workers of the soil,
Mindless individuals, lowest of the classes,
Tireless workers who make up the masses.
They work for a queen they've never seen.
Very dependable, yet totally expendable.
They scurry about for days on end,
looking forward to the company picnic.

David Edward Jetty

Love

It's said that there is a season
  for every thing that grows.
But love, too is a growing thing
As everyone knows...

And love can start any time,
Especially when it chooses to
Anyone who's ever loved
Will tell you this is true.

And if you've loved, you've surely found,
Love can not fade away.
'Cause when it's real, it lasts and lasts
  forever and a day.

Travis Radford

A Day To Rejoice

Valentine's Day.
A holiday invented to
celebrate the gift given to us by God,
a gift handed down from generation to generation,
a love that has existed as much
as the sun exists in our universe.
The gift of love.
A gift that makes us care and share and be merry.
It is this day
that we can rejoice in an emotion
so deep and wide,
that it exists all around the world.
It is the perfect holiday
for an emotion as perfect
as a full-bloomed rose.
It is a day for
everyone to yell with joy,
to laugh with pleasure,
a time where everyone loves.
This is a day to rejoice.

Meredith Curry

I'll Never Love Again

We fell in love in the fall saying our
love is like the seasons always
changing, we let the love
we once shared slip away.

I'll never love again the
way I gave my heart to you.

  The summer sun came along
ended on our love long ago, we were
too young to understand to ever know
that we were never meant for each other
and that's the way love goes.

  I'll never love again the
way I gave my heart to you

  At one time our love for one
another was so beautiful in every way when
I think of you I fall in love with you,
maybe our love will rekindle someday a love
so free, a love for you and me.

  I'll never love again the way
I gave my heart to you.

Deana Matesic

What To Think

Think about me, think about you.
Tell me what to think, you do it so well.
I should think about you, that's what you think.
What to think, what do you think?

Think, think, think.
A sound, not a word, a dripping faucet.
That's what I think, think, think.
Think, think.
A living thing, not a word, a heartbeat.
That's what I think, think.
Think.
Something people do, not a word, a curse.
That's what I think.

Think about me think about you.
Don't tell me what to think, I do it very well.
I should think about you, that's what I think.
What to think, what do you think?

Barbara M. Franey

Time

It was a time when dragons and sorcerers ruled the earth.
A time when kings and queens sat upon their thrones of gold.
A time when fair maidens fell in love with daring young knights.
It was a time when minstrels sang songs of old.
It was a time of wild flower crowns and dark colored silk.
A time of beautifully crafted swords and shiny suits of armor.
A time of white unicorns and mystical crystals.
It was a time of dark green forests and sparkling blue lakes.
It is a time that young girls dream about.
A time that young boys envy.
A time that fascinates the mind and is appealing to the heart.
It is a time that exists only, in myths and legends.

Erin Higham

Celestial Reckoning

Ne'er was the sky so brightly lit
That night of nights when He was born.
Each star from out its vast orbit
Brought forth a gem to Christ adorn.

From all these gifts, the Lord did choose
The purest, brightest splendor,
To show the way that wise men use
To find All-Love's extender.

Gerard A. Rossi

E Pluribus Unum

If I had several lifetimes, I'd be who I am.
I do science research, for wanting to know
The answers to questions of interest to man.

In one other lifetime, I'd live as a nun
To serve my community without a care
Except did I love them as God wills it done.

In another scenario, I'd like to write
The good news around me wherever I went,
Of little that's wrong, and of all that is right.

If there's reincarnation, then I'd like to dance
At every occasion to act out the role
Of ritual, mystery, death and romance.

If confined to one choice, I'd fit all into one.
To dance and to serve and to ask and express
The joy of it all, would leave nothing undone.

Maria Davis

The Wharf

When the Smokies cast their shadow
upon my simple home,
as the sun begins to set, and I am all alone
I can hear in the distance,
a faint Rebel yell
when the volunteers told the Yankees
to waste away in hell.

When I look out toward the river,
where the iris is in bloom
I can still smell the cotton
which now awaits the loom.

When my time has come
as the bells begin to toll,
the music of country
will gently soothe my soul.

Then place the sod above me.
Then tread there tenderly,
so I can rest forever
in Savannah, Tennessee.

Michael Patrick Singleton

Hope

I would like to think of hope as a glowing orb of light
floating in the dark sky, and brightening the night.

I would like to think of pain as something to be shared, a
compassionate hand reached out to lessen someone else's
burden, a gentle voice whispering words of comfort to a
loved one or a stranger in a time of fear.

I would like to think of love, as pure and yet contagious
a smile could spread it through a crowd, and though there
may be searching a vaccine would never be found.

Gazing out of my window, I let these thoughts sift through
my mind. Could these daydreams, in reality, ever possibly
come true?

Childish voices rouse me, and my ears are filled with their
chime-like laughter. I feel my lips turn up into a dreamy
smile. In the nearing darkness, upon the horizons edge, I can
almost see it, a blossoming, glowing orb of light.

Kelly A. Byers

Motherhood

"Motherhood" is something most any woman can obtain,
If willing to endure a certain amount of pain.

However, the true spirit that accompanies this title,
Cannot be found by attending a mere piano recital.

For it takes many long years of blood, sweat and tears,
And a calm loving voice to help children overcome fears.

"Motherhood" means that you are always there,
Your undoubting love shows you always care.

You have been there always through our bumps, cuts and bruises,
And helped to snuff out many long and short fuses.

As I sit back and recollect on all of lifes sorrows and pleasures,
I can't recall one without mother and on that I will treasure.

To measure the success of motherhood one only has to observe,
The reflection of love she receives from her children is the
Final and resounding curve.

Deborah D. Toole

Untitled

Silent the memories flutter
Not to be abandoned, but preserved obscure
as in each passing season,
a ritual of what has been

Memories of joy, sounds of laughter
echo in the distance, as if a call
to awaken the broken spirit

Heed them! We are one, man and time
children and dreams; seeking place
distant but rich with promise

Our hope is not denied
the savior of the masses, hope
ushering in a breath so pure,
when all else is lost.

Suzanne Douglas

Avast

Deny the avenue of deceit
Do not harvest avarice as if it were wheat
For if we do not avast
Away from the evil advocate at last
We will be dragged down by our guilty pasts

Rachel Summerhill

My Best Friend

My best friend's name is Jesus
  and he lives in my heart.
He really pleases me
  because of his great art.
He created the birds
  and the ocean's fish.
He made my family
  and the food in my dish.
He came to earth a long time ago
  and died on the cross to forgive our sins.
He was born in a manger
  that was in a barn.
That is my best friend
  and he is true to the end.

Sadie Rasmussen

My Broken Heart

Now that I accept our love has grown apart,
What does it take to mend a broken heart?

A little glue, a lot of time,
Waiting for you next day in the sunshine?

As time goes on your mind will play tricks,
Images of old times, they tend to stick.

Those snapshots are finished, don't let them stay.
You must make a plan to get away.

Burn the bridges so no one ever again crosses.
Abandon all hope, cut the losses...

Accept your old flame as a brand new friend,
And never fall in love again?

Oh, what drastic steps to take
To save the heart that one did break.

JC Payne

Four Walls

I sit behind closed doors with four walls surrounding me,
this room I have never left.

I close my eyes and I visit many places
that bring me happiness.

I walk through a waterfall as it cools my warm skin
this waterfall cleans out my mind of all that is bad.

I sit under a tree and feel the cool breeze blow
through my hair, I wish to grow roots to stay in
such a peaceful place.

I fly through the sky as free as an eagle, I spread
my wings never wanting to land.

These four walls I have never left, but they do not
allow my mind to sit still.

Gracie Sotelo

The Anger

Beaten down, getting raped, is it any wonder we are full of hate?
Men beating women, women killing men, two wrongs don't make a
  right,
so who will win?

Anguish, torn, and ripped, may I ask, "Why is the world being
  stripped?"
People beating people, kids killing kids, we should know by now,
the world is on its last bids.
Guns and knives let's just assume.
Put it all down for Jesus is coming soon!!

Chris Fuqua

Alice

Her mind took flight
one dazed, defenseless night.
"Geese mate for life, and chivalry is dead."
That was all she said.

Paranoia hobbled through the door,
and hobbled her evermore.
Schizophrenia tightened its grip,
and I heard her mind rip.

She was afraid in a crowd,
in her home, in her head.
Geese mate for life,
and chivalry is dead.

Pauline A. Landry

Growing Old

They tell me it's my birthday and I'm growing old.
Oh? Strange I don't know lest I have been told.
I have known the very sweetest treasures of life.
I have experienced heartache and bitter strife.
By the grave I have said good-bye to ones I love.
I have praised God with joy and blessing from above.
I have been given opportunities beyond my dreams.
And yet, the more I learn, the less I know, it seems.
I have been both blessed and cursed.
I have been loved and hated by the best and the worst.
I have shared with my wife joy and tears.
We have walked through bright happiness and dark fears.
Where work has been my pleasure and my goal,
I can say I have enjoyed it with all my soul.
Yes, I am getting old and much of life has slipped away,
But, it has been wonderful and great, what more can I say?
The passing of the years means not one thing at all.
For today I am 83 and I thank God I am still standing tall.
Oh yes, death will come as it most surely will.
But until then, I will live everyday with a thrill.

Thomas J. Rector

If

If everyone would work each day, within his home, he would find
There's always someone here on earth, most willing to be kind enough
To greet him everywhere, when brighter days appear,
And help him when he is in need, some voice he wants to hear.
Sure if little children can learn, the lessons that they write.
Of many various ways of life that are within their sight,
Others should seek work and pleasure right here, that they can do
With ordinary people who will welcome friends like you.
Good friends, I ask never forget the "If's " of every day,
So stop to see the friend in need; don't hurry on your way.
You may not know the heart-ache that some have shed
For they took care of others; when sick in bed.
They'll take you in with out-stretched arms, a grip that is
  much tighter
And you will know down here on earth their deeds are always
  brighter.
Don't drop a friend or listen to some stories you are told,
I'm sure you'll find him sweet and kind, when you visit his fold.

Frances Schroll

Who

Who thinks they can stop me from
doing what I choose to do? Excuse me
ma'am or sir is it you? Because if it
is you, you should think again, 'cause I'm
the key to my future and knock, knock,
I'm comin' in. I will think big not small
with ideas that keep growing tall. Let me
tell you something, nobody will stop me
from being me.

Samora Jones

For My Father

It's been five months since you're gone, how lonely it's been,
so much has happened yet I couldn't tell...

I wish I could tell you the weather has changed,
but since you're not here the smell is not the same.

Days are longer, nights are short,
wish you were here but sadly you are not.

I hope you've found comfort in your new place
and there are roses to fulfill your grace.

You need not to worry out there in your glory
for you have left five wonderful stories.

Each one a book with its own chapter
but if you read them it will bring you laughter,
Somewhere out there where you might be.
I hope you are looking, at the world and me.

I know you are resting no more pain, just how neat!
I miss you dearly and one day we will meet.

I'm sorry to tell you, that I've got to go now,
But I'll see you out there somewhere in the crowd

Anita Lamberti

I'm So Sorry Little Billy

I never knew that
15 minutes away from me lived a nine year old boy who had never
Been to a movie theater
This same boy had never
Seen doors open automatically or
Sat in a booth or
Seen a battery-operated doggy wiggle its tail

I never knew that
His shoes and socks were once cut off of his moldy feet

I never knew that
This boy had only two pieces of notebook paper left and
Did not own a single children's book

I never knew that
The school uniform and shoes I bought were
His only decent clothes

I never knew that
Last year all he wanted for Christmas was
For his mother to stop drinking

I am so sorry
I never knew that

Ruth A. Burton

Untitled

I want to tell you
that sometimes I
hear you crying, and
there is nothing I can do—
I want to say certain words
that I am sure will ease your pain,
and yet I know they won't.
I no longer believe in
cliques—they are deceiving,
and only prolong the loneliness—
Words are not a comfort,
but memories are, and
kisses shared, and dreams that have been lived.
Soul to soul, heart to heart, time shared, and spent
in loving shall comfort you in the dark.
Remembering the secrets, and the laughter; whispers of
your common truths, and all
the happiness from each yesterday
will provide for your strength
and hopes of each tomorrow.

Cathy L. Spier

When Wars Shall End

Crosses, markers, row by row
  Of those who suffered long ago
On bloodstained fields, tear drenched earth,
  Where vanquished all men's song and mirth.

Battle cries that once rang loud
  Amidst the tortured, madding crowd
Of soldier's wretched, writhing fears
  That death should take away their years.

Boys that overnight were men,
  Yet captive by the doubts within
That crouch behind each souls own door
  And lie beneath our earthen floor.

Wars that no one ever won,
  Battles that go on and on
'Til mothers' prayers have flooded heaven,
  'Til time and times again have ended.

Then with weary eyes we'll gaze
  Upon the Lord, oh ancient of days,
As lightening strikes form East to West
  To grand His peace, forever rest.

Wesley K. Curtis

Who Am I?

You wouldn't think I cause your tears,
You wouldn't think I cause your fears;
Or your depression and anxiety,
Or your recession from society;
You don't know all the evil I cause,
I have never broken your laws;
Society scorns me yet I go unpunished,
Those I command are soon to be finished;
Some of my followers break away,
For they have finally seen the way;
But most sink deeper into my spell,
By casting themselves into my hell;
Age makes no difference to me,
Young and old drown in my sea;
I'm not prejudice to any one group,
All my followers become just one troop;
All are my followers, loyal and true,
And none of them have the slightest clue;
Those who use me take the fall,
Who am I? Why, I'm alcohol!

Teresa Kathleen Thurman

Queen Summer

Summer is queen and rules with a zest
once the spring has decided to rest.
Then summer dazzles with her crown of fun
whose heat still throbs when day is done
if that's her mood just then.

She sparkles and teases to gently entice
all the adorers to her paradise
of radiant sunshine, pulsing green shade,
then whisks it away and showers each blade
'til her bower is a dismal den.

Summer dances, cavorts, a capricious lass
knowing full well her moods have class.
She'll warm you, then cool with freshening breeze.
She'll soak you, then dry with compatible ease.
Summer plays with her worshipping men.

Some folk seek summer, their manner bold,
while others rant weakly yearning for cold.
Queen summer will reign where ever she'll be
allowing each season to have its own spree
knowing all wait 'til she comes back again.

C. Rosalind Russell

If A Mothers' Dream Could Come True

If a mothers' dream could come true
Only good things would happen for you
No heartaches, no pain
No losses, only gain
You would always be happy and never blue
If a mothers' dream could come true

You would be healthy, wealthy, and very wise
There would be no sadness in your eyes
You would live in a mansion and drive a Mercedes Ben
You would never lose, you'd always win
Your life would be perfect, in all that you do
That is how it would be, if a mothers' dreams could come true

Jenny Sue Stafford

A Man Died On Television

A man died on television today, but should we know?
A generation, buckled at the knees, from seeing casualty in those
    who lead.
Into our quarters death is brought.
A father cried on television today, but why do they show?
In hopes that their future will be bought.

In that land, we are, when the gunshot rings.
And to the grave will that memory stay.
An image of people unknown, but still we mourn.
And somehow tomorrow manages to gray.

A man died on television today, but I do not know?
For the sun is still brilliant and the waters still flow.

Christopher Jones

And She Walked Away

For two years, we walked as friends, the very best
her words assured me that we would forever be
best friends. Many lovers she had held but a friend
a best friend she did need, and I was that to her.

There were times of trouble, difficult times, but then
she said that we would arise above and best friends
be, there for each other, always, for she and I,
gave unconditionally of our love always.

There were times of ecstasy, happiness, always
being best friends, being there for each other in
times of distress, heartache, grief, and anxiety.
She for me, me for her. Love for each we did have.

Then one day, she said I have something to tell you
for you see, you are no longer my best friend. For
another has taken your place. How sad my heart
did ache. Tears came to my eyes and pain to my heart

Because this, my friend, walked away never to
again say you are my best friend, today, forever.
And I miss her. And I love her.

Derald Walling

How Long Will It Be?

How long will it be before this world comes to an end?
How long will it be before I meet my only true friend?
How long will it be before we go?
How long will it be? Nobody knows.
How long will it be before I go home?
How long will it be before I see my father's throne?
How long will it be is the question I ask
How long will it be before I complete this worldly task?
There's no answer to this question as you can see.
The question, still remains how long will it be?

Ronnie Brown

Definitions Of A Friend

One who makes certain you have enough to eat
One who makes certain you have shoes for your feet
One who makes certain you have clothes to wear
One who makes certain the cupboard is not bare.

One who is beside you, in good times and bad.
One always there whether you are happy or sad.
One who you will never need to ask
To help you out with the worst of tasks.

People we know are referred to a lot
As a friend of ours when actually they're not
Although not an enemy they fail to possess
Those traits setting them apart from all the rest.

With no obligation as husband or wife
They are always beside us throughout our life
They will always be there right up to the end
My brother these are definitions of a person
    called friend.

Sam Wolaver

Shhhh

As I lie down upon my bed
and my Beloved is resting still beside me,
I will not awaken nor disturb my Love.

As I lay my head upon His chest and
my Beloved is resting still beside me,
I will not awaken nor disturb my Love.

I long to keep Him by my side.
In Him will I always abide.
My Beloved is mine and I am His.

As I hold Him close and whisper, "Peace, be still,"
this is where I long to stay, wrapped in the
arms of my Beloved.

As I arise and kneel down in prayer
and my Beloved is resting still,
I offer thanks and praise, for
my Beloved is mine and I am His.

Dorothy L. Bridges

Sing A Song Of Freedom

The songs that they sang had meaning to them
In the fields of white cotton, they'd blurt out a hymn
"Steal Away, Steal Away, Steal Away Home"
Gave Ol' Joe the message, it was his time to ROAM

Singing, "I Couldn't Hear Nobody Pray,"
Mammy told the field slaves she heard nothing that day

As she cleaned on the porch of the Massa's big house
She warned them to flee, but be QUIET AS A MOUSE

Then she'd sing out the order to "WADE IN THE WATER"
"Go down," she would say, "by the stream"
This let Big Luther know, it was his time to go
If he wanted his sweet freedom dream

They would sing with great MIGHT, "There's a meetin' tonight"
To this meeting how forward they looked
For they learned how to read, while the Master was sleep
And the BIBLE was their only book!

So, sing a new song, oh, sing all ye Saints
Let's "Lift Every Voice and Sing"
For the day, it draws near, when He'll wipe every tear
And His freedom to us He will BRING.

P. Mack

I Am A Child

I am a child, a newborn son.
The product of love, when two are made one.
My innocent age, is taken too fast.
I become a young man, and learn from my past.
I sweat and I bleed, and when needed I fight.
I'm just trying to live, and do what is right.
One day I find love, and for her love I try.
Together we laugh, and together we cry.
A family in time, is what our love brings.
I am just a poor man, with more wealth than all kings.
Our children they grow, and stray from the nest.
And I have grown old, too weary to rest.
I live my last days, inside of myself.
I await what's to come, others cry for my health.
The Lord hears my prayers, the last words from my breath.
And sends forth his hand, to greet me at death.
Heaven awaits, free as creatures run wild.
And now this old man, once again is a child.

Charles T. Prince

Love

Stronger than friendship
Oblivious to time
Caught like a zombie in the moment
Through which roses bloom in red
And hearts are fulfilled and caressed
By thoughts and with feelings
Of satin soft as velvet
Feeling rich with no money in pocket or hand
A feeling beyond happy
A warmth beyond believing
From the heart spreading
Till it seems my whole body burns in flame
Though there is no pain
Just pure joy
Illuminated by feelings inside
A light to shine
In the darkness of loneliness
Our blood binds together
And I am on a natural high.

Meridith Paterson

Dream Meadow

Come with me where the grass is deep
Where the crickets chirp and the field mice creep

Come with me to this wonderful place
Where we use to play, jump and race

Lay with me in the grass at night
Where we can see every star in sight

Come with me yes come along
Listen to nature's lullaby song

Come with me where its peaceful and calm
Where wild flowers grow to size of your palm

Come watch the wind whirl around
Where the leaves float softly to the ground

Where days never end,
Yes come with me my friend

Come with me side by side and hand in hand
Run away with me to this majestic land

Come with me where dreams never die
Where your imagination sore and fly
Oh come with me my friend

Inzie Reynolds

Resilience

In my resilience, I am able to walk away,
though I am with you always.
In my resilience, time will pass and fade my love,
but never my memories.
In my resilience, I will find another with whom I
can share my thoughts.
And in my resilience, after him there will be another.
I am resilience in its finest hour.
I shall wish no bad fortune, though it be wished on me.
I am a creature of God, and of his mercy;
and for these reasons, I am resilient.

Bonnie Jay Roberts

A Wedding Thank-You

Through the years, you have grown into our hearts,
Now that it's our wedding, we are glad you're taking part.

For all you help, we thank-you very much,
We could not have done it without you and we appreciate it a bunch.

You will always be remembered in a very special way,
For your friendship and your participation in our very special day.

Annette McLaughlin

Things That Go Bump In The Night

When was a little mite,
I would hear things that go bump in the night;
I was filled with such fright,
When I heard things that go bump in the night.

I would look around my little, dark room,
Did I turn on my night-light;
Should I get the broom,
For when things go bump in the night.

I raced to where my parent's slept,
But it was sure bet;
They wouldn't be up in such a fright,
Looking for things that go bump in the night.

I waited under the covers,
Crying for my dear mother;
I was afraid to look at the sight,
Of things that go bump in the night.

As my legs felt woozy,
I saw it was snoopy;
The dog filled me with such fright,
Thinking he was the thing that goes bump in the night.

Christopher Thorne

Forgive Me

Forgive me Lord, for I have sinned because I have
a Loyalty within. Sometimes stars sparkle in
my eyes, sometimes something sad will make me cry.
If I do something bad or wild, forgive me Lord
for I am still a child.
And as the days pass by and it is my turn to go.
Please let it be fast and not slow.
There still is a lot of time for me to grow,
and a lot of things I do not know.
For one thing I am sure of is the Lord is in my heart.
And as I let this poem rhyme I know on a clock there
is a time for everyone you see and there will be a lot of
time for me and as I let this poem fill in it — it
will be a part of me.

Anna Baker

The Demon Of Depression

It's cold and dark
It wants to take me
Sometimes I feel the need to let it

It kisses me with its frosted lips
It calls to me everyday, even as I sleep
I answer, I do not go, not yet

It controls my mind, pulling me closer
it makes me do evil things
For I am nothing, as it has made me believe

It takes me tight into its grip and holds me
between two worlds, for one, I don't want to be in

I stay, not for me, I live for others
As I sit here, I wait. I wait for death
To rape me of my soul
Then I shall be free.
Free from life.

Melissa Starr Eudaly

Snowbound

Oh how still the winter night
the city blanketed with snow
falling silently, discreetly,
covering the less perfect things we see and know.

Then drifting through this wonderland
come your face, your smile, your eyes
and, I am once again snowbound
as though your nearness descended from the skies.

Thoughts rush in of days gone by
nights of forgetting disappear
time reverses and again
I tremble as though you were here.

What is it in a snowflake
that makes me think of you
why is it in this long cold night
I can't accept what's true?

Perhaps, because subconsciously
I know reality will invade
and, the wonder of this misty night
as our love, with dawn will fade.

Elizabeth Harrison

Piotvor

To the believer and the skeptic
and the realist and the imagist
To the humanitarian and the fratricider
and the comforter and the vexer
To the striver and the quitter
and the extrovert and the introvert
To the leader and the follower
and the pathfinder and the concealer
Looking with anticipation for the solution to the problem
Peace Is On The Verge Of Rising

Vincent Christopher Steele

My Painful Soul

I am a buffalo, so large but gentle,
watch me run through the open plains and dry air.
I no longer can run with my family
in the beautiful fields of the west.
You have taken my land,
You have killed my family,
You have ruined my peaceful life.
Look into my eyes—See your reflection
Look into my heart—Feel my pain . . .

Tiffany Noel Frazier

Memories

Memories are created by yourself, gathered up
armful of flowers, stored within the heart and mind.
Sometimes they overflow into your eyes, your sparkling
stars, or golden sun beams in your hair. Tingling
in your arms, they touch your fingers, reach out
to touch another hand, create more memories to share.
They are like moonbeams, snowflakes, and pieces of
crystal ice. Memories are pieces of life , they
keep you going, when you feel there is no place to
go. They creep into every part of your being.
A part of you and others too. They linger and
sometimes grow, they scatter like the fluff of a
dandelion after the flowers blooms. As they scatter
they settle on someone else, and create more memories
dance like dewdrops on an early morn, they ride on
the crest of a wave, and are boundless. Like a big
piece of chocolate cake, to saver and carry within you.
To taste, to feel, they are pieces of love made over
the years. Made from fragile things, and giant dreams.
Your memories are you.

Edith Vetter

Do Not Be Sad - I Am With You

Don not be sad I am with you.
When you watch white clouds slowly
drifting across the blue skies - I am with you.
When new snow covers the earth with a
blanket of crystals glistening in the sun I am with you.

In thoughts held close inside your heart and mine - I am with you.
Time spent - love given are still a part of it all I am with you.

White daisies gently swaying in a summers breeze
I am there.
Fallen leaves, resting after giving shade to cool your brow
I am there.
Rain drops touching window panes washing dust away
I am there.
Watching, waiting, loving still,
I rest my head in the lap of Gods green earth.
But my soul has ventured forth and
is now a part of this entire universe.
My destiny fulfilled—I am at peace.
Do not be sad!

Ruth Petrasek

You

I have been waiting for this moment
now that it is here,
I wonder what you think
and what is your motivation,
and how you look so beautiful,
to everyone but you.
The curves of silk draped over a perfect body,
the eyes of understanding
all this and more
the person I see is beautiful,
gorgeous on the inside
elegant and divine on the out
the person I see is caring
and never to be taken lightly
strong and willed, firm and compelled
sweet and mild, delicate and sensitive
easily offended by unkind and untrue criticism
easily pleased by smiles and laughter
what words to use to convince you of you.

Justin T. Hesley

Love

Thine eyes are as jewels sparkling in the sunlight,
Your hair as the golden grains of wheat billowing in the wind,
One hair the less,
One sparkle the more,
Could not take away from the true beauty I see within you,

They say, "Beauty is in the eyes of the beholder,"
Well, when the blind beholder saw you he could see,
Yet he could not see you hair,
He could not see your eyes,
But he could see the true beauty that lies within you.

Chris Dabb

Carry On

A rather beautiful hillside
during a bright smooth moon.
Naked people run down its silent
green side like children laughing
during a parade
The sweet kiss made the souls dance

The sound of fall, and the crackle of wood
were all around in its infancy
Beneath the beautiful mist the
angels began to sing

Enter my sweet forest
Enter my hot dream and come with us
to discover the cool land
Dancing and dripping with warm pleasure

Gary Jerome

The Master's Gallery

I'll stop to gaze and listen
As this new day has begun
And night lets fall her darkened veil
Giving Passage to the sun
The first birds song, a signal
And life stirs across the land
A marvelous stage of miracles
Created with His loving hands
In the sights of life, sweet smells of life
His tender care abounds
And to please us even more
He added soft and glorious sounds
To see, to smell and hear the world
That God has made for me
Is each day a private viewing
Of The Master's Gallery

Julia L. Katolick

Millennium Sonnet

Inched we forward on the sands of time:
Never knew we all we thought we knew,
Reveled still we in our Cosmic Rhyme,
Imprecise, yet ever were we true.

'Tis our nature to define each star:
Meaning is our master, though our schemes be dashed,
Year by year, as travelers from afar
Bring back cargo of our dreams, rehashed,

Yet claim we our Godhead in the tempest's eye
Bowing not to Forces we acknowledge not,
Accept not the outcomes that our acts imply,
Certain we'll outrun the chaos we have wrought,

So we bring down Mercy as a God amused
At the opportunities we have abused,
Winds for us once more the Mill of Pain,
Lets our proudness gum the works again.

John Thompson

Saracen's Heed

I revelled in his smell for as long as I could
I kept my daydream of his face
filed along with all the others of his nature
I smiled when he told me to behave but I knew,
I just knew not to laugh cause he meant it.
I scratched his stomach to show him pain
and left him to teach him sorrow
I felt his eyes follow me around to the beat of the music
I fell into his smile
I held on
I let go
I let myself dream of him, talk of him, think of him
I let myself lie in misery without him
then I was silent and I knew why
I ached and hurt and I waited
I stole his expressions and buried them in my soul
I felt heat and insanity and irrationalness
I lusted and grieved
I let him be.

Karol Sheinin

Candle Daze

The days are melting like hot wax into the realm of
yesterday
Forming memories of variable shapes and sizes
    Casting into a solid structure of nothing to come again.

Tomorrow rises high like the flame of a burning candle
    heating the wax of time - dripping - sliding
disappearing into the vat of eternal past.

The future - burning bright - holds everything;
    all that minds imagine.
All the forces of reality are controlled in the seer's mind.

To live merely getting by
    is to extinguish the flame of tomorrow
But to apply effort is to feed the starving fire -
    to melt away the walls of
        wax that entraps the days ahead.

Michael Lanier

Untitled

You feel like home to me...

    ...The foundation built from love,
        will not weaken with passing time.
    And the walls (raised by respect)
        can withstand the flood of our fears.
    Its rooms are filled with feelings;
        sadness, hope, forgiveness and joy.
    Our roof, a blanket of dreams,
        shall guide us into the future.

You feel like Home to me!!!

Adam Schulz

My Innocence

As I walked the moon seemed to follow me;
the mist was all around.
The moon shined so bright,
it was hard for me to see.
I took each step carefully,
never knowing what lay ahead.
The wind howled, as if telling me to go back.
I kept walking;
I should have listened...
I never walked back.

Jennifer Harblin

What Would It Be Like

What would it be like to be a little girl
to run and play and laugh with daddy?
What would it be like to sit on daddy's lap,
look him in the eyes and say, "Daddy, I love
you!" with a big hug and kiss?
What would it be like to be a little girl
looking up to daddy as my hero?
What would it be like to dream of the day I
would marry my daddy?
What would it be like to see daddy come home
from work greeting him with open arms and a
big smile?
What would it be like on those scary nights to
have daddy protect and comfort me?
What would it be like to have grown up with this
man, my daddy?
What would it be like to not be so strange with
my daddy?
What would it be like. . .

Shileen Nixon

A Foe Or A Friend

With Time everlasting in darkness and dream,
To awake and be spoiled the end never seen.

The countless illusions play tricks with your mind,
As you lay there helpless, suspended in time.

Your fate never knowing the where or the when,
Is time everlasting a Foe or a Friend?

As daybreak is nearing the sounds of the dawn,
A feeling of danger, the memory lives on.

What could this be the message they send,
For I'll always wonder a Foe or a Friend.

Steven B. Thompson

Untitled

There's a time for every reason,
given you stick to the things you believe in.
At the discontent of all others,
a time for uniting all sisters and brothers.

Staring is love's vacant look.
How could have someone wrote the book,
of love, that is thought we must need,
yet how illiterate love is indeed.

If to give love away
just don't try not to play,
it's of no matter the colour you bleed.
And we can only feel lucky of love that is blind,
for still none of us know how to read.

Steve Phipps

Hold The Night

Look into my eyes, their fire burns,
Softly gazing upon you, please do not turn.
Night arrives softly driving away day.
Please turn toward me, at least don't turn away.
Look to my face, it hides the fire.
Darkness blots everything, hides deep desires.
The wind kicks up your locks, blowing them free,
The moonlight reveals your true beauty to me.
Time is unkind, stoically running course,
Giving and taking without remorse.
Still time has given us a moment alone
So what shall be done before it is gone?
  Give me your hand please, I'll hold it tight.
  Look as far as you can see I'll hold the night

Michael Lloyd Morris

Scared

Below the surface, within the heart
Lies the memories of a love once true
Together as one...
But now broken in two

A elegant vision, she thrusted my soul
The warmth of her soothing voice
Her peaceful and tranquil glow
Took me beyond the reaches of my mind
I was filled with the adeptness of her disguise

Fooled by the stunning elegance she possessed
Longing for....craving...the firmness of her breasts
The desire, the passion filled this empty heart of mine
She gave me a look I could not deny

Lost in the rush of my aching heart
The pain surely subsided
As we came closer together
It was my trust that labeled me a liar

No way out...I betrayed, I dishonored
Now living in disgrace
With this scar as a reminder

Norman Wong Jr.

Dakota Boy

I am born of the prairie.
I am son of the plow and the rake.
The north wind that bends the grasses
moans in my ears.
My mind burns like the dry August sun
when demons possess me.
When I am betrayed;
my soul cries like the
coyotes on the section line, and my heart
is as cold as the northern lights.
I am a Dakota Boy.
I hunger for the space between cities.

Samuel Lovold

Star-Child

I see, as was decreed before this day,
Horizon streaked with blood through dusk and dawn,
The heavens veiled by shades of sable gray.
I see the sky glow bright though light has gone
A star burns vividly, a light then dies.
And from this flash of fire a child I see
Clothed in whitish-grey, unseeing eyes.
Her hands unclasped, for beckons she to me
I follow her, this sister from my past
Departed babe of mother, never known.
She leads me to the valley at long last,
Takes she my hand, and chills me to the bone
  For though her grasp is cold, her hand is wet
  And in the light I saw it was not sweat.

Jennifer Cheng

Eternity

Walk beyond the Golden Door
To a life of forever more.
No more suffering, no more pain
No more of a world gone insane.
Just good times, nice and slow
No more racing, for there's nowhere to go.
No more appointments left to keep.
Now it's time for Eternal sleep.
To walk the Heavens till and end of time.
Though of Earth you'll be missed,
But the Lord felt it was time for your eternal bliss.

Michael J. Schwartz

Hands

My hand is what reaches out to catch you whenever you fall.
My hand will be there to grasp you when you call.
My hand is a white beam of bright light;
piercing through the dark, cold loneliness of night.
My hand is there to wipe away your tears
to help you find comfort from what you fear.
My hand will always caress the tenderness of your skin.
My hand feels the warmth coming from your heart within.
My hand knows the softness of your lips;
painting a red swirl on my fingertips.
My hand is there when ever we touch.
It is you and your love that I need so much.

Your hand is what reaches out to catch me whenever I fall.
Your hand will be there to grasp me when I call.
Your hand is a white beam of bright light;
piercing through the dark, cold loneliness of night.
Your hand is there to wipe away my tears
to help me find comfort from what I fear
Your hand will always caress the tenderness of my skin.
Your hand feels the warmth coming from my heart within.
Your hand knows the softness of my lips
painting a real swirl on my fingertips
Your hand is there whenever we touch.
It is you and your love that I need so much.

With your hand in mine
We have the strength to walk together...
Until the end of time.

Robby Vernon

Cigarette Butts

Cigarette butts, cigarette butts, lying all around.
Plummeted there by the smokers, thrown down to the ground.

Remains of momentary pleasure but everlasting intoxication
Not really being litter, but not being decoration.

They really serve no purpose, just sort of lie down there.
Each has its own characteristics, but only if you stare.

Getting trampled then blown away, taken to another place,
Gathered in a cluster but each with its own little space.

We are like these cigarette butts scattered all around.
You know God is the smoker, placing each of us here on the ground.

The Earth be our sidewalk, the place which we reside.
Then the wind blows us around
  and we've got a new place to hide.

God must be a chain smoker, yeah cigarettes are his fit.
One day he'll get cancer, then he'll have to quit.

Adam Goodwin

The Pattern Of Life

A leaf turns over, it is as green as can be.
But soon it changes color, for all of us to see,
The leaf is then stepped on or blown in the wind,
until this cycle of its life will end.
The leaf changes color deeper still,
nothing can stop it, but death soon will.
That same leaf that began as green,
now sits with others, and casts the image of a dream.
Brown and old they have all become,
but there is nowhere to go, nowhere to run.
They gathered into a pile and in a pile they will burn.
But as this cycle ends, another leaf turns.

C. J. Rotert

The One Who Walks My Dreams

My life I look for only one
To fill my heart and light the sun
I see her almost every night
In dreams I flee my troubled plight
I want someone to love and hold
To cherish me and not to scold
My dreams are filled with visions grand
My love and I walk hand in hand
My eyes are open just to see
The pain, reality can be
I want a love to transgress time
Someone to love, who will be mine
I don't believe the things I feel
Who can say what once was real
By day I see a troubled life
My dreams they come to end the strife
I look for one to end the pain
With the love I long to gain
A love I want, that's all it seems
None other than the one who walks my dreams

Marc Bennett

Cyberlove Ben

We never felt, we never kissed,
We loved each other from afar
We often laughed and often missed
Our timing was not up to par
CyberBen

Our online love was never really an affair
But we did care.
Our dreams, they seemed so real and yet
We could not touch, we have not met
CyberBen

My dearest there will be a day.
You'll come and I'll be here to say,
I love you, want you, need you to
Feel as I feel, real and true
CyberBen

And if we never meet at all
In our Web world, online call
Lovers destined to the fates
Of online romance cyberdates
CyberBen

Connie Berridge

Scattered Flowers

Scattered flowers singing alone
Humming their joy in a mellow drone

In dances of love their petals do shake
Their blossoms yawn like a mouth agape

A fragrance of the heavens perfumes the air
For you alone they do prepare.

Rolling back the clouds for the sun to shine
To proclaim that you are truly mine

And mine forever many a bird sings
As they float with the wind beneath their wings

Till the flowers close their blooms at night
And dream of the maiden all in white

Rosa Mendez

Small Wonders

The dew on the grass in the morning light
sparkles in the glow of the sun

Bubbles blown into the air from a wand
soap sparkling in the bottle
quickly disappear till there are none

Snowflakes falling ever so softly
quietly down to the ground

Clouds in the sky with their fluffy edges
floating, but there's no sound

Small wonders of beauty are these
filling the senses, give it a try

We should take each and day
and live it our best
don't let life pass you by

For these are what connects us
how fragile, how lovely
we know what is important
the simple things
Brenda Robinson

Floridana Farewell

Scattered on the winds above the water
And happy sands she held within her heart,
Her ashes, from the fingers of her daughter,
Dance, and dissipate, and then depart.
The sea is calm, it gently laps the shore
Behind the girl knee-deep in wet and warm.
Perhaps a ripple, surely nothing more,
To indicate there ever was a storm.
A verse her mother loved, the girl recites,
Then turns away to wade back to the land.
She's faithfully fulfilled the farewell rites,
And now her mother's one with sea and sand.
Then suddenly, in all that lack of motion,
That glassy sea, that seems so quiet yet,
A single wave, alone in all the ocean,
Knocks her down, and leaves her soaking wet.
She rises, laughing, as she turns to say,
"Okay, Mama. You've had the final word!
Goodbye, God Bless!" and as she turns away,
It seems a far-off giggling is heard.

Adolphus Lawson

Another Day

As he sits in the corner with a gun in his hand,
he asks himself softly...am I really a man?

His heart beats faster as he looks at the scars on his wrists;
Then softly he cries and clenches his fist.

Look what I've done to myself over the years.
What was the point? It is not very clear.

Now as he sits with the gun to his head,
Do I really honestly want to be dead?

Or is it a way to get rid of the fears,
To pass on the pain and pass on the tears.

Now he slowly pulls the gun away from his head,
he gets up walks over and lies on his bed.

He says to himself I have to move past scaring my wrists
and having outbursts like the last.

He closes his eyes and wakes to the day

The thoughts of last night have drifted away.

He drives off to work with a big grin;
He says this is a new day, a new day to begin.

Kathryn A. Beam

No Detente

As night falls
Silence calls
Loneliness waits in the dark
With screams soundless and dreams boundless
Another night without you.
We are apart
Because your mind and heart
Are separated by denial.
But beyond that wall
Your eyes tell all...
I know you're hurting, too.
Yet you continue to hide
Behind your stubborn pride -
You'd rather be right than be happy.
Tracey Hoffpauir

Chains

I feel as if trapped, in this misery enclosed
It's an uneasy feeling of stiffened and froze
That claustrophobic feeling of not breaking free
The surrounding knowledge of not being me
My senses are haywire, my brain's gone astray
The voices are saying that I die today
I can not live this life of pain
With everything to loose yet nothing to gain
You give and you get that's the way it's supposed to be
But this world that we live in is demented can't you see
Twisted and deranged is everyone's mind
It's the truth that I know and the truth I can't find
We live in this world so close yet apart
Where love once was now hate fills the part
Please come in my body take over my place
Take my pain and my sorrow yet leave me my grace
Give me the peace and security I deserve to have
Take from me the evil and the bad
You've taken control of my mind all memories now are of you
It's your pain I suffer with now what can I do
Amber Raeschel Conrad

Sweet Is The Ocean

Sweet is the ocean, lovely are the waves, I love the ocean,
I'm here everyday. Lovely are the seagulls, high in the
sky. I love to watch them go flying by. Soft is the sand, hot
is the sun. I love building castles because it's so fun. Sweet
is the air, smelling so clean picking up seashells. I feel
serene. Sweet is the ocean lovely are the waves, I love the
ocean, I'm here everyday.
Emily Carr

First Snow

Summer's over; now it is fall,
Everything's sleeping waiting for snow to fall.
That beautiful blanket soft and white,
Seems to come in the middle of the night,

It's so quiet and perfect too,
Not to enjoy it would be a fool.
Little footprints scattered 'round,
As they play, you don't hear a sound.

Birds and rabbits all alike,
Cats and dogs, they never fight.
It's so peaceful, heaven-sent,
You wonder where the hating went.

All these creatures must agree,
God gave tranquility for us to see.
Enjoy it
Suzanne M. Rassi

Seizures

I never thought I could feel this way,
Until seizures took my freedom away.
How could this happen and how long will it last,
It's hard for me to leave my pain in the past.
People say to me, "Just forget it and move on.",
But they don't really understand what's going wrong.
I'm scared, restricted, and sad,
Slowed down by medication, and just plain mad.
I'm mad because something's wrong with my brain,
And when I don't get answers or resolutions I go insane.
I don't know what results may come,
And I'm constantly taking medication to make my brain numb.
Time is just passing me by,
And there's nothing more for me to do except cry.
I'm crying because I'm scared of what the future may bring,
And if my seizures continue, the future may not bring a thing.
Nothing good, for sure, except drugs and tests,
And I just had surgery, that tops all the rest.
I don't feel good because I'm scared and mad as hell,
Maybe something positive will happen, only time can tell.

Renee C. Deyden

Up Stairs

So many memories just build
Like the layers of dust upon them
That old painting of father's father
The paper thin blanket from mom
Empty shoe boxes
A red fire engine with a broken wheel
The fake Christmas tree with long-lost branches
The damn guitar with the broken string,
    never could play it
Of course the rocking horse,
    spring rusted and stretched from long rides to the wild west
Oh, and that broken mirror
Lost in the back
Forgotten
But still reflecting

Michael J. Kohn

A Robin Named Karen

"I would not have written this if I didn't love you, Karen."
Spring is near and the Robins are coming back.
The Wood Ducks of winter still go quack quack.
Then you see a sparrow warming up an old nest
and below the oak a sleepy cat ends his fast.

But wait! There's something in the Southwest.
Yes it is! A beautiful Robin 4434 red breast.
But oh :(will she fly near.
For her cheerie up chirp I can hear?

She's off at a distance looking over and around.
Up in the air she soars and then back to the ground.
What is she looking for as a child I would say,
"Is it some place or someone she's reaching to stay?"

So I watch intently for the pattern of her flight.
I hope she'll find an oak tree to sleep tonight.
Then I see her coming closer; getting late now; time for bed.
And there she goes   :(to a neighbor's cedar tree instead.

So the next day I awake and hear a quaint familiar sound
the Robin song "Cheerie up" in my oak tree she found.
And there beside her a new companion happy and free,
"Cheerie up," he says, as if to day to me:
        "God takes care of the little things of life.
            Including giving a godly man a godly wife."

James W. Jennings

Tear Soaked-Faded Valentines

Fairy princess with broken wings,
tear-soaked faded valentines in her hands.
Remembering how things used to be,
before she lost her innocence.
When the world was a nightmare,
She was a dream.
When she danced lightly on rose petals.
Things were so pure,
so untainted then.
Fluffy and perfect.
It will never be again.
Since her wings are broken
and she still holds the faded valentines to her heart.

Amber Wright

The Music Stays Within

The "Hello's" my dear feline friend will no
longer be said.
But the goodbyes will always be in our memories
and still be repeated in our sorrowful hearts.
The day we had to let you go, no longer to
see you with us;
to give us the pleasure and joy we found and
always knew we had with you.
We will remember you Amadeus our dear feline
friend, for your frolicking ways to atone for
your soundless world, was like a Jester's way to
put musical sounds in our thoughts and hearts;
which will always stay to be played over and
over again.

Gertrude Sherwood

Am I?

I am and am not black and/or white
I see all in darkness and nothing in light
I wear the halo with the bulb burnt out
I smile brightest beneath my pout
I am justice with only one eye closed
I am the "what if" that is supposed
I can be repetition instead of rhyme
I can be repetition instead of rhyme
I am the ceramic angel with the broken wing
I am the phone that refuses to ring
I say yes to ifs, ands, or buts
I am the virgin dressed like a slut
I am the cookie that spoils the meal
I come back up again after the meal
I am the vegetarian that loves the veal
I am too numbed by sensation and cannot feel
I say fix everything with a pill
I don't say "oops," I say "God's will"
I will be there when you close your eyes to see
I am the part of you that you blame on me

Daniel L. Grant

Whisper

Did you hear me whisper
As you went to sleep last night?
Did you feel me kiss your cheek,
And tell you to sleep tight?

Did you feel me hold you?
I do that in my mind.
I can almost feel your skin against mine,
And our breath keeping time.

Did you hear me whisper,
I wish that you were here?
Did you feel a tear upon your cheek?
I think I left one there.

Diane Terrell

Nana, I Miss You

I remember the special love that could never die
The long late nights, so many words between us,
How I long for those years and your words of wisdom
Nana, I miss you.

Lingering luncheons that cling forever in my mind
Talking endlessly could never be forgotten,
for I dream of having just one more day, or hour
Nana, I still need you.

I stayed at your bedside and cried endlessly
Willing your wellness was something I just couldn't do,
Life will never be for me as it was without you here
Nana, I loved you so.

Every time I remember you the emptiness creeps into my soul
No time was sadder than the day you left this earth,
A thousand times I told you I loved you, meaning to say more
Oh Nana, I still love you so!

Diane L. Johnston

The First Of The Last

As I sit and wonder what my life will be
I think only of this tragedy.

A single tear rolls down my cheek
I wonder how bleak.

Then I hope and pray that your life
will be okay.

I dream that someday you will
feel the way you once did.

And I can be as happy as we once were.

Life has become such misery
I imagine it will become a drudgery.

Then I realize only God knows what's best
and meant to be.
I place myself in his hands and pray you will
do the same.

Mathew Minardi

Transients

Homeless inside a cardboard house,
I wakened to a train whistle.
The forlorn note of a midnight train
doplers up an alien scale then
in lonely creshendo retreats,
moaning as if searching thru infinite space
for a place,
any place.

I shiver in the winter sky
under stars shifted red, alone.

Lighted cars swiftly rise up, then recede,
racing in unreachable orbits,
worlds oblivious to mine, until
one car, one window, one person glimpsed;
our eyes connect for one relativistic instant;
a shared continuum of time and space.
An eternal instant in
a place called no place.

I shiver in the winter sky
under stars shifted red, alone.

David Brest

Golden Indian Girl

The golden Indian girl
who roams about the emerald forest of thy dreams
came to me in a vision one enchanted feathered night
swimming with the butterflies and dancing among the leaves

Can't take my mind from before her face
for what other glory on earth could capture my attention
as her sweet silvery smile, golden Indian summer soft skin
her eyes glanced down and whispered so soft in her affections
her own lips sheets of canvas in the rain flowing gently
through her hair so long and true

Clouds fly by and winds blow strong
rose fermented fragrance
Tulips, Carnations, Seraphs and Cherubs
stare in wrapped amazement
peer toward her again in wonderment
with wishful thoughts to one day be enclosed
within her gentle rain

Scott Leonhard

Ending

Visions of my Eternal Burning
Scare me so that I'm still yearning
To seek more of some gift of Love
And stay all alone hopefully up above

I scream to find the answer why
We were put on this earth to live and die
To give love off but take none in
So ashamed of a life of sin

Thought of Evil begins to bloom and scream
But all is blinded by your bright light beam
Which shine out You and I close my eyes
For all wise to who know who can hear all your cries

With no clue of what I begin to fear
But with my comfort I can always hear
"That is not dead which can eternal lie,
And with strange aeons even death may die"

Robert Burley

Gentle Beauty

Your eyes, deep enticing pools, that I might swim an eternity,
    Basking in the radiance of your beauty.
Your hair, a gentle flowing river of splendor,
    Skin soft as silk, and lips the petals of a rose.
Your hands so delicate they must have been woven
    From the clouds themselves.
Might luck shine upon this pauper,
    That he may sit with the princess.
For only royalty could carry such elegance.

John S. Weston Jr.

Assimilation

I look back over my shoulder
And see the thing that follows.
I determine to run harder,
    faster,
    faster.
My life depends on it.

How did this happen? What have I done to deserve this punishment?
The needles, the blood, the pain of becoming human.
I cannot resist any longer.

Jonathan DeLaughter

Test Of Time

Glistening crystal eyes Pierce through my mind
I'm confined to your ways and I pray for our time
All the while I lay Just relax Contemplate
A vision of two which includes you and fate
Tremorous aches through my heart and my soul
With the though I'd grow old without you to hold
Yet no futures foretold In effect I proceed
To look in your dreams and fulfill all your needs
Subtle thoughts are conceived Candlelight and red wine
Our worlds are combined Our attire's divine
New levels are climbed Destiny is the peak
Seven courses to eat Eloquent yet mystique
Love is oblique Understood in all ways
Serenade beauty's shade Enhanced by moon rays
That look still of Jade Most precious memoir
Style of hussar Hair flows like Loire
Avatar in your own All actions condone
Tonight and hereafter Our bliss is your home
Nothing atone We start with a new
Lend hearts to each other Our love will ensue

Kevin Bross

He

He is my Light Writer
streaking white my skies
through the night
burning flashes of searing passion
his lightning etches my stormy soul

And he
is my crashing waves
beating, pulsing thunders
against my soft white sands
scattering secret shells along shores
of my body - and I his lighthouse
guide him through the
fogbanks of pain

He
commands my universe of being;
my earths slave at his feet
and I am his comet of all galaxies,
screaming through the dark islands of love
my luminous tail
writing his name in time forever

Katalina Polzin-Elsasser

No Time For Good-Byes

I feel the tears swell up in my eyes,
I hear the words spill out as I cry,
I know I love you and I always will,
no one can change the way I feel

They tear us apart and take you away
they hold me back to make me stay,
they leave me alone, why should they care.
No one sees the fear, no one is aware

No time for Me, no time for You.
No time to cry, or be so blue.
I beg and plead, and ask them why,
all they can say is...

  "No time for good-byes!"
  Sara Beth Clark

Bonfire Of Bills

I have several bills
which I created in my youth

I make payments every quarter
and payments every month

I work, I toil to pay them
while they rear their ugly heads

And quench the fires of frivolous spending
where by it makes me sad

I vow these debts I'll settle
and then I'll celebrate

The night I'll use as kindling
these statements...

I can't wait!
  Marsha Louis

The Gift

Everybody has the gift,
All around the world.
Even the Magi had the gift,
But was really never unfurled.
It has a value that numbers can't count,
Yet it's free from every child.
It can't be purchased in a store;
And it certainly doesn't grow wild.
When times are darkest, it brings us hope.
It's the subject of many a song.
It's a gift you can give over again,
Every second, all day long.
You'll never know who needs it
or wants it at the time.
But those who do receive it,
sometimes say they heard it chime.
So read this verse very carefully.
Think it over for a while.
And the very next time you need a gift,
Give the gift of just your smile.

Bridget Foti

I Am

I am special and unique
I wonder why we came to be
I hear the voices of my conscience
I see the people dying
I want the world to get along
I am special and unique

I pretend to be a princess
I feel I want to cry
I touch people's hearts
I worry about life
I cry when I am criticized
I am special and unique

I understand we will all go someday
I say I'm going to succeed
I dream for no more hunger
I try my best at everything
I hope they will find a cure for all diseases
I am special and unique

Nicole Gonzalez

Untitled

At first you try and convince yourself that it's no big deal.
Everyone else is doing it, so why not you?
It's the greatest solution to a life full of problems,
The best escape you've found.
You know that you could never stop as your heart's beating fast,
And you know it's too late when it starts slowing down.
First the black darkness appears,
Then the images of all those empty lost years.
As the end is near, you can feel a sudden shot of fear,
Before the last breath you take.
And as you wake in a bright new place,
You clearly see the mistakes you make.

Elizabeth Lorenzen

My Very Own Garden

Inside me is a flower garden
A flower blossoming in each joyous moment
One dying in every rain drop that falls from my eye.

Sun rises in my heart, when I'm excited
Brightly shining on my garden
Setting when I'm afraid
Leaving my garden in a shivery night.

Anger growing inside me casts a dark shadow
Killing the flowers with its fearful temper.
Laughter opens a door nurturing the flowers.

When I am ill, it seems as if a flower is also sickly.
Even when I become healthy, the flower still suffers.
Courage and strength, that's what it takes
To save it from entering a dark hole behind a blanket of shadows.

Now you must be wondering
Whatever do I do
When my garden is drowning is a puddle of my tears.

Well, I really don't know
It must be magic
Which only the heart can understand.

Marissa DeAnna

Pain Left Behind

As I looked in her eyes, my heart fell into a place unknown.
No, my dear daughter, Norman's not all alone.

We tell each other, he's in a better place,
but the loss we feel, deeply shows on each face.

He was taken from us on his 15th birthday.
Oh Dear God we cried out, why does life have to be this way!

As the tears fell and hugs had no end,
caring and comfort love does send.

Children shouldn't have to deal with such pain,
yet their tributes and promises show there is much to gain.

There is no surprise with the strength a child holds,
there's only a strange beauty as it unfolds.

My daughter, his friend and others you see,
will cherish his memory and miss him deeply.

Today, one month long, they gather again,
to comfort each other and visit their lost friend.

Shirley Raymo

Through Our Lives

Sightful years have flitted, Through Our Lives,
ever increasing in intensity, that the pangs,
of Love pound, perpetually, pressed,
between the pages of images incessantly.

Rightful tears have silted, Through Our Lives,
never decreasing in density, so that the strings,
of Hurt stand, seemingly, stressed,
beneath the edges of derived diversity.

Frightful fears have filtered, Through Our Lives,
forever recessing in reality, so that the throngs,
of Hate hide, hideously, harassed,
believing the horror of reduced, reciprocity.

Spiteful spears have lilted, Through Our Lives,
ever expressing in eternity, so that the prongs,
of Burden bare, brazingly, bold,
around the brink of exceeded, eccentricity.

Triteful ears have listed, Through Our Lives,
never compressing in capacity, so that the things,
of Pain push, pressingly, poised,
amid the prose of perfection, permanently.

Frank Jenkins

A New Life

. . . As I gaze into her beautiful eyes,
 I can't help but to cry . . .

. . . To hold her in these arms of mine,
 It would be so divine . . .

. . .But then she walks away from me,
 So I fall down to my knees . . .

. . . I pray and pray that one day,
 She would come back in some way . . .

. . . But slowly as time goes by,
 I can no longer cry . . .

. . . Then one day she calls on the phone,
 It was a shock and I was blown . . .

. . . Especially when I received the shocking news,
 and in my mind it felt like a bruise . . .

. . . After thinking awhile I couldn't help but to praise,
 the one up above for giving my true love back
 with a new life that we will raise . . .

Julio Rodriguez Jr.

Lost Love

Please my love—my voice is pleading
 What is this thing we are feeling
Can it be love we both could share
 And is it only in deep despair?

We once were young with radiant laughter
 Without a thought of what love was after
Why, oh why, could I not see
 Time would not always be kind to me.

Our hearts were full and oh, how tender
 So easy to bleed with sweet surrender
What then—shall we never feel
 That love which beats within us still?

Reach for me, I'm pleading now
 Don't shut me out with all these doubts
It won't be long this time will pass
 When there shall be no love at last.

Mary G. Fields

In Silence

Many times,
You have come to me in silence.
My dreams are full of your being.
And now, while I long for you tonight
As always, you are softly becoming me,
Penetrating my love.

My dreams, searching,
Yearn to realize you.
Surrender your soul
Bring them strength and life.

Come, hold my hands,
Know by their warmth that I need you
And accept the love I gently offer you.

Open your fragile heart to me
And let me enter into it,
That I may be concealed in its tenderness.

Then, in the end,
when we are finally together,
Let us discover ourselves
And embrace this precious feeling because we love.

Edward F. Hayes

It's Beginning To Rain

It's beginning to rain,
Everyone is in a hurry trying to escape it,
Except for me.

It is sad,
How when some grow old,
They have no time for it.

For getting how it felt upon their face,
For getting how much fun the rain use to be.

I launched may a sea battle back then, on pop sickle
Sticks that became battleships, and the puddles the seven seas.

Maybe I am insane, maybe,
But I still like the feel of the rain upon my face,
I still wage war on the seven seas,
When the world is not watching.....

John Corkins

Untitled

Colors, colors, colors
Colors are bright and sometimes light.
Colors change from light to dark.
Colors make other colors darker or lighter.
Strawberries are red and blueberries
are blue and goose berries are
green and blackberries are black.
Colors are all different.
Green is a color that is used for the color
of money and the color of trees.
Colors are used all of the time in everyday.
The sun is yellow and bright.
The moon and stars are white and bright
  So have a good night.

Jaclyn Bradley

A Child

A child like a flower,
An infant like a seed.
The flower grows, as does the child.
When the flower blooms, the child has reached adulthood.
With each petal that falls, a memory of childhood goes too.
When the flower dies, so does the soul and the child inside.

Rachel Weiser

Decadence

All mighty Sunne, how the warmth of thee
Shall embrace us on this unique day for one?

Glistening she hast to me,
For now, my dearest Megara doest support the ring;
Within my chamber she will sing
And I, to have been proven but twelve times tonight;
Starved I most certainly be,
For a mere bite of Salmon had I you see.

We must now dyne, for us to survive
Upon the other bank she now resynes,
Hereby shadowy and senseless to me
My weapon is worn you see
Unable to replace this smoldering stub,
If only you would rise my dear Sunne!

I, but a wise fool
Crawling, groping this frozen scape of land,
Lets myne eye see Her A woman I can no longer stand,
  The whispering moonlight eye a hero, as my brother
While waking laughs this terrible mother
And off Her Arms slips the golden coils one after the other.

R. Shaun Ferenc

My God

I came before the preacher man
And said Sir, help me if you can
To find the place where God might be

I'm drowning in a sea of dryness and fear I may be losing my mind

The preacher man he frowned at me
Said Son, you and I disagree
That's not our latest theory

I fear you may have fallen behind, oh you're so far behind

So I ran into the church and prayed
And there upon the altar laid
My broken, twisted soul

I cried out to the Holy One,
If You exist then send Your Son
To come and make me whole

And in a silent shroud of ebony
In darkness there He came to me
And whispered in my ear
Child, I am here . . . as I have always been

My God, O My God, You descended from the skies
And tore the blindfold from my eyes

Jeffery Frank Edens Jr.

Untitled

Living in a world where love is a necessity
and rainbows are hard to come by.
Can really get a person down the sidewalk
kicking cans, catching rainbows from sun rays
in his hands.
But, four leaf clovers still grow in the grass
that grows in my botanical spot.
The grass is always greener on the other side
where the chicken tried painfully to get.
He had no success because he was hit, by my being
lost and found on the ground now I can have my dead
chicken gumbo?
I don't know the answer is so so me a garb with
gold spun by fools while babies drool on my shoes and
see I'm living in a world where love is a necessity
and rainbows are hard to come by.

Gwen Jenkins

My Great God

I held a little hair in my hand,
I saw a sparrow flying through the air,
I stood in the sand on a sea shore,
And I know my Great God was there.

I watched the seasons change in the springtime,
Summer, autumn and winter follow so near,
The sun shines, the rain falls and the snow drifts down,
covering the seeds as they sleep in the ground,
And I know my Great God is there.

Babies are born and grow up,
People grow old and pass from this life,
Going by clay, just like he said,
And I know my Great God is there.

Some people just refuse to believe,
Even though the Heavens do declare,
There has been a change in my heart,
And I know my Great God is in there.

Georgia P. Kelley

Autumn Interlude

The winding path in a gentle tease
Beckons my spirit beyond the trees.
Come and walk awhile with me.
Forget your cares, come be free.
Wander through my forest and stream.
Rest in the meadow, let yourself dream.
Your spirit will soar as the clouds drift by
While an explosion of color greets your eye.
A sunset heralds the end of the day.
With a joyful heart be on your way.

Lucille Nordlund, SFO

Untitled

The sound of music, the chatter of my peers
Things I've been listening to for quite a few years.
Airplanes overhead, birds chirping outside
flying and chirping are things that I've tried.
Parents driving in their cars, people skiing at the lake.
Things I would have died for a chance to take.
Growing up to be a famous movie star,
having a limousine for my first car.
Being an influence on someone's life someday, sometime.
Investigating a case at the scene of a crime.
Being involved in "little talks,"
taking several beach-front walks.
The best part of being a child would seem. . .
Children have the chance to dream.

Kelly Rinderknecht

Time

The seconds grow so slowly into time,
Reaching for the sky before they return
To change once again, in wait for the chime,
That disturbs my mind, so the day must learn,
'Tis how for I should go in time without
'Gainst how far I go not with time immense.
What shall I become if I were to shout,
At this time, at this world, of no suspense.
Look the hour in the face——the mirror.
The face in the mirror is in time's place.
The time stands still you can not see clearer,
But then it is gone, to the eyes disgrace.
So that's how it is, and that's how it ends,
For upon the time is where it depends.

Kevin O'Neill

Untitled

For so many years I have been looking for someone like you.
Now that I have found you, I pray our love will stay true.
So let's take our time and please tell me what you want.
I'll do anything, so I won't lose your sight.
To hold you tight, throw any kinds of fights.
So here I am and holding my baby boo.
Two young people, now knowing what to do.
Neither one of us has been where we are, so don't be scared of our
    fear.
I shall pray to the Father to help us on our way.
So scared, hoping you are here to stay.
So scared, of the thought of you leaving me.
So I decided to make a prayer, that you won't set my heart free.
Please tell me what I can do, for this dream to last 'til ever be.
The next time you close your eyes,
I hope you know that these arms won't ever let you down,
Or will my eyes ever tell lies.
You give me love, no matter what I do.
When I am sad, you are there for me and put on a smile.
I will do my best, to show you what has been in my heart,
And prove that my love, gets stronger since the start.

Marc Oiwa

Untitled

To my dearest Shawn,
In April 19, 1973
God gave a special gift to me.
He filled my life with joy,
And blessed me with a precious baby boy.
As the years swiftly past,
My baby boy grew up fast.
It is so hard to believe,
It seems like just yesterday he was here with me.
No sooner than I turn around,
There he stands in his college graduation cap and gown.
Precious memories I'll treasure so much,
For time goes by in such a rush.
And now as I take and hold his hand,
I realize my baby is now a man.
No greater love can a mother have for anyone,
than the love I have for my wonderful son.
  I'm so very proud of you and
  love you with all my heart.
  Always, your Mom

Victoria McGill

Life Support

In the chill of night I shudder
Gasping breath, my heart does flutter
Electric shock runs down my spine
Know I'm running out of time

In darkest depths dim light flickers
Clotting blood through veins flows thicker
Pulsing beat begins to slow
Survival level running low

Crowded faces look down on me
Who they are I cannot see
Voices speak though I can't hear
On my lips taste salty tears

Tubes are running in and out
Not sure what they're about
Nothing in the medical history
Condition still remains a mystery

Though it couldn't be explained
In the end there was no pain
Body performed one last twitch
At the flick of a switch

Ljubica Radovic

The Deadly Disease

Here I sit in a room full of strangers
Yet I seem to know them all too well.
Eyes full of pain, dreams of life before still hang in their minds.
Fragments and splinters of their soul traveling
On a journey that seems too far to ever find home again.
Here we are, a room full of strangers coming together
To fight, to be free from the deadly disease.
Fighting hard to stay on the come back trail from hell.
Grasping each word that is spoken
Pulling them in like a fresh drink of water
Trying to put out the fire from hell.
They say, "Look at me, see what I have become,
A broken spirit, fighting for my very soul,
My very life. I had it all, then it was gone."
The deadly disease crept ever so slowly into my life
Pulling me down, letting me down.
Listen to what I have to tell.
Hear my words, take them in. Maybe,
Just maybe, you will grab hold.
Take back your soul and fight the deadly disease.

Virginia Ann Ohman

God's Black Lace

The artist hand can ne'er replace
The exquisite beauty of God's black lace.

Trees devoid of leaves in the wintertime
Bring elegance to the northern clime.

Baring their souls against a pallid sky,
Their twig and limb artistry we cannot deny.

Each exhibiting a style and grace,
The intricate weaving of God's black lace.

Betty Frater

Life Immortal

How could I know when I awoke,
All the beautiful wonders I'd see!
Or this precious gift God gave me,
Would last through eternity?

And did I know this personal friend,
Who is always close by my side.
Who gave me the freedom to choose,
If I wanted Him as my guide?

How could I know what the beauty I saw,
Was part of His marvelous plan;
And expression of love, from the Master above,
Created precisely for man!

O the innocence wonders of childhood,
Comes with laughter, joy, and tears;
And helps to shape and mold a youngster,
Into his adult years.

The wisdom that comes from awareness,
Of some bigger and mightier than you;
And that every soul is accountable,
For what they say and do.

Nellie B. Saucier

Untitled

Oh my darling my love so true.
How I long to be with you.
To hold you in my arms real tight.
To kiss and thrill all through the night.
I'm wishing I may I'm wishing I might.
Have your love the rest of my life.

Rosemary Lesley

Caribbean Lightning

Have you ever seen lightning flash across the Caribbean Sea
On the Isle of Roatan,
Lightning streaking through the sky like chariots in the night,
What a beautiful sight to see,
Lightning lighting up the sky on the Caribbean Sea,
On the Isle of Roatan,
Memories of love, flashing through your mind,
As the lightning flash through the sky like sparkles in the night,
On a beautiful hot summer night,
Near the Caribbean Sea,
On the Isle of Roatan

Rene Flores

Toys

Toys, toys all around,
On the stairs and on the ground.
I see toys wherever I go
Like red rubber balls and pretty china dolls
Colorful building blocks and such.
When I play with these toys,
I like it very much.

Lauren P. Welkey

Love

I've known you since the second grade,
I think you're really cool,
I think you're really hot,
I think of you a lot and if you like me
and if you do, don't wait to tell me in
the month of June,
I know I hurt your feelings, I know
I broke your heart, but if you forget
about liking Dawn I'll take you instead.
I know you don't feel the same way as I do about you,
but if you are willing to be a little more
than friends I wouldn't mind at all,
we could be a couple like them all,
now that I'm old enough to know about love,
I can tell that I care and really like you,
so give me a sign, give me a clue so I can tell
if you like me too.

Julie Vincenzi

A Life Of Giving

A life of giving is worth millions, true;
A life of giving is valuable to you...:
It fills your life with happiness and joy;
It cleans the soul and makes you feel royal:
The birds in the air, no one can tell...;
The fish in the sea, they do well...:
The obsession with love, they tyranny of lust;
the joy of togetherness, which is a must;
I seek things of splendor, which to you may seem to be;
Small symbols and signs of reality:
But, let us not be hasty in crushing someone else's dream;
For a ray of hope is likened to a steel beam;
It holds together the frame work of life;
And prevents you from falling into poverty and strife:

Marvin Kenneth Keith

When Will You Always Be A Friendly Flower?

When flowers bloom in the spring,
When the sun comes out in the summer,
When leaves fall in the autumn,
When it gets cold in the winter,
When will you always be a friendly flower?

Kristin M. Hernandez

Break Out

I used to live my life as a wanderer, Now I'm just crazy
The space that fills my soul feels empty
I need a fill. $1.39 a gallon
Why not shoot myself with a hot substance
I'm just a man who wants to be a boy
I just sit back, take a drag and wait for my soul to take me
Take me to that place, the place that gives me life
Take me to my ecstasy
I am life,   I am life
I run from block to block,   waiting
I hear the ticking of the clock
I hear the cry of a warrior
But would rather be I a lover
I am now at the age of essentience
An age where I choose where I take my turns
My turns give me direction which no compass can ever show me
I am crazy, crazy with desire
Here I am alone
soul covered with this shell that gives me life
But keeps me from living.

F. Tucker Schade Jr.

Children

Two children...3 and 4, one black, one white
Laughing and playing, no fears...no fights
They share toys...make up games
To them, they're both the same
Oh this world, oh this place
Look at them.....look at their face
They don't care if one is from across the tracks
They don't care about the money the other lacks
They don't care if one is poor, or the other rich
If one studder or the other eyes twitch
They just want to be friends...friends who care
It doesn't matter if no adults are there
If only adults were like those children we see
Oh what a wonderful world this would be.

Vanessa Maith

Queen Of Luck

She always was a faithful one, a working day by day,
And toiled as hard as humans could yet never got her way.

Each morn she woke up with the dawn, her coffee was fixed cold;
Then sat and gazed into the dark and dreamt of days of old.

She was so rich, she was a queen, with all she ever dreamed,
'Twas beauty in its purest form, a perfect life it seemed.

She was well known throughout the land, all people knew her name,
But even through all this good luck, this was no simple game.

Too soon the treasure became lost, good luck withered away,
Her friends and fam'ly were so sad, she could not bear to stay,

She fled so fast, quick as the wind, she needed a new life;
But to erase all of her past, she had to take on strife.

She toiled much harder than the rest, but never was paid more;
The joys in life had gone away, her life became a bore.

She worked so many jobs a day while gazing at the time,
Sometimes her talent went unpaid, a nickel or a dime.

And when she came home late at night, her coffee was fixed cold;
Then sat and gazed into the dark and dreamt of days of old.

One day she vanished in thin air, she's no where to be found;
Nobody noticed she was gone, in Heaven she was crowned.

Stephanie Maximous

Untitled

I sit on the jagged rock,
as the waves lightly embrace my bare feet,
and remember the tragic boat ride
in which my love was never found.
O' waves,
you are like daggers
which cut into my heart and my soul.

I will never again be a whole woman.

Susan-Kate Heaney

My Valentine

Every day is Valentines Day when I'm with you.
   My heart goes flip flop a lot, and that is true.
Don't send roses, diamonds and candy,
   Just having you is oh so dandy.
Every day is Valentines Day, you know that too.
   Because I love you.

Every day is Valentines Day when I'm with you.
   Now here is something nice that you can do.
Send me roses, diamonds and candy,
   Then you will always be so dandy.
Every day is Valentines Day, it's plain to see.
   Because you love me.

Olga Jaryga

The Spirit Of Man

The Spirit of man, a great mystery you say;
What is it, my friend? You ask.
Where does it live, and what does it do;
Where does it come from, and where will it go?

Some say it's the conscience of man,
And some describe it as your most inner being.
For others, it's the quiet voice,
That speaks to you from within.

The Spirit of man, the human spirit,
is entwined to the body and soul;
And, like an inner light, it supernaturally shines;
The pathway of man, guiding his life.

That great Spirit of man, you say;
resides with man, and directs his life,
But, when it departs from the body and soul,
Tell me, my friend; where does it go, and what will it do?

Lynette Benjamin

Seniors

Where has everyone gone
Disappeared before my eyes
Left out the window
To a place called the world
Those young days don't last long
They're gone before you know it
A trader that used to be mine
Spoke to me of how he's grown up
This is a turn for the better
I'm proud for the change
It's such a relief to know
He's not the desperate he used to be
Now I have noticed from everyone left
We take things a little more seriously
Growing up is a part of life
Just remember yesterday is in our memories
To be activated at any given time
Soon I'll be out the window and I'll disappear
There will be another person
To feel what I feel next year

Jason Elschlager

It

On a cold and lifeless day.
Wherever the trees have
been striped of their beauty
and the sun has gone away.
We sat looking out our windows.
Wondering why it has passed us by
Did it not hear our hearts fall to its feet.

Can it not see the love on our faces
or hear our hearts beating at a faster pace.
Does it not see the longing in our eyes, that
someday we might meet.

They say it makes the world go around
Everyone wants it, we all say we deserve it.
We act as if it's grown wild underground.

Such fools, we all are to think
Because we say we need it.
It would come to us in a blink.

Well, I'm here to tell you all that it
Doesn't work that way, love must be earned.

Nancy J. Wood

Transformation

Dull dark armor shineless on the knight
Spectral voices sounding out of sight
Dim mournful faces forming in the night
Death is awaiting shunning all forms of light

A quick bite spells eternal rest
Razor like fangs to end life's jest
Watch thought and movement slow
Where fleshly shell fails to go

Immortal soul soars in love
From depths' descending worldly glove
To eternal spirits holy abode
Where truth's creator is fully known
As triumphant Son takes one home

Frank R. Sanchez

The Inheritance

I viewed the casket, teary eyed.
The pain was great. My Grandma died.
To a child nearly six, but still just five,
I needed her with me and still alive.
How could the God she had taught me to know,
Take her away when I needed her so?
She taught me to read, to spell, count and write.
She taught me the difference between wrong and right.
She taught me to reason, to think and to love.
She taught me respect, (sometimes with a shove).
She taught me patience with those around me.
She taught me of angels who still surround me.
Her laugh was infectious as well as her smile.
They remain with me after all of this while.
Money was scarce in those Depression years.
One day she told me, while wiping her tears,
"I've no wealth or possessions for me to give.
I've accomplished little in this life that I live."
Sainted Grandma, please know, wherever you be,
The gifts that you gave made a Lady of me.

Loretta M. Lee

Friends Forever

I will be your friend forever.
I know forever is a long time.
But I will always endeavor
To respect your feelings as if they were mine.

You always build up my self esteem.
I hope I am able to do the same for you.
Sometimes I backslide, it would seem
And think you would put me down, too.

Like I have been told so many times,
My old tapes cause me to feel that way.
Then I realize how many times
You have brightened up my day.

It is so easy to be a friend
To someone as nice as you.
My friendship will not end
Until my time on earth is through.

Rowena N. Smith

Marriage

Poets and Philosophers have been trying
with failure to analyze love in all its
many aspects.
Through centuries lovers have found
themselves coming together for one moment
in time and example. For this ceremony
is a clear illustration of the poets and
Philosophers missing link.
Two hearts joined as one in life, death,
and love. Two lives examples of maybe's
and what if's and dreams.
If only everyone could know the
accomplishment in such an idea then
the world would be undivided.
Until then all may receive a chance
to glimpse it in a star-crossed pair
chosen to stand in time and example
and understand the amazement and
the fantasy of love.

Martha Klick

The Man Within The Man

Fishing, hunting and farming was what he loved to do
He had mushroom spots that were only known by few
With all the playing that Jim did he still had time for his friends
No job was too tough, not for a man like him.
As a husband he was loving and caring — gentle but strong.
As a father he was a teacher, a confidant and always a friend.
There was nothing in the world he wouldn't do for them.

There was no "step" in this father for he treated us as his own.
He had no idea of the lasting impression he made on us,
or how he held us together like stone.

Oh, how we will miss him we all loved him so...
But please remember he would want us to know...
Life continues on and so must we. Although we no
Longer have him on earth, he will always be in our memories.

Katrina Newman-Turner

SO

Complete honesty will be exchanged
with every good night kiss

A false smile to an intricate story
the wind at the window to silent footsteps

Exposing all experience will complete
the circle creating an engulfing welcome

For each there is one to need,
one to understand, one to belong

Danelle Renne

A Wish And A Star

It happened on a starry night
This falling star fell just right
So I closed my eyes extra tight
And hitched a ride on this star in flight.

"Make a wish!" The star bellowed with glee,
"But from the heart this wish must be."
In my heart I dug down deep
And found a wish nearly half asleep,
"You must give the wish a life of its own."
So I nudged and dusted till it brightly shone.

I unfurled my heart and let it fly
Then gradually opened each eye
The star will see the wish to its destination
And return for one of yours that needs navigation.
Curtis W. Luttrell

From A Distance

Slightly less than a dozen different colored pine trees,
swaying in the wind.
The colors amongst them range from greens to browns,
with a touch of red here and there.
They stand tall and proud.
Under them, are bushes, and other smaller trees with no leaves.
There is a thin blanket of snow covering the ground, that seem to go
on forever.
From a distance, there are a few buildings, telephone wires,
and cars steadily moving by.
As a gust of cold wind blow by, one or two leaves falls off of an
almost bare tree.
From a distance, as far as you can see, everything looks peaceful.
Sarah Van Nostrand

Falling

I scream but there is no sound,
I breathe but there is no air,
I hear the howls, but there is no animals,
I feel the ice against my skin.

But there is no screams or howls,
no ice against my skin. Not even
air in this world.

In this world, there is only
Phantoms.
Crystal J. Lowry

Love's Poem

To a risen sunrise beneath a wide arena of open space,
Where intricacy paints the purple winged lace
Of love swirling, upon the ocean waves of air unfurling,
Blowing, blending, gently above.
Sapping trees sweep each other's feathered limbs in pure delight,
Amid the sweetly woven light
Of day and her brilliant display.
Cooling the calm leaving of night,
Dancing rays bubble in subtle warmth
Cleansing the gentle face, of Change.
Silks and scents pave the richness of color,
Tapestries of sound breathe into tune
To the fragrant falling of the whispering moon.
Fainting clouds disappear
As sharpening blue speaks, loud and clear.
Rivers still running cold, soothe thy tired toes,
As angelic rings dazzle an opening rose.
Sent by true love! The most precious gift,
All in the breaking of a most royal lift,
of day.
Jenea Zapparelli

Ode To A Gentle Woman

A graced-filled woman,
  this Mary Ruth.
A woman of faith,
  a woman of prayer.
Eighty-some years she walked this earth.
  But only three loves had she.
    God was supreme,
    Community and neighbor intertwined.
Her God espoused her
  with love divine.
Community and neighbor
  quietly immersed was she.
Everyone she met
  was stranger no longer, for...
    when she listened to your words,
      she heard your heart;
    when she looked into your eyes,
      she saw your very soul.
Be gentle with her, God, she was gentle with me.
Hold her close to you, as she did me.
Sarah Ann D'Amico

My Little Angel

  A cloud of golden, shimmering powder
appeared before me. The dust formed
the outline of a small child, like a constellation
on a clear, summer night. It moved toward me, and as
it did this, a little girl formed dearly, precious and pure.
  Her eyes were blue, then green, and brown. Her hair
was blonde, then red, and black. Her face was brown, then
yellow, then white, every one of her features showing beauty in
its own special way.
  Wings of gold and ivory downy feathers unfolded from her back.
  This wonderful creature faded away as it appeared, folding her
wings behind her, and gently closing her eyes.
  I never bid my little angel farewell, but I have found a little
bit of her in everyone I meet.
Angela Calchera

Now That I Have Multiple Sclerosis

Can I Find Poetry For This Life....

This life turned upside down.
Can I forget the life that I remember, life as I knew it.
Years of travel, excitement, adventure,
full of city talk, exotic places and finances.

I miss the city talk,
I don't know the words anymore.
What can I expect of this new life?
Will it be easy to find the new words?
Can I make a new road?
Turn this illness into my new self.

There is poetry in my new self
But it is a different theme...
a persistent heavy theme, with me constantly,
wearing me down
waking me to fear each morning
the hollow feeling that late afternoon brings
sometimes with a cane, sometimes staggering
stumbling and clinging to walls.
I am definitely a wall walker
as I head out to face my new self!
Marjorie Kamps

Beautiful Someone

You are the beautiful someone - the beautiful someone for me -
Smiling so sweetly - charming discreetly - you're Paradise-bound,
I suppose;

Like the dawn, your presence creates an illusion - exciting my
heart, heaven knows;
You're bloom on the flowers, that lingers for hours,
You're sweet, you're sublime, you're a rose.

And when the moon shines - descending through all the ages -
comes melody so pure and free of all insane illusion -
Then I am yours and you are mine - as we drift along the shores
of time - we kiss - and then it's bliss again, in quaint romantic
places:

Filled with bewitching enchantment - rememb'ring your eyes all
aglow - you are the beautiful someone, my dar-ling - for me -
and please remember - you'll always be so!

Charles L. Richardson

The Sub-urban African Alien

He walks down the quite street,
Faces never laughing or crying,
Stern they appear.

They trade with clean, soiled feet;
Some tainted, some with blossomed ideas.

He walks down the quite street,
A passing guest,

An alien like all his forebears,
With beautiful skin, black and kiln-dry.

Starring faces still on him.

He poises,
He trades softly with head highly raised.

Network news tells him black, white, blue,
People gazing at him wear,

But cars parked besides the mirage roadside,
Only he sees in color,

Now he understands why all the gazes,
An immigrant African - an alien,
Adorning his cultural signature,
The caftan, the cone hat and agbada.

Primus Chuks Igboaka

Injustice

I Inner city youths cry out; not by themselves,
　　but by all youth.
N Never has there been such confusion,
　　anger, loneliness, pain —
J Justice! For all people, races, age,
　　creed and nationalities Cry Out!
U Unbelievable sorrow
　　has overcome us.
S Strength, courage, honor, hope and faith —
　　sustains us.
T Tick-tock, tick-tock, tick —
　　we're running out of time.
I Infinity — nothing —
　　silence.
C Children! Wake up!
　　We have failed you.
E Every child and unborn child —
　　Hear our cry —!!!

Patricia Palmer

Hiding

All alone
Sitting in the dark
Hiding from the fears
That are in my mind
Waiting for the light
To come and swoop in and take me away
From this fearful place
So that I might continue to hide
From all the evil of this world
I shall never have the strength
To fight all that comes my way
So for now I hide hiding away in the dark
Hoping to reach some comfort
But always an arms length away
So you keep trying to hide deeper
In this new world you are trying to create
Hoping the more you hide
You won't have to face the world head on
So you dig deeper and deeper
Until it is too late and you cannot be saved

Jennifer Palmer

I Thought It Was Over

I thought it was over
I could not go on with life
The thought of losing you had entered my mind
As thoughts became reality I cry over you
So many times
So many times I couldn't sleep
So many things upset me
It was all because of you
I wish it was all a bad dream
That I would soon wake up
But you no longer live
The pain lies down deep
So many times I cry
So many times I wish it could all change
I wish upon a star as I cry myself to sleep
That I could have seen you once before you had to leave
I hear your voice talking to me
It's all over now
I'll let your soul rest
I love you and hope you rest in peace

Jennell Thurn

Secrets

As I think one day I wonder
what is a secret?
I suppose that no one knows
it is a secret
every secret is different
but what is the purpose?
I know
I am the only one who can know
and no one else can ever know
because I know
but if I am the only knower than what good is it?
I will have no reflections, or thoughts about it
If I merely forget it will end
so what are secrets for?
Do they make friends, or break them
make peace, or create war
hide hate, or destroy love
no one will ever know but me
for I have kept the secret

Mark Chakoian

Life's Contradictions

If a man does not live his life,
    Can he die?
If a lonely man is kidnapped
    Is he really missing?
If a man who lifts weights can't control his temper,
    Is he really strong?
If a man has no love for anything,
    Can he die of a heart attack?
If a man does not live his life,
    Can he die?

Derek Brigante

The Vagabond

A lonely vagabond was I until you came along.
Searching, yearning for someone to give my heart a song.
I trekked o'er every hill and dale and trudged through valleys deep.
Alas! I knew until I had found you
That I would not slumber or sleep.
I braced myself against the cold and braved the blistering heat.
I danced with death, faced dangers untold,
And struggled with thoughts of defeat.
A pitiful vagabond was I consumed with pain and grief,
Until you came like refreshing rain
And brought to me sweet relief.
You showered me with your precious love.
You gave me the joy I'd been missing.
You brought a bright twinkle back into my eye,
And convinced me that life was worth living.
I have no one to thank, save the Father above,
For allowing my dream to come true.
Oh, Heaven forbid if e'er I forget
What a treasure I have in you!

Amy J. Freemire

Love...

    Love is a special thing. It can't be
bought, stolen or denied.
    Love is an act of giving and receiving.
Everyone has love if they know how to use it.
    A child shows their love through
hugs and kisses.
    An adult accepts love through kind
words and deeds.
    Animals recognize love through handling
and cuddling them.
    Love can be said in many ways.
Candy hearts and flowers are all signs of love.
    Love can turn a tear into a smile.
Love can mend a broken heart.
    Love can be a song in your heart.
Love has many doors.
    Love can be given, received and
recognized through everyone.
    Love is a special thing.

Helen B. Matheney

Quest For Peace

I stare at the ocean as the sun rises from the east
As the water breaks quietly and rushes to my feet
I know for a second the ocean can become a beast
The water is brisk as chills go up to the top of your head
Closing your eyes to feel the air that is so fresh
you take a deep breath to taste the mist
your mind is at ease for you are at peace
A seagull in the background squawks as it flies for the ocean
It is at home where he is at peace in his mind
The sun warms my face as it climbs to the sky
another beautiful day in paradise
I look to the sky and not a cloud around for
my mind can only see Peace . . . Peace . . . Peace

Christopher J. Gambino

Steadfast Love

It seems so long ago, you were just a stranger,
so full of mystery and danger.

But all at once you become my friend,
always willing to step in.

You made me smile, you made me laugh,
you always kept me on the right path.

Through so many others, our friendship grew,
But what the future held no one knew.

Still for me you were willing to take a chance,
without even a backward glance.

So together, we set out to learn life's lessons,
but what we found was one true message.

Although you think one way and I another,
we really do compliment each other.

With all the world still to conquer, we have already won,
because today we join together as one.

Now until the very end, until the very last,
at your side I will stand - steadfast.

Brookie L. Crawford

To E:

In haste I spoke, with little kindness;
    You showed distress, - but too, forgiveness.

Thoughtless and careless, I scarred your heart;
    You hid the hurt and - in time forgot.

So was shown our Lord's forgetting and giving:
    That He blesses us oft. Both morn and ev'ning.

I tried proving love with gifts and things:
    You treasured most my touch, - my being.

Gently you mused of my many mistakes;
    Then helped me atone, and them erase.

Thus learned I, God guides, - makes plain
    Life's meaning, and His love delights our long betrothing.

David M. Hubler

Poetry, Poetry

Poetry, poetry, that might be the way
for me to get out what I have to say.
That I have come backwards to the study of DNA.

Phosphorus, Phosphorus, it is the light.
ATP= C10, H16, N5, O13, P3, He did it right!

The bugs have their antennas. We are not even looking?
Because then they would learn of all the oil we have been cooking.

The soul is electric, it's the battery I quest!
No artificial vanilla, only God's best.
So forgive them, Lord, they have not quite been told.
Let them wait for the book if I could be so bold.

Frannie Hebert

Pets

While looking through this and that the other day
I came upon a collar belonging to one I once loved
How quickly they seem to grow and fade from our lives
We remember and grieve for love lost, while our hearts
Rejoice in the memories dearly held
Snatched from our lives by natures cruel boundaries
Fate's unyielding paradox:
That to love one means to open your heart to all the love
And all the pain of having had them
And being master of nothing.

Stephanie McCaskill

Maternal Male

Maternal weight gain, unmerciful morning sickness
Accepting the guilt, for her spiteful rudeness

The sensuous enlargement of her breast
Responsive to her condition, to show my best

Precarious moods their enormous appetite
Allowing her to feel, she is always, absolutely right

Knowing when to be gentle and forgiving
The pickles, ice-cream, what a misunderstanding

Sensing when to be strong but weak
Our new life within, is hungry and ready to peak

Reminiscing, of all the pleasure she brings
Waiting to see him create baby bathtub rings

A soothing bubble bath and a chilled carafe of wine
Enchanted to reveal, she is worthy of my time

Back massage and rubbing of her precious feet
Ready to rave, to the people we meet

His opportunity to parade, their eternal love
Eager to bestow, she's as pure as a dove

Unbearable labor, miraculous delivery
Love for this wife and newborn baby. Maternal Male
G. J. Gentry

Tears Of An Angel

Long have we wept for humans.
Long have we wished for joy to your hearts.

An angel's tears
are for happiness
for each soul
who reaches out
to talk to us.

An angel's tear
is for sadness
for the despair in the
hearts of humans
who do not know
the love of an angel.

Long have we wept for joy.
Long have we waited for this day.

Angels who love you!
Ricky Cullipher

Untitled

Around a table, long and wide
forty people stared with eighty eyes
Doubting faces wondering, pondering why
images and questions racing through their minds.
Gathered around were those alike
yet different in a critical way,
Not gender, color or language known
their being there part of the scheme in play.
For no particular reason to be seen
they were chosen to make this round,
Tomorrow forty new people with eighty eyes
shall sit, stare as their lives abound.
Life's journey is blind to prejudice
cares not about things we know,
Life only cares that we give it a try
so that with our journey, life too grows.
Cathy L. Snyder

Old Friends

Our steps grow weary as we follow the familiar path,
Our sight grows dim to watch the golden sun
Peep over the far horizon or behold its glorious beauty
As it sinks behind the western hills.
The thousands of stars as they blink in the dark sky,
Or the silvery moon playing hide-and-seek
With the clouds on a stormy night.

Though our sight grows dim to the beauty around us,
Our mind's eye will see them forever.
The bushy tail squirrel eating nuts beneath the tree.
The beautiful red bird singing its praise for a new day,
The lovely rose unfolding to full beauty,
The familiar path we no longer follow.

A gallery of precious pictures,
All the happy things of by-gone years,
Bright and clear as yesterdays.
Our mind has a thousand eyes lest we forget
And grow old.
Frances H. Weidner

Me, I Am

A black man, doing the best that I can
in a world that seems not to care!
To me, it seems
if you lose your soul
to reach your goal
You still won't be anywhere,
for life is a game
a never ending game
that makes you believe that you've won
by the time you realize that your life was a lie,
Too late, your life's already done - for some.
Wake up
Shawn A. Emerson

I'll Tell You What Some Old Guy Told Me

I remember back in the good old days.
The wind would take us where we wanted to go,
and fear kept us close.
If we went to far from home we wouldn't return.
Either the monster would get us or we would fall off the edge of the
      earth.
Today people no longer fear these things.
They're still out there, hiding.
I think I saw one of them the other day, behind a 7-11 I believe it
      was.
Oh they're still out there, you just can't see them.
Joseph E. Grohoski

What If I Fall

   I know of your reasons. I know of your
hurt and pain. I know you don't want to try, but
What if I fall. Don't you think I've sent it, don't you
think I've been there before? They say its better to
have lost at love, than to never have loved at all,
but what if I fall?
Do you know me? Do you know of my hurt and pain?
She says; don't you think I've seen it, don't you think
I've been there before? What if I fell down on
my knees and begged you please. Would you bend
and touch my face, of would you keep pushing
me away?
   Now what if I Fall?
Lewis C. Alexander

The Wizards Whistle

The trees are fingers rising out of Hades
The stone tables lend me their inspiration
A checkerboard engraved in the stone table
A platform for war
Kings, queens and pawns battling to the end
A strange spirit takes over my surroundings
The wind begins to push stronger
The wizards whistle from the tops of the clouds
Obstacles placed before me
Conquer them and I shall be free
Free from all this turmoil
Free from all this confusion
Free from me
S. F. Angeles

The Victory Of Dawn

As the curtain of night did close,
An encore was called, and I, the dawn arose.
As I moved center stage, with ultimate grace,
My audience, in awe, reflected in the radiance of my face.

Did the dark of night really disappear,
As it does every day of the year?
Or is it a mystery that lies within each soul,
Waiting patiently, in the wings, to unfold?

Will the darkness claim the spirit and cannot be free?
Forever faced and sentenced to a dark eternity!

"Nay," say I, for I am the morning light,
I shall unfurl my wings, and plan my flight,
And soar and triumph, o'er the absence of light,
My victory claimed, o'er the dark, dark night.
Linda B. Van Hook

Our Uncle

How many times can a family say,
    There is a person living today.
One who is friendly, has feelings and cares,
    For the sake of others and all their despairs.

Someone so loving and eager to help,
    No thought of payment, no injuring welt.
Just one happy uncle, glad he is there,
    To help out his family in bad weather or fair.

It makes us feel joyous to know he's around,
    To keep us from sinking and up on high ground.
How many more words could we possibly state,
    For having an Uncle with love never hate.

The person we turn to, a smile on his face,
    In our hearts he claims a warm special place.
Sharon Gross-Culp

My Angel

Do we live life just to die?
Is talk of forever only a lie?
Now that he's gone we're forever apart.
Where is heaven? Where does it start?
Now he's my angel watching from above.
God, please say hello and send him my love.
Please give him back, it seems only fair.
I know it sounds selfish, but I don't really care.
When I talk to him I wonder if he hears.
Can he feel my pain, can he see my tears?
He didn't live his life, he never had the time.
Is being young and having fun such a crime?
I guess so because now he's gone away.
If I could say one more thing, what would I say?
I'd make him understand how much we really care.
After all, living life to die isn't really fair.
Sarah J. Pina

Reunion

I remember your smile, your friendship, your faith.
You were always positive, you could patiently wait.
You found good in things that were bad,
You could make me smile, no matter how sad.

You took care of your own, with endless love.
Showed your feelings, prayed to God above.
You always gave, no matter the need,
Be it food, love or just a strong sleeve.

I miss you more with each passing day,
needing your guidance to show me the way.
But I know in my heart, if I speak out loud,
You can hear my words there above the clouds.

When I am called by God above,
I will again be within your arms of love.
To talk and laugh and share our time,
Forever together in heaven divine.
Karen O'Bannon

Through The Looking Glass

As I look at you with comfort, no pain in you I see.
You are but a pale distraction, silent from the air you breathe.
Remembering the innocence, you had bestowed on me.
The laughter and compassion that lie within me, are but a
Reflection of the things you use to be.
Your kindness to the world you touched, the hope which you inspired,
Will forever mean so much.
Your painful struggle for life, afflicted by the hurt.
Symbolizes strength and relief for everyone to learn.
Anguished by your timely death, sadness in my heart.
I feel the sorrows in me, forever now we'll be apart.
Mourning is hard to do, for I feel you are still here.
It is hard for me to let you go because you were so dear.
I'll cherish all our memories, those days were full of grace, the
Way your were, in my mind, I shall always see your face.
As I look back, "through the looking glass", a mist appears in my
Eyes, for I will not forget you, as time passes by.
Diadel K. Ortiz

Ants

Ants,
Just ants,
Little black ants.
Sightless workers of the soil,
Mindless individuals, lowest of the classes,
Tireless workers who make up the masses.
They work for a queen they've never seen.
Very dependable, yet totally expendable.
They scurry about for days on end,
looking forward to the company picnic.
David Edward Jetty

Life

Life is strange,
to a point that's not real,
people walk down the streets,
and never show how they feel.
If people are angry, sad, or mad,
they just walk around, and pretend they are glad.
When people say thing's that are so mean,
Things that are rude, upset, and unseen,
they hurt people that do nothing wrong,
so they walk around and sing a sad song.
In Martin Luther King's I have a dream,
He dreamed that people would quit being so mean.
As my poem ends, the world's still the same
Life can be hard, and no one knows your name.
Chrisi Gigante

You'll Never Know What Your Love Meant To Me

I was just informed you don't want me anymore
If your love's a game I guess I never scored
I did everything that one man could do
Girl I tried my best to stay in love with you
But it wasn't good enough you made up your mind
You're with someone else so you left me behind
The nights we weren't together I stayed at home
You always knew where I was I never wondered or roamed
The nights we were together I felt your soft touch
Oh how I wish you'd come back girl I miss you so much
I don't have lots of money or a college degree
If that's what it takes I guess that takes care of me
But one thing I have I've had from the start
Only for you all of my heart
Don't worry baby please don't cry
I'll make it somehow or at least I'll try
Don't try to find me just leave me be
I guess you'll never know what your love meant to me.

James William Yeatts

Where Did All The Good Times Go

May you all have your special dreams
And I hope they all come true
For I love you all so dearly
As I think of all of you.
You are my reason for living
As I've watched you grow and grow.
I know you'll keep on learning
All that there is to know.
That will make me happy
For I love you all so much
Please be the best you can
Your reward will be a bunch
And as you love each other
I hope you will think of me
Just pretend that I am with you
It will be a great memory.
Bless you, my children,
Remember I'll always care, I'll love you forever
Even though I am not here.

Mary Bohl

I Played In The Mud

I was told to be quiet, be still, and sit straight
but I simply can't sit here, it's too long a wait

To act nicely and proper is just not my style
I'd rather run freely and play for a while

I played in the mud and made quite a mess
I had quite a pie but it fell on my dress

Mama called, "come on, we must go to church!"
but she couldn't find me, I'd climbed up the birch

"Get out of that tree! You'd better come down!"
so at the bottom I met her standing there with a frown

She looked at my dress, mud stain and all;
she needed a reason for the things that she saw

I have to excuses for the things that I did
all I could think of was I'm just a kid!

Laura Hackett

Heavenly Message

I am the way, the truth, the light
I'll always guide you through the night
You've always done whatever is right
With me, always in your sight
Believe me, I hear your every plight
Therefore, there is no need for flight
It's been a struggle, a long, hard fight
You've just about reached the height
For everlasting love, happiness and peace
With God's Eternal grace that will not cease
With only the possibility of absolute increase
This heavenly message sent from above
Is God's greatest gift of love
Sent directly from above
Which hovers as a white dove
To be worn as the perfect glove
With no need to push or shove.

Catherine Liebel

His Love

I know I still love him
Or like him a lot
I know I want another shot.
There's this thing about him
I wonder what it is
It turns out ok
Still thinking about him every day
I think he's interested
How do I know?
I wish I knew his feelings
I wish they would show
I know he means a lot to me
I need to know if we'll ever
We're friends no we've kept in touch
Every day I think of him, I miss him so much
Again I ask, what do I do?
I need his love pure and true.
I need to know how he feels.
One time I will until then I'll imagine
His love is still

Angie Menefee

Love, Why Does It Hurt So Bad?

As I sit here all alone, I often find myself
asking, why does love hurt so bad?
Unknown to me why I feel this way,
the question arises but no one can say, why
love hurt so bad.
Many deep feelings become involved and yet
the question remains unsolved, why does love hurt so bad?
The ins and outs, the ups and downs on
this carousel of love, I turn to the heavenly
skies above looking for an answer.
Amongst the clouds so broad and wide,
my feelings so deep I could not hide, the
tear that rolled down from my eye...
Why does love hurt so bad?
I say to myself just to ease the pain what my mother
has said to me, she said "my child, don't be so sad, for true love
hurts, you see."
This has been done to test the strength of people who are in
Doubt, if it's true love when things get tough only the
Strong can work it out.

Delphine Timmons

Bull And Finch

As we sit in the pub
we watch
as the fog marches in off the Thames
and drowns out the simmer of conversation.

And as if out of a dream
two figures
filter through the damp, smoky presence.
Hooligans from Brixton
attired in black
and shimmering like diamonds.

Glasses cease to clatter
Darts no longer fly
Dominoes fall
As our future is forced before us
through these defiant monsters
who want to swallow
the whole bloody island.

Christopher Oakes

Enough

Walking by, the forest whispers the time,
The time that time will stand,
And camouflage the sun.
But the sun will not disappear
For its brightness shines throughout.
Yet brightness is not quite enough,
Not for this time.

This journey seems to extend forever
And when will there be an end.
The trees age and brown and green fade to ash,
Yet the forest has still not passed.

As the night falls the air out there rushes
For the time has come-all too slow.
The forest has burned to a core
Leaving behind only a speck,
A speck of light radiated by the sun.
Perhaps time was not defined,
For the sun was enough to stand.

Melissa Marie Vasbinder

My Dad, Your Gramps

My Dad and your Gramps was a grand and noble man.
He worked so hard and tilled the land.
Frank H. Wolf was his name.
A Veteran of World War I, who suffered pain.

A farmer, a husband and father of four,
Was happy and proud, never asking for more.
He wasn't president nor owned a lot of land.
He wasn't a Yale nor a Harvard man.

To land and riches he laid no big claim.
For his family to be happy was his highest aim.
Gramps was witty, humorous and liked a good joke.
Always sympathetic and kind to all of his folk.

Yet so rich with the blessings from the Lord.
These were the blessings my Daddy stored.
This grand old man lived to be 79.
And hated to leave his loved ones behind.

To Daddy's type of riches I lay down,
Humbleness, Honesty, Kindness, all put on his crown,
But above all, an honored name.
Only wish that I could be the same.

Norma Jean Endris

Genes

Ashes remain
Warmth's reminder of mother's
Bittersweet belly
Bare beneath the sky
Ice-blue and begging

Mother whom I once knew and would not
Recognize again

A veiled faced memory
Dreams in black

Now I her child

In this unrelenting world
Of black eyes, black hair
Fractured memories
Powerful and unforgiving
Beat the rhythm

Hear the fear of death

Walks through me
Splinters my genes

Celia Panagopoulos

The Accused

You ask me, Sir, if I would kill
I have neither the desire nor the will
I have never aspired nor conspired
To slash a tire or set a fire
Nor have I had the indiscretion
To prescribe arsenic for his indigestion
And when I think of having fun
I do not get and load a gun
I have never contracted murder for hire
Nor bought insurance in order to retire
But if such thoughts from time to time
Have upon occasion crossed my mind
There exists Sir one great detraction
That prevents such thoughts from becoming action
Now you may think that I don't like jail
But the truth is Sir, I'm afraid of hell
No, I have reason not to kill
Always have, always will
You asked a question and I have answered
No! I will not kill that bastard!

Betty A. Burnett

The Summary Of Life

I am built on a foundation as solid as the fathomless
    depths of quicksand;
I am as predictable as the varieties of Mother Nature;
    I am as stable as a storm-tossed sea.

I have seen billions born and billions die;
I have witnessed the highest of triumphs and the lowest of defeats;
I have seen thousands of senseless wars and millions of
meaningless treaties.

I have seen the rise and fall of great nations and civilizations;
I have noted the resilience of humanity, as well as its
utter fragility;
I bear testimony to the wondrous miracles of God;
and the glorious miracles of science.

I am that which is timeless and inexhaustible;
I am the center of the universe;
I will always exist in some form, somewhere in the
limitless voids of space and time;
I Am Life!

Deborah A. Jacks

Degrees

There lies a gap between tough and tender
Compromise to surrender or race and gender.
From the heat wave to the freeze or the north
Winds to a cool breeze all she hears and
Everything he sees are weighed out into varying degrees.
As black and white turn into grey and nocturnal
Creatures meet the day innocuous axioms continue to
Sway, while countless nerve endings are beginning
to fray. Laughter swells to tears while faith gives
way to fears, emotional contusions are wrapped in
subterfuge and behold our days are years. Beyond
the sleep into the light hangs the thread which holds
our plight and feeds our need to identify, experiment
and classify from the morning we're born until the
night we die. The boundaries we've crossed always
shifting sometimes lost, keep us aligned and help
fill the void from what is kept and what is tossed.
So as we reach new fahrenheits, we'll strike a
chord into the sights of the very one's who were
afraid to look inside their centigrade. Mercury out.

Charles Carter Jr.

Christmas Day

Christmas Day is drawing near
Soon it will be Christmas Eve
Not long before Santa is here
Then gifts everyone will receive,

The trees are decorated so gay
The spirit of Christmas is in the air,
But everyone enjoys Christmas in a special way,
For everyone is joyous at Christmas-time,
Everywhere.

Christmas is for everyone
Young and old, rich or poor
For it is the birthday of Jesus;
God's loving son,
That the spirit of Christmas shall
Be cherished forever more.
Remember Christmas as a source
Of happiness
What it means and stands for
Is a guide to the Christmas spirit of gladness,
That will always be remembered ever more.

Joan D. Snyder

Thank You

I wish I was born twenty-four days earlier;
I would have met the man who was loved.
When he died, a saint was lost, and gained by God.
Some loveless beings treated him low;
Most loved him more than life itself.
One daughter never felt such pain;
when he could not walk she was his cane.

I wish I was born twenty-four days earlier
To meet the man who created her.
Maybe I did cross paths with him,
Him coming up and me coming down.
I am told I look like the man, my papa.
When I see him again I will say two things:
I'm sorry your life became an impossible test
but thank you for my mother, she's the best!

Robert J. Meier

Wind Rider

Time stood hushed in the tranquil, murmuring, morning mist,
Dawn hung golden, like a haunting, golden lullaby...
The melody chimed, dusk to day break,
With love of incandescent, irradiated light....
Spreading with the language of universal standing,
Expressions made luminescent, with heart flowers...
Each preferred passion of happiness shared,
Sparks of life, driven and housed within...
Wishes of the heart, are the patterns of love,
Patterns, shapes created by life experiences...
Like clouds of roving, white tossed by the wind,
Teasers of the living, dramatics in action...
Beholders, reflector of mirror images,
Thronged, pressed by hardship, endurance tested...
Nighttime hindrances, misted by clouded time,
Pegasus' flight, milky clear sky strung...
Love displayed like studded, diamond happy.

L. Catherine Snow

Compendium

So I've written it down
with all my discrepancies
it's a point of fact
sometimes I tried to be discreet
the discursiveness from sect to sect
has helped set me free
ideas that are pending
I could explain to a tee
the points that I have written
often scare me
Putting it on paper seems to me
to be a part of my stupidity
but no one else would hear
I fear they'd misunderstand
so I confided in thee.
I speak to the paper as though it where real
it has soaked up every word
of my little spiel
for that I commend and will continue to write
because a blank piece of paper can be a sad sight.

Tony Louderbough

Touch Me

My dreams come alive with you
Like autumn comes alive with color

You bog my sense with a touch
Caressing me in places no man has

My arms ache to hold you to my breast
To feel your breath upon my neck

My darling, I grow weary of time
Longing for your promise, holding the secret

I have no one but you
It is your touch that keeps me alive

Touch me again and again
With words of hope and comfort

I need you as much as you need me
Touch me.

Becky Ann Feltmann

Angel From The Light

The brightest light that can be seen
Shines from the heavens, beyond reality.
Purest of all forms that can ever be true
Was the angel of the light, who came and took you.

I sometimes stare into the sky at night
In search for the angel, that came from the light.
A dream of Elysian fields, reality for you
Reaching for nirvana, an existence come true.

Soaring through the clouds, aviating through time
Multitudes of angels, paradise in mind.
The starry skies of heaven, forgiving all your sins
Closer to the light, driven by the winds.

My field of dreams, forever to be
My guardian angel, to remain by me.
A faithful desire, being together again
Is a genuine wish, from the beginning to the end.

Terry Ann Shuman

Sadness/Happiness

The cheering crowds are gone
Beer pumps are idle
Popcorn machines have lost their sizzle
The other team has won
The game is over
Our team is grieving in the showers
The odds were wrong
The fat lady has sung

Sad is a stadium with no spectators
Sad is a field littered with paper wrappers
Alone in the stands I am looking at a bad score
Will I ever want to see more

I should not be unhappy
Saturday is the next kick off
Our team for sure will win the day
The crowd again will be hoping for the play off
My sadness I will not be remembering
As a true sports fan again I will be cheering

Yvette Eve Tetreault-Ducharme

Brother Jim

I had a brother, whose name was Jim.
A better friend no one could win.
I can't deny his past mistakes.
They were at times so very great.
But at this time. I choose to reflect
Upon those things I shall never forget.
Like days in youth with brother Jim.
And all the games we would try to win.
The yesterdays of fun and boyish laughter.
Such are the things that cannot die.
For they will ever be part of Jim and I.
But now what can I say to brother Jim.
While his form is so quiet and still.
Except to say. As I always will.
That brother Jim is my brother still.

Albert E. Leather

Winter Wonderland

Sharp winds blow fiercely across snow
covered fields,
Snowflakes dance wildly about,
Ponds are frozen over,
Rooftops are blanketed in freshly fallen
snow,
Trees silently sway with leaves long gone,
Winter is a wonderful season.

Kari Mizer

Fatherhood

Fatherhood is a beautiful reality,
Fatherhood is a touch of spirituality.
Fatherhood is a blessing to behold,
Fatherhood is a story that needs to be told.

Fatherhood means more than conception,
Fatherhood means more than alimony collection.
Fatherhood means more than bringing home the bacon,
Fatherhood means more than always an absence explanation.

Fatherhood is a gift given to special men,
Fatherhood is an example discouraging sin.
Fatherhood is to show unconditional love and care,
Fatherhood is simply a willingness to be there.

Fatherhood must be a sacrifice,
Fatherhood must be a willingness to pay the price.
Fatherhood must be more than just on the surface,
Fatherhood must be your dedicated purpose.

Fatherhood is an institution that is serious in nature,
Fatherhood is not something found on the headline of the paper.
Fatherhood is a message of eternity,
Fatherhood is the continuing of your legacy.

Chakiris M. Moss

Surrogate Saviour

To die on a cross is no small feat
Unbearable pain in the dust and heat
To feel the long nails driving into your palm, blood flowing down,
no salve or a balm. Rejected, turned on, no one to support
Disgraced, belittled, cruel retort
To see friends who know you turn and just run
After all that you have taught them and done
To do and bear all this because of your love
Not for a show but because of your love
Out of love for people who don't even deserve
Any mercy from the sentence that they have to serve
A people who have done everything that is wrong
Who deserve to be sentenced, yes, and then hung
But when God the judge opened his mouth to condemn
He was ready to pour out his wrath upon them
"Guilty as charged, I'll take their lives away."
Jesus stepped in and said, "For their lives I will pay
These people just need to be saved from their sin
My own life I'll give so that their lives I'll win
All that they need to do is just tell me they're sorry
And I will relieve them of all cares and worry
Will I force them to do this? No, they are free
To take it or leave it but my earnest plea
is that they would accept this present from me

Lesa M. Lawson

A Poem

It is the red rock bottom of the sea
Where no human can be,
Without a mask!
It is crystalline fishes,
Fire red,
Wagging graceful tails
'Neath whales of silver blue.
Snails and sea weed buried deep in yellow sand,
'Neath blue green waters...
Gracefully, the orange fishes
Thrust bellies, flap tails,
Circle the blue rocks
As the sun's rays play
Hide and seek with the shadows...
A poem is the fire red dance
Of crystalline fishes,
In the steel gray rocks at sea.

Naomi Cohen

183

Free To Be Me (About With Society)

So I wear my dresses short, and high-heeled shoes
  Does that make me a whore?
So I choose to wear my hair pink, blue or green
  Does that make me a freak?
What if I choose to not wear panties or a bra
  Does that make me weird?
Who are you to judge me, by the things I do or what
  I choose to wear...
I know who I am, and what I can be.

I can be anything I want to be, because I know who I am

I can be a doctor, lawyer or even a scientist
Because I know who I am
  How dare you! To tell me what to wear
Or how to wear it,
  That's not being me. That's being what and who
You want me to be.

But I am me, so let me be me.
  And as long as I believe in me, I'll be anything
I want to be.
Because I know me and I am free to be me...

Tyra Luckett-Robinson

My Two Lanterns

I have my very own lanterns
They're with me wherever I go
And I love to look at these lanterns
For they bring me comfort and hope

They were not bought at a store
For their value is worth more than gold.
They were shaped and made to perfection,
My two lanterns will never be sold.

They give light whenever I'm lonely.
They give light whenever I'm blue.
And the Father above gave them to me,
I'd need them, and he knew it, too.

They're unique and I'll keep them forever.
My two lanterns are wonderfully made.
Though they're different, they're always together.
In a storm they share their strength.

In case you have reason to wonder
Why my lanterns are so precious and rare,
Just look at my beautiful daughters
And the answers you need are all there!

Alma N. Garay-Guerrero

My Death Upon The Open Seas...

The pain pierces my heart
Like a rusty knife of old,
Leaving me there lifeless
With many stories left untold.
Nobody will find me
Nor do I wish to be found,
My being is suffocated
My feelings are bound.
In a world so full of wrong
I slowly sink into the depths of the sea,
And fill my soul with bitter tears
Tears that blend with the water around me.
It seems so odd to have tears come from my eyes
When I am surrounded in water,
But truth be told, nothing surprises me
Not even now.
The dreams I've dreamed
Have all since yielded,
And have become distant memories
With my death upon the open seas...

Michael Garippa

Sonnet In Black

My frustration is kept in quarantine
Isolation is easiest to obtain,
My blackened soul now feels obscene
Confusion becomes harder to sustain.
Always lost in the pit of loneliness
How I find my way out is the question,
Emptiness replaces feelings of bliss
Reality, a sad misconception.
Mental break leads to timely disaster
Field of pain is where I graze tomorrow,
Feeling depression brings anguish faster
There's no escape from the insane sorrow.
I've had enough of endless misery
It's time to return to serenity.

Vicki A. Policastro

Sweet Lindsey

After the news I sit and ponder
of sweet Lindsey with all her wonder.
She gave much joy,
when she played coy,
with a smile that brought delight;
a gift from God, an innocent angel shining bright.
When you first saw her in all specialness,
it was easy to look past the lack of normalness.
For she was a special child of love,
sent and now returned to God above.
There are no words that will express,
your loss of hope and emptiness.
My prayer, I hope you hear my voice,
is after grief, her life though short you will rejoice.
And when you do, imagine the face
that in our hearts has taken its place.
In the years that will follow, her memory will shine,
and live forever in those who loved her and mine.

Debbra Parsons Strobel

Chapel Of Love

In a tiny chapel
they said their vows
to love each other forever
starting now

Two lives joined as one
two hearts united
when at last
the unity candle was lighted

There were tears in her eyes
and a smile on her face
she had finally met the man of her dreams
that no one could replace

It all still seemed like a dream
as he stood there by her side
but she knew it had to be true
when the preacher said - "you may now kiss the bride"

Jodi A. Rieke

A Winter's Day

A few weeks ago it was Christmas,
I still feel that good cheer.
The season I'd hate very much to miss,
if only it could last all year

The sun is rising in the sky,
I see the birds begin to fly.
The animals in the forest begin to wake
My mother is in the kitchen, starts to bake,
until the sun again sinks and will die.

A. Walker

Spinning Moon

You and I, wrapped in the ivory light of the moon.
Delicate kisses, designed to set my soul on fire,
Liberating belonging, longing, wanting you,
Sweet, potent infatuation,

All spun together makes me slightly dizzy.
The intense warmth of your attention
Melts the wall around my heart and sets me free;
But not to run, to stay.

Bathed in the ivory light of the moon
Our love is good and pure, young and strong.
We hesitate to wonder at its power
Then fall into the passion of its endless depth.

Elaine Nefzger

The Beauty In Change

Magnificent sunsets like romantic afterglows
provide a renaissance of human feelings.
Radiant reds, tangy titians, and subtle saffrons
are encapsulated by coalescing navy flows.

Sunsets with Venus sparkling in her prime,
are reminiscent of life's bittersweet memories.
A sense of contentment becomes pervasive
anticipating other future transitions of time.

Then, stars gleam as jewels in darkest night,
illuminating until sunlight once more unfolds.
This elegant celestial cycle continually assures
beauty in change for those with acute insight.

Walter S. Polka

Heaven Sent

Those words flowed so freely from your heart.
In the midnight air your words touched my heart.

You spoke the words to the melody that reigned in my soul.
Neither of us knew the story that these words would unfold.

I laid and watched as your words lingered in the midnight air.
I watched as they encompassed every being, then embraced me there.

You've held those words so close and dear.
You protected them and hoped no one would ever come near.

Your feeling, those words were so young and new.
They took you back to your dreams of a love so true.

Your words gave me hope that my prayers were finally heard.
Your love in my life has truly blessed me, a gift from above.

When I met I knew with one look in your eyes that his could be.
God had sent me someone who would take the time to just love me.

I Love You Too.

Melicent Branch-Clarke

In Your Face

The dimension is one of many subdividing lines;
Hiding, running, fighting, heroism, sorrow,
Happiness, hardship, love, strength,
Weakness, life, hunting, death,
And finding soul to soul
That we all walk
As one.
This message has come across a generation,
Many thousands of miles, and on,
Via techno-miracle, to me,
A proud member of
The revolution
Of evolution.

Judy Harrington

An Answer

Remember asking me what you should do?
I really did not know what to tell you.
At night I sit and think about all my problems.
When a friend cannot seem to find an answer,
I think of that too.

I tell you to be strong,
but you always are.

I tell you to follow your heart,
but don't block out the mind.

I tell you to cry if you need to,
and to get back up if hurt.

But here is something I learned from someone special.
Something I never told you,
and should have many times.
It is to never give up your dignity,
What you have stood by and called you principles
for years you should never let go of.

Being strong is the first step,
your heart and your dignity need to come together
for true love, not self-sacrifice.

Jennifer May Buckwalter

Skydom

A whisper of lace, a touch of velvet,
How we look to the sky to aspire.
White peace and serenity, floats, offering
False placidity while we falter on two.
Towering infernos of storm allow
Us to remember our maker, but, alas
Clouds reign, the skydom alone exists.
A touch of love, a whisper of faith,
An end to a God, passing in the cloud.

Suzanne Patterson

Only He

Only He can love you infinitely.
Only He can feel your pain.
Only He can dry your tears.
Only He can hear the whisper of your soul.
Only He knows your pain.
Only He knows the desires of your heart.
Only He can love you without limits.
Only He can console you.
Only He can give you life and take it away.
Only He can give you real joy in your heart.
Only He can heal your injuries completely.
Only He, only He.

Kety Y. Hansen

A Lonely Moment

It is gray and rainy, winter is here to stay,
My heart is heavy with memories from another day,
How do you forget a loved one when they are in your heart and mind?
Do you pretend it never happened or how his face would shine?
Smiles, touches, scent, softness, sweetness and power,
Oh, how I would love to go back even for an hour,
I know I will never share another smile or thought with you
but perhaps in some private time you will miss me too.

Though you were mine only for a moment in this life of mine,
Warm memories are my legacy at this lonely time.

Shirley H. Wall

Tolerance

In history we've read about
  and still can see today,
the hatred that is in some eyes
  that could be there to stay.

How could anyone ever think
  that they were better than
their fellow being standing there
  and living next to them.

The pain and hatred can go deep
  but do not let it stay.
Just treat your neighbor with kindness
  and the hatred will melt away.

You're not better than your fellow man,
  God made you both the same.
Treat each other with great respect
  and God will treat you the same.

Tiffany McCammon

Cup Of Joe

I came to warm myself up with you,
I remember meeting you at
this same truck stop years ago,
You brought me great pleasure then,
Will you do the same tonight?
This is one of the last 80c
pleasures in the world.

Michael A. LaMagna

Could This Be Love?

My heart was pounding
When I first looked at you
Though I didn't know why
I felt kind of strange inside

As I looked at you again
I was somewhat surprised
Because to my amazement
You were looking into my eyes

I felt a chill go down my spine
Then I knew that you'd be mine
As you got up to leave
I felt my arm upon your slave

Then you took me by the arm
And led me to your car
As we drove away you said to me
"I think I love you, will you marry me?"

I was so surprised that first I laughed
And then I cried
As you might have guessed I said yes
And we lived and love for all eternity

Kimberly AnnEngle

Wild Cry

Man has landed, time to run
Now that he's here, is our time done?
Man destroys as man creates
We must leave now, or is it too late?
The fields are gone, it's time to cry
Buildings sprout up, more of us die,
No grass to eat, no trees for shade,
No natural life, it's all man made
I am the tiger, I am the bird
I am the whale with a dying herd
we tried to run, man is too strong
I am the wild animal
I used to belong

Michael Lynch

Fire and Smoke

As the world turns,
Forests begin to burn.
Everything in its path,
Burns to ash.

Towering oaks,
Fall in the smoke,
And all around,
Animals run abound.

All through the night,
Birds fly with fright,
Filling the night air,
With call of despair.

The animals dash,
To avoid the crash,
Of burning logs,
And the air filled with smog.

Suddenly, rain descends,
And the fire ends.
The animals now learn,
That the world will always turn.

Jennifer Jiang

Say Good-Bye

We are put on this earth to do a job
And when that job is done,
We are sent to a better place
Where there awaits another one.
Our time on this earth is priceless
For it can never be replaced,
And the time spent with your loved ones
Will never be erased.
Never again will you see them
No more kisses, no more hugs,
No more living in this world
Filled with violence and drugs.
So say good-bye, reach out to me
And I will take your hand,
And hand in hand we two shall walk
Through the gates of God's promise land.

Samantha D. Hernandez

Shining Love

Man and woman sharing love,
Fusing lives together.
Sacrifice and forgiveness,
Allegiance, fidelity.

Like a rod of hardened steel,
Love is fired in life's stress.
Day to day, from life's problems,
Strengthening bonds of their love.

From early years together,
To maturing times of life.
Friendship grew ever closer,
Separate hearts now as one.

Within life's frail existence,
Illness, death unforgiving.
Lessons form eternal pain,
Lessons of enduring love.

Heroes and heroines,
Unsung of their deeds.
Devoted to their lover,
Sacrificing self for love.

Douglas Bergman

My Darling Son John

My darling son
  I love you so,
But this much
  I think you know.
From little on,
  You were my pride,
And never did,
  I try to hide,
The feeling that
  I had inside.
For you alone
  Meant more to me,
I hope within your heart
  You'll see,
How very much
  You mean to me,
So John in closing
  I want to say
I love you more,
  With each passing day...

Rita Williams

The Never Demon

The never demon
Sits on my shoulder
And waits
For the word
Never
To come past my lips

As soon as he
Hears never
He cracks his whip
And says
"Let's get her boys"

The never demon
With his big ears
Will hear even
A whispered never

Beware the never demon
He may be on
Your shoulder too

Never say never
"Oops!"

Betsy King

The Rose

The life of a rose is like our love,
it grows with guidance from above.
If you give your love enough room,
like the rose, it too will bloom.

The rose begins as a bud so tight
but opens with the morning light.
Even though it started slow,
our love just like the rose did grow.

The rose will open its petals by day
to catch the sun's sparkling rays.
Love will open your heart, it's true,
to catch the joy that comes to you.

Although the rose's petals pass
its life continues to last,
as it drops its seeds upon the earth
so another rose may have its birth.

Our love like the rose will never die.
The two of us, we know why,
because God has caused us to be one,
to be together until our life is done.

Denise Bernard

My Friend. . .

A wall separated us
but our hearts broke through,
and over time, our feelings grew.

As more barriers are put up
love will endure,
Not even a mountain can come between
something so pure.
Marvella Phillips

When Love Becomes A Burden

A heavy heart
  brimming over with flooding tears
  overladen with accumulated fears
  tortured by regrettable memories and
  holding onto unforgivable histories
Sadly looking back,
  at the chipping away
  where lives now exist
  in a bittersweet phase
  which feels like
poisonous daggers
infecting and cutting
into the fragile and tender place
within the open heart
of the one
  who loved
  so much.
Tonetta Henderson

Autumnal Omen

When colored leaves fall and blow
Summer's warmth is swiftly bled
As winter winds bring cold snow.

Cold sharp nights crawl too slow,
Darkest nights that are daylight fed
When colored leaves fall and blow.

Whiteness sinks to shroud all below
The clouds, their levity fled
As winter winds bring cold snow.

And I, warm by my fire's glow,
Know that I've come to dread
When colored leaves fall and blow.

And outside, when I must go,
Mark well my hurried tread
As winter winds bring cold snow.

Frigid winter brings its old show
And chattered words will be said
When colored leaves fall and blow
As winter winds bring cold snow.
Thomas Terhune Jr.

Untitled

I met you at the waterfront
I chased you across the fields of
  California
I sat with you when your friend died
I slept beneath your chin to feel
  the warmth of your breath
I dreamed, hoped and cried with you
And watched you walk away without a
  sound
Karen Eason

Life Of Love

Yes the years have past
  so does father time.

Why, then worry our live's
  have been defined.

Now we can smile as we
  watch our children grow.

Delighted satisfaction, for we
  are grandparents you know.

To my wife I want to say, my
  love for you will always stay.

So even though the years have
  passed, we will be together
  to the very last.
Alfred Burton Snykers

Nature's Bounty

Off thru the woods
  I wandered one day,
    feet crunching the leaves
      as I passed squirrels at play.

Glancing upward thru branches
  windswept nearly bare,
    filling my nostrils
      with fall's clean, crisp air.

Sweet Nature wrapt round me
  cleansed my soul of all care
    'though my feet touched the ground'
    I floated on air.

The sweet chords of Nature
  touched gently my ear
    with the quick fleeting sound
    of a startled young deer.

'Twas ne'er a place
  where such beauty abound
    and my heart carried home
    the treasures I'd found.
LaVera M. Morris

My Poem Of Love

You can't see
the tears I cry
but it's there

You don't no
how deep my pain
but it's there

Our family tree
is like a rock road
we don't understand

It's like being
all alone out
here in a big world

Now time pass
giving me a chance
to grow

Unable to forget yesterday
I am living for today
as a color American

I say that to say this
I am going to hold my head up
Margaretreto Wimberly

Ostriches Telling Secrets

We saw Pelicans
  lightly napping

We saw a Peacock
  on a wall

We saw a crab eat lunch
  and go to bed

And Ostriches
  telling secrets

We saw a single file
  of boating

And boats
  and trailer hitches

We saw Blackbirds
  singing choruses

And Ostriches
  telling secrets
Leslie Ayn Jackson

She Didn't Know

She didn't know she was beautiful
Though her laugh brightened the room
And her eyes were warm and comforting.

She didn't know she was beautiful
Although her deeds gave others joy
And her hand was extended to many.

She didn't know she was beautiful
Even though her presence pleased people
And her words gave encouragement.

She didn't know she was beautiful
Though she was there when needed
And she didn't desire rewards.

Then, she saw herself as others had
A glow followed a smile
Now she too knew she was beautiful.
George Andrusin

Girl O' My Heart

I do believe that God above
Created you for me to love
He picked you out from all the rest.
Because he knew I loved you best.
I once had a heart tender and true,
But now its gone from me to you.
Take care of it dear, as I have done.
For you have two and I have none.
If I go to heaven and your not there,
I'll paint your face on a heavenly star.
So that all the angels may know and see
Just what you dear, have meant to me.
If your not there on judgement day,
I'll know you've gone the other way,
I'll give the angels back their wings.
And just to show you what I'd do,
I'd go to hell - dear, just for you!
Viola I. Davis

Untitled

Silken webs part the vision,
As inner crevices behold the light.
Come forth, mighty dawn;
The silent night weeps.
Pat Brown

Revenons (Let Us Return)

One moment only,
    to return.
Out of time I tread the path
    of rain and snow,
Toward the tall glow
    of your beckoning flame...

Archaic moment,
    touch me
With your rocks and stone,
    your artifacts
Gleaming in the frozen hoarfrost
    of another time...

Aeons! Cut loose
    these threads.
Send me on the path again,
    unaided and alone.
Nourish me with the blood
    of your fallen trees....

Revenons!

Paul M. Belbutowski

A Christmas Gift

    Christmas!
A special time of year.
    Christmas!
A time of giving to each other,
I give this special gift.
I give these heartfelt words.
Love and friendship,
Freedom, happiness,
Joy and cheer.
All this and more I give to
you, my dear, to have and
to cherish every year.
    Christmas!
Comes but once a year,
    Christmas!
I give to you this year.

A very Merry Christmas!
A very Happy New Year!

Phillip Zima

Labyrinth

Life is deceiving.
People are fake.
Everything is wrapped
In a package of lies.
A skeleton lives in every man's closet.
It's dying to get out
Along with the dust and dirt
That clings onto everyone.
You may think you know someone,
But you're only lost
In one of the many
Mazes that people are made of.
All of which lead the same place;
Confusion, doubt, misdirection.
People claim to know you
But don't.
No one really does
But yourself.

Schaefer M. Southard

Auntie's Secret

Her years were six
Going on sixteen,
She just knew she'd grow up
To be a Movie Queen!
Her blonde curly hair
Looked like spun gold
Her eyes were azure blue,
As she was so often told!
She was Daddy's girl
And Mama's joy—
She even conned her Aunties
Oh! She was so coy.
But her years I knew,
She did not fool me—
For when I tucked her in
I peeked you see.
So there's one secret,
That we share,
Asleep she cuddled
Her "Teddy bear"!

Marge Pickett

Precious Child Of Mine

Precious child, precious child of mine.
The time has almost come
for me to let go.
To let go more of you
to the world outside my heart.
Precious child of mine
it's almost time
to make your
own decisions
own mistakes
your own love,
that some day will be
Close to you in heart, spirit and soul
precious child of mine
Go forth
be brave and remember
that I'll always love you
be there for you,

Anntonia Franklin

I Give You Mother

I give you mother the golden crown
I cry for you and I miss you tonight
Mother so dear to me now I see you

In heaven with the golden crown
Upon your head no sorry can be
Here in heaven with God

I give you mother the golden crown
That I cry for you and
I miss you tonight my mother dear

Richard W. Reckart

Sand Castles

Sand castles,
Oh, fun to build!
But, how fragile they are.
They wash away, much like life.
And there's nothing to show
Who passed this way.
Except the thoughts of those
Whose lives were touched.
And even they
Are — sand castles.

Francis Killinger

School Of Joy

In this school of joy
With poems on the walls
Kids painting
Flowers in pots
Everything feels right.
And I write this poem
That comes from the heart
In this hour of peace
When the red rose on the wall
Reminds a new ocean
Of white waves
And little boats
Sailing in this afternoon of joy.

Gabriela Martins

Suppose Everything Is In Microcosm

Then
there's a universe
inside each pore
replicating
the galaxies
of our outside heavens

And the gypsy parent
of a sub-neutron
conceived inside a cell
today
could plot an
astrological chart
amid the stars
of my
anatomical skies

So welcome, new born
Taurus of my kneecap...

Donna G. Lerner

Portulaca

I'm a Portulaca,
Ross Moss is my nick name;
Yellow, peach, and apricot
Are my claim to fame.

Plant me in a sandy spot
And water me with care,
For if you don't "Alas, poor me
I will soon be bare."

Keep me in the sunshine
And in good health I'll stay,
For then I'll be as beautiful
As I appear today.

Janice A. Pitts

Candy Coated Box

Lying in my bed,
Just can't seem to get to sleep, so
I stare at the walls.
Disillusioned thoughts cross
My mind, do I even know
Myself at all?

Stuck inside my
Candy coated box, tastes
Too good to let go.
Trapped inside a world
So few around me know.

Nostalgia rings a tiny bell
Inside my head, the bitter
Sweetness keeps me here
Lying in my bed.

Evan Andrew Scott

In The Darkness

My sickness lies in the mind
Hidden from judges, jury and kind
Left alone for fear to grind

A losing war rages inside
Destiny has its own stride
Pressing for an extinguished light

A passion for nothing, obvious to me
This blind universe will never see
Nor care to face its own imagery

Robert Ryan

The Sign

The song of my heart
is light as a lark.
You sing to me in my dreams,
We are in love it seems.
I was sad to part,
In your eyes a spark.
Our souls gather like leaves
intertwined amongst the eaves.

Mindy Schreck

The Choice Is Yours

I look into your eyes,
and all I see is lies.
Coming from deep within,
screams your most recent sin.
I told you not to do it,
but then you went and blew it.
You went and did the deed,
and now you have a seed.
The seed won't be one for long,
you'll soon sing lullaby songs.
The choice you made was yours,
you went behind the doors.
I told you not to go,
and now you feel so low.
Will you keep the baby?
Your reply is maybe.
You have to decide,
there's no more time to bide.
You have to make a guess,
will it be no or yes?

Lauren Felder

Wine Baby

'I remember you were a
wine baby'
my brother said through beer-eyes,
smoke tendrils, and
the plastic smack of billiards.

'Mom would balance the crystal
on the curve of her stomach'
he said, and
when I would kick
red ripples ran like heartbeats,
wine-wake of crimson
on a dark sharp surface of birth

Strange entertainment
twenty years later when
a kick in the stomach
would never mean quite so much
and a womb holds more fear
than life

Megan Mulloy

In The Mourn

The shovel ascends
Hearts sink
Silence arises
Tears think
Shadowed vale
A proper place
For pain to rest
Through years of fight
The combination wore you down
But late at night's
Not the only time tears pour down
Sorry to lose you — happy for you
Misery resigned
Life impeded
Love undefined
Just what you needed
In solace
A rest after the struggle
We all bless
For you've touched many a soul

Phil Laws

Paradise Cove

In Paradise Cove,
Where the tides are high
In paradise Cove,
Where the birds all fly,
We go to see the sun set low
We go to share the things we know.
A secret passion
A sacred lust
We keep it inside
We feel we must.
A love that is so wonderful
And so bright
How can it be so wrong
Yet feel so right?
    So here we are in Paradise Cove
    To keep our secret hidden
    Here we are in Paradise Cove
    Because it is forbidden

Silver Moon

A Promise (Broken)

Summer, summer, drawing near
the sweet July scent flowers bloom,
and when I know you're coming near
I cannot help but be in love with you.

But when fall reigns its ugly head,
like a windswept juggernaut
I cannot help but feel its wrath,
the lonely knowledge you are gone.

I wait for you outside your window,
I am still my only friend
until the world crumbles around me
until my life is at its end.

I will sit here and wait
for the stars to come out,
and for this cold December chill
to be warmed by your love.

I am now what I always have been;
I adore you now as I always shall;
Don't forget that, please, Wendy,
until the end. Until the end.

Kevin Summers

Fever

Fever burning
In the night
Small face flushed
In moonlight
Glassy eyes
Piteous call
Cold compresses
Tylenol
Loving fingers
Softly stroke
Soothing stories
Softly spoke
Breath is even
Child's asleep
Quietly into
Bed I creep
All is quiet,
Boy, I'm glad
My heart aches
When they feel bad

Surie Fettman

Fall In The Woods

As I ride my bike
   along the path,
Birds circle overhead.
The leaves are crunching
   under my tires.
I come to a halt
Along the river's edge.
When I lie down
On the soft, sweet grass,
A white tailed deer comes
   to drink.

Nicole Burow

Day's End

The house is all quiet
Kids now are in bed
It doesn't seem that long ago
They laid down their weary heads
The house is all clean now
Toys all put away
Time to sit and relax
Reflect upon the day
Joey didn't want Teah touching him
and with his voice so hard
So what if Teah tried to feed
a dog bone to the bird
And so she put the cat in the toilet
it needed a bath anyway
It's okay, I took time out
Joey needed someone to play
I thank God for my children
and I'll do the best I can
For if not for the love of my children
I would be less of a man

G. P. White

Connections

As I search for the
essence of my being,
I find myself
reaching through
you to me;
you are humanity,
humanity is me;
harmony for me is
peace for thee.

C. N. Dozier

Imagination

I am the artist of the mind.
With vibrant colors,
I paint perceptions and ideas.
Some consider me quixotic,
Yet others perceive me as
the epitome of brilliance.
My canvas is the stark realms
of the human mind.
My brush,
empowered by thought,
fabricates images and
embellishes each creation
with the hues of life.
I dwell in the brain,
transgressing the boundaries
of conventional thought.
Every night I dream and
envisage the unthinkable.
I am the antagonist of realism.

Lorie M. Chapman

Wow (Words Of Wisdom)

Alone in the Dark,
In a room with no
boundaries and no limits.
Nothing around you, and
nothing below you.
As you sit in this state
of unconsciousness, filled with
an absence of light, sound, and
felling.
In a world where we
cannot be touched, or touch
others, without speech or sight.
It is in this void of life,
in the absence of being, this mass
of nothing, that we discover
who we truly are.

Shawn Thompson

At Sword's Point

Warmth spreads;
begins with just
a tiny prick.
Then it spreads slowly,
seeping along quietly,
seductively.
Lying there watching,
waiting for the bliss
that comes
from letting go.
Slipping away,
the warmth continues
outside, the coldness
inside,
'til they meet in
eternity.

Jamie Sloniker

Untitled

Angels, angels all around
from the heavens to the ground,
protect me from all evil harm
when I'm in reach of dangers arm.
Guardian angels dear and true
lift my spirits when I'm blue,
guide me to my destiny
wherever it is God wants me to be.

Julie Hammond

Rain

The clouds cover the sun
And it rains;
It's dark outside, and the sky is gray,
And it rains;
The water comes down,
The thunder crashes loud,
And the lightning's too bright to see.
Puddles form,
And the rivulets too;
Water's all around,
When it rains.
I walk outside,
And play in the water.
I see the world as it washes away.
The grass will grow,
And trees will too;
Flowers will bloom
Over me and you
cause it...
rained.

Christopher Anemone

Chocolate Cake Confusion

I can't take it
It's too much
So rich
My love for it
It slides in the wetness
Excites the senses
Gets stuck in my throat
Stop, Oh, bring it
On a platter with fruits and cream
To tantalize my mind
It screams
At me
So sumptuous
So perfect
Such sin
What could my repentance be
I reach
I grab
I hold in my mouth
Should I indulge in the dream

Ashley Gagnon

The Day I Die

Tell Faith that I am dying,
My hands are shaking,
And my eyes are feeble from pain;
Go tell God that I am dying,
So He can be my witness
Of those that hate me,
And those that love me;
Go tell my Friends of the news,
So they can come see my eyes closed,
Blind from the biz of the wicked world;
Go tell my Family not to worry,
That my body is lying still,
For one day I shall rise
From the glory of the Resurrection.

Steven Chu

Beware

I open the window,
and what do I declare.
The fate I see with my eyes.
I realize what I am aware.
But do I dare to suspect my fate.
I beware!

Kristin Noelle Carr

Heaven And Hell

When you touched me,
I didn't know what to do.
I felt so warm and comfortable.
Peace hit me smiles lit up the room.
I'm so confused on life.
Sometimes it really hurts.
Sometimes its really good.
But how do I deal with it?
Life, death, and Heaven, Hell.
Life is full of wonderfulness.
Death is too.
Heaven is wonderful.
Hell is not.
That's why life is worth living,
And Heaven is worth dying for.

Regina Williams

Untitled

Our friendship has expired
we can go our separate ways
I've set every thing on fire
No one's there for you today
I'm sick of all your apathy
but depressed to see it go
regret might catch up to me
but you'll always need to know
I could depend on you for support
but support found a new friend
I'd rely on you for comfort
now our friendship's found its end.

Alana Carso

We Fear Them

Once mighty now weak,
Great leaders of yesterday,
No longer before us,
No longer strong
Now so frail.

They sit in darkened rooms-dying!
Do we then help them?
Those who once helped us.
No!

We cast them away.
Like garbage, they're treated
No respect.

We keep them hidden
Because we fear,
Not what they were,
But what they are,
What we will one day be!

Leslie Asin

The Last First Time

My last first time is who you are
My strongest love, The brightest star.

There have been lovers in my life
Whose tender hands have stroked my skin
And touched the child that plays within.

And lips have lingered long on mine
with maybe not the taste of wine
yet women I have known were fine

There have been moments so sublime
that to repeat them seems a crime
But the moment that your eyes met mine
I knew that this would be
My last, First time.

Geddes Fielder

Untitled

Once upon a paper
  A pen did start to write
Expressions of a hungry mind
  Desires of a heart's plight.

Needing the knowledge of wisdom
  Seeking the mysterious answer
Of life's untold story
  And death's own true master.

Not knowing what it's writing
  Just knowing of its need
To express some of its anxiety
  And trying so desperately.

Unable to be the accomplice
  That the frustrated hand had hoped
The pen removed from the paper
  Praying someday it could cope.

Rhea Knoderer

dance with death

i want to dance with death
and visit immortality
i want to claim my
eternal birth right
but you do not
waltz with
death
or even fox trot with death
with death you must
dirty dance or not at all
death is supposed to be so
hot and cool
may be some could rub
off on me

L. Jaffe

The Bird Of Life

I must not weep for broken wings
  Or feathers I have lost
With each new day a pain will mend
  No matter what the cost

However cruel the world may be
  Forever I will fly
Over the hills, over the plains
  Across the boundless sky

My feathers all arranged in line
  My heard held high in pride
The world is my enemy
  Though always at my side

Margaret Mair

Time

Time flies quickly past,
Like a bird on its wings.
It hurries, never stopping,
Like a river, rushing to the sea.
It never pauses to take a rest,
To lie down and catch its breath.
It leaps faster and faster,
Like a hunted deer.
It is an everlasting sea,
Going on forever.
It is a jack rabbit,
Hurrying to its burrow.
Time.
Going on, forever.

Andrew Shields

Chaos

Wrap me in words that you wrote
That don't mean
Anything
You say I believe
The lies
Because they were
Your truths
That haunt me
As the wind
Does the skin
On my hands and knees
Crawling to who you never were
But so wanted to be
The one
You ran to
When you needed someone
Who was always there -
I was, but now...
He's gone.

Robert Brelsford

Life's Highways

As people walk down life's highways
My ways seem so unclear
To live one's life in such turmoil
is so unreal.

Are all the paths interwinding
Do all that come pass
Does life's end hold to never ending
When all must become the past.

Yet in the mirror, we all do hold
There is more than the past
It's the tomorrows that are
Not present, that provides the hope.

But hold not to tomorrows
that hold a hope
For life is never ending
And all must come to past.

For if life is interwinding
And all tomorrows become the past
Then all paths become interwinding
To the past on life's highways.

Thomasine Pursley

The Beach

I was walking on the beach,
So peaceful and calm;
With the red sun setting
  on the horizon
    of a deep blue sea!

The seagulls were flying high,
In the warm spring evening;
Gliding across the sky,
Like a feather in the wind.

My legs were getting tired,
For I had walked for miles.
So I sat down on the warm brown sand,
And watched the evening turn to night!

Christina Martin

The Fire Rose

Washed away in a flood of tears
thinning a vein with remorse
forgotten with time...
I choke on regret

We shared a booth
In solitude's parlor
We prayed to fight back
Punishing hatred with sin...

Secrets behind closed doors
Never sharing the same mirror
For fear of losing the other's gleam
Hope in the eyes of pain
Reaching through your rain...

Tim Cox

Empty Needle

I made your bed and I lied in it
Picked up my heart where I left it
Swallowed it back down
So at least I own it again

Swallowed down the choke in my throat
Too cold now to come out

Too cold here-pick up a needle
Make me warm, boiling blood
Make me pretty, make me dry
Empty needle make me fly

I'm on my knees begging
Hung over your white savior
There goes my heart into the water
Swallow it back down

Swallow down the choke in my throat
Too cold now to come out

Too cold here-pick up a needle
Make me warm, boiling blood
Make me pretty, make me dry
Empty needle let me die

Sarah A. Clark

Santa's Fright

Christmas comes but once a year
Of this we need have no fear
He lands on each and every roof
And very seldom has a goof

This year we had lots of ice and snow
And the wind did really blow
When Santa landed upon my roof
Rudolph really had a goof

His hoof slipped upon the ice
And what happened is not very nice
All the reindeer slipped and fell
And what a story we have to tell

Sled and all fell to the ground
And Santa jumped up with a bound
He put his finger upon his nose
And now this story will have to close

Sled and all rose to the roof
And Santa laughed at his big goof
He turned and said to all a good night
Merry Christmas - I really had a fright

Raymond W. Field

Music

Improvising
jazzercizing
soft rock licks
tantalizing
her grandson's music
is different
from her own

Opera and ballets
symphonies,
concerts with valets
music always has sweetened
her throne

Grandmother listens with pride
harmonic passion they don't hide
for music resonates deeply
in their veins

The generations are bound
by the agelessness of sound
a precious thread
that repeats in refrain

Sue Nosker

Love Heaven Sent

Peaceful morning, spring's blue sky
Holding back, just a little shy
Dreams shared, plans are made
Starting slow, the foundation's laid

Sunny afternoon, summer's true heat
Hearts are blind, passion leads
Intensely revealed, feelings felt
Destiny smiles, cards are dealt

Starry evening, cool autumn breeze
Holding hands, talking with ease
Color evolves, love matures
The long road, filled with blind turns

Wintry night, cold and bleak
Struggling smiles, tired and weak
In time, it is clear
Love can erase the darkest fears

Peaceful morning, spring's fresh scent
The seasons weathered, love heaven-sent

David S. Hess

Angel Of The Night

There's a presence
ever so slight,
Like a gentle breeze
blowing in the night.
A warmth that surrounds us from a far,
Like a beautiful
glowing little star.
A soft touch on the cheek,
A sense of being, but
doesn't speak.
A good feeling that
everything's all right,
It is the angel of the night.

Johnnie Brown

Dear Meme

You fill my heart with love
even though you're up above
I hope you're happy way up
there still I wish you were
down here I know if you
stay close to my heart!
I know we'll never part.

Crystal Kron

Elves

Elves are happy
Elves are kind
with pointy ears
and sometimes tears
Elves are caring
they love their job
and their boss, the Santa Claus
Elves are busy doing their job
scraping and gluing and
making toys for good little girls and
good little boys
Elves are into
Christmas cheer
and are in their workshop
each and every year.

Elizabeth Bishop

Untitled

Different
I think
If everyone were alike,
life would be dull.
W**e** are all equal.
Sex, color, religion, or race.
Not **e**xactly the same
Not good or bad
Not ri**g**ht or wrong....

Different!

Gwen Earls

For Lori M.

When I see her
I see a glimpse of the future
and a respite of the past
she looks at me
while I pretend not to notice
her eyes light me as a candle
in a dark tempest
each time she chooses to sit
and talk to me
I learn something new
which warms me like her smile.

A. L. Schwartz

True Friendships

Friendship is a priceless gift
    that cannot be bought or sold;
Its value is far greater than
    tons and tons of gold,
Because gold is lifeless and so
    cold it can not see nor hear
In time of trouble it is
    powerless to cheer.
It has no ears to listen
    nor a heart to understand
It cannot bring me comfort
    nor lend a helping hand.
So, when I ask God for a gift
    I'm grateful when he sends
Not diamonds, pearls or riches just
    the love of an honest true friend.

Sister M. Sharon Schaefer

Writer's Block

right
what?

eye

cc
aa
nn

k   t
 no
 no
k   t
even
v v
even
n n
thjink
. . . .
WRITE!!

Robin V. Abouzahr

My Flowers

The flowers in my garden
Were never meant to stay.
They brighten for a season.
Then gently go away.

My children are my flowers
A garden growing tall
One left me in his springtime,
Another in his fall.

God, please keep my flowers
only two are left to grow,
Give them both full seasons
And blooms worthy to show.

Shirley DeBerry

The End

Please don't look at me.
    Because you may love me,
        If you see beauty.

Please don't think of me.
    Because you might smile.

Please don't touch me.
    Because you may enjoy my
        Softness.

Please don't call me intelligent.
    Because you may envy me.

Please don't remember me.
    Because it may bring you pain.

If you do this, I will be unable
    to return your love, smile, touch,
        kind thought, envy, or pain.

Because my heart stopped beating
    when you said

    Goodbye

Sheila Bye

In Between Spaces

I'm here and you're there
Time is in between and everywhere
Shoulders laden down with care
A moment's quiet alone is rare
I take this opportunity to share
Not just the worries and the cares
But to ask you how you fare

Sharon Tomlinson

Ode To A Mosquito

To you who haunt the house at night,
You're so determined in your flight;
How can you be so indiscreet,
To torture people while they sleep?

How dreadful does your motor hum?
You must think we humans dumb,
To cuddle there in peaceful rest,
And give our blood at your behest.

You buzz the ear, you buzz the nose,
You buzz the face, and so it goes;
All you bring is discontent,
To satisfy your evil bent.

But Mr. Skeet be not deceived,
Your evil chores shall be relieved,
For we have pledged ourselves tonight,
To settle scores before you bite.

George H. Hizer

Fall

Green to red.
Red to orange.
Orange to yellow.
Yellow to brown.
Brown
to
the
ground.
Swirling
And
Twirling
Down
To
The
Ground...

Get your rakes,
Get your hats,
Get your wheelbarrows,
Get your jackets.

Fall is here!

Alex James Borgen

A Letter From Desert Storm

A hundred thousand,
Far too many to feed.
Too many to care for.
For them it's a dungeon of despair.
Children cry and wet their clothes,
Scratch their matted hair.
An evil king eats steaming pig
Not far from a starving child.
As he consumes his feast
He yells, "All Americans be cursed."

Mark Peters

A Hand To Hold

Here I am again
Looking back at where I've been.
Someone else wants to know
Where I plan to go.
I don't know what comes next.
I haven't seen the text.
I am full of fear.
I don't know where to go from here.
I don't understand God's plan,
But I know He'll hold my hand.

Tiffany Alexander

Telescope Of Hope

With a simple sigh,
I gaze into the sky;
Through the telescope
Of my hope.

I see from afar,
The gleaming of a star;
So distant yet bright
To my sight.

For through this device,
A vision so precise;
An enchanted view
Clear and true.

Thus of all the girls,
All the radiant pearls;
That shine with delight
In the night. . .

This One I behold,
Her great beauty so bold;
Through the telescope
Of my hope!

Mark Steven Fetters

Looking For Love

A task hard to understand,
for it's the one thing always
available and close at hand.
Still the world goes on searching
forever trying to find.

It is given freely
A price of the highest kind
The heart can't feel it
its depth is very deep
The mind can't comprehend it
yet the soul seeks

The task required
to have and to receive
A simple one it is

Only Just Believe

"God so loved the world
that he gave his only begotten Son"
and He lay down his life
For the sake of His Love.

Rachel Gillon

Untitled

Love is heaven, heaven
is the distance between
night and day.
The touch of someone's
hands, the courage you see
as you look into their eyes.
The happiness you
feel as you sit in front
of the fire side by side
with that special someone.
You feel no loneliness
anymore for the strongness
of your loved one, makes
you feel like SOMEBODY
once again.

Shelley Wheeler

Memories

For every moment we have cherished
throughout the years that have past
For every day that has gone by
that we wanted so much to last.

For all the weeks gone by
when all we wanted to do was run
For all the years gone by
when we had so much fun.

For now the time has come
where we must go our own way and depart
For all the memories we've gathered
will always remain in our hearts.

Good-bye for now,
but never forever
Even thought we'll be apart,
our memories will always be together.

Kara C. Klinger

Aryn's Dream

Where do I go?
What do I do?
I search for a place;
Filled with a calm pace.
Joy that abounds
Love that springs
And hope that lies in
All things!
Like a friend once said,
"Look up, over your head!"
But, I can only
It seems, look down on things.
Oh, how I long for
A ride on a birds wings.
To feel the beauty
In the soul of my being!
Oh, how I long for the day
When all my pain goes away!

Eric Braun

All Winter Long

Summer, oh summer
how I've missed you all winter long
I've missed your warm nights
on the back porch steps
I've missed your hot evening sundowns
and your misty morning sunups
I've missed you all winter long
I've missed your lightening bug ballets
and your whippoorwill serenades
I've missed your doodle bug cities
and your black berry fences
I've missed your honeysuckle breath
and your sunflower eyes
I've missed you
All winter long

Anita M. Dixon

Afraid

When I first saw you I was
afraid to meet you.
When I met you I was
afraid to kiss you.
When I kissed you I was
afraid to love you.
Now that I love you I'm
afraid that I'll lose you.

Natalie Elizabeth Parker

The Only Things That Are Good

In my wretched
life of depression,

where sadness lingers
like thick smoke,

little signs
of hope,

and the awareness
of the stranglehold

of life
are the only

things
that are good.

Pat Pauletti

He Sits

He sits.
He waits.
Waits in the silence.
Waits within himself.
It happens.
A stampede.
The door opens.
Everyone screams.
School's out.

Aaron J. Davidson

Poetry She Doesn't Write

Poetry she doesn't write
but she's a poet still.

Her smiles for me,
her kisses sweet,
all do a story tell.

So many years together,
I just forgot to look
for all those little things,
that write a treasured book.

Her hand upon my breast
as in the dark we lay,
is better than the kindest word
upon the printed page.

And as I turn in sleep,
close by me she will be,
to be a poem unspoken,
inscribed on me by Leigh.

Joseph L. Mole

Your Love

Lord, I saw Your love today.
I saw it when a sunbeam reached
  through the clouds.
I saw it when a friend found me
  in the crowd.

Lord, I felt Your love today.
I felt it in a smile on someone's face.
I felt it in a friend's warm embrace.

Lord, I heard Your love today.
I heard it in the chirping of the birds.
I heard it in a friend's caring words.

Lord, I needed Your love today
  and You gave it freely.
It was there for me to see and feel and
  hear
In everything that was near.

Tammy Smith

Marketing Of Beauty

Your beauty is highly demanded
  by the market of men.

A poor investor like me
  has no capital to invest,
    except my body and soul.

Interest increases along with time
  especially property claims
    rather than inflation.

Neither goal nor approach
  to meet your standard,
    Another word No qualifications
    to satisfy your demand.

Beauty is a moment
  Red blooms gray withers,
Take the opportunity to invest
  the market of stocks and bonds.

Dexter P. Do

A Man's Pride

As time rolls on
it's hard to hide
this callous shell,
this manly pride.
I stand up proud
though living in fear
that one may see me
shedding a tear.
Still wearing the mask
that's now peeling away
to adore the great beauty
of a warm summer's day.
So I'm up on the wall
that's surrounding my heart
which is now crumbling down
a new way to start.
So now day by day
I do the best that I can
to just be myself
and be my own man.

Robert J. Curran

The Power Of A Man

It is a hard thing to measure
The power of a man
You will not find it in his arms
It is not in either of his hands

You will not find it in his head
Thinking with his brain
Through all his years of schooling
His mind has been well trained

You will not find it in his wallet
Where his money lay
He is working for a living
That's how he earns his pay

You very well may find it
In his beating heart
This is quite the common place
Where the power often starts

To find the power of a man
That has been the goal
And if you look close enough
You'll see it's in his soul.

Al Roma

Love Rose

  Some say love, it is a river that
drowns the tender sea.
  Some say love, it is a razor that
leaves your soul to bleed.
  Some say love, it is a road that
never ends.
  Some say love, it is waking
that never takes a chance.
  It's the one that won't be
taking that never seems to give.
  Some say love, is for the
lucky, and the strong.
  Some say love, it is a dying that
never learns to live.
  I say love, it is a rose and u
its only seed.

Cassie Wolfe

The End Of A Paper Route

I deliver your globe
But now I am quitting
So I think a farewell
Would be quite fitting
Sometimes I'm sleepy
Sometimes I'm late
Sometimes my car
Isn't running so great
Sometimes the globe
Fails to pass on information
Sometimes I forget when
You come back from vacation
Sometimes the weather
Makes it hard to operate
Sometimes my substitute
Fails to cooperate
I've tried my best
To get the news to your home
If not a tip for my service
How about for this poem?

Scott Oddo

Life

Life little blesses
Treasures of the heart
A journey down life's highway
Take time,
make time if you must.

All in fleeting moments
A slide show at fast speed
A memory so quickly
there is hardly time
to breath.

Slow it down,
Oh, slow it down,
Make the journey last.

Barbara Allison

Tranquility

As I sit along the ocean's edge
the moon whispers to me,
"Peace and tranquility to you."
A tide comes to shore
and laps gently over my feet.
how wonderful it feels,
smooth and pure,
like a babies skin.
Oh, how wonderful.

Melissa Sue Zeller

Days Go By

At the dawn of each day
we all awake and say
Thank-you Lord for this day.

Beautiful and bright dreary or dark.
Each day I count like beats of
a precious heart.

So as the days go by some good
some bad.
We stop and think are we really
showing were glad.
Glad for the days we have!

When days go by so fast we don't
always stop and think how fast.
We always think we want them
to last.
Our bodies grow old when days go
By our hearts are meant to be gold.
As days go by.

Judy Swisher

The Shore

Sitting on my balcony chair,
the ocean breezes blowing in the air,
All the sudden what do I see,
but a purple sailboat heading toward me,
Seagulls soaring in the air,
It's probably not so boring up there,
Airplanes flying by,
way up in the sky,
A dog in the water,
swimming harder,
Having a lot of fun,
In the sun,
Chasing a ball,
while his owner will call,
These are all I see,
while sitting on my balcony.

Krysta Marie Berkich

Gods Little Children

Have you ever noticed
The little people on earth
They're just like us
But alike close to the turf

Their voices are small
Like their feet and hands
You'll usually find them
Making castles in the sand

They're joyous, they're carefree
God made them this way
To remind us daily
How we should stay

Trusting and believing
In all that they do
"In remembering"
God made us too

We're just a little bigger
We've paid our dues
Our hearts should be like children
Lets try to fill "their" shoes

Leslie Claire Mack

Although

Pain, sorrow and grief
  Be mine,
Within I too hold relief

  Always
Guilt, sadness and loss
  Each day,
Over my mind I do toss

  Between
Me, myself and I
  It's true,
Only birds are meant to fly

  Beyond
Pride, blindness and stars
  That passed,
Tomorrow you healed the scars

  Without
Faith, patience and you
  I know,
Future can't bring my just due

Gayla Lynn Barsch

Where Do I Belong?

As I pass from day to day,
looking for the right place to stay,
I can't help but wonder,
Where do I belong?

Is it possible when I came
to the fork in the road, I
went right when I should
have gone left?
Where do I belong?

I live in a house with many
things, but what do all
these things mean?
Where do I belong?

So many faces and so many names
so many hellos, good byes, how do you
do, and nice to meet you, but
Where do I belong?

Jennifer D. Colen

Texas

The sun
  shines on the range
The oil
  boils from the ground

The Grande
  streams to the gulf
The cowboy
  climbs on the horse

The Alamo
  spurs on the man
The capitol
  peers at the sky

The state Texas
  stands in the world
The Great Lone Star
  blooms in the soul

Myles Brandon Bogner

Peace

Today I sat under a tree
I did this just for me.

As I sat on the ground
With the wind blowing around.

With my mind and soul at peace,
The Lord gave me a new lease.

Tomorrow I may do it again,
Today it was just to begin.

Maedel Hearn

Siren Blow!

Siren blow! Siren blow!
Here comes the Mig attack;
Jump in the trench, save the luck,
Look at the Mig flying low.

Siren blow! Siren blow!
Thousands of burning stars;
Makes the sky smokey fires,
Gave a dive on the way.

Siren blow! Siren blow!
Sheets of tins started to flow;
Bombs the target, runway hollow,
Kills the human as a prey.

Siren blow! Siren blow!
Flees the Mig to the east;
Collapsed buildings are in rest,
Mig attack is so I know.

Siren blow! Siren blow!

Mohammed Hossain

Pansies

Little pansy children
Huddled close together
With your funny faces
Laughing at the weather

Dewdrops lie on satin
Like tears that heaven sent
25 with slightest breeze
Your tiny heads are bent

Some like orientals
With slanting eyes and small
Some like little kittens
Whiskers nose and all
Comics of the flower world
It surely must be true
God must have laughed in merriment
When he created you.

Melrose I. Riley

Snow

Snow, snow
it's so fun
it could never be outdone.
Snowball fights
dark, dark nights.
Snow on the ground,
snow all around.
Snow, snow
as we know
it is white.
Oh, I love snow.

Haley L. Close

Modern Woman

She stretches one arm
back to pull a moral
from the past

She stretches the other
forward to retrieve where
she's going

She cups her hand to hold
her child's head before
kissing it

She is home in time to
watch tomorrow in the
making

She changes the diaper
Finds a pail not yet
overflowing

And reaches for a pen
and pad in her office.

Rachel Gladstone-Gelman

I Expect Too Much

I used to expect too much
You said I'm a lunatic
I believed you

I used to be crazy for you
You said I'm a lunatic
I believed you

I used to be madly hopeful
Now I'm just mad
Because I believed you

A. M. Olson

Upon The Death Of My Father

The circle is broken
Scattered beyond repair
The wondrous golden circle

The heavens move
And all the land shifts
The circle has ended again

In another time,
In some other place,
It will form again

Until then the gods wait,
And the priests sit silent
Shrouded in mist.

Until the child lifts her eyes
And sees her father,
The circle waits.

Joan Blaies

Untitled

The beauty of nature
And reality of life
And the happiness of these children
So little it takes for them to survive.
Only we know what greed is
And what we want from life.
No satisfaction
Always more strife
Two different worlds
Two different lives

Florentina M. Walney

Imagined Time

Fooled by thy thoughts,
    Again I am lifted.
He that I seek is mine,
    Just for imagined time.

Counter-clockwise is our time.
    Pictured as before,
You are placed by my present side.
    Pictured as before,
I dream you into my world.

Reversed into the clock,
    I continue to dwell.
Happy in those thoughts,
    I try to bring here.

Deanna Royal

I Love You So Much

Until I Can't Stand You

What ever happened to our love,
that now we are cold as ice
towards each other.
Our words are so harsh,
We never have a kind word
to say to each other.
Nothing ever seems to go right.
I love your crazy self so much,
until I just can't stand you.
I think it's best you go on now,
because we aren't right for each other.

Shanika Nash

the farewell

i must leave you in this life, my love
do not live it looking behind you.
know, within the great circle of time
that i will find you.
i will find you.
i will find you.

for what was in the beginning
will come round again.
remember: time is a circle
without an end.

Rita Hsu Syers

Untitled

Hopes and dreams
Nurtured by time
And with time
the answers come
But will they come in time
One last chance at love
Before my heart will fade
One last hope
Of being loved
Before my heart turns black.

Theresa Swiderski

Untitled

Does anyone hold in the heart
A special spot reserved
For that one young love?
It may have lasted a short while —
It may have lasted longer.
But, sometimes, the heart opens
And, for a moment, the memory returns —
Beautiful! Treasured!
Doesn't everyone?

Margaret D. Burcham

Life

I am alive so people say.
A happy person from day to day.
Until the reality of life sets in.
It sneaks up on me from within.
I take a lot of pressure on.
Until at last I feel I've won.
Sometimes it burns like a candle.
And it's more than I can handle.
I cry and sigh and beg and plea.
Life a child's inside of me.
Someday I feel I'll understand.
But for now I'll do all I can.

Johnna Barron

Grandpa

Empty sandbox
Popped balloon
Dried up mud puddle,
Will it rain again soon?
Broken Barbie
Hung from the tree
Above the cross
Where the dog's buried.
The wilted rose
That lost its scent,
Its pedals were dry
Its neck was bent.
A shotgun shell,
Blood on the walls,
All that is beautiful
Dies in the fall.

Becky J. Quinn

Who Am I?

I'm proud to be an American,
    the flag I do display,

I'm proud to be an American,
    but didn't watch a Packer play.

Trust and honesty,
not money and fame.
These values I treasure,
    God bless the U.S.A.!

Janet E. Casper

Tears Of Love

In memory of Esther Mills
It happened so quickly,
    No smile or a word.
Knowing not what would be,
    "She's gone", is what I heard.

Sweet memories have I;
    None of her gentle touch.
So quiet, peaceful she lie.
    Oh, I love her so much!

Looking at her face so dear,
    Can that be a smile I see?
Through many a flowing tear,
    I knew it was just for me.

As if she said, "All's fine,
    I'll see you in heaven,
My sweet mother of mine;
    Where I'll say once again,
"I love you very much, Mom!"

Connie Reigel

My Dream

Would like to be a ship.
Sailing from shore to shore
Looking for you.
Tossed by the waves and wind most of the time,
Kissed by the sunlight and moonlight sometimes.
You will hear my thundering call when I come.

From the many footsteps that I felt, I knew it was you.
I rocked from side to side and back and forth as my greeting—Welcome!
Traced your footsteps till you reached your cabin.
Stay calm! When I heard you praying.
Do not worry, love! I will take you to your destination.

Days and nights, I felt your laughter, chatter and dancing feet.
I was enthralled and thrilled, too.
As if yours and mine enjoyment will never come to an end.
One day my captain shouted, "Prepare to embark!"
At the thought, I got lonely.
Goodbye, love! Here is your destination.
I will be here when you return.

J. S. Fernandez

The Realm Of Our Love

Destiny brought us together - unforeseen circumstances pulled us apart.
We loved, we laughed, and we cried as we touched each others hearts.
My emotions flowed rapidly when I found myself alone -
first, there was anger, then fear, and finally sadness when I
realized again, I was on my own. As time from an
hourglass I began to heal... now I cherish the beautiful
memories because I realize the love we shared was so real.
Even though we're no longer united - I consider our love a treasure-
something I will value forever and ever.
I can now spread my wings and fly away-
because I know we shall be apart of each other, not just
for yesterday but for always. I will forever remember the first
time we kissed- and I can now say to you what you've
always said to me..."Honey, you will be missed."

Kathleen Hollins

Questions Forever On My Mind

When I think about all of the times we spent together,
The laughs and the dreams, hopes and aspirations we hoped to achieve,
I am confronted with the knowledge that they will never exist again.
At this thought, pain sears through my heart breaking it into a
million pieces.

We had devised so many plans and formulated so many visions,
That our futures seemed to be full of possibilities,
People, places and adventures yet to see and do,
Until fate stepped into the light to deny us these experiences.

Why was he taken from me? I do not understand.
Why was I the one left behind to suffer?
Why was it that I could not go with him?
Why does my heart have to hurt so much?

I don't know how to begin living my life without him.
How am I supposed to when he played such a big part?
Getting through today is a struggle,
Looking towards tomorrow seems impossible,
Am I ever going to envision a future by myself?

I am sick of being angry and confused. Why am I angry at him for
leaving me, when I am so confused as to why he had to die?

Oh, why did he have to die? He didn't deserve to die!

Amy Sweeney

The Quilt

The quilt that I remember best,
In summer stored in cedar chest.
In winter time it kept me warm,
Snug in bed, from winter storm.

Squares of wool, both new and old,
Kept away the icy cold.
Cut from grandpa's old tweed vest,
Scraps from Mom's old "Sunday best,"
Dad's blue serge and grandma's, twill,
Bits of flannel filled the bill.

Blocked and feather-stitched together,
Perfect quilt for winter weather,
Comforters of fluffy down,
Coverlets that now are gone,
Other quilts of silks and cotton,
In my mind nearly forgotten.

The quilt that I remember best,
In summer stored in cedar chest

Bee Mitchell

Written Prior To A Divorce

I wept to see
The fox chew free
A leg its freedom cost

Then laughed and thought
For freedom bought
A leg - so small the cost

B. Foster

A Difference

Could we have made a difference
in some very youthful lives?
Could we have helped some little ones
for excellence to strive?
Perhaps we've held some smaller hands
and led them the right way.
That they might take a firmer stand,
and would not go astray.
Could we have had some influence
for good on younger minds?
That somewhere in the distance
a better world they'll find.
And if we have made a difference
on the path that we've walked down.
Perhaps we've caused a child to smile
or helped remove a frown
What would we leave these little ones
as each our leave must take?
Let it be - one "Precious Thought,"
What a difference they could make.

Rita J. Bowers

One Lone Hawk

Cold and dark with rains
that pound to the core of my heart.
The sounds of the storm echo in my ears and mind.
And I fall, fall to the ground as still as the trees.

But yet, the dark sky breaks up as the
Sun's rays touch the earth.
The gold hue shines to the ground
And bathes with rich life.

A lone hawk soars through the air.
Its wings spread with grace as it
glides its way toward my palm.
There it rests in such a state of peace.

Eddie Tieu

Playing The Game

I had established myself, was captain of the team and living my
dream. I was on top and nothing could stop me it seemed.
Playing the game gave me inspiration, at the same time I
could take out all frustrations. Everything personal I could hide on
the field like a gladiator encased in his impenetrable shield.
When I could no longer hide behind the gear things got confusing
and not very clear. Starting the endless, reckless ride that
ended up here. With new armor I came to play. I had established
myself and seemed to be living a dream, I was on top and
nothing could stop me it seemed. Playing the game gives me
inspiration and allows me to take out all frustrations.
  With my new shield, I am no longer on a playing field, but
in the game of life on a street filled with continuous yields.
I'm playing the game calling my last timeout, the opposition
wants a shut-out. Do I play for the tie or win for self
pride? With time running out I throw down my shield,
hiding from nothing and showing no fear, like a gladiator
leaving the bloody battlefield. I've established myself,
Living my dream, and nothing can stop me it seems.

Robert E.

Love
(Enlightenment Of The Self)

  There is a cry which comes from the depths of man's soul
that pleads to be heard.

  The mournful sound of a lone rose calls for understanding
to melt the crystallization of mornings dew upon its flesh
and warm the heart with the light of Love.

  Yet man hides from the very thing he thirsts for;
Although with him it has always been, seated upon the throne
of his Eternal Being.

  Freedom from winters chill stands within the peddles of
his own blossom, waiting for man to open his eyes to see the
spark of Life that glows with every beat of his heart.

  It is only then that the harsh frozen landscape of man's
Earth walk becomes fertile with the birth of spring;
when the waters of Life flow again, bringing change in Her wake.

  The song of Hope and Realization will come in place of
mournful loneliness, when the rose of empty despair can caress
the truth within and know the crystallized dew upon its flesh
is Her Love sprinkled as a blessing of Life on the unlit hearth
of man, before he looked to the throne of his Eternal Being.

Charlene J. Boush

Broken Hearted

The pain pierces my soul, sending lightning bolts of shock up and down my body.
The tears come pouring out, a regular downpour in the rainforest.
The love has been crushed, mercilessly, without a regret in the world;
and the broken heart is left unnoticed, unloved.

The jagged edges are left to prick whatever feelings have survived.
The joys have been erased, leaving no trace of any remains.
All I am left with is vulnerable, sorrowful, lonely love.

My heart is left broken, a cure not found.
No tool can fix it, for the one tool I had, loves me no longer.

Maria Pavelo

Why

Why oh why must it be sometimes I think things only happen to me
I always feel alone and afraid you see
Sometimes afraid to be alone and alone to be afraid
No one can say someone is there for them always and
they are never afraid but some people think that and they are
terribly wrong
I'm glad I don't cause it makes me feel a little strong,
strong to face the world each day and whatever comes my way
But I can't fight everything and win you see
I most lose sometimes and that's apparent to me

Abby Lynn Rathgeber

Our Love

To be a flower
is to wilt away
Don't let your life
be that way

Let the showers
Of our love
feed your soul

Then you will not wilt
but flourish
with happiness untold

For our love
will be with you
until the world grows old

For our love for you
will never wither
but grow and grow.

Nancy Morales

Spring Is Here

Spring is here let's give a cheer
we made it through the winter.
No more snow or bitter cold to put
us in discomfort. Spring is here let's
give a cheer for we know what is
coming. Sunny days and breezy nights
to make for comfortable living.

Lori Mulready

Remember

I hear her cry
I feel her pain
I am reaching for her
I want desperately to help her
I can't find her
Where is she?
The screaming is getting louder
Where are you?
Please help me
Someone, help me
I will save you
I will love you
Who are you?
Are you really here?
I can't remember
There is silence.

Dorreen Lyn Wojcik

Shoes

They were bought
They were needed
for tiny feet:
once upon a time.
Even when there
were just a few coins
left for the rest of the month.
We survived.
They were bought
for growing feet
"The kind the other kids have, mom!"
Even when money was short.
They were bought
over and over again,
As you grew
too fast for your own good.
One day I turned around,
and there was no reason
to buy
shoes.

JoAnn Scott

Secrets Behind A Letter

Gazing above at the world around me knowing what has occurred.
Who would of guess that around my aura there is neglect.
Don't pity me, learn about me, give me the respect that I
desperately yearn for.
Can you see the pain in my eyes —
The hidden - interior, the hidden tears.

Hand in hand go suffering and its little sin.
Known is what can never be spoken of.
See these hands - One over my mouth its companion on my heart,
where wrong doing has occurred.

Watch my next step — to the right, to the left, straight across an ocean.
Where I will go not even I know.
To escape the land of the mourning and dead to the land of prosperity and optimism.

Only a confession by the weakest person in town can save four lost
souls. The greatest sinner of all dies alone of neglect. The child
set free from a life long curse. I, never to meet my love ever again
in this life or the next. This revelation has taken any chance
of ever having a walk in the forest with you.

As I sign to...a kiss...death...in heaven forever, no more...

Sheila Nowfar

Untitled

As he gazed into her eyes and spoke she could hear nothing.
Her body shook inside, as if a volcano was about to erupt.
Her throat tight, like someone was tying a knot in a thick piece of rope.
The tears about to flow, but she tried too hard to pull them
back, so instead they dripped down her cheek steadily like a leaky faucet —
and he still spoke
and still she tried to hear the movements of his lips, like
a hand puppet's they moved in slow motion as if someone or
something was speaking for him.
But when all the words were said and done, she did hear every
last syllable spoken.
Still trying to fight back the tears, she somehow cracked a
smile through the solid stoned face that her cashmere-like
skin had become.
With a gentle touch he pulled her toward him, whispering
words that meant nothing, and as she pulled away she trembled
inside with anxiety as their lips gently touched one anothers'
for a soft kiss — not knowing yet if this would be their last.

Lonna Corso

A Christmas Story

Once upon a time in Bethlehem, there lived a piece of hay,
who thought it was his lot in life to be real bored all day.

He was for sure there was no fun, in laying in a feeder,
but what was he supposed to do, he never was a leader...

One night as he lay all still, (like he had a choice),
he heard from out of no where a loud and booming voice.

"Hay, you're going to be used, in my awesome plan,
you see I'm sending down to earth a really awesome man."

"Why me?" Hay asked, not fully comprehending,
"Because you will be nice and soft on the one that I am sending."

After that Hay understand and couldn't wait until he was needed,
(he just hoped the person came before the animals were fed.)

A few nights later as Hay was sleeping two people silently crept in,
and little hay didn't even know that the fun was about to begin.

Suddenly hay felt a presence so wonderful and so right,
and he knew that he was witnessing history being made that night.

The moral of the story, it is simple but so true,
even if you're only hay, God can still used you.

Stacie J. Gordon

City Playgrounds

Slowly rising to his feet
One arm extended out,
Then inches from the stroller
Drunk legs collapse the lout.

A 'homeless' waits impatiently
With precious plastic urns;
Kids hang from the drinking tap
Not giving him a turn.

Now quiet, whisky tainted
callused nicotine yellow,
Masturbating fingers move
Over the knob for flow.

He spits into the leakage
Where little spades scrape mud,
And flounders through the trash can;
Stubs make tobacco cud.

We traverse through the playground
Side-stepping condom crimes
And at the tap my heart stops-
Sam licks the knob of grime.

Marlene Strode

Yesterday's Baggage

I have no tears
For yesterday;
I'll not look back
On shadows of the past,
Or ruts encountered
On the way.
I'll not hold fast
The residue
Of yesterday's sorrow
Or regret.
It's unfettered
I must be,
Unencumbered,
Free.
Free to be alive,
Completely,
Exultantly,
To the wonder of today,
And the promise
Of the 'morrow.

Leonard Rochlin

Imprints

On her face
A veil of
Blush
Unfolded

Stars
Danced
In her eyes

Head
Swept back

Arms
Motioned
Upwards

She smiled

And love
Gazed in
Wonder

Marcelle Kerouac Crook

Keepsakes Overheard

Drowsily waking — to laughter from the kitchen; Little Carrie's here,
Narrating the escapades of her six children at the circus.
Or to concern, the softly serious French accent of Mrs. Barnard's
Momentously reporting of her son somewhere in Europe's WW II.

Later, swinging in the sun-warmed, still dew-drenched yard,
Pleasantly distracted by the sing-song chant of "Wa-ter-mel-on!
Wa-ter-mel-on for sale!" and the clip-clop on the pavement
Of the vendor and his horse-drawn, green-laden wagon.

Then the wondrous summons from across, up, or down the street,
"Can you come over and play?" All day long-lunch, a brief pause!
Squeezing hue and scent from sluggish four o'clocks not yet awake
Into bottles of water for the perfumery in "owning different stores."

Climbing the china berry tree to the roof to parachute, playing army,
Striding on stilts, building sandbox cities, playing jacks and statue.
Selectively sharing treasured Hedy Lamarr or Lana Turner paper dolls;
Wearing a starred paper crown until the bid to dinner ends my reign.

In the last light, shaking pink lace from the crepe myrtle to create
An exotic stage to dance, becoming Maria Montez of Arabian Nights.
Giving into bedtime, but not sleep, until the day's final sound,
That forlorn cry of the nine o'clock train, merely passing through.

Theda Burnett

My Wee Wee Woman

What's the matter, baby are you sick? Well
you just bring your fat self home where we love you.
This was 1988. I have always loved Momma Stella for her
wit and candidness. She will always be known to me
as my wee wee woman.
I shed my tears to water the thought of my
grandmother as a free and gentle flower growing wild, knowing
that she almost died as a child. But God saw fit not to take
her at birth and gave her some time here on this earth. So for
that reason I am here, because she gave birth to my mother who
is so very dear. I will forever keep the memories of my Momma
Stella alive, as I continue to live life and strive. Her quiet and reserved
ways of existence has given me a foundation for persistence.
Yes she is my window watching Granny, who took no heed to spank
my fannie. I only wish I knew what she could see, as she sat and
stared beyond the trees. Maybe she envisioned a better you and a
better me. So let us all be the best that we can be, and look forward to the things we cannot see.
I love you, Stella Mae, always, forever and a day.

Terri Barnhill

The Unknown Heart

Like an uncharted isle in open sea
There lies a heart no one can see
A heart that cannot express itself by signs or words
It rests inside undisturbed
Venturing out to the unseen world leading people in thinking that all is gay
Foolish people, all I did was put on a Broadway play
It's a heart that wants to speak and tell
Sometimes wishing that it were tears from an eye that fell
The heart's a world of joy but overshadowed by pain and struggles
Clinging to the hope of one day finding a double
The heart gets heavier by the passing of each new day
Tried sharing with a familiar face but he just faded away
He asked a question which was polite
But the manner in which he questioned just wasn't right
Told a little white lie which wasn't the truth inside
'Cause he didn't have the right frame of mind
Believe these words that a perfect match is difficult to discover
Where could it be, I often wonder
Until the day when God provides the clone
This heart inside remains unknown

Linwood Lee

The Question

Can we learn what we really need
   by living here on earth?
Are we given the gift of life
   from the moment of our birth?

Do we lift our heads each day
   in wonder of what is free?
Will dying give us all the answers
   of what we are meant to be?

Kimberly J. Sandifer

Heaven In My Hands

I had a touch of heaven in my hands
For just a few short years
But it left without my knowing
Leaving me heartache, grief and tears

I had heaven in my hands
And those years have passed me by
I loved you then, I love you now
By the grace of God, I wonder why

If I could turn life back in time
I would be happy as could be
Because I had heaven in my hands
But I was too blind to see

As I go on my simple way
Not certain of which way to turn
I let heaven slip right through my hands
But it's not too late to learn

Now, on the beach, I'm all alone
Sketching memories in the sands
I must look ahead, the future is mine
With heaven in my hands.

Beulah A. Reeder

The Beginning Of Tomorrow Has Ended Today

As pale as our reflections
As dark as our shadows
As regretful as our neglections
And more feared than our foes

More missed than our affections
More colder than the wind blows
More needed than our corrections
And more greener than the grass
grows

Headed in no direction
but following a glow
a place of collection
But where nobody knows

Phillip Boccelli

Not Today

Days there are when every puddle
Dries before you brink it
When every thought that could befuddle
Flies before you think it
And all things pay;
Bankers want to lend you money
Even when you need it
Your schedule runs as smooth as honey
Even when you speed it
But not today. . .

Gerald F. Fisher

His Eyes

I didn't know why I despised his deep dark brown eyes,
But when they glanced over at me, mine seem to connect with simplicity
Peacefully lost amongst the trans., searching for broken pieces of romance
My heart felt rapidly weak, as I could hear every single beat
Tingling through my body, touching the tips of my fingers so tenderly.
Our eyes wondered not but focused within, the curiosity could only win
His deep dark brown eyes, went on father than the bluest skies
As though looking in through the eternity's, an endless gaze of sincerity's!
No pleasant smile or frown of dismay, I never know what I should say
Desperately trying to figure out, what his thoughts were all about
Only made my mind roll, searching too far beyond his soul.
Feelings of emotions I didn't find, why was our love hidden inside
Never letting our true feelings free,
locking them up in search for a key
Love, passion, and hate, only the destination would lead to our fate!
A lost feeling of joy and pain, like the sun shining through the rain
Left my broken heart in affliction, to a gloomy sigh of confusion
I never felt this way before, I couldn't stand the suspense any more!
But what really hurt I tremble to say, is when his deep dark brown
   eyes looked away.
   Caira McFarland

Mom

   Mom, you gave me life when I was born.
Mom, you made me happy when I was sad.
Mom, you made me glad when I was mad.
Mom, you wiped my tears! When I cried.

   Mom, you gave me food when I was hungry.
Mom, you helped me through the good times and the bad.
Mom, you did good things for me.
Mom, you healed my wounds when I was hurt.

   Mom, you prayed for me when I needed your prayer.
Mom, you gave me strength when I needed it.
Mom, you gave me medicine when I was ill.
Mom, you did my hair for school.

   Mom, you dressed me when we went out.
Mom, you gave me wisdom to be smart.
Mom, you gave me all these things.
Mom, but I never thanked you.

   Mom, so now I thank you.
For the things you did for me, Mom, I love you.
Mom, thank you for the things you have done for me throughout my life.
Mom, you sparkled happiness into my life.
   Tiara Lopez

Meeting Love

A gentle touch light as a feather tickled my heart
The bold calm that emanated from your grace seemed to lay claim to
all other senses
The harmonious melody of the spirit seemed to exist for my ears only
The dance that evoked was not the tango but a rhapsody of moves that
entangled my soul
In that sacred dance I saw your face as you relinquished your love
and released the essence of you
The glow that had begun in me seemed to make gravity loosen its
grounding grip and I soared to the heavens never wanting to return
I asked who might you be that causes such overwhelming emotions that
no obstacle can be seen or imagined
The answer was given fearlessly and firm with the most gentle and pure touch
"I am the best part of you emerging as one by faith from the spirit
of God in you"
   Judith J. Baker

Arabella

To gaze upon beauty,
is to drink from the soul.
To feel her love everyday,
stirs emotion without control.

To breathe her kisses,
light upon the air,
to bask in sunlight,
is to touch her soft hair.

To live with passion,
is to evolve from pain.
The freedom of a fool,
who dances in falling rain.

To walk in her company,
is to never be alone.
To speak of her is poetry,
that sets words free to roam.

To love her is divinity,
an acceptance of fate.
The end of the search,
for the one true soulmate.
   Ashley Long

Unspoken Love

A love to share with each other
From the moment that we met
That grows within out hearts
Waiting to be expressed

You fill the space within my heart
That no one else can do
To be held in your warm embrace
And unspoken love for two

To be sheltered in your arms
For all the world to see
The glow that shines in your eyes
Is the love you have for me
   Lula Taylor

Expectant Parents

Wonder what our tot will be?
Dainty girl or handsome he?
Will its eyes be brown or blue?
Will it look like me or you?

Small pug nose or dimpled chin?
Coaxing smile or winning grin?
And hair upon its head?
Wonder—will it fit the bed?

Wonder how it's gonna feel?
Will it kick or will it squeal?
Will it know me when I look?
Are directions in a book?

Anxious parents in a whirl.
Waiting for our boy or girl.
Amusing others while we fret.
Wondering what we're gonna get.
   Elizabeth Krim

Not Fantasy

Purple, yellow, blue and white.
Flowers galore, in colors bright.
The road's edge is an eye's delight.
God's paintings are a lovely sight.
   Vehig S. Tavitian

A Life Alone

Solitary lengthening every moment to an infinity lacking measure.
Alone to such a degree the slightest sound brings a frightening pleasure.
Life was not always so empty, with so much despair and so destitute.
My scorned love was the delivering to such a deprived state of recluse.

The creaking of the door, the train with its loud roar,
The wind which crackles by, the birds song as they fly,

Any sound of any tone — Reminders of my life alone.

At night, I escape to a distant slumber with emptiness hidden deep.
Dreams of laughter, company of others bring fulfilling, invigorating sleep.
Suddenly, my eyes will close no more, forcing reality to awaken.
Consciousness, interrupting the peace, the truth of a dream forsaken.

The unfamiliar sky of a deepened blue, the faces of the crowd all anew,
The vast roads winding and long, the many turns I'd taken wrong,

Any sight which was unknown — Reminders of my life alone.

To be taunted for my hopes and desires, was the catalyst for my spirit to aspire.
Speaking upon many a heedless ear, no longer caused my soul to fear!

The ignorance of the oblivious intellect, the constant harping of the societal reject,
The degenerate not fit for a cage, the decay of humanity in this time and age,

Any depth to which humankind had grown — Strong encouragement for my life alone.

Ramona Spletzer

A Simple Twist Of Fate

Isn't it funny how much things can change in the simple wink of an
  eye? How lonely fears turn to light-hearted laughs, when you lose
  yourself in his smile.

How you expectantly wait for that first fateful kiss that you know
  will just leave you breathless, and the slow, dull, ache of your
  heart now sings to a beat that is restless.

And all your lonely nights turn full, even when he's far away; for
  every minute the clock slowly ticks...all you can see is his face.

How hollow dreams turn from empty vessels and the bittersweet
taste of wine, to an exciting place where your heart can run free on the endless sands of all time.

And after all the endless nights and cold dark rainy days, he's
  sitting right there...two heartbeats away...just as plain as the
  nose on your face.

A joining of hearts, a blending of souls, that you thought was lost
  in forever...who knew but a simple twist of fate could somehow
  bring you together.....

Bethany L. King

Hey Lord

Hey Lord...
  I'm young and I'm strong and on top of the world. I do anything
  and everything, and get all the girls. I'll be a doctor or lawyer,
  I know I've been blessed. No doubt about it, I'm as smart as the rest.

Hey Lord...
  Still handsome and smart, but college is tough, so many people with
  all the right stuff. Ned to try harder, and can't be a fool, I
  need a job when I get out of school.

Hey Lord...
  Got a family and kids and work all the time. Gained some weight,
  lost some hair, but everything's fine. My wife works to help pay
  some of the bills, Kids come first, save a little, there's not many frills.

Hey Lord...
  Kids are grown, on their own, we sure are tired. We're still
  working hard, trying to retire. Not so smart, not so strong, not
  so sure of it all, I wonder and think was this your plan after all.

Lord...
  We're old and we're weak, not well anymore. Had good times and bad
  but got through them all. My journeys had love, peace of mind,
  sadness too. Hope to see you soon...do I have questions for you!

Richard J. DeRose

Who's The Dancer?

She is...
That point on a stage
Where shadow
Becomes light

Her song is written
On a sheet without lines
The lyrics are her secret,
But her beauty plays the tune

She humbles the audience
With her show,
Then kneels...
To pick up roses

Vanishing...
Into a forest of dreams,
She evades capture...

The artist is the hunter

James Fucci

Some

Some are old and yet young,
Some are young and yet old,
Some are wise and yet dumb,
Some are weak and yet bold.

Some are unclean and yet accepted,
Some are uneducated and yet talented,
Some are ugly and yet loved,
Some are uncouth and yet pray.

Some are silent and yet care,
Some are quick and yet slow,
Some are right and yet hated,
Some are peasants and yet grow.

Who's to say what is right,
Some are black and others white.

Kenneth F. Temple

My Angel Dear

My Angel Dear
I know that you are near
But sometimes I need
A sight, a sound, a flash
of light
Am I wrong for such a
need?
Do you think less of me?
No!
You are there, I know
with all my heart
I take cover
I feel comfort
My angel Dear

Bina Kirschner

Our Love

Our love is like the rising sun,
like the fresh morning dew.
Together, honey we are one,
our love is forever true.

Our love is like the love song,
that birds once gayly sung.
Our joy will be forever long,
our hearts forever young.

Lora R. Waide

What Will You Do?

What will you do, when the whole world kneels before you?

You've circled the world, seen so many things, been gifted with glory, diamonds and things.

You've played for the finest chandeliered halls, played for the crowds
and loved the applause.

You've tea'd with a Queen, entertained Kings, then looked back to see,
yes, you're on the marquee. All glitter, all glamour, that's been
your call, just remember, my lost love, even Kings have their falls.

And what will you do, when the world no longer loves you?
What will you do, when you look back and see, it's not your symphony,
when the curtain has closed, you can only suppose, there's another they chose?

What will you do, when the gold in your hand has turned to sand?

So what will you do, when a new world kneels before you?
Not Princes nor Kings, with diamonds and things, no, not even painted on nobility.
But not quite a pauper, just one that can offer just me.

What will you do?

Jose A. Bustos Jr.

My Country And Me

I am an American
In the land of plenty and free
This land of opportunity
Was abundantly passed on to me
What does it means to be an American
To stand proud with honor and grace
This land of opportunity
For every creed religion or race
This country stands proud and ready
To fight for what it believes
Ready to give aide and assistance
To those who are in great need
Our promising Lady Liberty
Standing taller than most trees
The stars and stripes of Ole Glory
Blowing firmly in the breeze
The bald eagle flying high and mighty
A symbol of strength in this land
Makes you feel proud
Proud to be an American

Linda King

Nature Moment

As Mother Nature uncovers her white blanket of snow from the
moist Earth, and she slowly sheds her skin, like a snake, and winter
yawns, and it slowly goes to bed.

As the days get longer, and the noon-day sun warms the old woman's bones as she sits on her front porch.

As the daffodills pull themselves out of the hard earth to test life once again.

As still there is a chill in the air, for winter has yet not let go of her last breath.

As a newborn baby cries with his first gasp for breath, and the pasture grass pulls itself up from its winter sleep. And the young mother
cow's bags fill with warm, sweet milk, for her first baby calf is due in days.

As the young boy becomes a man, and gives his heart to his first love. And the winter clouds bid good-bye for another day.

As all living things bow their heads and give thanks.

As God has given them beauty of nature to fill their entire beings.

As we take time to enjoy nature in its full splendor, and nature gives birth to the coming of spring.

As animals' bellies are full with the upcoming of new life, and nature breaks loose with all its motherhood, so say the poets.

Give me life.

Give me life.

Shirley McCallister Vinson

Basketball - In The Paint

As the crisp, cool air and football descends, that's when basketball
begins. As the fans all hurry and bustle inside to watch their
favorite teams collide. The energy you feel in the air is better than
watching Fred Astaire.

The announcer is organizing his notes and stats to give the fans all of the facts.
The teams hit the floor and no one goes out the door. As the ball is tipped into the air,
fans' eyes grow big as if at a huge fair. Up and down the court they go, swoosh, swoosh,
each team scores. The crowd goes wild as half-time nears with the cheerleaders yelling
their favorite cheers.

One coach is happy and one is sad, because his team has played so bad.
As soon as the second half begins I started to dream about when. . . . .

On the basketball court, I am always a sport. I pass, dribble, and shoot so I won't get the boot.
On the free-throw line, I will always shine. Sometimes I'm high point man, always trying
the best I can. So one day my name will be in the Hall of Fame.

Regis C. Fox

Planet Earth

A work of art,
Created smart,
You have lots to offer,
Yet you are so fragile
The Threat to you is Real.

No sign in sight
That this Dark Night
Will ever come to pass.
The deck is stacked
Against you, Planet.

Or is it that only
We must go?
So we can stop
Torturing you?

When we'll be gone
You'll still be here.
Free of your Human Burden,
To support the more deservin'...

Maria T. Kenez

Lost Love, Never Lost

The evening is late, the sun has left the sky, twilight barely
lingers. Cool breezes, light as feathers, caress the coming night.
This beach place where one can be alone is a gift to one in need.

Looking far down this lonely place, I see the small figure of a woman,
head bowed, tears seeming to finally set themselves free. She feels
so alone. I see her shoulders racked in sobs, so long held in check.
I feel her loneliness and her hurtful heart. How can friend help friend?

Now the darkness surrounds quiet - can she feel a presence?
No, not yet. Slowly, the light of night is there, the appearance of the
multitude of stars shine down on this woman, kneeling in the sand.
Does she feel their warmth? Not, not yet.

Time passes, tears stop, sobbing is quieted, loneliness begins to
fade. Hat has happened? What has changed in this short span of time?
As she lifts her head her eyes see the stars and slowly she feels a warm awareness of
someone close by, touching this small woman in the gentlest way.
 She feels this presence, wraps herself in this joyful gift, her eyes are smiling,
her heart skips a beat as a warmth surrounds her, and she knows she'll never really be alone,
that her loved one's love is forever.
Yvonne Brittsan

Grandma's View

She likes to sit on the back porch and listen to the birds sing
So I cut the grass and pull the weeds so my Grandma can enjoy the view

She had a little postcard on her wall of a giant surrounded by
colorful flowers artwork by Matisse

So I painted her that picture in magnificent form so my Grandma can
enjoy the view

She never fussed about all of her aches, discomforts or challenges
But if I could I would endure her pain and suffering so my Grandma
can enjoy the view

She tells me wonderful stories of my greats and grands and how this
family came to be
So I close my eyes and live her words and I enjoy the view
Tika Juneja

He Asked Me

He watched the evening news with me and then he asked me why?
Why the father burned his house down so his wife and child would die.
Why the woman thought her only choice was that of suicide.

He read the daily paper with me and then he asked me how?
How could the teenager pictured there, drink too much wine and drown.
How someone could have killed that girl...strangled in her gown.

He listened to the radio and then he asked me what?
What happened to those people when all their jobs were cut.
What made that mother leave her baby on that filthy bus.

He took a walk thru town with me and then he asked me where?
Where did the homeless get their food, since no one seemed to care.
Where do the little children go, when home's too much to bear.

He sat down in the park with me and then he asked me who?
Who decided you're no good if your skin's a different hue.
Who would choose to hate someone because of different views.

He watched the sun go down with me and then he asked me when?
When would people get along. . .allow their hearts to mend.
When would the future be less bleak for children just like him.

He said a tearful prayer with me and then he asked me:
                              "Why"?
Sherri T. Watson

Inner Silence

Time stands still, vacuum tight
Feeling void, seeing no light

Heart empty, dull and dark,
Eyes looking, yet deep and narrow
Looking past, not focused,
Reaching out not touching
Stretching, straining, never complaining
Feeling tense things make no sense

Time stands still, vacuum tight
Feeling void, seeing no light
Melvin Levon Henson Jr.

Tears

Catharis needed
Way deep inside
Too scared
To let it flow
Who to catch the tearful blows.

Hurt,
Pain,
Buried, hidden
Silence screams
Fighting freedom.

Masked face
Before the crowds
Heavy heart behind the blouse.

Who stands at the heart
To hear the cries?
He does
Give Him a try!
Denise Thompson

Untitled

I lost my heart tonight
While gazing into your eyes.
Out of control, it careened into
the depths of your soul.
A topsy-turvey fall through
the canyons of your heart
Scraped away the layers of jaded
seclusion I had built around my core.

Stripped naked of my armor
my shield against broken promises
and dreams that never do come true
I lie trembling at your touch...
Praying God will not wake me from
this most perfect illusion.
Susan Mitchell

To Nancy

You say our Nancy's got the mumps?
Goodness gracious how she jumps!
She squirms and wriggles, fidgets, too!
Whatever will poor Mommy do?

Just tuck her in her little bed,
With books and crayons by her head,
And all her dollies at her feet.
Then give her something good to eat.
Nina Hudnell

Autumn Eyes

The sun rests soft upon the hill, there's a cool and drifting breeze.
It caresses softly the darkening land and gently sways the trees.
But in this hour of evening shade I know that there will be
Happiness with you always, as long as you're with me.
The days pass by so quickly now, life seems to rush by.
There's never time to think too much, no matter how I try.
But in these days as Winter nears there's warmth within the air,
For you're the sun within my soul, the dreams I long to share.
Autumn Eyes you're always here for me, you fill my days with cheer,
I never feel afraid when holding you so please stay always near.
For my treasure lies within your golden smile and the soft touch of your hand,
And Autumn Eyes I love you more than you'll ever understand.
You'll never know just what it means to be standing by your side.
You'll never know how my heart feels, how it suddenly opened wide.
The love I have comes pouring out and I give it all to you,
And Autumn Eyes the love I have will remain so pure and true.
Now Winter comes and Winter goes and soon turns into Spring.
Life has blossomed with Winter's pass, there's new song now to sing
But the memory stays within my head, for memory never dies,
I'll never forget my season of love, my days of Autumn Eyes.

Steve Sprigg

Jacqueline

Once our eyes met. . .it happened. Strange, nerve-tingling
sensations; disturbing heart beat's rhythm, endangering
My calm as the oneness of my self reached out for another.

My love's fortress of safety crumbled at the sanction of her
beauty. . .our shadows merged, permissively invading ritual privacies,
as I held in my hand the tapering roundness of her symmetry. She
sensed my desire and I guessed her heart. In my body she searched
the mountain for the sun reluctantly buried in its forest, in her body
I searched for the escaped boat adrift in the middle of the night.

Justifying moments' grammar, fate orchestrated its poetry
As eternity confined itself in our world of two. My void
Clung to the filling of her. Our presence was Mother earth's
Quiet time. She lent me her priceless virtue. . .I imparted my
Unspoken love. Her fragrance stimulated a certain joy
Embracing no reason within me. . .round about me and
Love became two minds blossoming in the other's brain.
I coveted her in my heart, craving her soulful love here and
Now. . .unafraid of whatever may arise, knowing that I have,
Enigmatically, come into my second self. . .come to love.

Preston Williams II

She Was Mine

The doddering old woman was once my daughter, full of hugs
    and smiles and laughter.

Treat her kindly in her age, for she was mine...yes, she was mine.

We grew together, she and I, through tears and fears, truth and lies,
parent-teacher conferences, projects, ribbons, praise...and smiles.

Treat her kindly in her age, for she was mine...yes, she was mine.

But now...the days of age do bind her, now...dark days will often find her
pinched with pain, bereft of care, a nursing home, a hopeless stare.

Treat her kindly in her age, for she was mine...yes, she was mine.

For now the winds of time do blow. For now dust fills each mortal soul.
Eternal time, immortal souls, in truth makes children of us all.

And I?...I swing on heaven's creaking gate, eternally, it seems, to wait,
for heaven's child and my best friend, I long to be with her again.
Down the country road of fate, at heaven's edge, I swing...and wait.
The air is still, no clock to stop,...and then I hear a bus far off.

Around the bend it winds, and winds, I see her face! And she sees mine!
Through the window panes I see, a sea of children just like me;
pixie faces, freckled skin, mushroom noses, wide-eyes grins.

Down the steps they bound with glee. But she is mine...eternally.

Barbara Grover

When The Bells Toll

When the bells toll
and time stands still,
When darkness never
touches the shore,
I will be in a place
where the moon never
dims and The Son,
shines bright evermore.
Where the sea of life
flows from Most High . . .
full of beauty that's
never been told.
There I shall live
and never more die
as the Glory of God
I behold!

Elizabeth Teasley Clayton

Sea Gulls

I saw a sea gull gliding by up, up into the blue,
One with the wind, the sea; so high
In unencumbered space to fly.
And when another came in view,
They bowed and swooped and danced those two,
Unmindful of the world where I
Observed their courtship in the sky.

Marion C. Smith

You Are The Warmth

How difficult to send a thought,
When all I felt was kept locked.
Such precious feelings that are fought,
Because of rules from those who balked.
How elegant a word may sound,
To distant ears who could not hear.
Once is darkness all around,
But now a source of warmth is near.
You are the warmth of whom I speak,
The energy that nourished me.
Someday I'll find the Truth I seek,
because of you, who set me free.

Sarah Adams

The Extremes Of Life

As deep as blood red
As high as a butterfly
As far as a star
As meaningful as a first kiss
It is the extremes of life
That show us who we are
As with love
You either love completely
Or you do not love at all
There are no in-betweens
In the extremes of life

Christopher Wonderly

Untitled

Traversing the vast flow of blood
shadows dancing crimson
the pontoon cradles slowly
underneath the opaque hood.

My vigor is not yet gone
I am not ready to go
yet the crippled ivory still twists
and the gnarled staff still rows.

Nick Naylor

And The Sun...

And these loveless shattered children are wilting on their faith. The
dying embers of the flame's final spark in the furious rage of
midnight's wind. Where the blows all come from the same source,
perhaps the west. Shadows dance around these blinding visions, and shade them from sight.
Crunching of Autumn leaves under infant in the middle of June, and this alien pleasure helps
(or forces) me to become my own worst nightmare. Filtered - And the whirlpool pulls me
under now, choking on that thick syrup another time.
And the sun.
As the sun, you are raising blisters on my flesh, or maybe it was the steps...
And I'm forced to breathe the nectar of
your passion once again.

To become a man, I am living your child, and this decision is not my
own. The searing heat of your icy fate (bestowed upon me) sheltering, nay tempering me to
the android you see before you now. Faulted ruin of your ever-loving dominion...
And the desire you felt me with. The flint, the tinder, the fire in you, and the direction in me.
I think I heard a crack. I heard the wrath of the wintery reservoir, as if I
could live forever. And I think the water was flowing from the east.
Yes, I'm funneling the wind and I believe I could sail the earth.
And the sun.
As the sun, you are raising blisters on my flesh, or maybe it was the steps...
And I'll never breathe the nectar of your passion ever again.

Brian Emershaw

Endings Rushing In

Endings rush in like madness before my tale has even begun.
I am wiped from existence with no chance of a start.
Words, details, and actions are cut short
in the absence of warnings.
I am left alone in my feeling, my senses,
my nightmare.

Laughter fills the air before I have a chance to hear the silence.
Shrieks of dying spirits and suffering hearts pierce the air,
awaking the darkness within me.
I want to hide in the black that arises from my soul,
but accusations flow in torrents,
drowning any hope of defense.

Emptiness flees my being before I have a chance to savor its comfort.
I want to feel, see, have, know, be
nothing.
I want to exist in my shallowness,
leaving a whisper of what once was
in the wake of the endings rushing in.

Breonna Redford

Go With God

I heard today that you weren't feeling well, death was oh so near.
I said a prayer in hopes that someone would care one man cared
enough to let me in
He told me your end was soon and now I am saying good-bye.

So I took his advice and now I am saying good-bye.
Please just go with God if you have to go.
If the light is near, walk towards it and don't fear for it the end
is near go with God.

I am saying good-bye to you before it is too late
for the end is painful and the road far too traveled
Yes, tears will come and go and pain will run ragged
But for I know one wish will come true
You will go with God and he with you.

As the end is now here, walk towards the light and grab the father's hand.
For he will hold you near and your memory will never fade.
For love runs deep and memories hold strong.
I know you love me and that I love you, so the end can come.

If I could have one final wish that if you must go
please go with God and run towards the light
for the end must come and love must go.

Julie Terrell

Waves Of Glory

I whispered bitterly
as you sang like the goddess
of the winter's magic.
I cried silently in the darkness as
you captured my
long flowing waves of glory.
My tears dripped to eternity.
You kissed my wounds and
dried my tears.
I held you close and
we dreamed for happiness once again.

Lauren Perna

Drummer

Did He play the hell out of those drums?
Feel the groove
Watch him move

Frown on his face
Watch his pace

Soulful groove
Watch the heat

Sonic boom in the room

Is he hot?
Watch him rock

In the lean
Moves so clean

Got the beat
Sexy heat
Drummer!

Yolanda Zesati

Hate

Our world is full of hate
as many may see
heavily increasing in rate
ease will be.

Rich or poor
hate knocking at your door
style or rep
being a prep
short or tall
stiff as a wall
slow at learning
quick at earning
being a nerd
choice of word

Our world is full of hate
as many may see
heavily increasing in rate
ease will be.

Christina Koyl

Deep Blue

From somewhere softly in the quiet
You looked at me and I at you
I drifted misty in the sea
Of your tranquil eyes
 —deep blue

In the waking of an instant
It was all that I wished to do
To stare at the eternity
Of your silent gaze
 —deep blue

Joseph Singletary

Shadows

Shadows across the ceiling, nothing on the floor below
Flaming logs so calm and warning with the air outside so cold.
Alone by the fire with time to think, reflect on all that's been
Slow motion across the screen in my mind where does it all begin?

I miss you more than ever; so much I want to say
I thought we'd always be together . . . why do you stay away?
Rain starts to tap on the widow revealing all my fears
I step outside into the night to mask my pouring tears.

I know that I deserve all this, I'm not a child anymore
I'm old enough to pay the price for mistakes I thought were right.
But in the middle of this rainy night nothing anymore seems right
And I don't know what to do except remember you.

Shadows now across the floor but I can't see them anymore
They've faded out behind the haze, haunting me in so many ways . . .

Over in the fire's eye, blue streaks within the red
With the sad sound of a songbird's cry, memories I thought were dead
Melissa Kardos Sanders

Friendship

Friendship means love forever no matter what goes wrong,
  It's like a candle that flickers on when the wind is strong.

Friendship is the wind that blows and sends the ship ashore,
  A true friend comes once in a while knocking at your door.

Friendship is the glue that bonds our love and trust together,
  It keeps us strong and powerful through dark and stormy weather.

Friendship is a pact for life that never can be broken,
  It's used to be carried on forever as our token.

Friendship (Our) will stay alive through all the hardships and pains,
  It has helped me get through life so far and all the joys I've gained.

Friendship (Our) makes me feel secure when all the hope is gone,
  It keeps me going and moving and helps me to carry on.

Friendship (Our) means the world to me and everything I own,
  It makes me feel total and whole and never feel alone.

Friendship is the cure to sorrow, sadness, and disease,
  It's always there no matter what end can never leave.

Friendship is the hope for peace and love throughout the world,
  It gives the feeling of love so true in a place that is so cruel.

Friendship is the key to life for whatever comes your way,
  It makes a place for love and trust for you to always stay.
Erin Kupcunas

River Of Love

Love is like a river,
sometimes smooth and sometimes rough.
Love is like a river,
surrounding all of us.

Love is like a river.
when damned it will surely die.
For love, love like a river,
must be free to flow on by.

Love is like a river,
as it seeks to be the sea.
If too much is taken from it,
it will cease to be.

Love is like a river,
sometimes hard like rapids often do,
and love, like a river,
slow and simple,
The way that I love you.
Samuel Gustafson

Somebody Turn Off The Light

It blinds me and binds me
To my humanity
It restrains me and chains me
To this reality
Somebody please! End this insanity...

It hates me irritates me
Mutilates till I bleed
Disgraces me erases me
Eliminates my dark creed
(But somebody's turned off the light)

Somebody turn on the light
It refines me but reminds me
Of my humanity
It surrounds me but grounds me
In this reality
This is what I've realized...

It knows me it clothes me
Shows me the dark side of me
The bright light makes me bleed,
But this is what I need.
Ian Blanche

Untitled

   You look into his eyes. . .Silence. You are lost when you dare to look into the chasm of his insanity. Lost in bloody tears and mangled illusions of who or what he used to be, he's trapped within an empty shell of someone who is light but still sits in darkness. Does he like it? Is this a need or a desire for him to be sleepy with angry dreams and live with angry nightmares? Lost soul will always be found but it would all depend on if his soul has the will to be caught.

   He is a floating dandelion, gliding along the winds of time, letting him go wherever the hands will take him. But with one slight glitch the hands that moved him are also the hands that let go. He disintegrates and falls into a shattered form of what he used to be.

   You look into his eyes. . .Silence once again. You can almost hear the screams of pain and anguish curdling around your ears. The screams will never be forgotten by me but are a living presence which is surrounding him throughout eternity.

   He is one of the unique. Whose bold eyes and sweet smile don't hide the lost and confused soul who is trying to fight and kill his way out of the labyrinth of his mind. The only thing that doesn't permit him to escape from the lulls and dying of his life and sanity is the confidence that there is no blood and death to fight for. If he would wipe his blood-drenched eyes and laugh at the illusions he so willfully wants to see. He would notice that instead of kneeling in the emptiness of darkness, he has always been standing in the compassionate glow of the light. . .
Tonya Hemmer

The Journey

As the crisp, northerly air blows away the last of winter's life,
There floats a feeling of anticipation in the air
For the warm air of Spring and the new life it will bring forth.

I, too, sense that feeling in the air
though mine is one of melancholy.
The times that have passed are haunting me now and seem to be
telling me that I should not move on, yet I cannot go back.
Caught in limbo, hanging on like the last desperate leaf that clings
to its branch during that first good snow, I want to fall,
But am not sure where that crisp Northerly air will take me.

I suddenly realize that I can hear the silence; Strange as it seems,
it speaks to me in the voice of a beautiful, young woman,
whose long blonde hair and piercing gaze envelop me
Like a cocoon that holds the secret to new life.

Here I am, warm, even as it is cold outside.
Problems are ever more distant and the passing of time
takes on irrelevant meaning.
So, when that crisp Northerly air has gone,
and I must leave this warm soft place,
I will, once again, be filled with that anticipation
of where the wind will take me. . .

C. W. Bonbright

For My Beloved Son-In-Law And Daughter, Doug And Stacey

My daughter's faith has brought her here today.
"Praise the Lord, the Lord be exalted", is all I can say.

The Bible says teach the young women in how they should go,
And through my love and actions, this I have tried to show.

In August of 1990, we were baptized together hand in hand,
And to God she prayed for a Christian man.

She wanted this day to be according to God's will and plan
So through trials and broken hearts, in obedience to God, she took her stand.

"God's ways are not our ways," I would say,
"He has someone better for you, "and we would pray.

On one very special night, Stacey prayed to our Heavenly Father above,
"Send me the man I am to marry, "and He brought her Doug.

She wanted a man who would grow in faith along with her,
And God was faithful, because together they study His word.

Doug also was being prepared by our Heavenly Father above;
And by his faith and obedience, he met Stacey and filled her heart with love

A marriage made in heaven? Yes, I would say,
Because God loves you so much, he works miracles when you pray.

Written by the Holy Spirit through Nancy M. Ott

What Will I Do Without You

I miss you next to me, and the way your hand is bigger than mine, the
softness of your touch, oh I miss you so much.

I feel I need you next to me, your arms around me, thank God I found thee.
I wish you would stay though we grew apart, I want you to know you'll
always be in my heart.
The love I feel for you will always be there, even if you don't still
care. Maybe we were never meant to be, maybe there was some
other purpose for me.

Yet I feel so confused, but I know I was not used, and while outside
I'm crying and inside I feel like dying, I still wish you were here
to end all my fear, and to make it somewhat clear, as to what I'm
supposed to do without you so near.

Jennifer Dorsey

Birthday?

I forgot
But I couldn't have
It was on the web site
each day came closer
closer
gone
How embarrassing
Hope it was great
out of this world
as my mind was
Maybe next year
I'll remember
but
Don't hold your
breath

Mary Mongan

A Teddy From The Past

Here's your teddy bear all brand new,
the one you cuddled the one you knew.

Even though we've been apart,
I've always kept you in my heart.

Memories are things that last,
things that hold and stay steadfast.

Memories have a way to stay,
in our hearts every day.

We will grow old as the years go past,
but the memories will last and last.

Here I am your teddy bear,
hold me close and keep me near.

Heidi Hanson

The Greatest Thoughts

Poets
Lost their
Greatest thoughts.
Through
The wind
They vanish,
To where
Memory knows
Not.
But
Birds sing
Them back,
In
A song
That thoughts
Cannot.

Linton Brown

The Fading Of Life

I felt the breeze
Upon my bare skin.
As the wind blew
I shuddered.
The chills swept
Through my body.
Soon, I started to die.
I was in a dark tunnel
With a light at the end.
The light became smaller
And smaller.
Within seconds
I was blind.

Shree Garnett

Pinnacle To Depths

Eternal flame
Haunt of men of talent,
Embodied in the spirit,
The halting place of the travelers,
The rendezvous of poets of acrostic rhapsody
The point to which all hopes are directed,
    veiled from time's inconsistency.

Simulated snowflakes celebrate our nuptials,
The hand of the lovely with sword and spear,
Whose feet spring upon you and trod on musk and camphor as
We pour forth gold for the sake of a pawn,

To have our name cursed and wrest from us,
When it seems impossible to remain steadfast and shake off the world,
When our sadness rages, and our only solace
    is found in the Eternal Flame, languished in chains,
Our deep sorrows unparalleled
    by tyranny and fierce cruelty,
We implore heaven for rain, but tears would suffice.
However, destiny's essence is a transformation,
So the tears cease and calm steals over.

Rachel Pinkerton

Generations Of Love

Once upon a time, Grandma and Pop Pop Threadgill loved
each other so much that they got married. They gave birth to a
beautiful baby girl. They loved her dearly. She was the "Apple of
their eye". They taught her the meaning of love and acts of kindness.

Once upon a time, that baby girl grew up and fell in love
with a man. They got married. They gave birth to a beautiful
baby girl. They loved their "Little Princess" more than the grains
of sand on the beach. They are teaching her to have love and
respect for her Heavenly Father and mankind.

Once upon a time, that baby girl will grow up and fall in love
with a man. She will get married and give birth to a beautiful baby.
They will love that baby more than all the stars in the sky.
They will teach their Sweetie the meaning of love, acts of
kindness, respect for our Heavenly Father, and all mankind.

Could this really happen? Yes, it could happen.
How do I know? Because this is my dream. This is my life. I am
that "Little Princess".

Ashley Rhodarmer

I Dedicate This Poem

I dedicate this poem to the people of this land
Who have been dealt a less than perfect hand.
To those of you who scramble to find
Freebies of all shapes, sizes and kinds.

To those of you who eat peanut butter and jelly
And as a result increased the size of their belly.
To those people whose hairline has advanced to the rear of their head.
They don't use hair cream but scalp wax instead.

To those people who have been hurt and have permanent scars.
To those people who have organs on display in glass jars.
To those people whose injuries have created limitations.
The real things are gone along with most imitations.

To those who through fate had their life cut short.
Wished their fate is destiny, their course in life would abort.
I dedicate this poem to all under achievers.
Who have becomes this world's best super believers.

And to all other people who feel they're excluded.
To all of the nerds of the world, I have also included.
So whatever shortcoming or troubles you're now going through.
Raise your head and cheer up. This poem is dedicated to you.

Virgil Brown

Untitled

My world
was
never pristine
or
dangerous
my used
world
traversed
in
infamy and
song
discovered
extra-terr(or)est(ist)rial
bliss
hubbley surrenders
its divinity
to
technogods

Stephen Strande

Will The Sky Again Be Blue

Dark Clouds pass overhead
Raindrops fall from the skies
You've broken my heart once again
Tear drops fall from my eyes

Will there ever be sunshine again
or this downpour continue on?
Will your rain dance finally cease
and I hear a happy song?

Will the sky again be blue
With clouds as white cotton?
Will I ever smile again
This heartache passed, forgotten?

Lisa Reyes

Forever My Love

You're my Love, my every need
Everything That I imagine
The need to make my life complete
You're my life, my guiding star
A star that burst forth from afar
Come into my heart
Make life a success
Lead the way to happiness
I need your Love
I need your Love
That is all I've even dreamed
I need your love so very much
Imbibe me with your powerful touch

Marguerite Campbell Bousley

Whispers

Darkness calls to me
As sunshine beckons others.
I set sail on a darkened sea
greeted by a veil of white.
Where others find discontent
I find warmth and comfort.
And as the noise of the day
is swallowed by night, I
lean back, close my eyes
and listen to her gentle
whisper.
For tho' I long to be the
mighty hawk, perhaps,
just perhaps, I should be
another.

Naomi Rodrigues

Pebbles

With Sadness on this Valentine's Day, one we love has passed away.
She gave her love so willingly,
To all she loved, not just you and me.

But if it is love we felt for her, for all the joy she gave,
We had to face the bitter fact; she would never be the same.
It is not your fault. It is not mine. There is no one to blame.

But now our job, as we move on, is to keep live her memory.
For without doubt, she will always live in the hearts of you and me.

The pain she felt is over now; she surely is with God.
For I am sure as she stands outside His gates, He will gently give His nod.

So don't remorse, and don't be sad.
But rather thank the stars above for all the good times we had.

She will always have a special spot in all who got to know her.
Her droopy eyes, her funny walk, her pretty golden fur.

I know it's hard to think real clear, but be thankful for the time we had.
And if that time was not good enough, then now we should be sad.

Her spirit lives in memory, her gentle goofy ways.
For when we're down, she will always help to make us laugh,
On even the gloomiest days.

Richard Pearce

Until I Have Known Of The Second Motherland, America

Many would refer to America as the blessed land of all people
Many longed for so, as the U.S.A. is the paradise of all immigrants
The starved landed here to survive just with bread and butter
The persecuted did here to win a certain freedom
The political defector did here to get granted asylum
The scientist did here to fulfill own technology
The jobless did here to win own livelihood
The African-Blacks did here to drudge at the Southern cotton plantations
And she landed here for her lavish dream; I landed here
For my literary dream
However her GI husband died game at the Gulf War, and my boo
manuscripts had been returned by all East coast publishers
She became hopeless in her long cherished dream
I came to standstill after strenuous efforts and perspirations
In short, she learned a vanity from his demise; I realized a reality
America is my second motherland, though my real motherland stood away
But I smiled in a whole week long due to a faith, because America
Is full of democracy and freedom
I speculate both in silence and candor which guaranteed above all
Blessed land meant a proven liberty in all .

Samuel Kimm

Frozen In Fear

The homeless man in the gutter slurring a continuous babble
If only someone would listen, the secret of the world would unravel
People walk by and look upon him with pity
What they don't realize is he was once a prominent scientist in their city
And what he knows is on the threshold of becoming more than a dream
Because he was there at the telescope when the others let out that blood curdling scream
Right before comet Hale-Bopp disappeared behind the sun
An anomaly appeared in the telescope lens, a most unusual one
And it was of unknown origin one could only guess
Then a radio receiver picked it up along with a message, that we were in eminent distress
The message told of a runaway celestial body
Rapidly closing in on the third planet beyond the sun now doomed to catastrophe
The message was sent in hopes, that if inhabited, the populous would hear
That by March 23rd, the final demise of our planet would be near
And if there was enough advanced technology to vacate
"Go for it now," before the approach is too late
The scientist is now mad, helplessly sitting in the gutter
And now that I know his secret, with similar fear I also shudder

Lorraine Stingle

In Loving Memory Of Samson

His eyes as blue as the skies
He is up at a pounce at sunrise.
He is my handsome boy
All so aloof and very coy
He is proud and mean and lean.
His vocals and senses are so keen.

He is my best of all friends my cat
And where I am - He is at
He is where the angels voices sing.
With me where the bell tolls ring

The bestest friend I ever had
Now in cat heaven where nothing is bad.

Leona Bell

The Downpour

The rain falls slowly
Like idle tears
That so many of us
Bottle up through the years.

The thunder crashes
Too loud to bear
For those of us who
Have no one there.

The lightening flashes
And lights up the sky
While some of us are
Down here, waiting to die.

But I'm not one of them
No, not anymore
I smile at life
And walk through the downpour.

Cynthia J. Firmingham

Love Lies

You said you'd love me always
You said 'friends till the end'
You said you'd wait for me
If I ever forgot.

You never said goodbye
You've moved on so well
We're not even friends now
I'm sorry I forgot.

I only forgot
Yet you still don't care
I dribbled our love
And my team lost.

I hope you're happy now
I hope you'll remember me
You'll live in my memories
And I'll love you till the end.

Gina M. Finocchiaro

From Melody

Don't cry for me,
I am not gone,
I'm in the wind and all around.

I did not leave you,
I would not go.
I still love you,
this you know.

Anita Pine

The Brief Meeting

Who knows who you might run into while walking down the street?
You'll smile, wave, say, "Hi", and, "Bye" to everyone you meet.
But on a rare occasion, there's someone you feel you know;
Someone who seems to look in your eyes, and then capture your soul.
There's a strange mystique about them, or the look upon their face,
Or sometimes it's just their aura that could never be replaced.
You never say a word to them 'cause there's no need to speak
And to everyone else they're ordinary, but to you they are unique.
This brief meeting won't effect you much, you'll go on with your daily
life Cherish all the joy it brings and deal with trouble and with strife;
You'll live through all the good times, and all the bad times, too,
But at least you'll go on knowing that there's someone for you.

Katie King

Shining Through

When your light seems to never shine and your load to heavy to bear
When surrounded by darkness you exist and enveloped you are in fear

When the cost of freedom seems to high and the roadblocks before you arise
When you feel like saying "I quit" but the voice says "No" from inside

When everyone seems to be your enemy and they laugh at you in their wealth
Your tears run down like a rapid because you can't even trust yourself

When your life of day becomes your dark of night and everything you've had is now lost
And you've tried your best to overcome. Now the price doesn't seem
worth the cost

When the funds are low and debts are high and poverty is a scream away and distaste of
defeat fill your mouth poisoned in the words way

When the price for happiness becomes to expensive and your bankrupt on the will to endure
You've now become a fallen hero washed up on a sandy shore

When they say your light's at the end of the tunnel whatever happens never bend
And you grit your teeth in anguish because the tunnel never comes to an end

So you proceed full blast down a dead end street, ready to bring it all to an end
Remember, holding on to the end of your rope may bring you the gold my friend

So give life the best you have, never say surrender
Defy defeat so life will never give you your dream back stamped Return to sender

And if everything you have ever loved suddenly disappears
You still have your life my friend so proceed with no fear!

Michael Goodin

A Leprechaun Tale

T'was such a nice day, one bright sun shining mornin'
I placed my hat on my head and turned twice around
Then wiggled my nose and hummed and sang some old Irish song to myself
Being Leprechaun day, today, I sang to myself
I'll kiss the Lass and Laddies and give them a green clover for good luck
As I placed, too, my overcoat on me, I turned twice around, and
Wiggled my nose and hummed and sang some old Irish song to myself
Being Leprechaun day, today, I sang to myself
I'll kiss the Blarney Stone and have good luck today and even forever
Then, I went to my door and went outside to a bright sun shining mornin'
And seeing some birds in the trees singing all about me
With fields of flowers and lovely out-of-door scenery all around me
I sang to myself—This is Leprechaun day, Today.

Elaine M. Johnson

To Bruce

Becoming at one with yourself so that you may bring happiness and
joy to your world and life is a lifelong journey. By slowly clearing
your own special path through the forest of life you open yourself up
to warmth, pleasure, and meaning. Day by day, step by step, breath by breath
you venture forward in search of a state of harmony and
inner-peace. You will survive, you will grow, you will shine with
loving energy and life. Cherish your hope and trust your internal
guiding light and all of life's rewards will be for you to share.

Wayne John Sullivan

Divine Devotion

I dreamt I was in Heaven
Among the angels; fair,
All of whom were beautiful
And all had golden hair.

I looked around for you my love,
But found to my despair,
To wherever I seemed to glance
I found you were not there.

But at last I turned around.
And to my complete surprise,
I saw you looking back at me
Directly into my eyes.

The seraphs now mattered not,
For I have my one and only.
I vow to never part with you,
I'll never leave you lonely.

Jason Korbus

To Wing No More

There once was known a little bird
Who flew away without a word,
She seem to be in search "a quest"
To find a place to build a nest.

In flight she found another way
Back to her love she flew to stay,
Back to the one she left in flight
She winged her way with all her might.

Accept me now she seem to cry
My love for you just wouldn't die,
My love grew stronger by the day
And in my heart you will always stay.

I'll never wing away no more
Or knock upon another door,
I've found the love I'm searching for
"I've found the love I'm searching for"

Katherine Smith Matheney

Me?

What is it about me
That makes me
Me?
What is it
That stands out
Defining
Establishing
Me?
Why this way
Not that?
Why do you love me
And not you?
What is it
And who is it
That decides
What is
Me?

Alice Rader

Modern Love

I shall not
lie to you anymore
flatter and scheme
so your heart, I can win.
Cause; I am what
I've never been before
both - lover and friend...

Sir Dionysus Cater

Vision

One night a man slept lonely in his bed
He dreams, visions the end of the Earth
A time without peace throughout the entire planet
A time that has been destroyed by hatred
Bursting bombs that sound like glass shattering on the Earth's surface
Young children scream like a missile's hum
Leaders fighting among themselves
Christians pray for forgiveness from God
Wondering what caused the destruction that is occurring
A light brighter than the sun then appears
Like a hand to pick up those believers
Everyone knows that the end is near
Those that come near the hand and are not true of heart
Feel their insides burn like a raging inferno
that is out of control in a forest
It is then that they repent for forgiveness
But it is too late, the man then sees himself inside the hand being carried above the Earth
Then a sudden boom occurs, and then the Earth is gone
Then the believers know that Jesus has come
To save his people from total destruction
It is then that they see the peace in Heaven forever

Amen

Daniel Ault

Old Christians Never Die

We laughed and cried the night you died as we remembered our life with you.
I'll never forget your words of wisdom of what we should or should not do.
You always told us to be strong you told us to always pray. This we still
Remember and we bow down everyday. I can see it all now as if it were
Yesterday when we were little children you taught us how to pray.
You were such a caring father in every sense of the word, those
words of wisdom you spoke-we were blessed to have heard.
We were all so proud of you - to us you were so strong.
All of the pain would go away when you would come along.
It hurt us so deeply to see our hero suffer we prayed so hard
To God to let your suffering be over.
May peace rest with you daddy - we'll meet again someday, old
  Christians never die they just sleep away.

Linda Logan

I Made A Wish

When I was but a little tot, I saw a shooting star
Closed my eyes, made a wish and sent it out so far.
To that place where angels dance and wishes all come true
Where children's hopes are precious gems, sparkling in the blue.

My wish was not for wealth or fame, though nice they both may be
I did not ask for perfect health, I had no fear you see.
I ask for ears to hear my chatter and laughter to make mine ring
I ask for eyes that smile out loud, children want such simple things.

I wanted acceptance to hold my hand, and arms of joy for hugs
I wanted compassion to wipe my tears and undemanding love.
I wanted security to be the lap that held me as I slept
I wanted forgiveness to be the heart that all my secrets kept.

I wanted encouragement to be the food that kept my dreams alive
I wanted faith to be the drink on which my hopes could thrive.
You see a child believes in miracles, things they don't understand
So I closed my eyes, made a wish and ask God for a friend!

Linda Lavender

The Little Light In The Pray Room

Oh I hurt inside as I sit and wait for God's answer
thru Jesus the truth and light of the world and weep with
anticipation as I kneel and pray to my God with Jesus.
The light in the prayer room still burning as I wept, for love is a gift
from God thru Jesus. Thru joy and spread
of sunshine that comes in the morning is a renew spirit.

Hattie Ware

Lost!

Have you seen Her?
Looking in the back streets
Lost in the fire
Over run by the masses
She's not for hire!

Do you know where to look?
Chasing a dream in time
Put to the test
Left for dead by millions
Scorned by the rest!

Are you the favored one?
Longing for the real answer
Last of the few
Smothered by nations
Left empty but new.

Do you care?
Her name is Freedom
She cannot be lost!

John Alexander

Lonely Winter

He left that night
awakened,
to touch his face in sleep
to touch
and of him he is thinking
a lonely winter
of poet's letters written
he left you that day
a morning's song
to keep you warm
and of him he is thinking
he left that night
to find his heart
in leaves and thorns
they said love was wrong
between like minds,
and he is leaving behind
his love, the night,
that winter
that lonely winter.

Kassi Ydris

The New Fear

The mild passions
of a blind society
the lonely way they
  cry out to me
aloud without sound
in their shallow graves
from the city walls
where rapture ensues
  and rushes all around
entertained by the muse
of a disastrous sight
host to the encrypted fact
  that the city sleeps tonight
under the wing of a
vigilant mother
killing the lies of burden
of the careful lover.

Kevin Overa

Convection/Conviction

Five tea bags and a gallon of quiescent water
Stand jar'd, energized by the sun; while Convection
Nature's most peaceful act of togetherness,
Creates, without turmoil, a most pleasing brew.

Five continents and seven turbulent seas of disparate ideologies
Stand jarred, energized by the sun; while Conviction,
Man's most warlike act of togetherness,
Creates, with constant turmoil, a most bitter brew.

Will humanity ever convert, the conferring of self-righteousness,
Through the conqueror's concussive Conviction;
To conveying to others, the righteousness-of-self
Through the conviviality of confleurent Convection?

Only the used tea leaves can tell, that mankind must learn to spell,
Using the new rule for peace... "I before E, except before C."
    John L. Smith

An Ode To The Temple Spire

From my window, in the Gatehouse
    I view the Temple spire.
It draws my eyes to'ward Heaven
    and my thoughts seem to aspire
Toward greater service on the 'morrow.

It calls to mind the Saviour's glorious promise,
    "That where I am, ye may be also",
And the goal of exaltation becomes more precious, as on I go.

The spire reaches up, so silently,
    pointing Heaven-ward, from whence it was inspired,
And all who come within its view,
    Find beauty, like sweet music from the lyre.

It prods the thought-chords of my heart,
    Reminding me of sacred work, within;
Of friends, who show they really care;
    of peace, and hope, and goals to win!

So, as I kneel, in humble supplication,
    And ask for blessings from above,
In gratitude, I thank my Heavenly Father, for Temple spires, my Savior
    and His Love!
    Mary Foster-Lamoreaux

Sadness In These Eyes

The news came so sudden, I never thought the day would come
My father's gone and I regret the things I hadn't done.
I can see the sadness in my family's eyes and feel their sorrow too
All that's left is coldness here and no one to run to.
As flowers bloom, I think about all the time we should have spent together
Walkin' hand and hand, never parting from one another.
I wouldn't know how the funeral was, I never got to go.
All that's left in my world is. . .
Sadness in these eyes.
Sometimes I ask my mom what my dad was really like
I think of all the loneliness and the hurt it caused inside
As time goes on I think I of how happy he may be up there
but all that will exist here is. . .
Sadness in these eyes
Sadness in these eyes
No happiness here but. . .
Sadness.
    Swanny Anita Bosch

Sand

Sand
Lining an ocean beach
Not knowing War
    Nor Death
        Nor Hunger
How I envy
And wish to be
Just one tiny grain of Sand
    David Spinner

Left Behind

You called me over
I knew what you wanted to say.
There was nothing I could do
No turning back, no running away.

You began to talk,
The words were so cold.
A tear slid down my cheek
as you looked deep into my eyes.

You saw the hurt,
'Twas impossible to hide.
My world was shattering all around.
"Why are you doing this?" I cried.

But no words would change your mind.
Now you pass by
As though we were never one.
I play your game without question.

Feelings deeply hidden
Make the nights so long.
Tomorrow, I hope you will see
The Love you left behind.
    Lynda Bowles

James

That pretty face,
so intent, so bright,
much love to give.
my son!

His eyes, bright blue.
they've seen so much,
but never fade,
James.

His time will come,
the future great.
True spirit, love,
will shine his fate.
He is loved.
My son!
James.
    Sally Kuhns

Peace, Beauty, Happiness

Peace, beauty, happiness
It is here, it's all around you.
When you look deep in a child's eyes,
You see it.
As you help a stranger in need,
You feel it.
As you help a stranger in need,
you feel it.
When someone says, "I love you".
You know it.
See it, feel it, know it.
Have peace, beauty and happiness
all around you.
    Kourtney C. Kocel

A Poem Poem

A thousand trains screeching to a halt . . .
A thousand headlights shining on my life . . .
A thousand gears grinding out the time . . .
(What? In a thousand years I'll never grasp the scheme.)
I cannot describe hate objectively.
(Hate is not objective.)
I cannot confess the reality of love.
(Love has no reality.)
I cannot compare death to blankets or saw blades or Pez dispensers.
Sex is not a cup of Irish Creme.
Poetry, parrot of the intangible, comes close but is not the real thing.
(You see?)
Poetry trembles, and poetry needs, and a poem is never the poem it seems.

Jeffery Johannes

What Do You Want To See

Tell me what do you see when you see me
Hopefully, my eyes hold the key
Or do you see what you want me to be see that together we are free
Is it your eyes you want to see on my face do you see my smile
The warmth that radiates a mile maybe you're looking for the tears
Tears replacing the smile seen over the years
Look here, see the smile on my face
Do you see my arms open to you - the best
Open as wide as far as the east is from west
Don't, see them closing the door
They are waiting to give you so much more
Come inside me, you will see a smile on my face
My love, do you see my open hands they are reaching out to understand
Take my hands, all of me will be there too
Counting fingers from one to ten, they belong to you
My hands will take you to the smile on my face
Can you see enough that you can touch my love
Does my love come from below or above
Take my love for now it is so very true
You will find my love passes the test too
Now tell me, you see the smile in my face

Terry Hite

To Love And Be Loved

Oh to love and be loved.
A snowstorm brings visions of beauty.
Raindrops are no longer depressing, they offer moments to reflect.
Continuing crises are no longer reasons to withdraw,
they somehow become manageable, and you're grateful for this wonderful life.
The sound of children playing,
Their thumping on the floor above my head seems almost melodic.
Then it's all gone!!!

You think you can't go on.
You're left emotionless. You can't feel for anyone or anything.
In moments of silence you can almost feel your loved one's presence.
You want to scream, to cry, to die.

And then reality strikes — you realize you must go on for those who remain.
For the love of your children, family and friends, you must go on.
You remind yourself of those who are less fortunate.
You give praise for that which you have, as well as the wonders of the earth.
You learn that you were blessed.
You were given the golden opportunity to experience true love.

In the midst of your tears, and in the midst of your fears, you
realize, you will be able to rise above this. You will, if only
in the distant future, be able to live and love again.

Vanessa C. Ford

Wind Sounds

The momentum
of life,
rushes through the wind,
frantic.

Joy and laughter,
spirit of being,
silence,
cries,
tears of pain
and suffering.

And songs
of love,
happiness,
adventure,
excitement
yet unknown,
waiting to be discovered.

We each make our own
sounds in the wind.

Joy Alexander

Wind Dancer

Up I went
On the wind
As it swirled around me
We danced
Like two lovers
Who knew no bounds
Around I went
With the wind
As it carried me
We danced
The wind and I
Like two friends
Who knew no time
I felt alive
So at peace
In the wind
I found release
As we danced
I felt as free
As the wind

Kimberly J. Gagnon

Heaven's Gate

Enmities of a vicious multitude
Savage words intended to mark
Leaving a man in weary solitude
To a world where daylight is dark

It's a cave with no sight
It's a grave dark as night
There cast a man who searched within
Wondering dreadfully to bitter ends

Cast as under serving beneath the earth
Cast savagely and tarnished with hurt
Since his birth the sun has shown
Yet in the dark he lives alone

Upon what ground do they reflect
Viciously and savagely to leave marked
Concerned not with truth but effect
To him that lives there in the dark

They pile stones where he might escape
Each one deceitful in its weight
To allow him to live it's too late
There he lives for Heaven's Gate

Clifton M. Wagley

On Top Of It

The breathtaking height makes my senses circle,
but the cold metal bar sticks firmly to my hands.
Reaching out to me, golden fingers of light
gently stroke my burning cheeks.

Finally, this last glimpse of warmth
hides behind the dark and serene mountains.
Being late, glowworms hum by and
follow the dim shine like the sweet scent of honey.

Powerful wind playfully entangles my hair, and I watch the city relax.
The smell of the giant gets carried away; it cannot reach me.
The approaching shadows strangle me, and moisture is crawling up my legs.
I return to all of you and know that there will always be a tomorrow.

Mascha N. Walter

Untitled

Color. Is that all people think about? It doesn't matter what color
you are, your sex or race.
 After all, isn't racism something we all have to face?
We shouldn't judge people by the color of their skin,
but what lies within.
Open your eyes and stop the hate and war! Can't you see?
People can't go on living like this much more.
Drugs and guns. Is that what the future's going to be?
I guess we'll just have to wait and see.
We can choose the future?
So what's it going to be?
Will it be a world in the clouds, with thunder and rain?
Or is there still something good this world can gain?

Julie Melissa Baker

I Am A Tree

Lo, I stand before you naked and bare for the cold wind has stripped me of all my finery.
But soon I will glisten in the sun covered in a veil of white for all to admire.
I sleep, I wait for there is a stirring within me for my buds are
restless to meet the world.
I have donned a dress of green.
I give shade to those that seek.
I hear laughter of children.
Birds rest on my arms.
What a happy time.
Lo, I know the cold wind will blow again and I will sleep dreaming
of another spring for I am a tree

Jean Kiefer

The Power Of Prayer

When I was just a little child, my mother said to me
If you ever need anything, get down on your knees...

I got down on my knees that night, and prayed in my own way
Lo and behold that next morning, I awoke to a brand new day...

A day no one had seen before, I didn't know what to expect
Amazed by this miracle, I had to see what was next....

My best friend got hurt that day, one heartbeat away from his grave
My friends and I got on our knees, hours later he was saved.

I had come to believe in the "Power of Prayer", until this particular day
My father got very ill, so ill, even with prayer he passed away...

"Don't turn your back on Jesus, my son," my mother said in a loving tone
"Your father is a child of God, and his father called him home...

Pass on to your children as I did, about the "Power of Prayer"
Just get down on your knees, and he will be right there."

He may not come when you need him, so keep that in mind
But as long as you pray and believe, he will always be on time...

Quinn T. Gibbs

Untitled

How can serpent words
roll off your tongue

bury me deep
bury me deep

Words were said sweet
then turned bitter
I believed what you said
could I believe what I read
Actions, words, mismatched

Love rolled in
and rolled out again
Beautiful shells shone in the warm glow
and ugly monsters ran deep in the sea

bury me deep
bury me deep

Tammara J. Williams

Angel On The Run

It's hard to see the angel
    When you're wiping up the gooh
And reaching for the little hand
    That pulls away from you

Your eyes follow his pathway
    As he darts across the room
He's gonna find a mess to make
    And he's gonna make it soon

They all say there's an angel
    Just around the bin
A darling child with sleepy eyes
    And a sheepish, funny grin

But give them a few hours
    Of noise and toys and gooh
And tiny pitter patter feet
    That run away from you

And their eyes will dance to music
    Of a slightly different hue
And your sweet, shining angel
    Will be returned to you!

Sharon L. Ricks

The Inside Me

They think they know me—
    my thoughts, my feelings.
I keep myself inside—
    my past, my future.
Forever behind a screen of happiness—
    my tear falls, my anger boils.
Forever behind an empty stare—
    my ambitions form, my dreams unfold.
Forever behind the sound of silence—
    my mind sings, my heart cries.
They know what I let them see—
    but they don't know Me.

Ayelet Marizan

Ode To A Slug

Get up you slug walk on erect
Stop crawling 'round so derelict!
You stupid thing, your slobbering
Makes me so disgusted!!!
Now, do you suppose a slug can walk
Because it's been instructed?

Ila Meyer

The Candle Flame

To some I am happiness, the promise of another day.
To some I am mourning, the knowledge that all must die.
To some I am serenity, the promise of something better.
To some I am life. To others I am death.

My life is short. My life is precarious.
And as they watch me, they cry, they love, they laugh, they pray.
My world slowly disappears.
And you can understand why? - Can you understand why?
I am bright for a little while
- like happiness
My light is not eternal
- like death
My light vanquishes the darkness - like prayer
I am subject to the wind and all its randomness - like life

Most of all though, I am warm and care for you, no matter who you are,
just because.
- Like Love

My flame will go out some day, but I will never forget you.
May Aeolus never touch you beloved one.

Geoffrey Aguirre

The Way Out!

I answered with my proverbial fine until the blinds of my eyes were
opened to feel the truth
Interesting how complex the mind to block in the pain
I'm sure I meant in
Sure that's what we are deceived to believe that with the walls up we
keep it out
Truth has shown we keep hurt in and salvation and healing out
To give it up seems to leave you vulnerable it's true
Oftentimes you would rather - at least the feeling is familiar
Let go though - it causes those we often watch and wonder about to
experience despair - to give up - to die from self-induced illness
No, I'm not saying they didn't believe enough
That it's their fault - I'm not saying they deserved it
What I'm saying is they didn't know the way out

A. M. McLaurin

Women Shall Live Free

Since the American Revolution we have been free to choose.
Choice is what we have lived for, fought for, died for.
Then why, now, in the end of the twentieth century do people
want to take my right to choose away?
I am a woman who has earned the right to live my life my way,
and this I owe to the many women who have come before me,
who have fought to be recognized as equal members of society.
Ignorant people do not realize that once you begin taking away our
rights, it opens the door to other oppressive laws, stripping away
everything history has given us.
Little by little, we will become faceless masses, prisoners once again.
No one but myself has the right to govern my body or my mind. I do
not support murder. I would never harm another for selfish needs, but
You who are opposed to choice are trying to murder me!
I will not let you take my life away! I will not be stripped of my
stars and stripes by the one-tracked minds of society!
Beware of me, and of other strong-willed women alike, together we will
put an end to your flaring hostility and innocent victims.
I am seen as an angry woman only because I speak the truth and
blatantly refuse to be pushed aside by stupidity and deaf ears!
I will butcher dictatorship with my pen, and I doubt the ink will
ever run dry.

Barbara Ann Belyski

Retrospect

On a cold and frosty morning
The children all go out to slide
With merry shout and voices ringing
I can hear them from inside.

As I watch them from the window
My mind goes back to bygone days
When I was a child, out playing
Childhood games in childhood ways.

From year to year as I grow older
Time is fleeting, so it seems.
Days go by so swiftly, passing
Just as time does in our dreams.

Children wish that they were older
But when older, wish for youth.
It's human nature to be wishing.
Isn't it the truth?

Muriel Lea Hartford

What Love Can Do

One day things will get better
One day people will know
That love is the only answer
It comes from God alone

Whispers in the morning
Prayers at noon
Helping others when you need it to
This is what love can do

Love can conquer hate
Love can change a life
Love can make it all work out
Yes this is what love can do

So when you are feeling down
When you are tired and weary
Remember God is still here
And He will not let you down

Because love can conquer hate
Love can change a life
Love can make it all work out
This is what love can do

Stavroula Angelopoulos

Sunrise

As the day peeks through
The sunrise the morning light.
So calming as a new breath of life.
See the sunrise.

Life for me is a challenge
Life for us was rewarding
Life without you is such pain
But like the sunrise.
I too rise to greet the day.

The love we shared was a blessing
The life we shared was the best
The loss of you is the pain
And that pain I will forget
For as the Sunrise
I will rise and greet the day.

I love you Johnny
and always will.

Toni R. Jones

Untitled

The artist lives everywhere
His unique blend saturates the air
The calling of his spirit echoes back as a mirror
would reflect our simplest dreams

The artist goes everywhere, no past, no present, or future
Just the formation in all three uniting as one
The deliverance comes through his hands, his feet, his eyes, his mind,
his heart. . .

There is no playground large enough to keep in the rapture
of the artist reclaiming his innocence
Graceful truth to bring forth through expression

He reflects and stimulates our senses
Both dark and light in creation
allowing the flow for aesthetic pleasure
to permeate our beings.

The artist lives everywhere
in nature, in the heavens, in the unknown, in his soul,
spell bounding, taking us to their world.

The artist lives everywhere
in all of us begging to expand and engage in our freedom
of who we really are. . . . . . .

Jodi Williamson

Suddenly Me

Peaceful in my mind I search for the being I sense I am.
My soul's quest for perfect expression has lead me on a path less
trodden by others; for becoming whole is a profound secret to be
revealed only in the closet of oneself - alone.

While gliding upon an outstretched wing, I listen and hear the angels
as they sing. The tune is so familiar - I feel at home in the rhythm
and harmony. Why do we wait so long just to listen? In stillness
and direction unprovoked, I feel a presence. My true being appears
like a sudden summer shower; washing away all my troubles of the hour.

I face the great Eastern Sun and bathe within its glow; its
streaming rays illuminate my soul and show me the way to go.
Truth lies shining in those brilliant beams of light. I follow them by
day and by night. As they move endlessly around the world, I share
in the pulsation that reaches forth with a warming touch to all
things. The rods of light are never out of sight, for even in the
shadows of darkness they reflect onto the gentle moon.

I cry out - "Oh wonderful swords of energy, pierce my heart with your
greatness and strength! Illuminate my being that I may shine as you!"
A beam of light shoots out from my faithful heart and pierces the lock
upon the door of my soul.
Peaceful in my mind, I search for nothing more.

Debra J. Mitchell

A Cry In The Dark

I reached out - no one was there; taking a few more steps -
  I tried again, 'is some-one there - anyone?'
Why isn't anyone taking my hand? Where is every one?
  'Try again', I told myself, surely someone is there—who cares?
Do they really? - Care I mean, then why am I alone?

'Hi, you called? I look up, but see no one—'why can I not see you?'
'Here take my hand.' She placed her hand in mine.
'Why can I not see you?'
'Oh, but you could! If you took time off to think of others,
To lend a helping hand, to share a smile, you would see.'

  It was difficult at first.
I started with giving a smile, and got one in return!
I saw that smile! And felt a lightening of my spirit!
A little time off - for those less fortunate, and then, I saw
Myself for the selfish person that I had been!

Diana Ratnam

A Call To Discipleship

This call is for all believers
  listen one and all
Won't you hasten to answer
  to the Master's call?

For he's calling all his children
  both you and me
To take the gospel message
  over land and sea

Yes' "come all believers
  just heed this vibrant call
Of spreading this good news
  to one and to all.

For this good news is life changing
  and oh" so seldom told
About its healing soothing balm
  to both the young and the old.

Monica C. Melville-Bacon

Here In The Dark

Here in the dark,
I sit, wondering,
Exactly where I belong.

Everyone says,
"Life is crazy" or,
"Life is hard."

I've heard all the expressions,
And I know all the sayings.
But one extremely important thing,
Is I don't know where I belong.

The clock keeps ticking.
The days keep coming.

Here in the dark,
I sit,
While the sun shines on my face.

Christina M. Capalby

Possibilities

I think of my death
I think of my life
I dream the millennium
With the smooth passing of night

I stare at the sunrise
I feel the fresh morning air
I remember my dreams
With joy and fear

I watch the children
I watch the animal life
I see with abandon
That they enjoy in this life

I turn back to the sky
I turn to the clouds
I see them drift
Wrapping around like a shroud

I think of my death
I think of my life
Like the dreams and clouds
The possibilities drift bye.

Nikki Williams

When Rain Falls

I haven't told you, about the rain
I haven't told you, How I feel when rain falls.
It's like my tears that he made when he left me.
It's the way my heart crushes when you said good-bye.
I think I'm dreaming, but when I open my eyes I still see him
leave me.
Why did I end up alone?
Why did you take this love away?
What did I do?
What did I say?
I thought we had forever.
I can't understand.
How were you so strong to leave me?
As all my rainy days turn colder and rain falls faster
I say to myself...
Let him go
I know one day it will be a shiny day again and
I will forget him, but for now
When rain falls so will my tears that were made the day he turned from me and walked away.

Maria Venicia Gonzalez

A Sea Of Turtles

Where the sun shines the whole year round and the rain rarely falls
upon the ground. There is no seasonal change and all the creatures
blend into the same.

Diversity seems to be like a blanket spread,
but if you look real close you will realize that it is all just in
your head. Drifting into this place you can easily be caught up in the flow,
each moment spent in isolation, it is no wonder you end up feeling so very all alone.

Cement kingdoms as far as the eye can see,
connected with many paths traveling to this way and that...with no

You may stop and question why this world attracts so many and spits back so few.
Some would say it is kind of crazy while others take a different point of view.

Shelled up or walled up, it is all the same. You are either a turtle
or you create your own game.

Adrianne M. Bell

A Star Winked At Me Last Night

A star winked at me last night
I never thought I'd know for sure when and where you'd get back to me
I never doubted your destination, only one it could be.

We weren't ready for you to leave and couldn't even say goodbye
Nobody in the whole world could stop you and knew better than to try.

You were always my Christmas, my Fourth of July, my New Years Day
You were always my cloud nine, my shining sky whether blue or grey.

Don't hurry me to join you, I'm taking my time but Will be there
I'll stand beside you, help you wink at those who see us, it's only fair.

A star winked at me last night and I winked back.

Ruby Line

Mother's Day

Today is not just any day; it's what we call our Mother's Day.
It's when we show the one we love; we're glad God sent them from above.
You know she's been there right from the start; and always has your best at heart.
She doesn't like to see you hurt; she'll wipe the tears, and even the dirt.
When you were sick, and had the flu; she kissed your face, and stayed with you.
She is always there when you need a friend; and is more than willing to lend you a hand.
She showed you how to be honest, and fair; to show concern when you really care.
There's no one in this great big world; who means more than Mom to this one girl.
For these, and many reason's more; I think she's the greatest that's for sure.
On this your day I give all my love; and hope you'll cherish the poem above.

Vicki R. Woods

Lonely Days

The sun has set before us
The day you passed away
Our spirit has been broken
With each new passing day
We cherish your smiles and laughter
And the memories of your life
With time our hearts will sing again
Our tears will turn to smiles
For your spirit will always be among us
And will live on throughout our lives

Jane L. Hicks

Untitled

Deep in her eyes,
she longs for freedom.
Deep in her heart,
she longs for peace,
there is none.

With thoughts,
dancing,
she wants to sing,
the lullaby of
a sweet rhyming hymn.

With her thoughts,
she must see, and
find herself, in
peace and be free.

Jennifer Judkins

For Once

Oh, for once I was an
infant that cried a
million tears.
Oh, for once I was a
child that had a
million fears
And now I'm a maiden
with a terror stricken
mind.
"Oh, God help me to
live, to be safer in
this spot than any
other wretched place."

Oh, someday I'll be humorous
and it won't be just a performance.
But for the present,
Fears,
Tears, and
Terror are all I know

Jesseca Goudreau

Alone In My Own Tears

Day's come. Still days go. No one
know's the sorrow and the sadness
that my heart holds. I'm alone in my
own tears. As I walk through this
life, time and time again I see
the true way God intended things
to be. Unity, love, peace and
understanding. Oh, wouldn't life be
so sweet. If no one ever got
deceive or beat. Oh to sit and think.
All the killing and surrendering.
That is why, I sit alone to
think. Then I can't hold back
I'm alone in my own tears

O'Rita B. Demmons

Precious Gems

The people in life that most often are neglected,
Are actually the ones that should be greatly respected.
It's the older ones that have gifts that money can't buy.
When others don't have time, it's always on them you can rely.
We often wonder, "Where lies the root of their knowledge?"
Some may have attended school; but most never went to college.
Yet, it's not a formal education that will result in a prosperous destiny.
It's the knowledge that you hold within your inner mystery.
You have emerged from the perilous huts of history's shame.
And come beyond a past that has been rooted in pain.
Never knowing that your nights of terror and fear;
Would make your children's, and grandchildren's days wondrously clear.
So we look to you as heroes that have never received their due recognition.
Looking back on your younger years, your body may not be in the same condition.
But, it's your mind that holds the everlasting key to our success.
Always knowing that the knowledge that you bestow to us is best.
So never should you feel that your living has been in vain.
The sacrifices you've made has shielded the next generation from pain.
You are loved in ways to express in words is quite complicated.
Because your love, wisdom and leadership is greatly appreciated.

Dana McKelvey

Forever Bound

The day you met her in a brief instance of time.
You both knew your souls would be forever bound until eternity.
She felt the respect, compassion, love you gave unto her so willingly.
She knew you would gently care for her without judgement.

She had the smile of an angel,
She had laughter that would light up the darkness ever so brightly.
She now is the angel that smiles.
She now laughs lighting up the heavens.

She is now forever sitting on your shoulder.
She is always going to be laughing with you.
She will forever be watching over you,
until the next brief moment of time that you both shall meet.

On that day she will be waiting for you,
with a smile and laughter.
For she is your guardian angel.
You know her name.

Ernestine Victory

Inyo Nationale

The water genuflects as I prostrate myself on this rock submerged
in water- the jagged stone shoreline dances with imagery, animal
and thirsty lives- flakes of mineral patiently waiting to give at
the emergence of a climber- finite trees, in rows, in harmony, so
abundant finite seems alien- I am thinking of humidity; mist blending
with perspiration as we watch Inyo's beloved waterfall run towards
liberation- through marsh, pond and to Lake David, of whom this
romance is addressed- while I am thinking, I am also hearing the
water trickle like mother's milk from its sinus- while I am hearing,
I am also seeing the same intimate portrait- the beaver makes his
damn of sierra pine longs- the fish inhale ripen mosquito larvae
(Grubbs)- the water ripples and stagnates by fallen timbers; tired
granite- the clouds drift slowly by in obscurity- I wonder if there'll
be an evening shower- the pines erect in rows without pattern,
arithmetic chaos - they exist- I perceive- the human braking branches-
foraging for combustible matter- alone without the sexual- the
chipmunk becomes a somewhat parasitic friend- these mountains, snow
capped and tree-line blemished with mounds of scattered white- O'
how accustomed I've grown- O' how could I hang my hat comfortably?

Joshua J. Lewis

Who Am I

She flew by lightly,
Imagining magic castles,
Winter lakes,
Spring stars,
A butterfly
A garden,
A bright yellow sun,
And summer dreams,

She flew up inside,
Wet winged.

Sun out today.

"who am I," she asks.

Night rain came,
Dark sky glows,
Slow music whispered,
Silent peace walked

Janalyn Lars

Sonnet On Waiting For Love

Daisies need some time to grow
And we shouldn't rush them at all
Too much rain or too much sun
Will make them wither and fall.
But if the daisies bloom just right
Their beauty will be seen
And all the world around them
Will be blue skies and grass of green.

I'll keep you always close to my heart
And wait anxiously for the time
When we can be together again.
I long for you to be my lover
And I thank God now
That you are my friend.

Bobbi Bergeron

Visitors Of The Heart

When he left her,
numbness settled
like a drop cloth of
protection against
her longing for his
return; and friends
who came to visit
offered no stage
for her to stalk
things out, or
have her pain
confirmed.

Instead, they came
to chat; unaware
that only Patience,
Compassion, and
Understanding,
can truly visit
a broken heart.

Madelyn J. Bell

Again

Tragic joy fills my heart
The masochist inside believes the dark.
My soul is empty, or so I thought
For love is a battle, not well fought.
Assailed by love, my mind recoils.
A stinging taste of kerosene oils.
I am confused about which way to go.
I do hate to love, but need to grow.

Brandon Kennedy

Stella

Besides Bangladesh, utterances stated, there is little to conclude.
   But life
Debated, goes against man, the rule that insists, calling himself
   fool, on
Patterns of an open end, menagerie of perversion where philosophy
   is now
And then crushed by a hobnailed will. The best ever said would
   have to melt
Caverns of wax, damp chaff combustible itself the fruit patterning,
   from the
Humming hamper filled with artificial dirt. Swindles splattered into
   the air,
Are made to beguile moments spared the obnoxious medium
   which admits of
Assumptions fixated and eradicating discussion. On ground this
   rainy even',
A mist hovering but cool, wet drops falling only sparsely, the
   Earth under
Combat boots brown, old, green everywhere, moving into a two-man
   tent,
Getting wet, reflect that nature is friendly, and with this common,
   innocently conscious
   James A. Miehl Jr.

Untitled

For every day that we watch the sun come up, we know we have been
blessed. Amidst all the ugliness around us someone gave us the
ability to find the beauty in this life. For every day that we watch
the sun set behind a cloud showering the earth with dazzling arrays
of color, gently easing into a starry summer night resplendent in its
own beauty and yet, so magnificently unpretentious that even the most hardened
among us have to sigh and quietly admit, we are blessed, because someone gave us the
ability to appreciate the beauty in this mess.

There are days when I don't see the sun coming up; there are times
when clouds obscure the beauty of the night. There are moments when
my heart is heavy with sadness and my eyes strain to hold back tears.

And as I am about to succumb to the insanity of this world I think
of the love that we share, which I hold onto so dearly.

The day will come when I will see the sun come up again and I will
take in its warmth; I will stand beneath a starlit sky and marvel
at its beauty.

And although the ugliness of this world may still be here, it is this
love of ours, this beautiful sweet love, that will always be the
blessing of my life.
   Lucille Wilkinson

My Father's Son

Black, curly hair crowns a brown-skinned skull holding
Chestnut painted eyes with gold speckled centers that
Radiate a well-worn smile.

He cups my small hand in his large hand as we walk into the theatre.
Pride filleth my tiny steps and love bathes my heart
As we share a double feature.

Then the memory dissipates and I puzzle at the change of scenery,
Not quite understanding the shifts of time,
My loneliness, my love for him.

My streaming tears beg for another chance,
No harsh words, silent calls, recriminations, rejections,
Just to be held, just to be in his company.

Sometimes in an unfinished tale,
Time's distorted and truth is untold,
Revealing the fetus aborted from its paternal womb,
Crying for nurturing in a tortured, masculine world.

I move through life rooms, regretting the past, fearing the future,
Existing in the present, yet, still, asking God to let me put
My small hands in his large hands because I'm my Father's son.
   Paul M.P. Silva

Untitled

Our angels have guided us
Marriage is our fate
I pledge love and friendship
To become your lifelong mate

Not just in body
But deep within my heart
Forever, I'll share my angels
To ensure we never part

Like angels in flight
And soaring high
Today we received our wings
It's our turn to fly

As the seasons change
And angels spread their wings
I promise to love you always
It's symbolized with a ring

I shall ask my angels
In prayer each morning
To guide us and protect us
To continue our love soaring
   Charlotte Sharkey

The Playful Princess

Amber flowing ponytail,
Heedless, oblivious, careless;
Reciting nursery rhymes.

Shadowy menacing danger,
Anticipating, Queen's henchmen.
Searching, seeking, stalking;

Flaxen skipping Princess,
Glances, approaches, knocks;
Enters thatched cottage.

Golden baking cookies,
Smells, sees, devours;
Sleeping, smallest bed.

Brazen Henchmen burst in,
Spy, seize, grasp;
Binding, sleepy princess.

Braided rope refuses,
Bellowing, snarling, screeching;
Awakens wizened sorcerer.

Furious ruthless henchmen,
Rushing, slashing, pouncing;
Attacking, composed sorcerer.

Unperturbed transformed sorcerer,
Courageous, strong, valiant,
Thwarting henchmen attack.

Subdued, groveling henchmen,
Profess royal allegiance.
   Mel Reader

Dolphins

Dolphins are sleek and agile,
Only seen for a little while.

Sometimes they put on a show,
When tired they let you know.

I like Dolphins, they're one of my
favorite things,
They jump real high and dive through rings.
   David Beard

The First Man In My Life

You were the first man in my life, who's been there through everything
You helped me to stand, walk on my own, taught me to deal with what life had to bring.
Your heart filled with love, your eyes shined with pride,
To watch all the firsts, you sat back for the ride.
A pillar of strength you stood fast and true,
To lend me a shoulder when I felt so blue.
The happy day came when another sought by hand.
You gave me to marriage without much demand.
To love, cherish, and accept me till death do us part,
Just as you had done right from the start.
Your child I am, my father you are,
Though we're miles apart, you'll never be far.
For together we've experienced all that life has to give,
You were the first man in my life and in my heart is where you'll
always live!

Beni Cogburn

November Wind

That November kiss that we shared
Only built a wall to climb.
An obstacle that we've had to bear
In and out of ties that bind.

A secret love that is scared
Of having the thought in mind
That one day when we become a pair
The dream will shatter and leave us blind.

Know this my vocal knight
My love for you is dear
Although we have times we fight
I do not shed one tear
Because the strength between us has a height
That cannot bring me fear
Of coping with what might
Occur if you or I turned the other ear.

Have faith in my love for you because through both thick and thin,
I will be there, tried and true - as a lover or a friend,
Whatever you need me to do. And never to be lost in the wind
My heart - that I give too, along with love until the end.

Chysawndra Lynnette Petty

Is There A Future In The Past?

Is there a future in the past?
This is a question that my heart must ask.
You say that you no longer love me, but I just don't really see
How you could just walk away from the love that we shared "yesterday"
I see you standing there and talking with your friends in the hall,
And they all have told me that I should give you a call.
But you seem to just need some time alone.
For I know that you do not have a heart of stone.
Though you have said I should find somebody new,
No matter what I do, I just can't stop thinking of you.
All I know is that I can't change the way that I feel.
Is this love for real?
There is a hole in my heart,
That will not mend as long as we are apart.
I feel that deep down inside you still care,
But the pain is just so hard to bare.
As each and every day goes by,
I don't see how we could just let our love die.
After being apart all of this time,
I still wonder will you ever again be mine?
If you were ever again mine, could we make our love last?
Is there a future in the past???

Sunshine VanVlerah

Lou Ann Give Me That Gum

The words the preacher preached,
Are as real as they can be,
That's why I came to praise the Lord
With my whole family.

The sisters started shouting,
'cause they got the message clear,
And happiness won't let them sit
In any kind of chair.

Now I just came to hear the "word,"
And praise the Lord you see,
But I kept hearing a smacking sound
That was distracting me.

My little girl was chewing,
And smacking with a hum,
And I turned and told her sternly. . .
Lou Ann, Give Me That Gum.

Clanthie F. Gordon

What If I Was Dead?

Lying on my bed
What if I was dead?
What would it be
That I could see
Could see if I was dead?

You cannot live forever
But dying ends with never
Who would have guessed
Which one is best
Forever or for never

Thinking through a thought
What price could life be bought?
Would it be right
To roam through night
With life who's price I bought?

Lying on my bed
What if I was dead?
A thought of scare:
Who would care?
So what if I was dead?

Joshua Beinke

The Touch Of Grace

Upon the shallow waters edge,
Lies a blanket of dew left unsaid
Yet stillness blinds beneath the bough
A willow cries, who's seeds will sow.

A skies embrace of homeward bound
Shall cradle so gently,
A sparrows sound.

And yet the wind, so strong, so bold
Shall keep the secrets
That life will hold.

Phillip A. Genchur

Untitled

A cold wind blows off the sea,
We huddle together to keep warm.
Dark clouds hold back moon beams,
Waves lap at our feet.

We watch as day breaks,
The tide rolls out with the past.
We are renewed,
Our beach is clear.

Ryan J. Kelly

Our Old Cat

He lays perfectly still on a pallet of old oak leaves in the garden.
Dappled sunlight twinkles down on him through the leaves of lilies,
iris, and azaleas. Sleeping, sleeping his golden days away.

So quiet is he that to the un-observant, he goes without notice.
Birds chirp overhead while squirrels romp along the fence and
yet he sleeps on.

First his eyes open like slits, then wide, to reveal a copper color
that is alive with fire, even at seventeen seasons gone by.
Like a king waking slowly and in his own time, he stretches
and comes to his full height.

How majestic his profile, so magnificent in his stance and
movement, his purring the regal drum roll of his own arrival.
All the majesty and joy and creation embodied in his frame.

Is it any wonder that we love and cherish him so, this, our old cat.

Rebecca Jane Coleman

A Blank Screen

A blank screen. A white cloud.
A lost love. In a dream. Then found again.
Forever is a long time, sometimes.
Together is a good thing, if you let it be. Life is full of
surprises. Surprises are full of life. Children playing in the rain.
Sun. A colorful rainbow. Like the crayon drawing of a five-year-old.
Growing up. Slowly, we think. Faster as we get older.
Silver lining, first in your clouds, then in your hair.
The man in the moon is watching. Who is watching him?
Lost in the forest. Darkness is around. Everywhere. Where to go or
not to. What if we find something we're not supposed to see?
What happens next?
Does anyone know? If they know, are they glad they do or ready to forget.
Can we ever forget our past? Do we want to?
Is it better to forget or to remember and learn?
A blank screen.

Sharon Williams

The Carlights Have No Name

As I sit in the back of my mother's car, I watch how the car lights
pass in the opposite direction.
As I watch the white light turn to red, I think of all my father said.
As I think of his immortal words, I think of how they twist and turn.

As I sit and reminisce, I think of those words my father dismissed,
"I will not ever see you again my son, and I love you no more."
As I dream of his returning to me, I dream of how things ought to be.
As I listen to the passing wind, my mind wanders and spins,
for I will never see my father, hear his words, or feel his sins.

As my mother drives the car, I think of all the things my father said,
and my mother shouts, "Say it in your head. Your father is gone and
nothing more, he is dead in my eyes and soon in yours.
You shut your mouth and close your mind, your father is dead and we will be just fine."

Jason Hood

Weeping Willow

I saw a man once sitting by a weeping willow
With his hands about his face and tears in his eyes,
His feet set in mud although it hasn't rained for weeks,
His clothes soaked although there is no water anywhere nearby.

Each teardrop carried with an echo silencing the night
And then the cricket played its sad song for the man with a weepy eye,
But not even the wind could dry his face tonight
For his broken heart refused to heal, despite the arguments from his mind.

He knew that there is nothing he could do to bring back the love he lost
But the memories of past joy didn't want to die.
As he looked up at the tree trunk he saw their names carved in thebark,
Once so fresh, clear, and bright, now old, brown, and dark.

Peter Pietruszewski

New Love

I can feel my heart beating,
Pounding, every second of separation.
Consequences of knowing you,
when I close my eyes,
you are what I see.
Unconsciously,
I begin to smile.
I remember your touch,
My body reacts. . .
breath catches,
pulse quickens,
chest feels hollow.
I am alive!!!
My days are a blur,
Only in your presence
am I whole. . .

K. D. Lunsford

Colored Folk Stand Up!!

You're black, you're smart, and God
made you, so stand up for who
you are!!

Stand up for your rights 'cause you
are somebody!

Stand up to the people who step in
your way and try to bring you down!

Stand up for what you know!

Yea, we're colored folk and we are
going to stand up for what we
know!

Stand up and be proud of who
you are!

Colored folk
stand up!

Tammy Anderson

Liberty

L and of people.
I mmigrants came here.
B efore I was born,
E ven now.
R eplaying instant memories.
T oday, yesterday.
Y earning to see family, but being free.

Erin Kane

Poisons Of The Soul

Stare now, into eternal fire.
The Abyss of suffering and pain
Thy maddening one.
Release me -
Death, darkness, desire.
Intrigue me -
Hate, anger, unjust.
Behold now,
The Poisons of the soul.
Life lost, pathetic dreams.
All, yes all
Lain to waste,
Within vile tombs
Of ill forgotten truths.
Ill truths that you -
Yourself have committed.

Steven Dwayne Spencer

Untitled

The sunflowers stood smiling as I hurried by
I saw myself among them, away from reality, rooted only to the earth
they look and seem like me and yet a common bond I cannot find
my thoughts which linger, which sway and die in time
are not approved of, are not the cliche of the world
the cracks, sealed with the sweet and tears of others—
others you call sister, lover, husband
my wall unfinished, unsealed, undone
unsure of whether to invite you in or hide beneath the airtight shelter
Once I was a Sunflower, rooted only to the earth
needing only a smile from the sun and a tear from the clouds
now as I wilt, an eclipse comes over my mother sun
the clouds laughing as they hurry past
I saw you, my hand stretched out
yet quickly did I pull it back
when I realized
your facade was complete

Kari E. Smith

Untitled

I sit on the floor of my room, in the dark
with my blanket wrapped securely around me.
The heat from my newly-fixed furnace
pushes up from the vent and spills out over my body.
It is hot and burns my toes but warms my arms and legs.
My body instantly grows still and sleepy, so full of heat.

I am five again, warm, loved and at peace.
The heat from the wood furnace two stories below
stoked by my father's hands finds its way
through the old heat ducts of my great-grandparents' home
and swirls under my homemade flannel nightgown.
My mother's hand-made quilt surrounds me.
My mind dances playfully . . . full of a happy five-years-old's thoughts. I am content,
secure, safe from the storm
that knocks on the windows outside.

My furnace switches off with a loud "click"
and suddenly I am grown.
I find my way back to bed, my own bed in my own home
and crawl under my store-bought blankets
that are so full of memories of you.
The chill of the night cannot penetrate the thickness of my covers, yet I am not warm.
I roll over and warm myself next to you
even thought you are thousands of miles away.

Merri J. Mattison

Willow

The willow is a tree that God has cursed as a depressant.
A willow is like an old man leaning and waiting to wither and die away.
Willow is a tree as wise as the oak yet, unwilling to share all that.
Knowledge gathered over all of those years.
It awaits the time for our Lord to bestow upon it eternal beauty to
    rise above all others.
However, in its own mourning it does not recognize the beauty
    that lies within.

Jesse Remillard

Summer Sky

The silhouette of robust pines
Against the summer evening sky,
The backdrop a maelstrom of citrus
Orange, desert reds,
Rest calmly on a cold, steel colored
Sea.
Harmonic sky, fragile moment,
A perfect memory,
Make me ponder of my life
This picture now a part of me.

Helen Ayala

A Story Untold

I am constantly at a ford in the road,
On it a sign stating, "a story untold."
I make my decisions,
Based on my visions,
Of what lies ahead,
And this I do dread.
I look for clues every day,
'Cause once on a road I cannot stray.
I am constantly at a ford in the road.
Making my life, my story unfold.

Nathan Petty

Tender Touch

I have so much I want
To say, life is a dream
a scene from a play

How can I find the words
to spark, to bring light in
out of the dark.

To fill your life with joy
and laughter, here today
and ever after.

A touch of grace and a warm
embrace, love and tenderness
for every race

Joy, and bless remember
    this

Linda Harrington

The Day On The Green

An end,
yet a beginning
Sadness,
yet excitement
Good-byes,
but new hellos.
Time - as fast as can be
Memories - always to treasure
Past - becoming future
Life - starting anew
Pulled - in separate directions
Heart - breaking in two
Can't it last forever?
Friends - drifting away
Love - passions subsiding
One - last time together
Turning - to face the sun.

Roseanne M. Nicolucci

Untitled

Awakened from a slumber, I still
find myself in the darkness.
Filled with guilt and unpure thoughts.
Waiting for death seems to be my
only escape. All my dreams
locked away in a keyless place.
Strength is what I need to open
the lock. Where are you with
your hurtful words, that wound me
from the inside out? Yet I ache
to hear your voice. Is it you that
I long for? Or is it the things
you say which push me deeper into
the grave that I have already
dug for myself.

Jacqueline Briggs

Snow

It is snowing very hard
Snow is covering up my yard
Snow is falling all around.
Snow is landing on the ground
    All the roofs are turning white
    It is snowing through the night
    All the water has turned to ice
    All this snow is very nice!

Risa VanAntwerp

Remembering The Light

You walked away
feeling you gave nothing.
How could I tell you,
"The light of a candle
seems small . . .
Until you've stood
in darkness."
And even though you're
gone,
I still remember your
light kept me warm
a little while.

Liz Cole Parker

Untitled

If all the world would healthy be and
All the poor folks rich
We know that there will always be -
The ones who have to bitch
Ones neighbor's hair is not quite right
Another skin is a bit too white -
Some family's children are too many -
others seem to have not any
They'll find a way we know full well -
to turn this Eden into a Living Hell.

Irene Savine

Oklahoma

Shifting winds and drifting sands
Empty places where life had been
Billowing smoke a belching hell
No time to turn, no time to wail
Empty arms with aching hearts
forever gone so early to part
innocent eyes closed in sleep
buried beneath the rubble so deep
evil and Satan will not command
they traveled to the promise land
beautiful pastures and streets of gold
no tears in heaven just earth below
   Tears will fall only awhile
when Moms and Dad unite with a child
Husband and wives will again meet
On Judgement Day we rise from sleep

Alice Lucille Bowens

Voices

There are voices in the street
echoing in the murky air below.
As the spirits congregate and meet
taunting words begin to flow.

There are voices in the hall
weaving silver webs of deceit.
And a cunning net begins to fall
about my crimson feet.

There are voices in the dining room
Their lies dripping in my ears.
Words of accusation, words of gloom
create despairing tears.

There are voices in the stairway.
Anger flows from each vehement shout.
Death is only a breath away
as my soul floods with doubt.

There are voices at my door
and I am filled with dread.
For the voices that I most abhor
are now within my head.

Nicholas D. Renninger

Untitled

Lying on a bed of satin
A rose upon your chest
your spirit is still alive
your body is at rest

The Demon won the battle
but you lost not in vain
fore in my mind and in my heart
your soul will forever remain

Many tears fall from my eyes
they land upon your cheek
you do not know that they are there
my heart is heavy my body is weak

I touch your hand one last time
and turn to walk away
Saying goodbye is hard my friend
but we'll meet again one day

Amy Ratajack

Like An Eagle

   Like an eagle
that never lands
flying to new horizons
   Venturing through the air
with her wings spread
letting the wind guide her
   Hands are like claws
grasping to her what is dear
never releasing
   Grip is strong, yet very tender
as she catches you
   Eyes are clear and bright
seeing the good in people
   Sitting high on a branch
overlooking the earth
watching with a twinkle in her eye
   Making responsible decisions in life
fighting for what is right
never giving up when things go wrong
   Like an eagle that never lands!!

Jennie Jobe

Burned House Casualties

   Coal black eyes stare
from the room dark and bare
   No more
   will words pour
   through the sagging door
From walls   of bone
The tenants   have flown.

Connie Sorrell

Kevin

Why did he have to go
Why did he have to leave
He was only 12 years old
He hadn't really lived
How can someone be so cruel
To rob a young boy's life
To take away the most valuable gift
Given to a person
His friends just left him there
How could they
Didn't they know
Didn't they realize
He would go to sleep
And never awake

Stefanie Nyhoff

Intimidation

I look at him, he looks right back.
He sets afar; on top a rack.
I glare at him, he stares at me;
for we both are trapped,
but I will be free.
I can walk but he can fly.
I despise and need him as days go by.
He is my enemy, he is my bondage,
but without him I am lost in all age.
I am not the only of his kept;
for some do work as others slept.
When I want he can be my friend,
but not until the days near end.
For when I rest he's at my side;
or in the day a raging tide.
And when your work is hard and long,
when troubles round you seem to throng.
Or when you're bored and may not talk,
you can not help but watch the clock.

Brian McCombie

The Storm

The day began so gray and cloudy
The wind rustled through the trees.
Briskly signaling the oncoming
Of a storm laden with snow.

Up above so close to the clouds
Thousands of cranes formed
A myriad of designs so clever
They seemed to have taken lessons.

I saw a dragon and a fish
I saw buildings and a ship
But mostly I saw the V-shaped
Formations they always hold.

Beautiful from large to tiny dots
High to higher altitudes.
In search of a landing place
To weather out the storm.

The Rio Grande Valley is just the place
So down they came at last!
The storm descended and passed
The sun come out to bid farewell.

Virginia Tellez Wayne

A Holiday Note

Dear Recipient,
My gifts aren't late this year;
they're sparse.

Today, they just push you aside,
even before you're ready.
Most employment is a farce!

Without the "greenstuff" coming in,
one can only recognize the season
when pulling on a scarf.

As I sit around,
with time to spare,
all I do is parse.

Now, having writ,
why not share it?
I think you'll get a laugh.

Richard A. Hanson

Death Of Summer

As Autumn winds blow briskly by.
One can almost hear summer's passing
sigh.
Soon the leaves will turn and fall.
A reminders of change to us all.
Summer days so bright and sweet.
Winters chill whispers death and defeat.
The colorful beauty so quickly gone.
Through winters cold we struggle on.
Till once again hearts and
brighten our view.
To lift the darkness from the earth.
We all eagerly await summers rebirth.

Kenda L. Siler

Whispers

Last night I lay, watching,
The tiny lines on your face,
As you slept so soundly,
Even your snores were erased.

I wondered what you were dreaming of,
As your lips slowly formed a smile,
My only wish was to hold you close,
Oh how divine

I gasped with pure delight,
As you whispered my name,
Lydia, Lydia, Lydia
You whispered again and again.

I leaned over yet closer to you
And swiftly brushed my lips to yours
I felt so alive and complete,
Honey, because I am all yours.

Lydia Griffith

One Little Question

A lifetime
of waiting,
for what?
for whom?

If this was
to happen,
why now?
with you?

No past,
no future,
a hidden relationship,
an unknown tie.

No reasons
or answers,
just one little
question...

Who are you
to me,
what am I
to you???

Adileh Sharieff

Today

From out of despair
   I must rise
Forget the past
   let the future rest
I owe myself
   the test
Of today

Jeanette jj Woodfin

My Friend Laura

In quiet moments, when I'm alone
I sit and think, now that she's gone
How much I miss my only friend
Who always had an ear to lend.

No matter what, if good or bad
This friend, Laura, I once had
Would stand by me and then advise
What I should do, as she was wise.

She taught me how to make the choice
Quietly now, I hear her voice
"Be good, be smart, have class and more
Be kind, considerate," she did implore.

To her alone, all credit will go
For most the good that I now know
Work hard, crawl to the top
Until your goal, you do not stop.

Good night, my friend, my mother dear
One sure thing you need not fear
Your guiding light will follow me
Until I die, my friend, you'll see!

Ann Kallios

Listening To A Clock

Have you ever listened to a clock?
Really listened, really heard?
In the silence of a lonely night
It seems to whisper but one word
Alone. Alone. Alone.

The old lady lay dying
Where once her husband lay so near.
The clock again was speaking
If only she could hear
Together. Together. Together.

Joyce Hoffman Bruce

I Have Consumed Destruction

I have swallowed the world's tears
and cleansed myself of sorrows.
   Immersed in the waters
   of amniosis and oblations,
I am purged of hope and terror,
   equal to existence
   (or perhaps annihilation).
A woman emerging and absorbing,
I can never be destroyed—
   I have consumed destruction.

Alexis Brooks De Vita

Penman's Ship

Sailing over windswept seas
Breaking through the waves with ease
My craft is in itself an art
My art is in itself a means
To let myself go
To fly as a dart
Then forced to come back
Reality attack
When dreams must part
To where they go
I wish I had some magical beans
To put at ease my aching heart
I'd visit the lands of fantasies
Sailing over windswept seas.

David Lynn

Dying Inside/Living On The Outside

I would keep my thoughts,
within myself, for the outside world
only brings pain and misery.
   What is love, I ask myself,
Love is a five letter word for
death. I've faced love, eye to
eye, and almost fell into the
evil spell of death. I would
never fall in love again.
   Only hatred, will bring me
close to one. For I would live
and walk another day.
   Do you not see?, do you
not understand?, that love
is deadly. For I would rather
hate than love. I would rather
live than die. I'm dying inside,
but living on the outside, can't
you see?

Hector P. Escalera

October

Weep no more
Summer's gone —
Our hearts rejoice
   in solitude.
The velvet depths of
battered seas
Envelop us
and stir our
   misgivings —
The sun weakly
reigns on benumbed
   chrysanthemums.
Weep no more.
Silver icicles cling
   and petulant
smoke stacks plume
   into darkness.
   We forgive
   We forget

Summer will come.

Nancy B. Craig

The Mourning After

Grandpa,

I really didn't know you that well
But the times we spent together
Will always dwell
In my heart always and forever.

I really wish
I had another day
To show you how much you're missed
In some special way.

Now I just hope and pray
That during this long peaceful rest
You will be blessed
And we can meet again some day.

God is with you
And so are we
So just go towards the light
To find an everlasting journey.

Love,
Your Grandson

Michael Fickett

Draw A Circle Around Yourself

Draw a circle around yourself. Every point
from yourself and the line around you has the same
distance. It begins and ends the same way and as
you stand in the center you ask yourself why. Why
do I end up the same way I started? Why am I so
distant from the world? Why am I in so much fear?
    Why is my heart so incomplete? And though the
planet has the same form as a circle, there is still
great distance within. Is being full and complete the
answer? Ask yourself why? Is an empty world filled
with joy? Is an empty heart worth living for? Open
the circle around you and let the power and grace of
people fill it with whole heartiness. Close the circle.
Don't look back. Draw and circle around yourself, but
only open it for the Spirit and the power of Grace.
Don't look back and ask yourself why. Accept the
power and spirit within and let it fill you with all
                    the ANSWERS.

Lila V. Miller

Twinkle And Gold

The glittery sparkles in the sky,
keeps a twinkle on my eye.

The sky is black as night,
but the stars guide with light.

But soon the sparkles disappear into the red,
time for the sleepiness to be gone and to rise from bed.

The golden ball of heavenly fire,
remains everyday's desire.

Then the sparkles in the sky
come out to twinkle on my eye.

I sit and wait all day long
to watch the stars twinkle among.

Janice Miller

For All Eternity

Our connection was instant
We were friends from the start
Our hopes, concerns, and dreams
Fused into one single part.

That first night that we talked
I knew you were the one
I felt I had always known you
And on that day our life together begun.

Your sweet smile and sparkling eyes
Drew me to your heart,
And your strong protecting arms
Told me that we would never part.

Our values are the same
Our thoughts so much in tune,
I see our children in your eyes
And the sun, the stars, and the moon.

You always keep me smiling
No matter what life deals to me.
My heart and soul are yours dear,
For all eternity...the way destiny meant it to be.

Holly Victoria Evers

What Color I May Be

I light this candle for the dead;
just in hopes no one has dread.
I touch this lamp for all to see,
look...someone is making fun of me.
I have no color, I have no shame;
toward my family or my name.
I'm no one special,
so please don't care,
people come from miles...
just to stare.
Stare and watch my head hang low,
the pain and agony...
it hurts me so.
I am not worried of what you think,
it's just my mind went a blank.
I am what I am and you have to see,
that you are you and I am me.
As I blow this candle out and turn this lamp off,
the dead are cease to be and no light to see...
what color I may be.

Samantha Brody

When We Meet Again

In the early autumn, when brown leaves fall
My heart will catch a glimpse of you.
God knows how much we love them
So he only takes a few
To make the place that we call heaven
A gorgeous place to view.
But when it's time to say good-bye
My heart will still ache for you
Though we are left behind
We must realize that God loves us too.
Angels are hard to find
But should you go to heaven and I remain
A thing I know I'll do
I'll walk slowly down that long dark path
for soon I'll be with you.
I want to know every step that you take
So I'll be sure to take the same
Because someday down that lonely road
I will hear you call my name.

Chrissy Abel

To My Valentine

Cupid's Arrow, so you've heard, goes straight to the heart
But we know that's a finish, it's never the start.
First you must pass through all the weird lines,
And share more than one of the many hard times.
You must live with some worry, with hopes torn apart,
And be ready to help, when it's not in your heart.
You must give till it hurts and you know that it will,
As your chest burns like fire, while climbing loves hill.
You'll pass through the brambles, with sharp little thorns,
That'll leave little scars, where your skin had been torn.
Through fire and flood and the hot searing sun,
Through winters deep snow and cold to the bone.
You wonder, "What's happened! What's Cupid done?!"

Then the soft touch of lips, that warms up the air,
Melts away the concern and eases the care.
Cupid's Arrow has gone through flesh, blood and bone,
And deep in your heart, loves found a new home!!!

Joseph Pass

Mirror Of Reasoning

When one reasons through the thoughts of others,
their perception is, without doubt, distorted.

Distortion brings about confusion, and
confusion leads to chaos.

Chaos brings about thoughts of perceptions without reason.

Without reason, one cannot perceive the thoughts of others.

Therefore, for another to perceive reason,
the thoughts of others will only be perceived
when they first reason the thought themselves.

When one reasons through the thoughts of others,
their perception is, without doubt, distorted.

Distortion brings about confusion, and
confusions leads to chaos.

Chaos brings about thoughts of perceptions without reason.

Without reason, one cannot perceive the thoughts of others.

Therefore, for another to perceive reason,
the thoughts of others will only be perceived
when they first reason the thought themselves.

C. Mark McKenzie

The Minute

What peace flows through my veins this day.
Just like that went all the dismay.

Tried soothing through readings and meditation galore,
seeking that comfortness and stillness we all adore.

The efforts to find constantly searching within,
my dear soul yearns for parts not of chagrin.

Believing the great teachers of knowledge and truth.
I struggle with principles there would be no need to disprove.

Accepting divination, uncomfortable as it may be,
if not of proof, to many is not worthy.

To surrender and rid all issues and answers,
we seek to endure more things of steadfastness.

When all that matters my inner soul sings,
the benevolent embrace to fasten all beings.

Lisa Dorman

Till Death Do Us Part

A thing of beauty
So full of life
It blossomed with every tender touch
It produced laughter, promise and hope
With every embrace, wink and smile
It grew.

Time passed and neglect eased in
A day without laughter happened.
The desire for attention was left unfulfilled
Disappointment and loneliness visited often
Causing blossoms to dry and petals to fall
It suffered.

Touches left bruises
Smiles turned into tears
Winks were replaced with frowns
No more promises were made
Hope diminished
Death happened.

Betty F. Haith

A Lady And A Sailor

She awakened this morning, no smile upon her face;
for today he would go away—far away from this place.

Gladly, she would give up all that she owns;
if she could but go with him to his new home.

It could never happen, she knew from the start;
still she was helpless, a prisoner of her heart.

She had loved him since the day they'd first met;
the memories would be treasured, with but one regret.

Never did they share that three-word phrase;
perhaps it would haunt her the rest of her days.

For she loves him with all of her heart and soul,
he makes the earth shake, lightning flash and thunder roll.

All along she knew they could only part as friends;
would, that she could, stand by him 'til the end.

But he has to go now and get on with his life;
she'd no longer be his woman, and never be his wife.

As he holds her close and they share a final kiss;
she knows that no other will ever touch her like this.

She fights back the tears when they say their good byes;
for her heart shall be heavy 'til the day she dies.

Anne Howell Watkins

She

As the crimson petals float to the ground
She reaches out, pleading to the sky
Pricked by the thorn, her sweet blood trickles down
She sees her strength slowly pulsating by
Her eyes well with tears for many a lost lover
With the rosy flush fleeting from her face
Tears tumble as she empties of her thunder
And swoons with the hopes to ease her disgrace
She quenches the richness of the thick summer air
Withered and frail, she lay in the leaves
With the acceptance of nature to ease her despair
Off does her life to with the breeze
With her body at rest forever anon
Her beauteous love forever lives on

Albert Lehrman

Darkened Rhythm

Alone I stand overlooking the sea,
It's a lot like me,
Deep, dark and never free.

I cried once, a long time ago,
My heart was ripped from me,
And that was a feeling I didn't care to know.

So within myself I disappeared,
Never to be seen again,
Never to shed a tear.

I have become lost in this sea,
Within my darkest hour,
The pain runs deep,
Knowing there is no one to care for me.

So, alone I stand, overlooking the sea,
It's like me,
Deep, dark and never free.

Mark A. Pierce

Dreams Of Peace

Dreams of peace throughout my mind
What it would be like to spend time in a world
Where people love each other, unconditionally!
Where children play without gun fire
Without drugs as the ruling power

Dreams of peace throughout my mind
Where good deeds stand the test of time
Never jealous or envious of others goals
Just a helping hand when one is told

In my dreams this day has come
For I believe peace has won
Juanita Thompson

A New Beginning

There comes a time when someone new appears on the horizon
Where once before my head would turn away from feelings rising
You entered in upon my life so unexpectedly
Now all my thoughts all through each day are with you lovingly
I see your smile, I hear your voice, I feel your gentle touch
Your flowers, your gifts, your cards, your notes have really
meant so much
To dance with you, to walk with you, or see you passing by
Completes the day and puts me on a supernatural high
But most of all I love to be held close in your embrace
And turn to see the love I feel reflected on your face
Phyllis R. Ziegler

Be A Friend...Be A Sweetheart

Call someone and say, "I love you" on Valentine's Day.
Remember, you can love more than one person in more than one way.

Love and friendship begin with kindness, with clarity
And by doing such deeds as donating to charity.

Remind your elders they're more important now than ever before.
Write a letter. Forgive a foe. Listen to a bore.

Don't be a snake in the grass. Don't be a stick in the mud.
Neuter a cat. Spay a dog. Donate a pint of blood.

You're not an idiot, you're not a fool
When you hug a teenager and say, "You're cool!"

Ask a doctor about donating your organs
When you're gone to save the lives of others.
Friendship and love include coming to the aid
Of your sisters and of your brothers.

Tell your relatives, neighbors and friends
You think of them now and then.
And don't wait until next year
To be a friend and a sweetheart again.
Stephen Bean

My Angel

As I looked out at my windowsill
I saw a beautiful little girl.
She looked at me with a smile
and said, "I'm staying for a while."
She had blonde hair and eyes of blue
and she said, "My name is Kimberly Sue."
Her voice was soft and clear,
my, she was such a little dear.
An angel face, so pretty and pink.
Then I began to think.
Why can God make such a beauty
that human voice can call her cutie.
She's more than cute or a little doll.
She's my angel, through it all!
Sue Wrieth

The Dance

The Dance. . .is Me.
        The Dance is . .You.

Loving, sharing a touch, a breath.
Perfume on the air
Perfect for you. . .Filling me with you.
We twine together, Laughing, sweating together
When drums beat our head,
And trip our feet, I see your
Strawberry hair flying in the night—
Where did you get fiery castañetas,
And who gave me this cape?
The night, the music, a river of sound
Has carried us away. . .
We dance on an ocean of darkling blue;
I cry you a softkiss, violins sing us a memory,
You swoon on my shoulder, I breathe your hair until
No other remains but us two.
The Dance is Me. . .Oh, The Dance is
                        You.

Dave Crosby

Heaven's Door

As I linger in the pitch of darkness
an ancient one appears to me
with the light of Christ in his eyes he proclaims
my soul is free and so too your own
in awe, I witness his ascent to heaven
yet again, I am imprisoned
in darkness

With precious words and prayers of the faithful

Heaven's door opens to me
glowing, warm, peace, love and joy fill my spirit
as an angel gifts me with grace

There is the hope of a love so true
it transcends the mere physical
to exist in the spiritual
so perfect and pure
it has been chiseled from solid rock.
Carla Martino

The Greatest Lesson Ever Learned

This is like a dream
Real it doesn't seem
All I do is wonder why
Oh why did you have to die?
The funeral's over,
The company's gone,
Many memories still in my head,
So many things left unsaid
Why did I wait
Until it was too late
To show the love
I feel for you?
Now all I can do is hope and pray
That you can hear all I say
And that you know what's in my heart
That I have loved you from the start
You have taught me many things to say
To love and laugh in many ways
And the greatest of these, this I know
Is to show what I feel Before someone goes
Shannon Schnepp

Twilight

Thinking on the twilight of my young life,
I ponder when a boy becomes a man,
Perhaps the time comes when he takes a wife,
Or when his hour is running low on sand,
The day will come when he is forced to act,
Take stock in himself like a company,
To see where time has been and where it's at,
Poised to think life is but a story,
Staring at the dawn of my own young sun,
I will find my destiny in the stars,
Boys will be boys to have some fun,
So where he goes, he'll never be to far,
The boy wonders when he will be a man,
Just look at love and take it by the hand.

Robert Sweeney

Grandmother And Me

My grandmother meant the world to me.
That's something that no one else could ever see.
We had great times together,
   even in stormy weather.

I thought she would live forever
Because she was very strong and clever.
On one particular spring day,
   her life was taken away.

Everyone told me it was not my fault.
I was young and helpless and didn't have a thought.
I would always sit and weep,
   with my head down to my feet.

One day a voice said, "Cry no more."
My heart began to heal its sore.
It must be Grandmother Aggie,
   telling me to come walk with thee.

Never have I forgotten her words.
I hear them each time I listen to the birds.
Now I know how things must be,
   but I'll never forget my grandmother and me.

Rachell Dockery

Beyond This Point

'Do not go beyond this point'
Flashes in my overused brain
'It is unnecessary to destroy myself
Or to step across irreconcilable boundaries'
As I slow - he groans
"Can't go beyond this point, huh?"
'Psychic or just scared?'
"Nope, I guess"
but even chaos has it advantages
And the bright lights bursting
above my head stop me
'Beyond this point - Danger'
Like the garbage cans lining
A freshly paved road
waiting to dry
crowding the bottle necked ashtray
where cars squeeze through
bumper to bumper
But I knock them over
   'Beyond this point'

Jenny Morse

Love Is Forever

Other things may come and go
But one thing that I'll always know
Love is Forever.

Families may split apart
Someone may have a broken heart
But Love is Forever

Countries may go to war
Your enemy now was your friend before
But Love is Forever

When everything seems to be falling apart
Between two people, something may start
Cause Love is Forever

Just remember when you're sad
Just when everything seems so bad
Love is Forever!

Dava Whitesell

The Children

So innocent and pure, they are bequeathed unto life
Unknowing and heedless of their ongoing strife.
Severe and relentless are the forces they face,
Life has now sent them on a brutally forged pace.
Screams from a house, or tears from an eye
Bring up harsh questions; we ask ourselves why.
Why have they grown, and failed to aspire?
Why have they failed at what we desired?
We know the answer, yet refuse to recall,
The fighting, the abuse; they saw it all.
The law has done nothing to enforce the due process,
Yet the longer we wait, the greater our losses.
These youths and small children are the ones who will pay
For the crimes we commit, day after day.
Children are beaten, within an inch of their lives,
And we refuse to listen, or to heed their cries.
We refuse to discuss it, or expose all the pain,
But we mask and conceal it; there is nothing to gain.
There is much we can do, and many we can save,
For we live a dream of freedom, in the home of the brave.

Sanjay Sinha

First Love

The wind - who runs his transparent hand through your hair,
The sun - whom you praise for his beauty and warmth,
The moon - whom you stay up late at night to stare at,
The stars - who reside in your eyes,
Jealousy.
Your car - in whom you find refuge,
Your couch - in whom you find comfort,
Your bed - in whom you find safety,
Your roof - on whom you find quiet,
Jealousy.
Your lamb - who you allow to console you,
Your dog - who greets you each time you return home,
Your family - who has watched you blossom and grow,
Your athleticism - in whom you find hope,
Jealousy.
The world - who holds you in his arms,
Your faith - in whom you have undying belief,
Our lake - with whom you find shelter and peace,
God - for whom you have unconditional love.
Jealousy.

Bryan Morley

The Mirror

I fell in love across a table.
He was a mirror reflecting me.
All my thoughts refracted through his words,
my feelings pushed through a glass.

I saw me, yet not I.
Images in light and sound, no substance.
A looking glass reflection,
made only of sand and heat.

I fell out of love with my looking-glass man,
the love of him only love of me.
Incomplete, only half of the whole -
His being only a carnival - glass reflecting me.

I want the one who isn't me.
Break the mirror, seven years of love.
Through a window, he sits.
Cold glass of separation
Step around. Come to me.

Elizabeth Pratt

The Love You Have For Me

To look into your eyes and see,
The love that's there just for me.
A love that touches deep into my soul,
A love that makes me feel whole,
A love that warms my body and lets it soar,
A love that leaves me wanting more,
A love I can not live without,
And that I know without a doubt.
If it left me I couldn't be,
Your love means everything to me.
You hold my heart in your hands,
So please Love, be gentle if you can.
Look into my eyes so I can see
The love you have there just for me.
And Dear One know this, please,
This love can make me happy or bring me to my knees.
So evermore hold my heart in both hands
To cradle my love that's unlimited as sands,
And look at me, please, never look away,
And our love forever will stay.

Wanda Kaynor

December's Epic

Relax my friend, sit back and listen
to the tale of a thousand souls
Not wind, nor fire, nor earthly desire
can change the way it goes
Many a year has passed with fear
that the farmer won't reap his crop
But time after time our thoughts turn sublime
and the feast seemed to never stop
The ground will shake and shimmer and quake
in denial of what we've done
But the vows we have taken are long since forsaken
And our souls will be cast into the sun
The sky will turn black and we'll never look back
at the ones we left behind
But we'll give them a day to remember the way
they found for their own kind
Children remember the chills of December
for your daddies have been sent to burn
The voices you hear should fill you with fear
Because you father will never return

Jeffrey Mitchell

The Dream

I'm standing near a tree in a park.
I can see a lot of people, but it's dark.
The environment is peaceful; I hear the song of a lark.
But I sense something different in the dog's bark.
It's a strangeness I just can't mark.
Confusion stings like the bite of a shark.

I'm surrounded by boys, girls, fathers and mothers.
I can see black, white, red, green, orange and many others.
But they all seem to treat each other like brothers.

I'm looking more closely to see if my eyes deceive.
I can see but am hesitant to believe.
The moment my eyes focus I start to grieve.
But I quickly extinguish my desire to heave.
It's a reality I did not want to perceive.
Consciousness returns like a novice trying to achieve.

The only reason they did not hate was because they could not see.
The only reason they did not fight was because they had no army.
The only reason they were at peace was because they had no memory.

Have you ever had that dream?
Too bad things are not always what they seem.

Shane Unrein

One Heart, One Sorrow

Death be not so proud to take the burning morn
With its defying darkness sprung up from Hades pit;
For as the clanging of Hephaestus' blade is constant
Similar so will the Sun rise twice relit.

A single tear drops with the Sun's darkened dip
As the span of ages passes in the night
And the fingers of Love and Cupid's gold
Caress the chilled finger's of old Frost's rite.

But lost to me this deepened sin
Of passion and death which passes below
For only my mind pertains to these
While my soul's deep troubles grow

My heart torn as my light dwindles down
And is lost in a bright scar in Pluto's flesh
As my Calliope is wrought from me,
And all my love is soon bethreshed

One Darkness, One light, One Deity, One Night
All of these their equal opposite belong.
A few who rule the many souls in their restraint
A few who rule on the wings of Calliope's song.

Jordan M. Lewis

Candles

Summer rises only to Fall
Tempest blusters only to stall
Morning dew glistens, feigning to fade
Candles listen, destined for shade.
 Green leaves whisper, give beauty to glen
Gold leaves flutter, dance the wind
Orange moon softens, grows into white
Candles flicker, ignoring the night.
 Clouds of silver, clouds of grey
Twisting, twirling, relentless sway
Blue sky deepens, loses, return
Candles quicken, darkness spurn.
 Seashore changes, forfeiting sand
Forest weakens, thinning to stand
Mountains falter, puny to time
Candles shorten, fatten and sigh.
 Mountain Laurel, wilted and sick
Adam and Eve...candlestick
Season changes, man must lie
Candles flicker, candles die.

Rickey Myhand

A Rose For My Lady

I rub the pale flower petals
flush against my skin
and inhale the sweet fragrance
given off as if only for me.

The supple flower grows to fullness
and strength, yet is filled with gentle
beauty and life.

The thorns on its stem protect it
from adversity and destruction,
yet bend to the tender and loving touch
of one who knows not to bring
harm nor pain.

The lover gently encourages and nurtures
the flower to maturity
so that it may bring beauty and pleasure
the one who cares and strokes it
to fullness.

Shellie Wagner

The Song Of The Harvest

I could hear the corn growing in the fields last night.
The wheat, too, stirred in amazed delight.
It, too, was reaching its natured heights.
The berries and gourds were moving along.
On vines and bushes close to the ground.
A pumpkin smiled as they all passed by.
The apples and pears in orchards grow soft and sweet.
As fruits of the fall nod their heads.
To the tomatoes, standing tall, in their deep-green beds.
The eyes of the potatoes watching it all.
While the leaves of the cauliflower and cabbages listen.
To the music and rhythms of the song of the fall.

Soon the farmer's thrasher will reap.
The summer harvest of corn and wheat.
And in Thanksgiving, we will all thank God.
For the bounty and splendor of the season of Fall.

Mary McGrath

Irony (The Dream World)

The Dream world thrives within the dozing mind
The host of Sleep's macabre and varied cast;
In strange and sinuous rhythms do they wind,
These characters of now, to be, and past.

I 'magine Freud would aspire to be King
And campaign for this "neurotic" Dream world's vote;
But if candidates could win upon one thing
It would not be the rule of textbook rote.

The world of dreams could never be contained
Within the bounds of philosophic thought;
The cast of players on stage within the brain
I fear would prove an uncontroll-ed lot.

And so to those who like the rules to keep:
It might be wise to never fall asleep.

Alicia Gonzalez-Greeley

Love Is Him

Love is intangible, yet it caresses me with each touch of his hand.
Love is warm, yet it shivers through my body when he approaches.
Love is shy, yet it boldly stares when he looks into my eyes.
Love is strong, yet it weakens my knees when he kisses me.
Love is alert, yet I miss out on the world when he smiles.
Love is jealous, yet it forgives when he walks in the door.
Love is patient, yet an hour seems too long away from him.
Love is open, yet only he holds the key to my heart.
Love is everything, yet is nothing without him.

Megan Way

So Long Ago

I remember oh so well, the day, the time...
My life, my world, became torn and tattered.
You took away my innocence....by force...
You took my trust, and gave me fear...

At night, I closed my eyes...relived your crime,
This soul, this heart, forever shattered...
Your life unchanged...without remorse...
Didn't you see inside my eyes, the tears?

So long ago, and yet your act remains sublime...
I have found true love...that's all that matters.
Your memory, your deed is slowly fading away, of course.
Replaced by love, so true and pure, is now what I hold dear.

Monica Ihlo

On A Dark Summer's Night

On a dark summer's night some hundred years ago,
When the dead walked and the moon hung low,
How odd it was when heard through the dark,
A whispered song, as beautiful as a lark.
Locked in a cell as tall as a tower,
Her song edged the night, every night, on the hour.
Her song was for him who died by the seas,
A story as haunting as Annabel Lee's.
He was thrown to the rocks, her beloved one,
Only to die by the light of the dawn.
How she wept, her eyes filled with tears,
For the loss of her love, to her, most dear.
"It is the curse," he had whispered one night by the moon.
"It came for my father, it will come for me soon."
She then understood, and ran far away,
But they had grabbed her, and told her to stay.
Her love they had pushed straight to his death,
Her throat they had slit, and the world went to rest.
But high in the tower, before the dawn's light,
You can still hear her singing, on a dark summer's night.

Rachel Stavis

Heaven

The moon shone
Rounded to perfection
Glimmering softly
I gazed upon it with wonder
The coolness caressed my body
Each drop of shimmering liquid silver
Looked as if a picture had been taken of it
Standing still, smiling upon me
I breathed in the clear, crisp air
Its sweet nectar healed my soul
Each glowing twinkle whispered in the wind
Peace, peace it said.

Cathryn Bales

Forever Only

A light touch from memory's god-wing inspired
a long-fallen tear from my Winter eyes.
And, through an emotion thought far retired,
a taste so lost sudden interests find rise.
I find that the night brings us closer now.
Within the walls of my mind I can, then,
only fear moments awake — oh yes, how
I embrace each cold soul-wind that you send.
In truth, I have know that, without you, life,
in its moments of pleasure and judgement,
has little room for joy, but width for strife.
that fading frost to fire was never sent.
But the old angel's touch is mine only,
and truth grips — I will forever be lonely.

Brandon Buehring

231

The Gift

The only gift that I recall
My Grandma gave to me
Was a seashell, brown and white, that she
Had taken from the sea.
She lived so far away from us,
So I never knew her well;
Yet there was a story in the gift
The seashell had to tell.
She loved the sea, my Grandma did,
And she listened to its song.
As she sat there in the sun and sand,
Its glory made her strong;
And she saw the beauty of that shell.
It was a work of art,
That still was one with the great sea,
Though now it was held apart.
I followed in my Grandma's steps
I treasure her gift to me—
And like my ancestor of old,
My heart is in the sea.

Jewell Clark

Poor Child

I watch as she grows fleetly. Innocence binds her bosom.
Quietly hunting for a plead she accepts all beings which
surround her. Objecting quietly, crying softly, yet she
laughs out loud - a mockery of life she makes it, evil child inside.
She used to be filled with terror, anguish, bidding what
would come next. Now its become clear, it's just a big
cycle, she's caught in the middle - can't breathe.
"Help me, `she cries', can't breathe!"
I watch as she longs to be free. Poor child, poor child
I wish I could help.
Tears fall untold with ev'ry step she takes and with ev'ry
words she dare speaks. It makes me so angry to see how she
hurts. She doesn't grasp just why. I've upheld as she's
tried to be perfect but the urgency is making her weak.
If I could take her back to when things were so mere, I'd
take her back to when love was clear and evil remained inside.
Evil has eloped and it halos her mind - I hate seeing this
happen - Just Stop! So I lash out and swing, the mirror
then breaks - Now, I can't see her no more.

Jeniffer Kocher

Rare Friendships!!

Friends are forever friends!
Their friendship never ever ends.

They are individuals but one,
without each other they are none.
Together they fall and stand,
each other they really understand.
Belief! Faith! And trust!
For friends are a must.

They love and they hate each other,
They console and they scold each other,
They share, they confide,
But yet have some things to hide.
Even if there is a difference of opinion,
Doesn't really matter to anyone.

Friends different yet similar,
Friends far away yet closer,
Friend! Oh Friend!
A person you can literally read.

A Friend in need
Is a friend indeed!

Roma Agrawal

Sandstorm

Blow North wind
Harmettan howl
Rustle my bones
Old now I cannot withstand your rage as in my youth.

At that portal that will transport me through eternity
I found a cleft in the rock where I may hide
The devourer took comfort
He had my soul.

But in the Winter of my life
The Rose of Sharon blossoms
A seductive fragrance draws me
Into a secret dwelling.

Latern ready
The bridegroom knocks
My lover grasps my wrinkled hand
Caresses my frail body and raptures me.

What is your prayer, my beloved,
His ear ever at my lips
That I may dwell with you forever my Lord,
Amen.

Olga M. Mike

A Lily In The Valley

A perfect lily stood in the valley
On a cool and sunny fall day,
He was bent with the cares of this world
And had spent a lot of time in his way.

God saw the lily in His garden
And remembered him from times of old,
God said, "It is time to gather
My child home from this world's cold.

When he was on his earthly journey
He spread love wherever he would go.
He treated all children as his own
And tried to prepare them for Heaven above.

I have watched my servant on his way
Amidst the evil of this world,
He kept the faith and continue to pray
And never wavered from his goal.

Today I will call him home
To walk these earthly journey, no more.
He will leave his family and friend behind,
But his life has shown them the way to go.

Betty Daniels

Endless Journey

It takes me to a winding road
in a desert land.
Twists and turns delude my mind,
try to escape that which binds
my infinite joy to my endless depression.
Cannot tell which from my expression
as I slither through a winding road
in a desert land.
An oasis appears before my eyes,
an end to fit my means.
I pick up speed for the Answer,
the Solution for my spiritual cancer.
But a mirage is all I find;
fate is rarely ever kind.
An oasis disappears before my eyes.
There is no end to this winding road.

Adam Schlesinger

We Are No Fools

We are no fools we go to school
there we are taught the golden rules
we pledge allegiance to our flag
carry our lunch in a paper bag
we go to learn right from wrong
as the teachers help us along
we listen to what the teachers say
as we love to go and play we don't need no more
rules, we are smart, we're no fools
drugs are just for fools, we don't need
them in our school, if some stranger says
come let's go, you're no fool, you say no!
Now this poem must have an end
The one who wrote it is your friend
All the words written are true
Stay in school be nobody's fool.

Dan Mueller

Live And Love Freely

Our lives are so precious, but few of us take the time
To live them to the fullest, while we still have a chance
Focus on the good things, don't dwell on the bad
Be positive and happy, not fearful or sad
Show those that you care for, your feelings each day
For none of us knows, when we'll be taken away
If you love someone say it, don't keep it to yourself
One day fond memories, may be all you have left
Don't be worried what others, may think of you
Express yourself always, it's the best you can do
Smile if you can, say I love you and pray
Then you'll find comfort, if your loved one goes away
You'll know in your heart, that your feelings were known
With love in your heart, you are never alone
So I say I love you, in a very special way
And no amount of time or distance
Will make my love go away
You can count on me, time and time again
I will always be with you, my most special friend.

Cheryl Kittrell

Almost Twenty Five Years Ago My Love

Almost twenty-five years ago my love
You became my wife
It's hard to believe even now
How much it has changed my life

I was an angry young man
The road I was traveling was bad
No one to show me the way
The ending could only be sad

The world was against me
So it seemed to me then
To ask for any help
To me would be a sin

The first time I saw you
I knew you had to be mine
What could I offer you, a heart of stone, a soul of ice?

But out of your eyes a light shone, it softened my heart of stone
And melted my soul of ice

And ever since then my love
As I lay in bed at night, I thank God above
For making things so right

Arthur W. Jennings

Untitled

I look upwards for understanding
I would suffer for supreme knowledge
but I am just a man; my education
given by a college.
Who am I to question the grief that we bare?
Who am I to anger, how could I dare?
I fear that I am wrong to question some things
but why does He destroy good people's dreams?
Is it a punishment for past sins
or is it to strengthen us, will it happen again?
I am taught to trust and live in faith
I am taught to forgive All
I try not to make judgments in haste
please You give me strength to
bear the burdens You give.

Curtis C. Viverette

Untitled

I feel as if I were a tree,
Transplanted at a mature age.
This is very harmful for trees,
If they are moved across oceans and continents.

First my leaves started to fall off.
Leaves were my old friends.
Some of them passed away, forever. Others are far away,
They do not nourish me anymore.

Winds of changes bent my trunk.
I tried to be straight and stretch to the sun.
But it is almost impossible: I cannot breath without leaves.
I gasp. A long and cold winter is coming.

My roots are weak to lean on them, and too unsteady.
New soil is hard and very frightening.
And there are different trees around me.
Different winds make them rustle in an alien languages.

But spring always comes.
Even if you have lost your hope.
New small green leaves appeared already,
And I believe that now I will survive.

Lucy Vilner

A Spring Day

The birds sing,
The bees buzz,
There is a little girl in the meadow, picking dandelions.
She selects them and pulls them out ever so carefully.
Like the world would dissolve
if she picked a wrong one or ripped one.
There is a house in the distance,
and I can see deer basking in the warm spring sun.
The little girl gets up and starts to skip back to her house
like she hasn't a worry in the world.
I suppose, these must be the effects of Spring.
because I never see this in Winter.
Spring seems to make everyone happy inside.
As I look through the window, I long to be outside.
I long to breathe the air of Spring,
and feel the warmth of the Spring sun.
I must leave this dreary house.
As I walk through the door, and step out into the sunlight,
I suddenly feel happy.
I twirl around and jump up and down, on this beautiful Spring day.

Conor Dirks

Twenty-One Bouquets

To Phyllis
She is honored by this tribute of Twenty-one Bouquets
Of very special flowers on twenty-one different days

Each bouquet squired by picture or special musing
To celebrate and honor the Lady of his choosing

Sweetbriar, daisy, carnation, and mistletoe with heather
All chosen to remember, all the different kinds of weather

The Love, the peace, shared when listening in the quiet
Was all the same as when the game turned to blessed riot

She was loved so much yet her due was unpresented
'Til time came when Her especial salute of
The Twenty-One Bouquets was invented

Don C. Craig

Hope, Joy And Faith

I sit and wait.
The radio plays an old Joe Cocker song.
The time slowly ticks by.
Memories flick through my mind like an old movie.
Dreams of what could be linger in the depths of my soul.
I can't seem to concentrate on anything but him.
His smile, his walk, his whole being invades my heart in a way
I've never known.
Will he stay?

My name is Hope!

I finally see him approach and my heart leaps from my chest.
He takes me into his arms and kisses me so gently I feel fragile.
His sweet, soft touch leaves his imprint on my heart.

Now my name is Joy!

He says something that makes me laugh.
My heart is so happy it feels as if it might burst.
I don't know how long we have together,
But love knows no time.

My name is Faith!

If it's going to last, I have to believe!

Belinda Eckert

What?

Pull my finger and you'll get a surprise
Hold out your hand but don't open your eyes
I'll bet you can't guess what's behind my back
It could be a Whopper or a Big Mac

What?

Today I got a package with no return address
Got a messy room somewhere under that mess
I'm the kind of guy I like to have around
Get off my grass, this is my playground

What?

I've got a headache but I don't know where it is
I may not be stupid but I'm no wiz
There's a car parked in the street pulling forward in reverse
I'm cursing in cursive, it must be curse

What?

The TV Is off while I'm watching my show
I like it here so I think I'll go
The hair on my nails is getting too thick
Better take my temperature, I don't feel sick

What?

Ben Bybee

On Awaking

In the gray morning light when I awake,
And find you lying there,
Neath rumpled sheets and wrinkled pleats,
The aroma of your hair.

I move gently in the stillness
So as not to disturb your rest,
But your tiny hands make strong demands,
Stirrings in my breast.

When we cuddle in the morning
And share our deepest needs,
Love knows no bounds and us surrounds,
With life's most precious seeds.

Doug Bates

In the City

What in the city is wrong today?
Our children can't go out to play
There are predators loose, just waiting out there.
Our most pressing problem? They are everywhere.

They hide in the rapist, murderer, thief.
Their most favorite place is the dark
Still you can find them on Main Street
In an alley, in school, at your park.

What in the City is wrong today?
Our schools are full of fears
When children get bruised, cut, broken, or killed
parents cry real tears.

Our skyline changes daily
What with Jacob's field, gate way, the rock hall
While in their shadows behind the scenes
Our children daily fall

What in the city is wrong today?

Mary Mechling Green

A Mother's Heart

A mother's heart is like a rose
Always opened with glee
It gives out a beat in life
That creates self-esteem.

A mother's heart is like a petal
It unfolds the reason for love.
She'll give the comfort to a child
That comes from heaven above.

A tender voice, the sweet caress
is always greatly needed,
And now I have my peace at heart
From a rose that has been seeded.

For all the mothers in this world
Should feel as they are one,
'Cause just a touch can make a difference
For what a mother's done.

Judith L. Warner

Confusion

A feeling I really hate-simply
  because I feel insecure.
There is nothing about which I am sure.
I cry a lot-which is something
  I hate to do.
But how do I stop it - I'm
  without a clue.
I really miss the things I had
I want to feel and do them again so bad.
Sometimes I feel like it's a big vision
But it's not, it's all my confusion.

Dwan Samuel

234

The Day When...

A day when people left their front doors open,
A day where children played unwatched,
A day when there was plenty of love and trust.
That is all a dream.

Now is a day when gunshots ring,
A day when it is typical to hear a scream,
A day when love and trust are rare.
So where are we heading?

We can turn our world around,
You and I can make a difference,
All of us can bring back the love and trust.
All we have to do is try.

So let us bring back the day when front doors are
left open,
The day when children play unwatched,
A day where there is tons of love and trust.
We can not and will not leave this all a dream.

Heidi Christensen

Singing

Singing is from the heart and soul.
Loved by the young and the old
From singing country to Pop
A little rhythm and blues.
Clapping our hands
Moving two by two.
Singing is like riding a bike
driving a car
Tying your shoe
You don't have to think
It's just something you do.
Singing brings happiness and cheer
to my heart.
From all of my song, back to the start.
Singing shows feeling, sometimes
Even a good tingling.
A good song like,
I have a good wife, but she's done me wrong.
You'll find out she done better in the next song.

Sheryl Hill

The Savior's Birth

Mary, a virgin, was with child
A woman, lowly, meek and mild.
She was God's chosen to give birth
Of the blessed Christ Child on this earth.

A stable in Bethlehem cradled a king
As a host of angels began to sing,
"Glory to God in the highest, peace on earth"
As they heralded the glorious birth.

Shepherds and wise men came from afar
To worship the Christ Child, led by a star.
He is Son of God and Son of Man,
He would fulfill God's salvation plan.

With hearts and voices let us sing,
"He is Lord of Lords and King of Kings."
On this silent and holy night,
Christ was born to bring us light.

Verna L. Funderburk

Spring

Why do I know it is spring?
Because I heard a robin redbreast sing.
A bluebird, harbinger of spring, is looking for its mate.
   That's why I know it is spring.

The sun is bright, the sky is blue, with fleecy white clouds.
Dark clouds hurrying along to cover the two.
   That's why I know it is spring.

A flash of lightning, a jolt of thunder rumbling.
Drenching the landscape with a shower.
It was heavy and short, and soon the sun appears.
   That's why I know it is spring.

The brown, naked branches of the maple tree
Standing stoically by the bubbling brook
Seemed to take a different look.
The buds start swelling and soon green leaves appear.
   That's why I know it is spring.

Birds singing, iris, daffodils, and tulips nodding their heads.
By the balmy breeze
Coloring the landscape.
   That's why I know it is spring.

Eugenia S. Reed

The Excellence Of Execution

To jump and soar and seem to fly
A bounce, a lift, you reach the sky
A spiral twist, a backhand flip
A graceful kick, a sidewind whip
A hit, a drag, a turn upside down
He's the "Best There is" this side of town

As the years go past and the champion still
His strength and might collapse under will
With a tumble, a spill, a horrible fall
"The Best There Was" they started to call
To them, he is a champion no more
They look down on the titles he wore
With a tear, a goodbye, and one final look
"The Best there ever will be" I write in my book.

Jamie Sudeikis

The Survivor

For only a second we were on this world together.
For only a second we stood amongst each other.

Some became the dominators of this world,
Others became the silence.

Only to be remembered by pictures in books,
And lists with "Extinct' written in bold ink
Above each name.
And only to be remembered.

But a soul survivor, the last of the innocents
Not yet bled by mankind.

Not yet skinned for its fur or slaughtered
For its tusks.

And so many more awaiting their time to vanish
In a simple heartbeat.

For only a second we were on this world together.
For only a second we stood amongst each other.

Jen Linder

Untitled

Here I am, there you are
Now what are we gonna do?
I said to you goodbye
But you only heard hello
I can't stay here for all the right reasons
I won't leave here
For all the wrong ones
You said to me don't go
That I was making a serious mistake
But which is worse
To stay for a chance to make a mistake
Or leave for a chance to make one anyway
I know the difference
From right and wrong
Between the truth and a lie,
Why do you think my decision
Was so difficult to make?
I need to learn how to love myself
Before I can be taught to love someone else
and I need to start living
Instead of always only surviving.

Charlotte Jean Davidson

The Ideal

And why do you turn your head from the multitude, o wanderer?
Perhaps to seek the lonely muse of thought,
As solitary as the morning star;
To grasp that spark she offers man so often in vain.
Is it hard, Apollo, to travel thus
Footsore, weary, in a strange land,
With only the faint flicker of a distant star
Holding you on this path?
Or is it so foreign to you who venture
All misty places where the last light falls fast,
Leaving no lingering sound of creature
Airy-winged or earth-tied?

Weep not, even brave wayfarer of this world,
For life is long, and you your star will clasp;
Where weary winds and tempest clouds pass by.
There, noble wanderer, will you find the rest
That fevered haste and burdened toil cannot extend to you;
Or any other so inclined prevailing against himself
In guise of love for labor unprofitable...

Marianne Lester Butera

Tom G.'s Rhyming Poem

I kept your memory in my heart
For all these years, right from the start
Imagined that my man would be just like you
But always wanted him to be you, too.
Come ridin' in on horseback, dressed in white
Pick me up and take me out of sight
Ever after caring for my life, and
Guiding me, perhaps, to be your wife.

I boldly want what I may never have.
My freedom calls me to its close demise.
What I am feeling cannot be denied,
Nor could it if I hadn't even tried.
But finding you has opened up my heart
And left me as I was upon the start.
In love with you, and wanting more
Hoping we'll walk through that door...

Together, this time...forever.

Brenda L. Reynard

Pain Dealt With

Though I know I feel pain, I know not what kind.
Who it was that broke my heart, I am sure to find.

Was my heart really broken, or was it just bended?
If it was that, why wasn't it mended?

Maybe because I showed them no pain,
For alone in my room I cried out in vain.

Who was it that taught me to hide all my fear?
Who was it that taught me to not shed a tear?

Whoever it was did a damn good job,
But my freedom to express they did rob.

I don't wanna die but the pain I must release,
When I make that small cut do the bad feelings cease?

The deeper I cut the better I feel,
But I can't help but wonder, is this relief for real?

When my friends see my wrists I don't plead the fifth,
I simply say it's pain dealt with.

Kayla Butler

Hiding From The Pain

I watch the girl with the long flowing hair,
And follow the tear drop down her face,
It stops at her chin,
As if contemplating the drop,
Till it hits the floor,
Collecting with the others in a pool of sorrow.

I watch as the girl wipes away the tears,
As if she could just wipe away the pain,
She pulls back her long flowing hair,
And fills her hands with warm tap water,
Splashing it on her face,
Camouflaging the tears.

I watch as she hides herself in makeup,
The tear stains disappear into Revlon and Maybeline,
Visene hides the red, bloodshot eyes,
And a smile hides the pain,
The girl looks different now but somehow more familiar,
And then I realize that the girl hiding from it all is me.

Katie L. Davis

Dreams By Starlight

I call upon my pentacle of hopes each night
I bare my heart to your glowing ears
I beg over and over
Your rays and beams build my hope
Tired of my tears wetting your back
Annoyed by my selfish requests night after night
You know I will not be loyal
I seek other dealers of dreams and wish on other phenomenon
Who could you blame with such desires as mine
To want those things she calls her own
To aspire for great things
Longing for green lawns and slender thighs
You laugh at my vanity
While I taunt you with a kiss
And persuade you with favors but you are not tempted easily
If you were the lady dancing on a star as they sometimes say
I would buy you gifts
And compliment you on your beautiful hair or dazzling teeth
Just for a taste of what she has
That other girl, you know, the one I wish to be

Rebecca Waller

The Lure

Why wait for medicine to show
  Ignorance and equivocation,
Venomous remedies by the score,
  Slighted by anesthetic minds no more,
Lofty merchants of gloom heave-ho.

Herbal magic may put us right
  On a naturalistic path of light,
Neophytes in a new age glow,
  The titans too pompous to know,
Detoxing is our reparation.

Why wait for medicine, we have no choice,
  In heady scorn, we purge and flout,
Indigenous life is ours, no doubt,
  Euphoric in our expectations,
Without pain, perhaps to bloom once more.

Rosemary Brunken

My Empty, Aching Heart

Alone in the darkness, the insanity will not end
That which deceives me, I used to call a friend
Nothing can ameliorate the aching of my heart
The mother I need close to me, you've driven us apart
Although time has lingered on, my heart is left to mend
My eyes have cried a million tears, yet unable to defend
I'll never understand why mommy said you were no real man
The orders you gave led to the distrust of your hand
She waved the gun into the air, as if she didn't care
The pain you caused her simply "was not fair"
Amongst her last breathe she whispered a soft good-bye
And to this day, I still cannot see why
Yet I never really heard her, I could only see red
It trickled down her porcelain facade, my mommy was dead
At her funeral you never shed a tear, I've wondered why
All you can offer is empty lies, why did she have to die?
On the town again, unable to offer a sympathetic tone
Yet you say you knew one day she'd leave you all alone
And yet here I stand, unheard every word I say
Missing my mother, comforted only by an ache here to stay.

Janelle Scheurer

I Wonder

  The night and its darkness envelop me
  stretching my soul to its breaking point -
I wonder...am I strong enough?
  The sweet taste of a luscious liquid takes over my mouth
  and controls all of my sensations -
I wonder...will I be awake long enough to savor this sweet
taste of oblivion?
  Day breaks and the world continues to whirl as I stand
  still. My senses fade and a burning fire engulfs me.
  My mind melts and I retreat into the depths of my soul -
I wonder...how long it's been since the world left me behind?
  As my final days unfold I wonder.
I wonder...am I'm strong enough, how long will I be able to taste
sweet oblivion, and how long has it been since the world left me
behind?

Christine Zeller

Beautiful Favor

With little time to mourn,
unto us an angel is born.
The silent soldier of new,
bears a burden that's sad but true.
With every smile he must pass our days,
destroying the pain and clearing the grays;
Although his job seems small,
He renewed our lives and saved us all.
So why this star became our savior,
God just granted us a beautiful favor.

Gerard D'Esposito

Flower Among The Thorns

Who is this flower I see standing proudly among the weeds,
Stretching upward ever so strongly?
Just to beat out that which would choke her roots from the soil,
Or to form a shadow to block her from the rays of sun light.
Does her fragrance warrant standing among the thorns?
Nay, for I say her outward beauty is dwarfed by that which
comes from within,
And the succulence of her sweet nectar that captivates the busy
audience,
Could, but does not cast a spell upon her friends,
Her moisture-clad petals appearing to be laminated,
It's just a cover to protect the softness from within,
For she grows among the boastful thistle,
Just waiting to bring her down.
Does she stand alone to conquer the pest and mites?
Or is there a gardener to help tend to this pestilence,
Fighting off the morning frost, searching for warmth,
She waits for the mighty hands to choose her from the ground.

Jamez Smith

Life's Tread

We run through life at a breakneck tread
Caring not who we push to get ahead.
Life's no fun when all you do is run.
And at the pace we're going there'll be no fun.
I wish all would for just a time
Slow down. Then we might, in harmony, rhyme.
Might feel the sun and the wind's caress.
Have you ever felt a breeze's gentleness?
It feels like true love which few ever know.
Few feel true love for we too often say, "No."
But no one can blame the dreambreakers
For the whirlwind of life all will alter.
In true nature we may be kind, yet if
We let the wind take us we grow stiff.

Patrick McCleary II

Getting In Touch With The World

Shhhh. Be quiet.
I am trying to listen to the world.
Listen to the grass beneath my bare feet,
Listen to the wind ruffle those bare sheets,
I am opening my ears
  and shutting out my fears.

Close my eyes.
I am trying to see the world.
See the love that builds foundations,
See the blood lost in confrontations,
I am opening my eyes
  by casting out the lies.

Settle down for now.
I am trying to touch this world.
Touch the spirit that guides us home,
Touch the sacred oak that has grown
all alone with me
  in this jungle of concrete.

Kevin Hulsing

The Little Light In The Pray Room

Oh I hurt inside as I sit and wait for God to answer
thru Jesus the truth and light of the world and wept with
anticipation as I kneel and pray to my God with Jesus.
The light in the pray room still burning as I wept, for love is gift
from God thru Jesus. Thru joy and spread
of sunshine that comes in the morning is a renewed spirit.

Hattie Ware

My Baby

What is something that is to me as good as gold?
I think it is something everyone should be told
Because if you decide it's valuable to you,
you will never need anything new
But, if you decide it's worthless
nothing could ever give you true happiness
it is not something easily thrown away
because a memory will always stay
What could it be
what could make me so happy
can't you guess
it makes a lot of sense
Would you like a clue
Should I tell you who
I will tell you what makes me happy
The answer to my question, my friend, is my perfect baby

Angela Ramirez

The New Kid In Town

"My caseworker's coming today, Mrs. Lee."
The little boy said with a grin.
I'm going to see my mom and my dad.
Should I be happy for him?

Timmy entered my life just a few weeks before
So timid and scared as a mouse.
He'd been taken from siblings, Mom and Dad
And placed in a foster-care house.

His own home had been too dirty -
Infested with rodents, feces, and such.
How was this allowed to happen?
Should I feel pity for his parents or disgust.

As I spent time with Timmy in our classroom,
He warmed up to new friends and routines.
The appreciation he showed was so touching,
And the love he shared was inspiring to be seen.

He hadn't learned these traits in a month.
Someone had showed him love and trust.
Maybe his parents weren't as I had imagined.
Maybe they needed help not disgust.

Rebecca Olechnowicz

Warm Sand

Peace and tranquility, finally found,
Blank face staring down.
Fragrant flowers in full bloom,
Stand before my open tomb.

My father taught me of the ocean and the sky,
Kindness for those who had less than I.
Of quiet sunrises over mountain tops,
And the soothing sound of rain drops.

A husband, cherished and true,
Always remembered to say "I love you."
Boys, girls, and laughter filled the air,
Pigtails, airplanes, and babes to care.

Sunflowers and thistles grew in the wild,
Breezes were warm and oh so mild.
But, I dreamed of life on an island far away,
Walking on warm sand, watching palm trees sway.

My body and lifeless heart,
Watch the carefree soul depart.
To finally in dreams be free,
Unknowing life was its reality.

Jeanne Hauze

Farewell, My Love

I wore a blue dress — Your favorite color.
With matching shoes that You adored.
My long, dark, hair that You were holding for hours,
I brushed so thoroughly, for You, today.
I'm wearing a smile, (while everyone's crying)
standing here, with all my beauty and beyond.
I'm here in the light, (while everyone's in the darkness)
holding a yellow rose above Your grave. . .
(lady in blue): ". . .no need for words, it is all in my heart."
(ghost): ". . .no words are needed
for even here in the cold and darkness of the ground,
I am warm and full and nourished by your sincere love. . ."
She smiled again. . .for one last time
And put the rose back in the ground.
She sat beside the stone of ghost
and whispered gently in a voice of sorrow:
"I died with You, my love."
. . .And the wind stopped. . .
for silence had spoken.

Irina A. Mosesova

Fragments

Gone are the pages that held the memories of my past.
For years my tortured soul has cried for the words
That once were, but now only shattered phrases remain.
Oh, how could I have shared the secrets of my very soul
With anyone who would rob me so?
Time has not yet healed the wound -
Of emptiness from this loss
Of anger.
I've longed for the remembrance of the words
That gave my past pleasures and sorrows life.
But still only fragments remain.

Marice Ann Piquette

A Child Searching

As another day begins, another night ends
Of visions and shadows of what could have been
A world of what was and what never will be
Of features and feelings only from a mirror I see.
A child, a chameleon, a clown of many faces
Playing their games and running their bases
I search for myself, for who I really am
I keep swimming in circles, can't get past the dam.
To some I am a rebel, a rebel without a cause
To others I am an angel, an angel with no flaws
To me I am a beggar, a beggar for my soul
To have the strength and courage to forgive those I do not know.
This stranger who bore me, then set me free
Is telling me she loves me, but how can that be?
Do I hug her, do I hate her, I don't know what to do
My world is full of confusion and a sky that is not blue.
My mind is in turmoil, my heart is in pain
Will I ever fit in or will I just go insane.

Gina Parish

Ebony And Ivory

Ebony and Ivory set on the board,
One is south, the other is north.
A sovereign fight is on.
Ebony and Ivory are sacrificed —
pawns for the gentiles,
   and gentiles for the Lords.
One moves south, one moves north.
Who will fall?
A pawn here, a gentile there,
   all to save the sovereign king.
Ebony and Ivory — their fate in a
game—
Fighting on.

Alexander Sadighi

Questions About Heroes

Does Batman ever wear his cape on a dog day afternoon?
When the sun burns down upon a city that's waiting for the moon?
Is he up for fighting battles when the humidity is high?
When criminals are at their worst, with murder in their eye?
Does Batman ever think of this in the coolness of the night?
Which seems to be the only time that he comes out to fight.
Do Batman and Robin wonder who quells the mid-day crime?
Are they so busy with the night, they never take the time?
Does anybody wonder who's there for us each day?
Well, save your care and wonder, just bow your heads and pray.
We all need heroes in our lives, who are chosen from our ranks,
Ones who win no matter what, from big time crime to pranks.
We put these folks on pedestals and idolize their strength -
Sometimes the idolizing goes an extra length.
So lest we should forget about the source from which we came
And start to idolize too much a certain hero's name,
Take a moment in the heat of day and stand beneath the fan
Remembering which is God, and which is just...a man.

Anthony Mangan

Age Of Sin

By God they're formed to live for him.
By faith they wait in peace to know:
the love, the life, the greatest gift,
the Father alone allows to grow.
But men with power come to assist,
the murder of the innocent.
The law of man says go, it's fine.
It's not a child, it has no mind.

Many could rescue but none dare attempt.
They turn and look down, they refuse to commit.
Those that never see the sun,
ask the Father: What's the reason?
It's hate and fear and ignorance,
Satan bred...and lacking sense.

What was sacred, man defiled.
For lack of faith, they kill the child.
But they will see the Son one day,
and beg forgiveness for sins they pay.

Susanna Griffie

Submit

Water rippling; one at a time
causing the pool to be distorted for a brief moment,
then gone.
Stillness.
Hypnotizing my senses; sending my mind
into a deep trance of mental sleep.
Silence.
No thoughts overcrowd by consciousness.
The voice of myself is dumb,
at least until I wake up.

Drip!
My senses are jolted back to the present,
and again the rippling trend continues.
Calming me.
Allowing me to sleep.
Leaving my mind;
lifeless.

Tricia McCarter

Best Friends

We all have friends,
We all have enemies.
But most of all we all have a Best Friend.
But what's so special about yours is you.
Also me and you are meant to be best friends.
Best friends is you and me.

Fallen Starr

Volunteer

If you're not straight with God, get straight —
Or yours will be a horrible fate.
I was lost with no light on my path
When Jesus came and I got a spiritual bath.

The power of the Holy Spirit is strong like steel,
And I wept at the altar in a kneel.
Jesus was the one love of my life
When I saw a light with Him in sight.

I searched for him, when it seemed like it was night,
Then I knew I couldn't play games with God.
Instantly I would find I would be the fraud.
I now approach God in a humble spirit.

So God, can you answer me and not discipline my rear?
Get straight with God and you won't have to shed a tear.
What you should have is this of the Lord: fear.
Sinning a lot makes you look like a smear.

Get close to God, get forgiven, get near.
When you pray take up your spiritual gear.
Build a relationship, don't be as a pioneer.
Help a friend with his walk; be a volunteer.

Daniel Wofford

Moments Of Happiness

Happiness a time of joy.
Your heart sours and you feel as if
You can touch the sky.
Your whole world begins to shine.
Sadness, a time of grief.
When tears fall down and your heart bleeds.
The clouds appear with the falling rain.
End your mind confines in the depth of pain.
Smiles, the kind on a old lady's face.
A smile that once a little child gave.
The kinds of smiles I wish I could give to everyone.
I wish I could be three years old again.
Not have any problems and worries.
I wish to be free.
Knowledge, I wish I knew now what that old lady knows.
Moments, I wish I could take the time of sadness
And hide it away.
I wish I could take two people in love.
And make them always stay together.
I wish I could feel a moment of happiness and keep it forever.

Ifra Yasin

Stormy Night

The night is dark with no visible moon
and the wind has a low, soft hiss.
I can smell the rain that will be here soon
and the trees are swaying in the mist.

Lightning streaks wildly across the black sky
and I shudder at the loud crackling.
I hear the tinkling of the windchimes I tied
while the rumbling thunder is seemingly laughing.

Through the darkness I see a blanket of clouds
as they float in fast and low in a mysterious way.
The clouds seem to cover the earth like a shroud
whispering as they pass and head toward the bay.

The rain hitting my brow is hard and cold
and with the wind is surprisingly harsh.
Thunder and lightning seem a bit more bold
and as it passes seems to linger over the bay marsh.

As the storm slowly vacates the land
and wanders off over the bay waters,
I hear a faint whisper saying, "I made my stand
and now will leave without anymore bother."

Sharon McIntosh Smith

Early, Earlier

If we could go back to an earlier time
And see the candles before they burned
Would we choose to light them as we did before?
Or to keep them new?
With no melting wax
Dripping down to their base
Standing upright and reaching high
Enticing with a giving of light the saving.
What to destroy, what to preserve,
What to settle with this thinking I enjoy?
Choosing one or not making a choice,
The answer is unimportant,
There's the greater question—
For what purpose would we return
To an earlier time?

David W. Rogers Jr.

Grandma

She never hit that five-foot mark,
But we all looked up to her.

She touched so many lives, it seems,
With her actions and her words.

She mothered eleven children,
One died in infancy.

She never questioned God's plan for her.
It was just all meant to be.

Her voice was never raised in anger.
She never saw the need.

We knew her words were always law.
It mattered not if we disagreed.

She taught us all what family means,
How we should love and support each other.

There will never be a better person
Than my precious loving grandmother.

I know she's looking down at us from heaven above.
And waiting there patiently with arms so full of love.

We miss her each and every day, those of us still here.
But heaven's got to be a better place, because my grandma's there.

Sheena Vaughn

One Minute In Time

The alarm goes off,
Push the "Snooze" button down,
Ten more minutes to savor sleep,
Hoping some magical feeling to reap.

Gazing at the clock as the minutes speed by,
I realize why my life has gone by like a flash,
I cry . . .
For all of the lost, wasted minutes
Oh God it's a crime to ever destroy
"One Minute In Time."

Sixty one years,
Thirty two million, sixty one thousand and six hundred minutes,
Have vanished from my life,
Minutes of joy and minutes of strife.

Oh to capture each priceless moment of time,
To have lived each minute as prime,
The blatant reality now has set in,
I still have a chance to win,
I will only move forward to achieve the sublime,
Living to the fullest each minute in time.

Barbara A. Welsh

No Money Down

As the days go by, I wonder, if my eyes will ever see
An end to bill collectors, using gimmicks for a fee.
It exceeds my understanding, how the world has gotten this way,
I enjoyed all this convenience, 'til the night returned to day.

Then there came the long procession, of knocks upon my door,
A salesman or collector to increase my worries more.
To demonstrate a gadget that I would seldom use or need,
To hook me line and sinker, with his 'no down payment' plea.

Oh boy, I was elated, I knew I had gotten the best,
I could keep up with the Joneses, and pass the acid test.
But that was, oh, so long ago, that I felt very blessed,
My furniture and all I owned, has now been repossessed.

I now live in a trailer, on the lower side of town,
I think of all the joy I knew, in terms of 'no money down.'
I now shop sales and auctions, as all good poor folks should,
I would like to beat the Joneses, but my credit is no good.

Nelson Williams

My Life

My life is so grand, the best it can be,
With so much love that surrounds me.
All my loved ones so dear to my heart,
My family and friends that will never grow apart.
I have so much going for me in this life,
It feels like I'm floating in the air like a kite.
I am just as happy as I can be,
I don't take life for granted, I keep positive thoughts-that's me.
I make the best out of what I have now,
I enjoy every minute - forever I vow.
We all have so much to be happy for,
In our wonderful world, you should be happy for sure.
When my luck is down and getting to me,
I pray for others with problems worse then mine, you see.
If people would realize, we really have a nice life,
And give all of their kindness to reach the highest height.
We would all be happy, like my life is for me,
And enjoy life to the fullest you can make it be!

Penny A. Troutman

Cracked Spheres

Cracked Spheres; dimensions of thine own.
Islands of solitude belonging to you alone.
Private world of fortune and poverty, Life and Death
Where the sole thought of self is Phoenix to the sphere.

However; these spheres are empty
they operate dysfunctionally
Other spheres would complete them
But wait! The difficulty

Of leaving one's own sphere and entering theirs
Thus requiring the allaying of fears
Of using your gifts to heal and share
A gentle love direly needed to repair

"No" one says; it's much too hard, and not worth the risk
'Tis better to remain an empty disk
And survive 'just so' and hope to conceal
Our need for a love so very real

What a world it would be
But just a moment to take off sword and shield
Amidst the strife, toils, and fears
To mend those broken, cracked spheres.

Dominic Patmore

Things Of Beauty

The butterfly, a clinging vine,
The color of a chablis wine,
Female eyes, translucent blue,
But dark and serious brown ones, too.

The huge oak tree, a babbling brook,
The darkest corner of a shady nook,
The myriad of colors that comes with spring,
Blending harmonics when bluebirds sing.

All these things are most divine,
And each fits in with God's own plan.
All with beauty, but none so fine
As the tolerant eyes of an humble man.

Charles M. Kirkpatrick

I, Cat

Sophisticated and aloof or obnoxiously loving
I can sit still for hours, then attack you for nothing!

The Googly Booglies only I can see
And your socks that really belong to me

Are traits of mine you've come to endure,
though exactly why you're still not too sure.

So you live with the chair where I made the gash
And you pay the Vet's Bill when I get a rash.

You wonder at times why you bother at all
then you suddenly find I'm a soft, fuzzy ball

I'm soft and I'm warm, I'll cuddle and purr.
I'll take your affection and I'll leave you my fur!

Cheryl Stamper

No Dad

No dad to greet me when I was born
No dad to greet me that October morn
No dad to hold my little hand
No dad to stand up and be a man
No dad to teach me my prayers
No dad to help me up the stairs
No dad to give me one silver nickel
No dad to buy me my first tricycle
No dad to teach me my ABC's
No dad to tell me about the birds and bees
No dad to read to me bedtime stories
No dad to share my dreams and worries
No dad to tell my troubles to
No dad to hear me say "I Do"
No dad to see his grandkids
No dad to see what his absence did
Longing to know what you was like
Wanting to know why you took a hike
Leaving mommy with seven little kids
"No" real "Father" does what this "Dad" did.

Ruth L. Walker

Uncle Timothy

Old Uncle Tim is the slyest old fox
He creeps in softly and he never, ever knocks.
He never lets you see him but you know when he's been there;
'Cause he, maybe, shoves a table or sometimes moves a chair.
Often it's a window that in haste he left ajar;
But there's always something, doors and windows though you bar.
Sometimes it's a shadow that goes scooting o'er the floor;
Sometimes out of silence the slamming of a door.
Sometimes when you're sitting in the house quite all alone;
You hear a padded foot-fall as the floor-boards creak and moan.
'Though things often seem peculiar and strange things you hear and
  see;
Don't let yourself get frightened, it's just Uncle Timothy.

Barbara J. Vogelgesang

Hana Ho Hana Ho

Hana Ho, Hana Ho, Sailing In The Night
  Vertical wings skyward ever seeking earth's
  breathy might

  Surging onward through the eerie night, through the
  eerie light beyond sight, to a distant shore.

  Snorting dolphins prancing in the silvered light,
  jolly fellows all, lifting spirits in the night,

  Clouds with dirty bottoms, clouds with strands of
  every hue, foretelling weather true.

Hana Ho, Hana Ho, Sailing In The Night
  Ever onward beyond the sea's clutching grasp, under
  diamond chips scattered as if by a gambler's toss

  Pitching, Rolling, Gliding, Hissing through the night.

  Borne upon earth's watery mantel, of ever changing
  sculptures by winds at night.

Hana Ho, Hana Ho,
  Sailing In The Night!!!!!!!!!!!!!!!

Richard G. Shawcroft Sr.

Little Liza James

Hello dear Liza, whom I've yet to meet
brief existence of one, old soul so sweet
what benevolence your parents have bestowed upon us
we're blessed and grateful to have you, and thus
we will help you and love you as on your way you weave
through this maze called life, and I sincerely believe
that this millennium next, will be a much better world,
as your talents unfold and your love unfurls
three thousand miles, much too far it seems
but I see you, know you and love you, in my dreams
I can feel you through the pictures your mom so graciously sends
there's a straight line connects us and I promise it won't bend
your "Grandma Jane" shines through your beautiful face
you have her love and beauty and grace
love and goodness go by many different names
but none hold more for me than Little Liza James.

Robert L. Hendon

The Moon

The moon again.
Last night she came to be,
pre full moon, in one of Miami Streets
- North Kendall Drive - she looked
like a teenager, shabby, careless
and vagrant - a little round piece
in heaven - looking "Mischievously" at me,
sexually pale, still beautiful
in spite of the astronauts violation.

She used the swimming pool
in my house as a mirror

O' moon you have been for ages
the go in between of many lovers
thankful or not - they still love you again
and again. I do - last night
my wife thanked God, for making you
so beautiful - your moonlight
it was a million times better
than any man made lights -

Humberto A. Gomez MD

A New Beginning

Like the snow melts away, and the temperatures rise,
A miracle is performed before your very eyes.
A long time we've all waited for a fresh new start,
His timing is precise. He promises to finish His great work of art.

He gives us His guidance and has laid out his tools,
He watches us carefully to see who obeys His rules.
He was crucified on the cross, and on the third day rose again,
He loves us so much, He wanted to forgive us our sins.

The new beginning is near, but you ask how does it start?
It begins with a prayer, just ask Jesus into your heart.
Accept Him as your Lord, repent, and submit to Him in every way,
Share with others "the good news of Christ" and pray they will be
saved some day.

Be prepared, for His judgment is at the end of the road.
Keep Jesus in your heart, and He will lighten your load.

Eric Patrick Eury

The Hoops Of Life

Make no mistake my beloved,
You must have a purpose in life today.
The way that you share what is given,
Will double when it returns your way.

Making constant mistakes robs your freedom,
Life becomes a burdensome load
So turn around while there is time,
And travel a different road.

Whenever you shoot for the hoops,
Center that throw on peace
Make sure it's intended to last always,
And not just to hold on a lease.

Show unity in the game of life,
Eliminate bitterness, hatred, jealousy and strife
Be original, create your own style,
Then joy will accompany and strengthen your every mile.

Now, you are very close to the basket
Love tells you it's all right to shoot,
There is no doubt as to whether you will hit,
Because you are now mentally and spiritually fit.

Bernice W. Honablue

His Precious Love

When were you last drawn to your Savior,
Could you say?
Was it while you were enjoying some pleasure,
As you went about your day?
Or perhaps when you were lying in pain upon your bed,
the thought of his great pain,
went reeling through your head.
It might have been when you were watching the moon up in the sky,
or saw a flock of geese gracefully fly by.
Perchance it was the sun, warm upon your face,
Children laughing eagerly, running in a race.
A tree in all its beauty, or a flower smelling sweet,
a scrumptious meal before you, oh what a treat!
Dear friends and family hugging with joy,
or a hand slipped in yours, by a shy smiling boy.
How many blessings does our Savior gives us each day?
Then should we not remember to pray to him and say,
We love you precious Father, for the many things you give,
And we will always love you, as long as we shall live.

Lee McCarthy

My Lonely Trials Of Living

Nothing I did was ever enough
Maybe I did not have the right touch
His kiss
Will I ever miss
Maybe it was not there
To let me beware
That in love time would pass
And then our love would last
I know I had weaknesses to bear
But he would always let me believe he was there
Why would he fake loving me
Just to let things be?
Now our kids would be his alone
And I would live without a happy home.
In love I did trust
That we would always be a family with true friends among us
Now today are there answers to find
If he was ever really mine
Love hurts
What can be worse?

Loretta H. Williams

What Kind Of Girl Are You?

What kind of girl are you?
You sneak out at night and get into fights
Your parents they care, But you always give them a scare
What kind of girl are you.

Do you think it's wise to smoke pot.
Don't you see it causes your friends to get shot.
What kind of girl are you.

What kind of girl are you?
When your parents come home, you live on the phone
They try to explain that you put them to shame,
If things don't go your way,
you're missing for a week and a day.
What kind of girl are you.

What kind of girl are you?
They hope and pray,
that you will change one day.
Dear! Life is not a game.

Jenny Richards

Baby Blessing

O Joy to whom is born
A baby—sweet, cuddly and warm
The parents' smiles light up the room
Dispelling from the home a feeling of gloom.

Parenthood had seemed an elusive dream
To this older, needy team
Patience, not time, was on their side
Together they took the losses in stride.

Careful plans were often hashed
Miscarriages intervened and hopes were dashed
But persistence played a major part
In creating the child Mom holds to her heart.

Family, friends, well wishers galore
Give praises, thanks and more
For this child whom all will adore
And God will bless for sure.

Alison Williams

Out Here

Out here in my element
Where the suns ray cannot find -
Where its warmth, ceases to shine
In the cold, blistering wilderness
Naked with my thoughts

There is a path leading to the perimeter,
The point where no where begins
And I am resting upon the giants head
My feet dangle before his eyes
The last of the snow rests in his hair,
It returns to empty skies

Where horizon meets mountain crest my dreams lie,
Somewhere between sea and sun, desert and moon,
Nestled -
In a starless night

Though I deny, I miss my summer orchid,
I am lonely out here,
Where whom walked though fields of thunder,
To an oak upon the wall,
As I lay in midnight locks - I do hear my wild loves call

James Dougherty

Traumatized Emotions

T-is for- Trashing of ones very soul.
R-is for- Rape of the mind or body.
A-is for- Assassination of spiritual and physical senses.
U-is for- Ultra fears set deep within.
M-is for- Melancholy at its lowest and severest.
A-is for- Attacked with out just cause.
T-is for- Trifles of life now so great.
I-is for- Inferior to most now.
Z-is for- Zest for life is dead.
E-is for- Escape there is none.
D-is for- Devastated to the very core.

E-is for- Errors in judgement to harsh.
M-is for- More pain then should be allowed.
O-is for- Opulence no more.
T-is for- Tears that never seem to stop.
I-is for- Ideas for life no longer comes to mind.
O-is for- Out going at one time, now silence takes over.
N-is for- Negativity which once was positives.
S-is for- Shy and inhibited for life.

Gloria J. Parker

Excessive Maturity Or Damage Report

Is the hair you wear becoming thin?
Each day you're finding "textured skin"?
It's increasingly hard to form a grin
  because your teeth feel funny?

And when you move, mysterious creaks.
Your sinuses spring unsightly leaks.
And when you talk, some words are squeaks?
  Your future isn't sunny.

Cheer up, dear friend, it isn't new
this experience that's happening to you.
It's something everyone goes through.
  Isn't that just crummy?

Despite the hope that we've been given
that as we age we'll still be driven
to expect the youth that we've been livin'
  it can't be bought with money!

Bobbie Thomas

Delilah's Rose

In veiled copse grows Delilah's Rose,
'Mid maze of brush and brier.
There, cruel God's prey, as fools foray
Labyrinths of desire.

Pure nectar drips from petal lips;
Sweet lies, with liquid ease,
And, redolence of heady scents,
Brings strong men to their knees.

Once, love besot, in vain, I thought
To pluck the bloom divine.
My breast was torn; wrest by a thorn,
And, withered on the vine.

For, man will head the primal need,
Despite the consequence;
Bereft by scorn, and, left to mourn
His loss of innocence.

Alas, fair swain, there's naught but pain
Of death, in passion's throes.
In lieu of hell; eschew the spell
Cast by Delilah's Rose.

Paula Jane Eastwood

Our Father

He was just an Honest and Humble man—
  Who worked real hard each day,
To support his wife and family he loved,
  Even though he didn't get much pay.

His hands were rough and calloused with age
  From the hard work he had done;
But he always had a smile for us—
  Each night when he got home.

He would take us children on his knees—
  And play and romp with us;
Yet no matter how rough and loud we got—
  He would never scold or fuss.

Then Mother would come from the kitchen,
  Read the Bible to us and we'd sing;
Then Father would lead family prayer;
  And it made our old home ring.

But all those good days are over,
  Both Father and Mother are gone,
Yet—in our hearts we'll never forget,
  How they worked to keep us a Home.

Louise J. Alexander

Untitled

When she, the woman I love, is not close,
How can I tell her she's the one
I love the most?
I cannot whisper it into her ear,
How can I tell her, when she's not here?
Waiting to kiss her lips of fire,
she's my fiancee, and only her I desire.
She will be here soon I anticipate and sweat,
walking down the aisle with first prize,
so she enters the room, it's Love
right before my very eyes.
She is a part of my life you see,
for the remainder of my days, I need her with me.
To wake in the morning, and to kiss her face,
I have her inside my heart, filling that once-empty space.
I'm inspired by her beauty, her beautiful eyes that light my life,
I could not be any happier,
She said yes, she would be,
forever, my wife.
(She's here.)

Kenneth E. Smith

Buy! Sell!

Why,
Measure my love in dollars
As if a thing
To be bought and sold.
I can do more for you
Than can gold.

Diamonds, am I to give,
When a chance is all I ask.
Fancy me your heart, I will give you mine
And like a diamond
Your everyday will sparkle, will shine.

Material things you know I can not afford,
Probably never will;
Your presumption, Yes, may hold true.
But truly great luxury lies in me,
In the things I can do.

And if such hidden value is forsaken,
The warning I cry out is for all:
Tragedy, not romance, will unfold
When one of the best things in life,
Love, is bought and is sold.

JoJo Raimondo

In The Beginning

There remains a Holly Spirit whom at the touch of His hand
Created a world that would be so grand
He created this world with love you see
This beautiful creation, in 7 days would be
With the breath of life came Adam, from his rib came Eve
A creation so glorious, some still don't believe
In the Garden of Eden they had lived in peace
The one day arose this deceitful beast
Disguised as a serpent, he had a plan
To take over the world, to destroy all of man
The trees of knowledge forbidden to touch
But the serpent convinced them, no harm to munch
Deceived, lied to, against what had been advised
The state of the world today . . . if only they realized
". . . For God so loved the world
that He gave His only begotten Son
That whosoever believeth in Him shall not perish,
but have everlasting life."
Amen.

Tina E. Malloy

I Love You?

What does this mean?
Is it just something that people say?
Is it like a blossoming flower that wilts away?
Is it like a deceased being sleeping forever?
Or is it something people think of as never?
What does it mean?

Dawn Delcourt

What If?

What if night were day and day were night?
Would that make all of our problems right?

What if here was there and there was here?
Would that make everyone far come near?

What if cold was hot and hot was cold?
Would that make shy people a little more bold?

What if this was that? Or he were she?
What if up was down? Or if you were me?

Would that change our lives a lot?
Maybe it would, maybe not.

Heather Fleckenstein

Kids Dying

A teenager, boy or girl
Mysterious keeps leaving this world
You always hear about a kid getting stabbed or shot
And worry about those who loved them a lot.
Moms, Dads, sister and brothers crying,
Wondering why are all the kids dying
Why?

Children are the future, they have their whole lives ahead of them,
It's horrible when someone puts that to an end.
We try so much to do our best to survive,
I'm staring to think no one wants us alive.
Children doing everything, trying and trying,
Why are all these kids dying? Why?

Kids don't go outside and play,
'Cause they're afraid they won't be there the next day.
Kids hope they have a future to look forward to,
Who ever thought it'll be like this in 1997?
Who knew?

Families crying;
Children trying;
Too many kids dying.

Michelle Ballard

Have I Told You Lately I Love You?

Sometimes it may seem we don't get
along. But for now we have to be very
strong.

For we are 2 different people sharing 2
different things. But we must always
remember the joy they bring.

So as for grown ups we must always
do our part. So our children will see
we love each other from the heart.
I Love You.

Jomero J. Booker

One Souls Journey

Once upon a time a child was born,
Born far far out in the place of no - time space
Then one day the earth summoned this
child, this child of peace and grace and
requested the smiling of his earthly face

The child smiled and honored this time and place
With the essence of his peace and grace
And when all seemed lost, bleak and meek
The prophets responded and sounded the
Horn resounding and then as fate had determined,
The child reappeared to
Illuminate the earth to its peak!

DE Carroll

I Need An Angel

I need an angel to be by my side.
Someone I can be open with and have nothing to hide.
I need an angel that can comfort and
care. One I know that will always be there.

I need an angel to be one to understand.
One that if I'm down, will hold my hand.
I need an angel that understands how I
feel. One that is not afraid and is someone very real.
I need an angel that will be there if I
call. One that will comfort me if my tears
start to fall.
I need an angel, I hope that you see. One that
I know will always love me.

Gymmie S. Spratley

Grandma's House

The old farmhouse stood empty, a look of despair.
Needless to say, in great need of repair.

A house with many stories to tell.
For three generations of my family there dwelled.

It's my turn now, I have to decide,
With who will this house now reside?

Thoughts of my grandma, my sister, and me,
As we played in the grass under the tree.

In the kitchen, remembrance of sweet smells of tea cake,
And stories of Dad, she told while she baked.

My daughter and family thought it would be
great to be part of this legacy.

We all got started for there was much to create.
Fresh paint, hard work, whatever it would take.

Time passes quickly, I'm not sure where it's gone,
Watching my grandchildren play on the lawn.

I sit on the porch in my old rocking chair,
sweet sounds of laughter everywhere.

The old house is not just a house anymore,
but the old farm house it was before.

Eugenia Wehr

I'll Never, My Angel

I'll never again see those sparkling, blue eyes.
I'll never again feel those big, strong arms holding me.
I'll never again feel those soft lips kiss mine.
I'll never again be able to sleep in the comfort of your presence.
I'll never again be able to look into those eye and
   see the beauty that was able to captivate
   me the way they did.
I'll never again be able to hear you say "I love you."
Nothing will ever be the same, because you're not by my side.
You're where you always thought you should be.
Where you thought you belonged.
You now watch over me from up above.
Now you are in heaven.
Now you are an angel.
Still you are my love.

Jessie Latham Meyers

A Change Of Heart

We're drifting apart like glass that is shattered.
Emotions flying about in multitudes of various directions.
Understanding is lost in the shuffle.
Comfort is sought in a friendly face,
A smile of sorts;
A ray of light showing me the way home,
But confusion does not melt...
Questioning the purest of hearts.

Tracy L. Boisvert

John R. Knott

The days are filled with long long hours
   And thoughts of you
I see your face in all the flowers
   At night the dew
Reflects from heaven a sacred light
   The stars soft gleam
And through the short sweet hours of night
   Of you I dream.

Betty K. Carr

The Great Land

When I sleep at night,
I sometimes dream about a land,
This place has a crystal clear river
running through it,

In this river are many of the fish known
to man; and they all live in peace,
It is a great view there,
There are mountains all over the horizon,
And I sit on a ledge watching below,

I watch the lions and sheep roam together,
All in peace and harmony,
Every time I go always leave,
Maybe one day I will not wake up,
And I will get to live in The Great Land,

Ryan Davis

Mothers And Love

Mothers and Love are so the very same,
Mothers are the picture, and love is the frame.
No matter if you're deaf, or cannot see,
No matter if you're ten, or fifty-three.
They all still love you, not just by chance.
Whether or not the circumstance.
I'd pay for my mother, no matter what the fee.
I love my Mother dearly, and she loves me.
And so we conclude, the difference is none,
Between a mother and love, since time begun...

Ryan Gelvin

Moods

Waves crash, clouds exume the night
Thunder claps post frightful light
Rains beat down in blind descent
Winds howl, billowing disastrous torment
Stars reclaim the blackness high
As heaven's peace calms the sky
Serene breezes hush the trees
Whence tranquil waves dance ashore from sea.

James G. Curry

Country Love

Country love is like the grass that's been
kissed by the morning dew.

Country love is what I feel
each time I look at you.

Country love is like a
soft summer breeze that
blows gently through the trees.

Country love is in the warm smile that
you freely give to me.

Country love is like the moon and stars
that are hugged by the darkness of night.

Country love is wanting you
to hold me oh so tight.

Country love is like the flowers
I hold in my hand.

Country love is because
I'm a woman and
you are a man.

Norma Kirby

Young Love

When it all started they were in love,
just like two angels sent from above.
They were so happy you could see on their face,
as they looked at each other, the peace and the grace.

They furnished their home with love, peace and more,
these two loving people who could live next door.
Each day their love grew, strong like a tree,
each year it strengthened for all to see.

But one day something happened no one could for-see,
they no longer smiled, they were not happy.
They walked with their head's down-their shoulders bent,
these two young people were no longer content.

The house built for two just isn't home anymore,
'cause love doesn't live there like it did before.

Helen Shea

Just Me

They brought you together
From four different places
And made you into a group
With recognizable faces.

You always made us laugh,
You taught us when to dream,
You helped us dare to love,
And showed how to set our minds free.

We were laughing and singing
And enjoying your voices.
But they tried to control things
So you wouldn't have any choices.

But they couldn't change what was inside.
You kept going, just as before.
The same heart then, the same soul now.
We don't want to be your puppets any more!

Enough is enough, as they would pass the cup
And you tried very hard to look the other way.
It's my life now and many never made it thru.
But hey, it's Just Us and we're here to stay.

Teresa Mechler

My One And Only

You are the sun, the moon and the stars to me,
But everyone says to let you be.
I'll never forget the fun we shared,
Together for those short years.
Thinking of letting you go always puts me in tears.
You will always be my life, my hopes,
And my inspiration for all that I do,
Forever and ever I'll always love you.
Whenever I was sad and lonely,
You were always my one and only.
I think about you night and day and sometimes I pray,
That one day you'll say, that you'll love me always.
I think of all your qualities
And how you're always nice to me.
I think of how you stole my heart,
And I wishthat we will never part.
I think of all the things we've been through,
Laughter, happiness, and crying too.
Your heart will always belong to me,
My one and only you'll always be.

Nicole Carpenter

What Is Love

Love is a funny thing, it comes and goes just like spring
First you will and then you won't, first you do then you don't
You tell yourself it must be true,
when you find you're lonely and blue.

You cry a little
You smile a little
You're happy and then you're blue
You ask yourself is this true
Tell me what is love

In the church together and words that were spoken
Vows that were made were not to be broken
In sickness, in health, till death do us part
These are the words that are left in your heart
The wedding is over, there is no more to be said
A year passes on, you wish you were dead
You go to court and tell your story
The judge looks at you and says
This cannot be, but your honor its true the only thing to do
We no longer care the love is not there
You must, you will set us free tell me your honor, what is love.

Clara Hoag

Crying In The Dark

To love you, is to tear a moan from the wild wind,
and steal a passionate kiss from emptiness;
it's to have a smile, from silence, as a gift,
and ride the sky, as a shooting star, bright and swift.

To love you, is to hide my tears amidst the shadows,
of cold and restless nights of sorrow;
tears of loss, doubt and pain,
clinging on to cloudy dreams in vain.

To love you, is to await that precious moment of finding,
that love astray, finally guided;
towards the port it once had fled,
to depart and stray never again.

To love you, has made me a warrior of life while dying,
and no one tends to see me crying;
'Cause I'm crying in the dark,
not one soul knew that you were lying...

Just this loser of a heart,
I've heard you say: "I love you";
a million times before,
yet no one, will ever see me crying...anymore.

Migdalia Garay

What I Miss

I miss the sound of your voice, soft and low.
The feel of your arms as you put them
around me, strong yet gentle.
I miss the feel of your hand,
as you softly touched my face,
the way you ran your fingers
thru my hair.
I miss the feel of your lips on
mine as you kissed me gently,
yet deep and demanding.
The way you touched me as you
slowly moved your hands along my body.
I miss the warmth of your skin against
mine when our bodies touched. And the way
it felt when we were together, like the rest
of the world disappeared and only the two
of us remained.
I miss us, but most of all,
I miss you.

Ronda Barnett

Of Love And Loss

The young girl and young man stand at the altar,
They promise to love if either should falter,
Off to the world their families are sending,
One life beginning, another life ending.

The job pulls him this way, the kids pull her that,
Her hair up in curlers, his middle gets fat,
Their separate lives they now separately tend,
The damage beginning, the start of the end.

The silence, the fighting, up sometimes till two,
And neither one knowing the right thing to do,
Each heart torn apart with no way to mend it,
The only agreement is that they should end it.

He packs up his suitcase, her ring she gives back,
She takes down the photos, the candle, the plaque,
They file the papers, the status now pends,
And few understand how it feels when it ends.

So off to a new life, they meet a new love,
They're certain that this one was sent from above,
The sad truth is each of them actually wins,
As one life is ending, another begins.

Lindsey Veldhuis

Making Of A Poem

A bygone-old bestial scream launches forth,
cry erupting ripples on a surface pacific,
sending surrealistic reality cascading,
like a wall of mercury-lined liars, pierced by a bludgeoning rock.
I the muzzled mustang ebony with rage tear away,
abandoning bejeweled fetters misnomered "evolved beings,"
in realization that I am not they.

The anvil-soul within greedily devours sense-ores,
leaving pure slag for storage in the mind-fort,
waves crescendo amongst gears of the god-machine, initiating action,
sprockets spin, culminating to maniacal frenzy.
From within emerges the ore ingots, amino acids for the living
creation, assembly line quickly produces the new piece.
As the work emerges inertia slowly sets in,
all activity degenerates, fading into,
the aquamarine Roman twilight.

Ravi Sankaran

The Dying Isn't There Yet

She sits beside him, sharing his fight.

Love has given her patience to sit at his bedside,
sharing the strength of a calm he needs to feel.

She holds his hand, his ground to life,
while breaths are raspy gasps for air.
He squeezes her hand to help fight the panic.

She looks at him, the center of her world
narrowed to how deeply he can breathe.

The life they've shared is tangible,
the closeness of years a presence.
With no time for tears, his pain is hers.

Expecting to share grandchildren and rocking chairs,
once life was a plan of foreseeable events,
Until what seemed just a detour,
a conquerable challenge, they fought to win.

Hope is gone. Each day is better than the next
with no promises until he breathes eternity's forever.
Outcomes of what have turned into when, and how
to face another night is the fearsome challenge.

But she still sits beside him, sharing the fight.

Carolyn Wearing

Jenni's Garden

I sit alone now, in your special place —
The garden speaking with your touch of grace,
Each plant responds as all who meet you do —
With joyous peace and confidence anew.

A bee draws nectar from purple hosta's bloom
To spread life next to another flowery plume.
Woodruff, fern, begonias orange-bright
Nestle 'neath young maples, seeking light.

Geraniums, azaleas, a Wye Oak, rose and grasses
Share space happily as summer's glory passes.
This treasured moment gives me hope once more
To fare if dark days lie beyond life's door.

Elizabeth Talbott Carter

If You Were Mine

If you were mine
My eyes would shine
As bright as the sun in the sky

My heart would sing
Bells would ring
And my soul would surely fly

I would nurture your heart
As I shared a part
Of your love, which makes me whole

I would ease your worries
and calm your furies
With a compassion fresh and new

I would awake each day
To kneel and pray
In thanks for the gift that is you

And the love that I know
Surely stronger would grow
With the coming of age and passage of time

If only you were mine

Bryant Joyner

Gloom

It preys on your life like a ravenous leech,
Drains you of your days, always out of reach.
A harbinger of doom, it tears at your
soul, bringing to your thoughts endless gloom.
Never ending misery and thoughts of death
dampen your days, your years, your last
breath.
The terror overcomes me, death is
now my wife, married for all times I
bid adieu to my life.

Joseph Mongioi

A Claim That A Train Killed A Hog

My razorback strolled your railroad track a week ago today.
Old twenty-nine came down the line, and snuffed his life away.
You can't blame me, you see, the hog slid through a cattle gate
so kindly pin a check for ten, this debt to liquidate.

Old twenty-nine came down the line, and killed your hog we know
but razorbacks, on railroad tracks, quite often meet with woe
Therefore, my friend, I cannot send the check for which you pine
Just plant the dead, place over his head, here lies a foolish swine.

Gaines M. Coker Sr.

The Best Is Yet To Come

He was a man of courage,
His spirit strong and bright;
When the doctor said "It's cancer."
He knew that he would fight.

As the pain increased and he grew weak,
That's when his family's loved reached its peak;
Those who loved him gathered by his side,
Prayers were said and tears were cried.

He knew they were of heavy heart,
They knew soon that they must part;
His love for his family was strong and true,
He knew that they were sad and blue.

Baby, you've been a wonderful wife,
There's no one I'd rather have shared this life;
We'll be together in spirit, death won't stop our love,
We'll all be together later in that beautiful heaven above.

I'll go on to heaven and check things out,
The best is yet to come - of that I have no doubt;
The fight that seemed lost was really won,
He knows that the best is yet to come.
Bonnie Douglas

Missing Africa

At last the hour had come
To leave the continent I'd come to love
For the one I would learn to love

The shores of continental Africa
To give way to those of America
A new life exchanged for the old
In a move quite so bold

Airborne, in the flight
My mind went into a fight
For it did not understand
Why I was fleeing my fatherland

Exhausted, I fell asleep
Only to see my friends beckon me from the deep
I shook myself from my sleep
Only for the plane to make a dip

I arrived to confront many a face
All moving at so fast a pace
That my mind was lost in space.
At last in America,
I began to miss, my Africa.
Benjamin Nwosu

If Tears Were Pearls

Verlane Walsh, a friend and neighbor
  Infectious smile for everyone.

Revered by wife and family
  Through suffering his reward he won.

If tears were pearls, we could weave a crown
of tears we shed for you.

Trust in God as a family
  He's waiting there for you

Garlands of flowers in remembrance
  soon will wither and die

But precious memories of his loved ones
  Live forever with him in the sky.
Judy A. Hitz

A Trip To The Zoo

I went on a trip,
It was to the zoo,
There were so many things,
I didn't know what to do,
I saw three goats,
Eating some oats,
And an elephant too,
Whose name was Sue.
I picked up a log,
I saw a green frog,
I called for some help,
And I began to yelp,
They took it away,
So I would enjoy my day,
After that I saw a bear,
And a horse with really long hair,
A lion was sleeping,
The birds were peeping,
Next time you go remember me,
And all of the amazing sights you can see.
Caitlin Elizabeth LeClair

Springtime Through Adam's Eyes

Springtime, springtime, springtime is here
I can smell the fresh scent of flowers in the air
Pink, white, red, green and yellow
Which is your most favorite springtime color?
I love the evergreen tree where the birds sit and sing
You can hear their most beautiful tunes at the beginning of spring
I love the beautiful trees with flowers that are white
My eyes look up to see a most wonderful sight
But springtime is also fun time for flying a sky high kite
In the tree in my back yard squirrels run and play
Up and down, up and down, enjoying a warm spring day
Making noise at the window is really their favorite thing
Waiting to see if to them the bread my mom will bring
Daisies are lovely yellow long stemmed flowers
We found and picked them after, walking for it seemed like hours
All the way home we enjoyed the fresh smell
And brought them in to mom with a big story to tell
I nearly forgot that the best time is to be
Bike riding, up, down, all around, underneath the flower tree
And zooming, zooming, zooming, with the whole blooming world to see
Adam Haynes

Spring

The sun as usual shows its face
Shadowy regions it does displace

Pairs of birds flitter about
Letting out their joyous shout

Cardinals, sparrows, robins and cats birds too
Make up part of our backyard zoo

Squirrels scampering about the trees
Topping telephone poles on their knees

Racing along the overhead highways
Phone lines provide the bi-ways

Silently daffodils face the sun
Their daily vigil just begun

Hyacinths and tulips on the rise
Open up their colorful eyes

The unruly grass is very green
Azaleas not yet to be seen

Numerous magnolias have burst forth
Often falling with the morning frost

Leaves emerging at random pace
Finalize the setting of this place
Maxwell Pevar

Colors In The City

Penny came downstairs one day.
She was dressed in blue.
Her mom said, "Change your clothes right now."
Penny said, "Why does it matter what I do?"

Joe came in from playing outside.
He was wearing red.
"You have to come upstairs right now
and change," his father said.

Colors in the city
mean much more than they should.
Groups of people are around today
who take away our childhood.

But Penny and Joe are lucky;
they received a warning.
Poor Billy went out in black and green —
he won't see another morning.

Jessica Bock

Thoughts from a Glass: The Celebration

Hey, bartender. Pour me a glass of my voice
and your ink. Let me buy you a libation,
so that we can dance to remember.
Bring me a bottle of your finest heart,
so that I might drink and be satisfied.

Hey. stranger my brother - let's get drunk
off of much sweat and sweet grape,
plunge deep into the eyes of a holy seer.
Let's a visionary give us a shot of his whiskey -
for that must be something to savor.

My friends, let's a moment with someone
who's been through it all.
Somebody who has the scars of immortal poetry.
Sweet poetry trickling down my throat.
And thirsty listener, tell us your tale.
For anyone with a heart for remembrance and
a mind for love can sit at this table.
Won't you join us?

Anthony Fondacaro

The Mystery

The journey we take will show us the way.
For the journey must each of us take to find the mystery.
To find the mystery is to find the answer.
To find the answer, first we must know the question.
Hence forth...the mystery.
Take heed for no journey is without its shadows.
Shadows, creations of our own fear, try to hinder our way.
They are our own for that we can control them.
No journey is ever so easy,
that it can be accomplished unconsciously.
We create the shadow, yet we create the light as well.
To embark on the journey one must face the shadow without fear.
In the light is the path we must all take.
It is the question and the answer.
It is the center of all knowledge.
None shall take this journey unless we can accept what we find.
What is the answer?
You tell me
You hold the answer yourself!

Gary VanBlaricum

White

Tastes like cool milk flowing down your throat.
Sounds like puffy cloud brewing in the sky.
Feels like a small soft feathered pillow cuddling next to your side.
Smells like a huge field of wild daisies singing with the wind.
Looks like winter with all snow covering the ground.

Lindsay Gordon

It Is The Years

I sit and ponder in my chair,
    the beautiful friendship we once shared.
What makes us the way we are;
    is it the trees, or is it that one star?
What made you change the way you were;
    can you tell me because my mind is a blur?
Was it the roads, or was it the sea,
    was it the weather, or was it me?
We both are going our own way;
    I wish, together we could stay.
From an unknown force far below,
    I see you walking by with a mere "hello".
What was the reason in the distance of our friendship
    can anyone give an answer to that one dip?
It is nothing that has already been said,
    because to me, in my head,
It is the years that go by,
    It is the years that have died.

Tracy Anderson

The Crash

All was quiet on a Saturday morning.
I sat in my lazy-boy and fought off yawning.
The grass to mow, the weeds to trim.
I was very relaxed and not ready to begin.
There was a noise outside that horrified me.
I raced out of my chair to see what it could be.
A plane had crashed from the blue sky.
If there were passengers inside I'm sure they would die.
The plane burst into flames right in front of my eyes.
My family in the background bellowed with cries.
As faith would have it all was ok
We were all blessed to see the light of another day.

Tony Fiore

Who Is This Living Soul?

Who is this living soul?
    Who is living in the heavens
    Above this beautiful earth.
    Who is this living soul?

Who is this living soul?
    Who is watching over us all
    And knowing what's next.
    Who is this living soul?

Who is this living soul?
    Who's eyes are the sun and moon
    And who's hair is the waves in the sea.
Who is this living soul?

Rebecca Mardelle Jackson, age 11

Teenagers

They are so young, and many think they know
The way of the world to go.
So young and very, very fast,
Never working to make their young days last.
Sex, drugs and violence are what they crave,
Living life in a virtual daze.
Parents and adults are but a bore.
Their experiences and trials go out the door.
A teenager's world is full of advantages for the taking.
But what kind of an effort are they making?
Their young world will be gone in a dash.
Opportunities will crumble as fast as a flash.
Oh, how they need to open their eyes,
So they can see that life is flying by.
So many need to stop before it's too late,
To take a hard look at the direction of their fate.

M. Buggage

A Thought

A Thought
A thought crosses your mind, what do you think about?
The way you play? Why do you sing?
Why do you think? (What a thought.)

Your Hands
They move. They touch.
They work. They write.

Your Mind
A place to be. A place to wonder.
A place to hide. A place to care.
A place to see. (What a place)

Your Heart
It feels. It hurts.
It loves. It beats. It flows.

The Brain
A work of art. Master piece.
A round thing. A learning tool.
A good friend.

My mind, my heart, my thoughts, and my brain, put my
hands to work to write what my soul feels.

Cathy Krause

Untitled

Would you leave my side on a dark gloomy night,
for you know I am scared of time spent alone.
In the dead of the night when I call out for you,
will you let me revel in pain and anguish?
If I weep for your presence to secure the night,
will you arrive to my rescue?
Do you see my inner self as one of power,
or does my imperfection block your vision?
My sense of adventure is intriguing to some,
or do you just see innocence growing up?
Can I hold on to your security,
If only I remain yours?
And if I ask you to step aside and let me brave,
will you?
If I ask you to leave and never return,
will you let me fall on my own?
Will you stay in my heart,
knowing without you I will be alone.

Aimee Mansfield

Test Of Love

Our distance from each other increases fast as a flying dove,
so too deepens the magnet of our love.
The phone booth at a distance gets closer by the step,
opportunity to hear your voice must be met.
Love for you and the kids is ever real.
Lord only knows the pain and fear we now feel.
Your soldier heads off to a far jungle land,
realization of death is a possibility at hand.
Acceptance of duty, too proud to say no,
the value of honor we as a family know.
Our love for each other was bonded while we were young,
this bond will make sure it is never undone.
Oh how we long for that glorious day to arrive,
when the battle is over and we as a family did survive.
Distance is now just a plane ride away,
our voices will be heard on this coming day.
To you precious darling, you are joined only by some,
thank God the end of the war has come.

Larry R. Moore

Untitled

Two people, with a new life,
together they start, a groom and his wife
soon comes a baby, a girl or a boy,
a little package, a bundle of joy...
they have taken their vows, from the heart,
and now their new life, is about to start
along the way, they'll start to have problems,
and it's up to them, to try and solve 'em...
finally, one day, it's gotten out of hand,
like a broken hourglass, out of sand
the more they're together, the further they grow apart,
and the taste of their love, has now turned tart...
so they decide to leave each other,
now their child is left with a father and mother
shipped back and forth for a couple of years,
the child grows up fighting the tears...
there's no one to blame, in all of this,
and this can't be fixed with a little kiss
an emotional scar that will last forever,
a memory that will be forgotten, never...

Nicholas J. Colontonio

The Dream

One night I had a dream
Of our family working as a team,
Everyone was full of bliss,
Something I couldn't possibly miss.

The baby was crawling on the floor.
He is someone I really adore.
Mom was cooking at the stove,
While Jon played with trucks he drove.

Amanda was singing lullaby,
While Pat kissed mom goodbye.
Kris was sitting and reading a book
So that she may have a better look.

I was crocheting on my afghan,
Saying " I will finish as soon as I can."
Everyone was in perfect harmony...
Something anyone would want to see.

Because we did what God has told
Us to do and be very bold,
He gave us a piece of mind..
Something with so much more than a diamond mine.

Serenity Lipinski

Confused Lily

The Easter lily outside my door,
One day became confused.
She should have bloomed in April,
But in October was enthused.
She slept right on through April,
And missed the Easter season.
When asked that she explain herself,
She really had no reason.

All summer long, her fertile bulb,
The rich brown earth had nourished
And now as she awakened,
It sprouted forth and flourished.

As October brought its wintry chill,
Her bulb was soon to burst.
I gently covered her at night,
But still feared for the worst.
Finally, I broke her stem, and carried her inside.
I hoped that she would blossom, thus to retain her pride.
She sat upon my desk and bloomed, I know she felt abused.
My silly little lily, so shy, demure - confused.

Gerda M. Johnson

Stranded

I had no choice,
When I heard the voice,
I had to land the plane.

The landing was tragic,
I wish there was magic,
So he would not have died.

I have to live,
So I can give,
My dad a great big hug.

My belt held my hatchet,
I hoped I could catch it,
The rabbit that passed on by.

No food did I have on hand,
Even though I was on land,
I did the best I could.

The fire was my friend,
It protected me to the end,
It saved me from my fright.
Weeks went by,
Without a plane in the sky, when will I be found?

Erica McKeon

My Michele

She hails from Ireland, the town
of Dundalk, in the county of Louth.
Her bright, sun shiny smile accentuates
the beautiful red lips of her mouth.
With eyes that are blue like a summer's clear sky.
Yes, my Michele is the fancy of every lad's eye.
She walks with the grace of a Queen.
My darling, my Michele, my sweet Colleen.
Her wispy shape glides with a majestic air
in rhythm with flowing strawberry blond hair.
I give all my love
to my sweet Irish Michele Cosgrove.

Thomas A. Phelan

This Silence

This silence that I've come to know
Always with a gentle voice
It comes to me in quiet times
And tells me what to do.

This silence that I've come to know
Calms all my fears and frustrations
It lifts me up to make me strong
Points the way I must walk.

This silence that I've come to know
Touches in ways so hard to learn
Like bare-backed trees it waits alone
To feel a warm Spring breeze.

This silence that I've come to know
Blows like wind in odd directions
Turns me inside out, upside down
Leads me to clear water.

This silence that I've come to know
I don't remember when or how
Only that it's a part of me -

How I love this silence that I've come to know.

Sue-Ann Commissiong

A Child's Possibilities

Give a child words,
    and he may learn to recite.

Give a child numbers,
    and he may learn to add, subtract, multiply, and divide.

Give a child ideas,
    and he may learn to follow.

But teach a child to think,
    and he may learn to lead.

Give a child anger,
    and he may learn to hate.

Give a child pain,
    and he may learn violence.

Give a child shame,
    and he may learn insecurities.

But show a child love and respect,
    and he may learn compassion and understanding.

Maria Liedtke

Daddy

I remember you, Daddy, your face and your smile
I remember you, Daddy, I haven't seen you in a while

I remember flying kites
And building model planes
Putting up Christmas lights
And hanging candy canes

I remember making angel food cake
And beating you at computer golf
I remember staying up late
Just so you and I could talk

I remember I'd make you proud
Just by doing little things around the house
I remember making you shout out loud
Just by doing little things around the house

I remember the day we had to let you go
After seeing the pain of emptiness in your eyes
I remember how it showed
That you needed to say "good-bye"

I remember you, Daddy, your laugh and your cry
I remember you, Daddy, but the memories will never die.

Susan Lynn Garfield

Silence

An empty void whispers to my heart
As we travel together, a world apart
For once in a life time, so long ago
Words of love like a river did flow
Now there is silence, that came this year
Fondly recalling the good times brings on a tear
What happens to love when your heart grows cold
For even the wisest are clueless so I am told
So what does one do to deal with this pain
and try to vanquish the thoughts of disdain
One wakes every morning and takes that first step
and lay no blame or thoughts of regret
For as natural as the passing of the seasons
change occurs at times without any reason
So be it resolved on this first new day
that the silence that came will soon go away

John Zawitoski

Intimate Moments With Jesus

Oh, how I yearn to be so close to
Jesus Christ, the anointed One.

How close can I get?
Closer

I walk and talk with my Saviour
And He embraces me with His love.

His love shines light in the inner parts of my heart,
Driving out any specks of darkness.

Now I can come to Him,
Soaring high and free in my spirit.

As I sit at His feet curled around His glory,
He deposits riches in my spirit.

What a burst of new life,
My dull senses are quickened with His creative power.

This is the time that I blossom
Like a butterfly radiant in the light.

I experience an elevated level of joy and peace when I am in
His presence.

This is when I know Him,
Not of Him.

Gloria N. Adams

Nicole

I have a little Granddaughter,
her name is Nicole.

She is so special I carry her always
in the depths of my soul.

It was for such a short time our sharing together,
but the specialness of these moments will never weather.

The years may pass, time will come and go,
but the bond between Grandmother/Granddaughter is
more powerful than many ever know.

Miles will keep us forever apart,
but the spirit and glow of this little girl
is etched in my heart.

Nancy Mell

The Meek And Humble Mother

She is so meek and humble,
and you'll never hear her grumble.
She wears a crown of Righteousness about her head,
Because this is how she is spiritually fed.
Her spirit is so quiet and sweet,
God is keeping her Lowly at His feet.
She is a virtuous women of today.
This is how we all see her in a pace.
She is never rude or dull,
because she get her counsel from above.
She is the mother of eight, and oh by the way.
Three sets of them were twins that she bore.
And God just keep blessing her but the more.
She worked hard to keep us fed,
And never was one of us begged for Bread.
She is a woman of God that we all love.
She is our friend. She is our mother,
She is all that a child can ask for in a mother.
We all love you Mom, we thank God for you.

Doris Hopkins

Denied The Right To Be Loved

Search my heart
and declare what you find,
A sea of forgotten hope
a field of remembered loves
that was secretly left behind

As I travel this desolate journey,
By ways of misery unknown
when words are denied freedom to escape my lips;
I have no expectations,
only reasons to moan
As sure as the eagles soar to the skies above
my heart knows it's been denied the right to be loved.

Katryna Gholston

Faith

Have faith, it's like the golden splash of dawn:
That light your soul, when hope is gone.
When hope's last desperate desire has fled:
And pride her haughty robe has shed,
Have faith, for God surely knows,
Each blade of grass that grows.
He knows the sparrow's fall from flight,
And sees the bad and good, both day and night.
Let not your soul be filled with dread,
For God knows, each hair upon your head.

Ruby R. Winegar

Here We Go Again

Alaskans are sad nowadays again...
They are sick with seasonal activity disorder,
Even sourdoughs are singing the same refrain...
"I'm sick and tired and down with cabin fever."
So, here we go again!

For gone are the sunny fishing days...
Of the day light saving time of summer.
Gone are the carefree weekend ways...
Vanished by the cold and windy winter.
Yes, here we go again!

Now hear this, a cheechako from the lower forty-eight
Came here for a year of fishing and hunting.
Said he suffered living-in-the-edge fright
But found the wilderness experience awe-inspiring,
And swore he will be back again!

Eulalio G. Maturan

Clean Up The Pollution Of Hate

When we walk in the "light" we we've got a job to do
To clean up the pollution of hate.
We can't do it by force, but we can let the light shine through
And clean up the pollution of hate.
Clean up the pollution of hate with love!
You'll get all the help you need from the "power" above.
It's up to us to put an end to wars and fights
And clean up the pollution of hate.

I'll begin by loving all the people close to me.
I'll clean up the pollution of hate.
Then I'll go on by loving those who live across the sea
And I'll clean up the pollution of hate.
I'll clean up the pollution of hate with love.
I'll get all the help I need from the "power"above.
Let's turn our backs on bigotry and racial strife
And clean up the pollution of hate.

L-O-V-E, love is the way
To clean up the pollution of hate.

Marie P. Nicholson

My professor said, "Write a Poem."

My professor said, "write a poem."
So I went home to ponder,
and found myself
quite all alone,
clueless
lost in wonder.

My professor said, "write of an experience."
So in my mind the wheels did turn,
and deep inside
my stomach churned.

Of life and death
I felt not moved.
What could I do?
Instantly I knew,
For
I've just described
the experience to you.

Mary Lee Reven

Missed

My grandmother died; I know not why
Her life was long
96 in all.

She gave birth to children
Two boys and a girl
Grandchildren she had
21 in all.

My grandmother was a queen;
African you see
Big, tall and strong; so we see
In her prime she ruled the land
Taming it was her plan.

She got married and loved it too
She was God fearing; I think He knew
Wisdom she shared, kindness she showed
Friends she had; few were foes.

Now she is gone; missed by us all
Her wisdom and kindness vanished from all
Our hope and prayer is that she'll be
In the presence of her savior; where she should be.

Dynsdale Anderson

Winged Shadows

Winged shadows
    colorless sky
winged naked ladies
    floating on by

Aphotic devils chained to the ground
the devils scream up to heaven
heaven hears not their sound

Retarded gnomes dance across a neon prairie
they come to a rainbow but dare not to tarry

A white silent angel gleams electric blue light
she flies toward the horizon and is soon out of sight

Vertical lines progress toward the sun
lovers were two...now they are one

Winged shadows
    colorless sky
winged naked ladies
    floating on by

Tom Spearman

Fulfillment

Do you ever doubt that your life is worthwhile?
Will you feel fulfilled when you walk your last mile?
Do you go to work with just one thought in mind . . .
Counting the days and watching the time
for an all-too-short weekend that wasn't so great,
and when things go wrong do you blame it on fate?

Only you can change your outlook on life;
not your mother, your lover, your brother or wife.
Take a look in the mirror—do you like what you see?
If not, then change to what you want to be;
and for those nameless faces you see every day,
give them a smile as you go on your way.

When you get to work, do what you have to do,
but give it your all and your skill will come through.
At the end of the day it wasn't so bad
if you know you gave it the best that you had.
Just give of yourself in all that you do,
and soon fulfillment will come to you too.

Eletha Davis

A Quilt For Caden

As you snuggle under your quilt of Love,
May the good Lord from above,
Watch you grow and make you pure,
Make you sweet and kind and sure.

Give you strength that will subdue
All temptations which come to you.
May you have wisdom to decide
To keep your faith what 'ere betide.

Your mom and dad will be with you,
Your four grandparents will help you too,
Your aunts and uncles and friends so true
Will help to guide and comfort you.

But all of these, as important as they are,
Can only help you to succeed so far.
Your life and future depend on God,
For He will be your Enlightening Rod.

Helen Burnett

Life's Disappointments

It is hard sometimes to accept
the fact what life may throw our way,
but if we look deep inside ourselves, we will find
the courage, strength and faith,
to face another day...

We must know that with each little hurt
and pain, that life sends our way,
is God
making us stronger and faithful to
receive his tender grace...

We can not always see the outcome or
understand often, of his ways...
but through his love and guidance,
we shall find peace from
day to day.

Carol T. Williams

Precious Memories

Memories are things you keep in your heart.
Memories are things that will never part.
Some are more precious than others.
Some that are about your fathers and mothers
That is why you never part with precious
memories that are within your heart.

Samantha Lee

More Powerful Than Death

As I grow, I finally see
what a great friend you've been to me.
You're always there whenever I need
A shoulder to cry on or a friend to believe.
You're very beautiful and talented it's true,
but I see more than an outside view.
A burning love for the Lord Jesus Christ
has helped me out through the darkest nights.
To do my part I feel I owe a lot in return;
I'd be willing to die, I'd be willing to burn.
I value every moment I spend with you
and cherish every word that we speak.
You are beyond the word "friend".
You're a best friend indeed.
I would follow you to the highest peak.
My love for you is more powerful than death.
I will love you beyond my very last breath.

Rebecca Gremmel

To Mary, With Love

A natural, yes natural desire
Oh God, so natural to have the maternal form
Draped before me on an altar,
High for safety, never chiding, encroaching,
Or siding with the others who don't care
To lend their credence to the dream
That one love, rising to this mark
Withdraws itself from the pit of need,
Withdraws to thee, Oh Mother star,
(Entry out of time, Oh daunting life),
A litany of giving, caring sorrow:
I feel you in the vaunting destiny
That takes me to your shrines.

Ann Cashwell Tuley

Do I Have A Future?

We used to hold hands,
But now we hold knives.
We used to aim at goals.
But now we aim at lives.

Where is the candy man?
Now we have cocaine bans.
The animals are dying.
So is hope.

There are cries of hunger,
But few cries of happiness.
How do we build the future
When you destroyed the tools of the past?

Nicole Tacchei

Only As A Friend

At first it was different, but now it's all okay
You're like a best friend and I don't love you
that way.
At first I was shy and you were too
But, now I'd do anything right in front of you.
You know I'd tell you anything and trust you
with my heart
And always remember I hope we never part.
I'll love you for a lifetime but
Only as a friend.
You're like an older brother
I know you understand,
That I'll love you 'till the end
But only as a friend.

Lyndse Thornton

One Season

Sitting at the kitchen window,
Looking at the beautiful, frozen land.
Gray painted on a white earth,
On a silent land.

Leaves impaled on lifeless trees
By the frigid wind,
Hang rigid in the late afternoon,
Illuminated by the setting sun.

Sparse shadows drift deftly on
The white earth covering a mute promise.
A blanket hiding a corpse
In a silent land.

Scoring summer from the canvas,
Consuming the frenzy of life;
Fulfilling the promise of fall
In a silent land.

The tall trees cower over
The covenant of renewal.
Waiting for spring,
Flowers lie helpless in the silent earth.

Thomas Essig

To Be Free

She sat on the hillside as the sun hid behind the tree,
the memory, seems only yesterday and the desire was to be free.
Warm tears came rushing by as the knelt upon the ground
Oh such desire to be set free, oh the pain that was found.

A sound like thunders rang throughout the land,
it seemed so loud but not to every man.
People rushed there and then over here,
the cars didn't stop as the ground received a tear.

A calmness came sudden and warmed the heart
her dream became true as she walked in the dark
The dark became light and then it appeared real
for she had been set free as she descended from the hill

Joe T. Massey

Husband Snatcher

She eloped with Steve and made him my ex
In spite of the grim message of the dream lusoria
Because the plot was not suspected with any index.
But this leech will dearly pay for my dysphoria
With chronic fantod, fights and fatigue from my hex.

In the final analysis, Juliana will have to flip the con
By buzzing his ears with an exotic and exhorting sound
Whose true meaning and origin are not in the lexicon
Until he listen, heeds and promptly turns back to town,
The sound of my fawning, cunning and beckoning leprechaun.

Called from my Vantage Press Inc. New York book
"Dream comes true."

Ofem I. Ajah

Family

F is for my forefathers of whom my country is
founded on
A is for all the battles that they fought for and won
M is for my mother and memories of my past
I is for my intelligence and intuition that tells me
that forever
    nothing lasts.
L is for the love that I always feel in my heart
Y is for all the years I've had on earth to do my part
Put them altogether, they spell Family
A word we all need but at times ceases to be.

Charlene Faye Tschopp

Translucent Door

Stairs spiral in an upward direction
Leading to where I do not know.
Awaiting decision of sheer perfection,
There now are stairs leading below.

Considering my options on through the night
Pondering the best route for me,
Viridescent stairs now appear on my right,
Their exact direction I'm unable to see.

To the left mostly certain I see even more
Captivating beauty has me locking in a trance
Replacing the stairs stands a translucent door
Including hieroglyphics on ritual dance.

Waiting for something to show me the way
Upward? Down below? The right? Or simply through?
Transparent illusions have nothing to say
Despite that they know what to do.

Decisiveness enters as dawn breathes hello
No questions unanswered confusion far gone.
Accompanying darkness, the stairs also go,
I pass through the translucent door to go on.

Amy Anderson

Caring Is...

Caring is a virtue
So often misunderstood,
It bears the fruits of empathy
Yielding forgiveness, as we all should.

Caring is a gift from God
Because His spirit lies within.
To care is unconditional,
From total stranger to closest friend.

Caring is universal
Regardless of race, sex, or creed.
Taking time to listen, extending a hand
To those in need.

Caring is like infinity
As boundless as the sky,
To care is to be non-judgmental,
Being cautious to question why.

Caring is an inborn trait
Often perceived as heaven-sent,
It must be developed, received, and respected
To emit its powerful intent.

Dwayne A. King

21st Century Knight

This is a poem of a 21st century knight.
His emotions inspired him to write.

Throughout life his peers would ridicule,
The subjects of which he wrote in school.

Everyone thought his writings a bore.
He continues to write, even though they ignore.

His ideas they all choose to eschew.
Still, for the hopeless, his words ring true.

When his muse stirs, his soul is set free.
Of the things he writes some consider heresy.

His way of writing only a few can relate.
Truth in words are his to enunciate.

He won't stop writing, a fact for sure.
Even if some still call him a bore

This was the poem of a 21st century knight.
Out crusading for his freedom to write.

Harry Racey

Conflict

I walked the redwood grove, so cool and still:
Green spires through-threaded by a tinkling rill,
The music for this mighty hall, which stood
A worship-place, cathedral of the wood.

I walked the redwood deck that I had built,
And tried to puzzle out my nagging guilt.
Unbidden, my thoughts turned to towering trees
Cut down for decks where men can take their ease,

Until each step from house to railed edge
Accused me silently of sacrilege,
And left me wondering: Which was worth the more,
A redwood hallow, or a redwood floor;

And, if selecting now between the two,
Which one I'd choose? Ah, conflict old but new!
For I'm devoted to outdoor relaxing,
But at the cost of a cathedral's axing?

Steve Mitchell

My Buddy

Carousel horses spend their time going around
    and around and around.
My horses buddy would much rather be in a parade
    marching through town.
His head held high, what a wonderful guy,
    as he proudly steps so fine.
He appears to be dancing along as he prances,
    head bobbing to music in time.
The children love Buddy as he marches along,
    they wave and clap their hands.
Buddy loves children, excitement and crowds,
    and the music of marching bands.

Janet Argent

The Prayer Of Life

As we get ready to sleep, we pray to the Lord that if we
should die, to take our soul to keep. We pray for the next
day, in hopes that the impressions will stay in those we
may have met. We pray for family, and homeless we can see.
The man with the sign, we wished we hadn't whined; when
our family gave him words of God's love. We pray for the
lost, yet we care about the cost — when it comes to giving the
money, we feel sort of funny. We pray for our friends, yet
don't care if they've sinned. We pray for some people we don't
really know, we really don't care if they come or if they go.
We just think it's the right thing to do, because we don't want
to look upon on you. Don't talk to them, because they're not one
of you. We pray for ourselves, cause we know we've done
wrong. The Lord hears our prayers before they are sung; so
think of the day you don't pray for some who needed it so.
Remember to pray, 'cause maybe one day if some one prayed for
you, it saves you from what you were about to do.

Laura E. Silvera

Soul Quest

I endeavor to journey
To the infernal world,
Which lays beneath me
Piteous and scored.
I intend to refurbish my soul and my light,
I intrigue myself, abruptly in fright.
The nocturne in music plays solemnly abrupt,
I struggle and I fight as I am cleansing thy
Soul.
Ominous litany flickers and burns,
Melodious refuge from consternation,
Absurd.
A rivulet of aberrations trickles in my mind,
The interloper is now a haze to entwine.

Remy E. Olson

The City Girl The Mountain Girl

Is there a difference between
The city girl and the mountain girl?

The city girl wakes up to booming music from her neighbor
The mountain girl wakes up to birds chirping
The city girl looks out her window to see kids looking tuff
The mountain girl looks out her window to see mother nature
working her stuff
The city girl wears baggy jeans and tiny shirts
The mountain girl wears decent jeans and layered tops
The city girl puts on a layer of make up
The mountain girl puts of a layer of bug repellent
The city girl eats whatever is laying around
The mountain girl eats a juice and cereal
The city girl looks at her dad mowing the lawn
The mountain girl looks at her dad chopping wood
The city girl turns on the TV to watch MTV
The mountain girl turns on the TV to watch the weather report
The city girl finds a lock to go on her door since tonight is the party
The mountain girl find sticks since tonight is the burning outside
Is there a different between
The city girl and the mountain girl?
(I would think so)

   Nicole Ortiz

The Garden Of My Sister

It is an oasis of beauty,
Lovingly created to be a welcome respite
From the cares and concerns of a mercenary world.

As cool bricks meander through soft, verdant grass,
Gnarled, timeworn maples magnanimously
share their leafy canopy.

Pink petunias overflow their tubs
In the joy of unobstructed sunshine.
Impatients expand their rosy territory
Delighting in the pine provided shade.

Sunlight dapples the wrought iron table
As culinary treats assault the appetite
And minty ice tea assuages summer thirst.

Faces, dear to the heart, light up
With the gladness of shared remembrances,
Future hopes and the contentment of the moment.

It is a haven, a Thoreauvian spot,
Bathed in the shades of Monet.
It is the garden of my sister.

   Ann Bevis

What Do We See In A Tree?

Do we see a cog in the wheel of nature, or just a place for shade?
Do we see a blending with the universe, or just wood for the fire?
Do we see the apple of the original sin, or just a snack to
   satisfy our hunger?
Do we see the beauty of the creation, or just a few branches and
   leaves?
Do we see the wonder of its existence, or just a piece of furniture?
Do we know the secret no one will tell?
Can we see the tree as heaven, or do we see it as hell?
All is in the eyes of the beholder
Do we see it through God's eyes, or one weak, earthly vessel?
The choice is yours, my friend.
It will make the greatest difference in the end!

   Carole A. Ingnam

These Sorrowed Seas

Godliness, her radiance, from the saints was she cast
O'er the seeping seas of sorrow, unto me was she passed
Oh! What blinding beauty bestills my beating heart
Divinity upon me, may our souls never part.
Burnished beauty in my heart, a love, a love so true
Yes! Bequeathed my love for thee, spoken unto you
Enchantingly, my love for thee, spoken in a vow
Teasingly, her vow for me seemed 'possibly' somehow
Oh did I wonder, yet in vain, what was meant for me
Relentlessly, I begged for she to love eternally
On the morrow came the sorrow, for my love had gone
Meagerly, on sorrowed seas, life must carry on
And the love sent from above, her love and mine for she
Never shall I lose that love, amidst these sorrowed seas
Cravenly, on sorrowed seas, I shall be adrift
Eternally our love rests here . . . everything must end.

   Donnie J. Burgess

Untitled

Life in its entirety is
somewhat agonizing, perhaps
because it is a day-by-day existence;
we know no other.
We only know what we live,
each line of thought as each day closes.
Tomorrow will bring sadness, we know,
sooner or later, even though this one
has brought smiles,
but it is bound to come,
deep tragedies that we cannot escape...
wondering, wondering when it will take place.
Only GOD knows.
We will be happy many days are
spent as such, some exhilarating, some quiet,
but with a smile on our face,
sense of beauty overwhelms us. Life is
good as each line of each day closes.
Only GOD knows.

   Deanna Jeanne Martinez

Untitled

Sunlight welcomed like a long lost friend
darkness fills the soul, almost near the end

Emotions rage as I search for a why
to this life that I'm living for this fear that I cry

Lost is this world of uncertain and deign
holding tight, letting go, what to do with this rein

Then you're blessed from above with no reason you know
giving light, giving meaning, giving all a new glow

From a seed to a flower all new things sprout
gives my reasons for why and what life's all about

A young one so tender, a soul that's so new
please give me guidance, let my actions be true

Then he's here and I know all the answers so clear
like the sunshine so welcome all his words that I hear

Just love him and guide him to the rights of your way
show him nothing but happiness, for this I do pray

Thanks for the sunlight, the way and the joy
thanks for this life and the life of my boy

   Jennifer Pratt

Childhood Flight

A teardrop fell in the night . . .
A child's cry
A kiss goodbye.

While ghosts that worship yesterday,
Lie silent in the shadowed room . . .
Silhouettes of life still linger,
Fragile
Waiting doom.

Echoes race down empty halls
In frantic search of someone's call.
While footsteps, still in endless quest for yesterday,
Will never rest.

Silence rules
And none can speak . . .
But all remember well,
A tear
That once fell in the night . . .
Witness of childhood flight.
Trisa Mason

Night

As I look through my window blind, out into the night,
Not one soul do I see,
The earth is covered in its
blanket of darkness, created by the one
and only creator God Almighty God.
The stillness of the night runs
down my spine, giving me chills of
all kinds,
Inside is where I will stay as
long as the night has its way. I lie
peeking through my window blind as the
night disappears into day.
I exhaust my self with a sigh
of relief at the rise of the sunlight
as I welcome the day.
The stillness of night has now
passed away.
Brenda F. Dickens

When God Takes You Home

As I knelt there quietly, I held her hand
Praying for it not to slip away, as if
Somehow I could keep her by holding her hand

Her beautiful face had grown dim
from the pain within

I looked to Heaven, and asked God to take her
Swiftly, where she would suffer no more,
and be young again

The loss I felt was unbearable, the tears
Were like torrents of rain
The days and nights filled with sorrow
For I knew I would not see her again

As I looked over the valley, it was so peaceful
And quiet—I feet her presence, ah for
Such a little while, I said Mama,
Then it happened, oh, so quickly, I felt her
Leave me, as if God had taken her
Hand, and said it's time to go Home again
Diana King

Problems

The hardest job about a problem is just to get a start;
I'm sure of all we have to do, this is the toughest part.
We often take our precious time and idle hours away,
Forgetting that we'll not succeed, with hands that only play.

Problems can be many things, friends we know and love...
Verbal problems and equations, snow-white clouds above;
Problems can be found everywhere, in this world of His...
All these things and millions more, that's what a problem is.

Solving problems is a trying task, and one we all defy...
We never solve a single step by only standing by.
The person who is up and going is halfway up the hill,
While we are planning what to do, we're only standing still.

The quickest way to solve a problem is soon to find your place;
'Tis true we'll only reach this goal by getting in the race.
You can not wait for someone else, you must be there yourself.
That knowledge doesn't mean a thing, that's stored upon your shelf.

So, this is your chance to do, and not some other time...
The longer that you wait to start, the tougher is the climb.
Beginning is the highest step, for when you've once begun,
You'll find the problem you dreaded so, is already halfway done.
Gladyse W. Harris

Just Say You're Sorry

Just say you're sorry, it's ok
You don't have to justify your actions
by bickering and feuding all day

I know you didn't mean it, that time before
when you turned around, bumped into it,
and it crashed to the floor.

If you had said you're sorry, it would have been OK
Not fuss and argue and blame me,
for putting it in your way

Now you've driven 50 miles out of the way,
cause you wouldn't listen, to what I had to say.
I told you 3 times to turn left at the light,
you said, no, you know where you're going, so you turned right.

Now we sit here, out of gas and out of money,
and as I turn to look at you, it's really kind of funny,
Everyone in life makes a wrong turn,
There's nothing wrong with that, That's how we learn,
So, it's all right to say your sorry, I promise, it's OK
Honest honey, trust me, I'll still love you anyway.
Loretta McDuffie

Just One Look

With just one look,
I felt a feeling like the earth shook,
Looked down at my chest,
Realizing my heart had been took.
Feeling part-high and part-paralyzed,
Is what I try to disguise,
As I lift my head from my chest
And gaze into her eyes.
My heart no longer beating,
But I am far from being dead,
As I start to get dizzy,
From blood rushing to my head.
I try to put up a fight,
But tonight's the night,
That I feel the effects of love at first sight.
She harasses my hormones when we are alone,
Whether in person or talking on the phone.
I have visited a place that not many have been,
If today was my end,
I would die with a grin.
James E. Jones Jr.

Untitled

Four Walls,
   shadowed by images of emptiness;
  One fine, dark grained door of beauty gently sways
    back
     and
      forth
Not leaving an impression or a hint of light into the room;
  A sense of dampness floods the room;
   sitting,
  swallowed by fear,
   alone in sadness.
I turn within to find comfort;
  Lie thy head down on the floor, and smile with wondrous
accounts
   of memories.

   Brian Bowen

Lovely Obstruction

I may never see a poem lovely as a tree
Unless it stands between a big bass and me.
I cast with all my patience and skill
Each limb I snag makes me mad enough to kill!

I may never see a poem lovely as a tree
But when it's between the green and my tee
And each stroke I make causes bark to fly
I send my club twirling through the sky!

Admittedly a tree is a beautiful thing
It just depends, at the time, on what I'm doing.
It's wonderful to enjoy its summer-time shade,
Oh yes, it's a beautiful thing my Creator has made!

   David H. Sloane

A Ghetto Mother Love

  A Ghetto Mother Love, where do it
come from?
It comes from way down deep within,
for a ghetto mom there so many things
she confronted with.
The first thing is no father there to help
raise her child. She pray's each day that
God will take away the sadness and the
unhappiness of her ghetto child!
And that one day no more will she have to
raise her, child in the ghetto and until
that one day.
The Ghetto mom will always love her
child, and pray that her child will never
have to raise a Ghetto Child.

  "A Ghetto Mother Love"
  Brenda L. Wooten

Final Exit

There comes a time in every man's life,
when the cold hands of death reaches for his soul.
And as his end approaches, he thinks about the things he has done,
the hearts he has broken and the mistakes he has made.
It seems funny that man would only think about this
when his end draws near.
And as he remembers, a smile crosses his face and
the memories warm his heart.
Given him the will to live one more second, one more minute,
one more hour, one more day, one more night.
Life is a precious thing to waste,
and he wonders why some give up without a fight.
Knowing that when he goes, it will be his Final Exit.

  Patrick C. Facey

My Vague Disposition

Float like a butterfly, sting like a bee
  I once met the great fighter Mohammed Ali
With all the king's horses and all the king's men
  I found a disposition which I cannot defend

Can you guess what I do with all my spare time?
  Write stupid little poems and play games with your mind
Merry Christmas to all and to all a good night
  I pushed Humpty Dumpty and he fell out of sight

My disposition is strange; it changes like sand
  I write crazy verses with a pen in my hand
In the evening I tire, so I go straight to bed
  But visions of sugar plums still dance in my head

On top of old smoky my disposition waits
  I sit on the toilet and ponder my fate
Float like a butterfly, sting like a bee
  What else can I do with a college degree?

  Bruce Green

Children Of Genesis

Harmony is shimmering from a kind morning sun
Bringing forward the saplings of genesis, once again

Behold, children basking in ponds of clarity
Breathing into them, cool, untainted winds

They feast upon the sweet fruits of nature
Nourished in the pureness of rain waters

Embracing the scents and sounds of forests
- Not yet burned by the fires of Man

Enchanted with the calls of untamed beasts
They are abundant, and live no longer in fear

Looking now onto flourishing golden fields
Man is humbled in the presence of rainbows

A journey has begun on a river flowing abroad
Through the canals of a world now reborn

A ship sets sail to endure oceans of vitality
To bring awareness unto all creatures upon the earth

  Melinda Mancini

Looking Back

There will always be a beginning, there will always be an end
So we have no way of knowing, which way your road will bend
Many times the paths we choose, all seem to be uphill
The agonies and ecstasies happen as they will
So who can tell with certainty what life is all about
The agonies and ecstasies will always be in doubt

When love seems lost and life seems dim
And happiness doesn't grow within
When the world grows dark and the nights grow long
And the memories aren't where they belong
When the teardrops fall and laughter fades
And misery pulls down its shade.
When your heartaches seem to just grow
You will learn and you then shall know

You need the tears, so you can hear the laughter
The sorrow, to know the happiness after
You need the bad times, so you know the good
Then you can feel the love that always stood
So looking back in time we should never come to regret
The moments or the memories, that haven't happened yet

  Ken Collins

The Sweater

The Sweater that I once wore as new
now faded and torn, how much it's been through
comfort, to me, it has always brought
another to its likeness could never be bought
each thread that's used to link it together
has been stretched and pulled, bleached by weather
it has forever protected me from the cold
its personality so strong so bold
now...though it's ragged and out of form
the Sweater of mine still keeps me warm.

John Thomas Pusateri Jr.

A Dream Of Tecumseh (The Great Indian Leader)

Such wisdom, at times, comforts us in sleep.
Let me describe my dream, as I lay under the stars—

In a deep ravine Tecumseh lay unseen,
A bullet in his side.
A mountain torrent thundered by,
In vain he waited for help.

Upon the dusty earth he lay,
Soon to be dust himself.
No one knew that he would die
And nothing came in view except

Two men just passing by who spoke his native tongue.
In a deep ravine he lay unseen; he languished, but they with glee,

Related the wiles of one brave man,
The alliances of "Tecomsee."
As he heard them speak of him so well,
He left in peace to ride the stars.

As I awakened I thought: when in my grave I come to rest,
And, as it was for him, that wanderers go passing by,

Perhaps their gentle words, as I end my breath and dreams,
Will make me run with deer or soar with eagles far and near.

Joseph E. Rouleau

Midnight Introspection

Love is a mystery, and so is my life.
Am I anything else, but a mom and wife?
When it comes to love, there's many a kind —
So, which one is it, am I out to find?

A love for myself? Well, I want that too —
But the love I seek, I haven't a clue.
I seek and I want, but what will I find —
A tangled mess of my heart and mind?

Of course I can see things I didn't before —
But will I believe, lift my wings and soar?
Or will I stay grounded, and wither away —
Because of no faith that I'll be okay.

Libby Jo Jorgensen

Lovers At War

We fought a long and bitter war,
My true love and I;
And in the end we both had lost
As times had passed us by.
As night fell on us
Our souls had died,
When after lost love our hearts cried and cried.
We fought a long and bitter war,
My true love and I;
We fought a long and bitter war,
Before we said Good Night.

Mirella S. Goben

Dear Friend

Dear friend, I need to talk.
As dear as you are to me,
As closely as we walk,
I'm not really what you see.

What you see is a reflection
of your own thoughts and schemes.
What you think I am is only a confection
of your own hopes and dreams.

I go with you through the forest,
Though in the open, I'd rather be.
I love mountains best,
While you...You love the sea.

The beauty of the sun makes you rave,
Yet I dream of stars and moonlight.
When the company of others I crave,
You want peace and quiet.

More unlikely friends I never hope to see.
Will you ever understand?
We're as different as can be
And yet we walk hand in hand.

Diana Lawless

Mothers' Reasons

The moon shines light upon their hair;
They sense that she is standing there.
And when her tears begin to flow,
For reasons mothers only know,
They taste the salt that fills the air.

Tomorrow has become today;
They sense it's time to move away.
And when she cannot say goodbye,
For reasons mothers often cry,
They hear the words she longs to say.

The stars provide their gentle light;
They sense why she was there at night.
And when they stroke their children's hair,
For reasons mothers are aware,
They feel the anguish of her plight.

Her passing fills them with despair;
They sense the salt that dries the air.
And when they cannot quench their pain,
For reasons mothers can't explain,
They thirst for tears no longer there.

Donna J. Carrara

Untitled

The cries of a broken angel
and the tears of a mending heart.
To wish to forget cannot mend a broken heart,
only faith can put it together while men take it apart.
Memories remain of such love and sorrow,
to remember the past is to know of a tomorrow.
Angels should never know of such mean and hateful things,
to love an angel is the song that every man should sing.
If the song of an angel were to be my last sound,
then it would be a moment in heaven with a lifetime on the ground.

Jeremy Dandron

The Little Light In The Pray Room

Oh I hurt inside as I sit and wait for God answer
thru Jesus the truth and light of the world and wept with
a anticipation as I kneel and pray to my God with Jesus.
The light in the pray room still burning as I wept, for love is gift
from God thru Jesus. Thru joy and spread
of sunshine that comes in the morning is a renew spirit.

Hattie Ware

Springtime

When winter ebbs and spring is near
The ice is slowly melting.
Change abounds for one to see
As the April rains are pelting.

The springtime warmth will melt the snow
As the trees begin to bud.
The birds put on a mating show
The roads all turn to mud.

Flowers come up in the spring
To add their beauty fair.
Any place that they can live
They'll be found growing there.

Life abounds, both great and small
The landscape turns to green.
The beauty of this time of year
Is seldom truly seen.

Spring moves on and soon will yield
Unto the other seasons.
It's still a favorite time of year
For all these wondrous reasons.

Harry Hardenburgh

Where Are You Now?

In the rhythm of your walk I am reflected
and in the peace of your eyes I sleep
and on waking, our gaze moves the clouds in a sweet dance
until there is a climax of infinite tenderness.

Your long lines, soft
as the beautiful sounds of a harp
produce and touching my skin
Vibrations
marvellous emotions leading
to the touch of our lips
bringing tears of
uncontainable happiness

You appear and disappear
like an enchanted firefly
and my feelings are stirred
revolutionizing my space
until I hear you speak
and see you in the doorway

Where are you, now?
I want to see you!

Patricio Carreno

The Drum

One day while under skies of gray.
I heard a drummer at play

This African, you see, didn't say a word,
but from his drum, many things I learned.

It spoke of palaces in far of places,
and of might kings and queens with black faces.

The drum spoke of great warriors with guns and spears
who invoked from many foes awe and fear.

The drum told me of empires great and wide
from Nubia to Ghana to the empire of song hay.

Then the drum whispered as the end drew near
This is your heritage, hold it dear

Now this is your heritage child of the black face
Shoot with joy and be proud of your race.

Jonathan Ellison

Mourning Of The Redbird

She sat, in subjugation on a lower branch
cajoling, wheedling her song of protest.

Lacking his crimson luster, humble in her coat
of brown, reddish hues highlighted her drab
tail feathers. A faint hint to her species.

Once, in feminine bravery she flew up to feed
on the opposite side of the cake seed.

He, in male indignation, cawed his rage
and angrily flapped her away.

She lit. Again a lower perch to his male domination
awaiting his allowance of her need to feed.

His appetite sated, he cawed and flew upward.
She cautiously mounted the perch and began her feast.

Her tail atwain, crown bobbing, searching,
alert to danger, she pecked and fed.
Not calmly, as he, but apprehensively.

And quitting, she flew to a lower branch.
Transfixed by the feeder,
in agony, wondering
"Have I done something wrong?"

Jane D. Harrison

To A Wonderful Lady

Here's to the lady, over whom that I dote
  So much I think of her, yet no poem have wrote
I am not alone in my praise, of this gem
  Friends, family and neighbors feel the same of this femme
Her daughter knows, she's a woman of grace
  And her kindness shows, just look at her face
There are stories and odes and tales of her praise
  And many would help, her halo to raise
To Kenny and Mark, she's Ma, or it's Mum
  She is still their mother, but also their chum
The grandchildren love her, they are at ease by her side
  They share my feelings, of my wonderful bride
All our love, upon you we bestow
  You're always in our hearts dear, I am sure that you know
Your character, no words or expressions could taint
  Your beauty, on canvas, only Michael Angelo could paint
And so life goes on, one year after another
  So God Bless this Lady, my wife and your mother.

Pater McEwen

The Master's Daughter

  This sailboat sailing through the water,
its beauty resembling the master's daughter.

  Being sturdy built with elegant lines,
going forth splendidly at all times.

  A most magnificent sight to see,
this sailboat whose sails number three.

Alan Peterson

Rare Roses

Roses bloom in fields of gold
Though some roses are very bold.
You can feel the air as the wind blows
You can see the sparkling water as it flows.
Gazing at the clouds you can see roses;
Rare Roses.
A rose feels as smooth as velvet
Because of its texture, not even a butterfly could tell it.
Roses; Rare Roses that bloom in fields of gold
Can not compare to its beauty and for being so bold.

Natalie Wilson

Father

I've watched your favorite movies, Father,
And I've listened to your favorite song
I've read your favorite books, Father,
And I've hugged your favorite son.
  I lie awake thinking of you, Father,
Weeping in abject darkness.
Unable and unwilling to reconcile, Father,
How little I remember of you.
  We have moved on in our lives, Father,
And for that I am glad.
Because of our loss, Father,
We shall be forever unwhole and forever sad.

Joseph M. Snyder

"God Sent!"

God sent Martin Luther King, Jr.,
As a ray of "hope"
Because he was filled with hope.
He loved God's people who had no hope.

In hope, he climbed the highest mountain,
Realizing he would never see the fountain.

Yet, he spoke of hope, in fiery words,
to all who would listen . . .
For the lowly and downtrodden, and all
would glisten . . .

Because God sent Martin Luther King, Jr.,
as a shining ray of "Hope!"

Cletus Watson, T.O.R., Franciscan

Memories

As I grow older, I ask myself why;
Why did I let the years fly by?
Fly too fast, much left undone.

Thought called, and spirit answered;
The journey was not to the realm of a star
But to the memories of yesterday.

Memories of loved ones lost from sight,
Of lives so shared and dreams so bright,
Of pain and sorrow, love and joy.

Just memories that linger from another time,
Beyond barriers unknown
By the limits of my mind.

Mary A. Schwenk

Castles Of Dreams

  Here I sit listening to the tempest
fade to a peaceful calm.
  Mollified sky, stars come shining
through.
  Castles in the air, how life has
changed.
  Lightning outlying the horizon, silent
thunder, another tree falls.
  Wayfaring steps, none justified others
personified.
  Neo abstractions turned imperfections.
Tomorrow another tempest may run
its course.
  Tonight I dream of castles in
the air.

Ed Trevino

Peace And Serenity

On the threshold of change is where we stand
In a world that has been dominated by man
Can you tell me what the future holds?
Am I able to stand proud and bold as I strive to succeed
It's not fame or fortune that I need
In a society where the majority rules
Why is so much detail paid to the ones who win and lose?
Peace is of the heart and soul
Serenity will never grow old
I mean what I say, and say what I mean
For only in having knowledge of self, can your life truly be clean

Tyrone Barner

How To Hurt Me

If you want to hurt me, then lock your door.
Because I know you possess the key that's on
  the floor.

If you want to hurt me, then love me no more.
Because I know you've done that to me before.

If you want to hurt me, then push me distantly
  far away.
Because I know you won't see me after that day.

If you want to hurt me, then use your hand
  across my face.
Because I know you'll leave without such grace.

Tammy Hickman

No Dad

No dad to greet me when I was born
No dad to greet me that October morn
No dad to hold my little hand
No dad to stand up and be a man
No dad to teach me my prayers
No dad to help me up the stairs
No dad to give me one silver nickel
No dad to buy me my first tricycle
No dad to teach me my ABC's
No dad to tell me about the birds and bees
No dad to read to me bedtime stories
No dad to share my dreams and worries
No dad to tell my troubles to
No dad to hear me say "I Do"
No dad to see his grandkids
No dad to see what his absence did
Longing to know what you was like
Wanting to know why you took a hike
Leaving mommy with seven little kids
"No" real "Father" does what this "Dad" did.

Ruth L. Walker

Uncle Timothy

Old Uncle Tim is the slyest old fox
He creeps in softly and he never, ever knocks.
He never lets you see him but you know when he's been there;
'Cause he, maybe, shoves a table or sometimes moves a chair.
Often it's a window that in haste he left ajar.
But there's always something, doors and windows though you bar.
Sometimes it's a shadow that goes scooting o'er the floor;
Sometimes out of silence the slamming of a door.
Sometimes when you're sitting in the house quite all alone;
You hear a padded foot-fall as the floor-boards creak and moan.
'Though things often seem peculiar and strange things you hear and
  see;
Don't let yourself get frightened, it's just Uncle Timothy.

Barbara J. Vogelgesang

Biographies
of
Poets

ABE, MARK T.
[b.] December 2, 1955; Reedley; [p.] Charles and Nancy Abe; [occ.] Accountant; [pers.] Would like it written: Mark Abe Reedley, CA, dedicated to my friend, Lillia.; [a.] Reedley, CA

ADAMS MFCC, SARAH V.
[pen.] Sarah Zea; [b.] October 23, 1955; San Francisco, CA; [p.] Helen and Marco Zea; [m.] Glenn Adams; March 22, 1980; [ch.] Mark, Elena and Johnathan; [ed.] B.A. and MA Gen'l Psychology, MS Clinical Psychology, MACL Theology, Psy A Candidate; [occ.] Mamafe Family and Child Counselor; [memb.] APA, CSPA, CAMFT, AAMFT; [hon.] Silver Eagle Award, Golden Eagle Award, Bank of America Award in Foreign Languages, APA Minority Fellowship, Samsha Fellowship; [oth.writ.] In process of writing doctoral dissertation which will be submitted for publication in the autumn of 1997; [pers.] I strive to help to improve one finality of life for humankind. I have been influenced by self-psychology theorist and romantic composes and poets; [a.] Covura, CA.

ADERMAN, DAPHNE M.
[pen.] Emily Gray Wolf; [b.] January 16, 1932, Kenosha, WI; [p.] Mr. and Mrs. James Anderson; [m.] Donald L. Aderman, June 18, 1949; [ch.] Pamela Marie, Deborah Ann, Christopher Scott and Kevin Craig; [ed.] Mary O. Bradford High School, Los Angeles Valley College, International Correspondence School; [occ.] Caregiver for Infants and Preschool Children, Grandma Daphne's Country Cottage; [memb.] North Phoenix Baptist Church, Gideons International; [oth. writ.] This is my first poem. I have the heart of a poet. I only hope I can put more of what is in my heart down on paper.; [pers.] To give honor and thanks to my God, Jesus Christ, for a loving family - many friends and a wonderful life. I only hope this can be reflected in my writings and bring hope to others for a good life.; [a.] Phoenix, AZ

AGUIRRE, GEOFFREY
[b.] October 2, 1977, Los Angeles, CA; [p.] Rodolfo and Beverly Aguirre; [occ.] Currently a student at the University of Montana; [oth. writ.] Currently putting together an anthology as well as writing a novel, "Jim Mazz."; [a.] Stevensville, MT

AJAH, OFEM I.
[b.] February 12, 1959, Adim, Nigeria; [p.] Ibiang Ajah, Obaya Ikwa; [m.] Francine Ajah, February 8, 1990; [ch.] Anijah 6, Tuniche 5, Achayen 2; [ed.] St. Brendan's Secondary School, Obubra, Crs. Nigeria, University of Ilorin Medical School, Nigeria; [occ.] Physician; [memb.] American College of Physicians, American College of Gastroenterology, American Gastroenterological Association; [hon.] Federal Government of Nigeria Merit Award, Intern of the Year, 1990-91, Interfaith Medical Center, Brooklyn, NY; [oth. writ.] Dream Comes True - a novel about a physician who falls in love with his nurse and elopes with her despite his jealous wife's attempt to prevent any such thing. The book will soon be released by Vantage Press of New York.; [pers.] There's enough in the experience of each of us to write a book. Time, the necessary but scarce ingredient, must be created for the endeavour.; [a.] Brooklyn, NY

ALBERT, ASHLIE NICHOLE
[b.] July 1987; Hays, KS; [p.] Paul, Melony and Bradley, (Granddaughter of Tom and Nadine Alber, O.L. and Elayne McGehee, Bill Rexroat, Lane and Diane Gooding); [ed.] "Drug Free" Honor Student, 4th grade, Avondale Elementary School; [hon.] "Talented and Gifted" Program, '96 TASS Math Academic Achievement Award; [oth.writ.] (Unpub) The Watermelon, My Mother and The

Beautiful Rainbow; [pers.] I want my family to be happy. I want to work hard: have a good attitude and keep a good relationship with God. I wish to inspire my Great Grandmother, Joshua Marie, who could charm the world with her command of the pen.; [a.] Amarillo, TX.

ALEXANDER, LOUISE J.
[b.] August 4, 1924, Meadow View, VA; [p.] Charlie and Mary J. Trent; [m.] Claude Alexander, October 9, 1969; [ch.] 6 by former marriage; [ed.] 7th Grade; [occ.] Retired, now homemaker; [hon.] Merit award for a poem titled "Dearest Mother," in 1965 for mother on her 69th birthday, June 7, 1965; she accidentally died from burning Jan. 11, 1966, father died August 3, 1967 of lung cancer.; [oth. writ.] Several poems over the years but none ever published as yet.; [pers.] My parents raised 4 children during the Great Depression as tenant farmers and on a small wage, so this poem although titled, "Our Father," is my tribute to them both.; [a.] Tampa, FL

ALEXANDER, MATTHEW LANE
[b.] November 14, 1982; Shelby, NC; [p.] Lane and Hope Alexander; [ed.] Student—Crest Middle School, Shelby, NC; [memb.] First Baptist Church, Shelby; [a.] Shelby, NC.

ALLANGE, STEPHEN V.
[b.] November 9, 1966; New Orleans, LA; [p.] Walter and Faye Allange; [m.] Stacey Allange; December 10, 1988; [ed.] Crescent City Baptist High School Metainie, LA; [occ.] Warehouse Manager Imperial Trading Co., Harahan, LA; [pers.] You control your own destiny. Make your own breaks in life, Open doors to your future that may otherwise remain close; [a.] La Place, LA.

ALLEN, JOE W.
[b.] Elsie, NE; [m.] Kathleen; [ch.] Mark and David; [ed.] Three College Degrees; [occ.] Classroom Teacher; [memb.] Wildlife and Environmental Org.; [hon.] Academic and education awards; [oth. writ.] Scientific reports, teaching materials; [pers.] I write for children so I write in rhyme and rhythm.; [a.] Muskogee, OK

ALTMAN, ASHLEY
[b.] March 11, 1988, Philadelphia, PA; [p.] Rodney and Sharon Altman; [ed.] 3rd Grade at Sewickley Academy, Sewickley, PA; [occ.] Student; [pers.] I enjoy reading, ice skating, piano and softball. I hope to become a journalist.; [a.] Ambridge, PA

ANDERSEN, AMY
[pen.] Silver Moon; [b.] August 17, 1982, CA; [p.] Terrie Fitzpatrick, Michael Fitzpatrick, Robert Andersen; [ed.] Currently in high school at South Hadley High School in Mass.; [occ.] Student; [memb.] Cheerleading Squad, Teacher for Math Superstars; [hon.] Honor student; [a.] South Hadley, MA

ANDERSON, TRACY
[b.] October 19, 1973, Plains, MT; [p.] Florence and Leon Anderson; [ed.] Graduated Plains High School. Attended FVCC - graduated with an AAS degree; [occ.] Work part time at Kalispell Grand Hotel and part time for an attorney.; [memb.] Pursuing membership with Trinity Lutheran Church; [oth. writ.] I have several other poems that I am going to see about publishing. This is my 1st publication.; [pers.] My poems reflect personal experiences of myself and those around me.; [a.] Kalispell, MT

ANDREWS, NICHOLE
[b.] July 10, 1981, Pittsburgh, PA; [p.] Nick and Debbie Andrew; [ed.] Still in High School—10th

grade; [pers.] I have an ongoing journal of poems that I have been writing for many years.; [a.] Lighthouse Pt., FL.

ANGELOPOULOS, STAVROULA
[b.] December 5, 1981; Silver Spring, MD; [p.] George and Mary Angelopoulos; [ed.] Riverdale Baptist School (not yet finished- 9th Grade year of graduation- 2000) This coming school year - 10th grade; [hon.] Creative writing award for the state of Maryland in 1993, Student Gov't. Award and many more. I am a member of the International Thespian Society; [oth.writ.] First poem I've had. I write songs, but nothing has been fully published before; [pers.] I write about what I believe and what I know is true. If this poem touches just one person my job is complete. This poem is in loving memory of my father; [a.] Lanham, MD.

ARGENT, JANET L.
[pen.] Janet; [b.] April 26, 1940, Glenndale, MD; [p.] Jesse and Martha Brady; [m.] Leonard A. Argent, January 22, 1960; [ch.] Lorrie Ann Shymansky; [ed.] Bladensburg High School; [occ.] Secretary, Davidsonville Elementary School; [memb.] Davidsonville Methodist Church; [oth. writ.] None published. "There is a New Guitar in The Heavenly Choir," "My Horse Taybor," "Brady's Hands" and "Midnight"; [pers.] What you are is God's gift to you. What you become is your gift to God.; [a.] Davidsonville, MD

ARGYROS, CHRIS
[pen.] Chris Argyros; [b.] July 21, 1956, Greece; [p.] Rev. John and Helen Argyros; [ch.] David and Sean; [ed.] Newfield HS. 12 grade-Graduate; [occ.] Bagel Lovers, Bagel Chalet Owner-Operator; [oth. writ.] The Other Is You, Search By Candlelight, Matter Of Compromise, I Need To Be Loved.; [pers.] Blood flows throw our hearts, thoughts flow throw our minds. The very essence of what we are is, "poetry."; [a.] Oakdale, NY

ATCHISON, STEFANI
[pen.] S; [b.] September 11, 1971; Orlando, FL; [p.] Gale and Steve Atchison; [occ.] Retail Office Clerk, Orlando, FL; [a.] Orlando, FL.

AUGUSTINE, REBECCA H.
[b.] November 1, 1950, Birmingham, AL; [p.] Ormond and Jean Howard; [m.] Divorced; [ch.] Elizabeth; [ed.] Newbury College, Boston, MA, Heald Business College, San Francisco, CA, Simpson College, San Francisco, CA; [occ.] Word Processor; [memb.] St. Luke's Episcopal Church; [oth. writ.] Several poems published as an elementary school student in Palo Alto Times, Palo Alto, CA; [pers.] I believe that everyone's life counts, that one's actions for good or bad have an influence on others. John Donne, my favorite poet, said it best, "No man is an island."; [a.] Birmingham, AL

AULT, DANIEL
[pen.] "Senior"; [b.] June 10, 1981, Woodbury, NJ; [p.] James and Brenda Ault; [ed.] Bingham Elementary School, Runn., NJ, Mary F. Vole Middle School, Runn., NJ, Highland Regional High School, Blackwood, NJ; [occ.] Graphic Arts Printer; [a.] Runnemede, NJ

AURAND, RHONDA J.
[pen.] Rhonda J. Aurand; [b.] December 4, 1977; [p.] Susan M. And Jeffrey H. Aurand; [ed.] Churchville Chili High School Monroe Community College; [oth.writ.] Sins, (others not published); [pers.] To be aware within yourself is the most important quest you will ever achieve; [a.] Maggie Valley, NC

AYALA, HELEN E.
[b.] January 23, 1959; LA; [p.] Jose Davila, Armida Davila; [m.] David; June 12, 1982; [ch.] Dylah and Damien Ayala; [ed.] B.A. in Business Administration, Whittier College, Whittier High School; [occ.] Homemaker; [hon.] Graduated with honor Whittier College; [pers.] I'd like to help people embrace beauty and truth. Thank you mom and dad, David, Robert Frost and my wonderful teachers Dr. Gregory Whirol, Carole Fritz, Mrs. Miguel, and Mrs. Groves, And my beloved Family; [a.] Carlsbad, CA.

BACON, MONICA C. MELVILLE
[pen.] Carmelita Melville; [p.] Melville, Lloyd and Muriel; [m.] Bacon, Wayne I; [ch.] Elwyn, Gary, Alexis, Jermaine, Tami; [ed.] Elementary school-Guyana, S.A., high school-Guyana, S.A., university and college-Guyana, S.A., Essex City College-Nwk., NJ, Rutgers University-Nwk., NJ; [occ.] Judicial Investigator/Social Case Worker (CSW); [memb.] Nat. Assoc. for Business and Prof. Women, Mt Baptist Church—Miss Society., Nat. Notary Assoc., Community Literacy Coordinator, Family Crises/Mentor Assoc.; [hon.] Outstanding Community Leadership Award. Dean's List U. of Guyana, Dean's List Essex City College and Rutgers University, Nwk., NJ; [oth.writ.] Several unpublished poems. Poems published in church's bulletin/magazines; [pers.] I strive to inspire, uplift, encourage and to touch lives everywhere through my writings.; [a.] East Orange, NJ.

BAILEY, ALMA
[b.] November 12, 1927; Wash. County; [p.] Byrolacy Elizabeth Lacy; [m.] Rev. James Balley; December 10, 1994; [ch.] Six; [ed.] 11th grade; [occ.] Retired; [memb.] Mainst M.B.C.; [hon.] I won an award for most grandchildren, won Certificate for Outstanding Worker in Lincoln District, won Coffee Maker, won Sewing Machine; [oth.writ.] 1 poem to the National Library of Poetry; [a.] Lyons, TX

BAILEY, DEREK
[b.] May 22, 1977; U.S.A.; [p.] Laura and Thomas Bailey; [hon.] Presedential Academic Achievement Award; [oth.writ.] Watch out, Lost, Missing, Crossing The Barrier, Emptiness For One Who Can't Be Seen, and many more...; [pers.] A day spent in Boredom is a day wasted; [a.] Irvine, CA

BAKER, ANNA
[pen.] Anna Baker; [b.] October 7, 1983; Melbourne, FL; [p.] Karla Baker; [ed.] 7th grade; [occ.] Student; [hon.] 3rd place in softball, 2nd place in Science Award in 6th grade. Art Awards. 7th Art Award for Jr. Art in Florida's Today newspaper; [a.] Fortpierra, FL

BAKER, JUDITH
[pen.] Judi Beard; [b.] October 30, 1955, Augusta, GA; [p.] Glenn and Mattie Beard; [ed.] 1978 - RN Associate Degree, 1988 - Bachelor of Science in Nsq. - USC-AIKEN, 1992 - Masters of Science in Nsq. Administration, Medical College of GA; [occ.] Nurse Principal - Ash Unit and Nurse Administrator - GA Regional Hosp. at Aug.; [memb.] Dept. Human Resources Leadership Program 1991; [hon.] Who's Who in the South and Southwest - 1997; [oth. writ.] Poems (2): (1) Faith Speaks, (2) The Garden - Answered Prayers published in Singles Outreach Deliverance Ministry Newsletter.; [pers.] The blessing is my life, the gift is living it bestowing love, the opportunity is to receive love with grace.; [a.] Augusta, GA

BALES, CATIE
[pen.] Catie Bales; [b.] January 7, 1983; NY City; [p.] Suzanne and Carter Bales; [ed.] I currently attend Green Vale School; [a.] Oyster Bay, NY.

BALZ, TIMOTHY A.
[b.] July 16, 1964; Freeport, IL; [p.] Tom and Carol Balz; [m.] Candy Balz; August 18, 1990; [ch.] Jeffrey and Megan Balz; [ed.] Ralston High; [occ.] Dispatch Supervisor for Ag Processing Inc; [memb.] Vice-President of Prairie Point Homeowners Asso.; [oth.writ.] This is my first; [a.] Omaha, NE.

BANDELOW, WALTER F.
[b.] January 2, 1913; Cleveland, OH; [p.] Walter and Irene; [m.] Christine Dean Colvard; June 19, 1943; [ch.] Peter Todd, Thomas Dean, Richard Walter and Christine Irene; [ed.] Walter Bandelow-Cathedral Latin High, Christine-Cleveland Heights High, Peter-Northwestern Univ. Thomas-Cleve. Sch. Of Electronics, Richard-Bowling Green State Univ. (ch) Christine Bowling Green State Univ.; [occ.] Retired; [memb.] Saint Francis Of Assisi Catholic Church; [hon.] Art Directors Clubs of: New York, Chicago and Cleveland for years 1950 through '88 and Santa Barbara Photo Forum; [oth.writ.] Family "Internal Journal" Monthly since 1972. Specialized Greeting Cards and Honorariums with verse, hand-lettering and art. Over 600 musical composition with lyrics; [a.] Mayfield Heights, OH.

BARNER, TYRONE
[b.] April 28, 1969, East Orange, NJ; [p.] Yvonne and Robert Barner; [m.] Shanette Thompson-Barner, October 15, 1994; [ed.] East Orange High School, Deury Technical Institute; [oth. writ.] Writings appear on cards for family and friends during holidays and special occasions.; [pers.] I love writing and reading because it is communication in its truest form. It also lets your imagination run free.; [a.] East Orange, NJ

BARRALE CATANZARO, BARBARA P.
[b.] October 19, 1964; Passaic, NJ; [p.] Robert and Patricia Barrale; [m.] Jim Catanzaro; August 28, 1988; [ch.] Michael James, Robert Patrick; [ed.] Garfield High School, Berdan Institute, Felician College; [occ.] Homemaker/adaptive parent; [hon.] Editor's choice award for outstanding Achievement in Poetry by the National Library of Poetry 1995," The other Mother; [oth.writ.] "The other Mother" published in "A Sea Of Treasures" Anthology; [pers.] My writing is influenced by my two adopted sons, who are multi-racial. I am proud to call us a family; [a.] Highland Lakes, NJ.

BARSCH, GAYLA LYNN
[b.] March 19, 1969; Columbus, OH; [p.] Don and Revel Archey; [m.] Jeff Barsch; [ch.] Jairica Archey; [ed.] BA in Psychology, enrolled in Master Level Classes, but undecided about next degree will earn; [occ.] Student; [hon.] Dean's list; [oth.writ.] I write a lot, but keep my poem ("Although" only poem I've written) and stories private; [pers.] Enjoy life; [a.] Delaware, OH.

BATCHELOR, HEATHER
[b.] May 3, 1971, Cookeville, TN; [m.] Mike Batchelor, June 26, 1993; [ch.] Brett; [ed.] Cookeville High School, Tennessee Technology University, University of Alabama in Huntsville; [occ.] Entrepreneur; [memb.] Huntsville Community Chorus Assn.; [hon.] Dean's List; [a.] Madison, AL

BATES, DOUG
[b.] December 5, 1948, Covina, CA; [p.] James G. and Velma Bates; [m.] Debbie Bates, June 6, 1970; [ch.] Ann Celeste, Abby Faith, Natalie Christine; [ed.] Lawrence County High School - 1967, Tennessee Technological University - 1977 MS : Biology; [occ.] President, New Day Maintenance Service, Inc.; [memb.] The Body of Christ, American Heart Association, Vietnam Veterans of America; [hon.] From his wife and children are many. He's a wonderful husband and father, his wife Debbie Bates. He doesn't know I put this in, I also submitted the poem for him. He writes me poems all the time. I have a bag full.; [oth. writ.] Articles for Herald Citizen newspaper, short stories for Tenn. Tech, poems for local creative writers.; [pers.] I use my poetry to encourage, lift-up and challenge the reader to reflect on their blessings.; [a.] Cookeville, TN

BECKFORD, LAURENTZ D.
[b.] October 29, 1970, Lynwood, CA; [p.] Linden and Odester Beckford; [ed.] San Dimas High School, 1 1/2 years of Pasadena City College; [occ.] Temporary Work; [memb.] (1) International Society of Authors and Artists, (2) International Society of Poets; [hon.] The Amherts Society's Award of Merit - Dickinson Award Nominee, Sparrowgrass Poetry Forum's Editor's Preference Award of Excellence Nominee - Quill Books $300, Editor's Favorite Nominee, 1997 North American Open Poetry Contest (semi-finalist), Award of Poetic Excellence Nominee; [oth. writ.] Various poems published in anthologies by Sparrowgrass Poetry Forum, Quill Books, The Amherst Society, Creative Arts and Science Ent. and The National Library of Poetry.; [pers.] To my fellow earthlings, let's open our minds and hearts. Love one another and God will bless us all.; [a.] San Dimas, CA

BEDARD, ELLEN LARSON
[b.] November 22, 1941; New Haven, CT; [p.] Elizabeth Ann Larson; [m.] divorced; may 5, 1962; [ch.] 3; [ed.] High school (Branford, CT); [occ.] Retired from Yale University (Senior Administrative Assistant); [oth.writ.] I have written other poetry. I am currently writing my life story.; [pers.] My mother had a nervous breakdown and my father was an alcoholic. Eventually I was in the same situation as my mother. I wrote poems village common.; [a.] East Haven, CT

BEDFORD, KIMBERLY A.
[pen.] Kim Kimmel; [b.] December 18, 1962, Beaver Falls, PA; [p.] Donald and Patricia Kimmel; [a.] Spencerport, NY

BELL, MADELYN J.
[pen.] Josephine Bell; [b.] September 16, 1943, Chicago; [p.] Fannie Dorsey and Ernest Bell; [ch.] Raymond Bell; [ed.] Master Social Work, Jane Addams College of Social Work - University of Illinois at Chicago; [occ.] Consultant, Haymarket House Treatment Facility, Chicago; [oth. writ.] Debut - "Visitors Of The Heart." Currently writing a novel.; [pers.] I am interested in depicting the raw essence of human emotions. I have been greatly influenced by Zora Neal Hurston.; [a.] Chicago, IL

BENFIELD, ROGER M.
[b.] Julyb 18, 1955; Frankfort, Germany; [p.] Joe B. and Gesila K. Benfield; [ch.] Justin M. and Joe B.; [ed.] N.B. Forrest High; [occ.] Visual information Specialist; [pers.] Infinity is such a limited concept; [a.] Alexandria, VA

BENJAMIN, GOLDINE
[b.] January 7, 1970; St. Thomas, VI; [p.] Errol and Lorna Benjamin; [ed.] BA in English and Education; Graduated May 1995 from the University of the Virgin Islands; [oth.writ.] I have written several articles for the Virgin Islands Daily News as well as other poems that were published in school newspapers bulletins; [pers.] This poem is loving dedicated to Anthony Gibson who always keeps me inspired. "All thanks and praise to the one true God."; [a.] Orlando, FL.

BERGMAN, DOUGLAS RENDEL
[pen.] Douglas Rendel; [b.] January 31, 1950; San Francisco, CA; [p.] Jess and Marie Bergman; [ed.] Dr. Chiropractice, Palmer Chiropractic College, B.S. Brigham Young University; [occ.] Chiropractor; [memb.] Omicron NU; [hon.] Dean's List, Palmer Veteran's Association Honor Award, Letter of Commendation U.S.M.C.; [oth.writ.] Books in progress, Heart Strings, Heart to Heart, Pictorial/Verse of the North West (untitled); [pers.] Life shiens in the warmth of love. Our inner most self the thrives on love. My work reflects this philosophy they touch heart and soul, and are shared from my heart; [a.] Puyallup, WA.

BERNARD, PEARL
[b.] February 17, 1926; Jamaica, WI; [p.] Mr. and Mrs Vassel, (both deceased); [m.] Deceased; June 16, 1961; [ch.] 1 Boy and 1 Girl; [ed.] Senior Cambridge Grade I - Exam set by the professors of Cambridge University England; [occ.] Companion to an elderly lady; [pers.] I do not wish to have this done - P. Bernard; [a.] Forest Hills, NY.

BEVIS, ANN
[b.] July 15, 1934, Cincinnati, OH; [p.] Tom and Florence Heywood; [m.] Charles Bevis, September 16, 1952; [ch.] Jeffrey, Leslie Jane and John Bevis; [ed.] Attended Aropohoe Community College, Denver, CO, College of Mt. St. Joseph, Cincinnati, OH and Saddleback College, Musician, Viejo, CA; [occ.] Housewife; [memb.] Hyde Park Community United Methodist Church, Taylor High School Alumni Association, Goshen, Ohio Historical Society; [oth. writ.] Upper Room, Cincinnati Euquirer; [pers.] It makes me very happy to write. I enjoy reading the Bible daily and keeping a prayer journal. My favorite book is Pilgrim's Progress.; [a.] Cincinnati, OH

BHAKTA, MAYA
[b.] April 22, 1975; Toronto; [a.] Los Angeles, CA

BLAIES, JOAN
[b.] February 6, 1934; Green Bay, WI; [p.] Mr. and Mrs. Clifford Swanson; [m.] Donald; November 19, 1955; [ch.] Sarah-John; [ed.] St. Lukes Hospital School of Nursing-RN Saint Francis College-BS; [occ.] Director of Nursing for Administration-Retired; [memb.] Amnesty International-AARP-Women's Club-Board Member Innovations for Indenpendent Living; [pers.] I am able to express myself better in poetry-I use it for myself as a way to release-I have loved poetry all my life; [a.] Mukwohago, WI.

BLEDSOE, FREDA DAWN
[pen.] Krystal Raine; [b.] November 14, 1980; Morehead, KY; [p.] Linda Jessie and Rickey Bledsoe; [ed.] Currently Attending West Carter High School, Olive Hill, KY; [memb.] Bald Point Church of Jesus Christ, Chess Club; [hon.] Won 4th Place out of 155 Cakes during bake-off, State Wide. First poem published at the age of 11 years old. Student of the month 10-91 and 1-92. Math Award 1992.; [oth.writ.] Articles published in local

newspaper. Have also entered 2 other poems in other poetry contests.; [pers.] I would like to thank Larry McKenzie 1956-1997 and Garnett Anderson for their inspiration, friendship and for giving me the courage to go for the gold.; [a.] Grahn, KY.

BLISS, CATHY A.
[b.] December 30, 1959, Fort Ord, CA; [p.] Gustave and Gracie Bliss; [m.] Divorced; [ch.] Chad Kelly, Rachel Lee, Clinton, Gustave, Sarah Ann; [ed.] Mt. View High, Central Arizona College; [occ.] Registered Nurse at Valley Lutheran Hospital, Mesa, AZ; [pers.] "Just A Soldier" is the first of my poems written and the only one that I've sent in to be critized by professionals, and published, as I have only shared it with a few family members. Needless to say, I'm pleased with the feedback I received.; [a.] Apache Junction, AZ

BLOCKER, SNAKE
[pen.] David Jason Blocker; [b.] Ontario, CA; [p.] James Madison Blocker IV and Nancy Dala Bloker; [occ.] Writer, Marhal Artist, and Helth Club Operator/Owner; [oth.writ.] I have been published in: "The Art of Emotions", which consists of over 100 of my poems. I have also been published in "A Lasting Mirage."; [pers.] The deepest love is not just words but actions to match; [a.] Rolling Hills Estates; CA.

BLOSS, NATALIE L.
[b.] January 8, 1974; [p.] Pauline Makl; [ed.] Bachelor of Science in Community Health Education, Temple University - Philadelphia, PA, Northampton High School, PA; [occ.] Director of Mental Health Services, Mental Health Worker, Physician Liason; [hon.] Dean's List, Dean's Athletic Academic Merit List; [oth. writ.] Personal poetry collection, songwriting collection.; [pers.] There are no guarantees in life so . . . love unconditionally, love passionately, love endlessly, love eternally.; [a.] Narragansett, RI

BOOKOUT, JAY MICHAEL
[b.] May 17, 1974, Fort Walton Beach, FL; [p.] Pamela Gayle Bookout; [ed.] Dora High School, Samford University, McWhorter School of Pharmacy; [occ.] Pharmacist; [hon.] Dean's and President's List; [oth. writ.] "To My Blue-Eyed Angel" published in 1994, several other poems published locally.; [pers.] I am a little voice whispering in the ear of society. Whether or not they listen is up to them.; [a.] Birmingham, AL

BOSWELL, LISA R.
[b.] July 2, 1976, Salt Lake City, UT; [p.] Craig Boswell and Lina Boswell Alabbas; [ed.] Graduated from Jordan High; [occ.] Administrative Specialist for Salt Lake County; [hon.] Honored in College Prep Class for Literary Excellence and Writing Ability; [oth. writ.] Have been writing poetry and short stories for many years, but nothing published as yet. (Besides in school newspaper).; [pers.] I am known as a "deep person" and I express my thoughts on paper. My life experiences have influenced me to write the way I do.; [a.] West Jordan, UT

BOUSH, CHARLENE
[pen.] Willow, Dragonfire; [b.] November 22, 1969; Norfolk, VA; [p.] Lyndel Landes and Shanon Baston; [m.] Divorced; [ch.] Victoria and Wayne Woodard Jr; [ed.] B.E.D. some Commercial Art and Phsycology... Life's experiences, mine and others; [occ.] Artist (visionary) and Writer; [memb.] None at the present time; [hon.] Honorable Mention by Poetry Forum, for "Her Frozen Journey." National Vocational-Technical Honor

Society; [oth.writ.] "Through Your Tears Of Sorrow" in Down Peaceful Paths, by Quil Books. "The Onyx Consumation" in Edios Magazine; [pers.] "Where there is life, there is love. Where there is love, there is truth. Where there is truth, there is wisdom, where there is wisdom, where there is wisdom, there is light, where there is light, there is life; [a.] Bradenton, FL.

BOWEN, DORIS A.
[b.] November 27, 1956, Augusta County, VA; [p.] George Washington and Margaret Louise; [ed.] Fort Defiance High School; [occ.] Cook with a world-wide restaurant chain; [pers.] I strive to tell a story in my writing that will make the reader think and feel, hopefully something they will enjoy and want to remember.; [a.] Verona, VA

BOWERS, RITA J.
[b.] December 10, 1939, Taylor, MI; [p.] Julia and Paul Leigh; [m.] James R. Bowers, December 13, 1990; [ch.] Doris Wray, Brady Elmore and Nicole Bowers; [ed.] 12th grade, Taylor Center High; [occ.] Retired; [memb.] Member of Church of Christ; [oth. writ.] Other poems; [pers.] Children, nature and religious beliefs influence my poems, I also like to write of imaginary places and people.; [a.] Elkmont, AL

BOWLES, LYNDA J.
[pen.] L. J. Bowles, Lynn Bowless; [b.] November 21, 1951; Radford, VA; [p.] Frankm and Martha James; [m.] John R. Bowles; September 5, 1970; [ch.] Laurie Katina, Ginny Marie; [ed.] Dublin High School, Radford College, ECPI of Norfolk; [occ.] Account Manager; [memb.] Now, Romance Writers ;[oth.writ.] "Missipy Novel, "Miranda" romance mystery", "Nitwit romance novel, collection of poems all unpublished; [pers.] Live to the fullest each day, for tomorrow will bring a new set of challenge; [a.] Hiwassee, VA.

BOYKO, ALISA DAWN
[b.] December 1, 1965; Brooklyn; [p.] Harvey and Barbara Horowitz; [m.] Richard William Boyko; July 16, 1989; [ch.] Richard and Samantha; [ed.] Still attending college; [occ.] Electrical Contracting and Real Estate; [pers.] This poem was written about a place I went with my husband. It's dedicated to my departed mother whom I loved very much.; [a.] Pearl River, NY

BRADLEY, JACLYN
[b.] May 15, 1981, Detroit; [p.] Christine Bradley; [ed.] High School; [hon.] I am on the Honor Roll. My grade point average is 3.0. I have won one medal for oratorical speaking, the silver medal. And I won a bronze medal for Medical Math in HOSA, Health Occupations Students of America.; [a.] Detroit, MI

BRELSFORD, ROBERT
[pen.] Robert Ford, Robert Giudicci; [b.] September 15, 1976, Houston, TX; [p.] Tony and Bonnie Brelsford; [ed.] Rice University; [occ.] English Major at Rice University; [pers.] The beauty of the heart is that it scars, heals and pleasantly remembers those things that tear it limb from limb. Growing up, I think it's called. I'm currently at work on my first novel, and amidst the chaos, editing my first collection of poetry.; [a.] Houston, TX

BREST, PATRICIA ANNE
[pen.] Pat Pabst; [b.] July 24, 1938; Hermosa Bch., CA; [p.] Jerome and Florence McElroy; [m.] David Brest; June 20, 1987; [ch.] Gayle, Shelley, Fred; [ed.] High school drop-out, California State University, Dominguez Hills Magna Cum Laude,

Interdisciplinary Studies, B.A., CSUDH, M.A. English 1993; [occ.] Graduation Evaluator, SCUDH, currently on disability leave, Hepatitis-C; [memb.] Past member American Field Service, Cal. State, Dominguez Hills Alumni Assoc., Academy of American Poets; [hon.] National Honor Soc, Phi Kappa Phi, selected to read at the 1984 "Poetry Alive Festival" by the Intellectual Life Committee at CSUDH. (The professional readers were Ann Stanford, Barry Spacks, Garrett Hongo and Thom Gunn); [oth.writ] Had my poem "Special Delivery" published in "Menya"-1988, Journal of Literature and Art, Cal. State Univ., Dominguez Hills. 14 Short stories (submitted for 4, got rejects); [pers.] "Till There Was You." "God's Grandeur," by Gerard Manley Hopkins and "The Second Coming," by William Butler Yeats are my two favorite poems. Rough Beast or Dearest Freshness? I write in an attempt to reconcile.; [a.] San Pedro, CA

BREWER, JEFF
[pen.] J.L. Brewer; [b.] April 10, 1957; Ogden, UT; [p.] Joe Brewer, June Brewer; [m.] Teresa Brewer, June 29, 1979; [ch.] Derrick Tyler, Mitchell Hamesom, Maygen Louise, Liesa Marie, Kimberlee Brooke; [ed.] Roy High School; [occ.] Welder, Loren Cook Co. North Ogden, UT; [memb.] Church of Jesus Christ Of Latter Day Saints, Roy 14th Ward Sunday School Presidency; [hon.] Eagle Scout-Boy Scouts Of America; [oth.writ.] A collection of poems and song lyrics available for publication to interested parties; [pers.] Life is a Rollercoaster you have to have the downs to enjoy the ups; [a.] Roy, VT.

BRIDGES, DOROTHY L.
[occ.] Paralegal Specialist; [oth.writ.] A Book of Remembrance; [pers.] All of my writings testify and speak of a redeemed life; [a.] Fairfax, VA.

BRIGGS, JACQUELINE A.
[pen.] Jacqueline Briggs; [b.] December 23, 1970; Tucson, AZ; [p.] Lisa and Jack Briggs; [pers.] Expression is a chance to grow. I welcome the opportunity. Strongest influence: my Grandmother, Lupita Samaniego.; [a.] Tucson, AZ.

BROCK, LISA CAROL
[pen.] Lisa Carol Brock; [b.] June 19, 1969; Lawton, OK; [p.] Jo Carol Kovae, Fred Lee Brock Jr; [ed.] University of Kentucky, Social Work still going (I've just started back); [occ.] Housemenger fen, Metro Group Home Inc. Work with Teens; [pers.] This is the first time I've shown any of my writing this poem is from a book I'me writing about my life; [a.] Lexington, KY

BROWN, LINTON
[b.] September 7, 1966; Samaica; [p.] Gloria Knight; [m.] Novelette Clark; September 21, 1995; [ch.] Tueze Brown, Garfield Shortdridge; [ed.] Nortland High, Miami Dade Community College, Florida International University; [a.] Hollywood, FL

BROWN, PAMELA R.
[pen.] Pammy; [b.] November 14, 1967; Savannah, GA; [p.] Minnie L. Hall and Late Rev. Charles L. Hall; [m.] Stanley M. Brown; June 1, 1996; [ed.] Alfred Ely Beach High Georgia Southern University; [occ.] Customer Representative, Kinko's Copy Center; [memb.] NAACP; [hon.] Who's Who Among High School Students, Dean's List, Ebony Promises Model of the Year; [pers.] I dedicate this poem to my husband who inspired me to write it. Also in memory of my father who supported everything I did; [a.] Savannah, GA

BROWN, PAT COKER
[b.] June 25, 1953, South Carolina; [p.] Milton Coker and Elnora Coker; [m.] Billy Brown, September 1, 1972; [ed.] Graduate of Palmetto High School, Williamston, SC; [occ.] Assistant Manager, Books A Million, Greenville, SC; [oth. writ.] Newspaper column, Reflections The Journal, Williamston, SC, Pleasant Boundaries, The Upper Room.; [pers.] I believe that within everything there is God's light, and no matter how great the dark, the light will shine.; [a.] Pelzer, SC

BUCKWALTER, JENNIFER MAY
[b.] Pennsylvania; [p.] John and Connie Buckwalter; [ed.] Future plans: college, presently: grade 11 Emmaus Senior High, Emmaus, Penna.; [occ.] Full-time student, athlete; [oth. writ.] Several writings have appeared in the school's collection of writing called, "The Collage."; [pers.] I started writing a long time ago when I was bored, now every time I pick up a pen I write because it's fun: "you see the true me in every piece of my work."; [a.] Macungie, PA

BULLETT, AUDREY KATHRYN
[pen.] Kitty Hill; [b.] February 12, 1937, Chicago, IL; [p.] Louis A. Hill and Eva Reed Hill; [m.] Clark Ricardo Bullett Jr. (Deceased), September 18, 1965; [ch.] Iris J. Hill and Grandson, Stanley Aaron Hill; [ed.] B.S. Public Administration, Ferris State University, 1984, A.A. Science and Arts, Ferris State University, 1983; [occ.] Metaphysical Minister, Writer, Counselor, Consultant, Reiki Master, Aromatherapy Practitioner, Retired Public Administrator, Retired Volunteer Fire Fighter; [memb.] Founder, Dawn's Light Center, Inc., Minister, Uriel Temple of Spiritual Understanding, Inc., Deaconess, First Baptist Church of Idlewild, National Treasurer, Idlewild Lot Owners Association, Inc., life membership, Lake/Newaygo Branch NAACP; [hon.] "Woman of the Year," First Baptist Church of Idlewild, Certificate of Appreciation, Idlewild Lot Owners Association, Inc., Certificate of Recognition, Yates Township Police Department, Twenty Years Service Award, Yates Township Fire Department, Victor F. Spathell Leadership and Service Award, FSU, Robert F. Williams Memorial Scholarship of Merit, FSU; [oth. writ.] Author, three books, Come Colour My Rainbow, You, Me and God, Sweet Marjoram, Life's Reflections as Seen and Expressed, Columnist, Lake County Star, Editor/Publisher, Crystalline View, Newsletter; [pers.] God has truly blessed me. I have a testimony about the goodness and love of a kind and generous Creator/Father. I allow my life to be directed by God and I am successful in all that I do.; [a.] Idlewild, MI

BUNCH, GAIL M.
[pen.] Abbie Gayle; [b.] September 4, 1941, Monroe County, MI; [p.] Henry and Mary (Lezotte) Laura; [m.] James W. Bunch, September 4, 1982; [ch.] "4 Bred - 2 Borrowed"; [ed.] St. Mary's Elementary School - Rockwood MI, Airport High School, Carleton, MI; [hon.] Elder of 9 siblings; [oth. writ.] Many poems and short stories, commentaries, etc. "Horses in the Trees," her first poem released, first published.; [pers.] Life has been a "trip" for me, and poetry has been a series of landing strips.; [a.] Sand Lake Heights, National City, MI

BURCHAM, MARGARET DICKINSON
[b.] June 28, 1923, Virginia; [p.] Maurice L. and Maggie Fuller Dickinson; [m.] C. R. Burcham Sr., August 9, 1969; [ch.] Richard L. McCluney Jr.; [ed.] E.C. Class H.S., Lynchburg, Lynchburg College, William and Mary, University of Virginia;

[occ.] Retired H.S. Teacher of English, Dramatics, Public Speaking, the Humanities; [memb.] American Assoc. of Univ. Women, Woman's and Garden Clubs, Dacend at Art Museum, Speech and Drama Assoc.; [hon.] Alpha Psi Omega for Dramatics, Sigma Tau Delta for English, Selected Outstanding H.S. Actress in Virginia, senior year in H.S.; [oth. writ.] Course of study for Dramatics in Virginia H.S. Social Column for newspaper. Research papers. More poetry.; [pers.] Reading/memorizing poetry has become a habit - a pleasure - a discipline in my life.; [a.] Richmond, VA

BURFORD, MARY
[ed.] Attended Emerson College of Self Expression, U.S.C. and Orange Coast College; [memb.] American Institute of Fine Arts; [hon.] Prize Winner in Los Angeles and County Poetry Contest of all Women's Clubs. National Gold Silver and Bronze Winner in Ballroom Dancing, a joyous hobby. I also enjoy gardening, and I am a compulsive reader.; [oth. writ.] I have had several poems published.; [pers.] I am inspired by the beauty in nature and personal observation.; [a.] Santa Barbara, CA

BURGESS, DONNIE
[b.] July 12, 1974; Roseburg, OR; [p.] Laurel Terill and John Burgess; [m.] Danielle Bandoni; [occ.] Butcher in local grocery store; [oth. wirt.] All other work is unpublished; [pers.] The most valuable lesson I ever learned is to thank all who stand in your way. Hardship and adversity bring creativity; that creativity brings solace and joy.; [a.] Florence, AZ

BURGESS, KRISTA LEIGH
[b.] March 7, 1980; Corpus Christi, TX; [p.] Anthony Frank Burgess, Kathryn Sellers; [ed.] I am currently a Junoir at H.M. King high School in Kingsville, TX. I have attended Kingsville public shools for most of my schooling; [occ.] Waitress at Sirloin Stockade; [memb.] Band in Junior High Candystriper for 2 years in High School, Basketball in Eight grade, Volleyball in eleventh grade; [hon.] Poetry award in 8th grade, perfect attendance and honor roll awards; [oth.writ.] I have written a full book of poetry including a few narratives and short stories; [pers.] Poetry to me is a very personal and emotional way of expressing your lifestyle and feelings. I hope that poetry will continue to grow and be appreciated by many to come; [a.] Kingsville, TX

BURKE, RUBY
[b.] August 30, 1914, Kanabee Co, MN; [p.] Joseph W. and Gladys Gruver; [m.] Goodwin E. Burke, June 20, 1934; [ch.] Bruce E., Wallace E., James M., Joseph A., Gerald G., Eugene A.; [ed.] One year college; [occ.] Homemaker; [memb.] Northwest Baptist Church, Denver, American Quilters Society; [a.] Arvada, CO

BURROWS, ELIZABETH MCDONALD
[b.] January 30, 1930; Portland, OR; [p.] Lord John Mac Donald and Gilbert du Motier; [ed.] Bachelor of Religious Education, Christian College of Universal Peace and Doctor of Divinity, Christian College of Universal Peace, 5 years of intensive study under the tutelage of Professor Edmond Bordeaux Szekely; [occ.] World traveller and international lecturer, author; [memb.] International Speakers Platform; [hon.] A recipient of the 1988 ABI Commemorative Medal of Honor, listed in Who's Who in Religion, Who's Who in Education, Who's Who in the West, Who's Who in the World, Who's Who in American Women, and Who's Who in America, published poet America Poetry Anthology, 1989, Publisher's Choice of Poets of the New Era, 1990, Distin-

guished Poets of America 1993, Treasured Poems of America, Sparrowgrass Publishing, and recipient of Cader Publishing's President's Award for Literary Excellence; [oth.writ.] Harp of Destiny, Odyssey of the Apocalypse, The Gospel of Peace of Jesus Christ According to John; [pers.] The inevitable destiny of our planet is peace. Therefore, the ability of mankind to work toward this common goal is extremely important. In achieving peace, hatred, malice, war, pain and sorrow shall pass away as shadows of darkness. Then, and only then, will the truly great age of mankind come into expression.; [a.] Seattle, WA

BURTON, RUTH A.
[b.] May 24, 1959, Fort Worth, TX; [occ.] Cosmetologist, founder My Kids, School Kids, Inc.; [memb.] Hair-America, National Cosmetology Association; [hon.] Commissions Business Recognition Award, Jefferson Award and over a hundred state, national and international hair and make-up awards; [pers.] I wrote this true poem from my heavy heart, with tears falling. God spoke and I listened.; [a.] Windermere, FL

BUSTOS JR., JOSE A.
[b.] March 3, 1947; Billings, MT; [m.] Marzene V. September 22, 1984; [ch.] Farythda Marzene; Renaldo Montigieu; [ed.] Military College USAF; Mt University; [occ.] Retired; [hon.] J.C. Penney Golden Rule; Music requested by churches; [oth.writ.] Easy Listening Lyrics, Melodies; Gospel; Children Songs. Would like to collaborate; [pers.] Inspired by Our Lord Jesus Christ. Lennon, McCartney, Harrison "What Will You Do?" Are lyrics to what is considered a moving, beautiful melodied song. Music composition my hobby, my work lyrical, so all is timed for music; [a.] Billings, MT

BUTERA, MARIANNE LESTER
[b.] February 5, 1931; Santa Barbara, CA; [p.] Herbert S. Lester, Elizabeth Sherman; [m.] William L. Stafford; December 12, 1950; [ch.] Jennifer, Barbara L. Stafford; [ed.] 3 years of College - UCSB (University of Cal. Santa Barbara) 1947-50; [occ.] Retired as machine bookkeeper in Beverly Hills, California in 1959; [memb.] President "One Dozen Roses"club when freshman at John Muir Junior High attended Katherine Branson School during freshman high in Ross, California...then Soph. and Junior High at Laguna Blanca before graduating at Santa Barbara High - 1st prize for poem in U.S. given in Hollywood in 1945; [oth.writ.] "Footprints in the Wind," "San Miguel Island and Other Poems";[pers.] was labelled Princess of San Miguel" (along with her sister Betsy) by the media throughout the '20's (her parents being labelled the "King and Queen of the Island at the time); [a.] Santa Barbara, CA

BUTLER, ASHLEY HART
[b.] October 22, 1985, Suffolk, VA; [p.] Jay and Debbie Butler; [ed.] 5th Grade, Nansemond-Suffolk Academy; [occ.] Student; [memb.] (1) 9th year dancing, (2) 5th year piano, (3) church choir, (4) rides horses, (5) 5th year at Camp Mont Shenandoah, (6) Happy Club (operation smile); [hon.] Forensics Team, Poetry Piano Guild, horse show ribbons; [oth. writ.] I write poems and stories almost every day. I once wrote the song about a butterfly that I played in my piano recital.; [pers.] I enjoy writing about my feelings, my experiences and new things I learn.; [a.] Suffolk, VA

BUTLER, DOROTHY
[b.] January 12, 1950; Hopkinsville, KY; [p.] Rosie Nell White, Elmo White; [m.] Malcolm Butler; July 9, 1968; [ch.] Cassandra - Malcolm; [ed.] High School, Christina County High; [occ.]

Lab Tech. American Contact Lens; [memb.] Greater Gethse Mane, Baptist Church, Gospell Chorus, Big Sisters of American; [oth.writ.] Several other poems; [pers.] Poem was dedicated to memory of mother.

BUTLER, KAYLA
[b.] October 17, 1982, Lima, OH; [p.] Sondra Humes; [pers.] All the poems I write come straight from the heart, for writing is my way of expressing pain, both emotional and physical. Every poem I have written has been dedicated to the victims of abuse, eating disorders, alcoholism and drug addiction.; [a.] Tucson, AZ

BUYS, JARRETT
[ed.] Graduate of Hubbard College of Administration. Data Series E valuator; [occ.] Founder and President of Safeguard Earth's Environment Foundation, 1239 S. Greenwood Ave. Suite 301, Clearwater Fl. 34616; [memb.] UCS member; [hon.] Built a castle in England; [oth.writ.] Articles published on environmental matters and his poetry published in numerous poetry anthologies and magazines.; [pers.] An educational environmental research entity devoted to prioritization of global environmental problems and mankind as stewards of Earth's ecosystem.

BYBEE, BEN
[pen.] Kolob; [b.] June 5, 1969; Earth; [p.] Mom and Dad; [occ.] Warehouse; [oth.writ.] At present, I am working on number 4 in a series of 5 volumes of personal poetry which I hope to have published someday; [pers.] The beauty of my poetry is that you can look at it and interpenate it any way you want and you'll never really know whether you're right or wrong. But it doesn't really matter. Or does it; [a.] Loma Linda, CA

BYUN, MICHAEL I.
[pen.] Ha-Jung; [b.] January 10, 1941, South Korea; [p.] Houng G. Byun and Soo Boo Lee; [m.] Soon Rye Byun, December 6, 1970; [ch.] Jin Sang Byun, Elizabeth Byun, Theresa Byun, Joon Sang Byun; [ed.] University graduate, business degree; [occ.] Restaurant Owner; [memb.] International Society of Poets; [hon.] 1) International Poet, 2) International Poetry Hall of Fame, 3) International Poet of Merit Award, 4) Recollections of Yesterday (Reflections), 5) A Lasting Mirage (Let The Spring Winds Blow), 6) The Other Side of Midnight (My Lady); [oth. writ.] 1) Reflections, 2) Let The Spring Winds Blow, 3) My Lady; [pers.] I love poetry. When I write poetry, the problems of the world disappear. I pray to God to help this world. I will always write poems.; [a.] Fredericksburg, VA

CALDERON, CANDIDA E.
[pen.] Candy Calderon; [b.] July 26, 1946, Puerto Rico; [p.] Monserrate and Blanca Negron; [ch.] Manuel, Jubetsy, Lisa and Denise; [ed.] High school diploma; [occ.] Store Clerk - Family Dollar Stores; [memb.] Hispanic Christian Church, "Disciples of Christ" —Church Elder/and Committee Member; [hon.] Certificate for course on Mental Hygiene/Way-to-go Award from Parkview Hosp. in Colorado for Volunteer Work. Award - from "Four Seasons Nursing" Center for volunteer work; [oth. writ.] Rec. certificate awards, "From Liberty's View" written 7/7/86, written 11/7/85 "War," written 3/27/88 "Farm Aid," published 11/ 93 "A Silent Prayer" and many more.; [pers.] In our troubled times, I try, in my writings to bring out a soft, sweet awareness of God's love.; [a.] Orlando, FL

CALIFANO, LISA MARIE
[b.] August 5, 1981; Ft. Lauderdale; [p.] Thomas and Deborah Califano; [ed;] Currently A high school Junior at Coral Springs High Schol and honor student in a Quantum Leap program and taking classes in high school, with college credits; [memb.] National Honor Society, Student Council Representative, Save Whats left Club , Adopt A Highway Club; [hon.] Principal's Honor Roll, Lettered in Varsity Swimmings, 100 plus service hours to the community; [a.] Coral Springs, FL

CAMPBELL, LINDSAY GENEVIEVE
[b.] July 24, 1980; N. Myrtle Beach, SC; [p.] Craig and Cindi Campbell; [ed.] North Myrtle Beach Primary on through high school; [pers.] The particular poem "Sadaam Hussein" written in this book, was written when I was 10 years old. My poetry is written about events that have happened in my life. I express my feelings, as well as myself through poetry.; [a.] Little River, SC

CARDONA, DENNISE S.
[b.] September 20, 1969, Rhode Island; [p.] Frederick and Paulette Martin; [m.] Hector J. Cardona, Manville Rhode Island, December 3, 1994; [ed.] A.A. Liberal Arts, Community College of RI, B.A. Public and Professional Communications from Rhode Island College; [occ.] Currently conducting a documentary in South America on Intercultural Communication Patterns; [hon.] Dean's List, Phi Theta Kappa; [oth. writ.] Co-editor of Community Expressions Magazine in 1994 for CCRI.; [pers.] I strive to learn as much about the world as I can and share this knowledge with those around me.; [a.] Lincoln, RI

CAROLAN, PATTY L.
[b.] August 28, 1956, Racine, WI; [p.] Raymond and Mary Carolan; [ch.] Benjamin - 12 and Sarah - 4; [ed.] BA in General Business from University of Wisconsin - Whitewater. Currently pursuing Dietary Degree at Sinclair Community College; [occ.] Mom/Student; [memb.] I have held a variety of volunteer positions at church, my children's school and in the local community of Dayton.; [hon.] Graduated Cum Laude at University of Wisconsin - Whitewater. Attained "Dean's List" status at Sinclair Community College; [pers.] Composing poetry is a favorite pastime of mine. I enjoy celebrating the beauty of my children and nature through this medium. Thank you for the opportunity to share this talent with you!; [a.] Dayton, OH

CARPENTER, JOANNE
[pen.] Joanna Todd; [b.] February 3, 1945, Ohio; [ch.] Three; [ed.] BS in Education from Bowling Green State University, Cambridge University, England; [occ.] Writer, Consultant; [memb.] Sigma Tau Delta; [oth. writ.] Positive notes, newsletters.

CARR, EMILY GROVE
[b.] July 5, 1987; Pittsburg, PA; [p.] Amy Carr, Doug Carr; [ed.] Currently in 4th Grade at Sinclair Elementary School, Manassas, VA; [occ.] Student; [hon.] Honor Roll Student; [oth.writ.] Several short stories for school; [pers.] I love the outdoors and nature. I especially love the ocean, to me it is a reflection of God's love for mankind.; [a.] Manassas, VA

CARRARA, DONNA J.
[pen.] Donna J. Scanlon; [b.] September 6, 1955, Saint Louis, MO; [p.] John J. Scanlon, Melba J. Scanlon; [m.] Peter K. Carrara Jr., June 18, 1982; [ch.] Jamie Rene, Matthew Ryan; [ed.] Parkway North Sr. High, University of Missouri—Columbia; [pers.] To my children, Jamie and Matthew,

I pray you'll always sense the infinite love I have for both of you.; [a.] Ballwin, MO

CASE, E. R.
[pen.] I M Unon; [b.] November 3, 1921, Long Beach, CA; [p.] Dolph, Edith; [m.] Verna Tot (Deceased), August 9, 1941; [ch.] Sandra, Tom; [ed.] Partial college, Kent State University, Ohio; [occ.] Retired (PAC Bell); [memb.] International Society of Poets, The International Poetry Hall of Fame; [oth. writ.] Eight Seconds, Pilot Error, Ashes To Ashes, God Was My Stand-In, I'm A Backyard Poet, Reflection, Ripples On The Pond of Life, A New Batch Of Spring, and many more; [pers.] Do what you enjoy, and enjoy what you do. Just be sure that it doesn't hurt anyone.; [a.] Warner Springs, CA

CAUDLE, THOMAS
[b.] January 16, 1934; Wadesboro, NC; [p.] Deceased; [ch.] Julie and Kristin Caudle; [ed.] BBA Wake Forest, MBA Wharton School of Finance and Commerce, U of PA [occ.] Commercial real estate broker; [memb.] DeKalb Board of Realtors; [hon.] President 1992 DeKalb Board of Realtors, Distinguished Member Int'l Society of Peots; [oth.writ.] Several real estate related articles in local real estate periodicals; [pers.] This is my 6th poem published by Nat'l Library of Poetry, and 4 have been chosen for Sounds of Poetry. I love to write about inspirational poetry and the inner beauty of man in his quest for God. I study the bible, Koran, and mystics Rumi, Kabier. Greatest influence is Meher Baba; [a.] Stone Mountain, GA

CHAPPELL, MORGAN
[b.] November 22, 1975, Summertown, TN; [p.] Gerrie Sue and Clifford Chappell; [ed.] Two years Diablo Valley College, currently at the University of Georgia in Athens; [occ.] Student/Reserve Fire Fighter; [memb.] Football at the University of Georgia, Red Shirt in Fall 1996 season.; [hon.] Wall of Fame at College Park High School in Pleasant Hill, CA, All League in Football, All Tyler Team two years in a row, League Champion in wrestling, Golden Foot in track.; [oth. writ.] "The Poor Young Junkie"; [a.] Pleasant Hill, CA

CHARLEY, MATIPA
[b.] January 22, 1984; Omak, Washington; [p.] William M. Charley Sr, Shirley Charley; [ed.] 7th grade Junior High; [hon.] Honor Roll, Basketball Awards, and in writing; [oth.writ.] Short stories for the school, and the young writers conference; [pers.] Well, I've always liked poetry. But in 5th grade one my teachers (Mr. Shell) encouraged me, and often I write; such things as poems. And also I would like to thank Mrs. Carlson too. And often I write of personal feelings found people I know; [a.] Okanogan, WA

CHARLEY, MATIPA
[b.] January 22, 1984; Omak, WA; [p.] William M. Charley Sr,Shirley L. Charley; [ed.] 7th Grade/Junior High S. Please Include on publishing the poem. Okanogan Junior/Senior High. Home of the "Bulldogs."; [hon.] Honor Roll, Basketball Award, Softball Awards and Writing Awards; [oth.writ.] Short Stories for the School; [pers.] Mostly the poems I write reflect my personal feelings toward certain people, or something I do at school to keep myself out of trouble. Like referals, because I like to talk alot; [a.] Okanogan, WA

CHASE, ALICE
[b.] Irvington, NJ; [p.] D. and Anna Smolyn; [m.] David M. Chase, January 21, 1948; [ch.] Two; [ed.] 2 yrs. college - studied with various Art Teachers, Dan Stone, John Rogers, Paul Wood,

John A. Grado; [occ.] Artist - working in watercolor and oils; [memb.] Art League of Nassau County, Guild Hall of East Hampton, Southampton Museum, Salmagundi Club, Independent Art League, National Art League, etc.; [hon.] 1st Prize Nat'l Art League, Award of Merit - CW Post College, 1st Prize Art League of Nassau County, Award of Merit - Independent Art League, Painting Chosen for East Hampton Town Hall, 1st Prize Floral Park Art League, etc.; [oth. writ.] "Summer Reveries," "My Love for Thee" and Untitled; [pers.] Everyone should try to express themselves whether it be by painting, writing poetry or even baking exceptional dishes. Use your God-given talents.; [a.] New Hyde Park, NY

CHENG, JENNIFER
[b.] October 7, 1981, Voorhees, NJ; [p.] Raymond Cheng and Kuntala Cheng; [ed.] 10th Grade in Boston University Academy, Study piano with Anthony di Bonaventura, internationally acclaimed master teacher and pianist, study music in New England Conservatory Extension Division; [occ.] Student; [memb.] Community worker (Tutor) for The Boston Public Schools, New England Conservatory Children's Chorus, high school news team; [hon.] MA State winner of Music Teachers National Association High School Piano Performance Competition, won second in the International Young Artist Piano Competition held in Washington, D.C., placed First in the Massachusetts Music Teachers Association State-wide Competition, First in the Manchester Young Artist Competition, Best Musician Award in Toronto Music Showcase Festival, Ranatra Fusca Creativity Award for composing the music and lyrics for her school team's performance in the Odyssey of the Mind Statewide competition, Honor Student in Boston University Academy; [oth. writ.] Several poems and short stories published in school magazines.; [pers.] I believe that literature, music and other arts, are necessary foods for the soul and mind so choose your spread wisely and have a feast.; [a.] Brookline, MA

CHLEBANOWSKI SR, MATT
[b.] March 15, 1936, Chicago, IL; [p.] Stanley and Clara Chlebanowski; [m.] Barbara Rogers, August 13, 1960; [ch.] Kenneth, Marlene, Matt Jr. Thomas; [ed.] St Joseph Catholic Elementary Sch., Chicago Farragut High, Chgo, IL Hadley School for the blind, Winnetka, IL; [oth. writ.] I see one manager farewell to our friend love they neighbor greetings from the grandparents I thank you Lord; [pers.] Interested in writing poetry from High School. Words of encouragement, from family and friends, to express my poetic talent; [a.] Downers Grove, IL

CLARK, SARA BETH
[b.] November 24, 1981, Louisville; [p.] Sharon and George D. Clark; [ed.] Attending high school; [occ.] Student; [memb.] Beta Club, JROTC, Concert Choir; [hon.] JROTC cheerleading trophies - blue ribbons for drawings, All-County Ribbon for flower arrangements; [pers.] I believe poetry is a way of expressing one's inner feelings and emotions.; [a.] Lebanon Junction, KY

CLARKE, MELICENT BRANCH
[b.] June 3, 1967, Tuscaloosa, AL; [p.] Millie English and Arthur Ivory; [m.] Derek Clarke, October 22, 1997; [ed.] University of Toledo and the Medical College of Ohio; [occ.] Physical Therapist; [memb.] APTA (American Physical Therapy Association); [hon.] It is truly an honor to have my writing recognized and published to other talented writers; [pers.] We all have talents or gifts given to us by God and the universe. It is our challenge to recognize what was given, share it and

watch it multiply. Believe in your gifts.; [a.] Dayton, OH

COCHRAN, GEORGIA ANNABELLE
[pen.] Annabelle Cochran; [b.] January 17, 1945, Swain County, NC; [p.] Inez Cochran; [ed.] Western Carolina University; [occ.] Retired Teacher—Elementary School; [hon.] A Certificate of Special Achievement from United States of the Interior-Bureau of Indian Affairs. For recognition of service performed in a manner exceeding the requirements of the teaching position.; [oth. writ.] Poems published in local newspaper and church bulletin.; [pers.] I am greatly influenced by the writings of Helen S. Rice. I am richly inspired by God and nature. I strive to reflect my thankfulness to God and mankind.; [a.] Bryson City, NC

COGDELL, DAISY
[b.] Kinston, NC; [p.] Dan and Daisy Cogdell; [ch.] Steven; [occ.] Staff Associate, Bell Atlantic Yellow Pages; [a.] Philadelphia, PA

COHEN, NAOMI
[b.] October 30, 1938, Jerusalem, Israel; [p.] Victor and Malka Shaer; [m.] Barnet Cohen; [ch.] Shira (Art Teacher), Didi (Clinical Social Worker), Jordan (an ER Physician); [ed.] M.A. English with Graduate Dean's List Honors, B.A. Summa Cum Laude; [occ.] Semi-retired as a Commercial Real Estate Broker; [hon.] Dean's List Honors, Summa Cum Laude, professional awards as a Real Estate Broker; [oth. writ.] Unpublished (unsubmitted poems).; [pers.] I believe in living a life that will strive to perfect the world. I believe in loving and being loved.; [a.] Huntington Beach, CA

COLONTONIO, NICHOLAS J.
[pen.] Nicholas J. Colontonio or N.J.C.; [b.] November 15, 1972, New York; [p.] Gerald and Jean Colontonio; [ed.] Some college, Iona; [occ.] Mechanic at Yankee Stadium; [oth. writ.] None that have been published.; [pers.] It's unfortunate, but I find nothing good to write about. If you don't know what I mean, just watch the news.; [a.] Bronx, NY

COMMISSIONG, SUE-ANN C.
[b.] December 24, 1962, Trinidad and Tobago, West Indies; [p.] Michael and Debra Mohammed; [m.] Anthony L. Commissiong, September 28, 1986; [ch.] Miguel - 9; [ed.] Petit Valley Girls Catholic (Elem.) School, Providence Girls Intermediate, Corpus Christi College (High), Trinidad, WI, College of Staten Island (current college); [occ.] Secretary - full-time, Freelance - part -time; [memb.] Trinidad and Tobago Working Women's Association (NY), Northern Lights (NY), Church of the Nativity Choir (Trinidad, WI), Youth Counsellor (Trinidad, WI); [hon.] Dale Cornegic: How to Win Friends and Influence People/Effective Speaking, Student Head, Miss Providence 1979, Miss Corpus Christi 1981, Writing Award 1981 (Trinidad, WI); [oth. writ.] Poetry Writer's Digest, Articles—Caribbean American Newspapers, short stories, Writer's Digest, Caribbean Contact Newspapers, other magazines.; [pers.] I believe that people are delicately made, soft and yielding—deserving only to be loved.; [a.] Staten Island, NY

COOK, CHRISTA
[pen.] Fiel Amiga; [b.] January 19, 1979; Dallas, TX; [p.] Susan and Michael Cook; [ed.] John Tyler High School, Central College; [occ.] Student; [oth.writ.] Over 100 poems as well as several short stories; [pers.] God is my inspiration, the Guider for the words that flow from my pen, Amor en Cristo.; [a.] Tyler, TX

CRAIG, NANCY B.
[pen.] Nancy Craig; [b.] October 5, 1934, Portland, ME; [p.] Elizabeth Webster Cushman and Eric Berg; [m.] Robert Sanderson Craig, June 11, 1955; [ch.] Robert S. Jr., Charles and Christopher; [ed.] Smith College, B.A. 1956, Portland Conservatory of Music (now studying there).; [occ.] Home Manager; [memb.] Cumberland Mainland and Islands Trust, Friends of Cases Bay, Portland Museum of Art.; [pers.] Living on the coast of Maine, I find inspiration in the ocean and the seasons. The study and enjoyment of music (piano) influences my poetry.; [a.] Cumberland Forside, ME

CRAWFORD, BROOKIE L.
[b.] January 9, 1972, Crawfordsville, IN; [p.] Diane Hoefakker and Samuel Davis; [m.] Robert S. Crawford, September 7, 1996; [ch.] Two dogs - Jasper and Brownie; [ed.] Bachelor of Science in Mass Communication and Psychology from James Madison University (1994), Granby High School; [occ.] Webmaster for Apollo Internet Solutions, a company I founded and a co-owner in AIS - specializes in putting small companies on the Internet and marketing success.; [oth. writ.] Several unpublished poems and short stories, news articles and features for several newspapers and magazines, public relations work and content on websites.; [pers.] "Steadfast Love" was written for my husband. It was read to him as part of our wedding ceremony.; [a.] Richmond, VA

CRONIN, ROBERT
[b.] September 29, 1922, Terre Haute, IN; [p.] William F. and Gertrude Cronin; [ed.] B.S. Degree from IN State University; [occ.] Retired; [memb.] Veterans of Foreign Wars post 972

CROSBY, DAVE
[b.] June 10, 1945, Phoenix, AZ; [p.] Edward Ellis Cosby, Linda Thompson Crosby; [m.] Sherrill Dean Seagle Crosby, October 21, 1995; [ch.] Glen Ellis Crosby, Ted Ellis Crosby; [ed.] B.A. English and Spanish, Brigham Young University, M.A. English, Brigham Young University, M.B.A. Golden Gate University; [occ.] Vice President and Corporate Account Manager, Millennium Bank, San Francisco, CA, Secondary: Dance DJ; [memb.] Past President, Rotary Int'l., Pinole, CA, Contra Costa Basketball Officials Association, Licensed Amateur Ham Radio Operator and member of the Contra Costa Communications Club, Adult Leader in the Boy Scouts of America; [hon.] Rotarian of the Year, Pinole Rotary Club, 1991, graduated from Woodbadge Program, BSA, 1993; [pers.] A theme of my poetry (as in "The Dance"), is the encouragement of couples to develop dynamic influences that keep them romantically and lovingly together in a divisive world.; [a.] Fresno, CA

CRUEA, LAURIE ANNE
[b.] November 5, 1975, La Grange, IN; [p.] Michael and Mary Cruea; [ch.] Glenn Dale Fisher II; [ed.] Burr Oak Community School, graduated 1994, Davenport College; [occ.] Administrative Assistant; [hon.] National Honor Society, Dean's Scholar List; [oth. writ.] Two poems published in high school publication, I am currently at work on a suspense/romance trilogy.; [pers.] I have always dreamed of being published, though I never thought it would happen. This proves that anything truly is possible.; [a.] Burr Oak, MI

CULLER, MARGARET W.
[pen.] Margaret W. Culler, Margie Culler; [b.] September 24, 1930, Pittsburgh, PA; [p.] Ellis and Inaogen Wilson; [m.] Arliss, March 26, 1951; [ch.] David and Richard; [occ.] Retired Nurse; [memb.]

G.B. Presbyterian Church; [oth. writ.] Several unpublished.; [pers.] There are three things that bring me peace, they are prayer, reading the Bible and writing poetry.; [a.] Chesapeake, VA

CURRAN, ROBERT J.
[pen.] Robert J. Curran; [b.] May 2, 1962, Jacksonville, FL; [p.] Jim and Margaret Curran; [ed.] High school graduate; [occ.] Purchasing Agent for the Duval County School Board; [memb.] Capal Music Industry, Leukemia Society; [hon.] The National Library of Poetry, The Nassau County Writers and Poet Society, The Poetry Guild; [oth. writ.] Personal material not yet published.; [pers.] I'm in hopes that my expressions will be enjoyed or heartfelt by one that understands the meanings of my art. True life events are my motivation or inspiration to write.; [a.] Jacksonville, FL

DAHLEM, IRENE BROWN
[b.] September 13, 1927; St. Louis, MO; [p.] John Wesley and Flossie Irene Brown; [m.] Wiliam J. Dahlem Sr; April 16, 1960; [ch.] John D. Hostert and Kevin and Michael Hostert (both deceased); [ed.] Sparta Township High School, Belleville Area College; [occ.] Retired Secretary; [hon.] Outstanding Achievement in Poetry, The National Library of Poetry, 1996; [oth.writ.] Analysis of Time, The Mind is a Most Woderful Machine, Mediation, Flirtation With Winter, Goodbye To A Son, Shattered Image; [pers.] We were put on earth for a purpose, that purpose is to give of ourselves and help others.; [a.] Sparta, IL.

DANDRON, JEREMEY SCOTT
[b.] February 12, 1971; Bellville, KS; [p.] Tom and Paula Akin; [m.] (Fiance) Denice Meyer; [ed.] Glendale High School, Glendale AZ, Military Intellegence School Ft, Devens MA. Tide Water Community College Chesapeake, VA; [occ.] Seargent, United States Army; [oth.writ.] Several poems written not never published but if it was up to my mother they all would be published; [pers.] This poem was written for Denice Meyer who I love and will always love. My dear, to know me is to know my writings. Thanks for the help mom, love you; [a.] Virginia Beach, VA.

DARRELL, LAWRENCE
[b.] February 24, 1928, New York City; [p.] An Abandoned Infant; [m.] Eleanor (Lang) Darrell, December 27, 1981; [ed.] High School, College Experience - Limited; [occ.] Retired/Astrologer; [memb.] Presbyterian Church; [oth. writ.] Poems unpublished i.e.: "Humboldt Paths," "Passing of a Leader," "You Who See Now," "Another Turn, You See," "The Little Chinese Boy," "Comparison," "Silence," "Leonines, Here and There," "Love - Mundane and Universal," etc. many of the above, written in the 1950s.; [pers.] Favorite writers: Shakespeare, John Keats, Emily Dickinson, Walt Whitman, and Robert Frost. The joy is in the writing of poetry and sharing same with others.

DAVENPORT, MARIE
[pen.] Tockey; [b.] August 13, 1937, Utica, MS; [p.] E. G. Davenport and Will Ann Davenport; [ch.] One - Maria Hodge; [ed.] Attended the University of Maryland; [occ.] Teacher Department and Defense (overseas); [memb.] ASCD (professional organization), member National Honor Society; [hon.] Teacher of the Year, excellent award for the past five years as a Teacher, community awards; [oth. writ.] Consultant for the TV Guide and television performance; [pers.] You must never give up. The possibility is always there. Influenced by: Maya Angelou.; [a.] Apo New York, NY

DAVIDSON, CHARLOTTE JEAN
[pen.] Charlotte Jean Davidson, Charlotte Jean Sargent; [b.] October 10, 1967, Berwyn, IL; [p.] Rodney Davidson and Betty Emericks; [ch.] Thomas and Colt; [ed.] Gov. Thomas Johnson High, Abbie Business Institute; [hon.] Editor's Choice Award, 1993 by The Nat.'l Library of Poetry for the "Untitled" poem by Charlotte Jean Sargent; [oth. writ.] One person published in the National Library of Poetry's 1993 anthology, "A Break In The Clouds" p.205; [pers.] Since the writing of "Here I Am, There You Are," I've become engaged to John Charles Newton and it is with his continued love and support I hope to always speak with my heart when I speak with my pen.; [a.] Sharpsburg, MD

DE VITA, ALEXIS BROOKS
[b.] May 23, 1958, Los Angeles; [p.] Wilbur Perry and Beulah Brooks; [m.] Joseph De Vita; [ch.] Joseph, Ceschino, Novella, and Johnea; [ed.] Palisades High, B.A. in Comparative Literature at U. of Vermont, M.A. in Comp. Lit. at C.U. Boulder, Ph.D. in progress.; [occ.] Dissertation research and writing; [memb.] Baha'i Faith; [hon.] Ford Foundation Fellow, U. of Colorado Fellowship, Academic Excellence at U. of Vermont, Mensa, Mortar Board, National Honor Society (Golden Key); [oth. writ.] Poetry and short fiction published by Guild Press, literary theory and criticism published by The Griot, seeking a publisher for my novels.; [pers.] I hope my writings lead toward multi-ethnic understanding and empathy.; [a.] Boulder, CO

DECKER, AMY DANEEN
[b.] May 6, 1977, Newton, KS; [p.] James Decker, Nancy Decker; [ed.] Edmond North High School; [occ.] Student, Univ. of Central Oklahoma, Edmond, OK; [pers.] An eyelash is in the eye of the beholder. Humor is a necessity.; [a.] Edmond, OK

DEDMOND, LAURA
[b.] September 26, 1984; [p.] Jimmy and Cindy Dedmond; [ed.] Prince Edward Schools (pre-k - 6 grade), Age - 12 yrs. old; [hon.] Honor Student since fourth grade; [pers.] I want to dedicate this, and all my poams to my parents, brother, grandparents and other family members, whom I dearly love.; [a.] Farmville, VA

DELAFIELD, CORRINE C.
[b.] August 19, Kauai, HI; [m.] Divorced; [ch.] John - writer, Debora - Production Manager, Musician; [ed.] Takoma Academy, Columbia Union College, Univ. of MD, Westminster Choir College; [occ.] Music Educator, Pianist, Vocalist; [memb.] MMEA, NEA, MCEA, Oratorio Society of Washington, Music Director - Hermon Presbyterian Church; [hon.] My children's choir is singing a song I wrote to the soldiers in the Gulf War on National Television. Earlier singing a Christmas song I wrote on TV; [oth. writ.] Several poems published, "Childhood Caprices," book of piano compositions, many love songs written with lyrics and music.; [pers.] I hope to bring out the beauty of life through my music. My poetry reveals my inner self and flows quickly when there are important events in my life.; [a.] Gaithersburg, MD

DELLABELLA, SCOTT
[b.] November 5, 1970; Cuba City, WI; [p.] Richard and Betty Dellabella; [ed.] Bachelor of Arts, University of Wisconsin Arts. Cuba City High School; [occ.] Computer Consultant; [hon.] Dean's List; [pers.] Poetry runs deep towards that place of "Otherness." It sits silently at the edge of the abyss where one becomes both the "other" and the "one." It evokes a strange and eerie nostalgia

which can be pointed at but never fully apprehended, for each moment slowly unfolds to become a new point of departure.; [a.] Cuba City, WI

DELUCA, JULIA
[b.] April 20, 1985; Glendula, CA; [p.] Paul DeLuca, Vicki DeLuca; [ed.] Balboa Elementary School; [occ.] Babysitter; [memb.] Shakey Softball Team, Balboa School Choir, Balboa School Orchestra; [hon.] Orchestra Violin Award for hardest effort, Little Shark's Soccer Trophie, Razzle Duzzle's Soccer Trophie, Party Line Pal's Soccer Trophie, Eagle's Soccer Trophie, California Style Soccer Trophie, Blockbuster Tee-ball Trophie School Choir Plaque, School Orchestra Plaque; [pers.] In each biography, there is no dull story of anyone. Even the dullest person has a drama, a comedy, and a tragedy in his or her life; [a.] Glendale, CA

DEMMONS, O'RITA BELLE
[pen.] O'Rita Belle Demmons; [b.] July 5, 1957, Richmond, IN; [p.] Orville Jett and Virginia Dixon; [ch.] Markal, Michael - 18, Monique and Monay (twins - 16); [ed.] High school only; [occ.] Home provider; [memb.] Emmanuel Baptist Church; [hon.] Only my family; [oth. writ.] I have about 33 other poems. I'll only name about four of them, I Know Not Why, Yearning For Your Love, Safe In Your Embrace, Our Undying Love; [pers.] I love to write poetry. However it is somewhat hard for me because I have Dyslexia.; [a.] Dayton, OH

DEROSE, RICHARD J.
[pen.] R. J. DeRose; [b.] November 19, 1942, Philadelphia, PA; [p.] Richard DeRose, Antoinette Lombardi; [ch.] Rick, Dean Scott; [ed.] BS Finance, St. Joseph's University; [occ.] Retired; [oth. writ.] "Why Love?", "The Phantom," "Life," "Class," "Florida" and "200 Years"; [pers.] Good things happen to good people.; [a.] Boca Raton, FL

DICKENS, BRENDA
[b.] January 5, 1957; Pinetops, NC; [p.] Jack T. Sdaton and Sophia Sdaton; [ch.] Jimmie L. Dickens/Justin M. Dickens; [ed.] Prusing a diploma from Long Ridge-Writers Group/Breaking Into Print Out of West Bedding Ct-06896-0801; [occ.] Special Security Officer/Alpha Security Inc. Ft. Washington, Maryland; [oth.writ.] "Something For Everyone" children's book-submitted for publishing by Carlton Press New York City. Note, I didn't have the money to pay to have this work published; [pers.] I actually like my readers to place themselves into my words of poetry, to become a part of my thought to let my words encircle them with pleasure, as they read my work. My gift to write is God given; [a.] Forestville, MD

DIRKS, CONOR
[b.] January 7, 1985; Washington, DC; [p.] Tim Dirks (father) Kerry Delaney (mom); [ed.] Currently in 6th grade attending Bates Middle School in Annapolis, Maryland; [occ.] Student; [memb.] Annapolis Soccer Club, Annapolis Baseball Club; [hon.] Presidential Fitness award Recipient-five times. Honor roll every marking period, and received an excellent plus rating in the National Guild Auditions; [oth.writ.] Several poems including "Tomorrow", and "A Warm June"; [pers.] I believe that everyone has the right to pursue a good education and that quality education is a good investment for the nation; [a.] Annapolis, MD

DOMONDON, CORNELIA B.
[pen.] Connie; [b.] September 16, 1921; Manila, Philippines; [p.] John Brown and Bernardina Brown; [m.] Dr. Oscar Domondon, DDS. (Divorced); December 24, 1952; [ch.] Samuel Nino,

Carolyn, Catherine and Oscar Jr; [ed.] Santo Tomas University, major - Home Economics and Art; [occ.] Nurse Assistant, Private Home Nursing; [memb.] 7th Day Adventist Church; [hon.] From St. Paul's, 1939 received Gold Medal for Conduct; [oth.writ.] "The Two Orphans" and "I Shall Return" (War In The Philippines) unpublished; [pers.] Do not procrastinate and don't quit, go forward and march.; [a.] Garden Grove, CA

DONNELLEY, MATTHEW A.
[pen.] Birdie O'Riley; [b.] August 17, 1977; Silver Spring, MD; [p.] Joseph Lee, Jr and Alice Christine (Donnelly); [ed.] Holy Redeemer School (K-8) Gonzaga College High School, University of Maryland, College Park Montgomerry Community College, Rockville; [occ.] Student; [memb.] Zeta Psi Fraternity of N. America, Phi Epsilon Chapter; [hon.] Eugene, O'Reilly, Award for Dramatics 1995, Parkmont Poetry Finalist 1995; [oth.writ.] "Sink Chating", "Car Troubles"; "Three Minutes Too Early (Three Years Too Late)"; [pers.] The meaning of life comes directly with what you love; [a.] Kensington, MO

DOPWELL, ARLENE
[pen.] Dawn; [b.] January 28, 1960; Kingston, Jamaca, WI; [p.] Mr. and Mrs. Wilfred Hector; [m.] Peter Dopwell; July 14, 1984; [ch.] Daniel, Deval, Deidreann; [ed.] Kingston Secondary High School, Borough of Manhattan Community College, Superior Carreer Institute for Nursing; [occ.] Medical Assistant; [memb.] The Church of Jesus Christ; [hon.] I was never rewarded for my poems, song, and skits. I gave them away to family and friends. They realy like my work, so I guess that's the best reward; [oth.writ.] My autobiography, songs, skits and short stories; [pers.] My greatest inspiration to write comes from the Bible, also when I see the need to bring out the good in people and things, I'm the life of any party.; [a.] Rosedale, NY

DORAN, CHRISTINE
[b.] November 13, 1961, New Castle, PA; [p.] Virginia and John (Deceased) Malandro; [m.] Timothy Doran, September 2, 1989; [ed.] High school diploma, Laurel High School, New Castle, PA; [occ.] Bookkeeper; [memb.] Writer's Digest Book Club; [hon.] I have been chosen by the Institute of Children's Literature for the opportunity to enroll in their course. My aptitude test and essay entitled, "The Pond", impressed them.; [pers.] I have always had an interest in writing and plan to pursue it further. I really just began to attempt writing a couple of months ago.; [a.] New Castle, PA

DORSEY, JENNIFER S.
[b.] June 25, 1981, Huntington, WV; [p.] Jon Dorsey and Elaine Dorsey; [ed.] Currently attending Fairland Middle School in Proctorville, Ohio; [occ.] Student; [oth. writ.] Several poems and short stories in my personal collection.; [pers.] Light cannot strive without darkness, the darkness makes you appreciate the light.; [a.] Proctorville, OH

DOUGHERTY, CHRISTINA
[b.] February 7, 1980; Pendleton, OR; [p.] Richard Dougherty, Loreen Dougherty; [ed.] Will soon complete the 11th grade; [occ.] Student at Auburn Adventist Academy; [memb.] Explorer Search and Rescue; [pers.] Don't be so caught up in your busy life to realize that you're not the only one with problems and always be willing to help.; [a.] Tacoma, WA.

DUCHARME, YVETTE EVE TETREAULT
[pen.] Yvette Ducharme; [b.] October 24, 1939; Granby, Quebec, Canada; [p.] Lindor Tetreault;

[m.] Irene Laberge; [ch.] none; [ed.] Baccalaureate Arts- Brebeuf College, Montreal, Law Degree-University Montreal, Security Teacher- Concordia University, Public Relations Degree; [occ.] Security Officer and Trainer; [memb.] Canadian Olympic Academy - Canadian Bar Association, Academy of Security Educators and Trainers, Unitarian Universalist Church; [hon.] Governor General of Canada for participation in 1988 Olympic Games; [oth.writ.] Law articles- security manual- magazine comments, local church paper, articles on political events, published in USA and in Canada; [pers.] Higher, stronger, farther too strong will not break; [a.] Quebec, Canada

DUERSON, LAWRENCE W.
[b.] November 13, 1917, San Antonio, TX; [p.] John and Anne Mae Duerson; [m.] Sally (Deceased), June 13, 1942; [ed.] B.A. Degree, Our Lady of the Lake, San Antonio, TX; [occ.] Red Cross Volunteer, Brooke Army Medical Center; [memb.] AFAR Temple Shrine; [oth. writ.] History of Riverside City, Texas Handbook.

DUNNELLS, KRISTIN ANN
[b.] December 8, 1987; Farmington, Ct; [p.] Mark and Patricia Dunnells; [ed.] Completed 3rd grade; [pers.] This poem came about because a little girl at the age of nine was being teased and did not want to fight. Win or lose, the poem should be published; [a.] Waterbury, CT

DUNSEITH, MELISSA
[b.] May 10, 1971; West Union, OH; [p.] Jasper and Jill Humphrey; [m.] James Dunseith; May 25, 1989; [ch.] Amanda, Amber, Colton; [ed.] 1990 Graduate of Lynchburg - Clay High School in Lynchburg Ohio.; [occ.] Housewife; [memb.] Penecostal Church of Hillsboro, Ohio; [oth.writ.] I have several poems, I've written but have not had them published.; [pers.] I put all of my feelings in my poem. The love I receive in this world has a great deal to do with my poems. Thanks to Jim (my inspiration); [a.] Sardinia, OH

DUNTLEY, LIESL
[b.] September 18, 1971; Plattsburgh, NY; [p.] Lydia Pascual; [m.] Carlos R. Pico; March 8, 1996; [ch.] Leilani, Alessandra; [ed.] Sunset High, Miami Dade Community College; [occ.] Housewife; [oth.writ.] Articles published in a local magazine, story in college paper and a poem in a town paper; [pers.] I wish my writing will touch and enrich lives. The greates inspiration comes from love instilled and pond memories; [a.] Miami, FL

EASON, KAREN
[b.] November 22, 1945; Paton, IA; [p.] Robt Eason, Jessi Buchman; [m.] June, 1967; [ch.] Bret William Giltner; [ed.] Jefferson High, Sun Prairie High, Napa College, Chabot College; [occ.] Animation Artist; [hon.] Recognition of Art Association for Youth Rehabilitation, cover design for medical research, University of Tennessee, 1996; [pers.] "To touch one's heart is to know yourself."; [a.] Paton, IA

EASTWOOD, PAULA J.
[pen.] P. J. Eastwood; [b.] February 9, 1944, Boston, MA; [p.] Everett O. Rowell and Doris B. Rowell; [m.] Arthur Eastwood, August 25, 1990; [ed.] SMTC, University of Southern Maine; [occ.] Freelance Photographer; [memb.] USM Alumni Asc., Southern Maine Craftsman's Society, Eastern Star, Riverside United Methodist Church; [hon.] Honor Society, Dean's List; [oth. writ.] Several short stories, anthology of personal poetry; [pers.] "Poets are dreamers, and dreamers

change the world." I have been most influenced by my late father, Everett O. Rowell, a very great poet and dreamer.; [a.] Biddeford Pool, ME

EDENS JR., JEFFERY FRANK
[b.] December 19, 1973, Pensacola, FL; [p.] Paula J. Hughes, Jeffery Frank Edens; [ed.] Meade Sr HS, Fort Meade, MD '92, 1st yr University of Oklahoma, Norman, OK, 2nd yr Anne Arundell CC, Arnold, MD; [occ.] Linguist, US Air Force; [memb.] Episcopal Church; [oth. writ.] None published; other poems, one novel.; [pers.] In our struggle against ignorance, oppression and all human evils, beauty is a weapon.; [a.] Fort Gordon, GA

EDGE, LINDA MARY
[b.] July 18, 1953, Webster, MA; [p.] Edmond and Patricia Montville; [m.] Larry W. Edge, June 1, 1973; [ch.] Ryan, Deron, Michael Edge; [ed.] Oak Ridge High; [occ.] Housewife; [memb.] St. Jude Catholic Church; [oth. writ.] Poem published in local newspaper, article printed in The Criterion; [pers.] I would like to dedicate "The Promise" to my father, who was my hero. May he rest in peace.; [a.] Indianapolis, IN

EDWARDS, DEBBIE
[b.] July 20, 1963, Pueblo, CO; [p.] Ronald K. McBride and Barbara J. McBride; [m.] James L. Edwards II, December 27, 1996; [ch.] Dawn Heck, Nick Heck, Amanda Heck, Michaela Edwards; [occ.] Housewife; [pers.] I have always had a hard time voicing my words. My poetry is my voice. I am so glad to be able to share them.; [a.] Saint Charles, MO

ELLIS, DELORIS N.
[b.] November 2, 1946; Picayune, MS; [p.] Ray White, Essie White; [m.] Willie Ellis; August 13, 1966; [ch.] Tattanie Ellis, Dezron Ellis, Kamesha Ellis, and Kellona Ellis; [ed.] George Washington Carvey High, Southern University; [occ.] Personnel Staffing Specialist, Naval Oceanographic Office; [memb.] Christian Community Helping Youth (CCHY); [hon.] Dean's List, President's List; [pers.] My writings are guided by my heart.; [a.] Picayune, MS

ELSCHLAGER, JASON
[pen.] Jasin; [b.] March 22, 1979, Parkersburg, WV; [p.] Randy and Jane Elschlager; [ed.] Senior at Belpre High School, early enrollment at Washington State Community College; [memb.] Art Editor for "The Talon," Belpre High School newspaper, and the Mentorship Program, Junior and Senior yrs.; [hon.] Honor Roll; [oth. writ.] The "Poetry Corner," "Eagle's Eye View" and music reviews for The Talon, HS newspaper; [pers.] My writing reflects individualism, my inner thoughts and feelings of real life experiences.; [a.] Belpre, OH

EMERSHAW, BRIAN
[b.] September 14, 1976, Kingston, PA; [p.] Diane and Steve Klem; [ed.] Dallas Area High School, Luzerne County Community College; [occ.] Student (Computer Graphic Artist); [oth. writ.] Published 5 issues of my own poetry magazine, "Closed Door," and am currently hard at work on "Exmortus" issue #1 with a partner.; [a.] Dallas, PA

EMERSON, SHAWN ANDRA
[b.] February 5, 1973; Greensboro, N.C; [p.] Mary Ann and Harry James Emerson; [ch.] Natiah Hyacinth Tyndale; [ed.] Walter Hines Page Sr. High,Johnson Community College; [oth.writ.] My seed, to thee I owe, give my praise, dedicated, and love song; [pers.] It is was for my Lord an Savior and my daughter, whom both provided me with a much needed "wake up" call, I would not be here today! All thanks and praise to Jesus, and all my work is dedicated to Natiah; [a.] Greensboro, NC

ENTENA, CATHLEAH V.
[b.] Manila, Philippines; [p.] Dr. Monchito and Annie Entena; [ed.] Woodburn High School, University of Oregon (B.S.), University of San Fransisco(M.B.A.); [pers.]Never stop at what we may believe is our potential, but always dream of being more. Poem ("Dream") dedicated to Chatham L. McCutcheon.

ESCALERA, HECTOR
[pen.] Justice; [b.] April 6, 1977, New York, NY; [p.] Felicita and Hector Escalera; [m.] Aracelis Manqual, in the near future; [ed.] Louis D. Braders High School, then attended Earle C. Clements Job Corps Center, now attending the New York Restaurant School; [occ.] Student; [memb.] Grand Billiards, located in the Bronx. City Wide Community Workers Organization located in Manhattan; [hon.] Top of my mathematics class, won two awards. Top of my history class, won two awards; [oth. writ.] Other poetry, yet to be published in the near future.; [pers.] Due to the fact that my past has brought me great pain, I try to teach others the reality of life. But my mission is not yet accomplished.; [a.] New York, NY

ESSIG, THOMAS
[b.] November 1, 1951, Philadelphia; [p.] Thomas and Elizabeth; [m.] Deborah, May 6, 1978; [ch.] Michele, Mary-Liz, Thomas; [ed.] BA English Literature; [occ.] Commodity Logistics Specialist, Supervisor; [pers.] Sometimes, I know what the thunder said.; [a.] Philadelphia, PA

ESTRADA, LUESA
[pen.] Child of God, Lui; [b.] December 12, 1972; New Jersey; [p.] Ricardo Perez and Luisa Lopez; [m.] Manuel A. Estrada; August 23, 1991; [ed.] Currently attending Nova Southeastern University of a Bachelor's in Special Education; [occ.] I am a substitute teacher during the school year; [memb.] I am an active member of the church of the Nazarene "The Good Shepard" in Hialeah, Florida. I also teach Sunday School there; [oth.writ.] I have several other writings but, none have ever been published. I entered this contest for the fun of the possibility of being published; [pers.] God's grace and mercy is greater and deeper than any universe in existence! The proof is all around us if we'd only open our eyes to see; [a.] Hialeah, FL.

FABIAN, DIANA
[pen.] The Mind; [b.] June 16, 1977; N.J.; [p.] Jose and Nida Fabian; [ed.] Homestead Sr. High and South Dade Adults Center Then, Miami Dade Studying for Veterinary Assistance; [occ.] Working at Domino's Pizza (Fl.); [hon.] Some of my others writing has been publishes in school newspaper and other poetry contest in Iliad press; [oth.writ.] I'm in the process of writing a book, the book is about how to understand your feelings; [pers.] I have been greatly influenced and blessed by reading many books and romantic poets; [a.] Homestead, FL.

FACEY, PATRICK C.
[b.] August 18, 1970; Kingston, J.A., WI; [p.] Mr. and Mrs. Facey; [ed.] GED One year of College for Audio Engineering; [occ.] Production Machinist at a Pharmaceutical Company; [oth.writ.] Songs: Ballads, R and B, Pop, Reggae, Rap; [pers.] Live, Love, Life, try to share in all three; [a.] Amityville, NY.

FELDMAN, JACK ALLISON
[pen.] Jack A. Feldman; [b.] December 19, 1923, Amsterdam, NY; [p.] Leon Feldman and Anna Esther Olender Feldman; [m.] Margaret Waldman Feldman (Deceased); July 19, 1946; [ch.] Robert Louis and Diane Lynn; [ed.] High School and Valedictorian of Electronics, Naval Air Apprentice School 1948-1952 (7588 hours), also taught math in school of study; [occ.] Retired from 35 ½ years with Naval Air Station; Electrical Engineering Tech., set-up Electronic Standards (World-Wide); [memb.] "Senior Engineering Technicians" by "National Society of Professional Engineers", Member of "Jewish War Veterans of America", Medic in World War II, Platoon 7, Battalion D; [hon.] World War II; Two Battle Stars, Asiatic Pacific Ribbon, American Area Ribbon, Philippines Liberation Ribbon, "Honorable Discharge", (Navy), While working in Electronic Standards Laboratory, I won several money awards for inventions in calibrating electronic standards in Electronics all over the world as well as The United States., [oth..writ.] As Senior In Wilbur H. Lynch High School, Amsterdam, New York, I won first prize in city, and honorable mention for state of New York and a certification for an essay titled, "How the Spanish American War Helped to Influence Our Present Latin American Policy"; [pers.] I was inspired in poetry by Robert Frost, William Shakespear, Virgil and Homer (Greek Poetry) Inspired by my deceased wife, Margaret Alice Waldman Feldman, by my present wife, Shirley Elaine Gray Wachtler Feldman, and her friends as well as my friends; [a.] Norfolk, VA.

FELTMANN, BECKY ANN
[b.] April 5, 1961, Glencoe, MN; [p.] Richard and Ardene Begaouette; [m.] Scott Feltmann, October 4, 1980; [ed.] Central High; [occ.] Homemaker; [pers.] I believe in having faith within yourself. This in return will bear fruit ir one's life and work.; [a.] Hamburg, MN

FETTERS, MARK STEVEN
[b.] May 29, 1976; St. Louis County; [p.] Earl Don Fetters, Bernice Fetters; [m.] Not married; [pers.] A person who does love and trust God, shall have a life most fulfilling in every aspect and way; [a.] St. Charles, MO

FETTMAN, SURIE
[b.] June 25, 1969; [m.] Jacob; [ch.] Four; [occ.] Pre School Teacher; [oth. writ.] Children's book - My Shabbos 123's - published by Ha Chai. Several articles for the Jewish Press and local publications.; [pers.] My greatest pleasure is to watch children develop and learn, and to help guide their emotional and creative growth. They inspire much of my writing.; [a.] Brooklyn, NY

FICKETT, MICHAEL
[b.] October 8, 1981; Portland, ME; [p.] George and Jeanne Fickett; [ed.] Student at Orange Park High School; [pers.] This Poem was written in loving memory of my Grandfather, Ralph Achorn who passed away in June 08, 1996; [a.] Orange Park, FL

FIELDS, MARGARET
[b.] February 20, 1919; Davies County; [m.] Lewis D. Fields; June 17, 1945; [ch.] 2 Daughters; [ed.] High School, 1 yr. plus 1 summer, (Indiana Central) now University of Indianapolis. Grad. From: Indiana Central Beauty College; [occ.] Retired from, Indiapolis L. Sayre's; [memb.]MT. Olive, United, Methodist Church; [oth.writ.] My memories (Only for family); [a.] Indianapolis, IN

FIELDS, MARY GUTHERY
[b.] April 16, 1936; Madison County, AL; [p.] John W. Guthery, Rubie Potts Guthery; [m.] Ray J. Fields; [ed.] Riverston High School, Alverson and

Draughan Business College, Charm Teacher at Platt College; [occ.] Electronics Tech. III; [pers.] Writing poems, songs and short stories is one of my many hobbies. It's a great comfort to me to be able to put my feelings on paper even if I'm the only one that may ever see them.; [a.] Scottsboro, AL

FINNEY, SHIRLEY L.
[pen.] Shirley Lee; [b.] July 29, 1935, Yellow Springs, OH; [p.] Virgil Crabbe, Susie Crabbe; [m.] Divorced; [ch.] Craig L. Finney; [ed.] Springfield High School, Class of 1953, Springfield, OH; [occ.] Retired Utility Employee; [memb.] Clark County Republican Committee, Miami Valley Military Affairs, Community Beautification Comm., Clark County Volunteer Services, Clark County United Way Volunteer, Northridge-Methodist Church; [oth. writ.] Many unpublished poems and short stories written for my own pleasure and satisfaction.; [pers.] Since I was a very young girl, I have enjoyed writing. I am a very sensitive person, and when I feel strongly about something or someone, I express myself through writing.; [a.] Springfield, OH

FIORE, TONY
[b.] June 15, 1965; West Islip, NY; [p.] Robert A. Fiore Sr., Rose Ann Fiore; [m.] Lori L. Fiore; October 26, 1985; [ch.] Ashley, Tyler, Alexis and Alicia; [ed.] Sabino High, Pima Community College; [occ.] Manager, The Home Depot; [memb.] LDS Church, Boy Scouts of America; [hon.] Community Service Award for the Homme Depot West Coast; [pers.] We are all blessed with great talent. Sek your Heavenly Fattler and Jesus to expose your gifts from heaven; [a.] Scottsdale, AZ

FLORES, FRANK G.
[m.] Magelende M. Flores; [ch.] Mylene Frances, Emil Francis; [ed.] D.Ed. (English Language and Literature), University of Michigan; [occ.] English Teacher, National Graduate University; [hon.] Certificate of Merit, Nanjing University, Nanjing, China, Presbyterian Board Scholar, United Board Scholar, Gold Medalist, essay writing contest, Silliman University, Philippines; [oth. writ.] Several language books, essays; [a.] Falls Church, VA

FLORES, RENE
[b.] January 15, 1944; [p.] Mr. and Mrs. Rene E. Flores Sr.; [ch.] Damion Flores; [ed.] Graduate of Dillard Univ., B.A. in Education, M.A. from Xavier Univ. in Administration; [occ.] Teacher; [hon.] I am the 1994 Masters Track Champion in the 100 yd. and 220 yd. dash. Broke existing record in 1994; [oth. writ.] I will be publishing a poem book titled, "Roatan's Reflections of Life," in the near future.; [pers.] Roatan is an island where my father and forefathers lived. I wrote the poem book, "Roatan's Reflections of Life," in tribute to my father, Rene Flores Sr.; [a.] New Orleans, LA

FLOWERS, J. C.
[pen.] Bouquet Kid; [b.] November 16, 1948, Broken Bow, OK; [p.] Edward Lloyd Flowers (Deceased), Tilda S. (Goodman) Flowers; [m.] X-Ethel Jane Sanders, September 4, 1969; [ch.] Kevin Lane, Lloyd Dale (Deceased), Jason Charles, Melissa Dawn, Jeffrey Gregory; [ed.] Holly Creek Elementary, first through eighth, Isabel Gray High, ninth through twelfth; [occ.] Supervisor at Pilgrim's Pride Poultry Processing Plant in Dequeen, AR; [memb.] National Library of Poetry Honorary Charter Membership - 1993; [hon.] Eddie Lou Cole's World of Poetry - Honorable Mention in 1991 three times, Honorable Mention in 1990 two times, Honorable Mention in 1989, 1985, 1984 one time, Golden Poet Award in 1991, 1990, 1986, 1985, Silver Poet Award in 1989,

International Society of Poets, Honorary Charter Membership in 1993, National Library of Poetry Editor's Choice Award in 1993, 3 in 1994, 3 in 1995 and (thus far) 1 in 1996; [oth. writ.] Several poems published in books by Eddie Lou Cole (Patience or Patient, Simple Advice, Little One's Control, Hobo's Relief, A New Horizon, He's Alive, Father, Mom and Dad), song lyrics composed with music by Country Creations, Nashville, Tenn., Royal Master Recording Company, Nashville, Tenn, songs on albums of Hit Songs of Tomorrow (Loose and Free, Are You Lost) and Peace Through Love and Song (Life is a Task, Jesus' Sacrifice), Nashville Sound, Nashville, Tenn. (Feelings, I'm Listening, Drinking Beer, Are You Lost, Mama (The Woman That Cares), etc.), songs on album American Sound Celebration (Feelings, I'm Listening); [pers.] Without God nothing would exist. He is the Creator and Father of all things. No need to question His works. Many people believe things done or said are from self alone. This is not so. I believe God's purpose or reason for happenings is to teach all. Ideas and thoughts with knowledge and wisdom come from the Almighty God. Any burden or hindrance (all obstacles in life) can be overcome for God is there when no one is. I thank God for life above all things and know without Him I would not be on earth. No offense, friend, but it is something to think about while living on earth. Mistakes occur in life. With faith, trust and belief, obstacles in life are apprehended on earth. Goals set are obtained using three steps: 1. strategy, 2. effort and 3. reliance on God (the important one). So rely on God and strive for the hereafter while on earth and a reunion awaits for the soul in Paradise. A Higher Power does exist - No Doubt. If this was not so, life for each would never begin. Something unique for all since we are sisters and brothers in His eyes.; [a.] Broken Bow, OK

FOBERT, GLORIA F.
[pen.] Gloria F. Fobert; [b.] January 17, 1926; Salt Lake City, UT; [p.] Florences Thomas, Marvin Blain; [m.] Edward L. Fobert; April 30, 1944; [ch.] David B. Fobert, Daniel Fobert; [ed.] West High School - S.L.C., Utah, Salt Lake City Trade Tech. Inst., graduate in Cosmetology; [occ.] Retired; [memb.] Garden Club; [oth.writ.] Friendship, Progress, My Valley, To Be; [pers.] I garden, paint and write poetry to amuse my inner self. The ways of human nature fascinate me.; [a.] Minibres, NM

FORSTER, STEFANIE ANNE
[pen.] Stefanie A. Forster; [b.] November 8, 1977, New Jersey; [p.] William and Mary Ann Forster; [ed.] Walnut Hill School for Artistic and Academic Excellence, Eugene Lang College; [occ.] Student; [oth. writ.] Several poems published in an anthology and small press publications.; [pers.] I wrote "Angel in the House" about and for my best friend, my mother.; [a.] Ridgefield Park, NJ

FOTI, BRIDGET
[b.] December 10, 1950, Milwaukee, WI; [ch.] Shawn, Craig and Neil; [ed.] WCTC Apprentice, Tool and Die Program; [occ.] Tool and Die Maker; [pers.] Most of my poems reflect emotion and the issue of kindness at all times.; [a.] Elkhorn, WI

FRANCIS, MAY R.
[b.] December 24, 1906; S. Williamsport; [p.] William and Sarah Reasor; [m.] Paul A. Francis Sr. (Deceased); September 2, 1959; [ch.] 2 Daughters; [ed.] S. Williamsport Schools Williamsport Technical Institute Wheaton's Business School; [occ.] Retired; [memb.] Covenant Central Preasbyterian Church Past President of Alice Hughes Story League; [oth.writ.] Poem in Williamsport Gazette, 2 Poems in Knights of Malt a monthly

bulletin; [pers.] Writing (Stories and Poems) are mostly on the nature and spiritual themes; [a.] Williamsport, PA

FRANGIA, PETER
[b.] January 24, 1921, Wilmington, DE; [p.] George and Sapeu; [m.] Anna, February 22, 1948; [ch.] Two, Dr. Maria Rayias and James; [ed.] High school, 2 years college; [occ.] Retired; [memb.] Army Air Corps - 352nd Fighter Group Air Corps - 351 Bomb Group Association, UFW - American Legion; [hon.] International Society of Poets, International Hall of Fame; [oth. writ.] Poems: International Society of Poetry - God Why Me, Just a Walking, First Love, To Me, Nurses, Did You Pass Them By, Friend. Sparrowgrass Poetry - Kiss. Iliad Press - The Thoughts of an Old Man, Danielle, Someone is Calling Me, Squirrels, My Dad, My Ma. The Poetry Guild Contest UB133 - "Sky". Creative Arts and Science Enterprises - "Fireflys". Novel: "Does She or Doesn't She: Only a Milkman Knows," "Heather".; [pers.] I have been writing poetry since 1992, I always try to write what is in my heart, if I am sad I write sad poems, if I am happy I write happy poems. I always carry a piece of scrap paper and pencil with me, you never can tell when a poem will flash in your mind. My philosophy in life is this, "Always try to help and lend a helping hand to some unfortunate soul, it will always come back to you a thousand fold."; [a.] Wilmington, DE

FREED, DAVID A.
[b.] May 7, 1926, Beloit, WI; [p.] Adolph and Marguerite Freed; [m.] Marian H. Schuchardt, December 22, 1951; [ch.] Alan, Kristin, Eric and Gretchen; [ed.] University of Wisconsin - BS 1949, University of Wisconsin Medical School - MD 1952; [occ.] Retired "Country Doctor," practiced medicine 40 yrs. West Union, IA; [memb.] American Medical Association, American Academy of Family Physicians, Iowa Medical Society; [hon.] Phi Beta Kappa - U.W. 1949, Alpha Omega Alpha - U.W. Med. Sch. 1952; [oth. writ.] Book - "My Case for Freedom" - Naylor, 1962, medical journal articles - "Will We Be Priced Out of The Market" - Medical Times, June 1965, "A Cross-Cultural Study of The Oath of Hippocrates," The Gundersen Medical Journal - December 1991.; [pers.] Recently retired from the busy life of a country family doctor, I look forward to more leisure to reflect and write.; [a.] Walker, MN

FREEMAN, CAMBRI LYNETTE
[pen.] Cam; [b.] July 22, 1973; Paso Robles, CA; [p.] Danny and Linda Horton; [m.] Scott Freeman; October 8, 1993; [ed.] Templeton - grade 1-12; [occ.] Housewife; [memb.] Poetry Editor for High School News Paper; [hon.] Several Poems published in High School News paper and not because I was Editor. We voted on them as as class; [oth.writ.] "The man who walks alone," " A Living Poem," "My Moon, My Cloud, My World", "In this Lifetime", "Life Changes", "A Rose and a Dream", Dark Shadows," Moon, Sun and Stars", "Gamblers Annonymous", "Heaven On Earth", plus several more; [pers.] Poetry doesn't come from your head and hands, it comes from your heart and soul. Its not a contest, it's an honor to create. Be open minded and let your spirit be free; [a.] Paso Robles, CA.

FREEMAN, NANCY
[b.] October 9, 1961; Shelbyville, TN; [p.] Mary and Boyd Warren (deceased); [m.] Glen W. Freeman; November 21, 1992; [ch.] Charlotte Elizabeth Chrystal Dawn, Lisa Shyvonne, and Glen Jr; [ed.] 8th Grade drop out, went back passed GED; [occ.] Sales Associate; [oth.writ.] Several poems

published in local newspaper; [pers.] My poems are written as a way to express my feelings. And I thank my mother for the encouragement she gave me to continue writing poems; [a.] Shelbyville, TN

FRENCH, TAMARA
[b.] February 15, 1983; Cottonwood, AZ; [p.] Robin and John French; [ed.] West Sedona School, currently in 8th grade; [occ.] Student; [hon.] 1st place in Reflections Contest, 1st place in school poetry contest, many Honor Rolls, a few Superior Honor Rolls, Wildcat Awards, 1st place spelling bee, 1st place state for poetry (AZ); [pers.] Follow your dreams no matter what, never give up and stick with it. You can do it.; [a.] Sedona, AZ

FUCCI, JAMES
[b.] May 12, 1952, Massapequa, NY; [ed.] A.G. Berner H.S., Massapequa, NY, University of New Orleans; [pers.] There are no metaphors to accurately describe the creative process, it happens so differently each time.; [a.] Covington, LA

FULTON, PHYLLIS BURCHFIELD
[pen.] Phyllis Burchfield; [b.] June 15, 1912, Titusville, PA; [p.] Samuel N. (MD) and Isabelle Burchfield; [m.] George Preston Fulton, October 11, 1942; [ed.] High school and Jr. college and Flight training for Commercial Pilot and Flight Instructor Ratings; [occ.] Breeding and showing German Shepherds and growing Tall Bearded Iris from my own crosses; [memb.] WASP (Women's Airforce Service Pilots), German Shepherd Dog Club of America, American Iris Society, Humane Society of the United States, National Wildlife Federation; [hon.] Member of the WAFS (Women's Auxiliary Ferrying Squadron), we were the first 25 women to fly for the Air Force. Later integrated into the WASP.; [pers.] I have found strength for my life in the message of the poem, "Footprints."; [a.] Old Washington, OH

GALLAGHER, BEATRICE SHEPHERD
[pen.] Beatrice Shepherd; [b.] October 2, 1910; Needham, MA; [p.] Ellen Vokes Shepherd - Norman S. Shepherd; [m.] Patrick Frances Gallagher II; 1945; [ch.] Dorothy E, Patrick F. III, Jayne M.; [ed.] Haverhill High School, MA 1928, Framingham Teachers College, MA 1932, Grad. work-Bost., Univ., Harrard Ext., MA 1932-1945, VCLA, Loyola Univ., USC CA 1952-1975; [occ.] Retired after 21 yrs 1st Gr. Teacher. 11 yrs Reading Specialist, CA; [memb.] MTA, CTA, NEA., Girl Scout Leader, Campfire Girls Leader, Boy Scout Leader, Cub Scout Leader; [hon.] Several Awards during my teaching career for outstanding. Contribution to children and youth by CTA, Masons and Lennox Teach. Assoc.; [oth.writ.] Busy writing childrens stories and poetry and traveling! School volunteer as Aide; [pers.] Keeping active keeps one young! I am 87 and still enjoying life to the fullest with traveling and my children and grandchildren and one great grandchild. Youth of our Country is our future.; [a.] Arroyo Grande, CA

GALLUS, FELICIA ANN
[pen.] Felicia Cerankowski; [b.] October 29, 1950; Philadelphia; PA; [p.] John Cerankowski, Ann Cerankowski; [m.] Joseph William Gallus; May 20 1987; [ed.] Saint Katherine of Siena Philadelphia, PA, Saint Hubert's High School Philadelphia, PA; [occ.] Housewife; [memb.] Wissinoming Historical Society's, Wissinoming Bible fellowship Church, Aid for friend's with trust in God founded in 1974 Organization; [oth.writ.] Here are other poem's that I wrote recently rough the years (1) Last to find out and the first cry, (2) My song, (3) Tell him now; [pers.] I am a quite and free spirited person, I am a Christian and believe in the Lord, also believe in the power of prayer, when I was in

school I always like all kind of poems. Now as I look back through the years I feel that the Lord as inspired me to write poems now; [a.] Philadelphia, PA

GANTT DANIELS, BETTY H.
[b.] April 15, 1947; Saluda; [p.] Mr. and Mrs. Curtis and Bessie Gantt; [m.] Mr. Terry J. Daniels, Sr; [ch.] Curtis, Terry, Jr., Bessie LaCheryl; [ed.] BA - Benedict College Graduate Hours from: Lander, Clemson, and the USC; [occ.] Media Specialist; [memb.] SCASL Delta Sigma Theta Pyramid Eastern Star - Satterwhite/Brown Ph: Delta Kappa; [hon.] Valedictorian from Riverside High School Honored student and Benedict; [pers.] I believe there is beauty in everything and that death is only the gate way to heaven I believe that man is only required to love one another; [a.] Saluda, SC

GARDNER, MARGARET
[pen.] G. Baby; [b.] March 10, 1964, Chicago, IL; [p.] Georgia and William Gardner; [m.] Brain Shelby Taylor, September 13, 1993; [ch.] Shelby Taylor; [ed.] 49 College credits earned at Kenny King College, Chicago, IL.; [occ.] U.S. Navy and Mother; [memb.] National Coalition of Blacks for Reparations in America (N'Cobra); [hon.] A beautiful son and husband; [oth. writ.] "Who Am I"; [pers.] Give a small gift to someone every day to make the world a more generous place.; [a.] Hampton, VA

GARTEE, BEATRICE
[b.] November 6, Chattanooga, TN; [p.] Cullen Maddox, Lela Maddox; [m.] Theodore Gartee, June 17, 1977; [ch.] Hope Prater, Ralph McCurdy, Cheryl Gruenefeld; [ed.] LaFayette High, Shorter College, West GA College Masters Degree in English and Education; [occ.] Retired Teacher of English, Freelance Writer, RVer; [memb.] Wesleyan Service Guild, Russel Park Baptist Church, Book Clubs; [hon.] Dean's List, several prizes and Honorary Mentions; [oth. writ.] Several poems published in anthologies, poetry magazines, and articles in a local newspaper. I have written many short stories and three novels, plus a chapbook of haiku - Hogache Haiku.; [pers.] I am a Christian who believes that each day is a gift from God and should be used in worthwhile pursuits. Life itself is the opportunity - make the most of it!; [a.] Fort Myers, FL

GELMAN, RACHEL GLADSTONE
[b.] June 12, 1961; Manhasset, NY; [m.] Jonathan; September 3, 1989; [ch.] Grace, Isadora; [ed.] M.A. Teaching English to Speakers of other Languages; [occ.] Domestic Engineer, Poet; [memb.] International Society of Authors and Artist; National Poets Association, Academy of American poets; [hon.] Editors challenge Award from Starburst, Accomplishment of Merit Awards from Creative Arts of Science Enterprises; [oth.writ.] ESL Articles review numerous poems and short essays in anthologies, poems appeared of fortcoming is Starburst Electric Rainbows, The tale Spinner Rag Shock, Black Buzzard Review, Poetry in Motion Poetry Motel; [pers.] I am grateful to Jonathan for his encouragement and grace and Isadora for their inspiration; [a.] Brooklyn, NY

GHOLSTON, KATRYNA
[pen.] Tahjee; [b.] May 23, 1970; Montgomery, AL; [p.] Annie Reeves and Reginaldi Britton; [m.] James Gholston; March 27, 1987; [ch.] (5) Decorey, Jasmyne, Tianna, Jarod, Jade; [ed.]Sequoyah High, Technical College, Data Professionals; [occ.] Homemaker, Aspiring Poet; [memb.] Alliance for responsible individual choices against HIV/AIDS, Literary Club Poet's Society; [hon.] National Library of Poetry, acknowledge by Nikki Giovanni;

[oth.writ.] Poems-Dying In Silence Five Reflections Of Me, Forever My Friends and many more; [pers.] My Goal is to share the talent that God has blessed me with.

GHOSTON, CARRIE LOUISE
[pen.] Louise Ghoston; [b.] July 6, 1936; [m.] Divorced; [ch.] Three; [occ.] Retired child counselor; [oth. writ.] To The Ostrich, a fiction story for children about a young ostrich who lives in Africa. I would love to have it published someday.; [pers.] I have always enjoyed writing since I was a child. I never realized I could make money doing something I love to do.; [a.] Milwaukee, WI

GIBBS, QUINN T.
[pen.] Q.T; [b.] February 14, 1966; Yazoo City, MS; [p.] Barbara J. Gibbs and Ernest Gibbs, Jr; [m.] Kelly L. Washington - Gibbs; September 24, 1994; [ch.] Quinnesha (6), Kelsey (2) Gibbs; [ed.] Yazoo City High; Central Texas College and Intraspection Institute; [occ.] Ultra Pure Water Technician, Intel Corp., Hillsboro, Oregon; [memb.] United States Navy's Enlisted Surface Warfare Specialist (ESWS); [hon.] Desert Storm Veteran; [pers.] In order to get a true sense of your own self-worth, one must draw from his/her own talent, perfect it and share it with others.; [a.] Beaverton, OR

GILBERT, S. OPAL
[b.] May 28, 1929; Stokes, County NC; [p.] Jim and Ada Martin; [m.] Bill Gilbert; November 7, 1948; [ch.] 4, 2 boys, 2 girls; [ed.] Radford University Radford, VA; [occ.] House wife; [oth.writ.] Across the hills from Bell Spurr (300 page book) Owners Manval (Article-Christian writing) Best place (poem) Ach-choo (poem) Grief (brief writing-poetry?); [pers.] I'm really thankful for my many blessings in life, I give God thanks and what to honor Him in all I do; [a.] Martinsville, VA

GILCREASE, LARRY
[pen.] (Truman Patch); [b.] February 1, 1950; Houston, TX; [p.] Marvin and Roseva Gilcrease; [ed.] M.Ed. (1982) U. of Houston, M.A. (1989) Dallas Seminary; [occ.] School teacher; [memb.] American Federation of Teachers) Nat' Asso. of Realtors; [hon.] Cum Laude (1989) Dallas Seminary; [pers.] A poet is simply one who, being attuned to words, tops in to the infinity of language; [a.] Houston, TX

GILLON, RACHEL M.
[b.] August 16, 1964, Tulare, CA; [p.] Josephine Carter and Robert Gillon; [ed.] Graduate of Delano High School in Delano, CA, 1982; [occ.] Medical Asst./Phelbotomist; [pers.] God is Man's only need; everything else is a want.; [a.] Pixley, CA

GIROUARD, RICHARD J.
[pen.] Richard J. Girouard; [b.] January 16, 1935; Newark, NJ; [p.] Louis J. Girouard and Laura Girouard; [m.] Carole Girouard; June 21, 1955; [ch.] Dona, Steven, Richard JR, Karen, Barabra; [ed.] Leominster High School, Leominster Mas.; [occ.] Real Estate Salesman, Free lance writer; [hon.] Former Mayor of City of Leominster, Mass population 35,000 between 1982 and 1988 Won numerous achievement awards during tenure; [oth.writ.] Written numerous Golf articles and a novel entitled "Were Nuts" yet unpublished; [pers.] I believe all writings should be a reflection of one's own conscious and not be burdened by social acceptance. To write without judgement as to create without fear of rejection; [a.] Sarasota, FL

GOMEZ M.D., HUMBERTO A.
[b.] November 30, 1928; Granada, Nicaragua; [p.] (M) Julieta Rosales (P) Evaristo Gomez; [m.]

Cristina S. April 30, 1982; [ch.] 3 from first Marriage, 6 stepchildrens from second marriage; [ed.] MD Universidad Nacional de Nicaragua 1956, Postgraduate in Anesthesiology, Massachussett. (Holyoke, Boston, Springfield); [occ.] Anesthesiologist - Active Staff member of the Anesthesia Group (CAS) at Columbia Cedars Med. Ctr. Soc. of Anesthesia - Dade County Med. Assoc. Intl. Anesthesia Soc. - NY Academy of Science - American Assoc. for the Advancement of Science; [pers.] I try to be close to nature and the Universe that's why I been influenced by Ruben Dario a poet from my country Nicaragua. (He was called "The Prince of The Castillan Language") Pablo Neruda from Chile -Walt Whitman from U.S.A; [a.] Miami, FL

GOMEZ- BRACETY, MIRIAM
[b.] June 16,1949; New York; [p.] Juan and Ramonito Rivera; [m.] Joseph M. Bracety; July 8, 1988; [ch.] Jose, Javier, Jorge; [ed.] Inter American University of Puerto Rico; [occ.] Presently Notary Public, former English Teacher and Secretary; [oth.writ.] "My Lord, Thank You" published in Essence of a Dream and several other poems and articles yet to be published; [pers.] There is a rainbow at the end of the storm.; [a.] North Bergen, NJ

GONZALEZ, MARIA VENICIA
[b.] May 29, 1978; [p.] Margarita and Alfonso Zarate; [ed.] Arvin High, Bakersfield College; [pers.] I would love to continue writing poems and one day reach the step of a true poet.; [a.] Arvin, CA

GOODIN, MICHAEL
[pen.] Lone Wolf; [b.] November 3, 1970, New York; [p.] Deborah and Owen Goodin; [ed.] One year of college at Suny Farmingdale; [occ.] Mail Clerk at Marine Midland Bank; [pers.] Life is pain and through my poetry, I try to reflect it by means of personal experiences or things I've seen. However, I offer a solution . . . endurance.; [a.] Saint Albans, NY

GORDON, CLANTHIE
[b.] Savannah, GA; [p.] Chatham Ferguson Sr, Clanthie Ferguson; [ch.] Three children - two grandchildren; [ed.] Attended Beach High-Savannah State College and Harris Area Trade School, Savannah, GA; [occ.] (Pre-school Poetry Teacher) work with pre-school children promoting self-esteem through poetry and skits; [hon.] Received an award from the state representative for volunteering my talent and time teaching poetry recitation and dramatic skills to young children at a city library; [oth.writ.] Publication in a book of poems, "Indige'ne," and local newspaper; [pers.] I am a dramatic speaker. I write prose and poetry skits, and organized a drama group, "Bay and Co." The poem - Lou Ann Give Me That Gum - is also a skit. I strive to share the gift God gave me with others.; [a.] Philadelphia, PA

GORDON, ELLEN K.
[b.] July 24, 1960; Covington, GA; [p.] Nelson and Jeannie M. Kelly; [m.] James R. Gordon; August 25, 1979; [ch.] Ryan Corey and Abram Joshua; [ed.] Newton Co. High, GA Southern College; [occ.] Volunteer Services; [memb.] Faith Christian Deliverance and World Outreach Centers, Helping Hands Ministries; [hon.] The International Poetry Hall of Fame, The Ellen Gordon Poetry Exhibit - address http://www.poets.com/EllenGordon.html; [oth.writ.] Several Poems Published, Manuscript in Winter '97; [pers.] It is my hope that this particular poem speaks to the heart of black men and all people; as well as encourage human beings to open doors, not close them; [a.] Decatur, GA

GORDON, LINDSAY
[b.] July 27, 1984; Gaithersburg, MO; [p.] Alan and Karen Gordon; [ed.] New Market Middle School - 7th Grade; [occ.] School; [hon.] I get on the honor roll and I get good grades in school; [a.] Mt. Airy, MD

GRAVES, JANET L.
[pen.] J.D.; [b.] October 2, 1944, Abington, PA; [p.] Charles L. Duke, Edna S. Duke; [ch.] Roy Duke, Adrienne and Carl L.; [ed.] Our Lady of Peace High School; [occ.] Teacher, Edna Maguire Elementary School, Mill Valley, CA; [memb.] Hospice of Marin, Muscular Dystrophy Association, Edna Maguire PTA, Children's Home Society; [pers.] I like to write poems that come from my heart. I'm a very spiritual person. I love working with children.; [a.] Mill Valley, CA

GREEN, BRUCE
[b.] February 10, 1964, Cheverly, MD; [p.] Bernie and Adele; [ed.] History BA 1997 UMCP; [occ.] Optician; [memb.] School of hard knocks; [oth. writ.] Nowhere Left To Go (currently an unpublished novel); [pers.] I think there are a lot of very serious people out there and I'm glad to not be one of them.; [a.] Annapolis, MD

GREMMEL, REBECCA
[b.] October 21, 1982; Portland, OR; [memb.] High on Life club, Harvest Baptist Church, Smithfield Middle School Show Choir, Smithfield Middle School, Cross Country and track team; [hon.] Made the all Region Choir, many metals is solo/ensemble contest; [pers.] This poemm is dedicated to my role model, inspiration, and friend, Twila Paris; Also, to my Lord and saviour, Jesus Christ, for always watching over me and never letting go; [a.] North Richland, TX

GRIFFIE, SUSANNA
[b.] July 18, 1959, San Manuel, AZ; [p.] Ronny and Judy Dennis; [m.] Divorced; [ch.] Mitchell Ryan Clark, Matthew James Griffie; [ed.] Safford High School, Safford, AZ, Mountain States Tech. Inst., Phoenix, AZ, Pima Community College, Tucson, AZ; [oth. writ.] Non-fiction book in progress entitled "The Greatest Gift"; [pers.] My writings are inspired by God the Father, for the purpose of educating and edifying my readers, as well as to glorify my personal Savior Jesus Christ. The message is clear: Life is a gift. All Life!; [a.] Glendale, AZ

GROVE, JO ANN
[b.] March 3, 1926; Clearfield, PA; [p.] Mr. and Mrs. Raymond Bohrer; [m.] Roger W. Grove, deceased March 17, 1988; November 26, 1942; [ch.] Son Gary D. Grove, Karen Grant daughter; [ed.] High school, Correspondent Real Estate Banking, Computer, etc. Enclosed my first poem written at age of 10, also Upon Yon Hill, writen the same time I wrote, Jacqueline; [occ.] I am co-owner of a cocktail and restaurant with my son; [memb.] Board of Realtors Fla., President of my business assoc., also American Legion post Wom Ax, 305 Fla. President Club, City Council, previous member Palaceiers rollerskating and dance club, boating and water skiing, play organ and amature oil painter; [oth. writ.] "My Mom," writen at 10 years of age, "Upon Yon Hill" writen in 1962 at the time of President Kennedy's death; [pers.] I have been a career woman all my life, I love working with people of all walks of life. I have been in banking, office, motel and cocktail lounges most of my working years, someday I hope to sit long enough to write a book.; [a.] Rochester, NY

GUERRERO, ALMA NYDIA GARAY
[b.] August 6, 1948; Santurce, PR; [p.] Irma R. Benitez, Gregorio Garay; [ch.] Roberto, David, Epi, Oscar, Beatriz, Adriana, Justin; [ed.] Associate Degrees in Alcohol and Drug Counselling, Legal Secretary, Certificate as a "Breathe Free" Instructor; [memb.] Member of the Ellenville S.D.A. Church in New York; [hon.] I am proud mother of 7 children and 9 grandchildren; [oth.writ.] Several other poems, story in True magazine for women, helped publish a church magazine called "Power Light" for youth; [pers.] I want to help young people find their true potential and show them there is no other friend like Jesus.; [a.] New Bedford, MA

GUIDRY, STEPHANIE
[pen.] Ashley K. Jackson; [b.] May 22, 1960, Philadelphia, PA; [p.] Delores Stewart; [m.] Steven Guidry, December 1, 1990; [ch.] Tiffany, David, Raheem, Antiole and Aaron; [ed.] Bok Vo-Tech High; [occ.] Caterer of Twice the Spice; [pers.] My poetry is of my heart and of my soul. Without the joy and pain of my love and lust experiences, my words may never have been heard.; [a.] Philadelphia, PA

GUSTAFSON, SAMUEL F.
[b.] March 1, 1963, Boulder, CO; [p.] Don Gustafson and Mary Fleming; [m.] Janet Gustafson, September 19, 1985; [ch.] Amanda - 19, Scott - 17; [ed.] Hughes High School, University of Cincinnati; [occ.] Carpenter, was an inner city school Teacher for 3 years; [memb.] S.C.A. (Medieval Recreation Group); [hon.] Dean's List, BS in Mathematics; [oth. writ.] Assorted poetry for my wife; [pers.] I wrote this poem for my wife as a Christmas present, to express my feelings for her and our love of 15 years. Love makes life bearable . . .; [a.] Salt Lake City, UT

GUSTAVE, PIERRE-MARIE
[pen.] Darlin; [b.] April 12, 1971, Haiti; [p.] Jacques Charles, Eva Charles; [ed.] Westhill High, Southern Connecticut State University; [occ.] Junior in college; [oth. writ.] Several poems to be published; [pers.] I have been greatly influenced by the early English poets and my literature teacher, Dr. Corinne Blackmer.; [a.] Stamford, CT

GUTIERREZ, SUZETTE
[b.] June 14, 1962; Ohio; [p.] Eurett Hudnell, Sr; [m.] Sandra Hudnell; September 11, 1961; [ch.] Everett and Suzette; [ed.] High School Deploma; [occ.] Father is peralegick mothe city employ for park and recation. 20 years; [hon.] Grand Father fought I World War II, Grand Mother song wrighter Ensterminta'l, Seamstress, writer, mother; [a.] Tampa, FL

HAMILTON, CARLINE
[pen.] Catty -Cat-Cat; [b.] January 18, 1970; Bronx, NY; [p.] Born in Jamaica, WI; [ch.] (2) Two Children Yashti - P.J; [ed.] Institute of Children's Literature, Monroe College; [occ.] At home Mom; [oth.writ.] Songs and poems made to fit anything you are feeling or anyone you had in mind. Aspiring singer and songwriter; [pers.] The reason that I am misunderstood is not clear for all to see. But my steps are written and marked by God, for he controls my destiny; [a.] Bronx, NY

HANSEN, CLAUDINE
[b.] September 9, 1974; Seattle, WA; [p.] John Hansen and Eva Kabbe Hansen; [ed.] Associate of applied Arts degree at the Art Institute of Seattle in 1995; [occ.] Freelance Illustrator; [oth.writ.] "A tale from treselby" an illustrated children's fairy tale yet to be realeased; [pers.] "Let your heart lead you in your task"; [a.] Seattle, WA

HARMAN, GERRIE
[pen.] Gerrie Harman; [b.] June 30, 1935, Hopewell, AL; [p.] Henry Clinton and Eva Watson Snow; [m.] Jack Dean Harman, November 3, 1957; [ch.] Rhonda Deese Rory and Forest Harman (Deceased September 14, 1996); [ed.] 1953 graduate of Cleburne CO High School, Heflin Anniston Business College, took a course in writing for children; [occ.] Homemaker, work some in niece's store; [memb.] Old Hopewell Baptist Church; [hon.] I have been published four times and received Writer of the Year awards from The National Library of Poetry also published for other poetry contests.; [oth. writ.] I have written several stories almost two thousands poems and have three songs put to music. Also written poems just to be used in church services.; [pers.] I am a Christian and want to share the love of God through Jesus Christ to everyone. There are many who are lost and don't even know it.; [a.] Heflin, AL

HARRINGTON, KEVIN J.
[b.] March 22, 1934, Boston, MA; [p.] Francis Harrington, Alice Harrington; [ed.] Bachelor of Philosophy, Laval University, Quebec, Master of Arts, Boston College; [occ.] Freelance Writer; [memb.] Non-Commissioned Officers Association, The American Legion; [oth. writ.] Articles published in several newspapers.; [a.] Westwood, MA

HARRIS, GLADYSE W.
[b.] September 24, 1937, Madison, GA; [p.] George White, Bennie M. White; [m.] Samuel B. Harris, June 19, 1960; [ch.] Anthony Orlando, Andra Oliva; [ed.] Morgan County High School, Savannah State College; [occ.] Instructor, Savannah Voc-Tech - Hinesville, Georgia; [memb.] Georgia Retired Teachers Association, Alpha Kappa Alpha Sorority, Inc., Midway Congregational Church, UCC, American Cancer Society, American Heart Association; [pers.] I try to do a good deed for someone each day and strive to treat others the way I'd like to be treated.; [a.] Midway, GA

HARRISON, JANE D.
[oth. writ.] "Gypsy Underground" unpublished; [pers.] Women continue to seek the words which enable them to present the truths necessary to tell the many sides of endured injustices.; [a.] Saint Louis, MO

HARTFORD, MURIEL L.
[pen.] Muriel L. Hartford; [b.] September 8, 1911, South Shields, Durham City, England; [p.] Rev. Fergus Lea and Violet Lea; [m.] D. W. Hartford Jr. (Deceased), July 20, 1931; [ch.] Three daughters: Jean Marie, Glenda Lea (Deceased), Donita Joan; [ed.] Columbia Falls High School, University of Maine, Machine, ME; [occ.] Retired; [memb.] Maine Teachers Assn., National Education Assn.; [oth. writ.] 50 poems published in various other publications. Currently work on my memories.; [pers.] "I'm going to wear out, I'm not going to rust out." "Respect" was written at mother-in-law's in 1945.; [a.] Columbia Falls, ME

HAVENER, ROXANN M.
[b.] August 3, 1980; Gilmer, TX; [p.] John and Tamara Havener; [ed.] Jr high school - Liberty Hill, TX; [occ.] Guardian Angel; [memb.] Nat'l Jr. Honor Soc., Girl Scouts of America, Liberty Hill 1st United Methodist Church, Journalism - PALS (teen support group), volleyball - track - softball - basketball; [hon.] Honored as Valedictorian at her 8th grade graduation. Straight A's her entire 6th grade; [oth.writ.] Have several other poems and short stories; [pers.] Roxann died in a car accident March 16, 1995. Roxann was a much loved part of our lives. She helped tutor many younger children. She is now in heaven with Jesus

watching over us with love.; [a.] Liberty Hill, TX

HAYES, EDWARD F.
[b.] September 8, 1951; Taunton, MA; [p.] John B. Hayes, Mary M. Hayes; [m.] Patricia L. Hayes; May 26, 1996; [ch.] Christopher Keith, Steven Keith; [ed.] Bridgewater State College, B.S.; New England Institute-Assoc. Mortuary Science; Stockbridge Agricultural College-Assoc. Turf Management; [occ.] Firefighter, Taunton Fire Dept., Taunton, MA; [a.] Taunton, MA

HAZELWOOD III, JOHN J.
[b.] February 20, 1957, Richmond, VA; [p.] John and Margie Hazelwood Jr.; [ch.] Michael Robert, Marie Aleen and Rose Amanda; [ed.] Manchester High School (1976); [occ.] Security Officer, Pinkerton Security and Investigations; [memb.] American Diabetes Association, American Heart Association, Emergency Cardiac Care Provider; [pers.] I write only from experiences and love of one woman.; [a.] Richmond, VA

HEARN, MAEDEL
[b.] September 20, 1942, Gonzales, TX; [p.] Donald and Billie Howell; [m.] Divorced; [ch.] Debbie, Bill, Don; [ed.] Business college; [occ.] Data Entry Supervisor for Tan It All/Future Firm; [pers.] I love writing poetry and look forward to having time to write much more.; [a.] Austin, TX

HEINKE, KATRYN
[b.] October 5, 1916; Goldbar, WA; [p.] Glady's and George Cross; [m.] Ray R. Heinke-deceased; January 24, 1933; [ch.] Ronald Heinke-Arlene Heinke Miller; [ed.] Grad-Everett High School Class of 1934; [occ.] Retired-Wash State Insuranee Agent; [memb.] Rhododendron Chapter Eastern Star; [oth.writ.] Poems for Relatives and friends birthdays-family Geneology; [pers.] Most of my time is spent reading, writing, knitting, crocheting and craft projects enjoy traveling with friends; [a.] Tacoma, WA

HENDRICKS, SCOTT H.
[b.] March 22, 1949; Sacramento, CA; [p.] George H. Hendricks and Beatrice B. Hendricks; [m.] Lynda S. Hendricks; June 7, 1975; [ch.] Renee and Michael; [ed.] Rio Americano H.S., Simpson College; [occ.] Special Agent and Registered Representative, Prudential Preferred Financial Services; [memb.] Junior Achievement, MS. Society of South Dakota, St. John American Lutheran Church Board of Outreach Church Chair and Council member; [oth.writ.] This is my first experiences at being published. I have written numerous poems and short stories yet to be published; [pers.] I strive to investigate the struggles and victories in life and my personal faith. I've been in fluenced by the early English poets and Rebert Frost; [a.] Sioux Falls, SD

HENLEY, SHAWN
[b.] September 11, 1971, Toledo, OH; [p.] Johnnie Mae Henley, J. B. Henley; [ch.] One - Shawn Annise Henley (Daughter); [pers.] I owe my accomplishment to God. Also Paul Lawrence Dunbar's poems inspired me to write poetry.; [a.] Toledo, OH

HERNANDEZ, KRISTIN M.
[b.] August 19, 1989, Plantation, FL; [p.] Dr. and Mrs. Joseph and Marilou Hernandez; [ed.] Grade two; [occ.] Student; [memb.] Brownie, Girls Scout #63 St. Anthony's Church Choir; [hon.] Excellence in all Academic Areas Feb. 7, 1997, Outstanding All-Around Student May 1995, Excellence in All Academic Areas Feb. 2, 1996, Excellence in Spelling June 14, 1996, Excellent Reading Skills June 8, 1995, Student of the Month for

Attendance and Punctuality April 1996, Student of the Month for Service Feb. 1996; [oth. writ.] In Oct. 1996 poem submitted to the Anthology of Poetry Inc. has been accepted for publication. The poem will be in the 1997 edition of the Anthology of Poetry by Young Americans which will go to print on March 31, 1997, St. Anthony Catholic Church weekly newsletter published 2 of her poems on third Sunday of Eastern April 13, 1997 entitled "Easter Eggs," "Easter."

HERNANDEZ, SAMANTHA
[pen.] Sam; [b.] February 6, 1981; Ipa, FL; [ed.] Gaither Highschool; [memb.] Tampa Bay All Stars; [hon.] Jr. Beta Club, Captain of cheerleading squad, gymnastics, peer mediator who's who; [pers.] My writing is a reflection of strong emotions and reality which touches the heart ofmany; [a.] Tampa, FL

HIBBS II, ROY
[b.] November 20, 1974, Chattanooga, TN; [p.] Roy Hibbs, Ruth Hibbs; [ed.] University of Tennessee at Chattanooga; [occ.] Working toward BS Chemistry Degree; [oth. writ.] Many poems and other writings in personal journals.; [pers.] That which is far off, and exceeding deep, who can find it out?; [a.] Jasper, TN

HICKMAN, TAMMY RENEE
[pen.] Tammy Renee Hickman; [b.] August 4, 1977; DeRidder; [p.] Charles and Teena Myers; [ed.] Freshmen standing at NcNeese State University in Lake Charles, Louisiana; [occ.] United States Tennis Association; [oth.writ.] Many written, but unknown and not published; [pers.] Most of my writings are based upon personal experiences. The animals killed today are the animals that are gone tomorrow; [a.] DeRidder, LA

HILL PUTNEY, MAXINE ALLEN
[b.] December 10. 1928; Covington, VA; [p.] Ruth and Jack Allen; [m.] Frank Putney; [ch.] Edward, Webster, Curtis; [ed.] B.S. VA. State (1950), Bowie State (Masters); [occ.] Retired (1990) P.G County Public School; [memb.] MRTA, Pecrta; [oth.writ.] None published; [pers.] Working with mentally and physically challenged youths has taught me to love unconditionally. I hope I have passed it on.; [a.] Washington, DC

HISCOX, STEPHANIE MEGHAN
[b.] July 24, 1979; Coffeyville, KS; [p.] Christopher Hiscox; [ed.] Sturgis High School, Glen Oaks Community College; [occ.] Restaurant Worker; [oth.writ.] A Love Story, I Can If I and Ponies of Thunder; [pers.] I try to reflect human nature in my writings. I wish that everyone could write to clean the soul; [a.] Sturgis, MI

HITZ, JUDY A.
[b.] April 14, 1951; Hershey, PA; [m.] Guy M. Hitz; August 26, 1972; [ch.] Christopher, Adrian, Justin, Colleen; [ed.] Harrisburg Area Community College; [occ.] Account Manager, MBNA New England; [memb.] American Cancer Society, Billy Graham Crusade, First Free Baptist Church; [oth.writ.] Poem published in Farm Wife magazine; [pers.] Enjoy writing poetry depicting personal stories of friends and relatives.; [a.] Bridgewater, ME

HOFFMAN, DEBRA
[b.] February 20, 1963, Port Jefferson, NY; [p.] Paul and Elaine Hoffman; [ed.] Sullivan County College; [occ.] Promotional Purchasing Manager, Harper Collins Publishers, New York, NY; [pers.] I always looked up to my father, he was a great inspiration. This poem is dedicated to Paul J.Hoffman, my "Dad."; [a.] Port Jefferson Station, NY

HOLLINS, KATHLEEN Y.
[b.] July 1, 1953; Wichita, KS; [p.] Louis and Martha Hollins; [ch.] Angel Lanette and Tristen Le' Mout; [ed.] Heights High and Central Business College; [occ.] Customer Service Rep. PNG-Energy One - Wichita, KS; [memb.] United Way, NAACP, Wichita Urban League; [oth.writ.] Poems and greetings card for relatives and very special friends; [pers.] Through my poetry, I have touched the hearts of many. I will continue to share my feelings with others; [a.] Wichita, KS

HOLTGREFE, PAUL
[b.] July 30, 1980; San Bernardino, CA; [p.] Martin Holtgrefe, Cynthia Holtgrefe; [ed.] Kimbark Elementary, Shandon Hills Middle School, Cajon High School - Apple Valley High School; [occ.] Full time student; [oth.writ.] I have over a hundred poems that hopefully in the future could be published, I look forward to it. [pers.] Give yourself some morals to live by, and stick by them, "they give you a little extra to live your live for." [a.] Applevalley, CA

HOOVER, JANET D.
[b.] August 6, 1952, La Crosse, KS; [p.] William E. and Barbara Baus; [m.] Gary B. Hoover, February 26, 1988; [ch.] Celi, Chad, Cari, Casey, Bryan and Tiffany; [ed.] La Crosse High School; [occ.] Mother, Co-owner of "Executive Limousine Service, Inc."; [hon.] State medals for speech and oetry at high school level; [oth. writ.] I have started a book of poetry that is not yet finished.; [pers.] My poetry conveys my deepest emotions and experiences through the joys and tragedies of my life. Poetry allows me to put my feelings into words.; [a.] Wichita, KS

HOPKINS, DORIS
[pen.] Dot and Doll Baby; [b.] December 15, Macon, MS; [p.] Mr. and Mrs. Lula Ruth; [m.] Doshie Lee Hopkins; June 6, 1971; [ch.] 5; [ed.] After graduating from R.J. Kirksey High, I continue my education at Brewer State Junior College, in Business Education from 1970-1975; [occ.] I'm presently working at Golden Flake Snack Food as a corn chip packer; [memb.] I'm a member of free will church of God in Christ in Birmingham, Alabama; [oth.writ.] "Trouble Times", "A Mother's Love", "The Eyes Of My Mother", "Satan vs. Evils", "The Lord Is My Everything", "An Angel In Heaven"; [pers.] I strive to reflect the goodness of God in my writing; [a.] Birmingham, AL

HOSSAIN, MOHAMMED N.
[b.] March 4, 1962, Bangladesh; [m.] Nahid Rumana, March 17, 1995; [ch.] Mohammed Nafij Hossain; [ed.] Graduate from Air Force Academy, Bangladesh; [pers.] My poem was published in the Bangladesh Air Force Journal when the cold war between East and West reached its peak. I survived in a war and wrote this poem; [a.] Philadelphia, PA

HOTUJEC, EDWARD
[pen.] "Swift Eddie"; [b.] June 1, 1928, Kansas City, KS; [p.] John and Mary Stimec Hotujec; [m.] Mae (Griffith), July 10, 1971; [ch.] John Hotujec; [ed.] Bishop Ward High, St. Benedict's College, Rockhurst College, Elgin College; [occ.] Retired - 41 years, Armour-Swift Eckrich - Materials Control Mgr.; [memb.] Order of Moose, American Legion, St. George Society, International Society of Poets, Disabled War Veterans; [hon.] Bronze Star (Korea) 1951-52, Chief Medic 3rd Inf. Div., International Poetry Hall of Fame, award for poetry; [oth. writ.] Wrote a book of unpublished poems, as a hobby. Editor of a church weekly.; [pers.] Fond of the beauty of nature and the outstanding characteristics of mankind. I believe in world peace. I hope for an end to all wars.; [a.]

Saint Charles, IL

HOUK, CHRIS
[b.] May 30, 1984; San Francisco, CA; [p.] Randy Houk, Crystal Houk; [ed.] 1996-1997- 7th Grade; [occ.] Student, St. Mary's School, Walnut Creek, CA; [hon.] 1996 Grand Prize Diocese of Oakland Young Author's Fair, 1996 Editor's Choice, Nat'l Library of Poetry, 1997 Grand Prize Diocese Oakland Young Author's Fair, 1997 Editor's Choice, Nat'l Library of Poetry, 7th grade California Junior Scholarship Federation; [oth.writ.] Books of poetry titled, "Nature's Song" and "A Precious Gift- My Feathered Friends." Several poems published in Nat'l Library of Poetry: "Peace," "Lord of the Air," "Guardian Angel" and "Shadow"; [pers.] Special thanks to my teacher, Mrs. Irene Lovett, who introduced me to The Nat'l Library of Poetry. My mom and dad for their love and support. My mom who is my inspiration and friend.; [a.] San Ramon, CA

HOWARD, WILLIAM D.
[b.] December 12, 1948, Fernandina Beach, FL; [p.] Mr. and Mrs. Charles W. Howard; [ed.] B.A. Philosophy, Master of Arts History, University of South Fl and Jacksonville University; [occ.] Teacher Honors World History, Stanton College prep (a national model school), part-time Professor Western Civilization at Florida Community College, Jacksonville, FL; [hon.] Published college poet, Dean's List, Co-host TV show Ideas Alive: script written by author on the lessons of history; [oth. writ.] Essays: on religion, politics (one received a letter of congratulation from the U.S. Senate).; [a.] Jacksonville, FL

HUBBS, CHERI A.
[pen.] Cheri Ann; [b.] August 31, 1961; Ayer, MA; [p.] Matthew and Sheila Wick; [m.] Kelly W. Hubbs; Novemver 4, 1989; [ed.] Eastport High School, University of Maryland; [occ.] Conversational English Teacher; [memb.] American Quilter's Society; [hon.] Phi Kappa Phi Honor Society, Navy Unit Commendation; [pers.] My writing reflects what it is like to be me; [a.] Norfolk, VA

HUGHES, SUSAN LEE
[pen.] Suzzi Lee; [b.] December 16, 1946; St. Paul, MN; [p.] Edward M. Lee and Eleanor Trudeau Lee; [m.] Divorced; October 1, 1966; [ch.] Randal Eric, Corey Garrett, Tanya Suzann, Nichole Lee; [ed.] White Bear School class 1964, Part-time student Century College; [occ.] Writer, single parent, student; [memb.] Valley Writer's Guild , St. Croix Center for the Art, Courage Center of St. Crois CFIDS Assoc. of America CFS Assoc. Minnesota open "U"; [hon.] Five Editor's Choice Awards 1995-1997; [oth.writ.] Six poems prviously published by the National Library of Poetry included in following: "East Of The Sunrise", "The Voice Within", "Forever And A Day", "Best Poems of 90's", "Essence Of A Dream", "Best Poems Of 1997", publication due August 1997 with Sparrowgrass Poetry: "Treasured Poems Of America" Several of my poems are currently being used by the local high school, also several articles (newspaper, etc.); [pers.] Sharing from my heart, I hope to touch others with a measure of encouragement, love, and sempathy. I am inspired by such poets as Emily Dickson, James Kavansugh, John Clare, Robert Browning, William Butler Yeats, Maja Angelou, Catherine Marshall, the Bible; [a.] White Bear Lake, MN

HUNTER, CHRISTOPHER R.
[b.] August 25, 1961; Encino, CA; [p.] Robert Hunter and Carol Callahon; [m.] Linda Hunter; August 18, 1996; [ch.] Jennifer Lynn, Bryan

Adam; [ed.] Palmdale High, Cryogenic Technician School through U.S. Navy; [occ.] Machinist Mate First Class, U.S. Navy, currently stationed aboard USS Kitty Hawk (CV63); [oth.writ.] A betting guide, "Rule at Roulette"; [pers.] When you find that special someone, share everything.; [a.] Chula Vista, CA

HUNTER, KENT
[pen.] Hunter; [b.] January 2, 1962, Jordan, MT; [p.] Wayne and Rose Hunter; [ed.] Garfield Co. High; [occ.] Self-employed; [a.] Jordan, MT

HURTADO, DEBORAH
[b.] April 28, 1959; Oakland, CA; [p.] Robert and Dorothy Bales; [m.] Hugo Hurtado; September 21, 1985; [ch.] Randy, Fernando, Madonna; [ed.] San jouquine Valley Colleage, California and Clark County Community Colleage Nevada; [occ.] Phlebotomy Tech; [memb.] Christian Life Community Church; [hon.] Recipes published in hometown paper, won awards in city cookbook; [oth.writ.] Poems about fathers, given to family members memorial leaflet about father; [pers.] The only things we leave behind are the children. We must remember to take time for them; [a.] Las Vegas, NV

IGBOAKA, PRIMUS CHUKS
[pen.] Chuks Primus; [b.] August 3, 1960; Nigeria; [p.] Chief and Mrs S.M.R. Igboaka; [m.] Mrs. Vicky Igboaka; July 7, 1991; [ch.] Somto (5 yrs) and Ifeanyi (1 yr 3 months); [ed.] Higher National Diploma (Equivalent BSC) Mass Communications (Nigeria), Non Degree MBA Student (Cleveland State University 1995); [occ.] Correspondent, African Weekly News, Charlotte North Carolina, Freelance Writer (African Union Of Journalists); [memb.] Nigerian Union of Journalists (NUJ) International travel/tourist journalists (former conference coordinator, Nigerian Chapter; [hon.] 1985 National Youths Service Corps (NYSC) Award, Award for outstanding leadership, National President and Chapter President, Association of Mass. Comm. Students Secretary, Nigerian Federation of Catholic Students (IMT) Chapter; [oth.writ.] Everyday Collections of African Alien, Unpublished poems by author. Published over 5,000 articles stories in "National Conconrd" News Papers - Nigeria's most circulated newspaper, African News Weekly, Author of Unpublished Manuscript, "Africa Beyond Disasters"; [pers.] "Do unto to others as you will like them do unto you" Communicating to exchange ideas and improve human relation/ race relations in a global village; [a.] Cleveland, OH

IHLO, MONICA
[pen.] Rosali; [b.] March 10; Germany; [ch.] Jeannette-Marie, Dianna-Josette; [ed.] Now-working on an Associate degree in Network Systems Administration; [memb.] "Make a Wish Foundation," "Pine Meadows Homeowners Association."; [oth.writ.] Have published several other poems in magazines; [pers.] One soul is shared by 2 people who are good friends and have a great deal of understanding and respect for each other. My best friend, Todd, has inspired me to write; [a.] Aurora, CO

IRISH, CHARLES KENNETH
[pen.] Charles Bubba Irish; [b.] March 4, 1979, Nashville; [p.] Kay and Earl Irish; [ed.] Still in school at this point.; [a.] Murfreesboro, TN

JAQUINT, HOLLY A.
[b.] August 28, 1975, Cedar Rapids, IA; [p.] Joe and Joan Grissel; [m.] Matthew D. Jaquint, September 7, 1996; [ed.] University of Iowa, Kirkwood Community College; [occ.] Assistant, Campfire Boys and Girls; [hon.] Dean's List; [pers.] As my first

publication, I dedicate it to my family for all of their encouragement over the years, and hope it is merely the first of many yet to come.; [a.] Albuquerque, MN

JENKINS, GWEN
[b.] June 19, 1975; Wilmington, DE; [p.] Sherlenne Jenkins, Late Steve Wilson; [ed.] High School-John Dickinson, Life Elders and the occasional bum, bus driver, or fortune cookie; [oth.writ.] Currently working on getting two books published. Help me find myself the other remains untitled; [pers.] It's seems so strange I'm happiest when I'm writting and I write my best when I'm depressed so as "ironic " as it may seem I'm happiest when I'm depressed; [a.] Wilmington, DE

JENNINGS JR., JAMES W.
[pen.] Bard Jacob; [b.] March 23, 1952, Lynchburg, VA; [p.] James Jennings, Virginia Jennings; [ed.] B.S. E.E. Virginia Polytechnic Institute; [occ.] Electronic Technician; [pers.] Proverbs 16:3: "Commit thy works unto the Lord, and thy thoughts shall be established."; [a.] Lynchburg, VA

JEROME, GARY D.
[pen.] G. D. Jerome; [b.] March 22, 1959, Dallas, TX; [p.] Duane Jerome and Jean Jerome; [ed.] J.J. Pearce, Richardson, TX, Texas Tech University, Lubbock, TX; [occ.] Mortgage Banker; [memb.] Sigma Chi Fraternity; [hon.] Texas Tech University's Dean's List; [oth. writ.] Numerous writings in my own personal collection.; [pers.] I wish to thank Cary Larson for being an inspiration to me, and the beautiful area of Lake Tahoe, California.; [a.] Austin, TX

JETTY, DAVID E.
[b.] September 11, 1959, Auburn, NY; [p.] David Jetty, Jean Jetty; [m.] Brenda Jetty, September 12, 1987; [ch.] Matthew David and Emily Marie; [ed.] Auburn High, Cayuga Comm. College; [occ.] Consultant, Trainer; [a.] Auburn, NY

JIPSON, SHARON M.
[b.] November 7, 1957, Wilmington, DE; [p.] Mæ and Carl Grose; [ch.] Maria and Timothy Jipson; [ed.] Christiana High School, Goldey Beacom College; [occ.] Human Resources Assistant, NCS Lawrence, KS; [memb.] Professional Secretaries International, National Association of Legal Secretaries; [oth. writ.] An Empty Soul; [a.] Lawrence, KS

JOBE, JENNIE
[b.] September 30, 1980, Blooming, IL; [p.] Tim/Janice Jobe; [ed.] Parkside Jr. High, Normal Community West High School; [occ.] Housekeeper at Jumer's Chateau; [hon.] American Legion Award (8th grade); [oth. writ.] 20 poems and 2 stories; [pers.] I intend to write my poetry and stories based on reality and what is important to me. I have been influenced by many people in my life and would like to thank them all for their love and support.; [a.] Normal, IL

JOHNSON, ELAINE M.
[pen.] Elaine Johnson; October 8, 1949; Medford, MA, USA; [p.] Laurence M. Hall and Virginia E. Hall; [m.] Roy E. Johnson; September 21, 1985; [ch.] None at present; [ed.] Malden High School, St. Mary's of the Assumption CCD, Malden Business School and PE Newman Preparatory School, John Robert Powers School; [occ.] Housewife and Retired Secretary and Minister; [memb.] Professional Secretaries International; [hon.] Upper fifth in the class at Malden High School, 2nd in the class at St. Mary's CCD School, 2nd in the class in French at Newman Preparatory School; [oth.writ.] Some writings in a few magazines, also, in school

I wrote much and many writings when I was young; [pers.] I write as if this is what I see in life, at times, and have been influenced and read poems and stories from many great poem writers; [a.] Malden, MA

JOHNSON, EMERSON
[pen.] Emy or Emerson; [b.] February 9, 1972; Santa Barbara; [p.] William and Bernadette Johnson; [ed.] Cabrillo H.S. El Camino College; [occ.] Retail Clerk Vons; [memb.] St. Philips Ame Church Son of Pastor William and Bernadette Johnson; [oth.writ.] Yet to be published, especially you. I'll just love you today. My thought of the day. Ideality; [pers.] Fulfillmennt Passion must always remain, because condition will always change, while perspective should always fluctuate; [a.] Compton, CA

JOHNSON, JOY
[pen.] Joy Unique; [b.] January 22, 1950, New York City, NY; [ch.] Laurence T. Johnson; [ed.] Wm. H. Taft HS, CCNY, CW Post - LIU; [occ.] 1st Grade Teacher; [memb.] International Reading Association; [hon.] Presidential Scholar, Dean's List; [pers.] I desire to bring joy into people's lives.; [a.] Bronx, NY

JONES, BETTY JEAN
[b.] January 27, 1932, Meridian, MS; [p.] Henry and Nellie Key McGlothin; [m.] Johnny Rowe Jones (Deceased), October 1956; [ch.] Van Rowe Jones and Bray Rowe Jones (Sons); [ed.] T.J. Harris High, Mdn., MS, Jackson State College, Jackson MS, attended Amer. U, Catholic U./ and Northern Colorado U.; [occ.] US Government Retiree, Wash., D.C. US Dept. of HUD (Housing and Urban Development, Office of Personnel); [memb.] Ward 5 Civic Association - American Assoc. for Retired Persons, member of Bible Way Church, Helping Hand Fellowship Club, Missionary Board World Wide, Bible Way Church; [hon.] Excelsior School of Music, DC, Employee Suggestion, US HUD, awarded Employee of the Year US Dept. of HUD, Award for Outstanding Fingerprinting for Dept. of the FBI (job-related), award for other training and also awards for Sunday School participation.; [oth. writ.] Class essays at the American University. Have written 13 Gospel songs and performed in concerts. Sang one of them on Broadway -(McDonalds lunch-time Bible Study class) assist in writing obituaries at my church.; [pers.] To share an opinion, I believe, is a God-given opportunity . . . and sharing mine with you is a delight. My opinion: "The world is wide, long deep and tall. There's enough room/here for all.; [a.] Washington, DC

JONES, JACQUELINE
[pen.] Jackie Burns; [b.] October 11, 1971, Texarkana, TX; [p.] Bertha Burns, Jessie Hamilton; [m.] Larry Jones, February 12, 1993; [ch.] Larry Jones Jr, Christopher Jones, Crystal Jones; [ed.] Liberty - Eylay High, ICS School; [occ.] Student, studying college degree in Accounting and I am a housewife; [memb.] DECA Club; [hon.] Volleyball, Band; [oth. writ.] Just recently started publishing my poems.; [pers.] I'm greatly influenced by the grace of God, and by the support of my husband and family.; [a.] Texarkana, AR

JONES, SAMORA
[b.] June 8, 1985; Montclair, NJ; [p.] Constance Jones, Geoffrey Taylor; [ed.] Edgemont Montessori Elementary Mt. Hebron Junior High; [occ.] Student; [memb.] Junior Bridge Club, Unique Stomper Drill Team, Mt. Hebron Sixth Grade Chorus; [hon.] "A" average student; [Oth. Writ.] Please See,"Imaginary World" "Wish Poems"; [a.] Montclair, NJ

JONES, TONI RENEE
[b.] July 19, 1948, Tacoma, WA; [p.] Charles and Rose Miller; [m.] John Walter Jones (Dec'd), April 15, 1967; [ch.] Renee A., Kristein J. and Rickie M.; [ed.] Placer High at Auburn - CA, Sierra College at Rocklin, CA; [memb.] St. Paul's Lutheran Church - Calif., Lifetime Member Vol. Fire Dept. of Meadow Vista; [oth. writ.] Never been published but for years have written songs and poems and short stories.; [pers.] No matter what life deals you with faith you can endure all the pain of losing your loved one. There is a light at the end of that dark tunnel.; [a.] Tracy, CA

JUDNICK, ROSE
[pen.] Rose Marie; [b.] August 31, 1938, Chisholm, MN; [p.] John Strukel, Agnes Laurich Cooper; [m.] John Robert (Jack) (Deceased), September 8, 1956; [ch.] Debora, Donna, Barbara, Robert (Bob), 9 grandchildren; [ed.] Chisholm HS, AAS - Mkt/Mgmt Mesabi CC, AAS - OFC Tech Mesabi CC, BA Comm/Art UMD, Univ of MN - Duluth; [occ.] Quality Improvement, Fingerhut; [memb.] International Poetry Hall of Fame, International Society of Poets; [oth. writ.] "Perception," "Love," "Fog," Semi-Finalist Nat'l. Lib. of Poetry "Sunday's Sun," semi-finalist Sparrowgrass Foundation.

JUNEJA, TIKA
[b.] October 24; Oklahoma City, Ok; [ed.] B.S. Computer Sciences, University of Maryland; [occ.] System Analyst; [oth.writ.] My Bald head friend (Short story), And then he said...;[pers.] To helps we are headed in different directions, but striving for the same goals..expressing ourself within. Forever 1024; [a.] Cottage City, MD

JURY, BRYAN L.
[pen.] Bryan L. Jury; [b.] February 1, 1928, Canton, OH; [memb.] BMI; [oth. writ.] "Outlaws Bonnie and Clyde," "Memories," "White Freightliner," "California Blues," "Lock The Door When You Leave," "Call Me," "Don't Come Home Too Late From The Party" and "Lilly Lackwana Blues"; [pers.] I write country/western song lyrics and music.; [a.] Lakeside, CA

JUMP, GLADYS J.
[b.] April 20, 1927; OliveHill, KY; [m.] Divorsed; [ch.] 5; [ed.] Completed the 5th grade of Elementary School in Kentucky Aden, Fultz, Sadieville, Dry Runt Oxford; [hon.] I received award for reading the Holy Bible from the beginning to the end. Also read the book of Mormon all the way through and received award for that two; [oth. writ.] I only write poems and songs; [pers.] I relie a lot on prayer for my work, I usually personalize my writings and yet it can relate to lots and lots of other people. Some peoms are real dreams; [a.] Chandler, AZ

KALLIOS, ANN
[b.] December 26, 1922; Lucien, Mississippi; [p.] Robert and Laura Kennedy; [m.] George Kallios; [ch.] Frank, Joseph, Patricia, Cynthia; [ed.] Franklin Country High School, CoPiah- Lincoln Community College, both in Mississippi; [occ.] Retired from finance and accounting, federal govt.; [memb.] First Families of Mississippi; [hon.] Numerous awards during my wt years with the Dept. of Army as a civilian employee, 1941-1972; [oth.writ.] Contribute to several articles in newspapers regarding my deceased mother, Laura, latest in Arkansas paper with title "Women like Laura Kennedy Helped with the War"; [pers.] My mother, Laura Kennedy JiGouLeff (1903-1990), was born before her time and was "one of a kind." I am starting a book about her life.; [a.] Hemet, CA

KANSAKI, ONAM (KYONG)
[b.] May 4, 1963; S. Korea; [p.] Onaesik and Yi Yong Suk; [m.] Eric Kansaki; July 14, 1983; [ch.] Christopher Kansaki; [occ.] Writer; [pers.] Serenity eases my mind. Nature ties my good and bad experiences together and enables me to expres my thoughts and my feelings; [a.] Honolulu, HI

KATZ, NETTIE
[b.] June 3, 1927; Germany; [m.] Widow, March 9, 1948; [ch.] One son; [ed.] In Sweden, 1947; [occ.] Housewife; [memb.] Diabetes Association, AARP; [hon.] Volunteer in 3 nursing homes; [oth.writ.] I am in a book, "Vanished World," by Roman Vishniack, page 175; [a.] New York, NY

KEITH JR., MARVIN KENNETH
[pen.] Teddy Bear; [b.] July 17, 1949, Milam County, Cameron, TX; [p.] Mr. M. K. and Orlean Keith; [m.] Mrs. Gladys J. Keith, October 20, 1979; [ch.] Three children, 2 grandchildren; [ed.] 2 1/2 years Temple Junior College, 1 1/2 years at North Texas State Univ., Denton, Texas; [occ.] Medically Retired, Medical Technician; [memb.] Member and Asst. Minister, MT Zion Baptist Church - Cameron, Texas; [oth. writ.] Nightmares, Kenndall Keith's Video Treasure. At time working on book. We must be going to heaven because it's hell being black, a minority or poor white.; [pers.] Love everyone, in spite of their beliefs. You dislike a person's behavior but not the person—The Battle Is Not Against The Flesh.; [a.] Cameron, TX

KELLEY, GEORGIA
[pen.] Georgia P. Kelley; [b.] July 24, 1916; Anderson, CO; [p.] Hoyace Russell, Janie; [m.] James G. Kelley; March 27, 1937; [ch.] 6; [ed.] Some finished High School (10th grade) some didn't we had 3 sons who took schooling in U.S.A.; [occ.] Retired; [memb.] Charity Baptist Church "Where Every body is Somebody" of Clinton Tenn; [hon.] Lifetime Scholar (Bible); [oth.writ.] Several songs, "My Thoughts On Paper" and 200052 pages on the Holy Bible. From Gen. Revelations including quotes and comments; [pers.] I'm happy all the time, I love every body animals, beautiful sunset and flowers. If I can change things for the better I do if I can't I don't worry about it; [a.] Clinton, IN

KELLEY, JERIANN
[b.] September 25, 1963; Southington, CT; [p.] Joseph Orofino, Dorene Orofino; [m.] Michael Patrick Kelley; August 14, 1982; [ch.] Tyler James, Ryan Peter; [ed.] Horace C. Wilcox Regional Vocationl Technical High School; [occ.] Homemaker; [a.] Superior, WI

KELLY, DOT
[b.] Clover, SC; [p.] Danile Noah and Margaret Pendletop Platt; [m.] Lawrence J. Kelly, October 8, 1994; [ch.] E. Eric Hutchinson, Karen Hutchinson McRae; [ed.] Specialist in Administration 1986 - Winthrop University, Rock Hill, SC: Master of Arts in Teaching 1972 - Winthrop University, Rock Hill, SC: Bachelor of Science in Elementary Education 1964 - Winthrop University, Rock Hill, SC: Rock Hill High School, Rock Hill, SC - Diploma 1950; [occ.] Temporary Instructor (EDU 449) 8/1995 - Winthrop University, Rock Hill, SC - also serve as Winthrop Area Coordinator for Interns; [memb.] South Carolina Association of School Administrators, South Carolina Elementary and Middle School Principals, Palmetto Reading Council, Association for Supervision and Curriculum Development, First Presbyterian Church, Rock Hill, SC; [oth. writ.] "Rear View Mirror" (in sunshine and day dreams, "Celebration" (in colors of

thought), have just completed manuscript for a children's fiction book.; [pers.] Given the interest, imagination, recollections, desire, and motivation to write, thoughts and ideas can be organized in a form that provides for great personal satisfaction.; [a.] Rock Hill, SC

KELLY, RYAN J.
[b.] March 17, 1972; Spfld, MA; [p.] Laurence kelly, Kathleen Kelly; [ed.] Cathedral H.S., Bates College; [occ.] 7th Grade Teacher, St. Matthew's School Spfld. MA; [a.] Springfield, MA

KILLINGER, FRANCIS
[b.] May 11, 1936, Johnstown, PA; [p.] Francis and Ella O. Killinger; [m.] June Mara, May 18, 1985; [ch.] 16 children; [ed.] Dale H.S., Johnstown, Juniata, Penn St., Orange Coast Jr. Coll., Southern Calif. College, West NV Comm. College; [occ.] Teacher at Rite Passage, Baptist Minister, Safety Officer Walker Lake VFD; [memb.] Life Member Cal. Assn. of Animal Control Officers, Animal Control Dir. Assn. Westminster Police Off. Assn., Amateur Bowling Tournament Assn.; [hon.] Life Achievement C.A.A.C.O., Poet Laureate. 1996, Nat'l. Honor Soc.; [oth. writ.] The Perfect Gift, The Christmas Life, The Souls We Seek, From Nowhere, I Came, Angels and Strangers, There's No Other One, Serve The Lord, To Worship, Love Unrequited, The Quest, The Traveler, etc.; [pers.] My gift comes from God, I can scarcely take credit for my writings. I'm only aware and ready for the next offering.; [a.] Walker Lake, NV

KING, GARY W.
[b.] August 16, 1952; Okla. City; [p.] Albert and Lorene King; [m.] Christina King; Autumn of 1997; [ch.] Danielle and Cody, step-children, Brandy and Brad; [ed.] Highschool; [occ.] Salesman; [oth.writ.] Sister, published in the rippling waters; [pers.] I like thinking maybe 100 years from now someone will read one of my poems. And just possibly think that's alright, and wonder who Gary W. King was; [a.] Topeka, KS

KING, KATIE
[b.] September 26, 1982; Torrence, CA; [p.] Debbie King, Marvin King; [ed.] Currently attending St. Joseph's Academy High School; [occ.] Student; [memb.] Duke University Talent Identification Program; [oth.writ.] Poems published in other anthologies; [pers.] I try to write about things people can relate to; I find it makes the piece much more appealing; [a.] St. Louis, MO

KING, LINDA GLASPER
[b.] December 22, 1951, Wilson Co., NC; [p.] Robert and Vernell Glasper; [m.] Carl Lee King, July 21, 1974; [ch.] Kenyatta, Carla, Christopher; [ed.] Springfield High, Institute of Children's Literature, Wilson Co. Technical Institute; [occ.] Postal Clerk; [memb.] Society of Children's Book Writers and Illustration, First Baptist Church, Lucama, NC Choir, Pastor's Aide Club, Floral Club; [hon.] Diploma basic writing, Institute of Children's Literature Advanced Writing diploma, Institute of Children's Literature; [oth. writ.] I do poetry for church programming events.; [pers.] "If I can encourage anyone through my poetry or writing, let it be done to the glory of the most high."; [a.] Raleigh, NC

KINZIGER, NOLA J.
[b.] September 6, 1940, Menomonee, WI; [p.] Emary and Florence Blosmore; [m.] Charles N. Kinziger, February 18, 1961; [ch.] Two; [ed.] High school and beautician school, became school instructor; [occ.] Retired; [oth. writ.] Recently published poems (Grandma's Advice, Little

People) with Writer's Cramp and Expressions Journal. Two other poems currently being published.; [pers.] Relate stories of human and emotional experiences through poetry.; [a.] Lannon, WI

KIRKPATRICK, CHARLES M.
[pen.] Charles M. Kirkpatrick; [b.] June 9, 1919; Cordova, AL; [p.] Melvin and Sarah Davidson Kirkpatrick; [m.] Dorcas G. Kirkpatrick; January 26, 1946; [ch.] Melba Belinda Kirkpatrick Gurley; [ed.] College-University of AL; [occ.] Deceased-T.V. Engineer; [memb.] Member Magic City Writer's Club, International Brotherhood of Electrical Workers, University of Alabama Alumni Association, Veterans of Foreign Wars and Disabled American Veterans; [oth.writ.] Beachheads: Alabama to Angio—covers troublesome times from early 1900's until 1946, as seen through the author's eyes—historical flames of life—surving the odds; [pers.] Always bound to the past, battle is etched within my soul, things of beauty, preordained rendezous, playful plays, points in time, God's creations.; [a.] Adamsville, AL

KNODERER, RHEA E.
[b.] September 28, 1943, Hermosa Beach, CA; [p.] Samual Payne Jameson, Hallie Graves; [m.] Elmer Knoderer, December 19, 1970; [ch.] Derek Vinson; [ed.] Ridgway High; [oth. writ.] Numerous poems, unpublished.; [pers.] I've been writing poems since childhood but was too timid to share them outside family and friends. To be published "the first time out" is exhilarating.; [a.] Warrenton, VA

KNOTT, JOHN R.
[b.] October 27, 1897, Oxford, NC; [p.] Samuel Waite Knott and Betty F. Buchanan; [m.] Amy Rue Perry, June, 1924; [ch.] Mrs. Robt Knight, Mrs. Luther Carter; [ed.] Law Degree, Wake Forest University, Winston Salem, NC; [occ.] Deceased in 1969, Vice Pres. and Co-founder of Home Finance Corp.; [memb.] Pres. of the State Life Underwriters Asso., Chm. of the Board of the NC Baptist Hospital, Board of Directors Charlotte Chamber of Commerce, Pres. Charlotte Art Council, Director Salvation Army, The Better Business Bureau, The National Consumer Asso., helped organize Myers Park Baptist Church of which he was Life Deacon.; [pers.] Mr. Herbert Bridges, who was associated with Mr. Knott in the founding of Myers Park Baptist Church and Charlotte Arts Council, said of him, "He was active in everything good for the city of Charlotte. I never knew a finer Christian gentleman."; [a.] Charlotte, NC

KOCEL, KOURTNEY C.
[b.] September 19, 1984; Elyria, OH; [p.] Stanley D. Kocel, Deborah L. Denes Kocel; [ed.] Currently attending Keystone Middle School, 6th Grade; [occ.] Student; [memb.] Girl Scouts 6 years, 4-H 4 years; [hon.] Honor Roll at Keystone Middle School; [a.] La Grange, OH

KOCHANSKI, BEVERLY W.
[b.] February 23, 1935, Bennington, VT; [p.] Bill and Hazel Wright; [m.] Joseph M. Kochanski, August 26, 1961; [ch.] Debbie, Mike, Jim; [ed.] Bennington VT High School; [occ.] Retired; [oth. writ.] Songs and poems for W.O.T.M. Club; [pers.] Dance teacher, love of arts and music; [a.] Brandon, FL

KOHN, MICHAEL
[b.] March 13, 1971, Evergreen Park, IL; [p.] John and Rita Kohn, Dennis and Barb Gackowski; [ed.] Carl Sandburg High School, Moraine Valley Community College, Northern Illinois University; [occ.] Bartender/Waiter; [oth. writ.] Poem published in high school magazine; [pers.] I was adopted as an infant and eventually found my biological family.

I would like my poems to help others cope with life's adversities.; [a.] Orland Park, IL

KRAMER II, JERRY
[b.] June 1, 1973, Washington, DC; [p.] Jerry and Katherine Kramer; [m.] Odeana, August 19, 1994; [ed.] Associates in Advertising Art, Prince George's Community College; [occ.] Freelance Graphic Designer and Territory Manager of a coffee company; [pers.] I'd like to dedicate this poem to my "Brother," James Vernon Marshall, without whom this poem would not be possible. I would like to also thank my wife and mom for their continued support.; [a.] Laurel, MD

KUBIAK, GREG D.
[b.] December 12, 1960; McAlester, OK; [p.] Curtis B. and Pearl Kubiak; [ed.] Mt. St. Mary H.S. Okla City, BA in Political Science, University of Oklahoma, Norman; [occ.] Domestic policy analyst, sydicated columnist, writer; [memb.] The Authors build; National City Christian Church; [oth.writ.] Political colums synadicated by continental Features, "The Gilded Dome" (Univ. Of Okla Press ISBN: 08061-2621-3); [pers.] My current work includes a stage-play "Layone in Atlanta", a novel of a collection of short stories, and compilation of poetry; [a.] Washington, DC

KUHNS, SALLY
[pen.] S. Kuhns; [b.] June 20, 1950; New Castle, PA; [p.] James Frazier; [m.] Mary (Pill) Frazier; July 2, 1988; [ch.] James, Price, Patty and Rich Kuhns; [ed.] Union High School, Lawrence Co. Vo-Tech School; [occ.] Pharmacy Technician, Burns Drug Co. in Connellsville, PA; [memb.] Woman of The Moose Auxillary - Lodge #16 Juvenile Diabetes Assoc; American Diabetes Assoc; [hon.] Academy of Friendship, Women of the Moose; [oth.writ.] Several Writings Locally - Exchange Writings With Other Unpublished Poets; [pers.] I draw my strength from writing and was greatly unfluenced by my brother Craig - who taught me to write at an early age; [a.] S. Connellsville, PA

LABRIE, JOAN
[b.] December 29, 1960; Manchester, NH; [p.] Mr. and Mrs Leon H. Rice; [m.] Paul Labrie; July 22, 1984; [ch.] Courthey and Sarah; [ed.] Graduated from West High School. Went to Bay Path Junior College in Longmeadow, Mass., also attended New Hampshire College.; [occ.] Catering for Castle Caterers; [memb.] Daughters of the Revolution-Molly Stark Chapter; [hon.] Graduated from Barbizon School (modeling school in Boston); [oth.writ.] I wrote essays for contests two of them were published in a local newspaper.; [pers.] My 6 year old daughter Sarah inspired me to write this poem.; [a.] Manchester, NH

LAHOOD, JULIE A.
[b.] May 31,; Marter's Ferry, OH; [p.] Thelma and Joseph La Hood; [ed.] St. Mary Academy, Monroe Mich. Layola University, Chicago, Del.-Theatre, Fine Arts, Classics-Ray College of Design-Chicago, IL; [occ.] Owner of Historic Properties Monroe, Mich-Monroe is Hometown of Libbie Custer; [memb.] Monore County Historic Soc. Chicago Historic Society Nat'l-Trust for Historic Preservation; [hon.] Piano and vocal awards-Runner Up-Miss Toledo Talent Contest. Modeling School Awards-Ray College of Design-Chicago; [oth.writ.] "Winter Days"- Editor's Choice Award-"Summer Hood", Editors Choice Award-"Custer-Golden-Hair-"Best Poems of 1997-Nat'l. Lib. of Poetry; [pers.] Libbie Bacon. She followed her husband, Gen. Custer, through many hardships, and is a beautiful role-model for women; [a.] St. Charles, IL.

LAMBERTI, ANITA M.
[b.] August 11, 1955; San Juan/PR; [p.] Jaime and Anita Gomez; [m.] Vincent Lamberti; July 14, 1979; [ch.] Raquel and Nicholas Lamberti; [ed.] College Degree/Arts and Science P.R. Junior College, San Juan University of Miami, Coral Gables, FL; [occ.] Self-Employed; [memb.] Member of English Literary Club Member of Homecoming Publicity Committee Univ. of Miami, Member of Circle K-(Univ. of Miami); [hon.] (Community Organization) Art Director for "Hurricane" Univ. of Miami newspaper, Awards: English Literacy Contest College Level-(2nd Prize)-Poetry; [oth.writ.] Several articles published in local newspapers; [pers.] I write to reflect true feelings of love, happiness and life. And perhaps to leave a trace of the purpose of my life. I have also been influenced by great romantic poets; [a.] Plantation, SC

LANDRY, PAULINE A.
[b.] September 17, 1941, New Hampshire; [p.] Alice and Adrien Landry; [ch.] Daughter, Susan, granddaughters, Heather and Emily; [ed.] 12 years, Catholic schools; [occ.] Legal Secretary; [pers.] We cannot consciously hurt someone in our quest for happiness/journey through life. Spirituality (or religion) is not a bad way to travel through life's moral land mines and challenges.; [a.] Phoenix, AZ

LANE, ELDWIN KENDALL
[pen.] E. Kendall Lane; [b.] September 15, 1930, Bath, ME; [ed.] Flunked out of 11th grade due to dyslexia. Served four years in Navy and two years as a missionary for Mormon Church; [occ.] Realtor (since 1965); [oth. writ.] Booklet on how to write ads for selling property and a slew of children's poems.; [pers.] I had a learning impairment (dyslexia) but I have not let it impede my chances for development and success in life. I have worked around it.; [a.] Pleasant Grove, UT

LANIER, MICHAEL E.
[b.] November 26, 1969, Montgomery Co., NC; [p.] Ardyth M. Lanier and Robert E. Lanier (Deceased); [m.] Patti A. Lanier, May 14, 1994; [ed.] BA English Literature; [occ.] Textile Manager; [oth. writ.] Several poems published in College Art Magazine.; [pers.] I believe that Love and Faith will conquer all.; [a.] Winston-Salem, NC

LARSON, IRENE MARY
[b.] September 19, 1921, Lynd, MN; [p.] Andrew and Mary Larson; [ed.] High school graduate

LAWSON, ADOLPHUS D.
[pen.] Tad, Tagady; [b.] April 13, 1926, Clinton, SC; [p.] Paul R. Furr, Edna R. Furr; [m.] Gay Carpenter (Deceased), April 12, 1951; [ch.] Daniel Leath, Bjorna Erika, Thomas Russell; [ed.] Cristobal High (C.Z.), Okla A&M College, Air University Command and Staff School; [occ.] Retired - Tech Writer/Editor (various); [memb.] U.S. English, National Geographic Soc.; [oth. writ.] Light Verse, Stars and Stripes, Reader's Digest, local newspapers. Technica Manuals: various aerospace mfrs. and Kennedy Space Center. Pattern making and design textbooks - Dell Publishing, NY.; [pers.] I've lived 70 years, and paid attention each of them. Dum Spiro Spero.; [a.] Santee, CA

LAZARE, DANIEL
[pen.] Ti-Jean, De Admiral; [b.] October 24, 1967, Dominica; [p.] Stephen J. Caesar, Sylma Lazare; [ed.] A 1985 graduate from High School, named the Dominica Grammar School; [occ.] Painter; [memb.] People Action Theatre (PAT), The Seventh Day Adventist Church; [oth. writ.] Short Story, Prose, Poems mainly, "A Lamentation" which I hope to

submit in next years Poetry Contest. A Lamentation depicts my personal experience in abstract language; [pers.] Speech impediment hinders my eloquence in speech dynamism. Poetry is my channel to express inspired feelings, styled with artistic quality which hynotizes and arrest readers attention, journeying their minds to my world of creative imagination!; [a.] Charlotte Amalie, VI

LEATHER, ALBERT E.
[b.] March 30, 1920; Kokomo, IN; [p.] James and Margaret Leather; [m.] Beverly Jean Leather; December 31, 1950; [ch.] Jeffrey, Melinda, James; [ed.] High school. A lifetime educational achievement in the study and research of God's written word, The Bible; [occ.] Ordained Minister in the New World Society of Jehovah's Witnesses; [oth. writ.] Newspaper articles pertaining to the ministry of Jehovah's Witnesses. Newsweek mag article on the environment. Currently writing book on our ministry entitled, "To The Ends of the Earth."; [pers.] "Fear the true God and keep His Commandments, for this is the whole obligation of man"— Ecc. 12:13.

LEATHERS, JODI KELLEY
[b.] December 1, 1965; Washington, DC; [p.] Sally McIntyre-Kelley and Jack Kelley; [m.] Richye Leathers; June 10, 1995; [ch.] Jesse Patrick, Sara Elizabeth, Jonathan Lee; [pers.] I believe writing should reflect the inner self; [a.] Pasadena, MD

LEE, BETTY J.
[pen.] Betty Lee; [b.] September 9, 1934, Columbus, MS; [p.] Ross and Pluna Owens (Decreased); [m.] John Gaynor Lee, June 24, 1961; [ch.] Teresa Angela O'Malley, Ronald Owen Jaynes, Pamela Kay Lee and four grandchildren. Host parent, Youth for Understanding. Effie Sevastopoulou, Thessaloniki, Greece, Millie Delgado, Caracas, Venezuela January 15, 1997; [ed.] New Hope High, Front Range College, Denver, CO, MS Univ. for Women, Columbus, MS; [occ.] Trying to learn how to be retired after having been Art Instructor and Owner of Betty Lees Art Studios, owner of Hansel and Gretels Young Fashions and International School of Modelling and Charm.; [memb.] TX Who's Who in Art, American Heart Association, Association of Outstanding Business Women, El Paso, Texas, Women in Banking and Finance State of Miss., Alpha Gamma Zeta, Christian Women's Association, International Society of Poets, The International Poetry Hall of Fame, Distinguished Member of International Society of Poets; [oth. writ.] The editor of a company newsletter. Poetry published in several anthologies.; [pers.] My favorite author is Maeve Binchy. I wish to be remembered as a contributor and not just a taker. To radiate a positive shadow on my surroundings. I have a wonderful, healthy life and I give God all the credit. My many talents help to make my life very colorful.; [a.] Columbus, MS

LEE, BETTY JEAN
[pen.] Betty Lee; [b.] September 9, 1934, Columbus, MS; [p.] Ross and Pluna Owens (Deceased); [m.] John Gaynor Lee, June 24, 1961; [ch.] Teresa Angela O'Malley, Ronald Owen Jaynes, Pamela Kay Lee, and four grandchildren. Host parents, Youth for understanding, effie Sevastopoulou, Millie Delgado of Venezuela; [ed.] New Hope High School, Front Range, Denver Co. MUW, Columbus, MS.; [occ.] Retired. Post: Art Instructor, El Paso, Texas. Owner: Betty Lees Art Studio, El Paso, TX, Owner: Hansel and Gretel Young Fashions, El Paso, TX, Owner: International School of Modeling and Charm; [memb.] Texas Art Association New Mexico Art Association, Midfield, Al. Baptist Church, Alpha Gamma Zeta, American Heart Association TN.; [hon.] Texas Who's Who in Art,

American Heart Association for community service, El Paso, TX Outstanding Business Women, Women in Banking and Finance State of Mississippi, Alpha Gamma Zeta, Valentine Sweetheart Air Force Squadron #157; [oth. writ.] The Editor of a company news letter. Poetry published in five publications.; [pers.] My favorite is Maeve Bitchy. I wish to remembered as a contributor just a taker and to radiate a positive shadow on my surroundings.

LIEBEL, CATHERINE
[b.] January 19, 1954, Latrobe, PA; [p.] Edward Kralik, Ann Kralik; [m.] Paul Liebel, October 19, 1974; [ch.] Kellie Ann, Jolene Ann; [ed.] Greensburg High, Westmoreland Community College, University of Pittsburgh; [occ.] Hostess, Cracker Barrell, Inc.; [memb.] Zion Lutheran Church, PA State Police Assoc., PA Sheriffs Assoc., Book-of-the-Month Club; [oth. writ.] Personal poems, poems of love, college articles, managerial writings; [pers.] I strive to generate "love" throughout the world in my writings, with the greatest respect for human life. I have truly been inspired by God and grandfather. "The Other Side of Midnight" in my writings.; [a.] Greensburg, PA

LINE, RUBY J.
[pen.] Ruby Line; [b.] August 26, 1914; Cherokee Co, OK; [p.] Leonard L. and Nancy Ann Cunningham; [m.] Dale A. Line; June 24, 1933; [ch.] Judy Jennings, Chris, Larry, Mark Line; [ed.] Bartlesville schools except one year and a half in OK Oilfield, Bartlesville Business College; [occ.] Cat watching, TV sassing, antiques researching, saopbox stumping and aspirin swallowing; [memb.] The human race, all others are history except the church; [hon.] Many were received in all the years of volunteer work with school, church, political party, concern and hospital; [oth.writ.] Poems, one-liners, essays for a (former local) newspaper; [pers.] For forty years or more when I wanted to memorize, I propped the copy above the sink. That's also where I brain stormed. Then I became known as the dishpan philosopher.; [a.] Bartlesville, OK

LOGRIE JR, ROBERT
[pen.] Robert A. Logrie Jr.; [b.] February 5, 1944, New Orleans; [ed.] Live Oak Jr. High and Elementary, Alcee Fortier High School, U.S. Naval Clerical Schools; [occ.] Retired; [memb.] National Park Trust, The H.S.U.S. Wildlife Land and Trust, North Shore Animal League; [hon.] High School Poetry Anthology winner 1964, year book Rep. and Newspaper Editor Jr High School, winner 1978 Mardi gras for best over-all costume design and presentation; [oth. writ.] Poem "In Life" published in 1964 collection of poetry entitled "Sermons in Poetry"; [pers.] When I do write, I draw from my own personal experiences, and try to express how those experiences have touched heart and soul. Nature and the out of doors, has been a great source of influence on my writings.; [a.] New Orleans, LA

LOPEZ JR., LUIS A.
[b.] November 19, 1968, Aibonito, PR; [p.] Luis Lopez and Maria Rivera; [ed.] Carroll College, Waukesha, WI, Dr. Jose N. Gandara High, Aibonito, Puerto Rico; [pers.] Get up and spread love!; [a.] Milwaukee, WI

LORENGO, JAMES M.
[b.] February 23, 1973; Butte, MT; [p.] Victor S. Lorengo, Nola A. Lorengo; [ed.] Continuing my education in Chemistry at the University of Nevada. Also I am starting my degree in English; [occ.] Laboratory Tech (Analytical) [oth.writ.] Working on many other short stories hoping for

a sell just recenly I made my first story submission. (I write horrors, mustery, suspense stories); [pers.] The pain of an irretrievable loos is made most unbearable, when it lingers before you just out of reach; [a.] Reno, NV

LOUDERBOUGH, TONY
[b.] July 29, 1979. Alb. NM; [p.] Rick Louderbough, Susan Weeks; [ed.] Del Norte High School (I'm Almost Out!!!); [oth.writ.] I've written many poems once of which was published in a school anthology. Never did I think my work would be published never did it matter; [pers.] "Never mock a wondering man, none is so good that they lack all faulty none so wretched that tehy lack old virtue." Anonymous. "A man about to speak the truth should keep one foot in the stirrup." Mongolian saying; [a.] Albuquerque, NM.

LOWERY, KERRY
[pen.] Kerry Lowery; [b.] January 4, 1972, Fresno, CA; [p.] Dale Lowery, Barbara Lowery; [m.] Allen Garvin; [ch.] Alex Garvin; [ed.] Clovis West High School, Heald Business College, Fresno City College; [occ.] Mother, Homemaker; [memb.] Childhood Education Assoc.; [oth. writ.] Several poems for family and friends at special occasions.; [pers.] I write from my heart, choosing things that have very personal meaning, and as a result my poems effect people in a people way. The greatest joy in my life being a mother.; [a.] Fresno, CA

LOWRANCE JR., THOMAS LEE
[pen.] Benjamin Hurtt; [b.] October 1, 1971, Waco, TX; [p.] Thomas and Gail Lowrance; [ed.] Connally High, McLennan Community College, Baylor University; [occ.] Writer; [oth. writ.] Recently published "My Vessel" from a compilation of my works. Ready to published Words Of A Dreamer—a book of poetry.; [pers.] To those persons who were a part of my life, but are no more, may these words say what I failed to. Thank you.; [a.] Waco, TX

LOWRY, CRYSTAL
[b.] March 13, 1983; Portland, OR; [p.] Katie Lowry, Steve Krebs; [m.] Tim Johnson; [memb.] Rose City Nazarene Church; [hon.] Citizenship. honor roll, honor roll. All American scholar. United States National Mathmatic Awards; [oth.writ.] I have just began my enjoyment in the wonderful world opf writing my teen years; [pers.] I enjoy expressing through my writing, and I hope to succeed in writing all through my adult years; [a.] Porland, OR

LUBECKE, JANICE A.
[pen.] Jan; [p.] Gregory and Elizabeth Lubecke; [pers.] I was going through some hard times when the Lord helped me reflect upon scripture and turned it into poetry. "Stick in my Eye" correlates with Luke 6:41-45. All of the poems I've been blessed with reflect scripture, and it seems it should be shared. "Praise the Lord."; [a.] West Allis, WI

LUTTRELL, CURTIS
[p.] Cecil and Ileen Luttrell; [m.] Nancy Luttrell; [ch.] Matthew and Jennifer; [a.] Wichita, KS

LUTTRELL, GEORGE MILTON
[pen.] G. Milton Luttrell; [b.] November 11, 1939, Brooksville, FL; [p.] Alfred Wilbur Luttrell - Lucy Webster Luttrell; [m.] Betty Albright Luttrell, December 27, 1961; [ch.] Daniel T. and David T. Luttrell; [ed.] Associate Arts St. Petersburg Junior College, B.S. Florida State University, Tallahassee, MED University of Florida, Gainesville; [occ.] Environmentalist and S.M.S. Contractor; [memb.] International Society of Poets, Florida State Po-

etry Society, Tampa Bay Poetry Council - Wanderlust Chapter - Florida Water and Pollution Control Operators Association; [hon.] Golden Poet "World of Poetry" 1982. Semi-Finalist Mid-Winter Oral Poetry Contest sponsored by T.B.P.C. at University of South Florida 1997.; [oth. writ.] Approximately 100 poems and short narrative prose constructions; [pers.] "The future is now. Take time to enjoy it."; [a.] Saint Petersburg, FL

MACK, LESLIE CLAIRE
[pen.] L. C. Mack; [b.] July 8, 1947, Berkeley, CA; [p.] Lester and Corinne Selan; [m.] Augustus F. Mack III, May 3, 1992; [ch.] Joseph E. Olstad; [occ.] Wife and Christian Steward; [memb.] Seventh Day Adventist Church; [pers.] I started writing poetry 12 years ago. Always loved poetry and asked God for the gift of writing. He graciously granted my wish. I write personal poetry of people's lives, birthday cards and experiences I knew. All writings I thank God and to His Love.; [a.] Pinon Hills, CA

MACK, PATRICIA H.
[pen.] P. Mack; [b.] March 27, 1949, Wash., DC; [p.] Alice L. Holmes (Deceased), Benjamin J. Holmes, Sr. (Deceased); [m.] Clinton Mack, June 12, 1971; [ch.] JaJuan D. Mack (Daughter); [ed.] McKinley Tech. High School, Strayer Business College; [occ.] Legal Secretary and Conference Planner; [memb.] Member in good standing at the Glendale Baptist Church; [hon.] Nominee for Sunday School Teacher of the Year in 1995; [oth. writ.] Numerous poems, inspirational writings and letters, poems for special occasions and family members.; [pers.] I believe that God blessed me with the special ability of creative writing. My ultimate goal is to one day write lyrics for a song to be sung by a choir at the Glendale Baptist Church, which is my home church.; [a.] Hyattsville, MD

MAFUTA, DIASONAMA
[b.] October 15, 1953; Luhombo; [p.] Wafid-Mafuta and Malata Lumingu; [m.] Kim Luvuma; December 17, 1983; [ch.] Ikiese, Benedi, Miliya and Dise; [ed.] Bangui Graduate School of Theology (1977-1982). Westminster Seminary ('91-'93). Eastern College (94-Present); [occ.] Student, Art and French, Teacher, Philadelphia; [memb.] Association des Ecrivains de Kinshasa (ZAIRE); [oth.writ.] (1) NE RATE PAS TES FIANGAILLES (Kinshasa: Edited by CEDI, 1987). (2) HERESIES AUTOUR DU MON DE JESUS-CHRIST (Kinshasa: Edited by CEDI, 1979); [pers.] Culture is live wire that propels the social soul of a given people. No ethnic group can survive without it.; [a.] Philadelphia, PA

MANCINI, MELINDA
[pers.] Children of Genesis came to me with the influence of an environmentally conscious intenational organization. Inspirations for present and future writings are, and always will be, from the hearts of disadvantaged children from all corners of the world; [a.] Colorado Springs, CO

MANNING, EDWARD
[pen.] Vagabond Ed; [b.] October 11, 1923, Ordway, CO; [m.] Barbara, February 14, 1945; [ed.] High school, Class of 1942, Cal State, San Bernardino, California for Technical Credentials; [occ.] Retired; [memb.] Retired Teacher's Assoc., V.F.W., American Legion, Navy Memorial Foundation, former Rotary, member of International Society of Authors and Artists, member of International Society of Poets; [oth. writ.] Book, "Musings of a Vagabond," book, "Made in Montana," book, "Tin Can Tales And Vagabonds," "On The Hillside," published in the Evangel magazine, "The Lone Sailor," published in the Lone Sailor maga-

zine, "The Old Man And The Ship," published in The Tin Can Sailor newspaper. "The Glory Road," published in The Grizzly magazine. Also in the following anthologies: Chasing Rainbows And Ribbons, Great World Treasury of Poems, The World's Great Contemporary Poems, Today's Great Poems, The Space Between, Journey To Our Dreams, Promises To Keep, Our Captured Moments, Best Poems of the 90's Editor's Choice Award. Featured as the Elite Award Winner, with 22 works in the anthology, "Voices of Many Lands," published 1995. Editor's by-line columnist award for "Manning Moments," to be featured in Starbust Journal. Other awards beginning in the 1950s through today.; [pers.] "As a former educator I have found that simplicity is the key to teaching others to enjoy reading. I write in simplistic terms and phrases so that beginners are aware of what is being said without the need of a dictionary for deciphering. Each verse is, in effect, a complete short story, simple to understand."

MANSFIELD, MARION H.
[b.] February 27, 1968; Waycross, GA; [p.] Michael Highsmith, Gail Crumbley; [m.] William R. Mansfield II; November 19, 1988; [ch.] Tres Mansfield, Jon-Michael; [ed.] Ware County High (degree), Valdosta State University, Tallahassee, Community College; [occ.] Server; [memb.] Cornerstone Presbyterian Church, Song Teacher for Cub Scout Pack #112; [hon.] Senior Superlative-Most Friendly, Who's Who in American High School Students; [oth.writ.] "Lines and Shadows" in high school, published a few poems; [pers.] Honor God and listen to what people say. I have no certain reason to write poetry, when it comes I just write, of course this poem is inspired only by my mom.; [a.] Tallahassee, FL

MARKS, EUGENE
[b.] 1962, Washington, DC; [hon.] Nominated for Congressional Award for Creativity in Community Service, 1989; [oth. writ.] Lemonade Gravy, first book, includes "His Very Burden."; [pers.] "Understanding" is far more worthy a goal than "comprehending." The first is a gift, the second a myth.; [a.] Charlottesville, VA

MARLOWE, BRANDON
[pen.] Brandon "Single Crow" Marlowe; [b.] March 24, 1978; Memphis TN; [p.] Bob and Arlieta Marlowe; [ed.] Graduated high school in '96 and is currently going to college at Middle Tennessee State University studying Computer Graphics and Acting; [occ.] Student; [oth.writ.] I have written many unpublished works that I have titled Sacrificed Love, pts 1-4, and one untitled work; love is what has inspired this poem. I believe love is one of the most powerful emotions that exist. "True Love Is Forever."; [a.] Hendersonville, TN

MARTIN, ANDREW AYERS
[pen.] Martin A. Ayers (Mart Ayers); [b.] August 18, 1958; Toccoa, GA; [p.] Mr. Wallace F. Martin, Mrs. Dorothy Ayers Martin; [ch.] Malorie Ayers Martin; [ed.] Stephens County High School: Toccoa, GA Emory, BA, (English), Emory M.D. (Medical Doctor), Duke, J.D. (Juris Doctor) Tulane: Pathology Residency; Baylor Houston: Surgical Pathology; [occ.] Physician (pathologist) Attorney at Law; [memb.] American Medical Assn. Louisiana, Mississippi: Medical Societies Fellow, College of American Pathologist Fellow, American College of Legal Medicine American Bar Assn; admitted California Bar, Louisiana Bar, District of Columbia Bar; [hon.] Who's who in World, Who's who in America; Who's who in American Law; Stephens Co. High School Hall of fame; GA State Star Student 1976 (higher SAT in state), National Merit Scholar, Phi Betakappa, Eta Sigma Phi,

Sigma Tan Delta (English honor), Latin, Greek honor, National Society of Collegiate Journalists, Member, Editorial Board, Duke Law Journal, Outstanding Student Activities, Duke University, Brown Belt JuJitsu; [oth. writ.] Reflection on Rusted Chrome (book of poetry) Discrimination in Aids and Marijuana Biochemical Testing (Duke L.J.), numerous medical publications, including Lancet, Cancer, Am J. Pathology; [pers.] A life lived well is the best poetry; [a.] Lake Village, AR

MARTINEZ, BOB G.
[b.] June 7, 1949, New Mexico; [p.] Mary Jane Martinez; [m.] Annette E. Martinez, February 10, 1973; [ch.] Lita, 20 yrs and in college; [ed.] High school graduate of North High School in Denver (1964-1968); [occ.] Security Officer of Denver Merchandise Mart; [memb.] Distinguished Member of ISP-NLP, Mile High Poetry Society and the Columbine Poets of Colorado; [hon.] Honored to receive many Editor's Choice Awards among a plethora of publications; [oth. writ.] My Time To Rhyme, my life's story from 1949 to 1994 (single unbroken poem . . . 302 pgs.) and Sidetracks, a compilation of my favorite poems; [pers.] I find that when I am ready to write, it's often the other side of midnight.; [a.] Denver, CO

MATESIC, DEANA
[b.] February 22, 1973; Pittsburgh; [p.] Darlene Matesic; [ed.] Steel Valley High School, CCAC; [occ.] Child Care; [memb.] For Volunteer Ambulance Service; [oth.writ.] Wrote two books, waiting to get published. Wrote other poems; [pers.] I strive to reflect the goodness of mankind my poems to be open and honest with yourself and others around you; [a.] Munhall, PA

MATHENEY, HELEN
[b.] January 31, 1945; Chicago, IL; [p.] Joseph and Joan Mastalski; [m.] Kenneth Matheney; June 17, 1967; [ch.] Steven, George, Christina; [ed.] St. Pete High School, St. Pete, FL; [occ.] Teaching Asst. at Blanton Elementary, St. Pete, FL. in 3rd gr. SLI (Severly Language Impaired Students); [pers;] I just want to say my heart and soul lives for children. I enjoy being around all kinds of people—young and old.; [a.] Pinellas Park, FL

MATTIX, SR., SAM H.
[pen.] Sam; [b.] June 2, 1931; Crockett, TX; Mr. and Mrs Houston Mattix; [m.] Mrs. Bessie Marie Mattix; [ch.] Sam Jr, Carolyn, Lashon, Joel; [ed.] Finished at Carver Junior High Kountze, TX. Finishe at Inaldo Matthew Sils Bee TX, Finished at San Jacinto College; [occ.] Roofing and Interproffing Equipment Operation and maintenance, but on June 15 1974 was Roofer Local Union #116 I was retired; [memb.] Baptis Church; [hon.] Brotherhood Award Dad of the year award, Choir award rep. the Roofers in a magazine called A Building Future; [oth.writ.] 2 Books unpublished, lots of poem and new songs; [pers.] Thank God who is the head of my life and all of the wonderful people who believe in me thank you; [a.] Houston, TX

MATTISON, KIM A.
[b.] April 29, 1966, Denver, CO; [p.] Terry Jackson; [m.] Hieu Mattison, March 13, 1988; [ch.] Ryan Boyles, Daniel Mattison, Nikayla Mattison, Liana Mattison; [ed.] Some college; [occ.] Total Images Desktop Publishing; [pers.] I love writing - I can convey my deepest feelings through the written word as well as touch others' lives.; [a.] Clifton, CO

MCAFEE, DEREK
[b.] September 28, 1975; NY; [p.] Laura and Pete McAfee; [ed.] Grover Cleveland High School,

Queens College; [occ.] Blue Collar Worker; [pers.] Who needs humor? I have life; [a.] Elmhurst, NY

MCBRIDE, MICHAEL D.
[pen.] Douglas Thornhaven; [b.] December 6, 1979, San Jose, CA; [p.] Douglas McBride and Carol McBride; [occ.] Student at Archbishop Mitty High School; [hon.] Honor Roll; [oth. writ.] Poetry published in school poetry magazine; [pers.] "They" are among us.; [a.] San Jose, CA

MCCASKILL, STEPHANIE
[b.] November 30, 1956, San Angelo, TX; [p.] Patrica O. and Ray E. Stratton; [m.] C. Blake McCaskill, October 9, 1988; [ed.] Clear Creek High School, San Jacinto Jr. College; [occ.] Secretary, Office Mgr., Solicitor of Insurance; [memb.] Life Underwriters Training Council Fellowship, Thespians, Girl Scouts of America, Humane Society; [hon.] First place in poetry contest, District of South Houston (73-74), high schools, Honorable Mention in State of Texas High School (73-74).

MCCLUNE, TAMIRA DAWN
[pen.] Fireskies; [b.] April 26, 1978, San Diego, CA; [ed.] Sheepshead Bay High School, Baruch College; [hon.] English Honors, Isador Strauss Award, Certificate of Merit; [oth. writ.] Several poems published by The National Library of Poetry and the Poetry Press.; [pers.] Never walk away from those you love!; [a.] Brooklyn, NY

MCGEARY, FRANK L.
[b.] February 14, 1927; Verona, PA; [p.] Martha and Charles E. McGeary; [m.] Doris Anderson McGeary; 1947; [ch.] Greg, Kevin, Erin; [ed.] B.S. - MET. Engineer Carnegie Institute of Technology various post-grad courses in materials quality, Management at several Schools and Universities; [occ.] Retired Engineering Consultant; [memb.] Sigma Xi, American Society for Metals, National Association of Corrosion Engineers, Professional Engineer-California, American Legion; [hon.] Scientific Research Society, President, Local Gov't Council; [oth.writ.] Writer or contibuter to many technical papers and several books. Editor newsletter "Materials Digest". Poems published in several books and articles.; [pers.] Poetry "Speaks" my unspoken and emotional communication to self and those who are sensitive to life's vagaries; [a.] Melbourne, FL

MCGEE II, GLENDA M.
[pen.] Bumble Bee G Money; [b.] September 5, 1960; Los Angeles; [p.] Lula M. Magness; [m.] Teri Lynn Bailey McGee; April 15, 1983; [ch.] Glendon III; Amber Nicole, Markus Daniel; [ed.] Centeniel H.S.; [a.] Compton, CA

MCGOWAN, JENNIFER
[b.] October 18, 1980, Paris, TX; [p.] James and Mary McGowan; [ed.] Currently in 10th grade; [occ.] Hostess at Italian restaurant; [pers.] I didn't think I would ever have someone notice my poems. Someone who cared made me believe. To: Freddie, thanks.; [a.] Charlottesville, VA

MCKELVEY, DANA Y.
[b.] February 2, 1980; Charleston, SC; [p.] Henry McKelvey, Alvarnia Mckelvey; [ed.] R.B. Stall High School; [occ.] Student, R.B. Stall High School; [memb.] Academic Bowl Team Debate Team; [hon.] Erskine Scholar Academic Bowl Team High Scorer Solo and Ensemble Award for violin; [oth.writ.] Several poems and essays written for school and country competitions; [pers.] I endeavor to shed light upon others as Maya Angelou and Nikki Giovanni have shed light upon me. So all writers who come behind me will never

have to walk in darkness; [a.] Charleston, SC

MCKENZIE, C. MARK
[b.] December 14, 1960; Ashland, KY; [p.] Ray and Wilma McKinzie; [m.] Martina C. McKinzie; January 10, 1990; [ed.] University of Central Oklahoma, B.S. Industrial Safety, Environmental Engineering; [occ.] Inventory Analyst with Boeing Aerospace Operations; [memb.] Phi Theta Kappa International Honor Society, American Society of Safety Engineers; [hons.] Who's Who Among Students in American Junior Colleges, The National Dean's List, Swam English Channel - July 1990; [pers.] Say what you want to say, do what you want to do. For those who don't accept what you do or say, their opinion is not relevant to your purpose. Writing mentor—Jean Binkley, Professional Rose State College; [a.] Midwest City, OK

MCLEOD, LOIS
[pen.] Lois Starr; [b.] June 24, 1920, Lafon, CA; [p.] Lela (Moody) Starr and Kenneth; [m.] Donald McLeod, September 24, 1939; [ch.] Two daughters, two sons; [ed.] High school, San Jose, 1/2 year college; [occ.] Retired Occupation Dairy Woman; [memb.] Society of Friends, Friends of Orland Library, Orland Historical Society, Friends unto Neighbors Women's Group, Orland Music Supporters; [hon.] None for writing, ribbon at local fairs for art work and flowers; [oth. writ.] Two children's stories, published several poems published locally, many poems unpublished and stories.; [pers.] I believe poems should reflect an idea as well at descriptions, I am a Christian of the Quaker denomination.; [a.] Orland, CA

MCMILLAN, BOBBYDYNE H.
[pen.] Bobby, Bobbydyne Hicks, and Bobbydyne H. McMillan; [b.] September 14, 1949, Oxford, NC; [p.] Carnell and Catherine Hicks; [m.] Divorced; [ch.] Tonya, Tinea, and Tanika; [ed.] E.E. Smith Senior High School and Fayetteville State University; [occ.] 5th Grade Teacher, Cumberland Road Elem., Fayetteville, NC; [memb.] First Baptist Church Choir, E.E. Smith Alumni Association, E.E. Smith PTA Executive Board, and E.E. Smith Band Boosters; [hon.] Third place winner and two honorable mentions, in the Writer's Ink Guild, Fields of the Earth poetry contest; [oth. writ.] Several poems and short stories (unpublished); [pers.] My genuine concern for all mankind has inspired me in my writings. If through self-expression, I could correct all the wrongs, this would be a flawless world.; [a.] Fayetteville, NC

MECHLER, TERESA
[pen.] Teresa Stack; [b.] October 30, 1961, Pomona, CA; [p.] Bernard and Dolores Stack; [m.] Laszlo Mechler, May 21, 1988; [ch.] Matthew Joseph; [ed.] Revere High, University of Akron; [occ.] Office Manager, P-D and Assoc., Cleveland, Ohio; [memb.] OOEA, IMRA, Nat'l Honor Society; [hon.] YWCA Future Career Woman of the Year; [oth. writ.] Compilation of many personal writings.; [pers.] Dare to find that ideal place somewhere between reality and the imagination!; [a.] Streetsboro, OH

MECK, JESSICA
[b.] February 26, 1981; Spokane, WA; [p.] Patty and Randy Meck; [ed.] John R. Rogers High; [occ.] Receptionist; [memb.] Chamber Choir, Shivesen Choir, Pirate Gold Choir; [pers.] I wish to say thank you to my parents for always supporting me and loving me. I hope I make a difference in the world and touch someone somewhere. Thank you to all who supported me; [a.] Spokane, WA

MELL, NANCY
[b.] October 31, 1940; [m.] Jerry Mell; [ch.] Charles, Mark, Jeffrey, Jerry and Colleen; [pers.] I wrote the poem, "Nicole," for a very special granddaughter, who lives in Scotland.; [a.] Omaha, NE

MIEHL, JR., JAMES A.
[pen.] Poe Van Morn; [b.] March 24, 1944; Buffalo, NY; [ed.] B.A., M.A., Canisius College, Buffalo, NY; [oth.writ.] Refugee's Vision," a play, @ 1977, Exposition Press.; [pers.] I could use some editorial help, Bio-Sketch, including my Mom, who is dying. I want her to see her own name on my poem.; [a.] Dyndee, NY

MIKE, OLGA M.
[pen.] HS; [b.] November 15, 1948; Greenville, NC; [p.] Charles Mike, Mary Mike; [ed.] M.A., New York University; [occ.] Nurse; [pers.] To God be the glory.; [a.] Winterville, NC

MILLER, LILA V.
[b.] May 9, 1963; Rockland County, NY; [ed] Center for Media Art) Advertising Art, Fit; [occ.] Drafpesin; [a.] Brooklyn, NY

MILLER, MARY ANN
[b.] November 7, 1964; Stana Clara; [p.] Stand Hope Howard Miller, Ruth Alee Shaney; [m.] Noel Howard Lowe; November 8, 1997; [ch.] (4) Three Girls and One Boy; [ed.] Milpats Cont. High School, Milipats Darlmouth Jr. High School, San Jose Rose Mary Park Elementary School San Jose CA.; [occ.] Homemaker; [oth.writ.] None, personal Journal.; [pers.] I truly am very happy you loved my poem and I am thinking on writing a short Sci-Fi novel and would love someone to help out on it. Like how to lay-out the work.; [a.] Santa Cruz, CA

MILLIGAN, TAUNYA A.
[pen.] Taunya A. Haag; [b.] December 27, 1975, Granger, UT; [p.] David and Pam Haag; [m.] Michael Milligan, June 3, 1995; [ch.] Nicole Marie, expecting August, 1997; [ed.] High school graduate, Tooele, Utah; [occ.] Homemaker; [pers.] My greatest influences are my parents, high school associates, my beloved husband and my children.; [a.] Virginia Beach, VA

MITCHELL, ANGELA BAGBY
[b.] August 8, 1971; Griffin Spaulding Co., GA; [p.] Henry and Gail Bagby; [m.] David Paschael Mitchell; December 9, 1995; [ch.] Giselle, Cookie; [ed.] The University of Georgia, B.S.E.D. in Secondary English, "No Fear Shakespeare" offered by the Ga. Shakespeare Festival; [occ.] Teacher, English and Art; [memb.] Golden Key National Honor Society, Kappa Delta Pi Honor Society, S.C.A. (Society for Creative Anachronisms); [hon.] Dean's list, Presidential Scholar Award-U.G.A.; [oth.writ.] "Ophelia's Barge" "The Courtesy Of Nature," "The Rainwoman"; [pers.] My influences include the early romantic poets (especially Shelley) Shakespeare, and C.S. Lewis. I strive to help others find the beauty in nature, and the joy the creator has placed within our own souls; [a.] Jackson, GA

MITCHELL, JEFFREY
[b.] March 28, 1981; Lawton, OK; [p.] Keithand Terri Mitchell; [ed.] Sophomore at Frederick High School, high school diploma pending graduation; [occ.] Independent Writer/Student; [memb.] Member of National Honor Society, National Jr. Honor Society, Fellowship of Christian Athletes, Oklahoma Honor Society, First Baptist Church; [hon.] 4.0 GPA, 8th Grade Valedictorian, Hugh O'Brien Youth Ambassador, Recipient United States National Mathematics Awards ; [oth.writ.] Previously unpublished independent journals and recordings; [pers.] My poetry's sole purpose is to take the reader places they never thought they could go and think in new and revolutionary ways.

MONGAN, MARY KATHARINE
[b.] May 8, 1967, Milwaukee, WI; [p.] Dennis and Marilyn Mongan; [ed.] Wauwatosa East High School, Mount Mary College; [occ.] Records Administrator at Mount Mary College Fund Raising Department; [memb.] Wilwaukee Alumnae Chapter of Mount Mary College, Peanut Gallery Email Society at Mt. Mary College; [pers.] Poetry starts out as prose, you must edit it down to get to where you are going.; [a.] Wauwatosa, WI

MONTEFORTE, MERLE A.
[b.] August 26, 1938, Brooklyn, NY; [p.] Myrl and Theresa Morgan; [m.] Al Monteforte, September 24, 1975; [ch.] Diana Lynn and Sandee Risa Dominick Amilynne Ashley; [ed.] Manual Training High School, Mandel School for Medical Assistants, graduate of Children's Institute of Writing; [occ.] Medical Assistant; [memb.] Forest Oaks Lutheran Church; [hon.] Top Award in Mandel School for Medical Assistants. Received highest average of class. Received gold pin on graduation from high school and medical school. Also on Dean's List in medical school.; [oth. writ.] Short stories and articles on various subjects, and various poems.; [pers.] If one person reads my poems or articles and feels the way I did when I wrote it, then I have achieved my purpose for writing it.; [a.] Spring Hill, FL

MONTFORT, JULIE
[b.] July 30, 1959, Port-Au Prince, Haiti; [p.] Philipe Charles and Julie B. Charles; [m.] Jean Edwing Montfort, December 22, 1984; [ch.] Olivier Montfort and Deborah Montfort; [ed.] Elementary and high in Haiti, College: Miami Dade Community College; [occ.] Tutoring at E. L. Doctor Whigham Elementary School, also working toward an AA degree; [hon.] First Paras of the Year in my work place.; [oth. writ.] Many other poems but never published them.; [pers.] Watching my son growing up inspired me to write the poem. And I came to the final reasoning to never judge mankind on their first appearance.; [a.] Miami, FL

MOORE, (MARVIN) ERIC
[pen.] Memoore, Mem; [b.] July 31, 1973; Pinehurst, NC; [ed.] Garner Sr. High Sophomore status and North Carolina State University; [occ.] IBM (Customer Set-Up Auditor); [hon.] Various awards outside of poetry or writing (ex. church, bowling, academic, computers, work-related); [oth.writ.] David's 121st in his hands to the Family (Poem to Grandmother) (Mother's day Poem); [a.] Cary, NC

MOORE, KAY FRANCES
[pen.] K.F. Moore, Kay Davis; May 25, 1939; Tom Bean, TX; [p.] Oneta Elizabeth Turner Davis, William Hoyt Davis; [m.] Robert Paul Moore; New Year's Eve 1965; [ch.] Sherry, Jason, Lisa and Ryan; [ed.] Went to schools in Whitewright, Texas, Jacksonville, Florida and Honolulu, Hawaii; [occ.] Freelance writer of short fiction; business card and greeting card designer; [memb.] Save the Manatee Association of St. Petersburg, Florida; [oth. writ.] Have published column regularly in several (weekly) newspapers in Oklahoma and South Carolina; [pers.] My family has sacrificed much while I was writing. My children turned out terrific in spite of it. I'm so very proud of them.; [a.] Mustang, OK

MOORE, LARRY RAY
[pen.] Sherwood MacArthur; [b.] August 8, 1940, New Harmony, IN; [p.] Albert and Goldie Moore; [m.] Rose Marie Moore, November 19, 1960; [ch.] Gregory Scott and Kimberly Diane; [ed.] BS Law Enforcement and Corrections, MS Criminal Justice, Post Graduate Studies completed Dr. Health and Safety; [occ.] Multi-plant Emergency Management Exercise Director; [memb.] International Association of Chiefs of Police, Institute of Certified Managers; [hon.] National Police Honor Society, Presidential Unit Citation (Combat-Vietnam), 2-Purple Hearts, Combat Infantry Badge, Lockheed Martin Energy Sps. Presidents Award, y-12 Plant Award of Excellence, (LMES); [oth. writ.] 17 magazine (trade) articles published in "The Police Chief," Security Management, Professional Safety, Military Police Law Enforcement Bulletin, American Operating Room Journal.; [a.] Knoxville, TN

MOORE, STELLA
[b.] July 12, 1951, North Carolina; [p.] Velner (McKnight) and Jeff Sharper; [m.] Terry Moore; [ch.] Antonio, Curtis, Angela, Alex and Tiana; [ed.] Franklinton High, Montclair State College, Essex County College, attended college two years, no degree. Both colleges are in New Jersey; [occ.] Train Operator with the New York City Transit Authority; [memb.] House of Prayer At The Gate called Beautiful Church, Building Fund Committee, Sunday School Teacher, Church Trustee, and a Registered Bone Marrow Doner.; [oth. writ.] None published; [pers.] I always try to put God first in my life, and do unto others as I would have them do unto me.; [a.] Teaneck, NJ

MORAVEC, ANDREA
[b.] July 3, 1983, Faribault, MN; [p.] Gary and Jan Moravec; [ed.] K-7 at Trinity Lutheran, 8th grade (1996-1997 school year) at Faribault Junior High School; [hon.] Editor's Choice, published in A Moment to Reflect; [oth. writ.] "It Does Me Just Fine" has been published, other short stories and poems haven't been published yet.; [pers.] Ever since I was really little I've wanted to do many things. One of those things was to become a published author/poet. I began writing stories and poems in 4th grade.; [a.] Faribault, MN

MORGAN, OLIVER L.
[b.] July 9, 1909; Spring City, PA; [p.] Titos Morgan and Annie Keffer; [m.] Mary (Deceased); [m.] Aprox. January 25, 1935; [ch.] 4; [ed.] High school only; [occ.] Retired; [memb.] None except, AARP, PNX Senior Center; [oth.writ.] My ideal mate no poem here, what do you think? Did you receive a couple of other poems I sent a fews days ago? [pers.] This is only a profile of my life; [a.] Phoenixville, PA

MORRIS, MICHAEL LLOYD
[b.] June 8, 1975, Corbin, KY; [p.] R. C. Morris, Sandra Morris; [ed.] Williamsburg High, University of Kentucky; [occ.] Theater Undergraduate Student; [oth. writ.] Flowers in the Wind; [pers.] There is but one magic: love.; [a.] Williamsburg, KY

MOSESOVA, IRINA ALEXANDRI
[b.] August 28, 1978; Azerbaijan, USSR; [p.] Nana Mosesova, Alex Mosesova; [ed.] Currently enrolled in High School (Graduate of '97); [oth.writ.] Several poems written, But none were published; [pers.] To me poetry goes beyond understanding on to feeling and relating to yourself; [a.] Ames, IA

MOYER, ERIN C.
[pen.] Erin Moyer; [b.] October 27, 1978, Pittsburgh, PA; [p.] Kathleen and Barry Moyer; [ed.] Hampton High School Class of 1997; [occ.] Student - Athlete; [hon.] 4 Year swimming letter winner, symphonic and marching band letter winner; [oth. writ.] All other writings have been left unpublished.; [pers.] Follow your dreams and listen to your heart for they are your true guides in life.; [a.] Allison Park, PA

MUELLER, DANIEL B.
[pe.] Dan Mueller; [b.] June 16, 1937; Clark, Co. WA; [p.] Mr. and Mrs. Raymond Moeller; [m.] Joyce E; September 23, 1957; [ch.] 3 boys Timothy, Rusty, Chris; [ed.] Grades 1-8, Veefkind Elm. Clark Co. WA, High School 9-10 Spencer high 11-12, Monroe High, Monroe WA; [occ.] Machinest; [oth.writ.] Unpublish songs; [pers.] I would like this ppoem dedicated to all children hoping they heed the message and strive for a better and Holsom life; [a.] Queen Creek, AZ

MULLER, BRITTANY
[b.] July 4, 1986; Ft Lauderdale, FL; [p.] William E. Regina; [ed.] Student at West Minster Academy 5th Grade; [occ.] Student; [hon.] Terrifoc Kid (Kiwanis International Award) Twice High Honor Roll 2 years straight (4th and 5th grade); [oth.writ.] Song writing: Christian, Country, and Love Ballads; [pers.] I do all my writing for the Lord Jesus Christ; [a.] Pomp. Beach, FL.

MURRELL, JAMES E.
[b.] May 29, 1958, Blooming, IL; [p.] James L. Murrell, Marge Murrell; [ch.] Elizabeth, Alan, Grant, Taylor; [ed.] Lincoln High, Lincoln, IL, Chesterfield Marlboro Tech.; [occ.] Carpenter; [hon.] Dean's List, Golden Poet Award; [oth. writ.] Complete book of poetry, several poems published in local newspaper.; [pers.] I try to put myself in another person's shoes and write a poem from their viewpoint. Feeling what they feel, seeing what they see good or bad.; [a.] Bennettsville, SC

NAIRN, THOMAS F.
[b.] March 25, 1937, Washington, DC; [p.] Walter and Margaret Nairn; [m.] JoAnn F. Serowick (Nairn), February 15, 1958; [ch.] Thomas Jr., James and Susan, Danamarie Daughter-in-law; [ed.] Anacostia High School, Ben Franklin University, International Correspondence School, Pepco Computer Course; [occ.] Lead Cost Analyst, Potomac Electric Power Co.; [memb.] Knights of Columbus, Calvert Memorial Hospital Aux.; [oth. writ.] Several poems, only one published.; [pers.] My poetry is an expression of my love and gratitude for my wife, family, relatives and special friends. They were there when I needed them after my two heart transplants.; [a.] Huntingtown, MD

NANDRESY, DOROTHY
[b.] April 19, 1911, Parkersburg, WV; [m.] John A. Nandresy (Deceased), February 15, 1936; [ch.] M. Sue Mortensen and Kitty North; [ed.] High school and Fairmont College, WVA, Universities of California at Berkeley, Hayward, San Diego, degree from San Francisco, a degree in Psychology and Social Sciences; [occ.] Retired; [memb.] Methodist Church, Bristol, FL, American Asso. of University Women, Eastern Star of San Lorenzo, CA; [oth. writ.] School Educator, Music Language Arts, Counselling; [pers.] Reacts to "beauty" of people, music, art and written and spoken words. Believes persons can accomplish much more than they do by having a positive attitude and striving to develop their potential.; [a.] Hampton, VA

NATAL, MARYCELIS
[b.] October 17, 1977; New Jersey; [p.] Carmelo and Reyes Natal; [ed.] A.C. Redshaw School, New Brunswick High School; [occ.] Sales/ Stock/ Cashier at shoe store; [pers.] My poems reflect who I am, and by reading them you get to know me.; [a.] New Brunswick, NS

NEITZ, LAURA M.
[b.] March 4, 1933; Philadelphia, PA; [p.] Mary and Walter Krzaczek; [m.] Brig Gen Robert H. Neitz, USAF (Ret); November 1, 1952; [ch.] Virginia, Carol, Laurence; [ed.] Frankford HS, Phila, PA; AA Troy State University; BA University of the State of NY; Fleisher Art of Memorial Phila; Defense Information Sch., Ft Benj, Harrison, IN; [occ.] Artist and Interior Designer; [memb.] Old Presbyterian Meeting House, Alexandria, VA; [hon.] Top 10% of high school's class; Outstanding Performance Awards from Department of Defense; Legislature of Guam Proclamation for Community Involvement, including species of water colors of endangered species of birds of Territory of Guam; [oth. writ.] Hundreds of articles published in Pacific Stars and Stripes; Award for article published in Soldier's Magazine, news releases for Dept of Defense to all major newspapers, several poems published in military magazines; [pers.] Wish to travel through life with grace and dignity, enjoying family and friends.

NELSON, CONSTANCE M.
[b.] August 21, 1938, Emmaus, PA; [p.] Leo and Bid Nelson (Deceased); [m.] Divorced; [ch.] Jane-Frances and Gregory; [ed.] Allen High School, Writers Digest (correspondence); [occ.] Retired due to illness; [memb.] Shiloh Bible Church, Monroe County Bible Club, CMA, Christian Motorcycle Assoc.; [hon.] Monroe County Bible Club; [oth. writ.] Couch Correspondent, Democratic Convention, published in local paper.; [pers.] Incurable romantic who loves the Lord and all His creations and people. I hope to praise and honor Him.; [a.] Bloomsburg, PA

NELSON, MADGE HAINES
[b.] 1906; Mt View, Ca; [p.] Mr. and Mrs. A Haines; [m.] Mr. Axel Nelson - 104 age; 1982; [ed.] MA. in Children Literature; [occ.] Retired school teacher; [oth.writ.] Fighting Africa's, Black Magic, When My World Crashed, You Too Can Find Peace, Lewis and Clark Exporers to the West, The Wright Brother, First to Fly, Angel Stories of the Bible, Stories Jesus Told, David and His Harp, Between Sea and Mountains, Fun and Health, Happy Children, Peter and Pan; [a.] Angurn, CA

NICHOLSON, MARIE PINKERTON
[pen.] "Aunt Pinkie"; [b.] December 20, 1922, Philadelphia, PA; [p.] William and Anna Marie Pinkerton; [m.] William Nicholson, September 7, 1945; [ch.] Deborah, William and Robin; [ed.] Hallahan Cath. Girls High School, Fleischers Vocational Business College; [occ.] Song Teacher at "Wee Love" Day Care Center; [memb.] Board of Directors of "Wee Love," a non-profit learning center. I receive my poems complete with melodies, so they are sung by 130 preschool children of "Wee Love"; [hon.] Prayer poem published in "Spiritual Frontiers Fellowship" quarterly; [oth. writ.] "Divine Energy," "Children Bloom With Love," "Love Makes You Beautiful," "'Ne Mae' Means You're Beautiful," "The People Of The World," "The Silver Rule" (Don't Waste Time and Energy on Hating) and "It's Your World."; [pers.] "Wee Love" is a public institution as we can't sing about God, so we sing about the light, love and joy within each of us. My works promote spiritual awareness.; [a.] Maple Shade, NJ

NITSCHE, J. NEAL
[pen.] J. N. Nitche; [b.] October 10, 1963; Dallas, TX; [p.] James F. and Anita Wardrup Nitche; [ed.] Lake Highland High School; American Trades

Institute (ATI) ACAD Degree; [occ.] Unemployed (Disabled); [memb.] First United Methodist Church, Dallas Saltillo Methodist Church, Saltillo, TX; [oth.writ.] Several, just never have found out how to get published, or if there was a market for it; [pers.] I hope my poetry reflects what is truley important in the world; love, peace nature. I also hope that the reader finds a little of him/herself in what they read and they enjoy what they read; [a.] Dallas, TX

NIXON, SHILEEN
[b.] February 18, 1961; Fostoria, OH; [m.] Don Nixon; July 9, 1983; [ch.] Justin Andrew, Austyn Jacob; [ed.] Mechville High School; [occ.] Full-time Home school Mom; [pers.] My Christian faith is the major influence of my life which naturaly filters through my writings.; [a.] McMurray, PA

NOLFI, KRISTEN
[b.] March 14, 1972, Bridgeport, CT; [p.] Catherine and Richard Nolfi; [ed.] Fairfield High School, Western New England College, American International College; [occ.] High School English Teacher; [pers.] This poem is dedicated to the memory of my brother, friend and hero, Richard F. Nolfi (8/2/77-6/30/95) . . . and David Tippet (6/30/77-6/30/95). These young men have given myself, Robert, Mom and Dad (and many others) innumerable valuable lessons in life. Rich and Dave, you will always shine on!; [a.] Agawam, MA

NORCUTT JR., O.L.
[m.] Kathleen Viola; February 14, 1991; [ch.] One son Okey Mason; [ed.] Graduate of Radford University with a degree n Journalism; [occ.] Police Officer for the City of Danville; [memb.] Veteran of Foreign Wars; [pers.] My poems and writings reflect the world I see around me; [a.] Gretna, VA

NORTON, NILE
[b.] February 24, 1922, Decatur Co, IA; [p.] Mr. and Mrs. Earl Norton; [m.] Mary Joy Norton, January 15, 1949; [ch.] Susan, Michael, Brenda; [ed.] PhD Univ Denver; [occ.] Retired; [hon.] NEH, Military Decorations, St. Mary's Univ distinguished lecturous program; [oth. writ.] Non-published: Hist. Lone Star Brewery, Agrimurder (fiction): Published MA and PhD thesis and dissertation; [pers.] Poem written on July 18, 1945. I believe this test to be the most all invasive event of the 20th century.; [a.] San Antonio, TX

NOSKER, SUE
[pen.] Sue Nosker, Bearfire; [b.] November 26, 1952, Burbank, CA; [p.] Lawrence Anderson, Ermal Huffman; [m.] Richard E. Nosker, March 26, 1977; [ch.] Sebastian, Zachary and Kalela; [ed.] B.S. Geology - Sonoma State University, M.S. - Geology - MacKay School of Mines, University of Nevada, Reno.; [occ.] Geologist/Tour Director; [memb.] Geological Society of America, Sigma X, Research Society, Business and Professional Women; [oth. writ.] Brand new poet . . . first time submitting anything. (I've written 150 poems this year); [pers.] Find the joy in each special moment of now . . . rejoice in the rich sweetness of today!; [a.] Sebastopol, CA

NWOSU, DR. BENJAMIN
[pen.] Apex; [b.] August 31, 1970; Igbo-Ukwu, Nigeria; [p.] Godfrey Nwosu, Mabel Nwosu; [ed.] Agulu Grammar School, Nigeria College of Medicine, University of Nigeria, NSUKKA; [occ.] Resident Doctor, Howard University Hospital, Wash, DC; [memb.] Silver - 88 - League; [hon.] Distinction prize in Human Anatomy, University of Nigeria, 1991, Best creative student, Agulu Gram-

mar School, 1985; [oth.writ.] Various poems in other anthologies. The One-Eyed Man, a novel in print; [pers.] I am inspired by God, my environment and my dreams; [a.] Hyattsville, MD

ODDO, SCOTT
[pen.] Scooter; [b.] June 1, 1964; [p.] Robert Oddo, Geraldine Oddo; [ed.] Maryvale High School, Alfred State University, Bryant and Stratton; [occ.] Self-employed Tree and Home Services - Taxi Driver; [pers.] When something jumps in your mind and it feels right - go with it until it works out.

OHMAN, VIRGINIA ANN
[pen.] Annie; [b.] July 21, 1942, Seattle, WA; [p.] Edger and Ruth Vassar; [m.] Paul Ohman, March 8, 1986; [ch.] Four, Ralph, Victoria, Darren and Robert; [ed.] High school; [occ.] Aerospace Coordinator; [pers.] My writings come from my heart. Wether it's about the homeless woman wrapped in a thin blanket lying on the sidewalk, or the birth of my grandchild, there is a story to be told. I write about life. The beauty of it and the sorrow of it.; [a.] Lake Forest Park, WA

OLIN, ASHLEY
[b.] December 10, 1983; Warren, OH; [p.] Nancy Olin; [occ.] Student-7th Grade; [hon.] O.M. - 3rd division - 3'D three 5th (Odessy of Mind) U.I.L.- 3rd thru 5th won awards for writing, acting and music. 2nd Band (trumpet); [a.] Garland, TX

ORTIZ, NICOLE
[b.] November 5, 1984, Santa Clara, CA; [p.] Debra Ortiz; [ed.] Presently attending El Portal Middle School, 7th grade; [hon.] 1. D.A.R.E. essay, 2. Best of the Writing Fair Award, 3. Rolling Hills Scholarship award; [a.] Escalon, CA

OTA, CARLA LEE
[b.] November 12, 1954, Portsmouth, OH; [p.] Norman Adkins, Sylvia Adkins; [m.] Edward I. Ota, October 10, 1987; [ch.] Derrik E. Farmer, Chris A. Ota; [ed.] John Glenn High School, Cerritos Jr. College; [occ.] Word Processor, La Mirada, CA; [memb.] Parent Teacher Association, International Society of Poets; [hon.] Several Editor's Choice Awards for poetry; [oth. writ.] Poems published in: "A Moment to Reflect," "The Nightfall of Diamonds," "Through Sun and Shower" and "The Best Poems of 1997."; [pers.] My writings are inspired by love and written from the heart.; [a.] La Mirada, CA

PADILLA, SOPHIE
[b.] July 5, 1930; Ovid, Colorado; [p.] Manuel Don Padilla, Margaret Martinez; [m.] Archibald A. Gonzales; January 20, 1948; [ch.] Denna Gonzales, Julie Gonzales; [ed.] Sacramento Senior High (Graduated) Vocational Schooling: Hair Styling; [occ.] Several in local newspapers articles, pursuing writing children's stories and poetry; [memb.] Suburban Writer's Club (Poetry Center Club) Sacramento, CA City of Sacramento Society of Poets; [hon.] (7-times) Awarded-Golden Poets of Awards of the Year; [oth.writ.] "Isaac" New Teeth, Indian Treasure, Indian Medicine Man; [pers.] In my being handicapped and certified to go blind, my quest is to write poetry that reflects people in all walks of life; [a.] Sacramento, CA

PALMER, CAROLYN Y.
[b.] June 19, 1963; Olol Hosp. (BRLA); [p.] Mr. and Mrs. Carroll Palmer; [ch.] Michael T. Jemone D., Donavan T. Palmer; [ed.] High School Diploma May 18, 1981, Delta College Clerical Business Cert. 1988, LA Tech. College - Welding Student 1995; [occ.] Homemaker; [memb.] Active member of the Church of Jesus Christ of Latter day

Saints, Serves as Single Adult representative, and activities committeee chairperson; [hon.] Editors Choice Award 1996, Editors Choice Award 1997; [oth.writ.] P0391404-049, Some Like it hot some like it, "Seeds" (Quill Books), Welder, P0391404 -019; "Happiness; [pers.] I Carolyn Palmer, would one day like to earn a law degree. I would also like to write children stories; [a.] Baton Rouge, LA

PALMER, PATRICIA
[pen.] Ms. Trish; [b.] September 22, 1953; [p.] Charles and Helen Baskerville; [ch.] Shnalyna '72', Kalvan '24', Dishan '76', Barbara-Lee '81'; [ed.] Graduated college; [occ.] Mother, Daughter, Sister, R.N. and friend to all. [mem.] Enoch Chapel Baptist Church, Paralyzed Veterans Assoc., National Parks and Conservation Assoc., Noetic Sciences, Southern Poverty Law Center; [hon.] It is an honor to be a child of God; [oth.writ.] Yet to be published. See King Publisher for publication of my book of poems; [pers.] I am a holistic spiritual being. God loves us all.; [a.] Hampstead, NC

PALSER, SPRING
[pen.] Skp; [b.] March 25, 1980; Valley Stream, Long Island, NY; [p.] John and Diane Palser; [ed.] William L. Buck/Memorial Junior High School/ Central high school; [memb.] NRA; [hon.] NYSMA violinist (Grade Level up to 6) Winner 3 years (metals) New York State Music Association; [oth.writ.] Destiny, Sugar Plum, "The Book of all Books" - A book with some of my best poetry ever written Impend, some work published in school paper; [pers.] "When you find yourself questioning your own sanity, then you will always know you are never really crazy to begin with-just live life to the fullest, Forget what people want you to be, -Just be yourself"; [a.] Valley Stream, NY

PAPE, MORITZ E.
[b.] December 14, 1903; Brookline, MA; [p.] Eric and Alice Pape; [m.] Doris Pape (deceased.); [ch.] Barbara Lynn Pape; [ed.] Tamalpais High School Mill Valley, CA; [occ.] Retired Accountant (now a writer); [memb.] Commonwealth Club of Calif.; Institute of Management Accountants (Past National Vice President) Knights of St. Cecilian's Church (Secty. 8 years.); [hon.] Emeritus life Associate of Inst. of Mgmt. Acctnts.; [oth.writ.] "The Schemees", "Poetic Variables and other Thoughts", "The iLost Gospel", numerous poems, short stories and non-fiction articles— see attached; [pers.] Many thanks for all the poems previously published by you over the years; [a.] San Francisco, CA.

PARKER, ELIZABETH
[pen.] Liz Cole Parker; [b.] June 5, 1942, El Centro, CA; [m.] Robert J. Parker II, March 17, 1973; [ch.] Keely Parker and Charlie Parker; [ed.] B.A. from Okla Northwestern, State University, graduate work at University of Central Okla.; [occ.] Speech and Drama Teacher in junior high for 33 yrs.; [memb.] Okla Education Association, National Education Association, Board of Examiners for National Council for Accreditation of Teacher Education Programs; [hon.] Outstanding Young Speech Teacher in Okla., Outstanding Jr. High Speech Teacher in Okla, Distinguished Service Award from Mid-Del School District; [pers.] You share your heart when you share your poetry.; [a.] Midwest City, OK

PASS, JOSEPH
[b.] March 18, 1953, Franklin, IN; [p.] Ed and Mayme Pass; [m.] Linda Lee Pass, October 28, 1978; [ch.] Wanda, Cindy, Heather, David; [ed.] 1 yr college; [occ.] Own Construction Company; [pers.] My writing allows me to express myself in

a way or depth that I would otherwise never allow.; [a.] Franklin, IN

PATTERSON, CHARLENE
[pen.] Charlene Patterson; [b.] June 13, 1917, Burkettsville, OH; [p.] Deceased; [m.] Deceased; [ch.] Three; [ed.] Walter, French, Lansing High, Mich-Holt-Mich and New Holland - OH Business Course; [occ.] Retired, "Now-Writing"; [memb.] United Meth. Church, United Meth. Women; [hon.] 25 yrs. School Teacher, 14 yr President U.M. Women, Plaque of 1st book; [oth. writ.] Poetry and prose, 1st book Dec., 1996, all poetry for Church for 50 years.; [pers.] I have recovered from a serious illness after losing my right leg.; [a.] New Holland, OH

PAUL, SOPHIA SONIA
[pen.] Sophia Sonia Paul; [b.] May 28, 1974; Trinidad; [p.] Molly and Theophilus Paul; [m.] No date; [ed.] High School, GED and (vocational) Child Care Diploma. Presently attaining Master Art Diploma and one at the Children's Literature Institute; [occ.] Pre-School Teacher at Linden S.D.A. Day Care Center; [hon.] (none) Just High School for good work; [oth.writ.] I have forty-five to forty-seven other poems written, but never published in newspapers or small books or magazines; [pers.] I believe that reading and writing are the keys to knowledge and the power to success. I started to write from a young age and got my inspiration from love, nature and people around me. Expressing myself in writing is the most treasured talent given to me by God; [a.] Bronx, NY

PENDLETON, JERRY
[pen.] Just - People; [b.] March 2, 1954, Philadelphia; [p.] George and Louise; [m.] Louise; [ch.] 5 girls and 4 boys; [ed.] 12th Grade; [occ.] Salesman; [pers.] Always love to write but never entered competition; decided to enter while reading your advertisement in Sunday paper.; [a.] Philadelphia, PA

PETERSON, MICHAEL MOSES
[p.] "Mosses"; [b.] June 10, 1975; Austin, MN; [p.] Ruth Vale, Jeff Peterson; [ed.] Hayfield H.S., Hayfield, NM, 3 years US Army infantry, 25th ID Hawaii, Combat Lifesaver course, Anti-Armor Warfare course, Air Assault; [occ.] Cutter Operator, Schmidt Printing, Inc., Byron, MN.; [hon.] Air Assault Badge (Army), Overseas Service Ribbon (Army), Expert Rifle Qualification; [oth.writ.] Drawing published in local journal, poem published in "Of Diamonds and Rust, Volume 2"; [pers.] My poems are inspired by life's many conflicts, comedy and tragedy, smile now and cry later.; [a.] Hayfield, MN

PETRASEK, RUTH E.
[b.] April 6, 1933, Pawtucket, RI; [p.] Dora H. and Georg Max Richter; [m.] 1st marriage May 10, 1952 (divorced and later remarried); [ch.] Michael B. Burke, Richard A. Burke, Randell F. Burke; [ed.] 6 yrs Cottage St. School, 3 yrs Goff Jr High, 3 yrs East Sr. High School, all in Pawtucket, RI, graduated with honor in 1950; [occ.] Retired - formerly Sr. Tax Investigator City and County of Denver; [memb.] Advisory Board Stout St. Foundation for several yrs., on Family Council for a yr. at Iliff Care Center, started no smoking policy in city bldgs with co-worker Billy Burleson; [hon.] Employee of the Month City and County of Denver, Certificate of Appreciation for Outstanding and Dedicated Service at Stout St. Foundation; [oth. writ.] In high school won prize for essay written in competition for all jr. high schools in area. Prize presented by Mayor of city.; [pers.] Life is an adventure but one never dies - our souls go on forever. I have written many poems but this one was written prior to emergency brain surgery as I wanted the grandchildren to feel I was not gone and never would be.; [a.] Denver, CO

PETTY, CHYSAWNDRA L.
[b.] July 4, 1977; Belleville, IL; [p.] Steve A. Petty, Cynthia L. Harvey; [ed.] Charter Oak High School, Cal State Fullerton, Chaffey; [occ.] Office Manager and Food Server; [memb.] Ice skating Institute of America, First church of the Nazarene, Pasadena; [oth.writ.] Several poems unpublished, several biographies; [pers.] Thanks to my past both good and bad for without that, I would have on inspiration; [a.] Chino Hills

PEVAR, MAXWELL
[b.] April 2, 1924, Philadelphia, PA; [m.] Shirley Pevar, June 12, 1949; [ch.] Jeffrey, Joel, Karen; [ed.] Bachelor of Art in Metallurgy, Master of Metallurgical Engrg. at Univ. of Penna.; [occ.] Retired - Part-time Consulting Engineer; [memb.] American Society for Metals, American Soc. for Non-Destructive Testing, Disabled American Veteran WWII; [hon.] Fellow in Am. Soc. for Non-Destructive Testing; [oth. writ.] Contribution to Metals Engrg., Merit Badge - Boy Scouts of America, children's book - self-publisher "Impy The Mutated Dinosaur"; [pers.] Each child has two children: Jennifer, Davo, Sarah, Michael. Karen has twins Aliza and Jonathan. I wish them a world in peace.; [a.] Elkins Park, PA

PHELAN, THOMAS A.
[b.] January 20, 1928; Manhattan, NY; [p.] Deceased; [m.] Deceased; [ch.] iThomas, Theresa, Barbara, William; [ed.] Bergen Community Coll. Thos. A. iEdison Coll. U.S. Marine Corps Inst.; [occ.] Priv. Inv. Karate Inst. iProducer/Director Murder Mysteries; [memb.] NYPD Detective Endowment Assoc. iInt'l Bodyguard Assoc. Poetry Soc. America, North Jenseiy Poetry Group, iKenneth R. Balter Poetry Foundation; [hon.] "Author's Award" N.J. Institute iof Technology. Nominated for "Pushchart Prize" by published! Magazine, i"Editor's Choice" National Library of Poetry." Featured in NY Times "On Books" column; [oth.writ.] Poems and short articles published in newspapers iand magazines throughout the U.S. and in Ireland. Poetry books: A Point iBeyond Silences Diamonds Into The Sun, novel "Code Name: Octopus."; [pers.] iWriting poetry has calmed my storm; [a.] Bergenfield, NJ.

PHILLIPS, MARVELLA
[b.] July 26, 1964; Norfolk, VA; [p.] Forrest and Alberta Phillips; [ed.] Attending Norfolk State University majoring in Business Administration; [occ.] Procedures Coordinator; [memb.] Member of the United House of Prayer For All People, Young Adult Choir, Ski Breeze, Naitonal Black Women's Congress; [pers.] I can do all things through in Jesus Christ who strengthens me; [a.] VA Beach, VA

PHIPPS, BRADLEY JAY
[b.] December 17, 1956, Fort Dix, NJ; [p.] M. Jay and Jean Phipps; [m.] Trisha Lynn Phipps, November 10, 1985; [ed.] B.F.A. University of Memphis, White Station High School, Memphis, TN; [occ.] Paramedic at Mercy Medical Center, Durango, CO; [oth. writ.] 1) The View from Purgatory Flats (a book of poetry), 2) The Imaginary Can Rise (a children's book), 3) "Me Not Connor, Me Helmet Boy" (a children's book); [a.] Mancos, CO

PIERSON, SHAWNA
[b.] September 15, 1978; Vincennes, IN; [ed.] I am currenlty a student at Vincennes Univesity and studying Journalism; [occ.] Student; [oth.writ.] I have been writing since age 10. I have a complete porfolio that I designed and laid out myself. I have been on two different newspaper staffs, serving as an editor; [pers.] Follow your heart. Love the children of this world; [a.] Vincennes, IN

PINARD, GILBERTE
[pen.] Gilberte Brown; [b.] June 24, 1924; Chantilly France; [p.] William James Brown ; [m.] Suzane Bizet; September 15, 1945 (France); [ed.] Gramar School High School 2 years College, 2 years business College, 4 years design, 1 year (hairdressing); [occ.] Poete; [hon.] Best Prize for application in studie first prize indesign (fashion and decoration.) Diploma for hairdressing with 30 years of practice; [oth.writ.] Essay book memories ironce essay; [pers.] I like to write with emotion a little bit like Sappo (grecgue poetesse) reflecting all the goodness and noblesse in life; [a.] Manchester, NH

PINNEGAR, STEPHANIE
[pen.] Stephanie Ann Pinnegar; [b.] October 18, 1974; Arkansas Blytheville; [p.] Jim Pinnegar, Kim Pinnegar; [ch.] Darby Yarnell; [ed.] Washington High School; [oth. writ.] Poems written and published by local school.; [pers.] I believe that one of the greater beauties in life are the gift of words, once spoken trey can mean so much to ourselves and others.; [a.] Riverdale

PIQUETTE, MARICEANN
[b.] December 8, 1954, Lowell, MA; [p.] Donald R. and Florence L. Janow; [m.] Jean C. Piquette, August 22, 1972; [ch.] Renee, Laura; [ed.] B.S. Univ. of Central FL., M.S. Nova Southeastern Univ.; [occ.] Special Education Teacher, Rogers High School, Newport, RI; [memb.] Teacher's Association of Newport, School Improvement Planning Committee, Keylife Ministries, African Inland Missions; [hon.] School Improvement and Educational Enrichment of Fl. Schools, Golden Apple Award, Outstanding School Volunteer Coordinator, Innovative and Best Practices in Integrated Curriculum for County Curriculum Fair; [oth. writ.] Publication of educational research practicum - ERIC and bound publication by Nova Southeastern Univ.; [pers.] Writing reveals the innermost feelings and thoughts that I have. In sharing I hope that the reader and I will share a common thread and touch with our hearts.; [a.] Portsmouth, RI

POLICASTRO, VICKI ANN
[b.] May 30, 1976, Brooklyn, NY; [p.] Jim Policastro and Paulette Ferdaise; [ed.] Western High School, Nova Community School, Broward Community College. Books - I am a self educator; [occ.] Reception/payroll/sales for First Class Sounds and Video; [hon.] High School Honor Roll, some writing awards, poem submitted in a collection of writings in school; [oth. writ.] Several hundred unpublished poems and lyrics, short story called, "False Desires," and journal writings. Also currently teamed with a professional astrologer to create written material for personalized charts and planners.; [pers.] My belief is that everybody has a strong power within themselves. We are all guided by our soul, and it will bring much achievement and happiness to those who seek to find it.; [a.] Fort Lauderdale, FL

POLKA, DR. WALTER S.
[pen.] Dr. Walter S. Polka; [b.] November 5, 1945; Niagara Falls, NY; [p.] Franklin W. and Josephine B. Polka; [m.] Victoria M. Homiszcak; August 3, 1968; [ch.] Jennifer M. And Monicajo; [ed.] Lasalle H.S. B.A. - S.U.N.Y. and Bufallo, Post Doctoral Studies - Harvard V. Florida State V; [occ.] Superintendent of School - Lewiston - Porter Central

School District, Youngtown, NY, 14174; [memb.] President of International Society of Educational Plans, member - American Management Association American Association of School Administrations, New York State State School Superintendents, Kiwams Club of Lewiston, Lower Niagara Lodge; [hon.] 1997 New York State Council for the Social Studies/Sirs. Academic Freedom award, 1996 Niagara University Adjunct Proffessor of the year award, 1989 Filene Foundation Fellowship for Harvard University, 1968 Niagara University graduate school scholarship; [oth.writ.] Weekly column "Superintendent's perspective" in the sentinel - a Niagara country publication with a distribution of 15, 500. Weekly poems published by sparrowgrass poetry forum, and Medaille college literacy magazine - prelude; [pers.] My poems reflect my achivements with advice people, things and ideas. I strive to capture the essence of the moment in the most approrient verval manner; [a.] Youngtown, NY.

POLLOCK, NOAH
[pen.] Noah Pollock; [b.] October 3, 1975; Racine; [p.] Mark Pollock, Debbie Esway; [occ.] Student; [hon.] Dean's list at Akron University; [oth.writ.] One short story published in College Newspaper; [pers.] Necebaho; [a.] Akron, OH

PORTER, KAREN
[b.] October 16, 1980, Cortez, CO; [p.] James and Dorothy Porter; [ed.] Currently a Sophomore at Montezuma-Cortez High School; [occ.] Student, in summer I help with parents' farm and babysit; [hon.] Ranked first out of my class academically because of my 4.0 average. Achievement awards because of my grades. Second in science fair at the county level.; [pers.] Writing, to me, means an escape of reality to focus on your dreams, morals and goals. Poetry just deepens the meaning of life even more.; [a.] Cortez, CO

PREDA, LUCIA
[pen.] Lusita; [b.] November 5, 1978; Romania; [p.] Constantin and Mariana Preda; [ed.] Graduated from Forest Hills High School in Queens N.Y. and now going to college to New York Institute of Technology; [occ.] College Student; [hon.] Poetry Awards; [oth.writ.] I had a peom published in a book named Daybreak on the Land; [pers.] My education is the most important thing in my life along with my parents who support me on everything I do; [a.] Rego Park, NY

PUCKETT, CHRISTA R.
[pen.] Christa Puckett; [b.] September 26, 1971, Nashville, TN; [m.] Kevin E. Puckett, April 8, 1995; [ed.] Georgetown Jr./Sr. High, Southern Hills Career Center, Army Ordinance Center and School, Southern State Community College; [occ.] Administrative Assistant, FRP Incorporated; [pers.] I give great thanks to my husband for giving me the inspiration to write, so that I may touch the souls of many people and bring to life the emotions that are forgotten with time.; [a.] Seaman, OH

QUINN, BECKY JEAN
[pen.] Q; [b.] September 28, 1974; Butler, PA; [p.] Nancy Shearer (Sopher), John W. Quinn; [ed.] Butler High School '93, Bradford School, Graphic Design; [occ.] Artist; [hon.] Highest Honors, Bradford School; [oth.writ.] "Dear Mister" NOMAAC, 1989, "The Troubles I've Seen" NOMAAC, 1990, "Shadow" Creative Illusions, 1991, "Thank You," NOMAAC, 1992; [pers.] I find the only thing for me to do whem my purple fades to blue is to get out my red and fix it.; [a.] Jackson Center, PA

RANDOLPH, BRADFORD EARLE
[b.] April 18, 1947, Boston, MA; [p.] Walter and Emerald Randolph; [ed.] Ed.M. Boston University, BS Chemical Engineering - Northeastern University, graduate of Defense Language Institute, Monterey - German Language, Computer Science - Cal State Hayward; [occ.] High School Teacher and Computer Specialist; [memb.] Black Data Processing Associates; [oth. writ.] "That Computer Programmer Is Berserk" by Silicon Sam and the Chips (a comedy album), "I Used To Spy" (book, fiction) plus several song lyrics and comedy routines; [pers.] These song lyrics were written for Ms. Annie Parms for Valentine's Day 1996, she's the hardest working woman in the parent business! I'd sure appreciate it if someone would compose the music.; [a.] San Leandro, CA

RANDOLPH, BRADFORD EARLE
[b.] April 18, 1947; Boston, MA; [p.] Walter and Emerald; [ed.] Masters in Education from Boston University; B.S. Chemical Engineering from Northeastern University; [occ.] Computer Specialist and Educator; [memb.] Black Data Processing Associates San Francisco Bay Area Chapter; [oth.writ.] Comedy Album "That Computer Programmer is Berserk" by Silicon Sam and The Chips. "I used to Spy" A Novel Intended to Reunite Bill Cosby and Robert Culp; [pers.] "Nineties Woman" was a 1996 Valentines Day song written for Annie Parms, the Hardest Working Woman in the Parent Business. I'm still looking for a composer; [a.] San Leandro, CA

RASSI, SUZANNE M. (FALETTI)
[b.] March 22, 1948; Springvalley, IL; [p.] Margarette Faletti and the late Lawrence Faletti; [ch.] Robert C. Wales III; [ed.] Hopkins High, IL, Valley Community College; [occ.] Not employed at present; [memb.] March of Dimes, North Shore Animal League; [oth.writ.] This little church of mine published in church paper. Dad's love publisehd with the National Library of poetry; [pers.] I have to feel my poetry. It has to come from the heart; [a.] Granville, IL

RAYMO, SHIRLEY JEAN
[pen.] Shades of Sadie; [b.] December 2, 1953; Witchataw Falls TX; [p.] James Cady and Pearl Wiech; [m.] Randy Raymo; May 12, 1995; [ch.] Kimberly Michelle Addy - Michael Jason Addy - Jessica Lee Beech; [pers.] Sadie Tex was a name given to me on the day of my birth by my grandfather Gret Cady. Early years found my love for writing so I selected Shades of Sadie as my pen name. This name inspire me; [a.] Petersburg, MI

REBECK, BETTY K.
[b.] November 28, 1954, Logansport; [p.] James and Olive Carson; [m.] Charles Rebeck, July 2, 1977; [ch.] Matthew, Anne, Karl; [ed.] B.S. and M.S. Indiana State University, Terre Haute, Indiana; [occ.] Jr. High Special Education Teacher; [memb.] West Central Classroom Teacher's Association, ISTA, NEA, St. Joseph's Christian Mothers; [pers.] I try to make my poetry imitate human speech. I have been greatly influenced by e.e. Cummings.; [a.] Winamac, IN

RECKART, RICHARD WILLIAM
[pen.] William; [b.] January 12, 1946; [ed.] 7 grade; [occ.] grave digging [a.] Oakland, MD

REDING, EUNICE ABBY
[b.] January 13, 1916, McKees Rocks, PA; [p.] William Henry and Eunice Wyres Ward; [m.] Richard Wallace Reding, August 28, 1937; [ch.] Barbara Ann and Richard William; [ed.] Warren G. Harding Senior High; [occ.] Reading, writing po-

etry, enjoying grand, great grand, and great great grandchildren; [memb.] St. John United Church of Christ, The National Library of Poetry, U.S. Coastguard Auxiliary, AARP, Philatelist Commemorative, Diabeties Society; [hon.] Poems printed in anthologies of The National Library of Poetry, Editor's Choice Awards; [oth. writ.] Invisible Enigma, Lasting Happiness, Travel Dreamer, Mystery of the Lost Words, What's Good What's Not, Reluctant Regrets; [pers.] Sharing my thoughts and the appreciation of my poetry gives me better insight to others and their ideas, which is most rewarding.; [a.] Strasburg, OH

REED, EUGENIA
[b.] January 11, 1901, Howard Co, MD; [oth. writ.] "In Her Honor," "A Sonnet" and "Dawn" published in College of Sequoias anthology.; [pers.] I have been writing poetry all of my life and still enjoy it in my nineties.; [a.] Visalia, CA

REID, ELEANOR PINNELL
[b.] October 24, 1937; Gauley Bridge, WV; [p.] Lois McDonald Pinnell, William Perry Pinnell Sr.; [m.] Divorced; [ch.] Maria M. Murphy, Frederick P. Reid, Donna K. Moore; [ed.] Buckham Upshur HS-1955 WV Wesleyan College- 1 year, Glenville State College 2 years, Fleet Business School 1 years; [occ.] Retired Secretary; [memb.] Heart to Heart Fellowship, Mt. Zion United Methodist Church, Lothian, MD. Hackers Creek WV Pioneer Decendents-Geneology, French Creek WV Pioneers; [hon.] Editors Choice Award, Elected to International Poetry Hall of Fame, Distinguished Member International Society of Poets Poet of Merit, Nominated Poet of the year by International Society of Poets and The National Library of Poetry; [oth.writ.] Have collection of thirty poems since January of 1995; [pers.] I was surprised with gift of poetry from God in 1995. I continually strive to reflect the love of God that I have experienced through life's trials and my faith in God. Dedication: To the women of Mt. Zion Women's Retreat of 1995; [a.] Lothian, MD

REIGEL, CONNIE
[pen.] Lou; [b.] August 8, 1949; Muncy, PA; [p.] Wilbura Esther Mills; [m.] Don Reigel; June 5, 1971; [ch.] 4; [ed.] R.S. Elementary Education, Bloomsburg University; [occ.] Housewife, Dietary Assistant at Nursing Village; [pers.] "Tears of Love" is about the recent loss of my mother. Not expecting it and sudden I needed to do something for her, I miss her so and love her more each day; [a.] Lewisburg, PA

RENALES, RICHARD F.
[b.] May 17, 1952, New Jersey; [ed.] B.A. Trenton State (1974), M.A. Kean College of NJ (1981), M.A. Kean College of NJ (1983); [occ.] Writer; [oth. writ.] Cooking and Living with Passion, A Guide, Volume One Library of Congress: 4-360-300; [a.] Milford, NJ

RENNINGER, NICHOLAS D.
[b.] August 12, 1980, Lewiston, PA; [p.] David and Cynthia Renninger; [ed.] I am presently a senior in high school. I home school. I correspond with ALS Academy in Allentown, PA.; [occ.] Student; [oth. writ.] I have had several poems and short stories published in school newsletters.; [pers.] I believe that the Lord has given me the ability to write and I strive to give glory to Jesus Christ in all that I write.; [a.] Williamstown, VT

REYNOLDS, INZIE
[pen.] Inzie Reynolds; November 4, 1981; Muskingun County; [p.] James-Mary Reynolds; [ed.] Freshmen at Janesville High School; [memb.]

A member of the Janesville Blue Devilettes Drill Team Dance Squad; [oth.writ.] Poem published in National Library of Poetry Book Spirit of the Ages; [pers.] I love to read poetry as well as write it, I like to express my feelings in my poetry, I'm also a lover of classical films and music; [a.] Janesville, OH

RICHARDSON, WILMA
[b.] August 5, 1940, Tulare, CA; [p.] Raymond and Naomi Morris; [m.] Jack C. Richardson, January 7, 1963; [ch.] 6 children, 11 grandchildren; [ed.] Chula Vista High, Chula Vista, CA; [occ.] Housewife (write poems for family), 2 booklets; [oth. writ.] Range Pollution; [pers.] I have written over 200 poems (2 booklets) for children and grandchildren as keepsakes for when I'm no longer here to comfort them!; [a.] San Antonio, TX

RICHMOND, BEN
[b.] October 25, 1949, Hinton, WV; [p.] Ben C. and Dolly Sue; [m.] Wendy A. Richmond, March 20, 1971; [ch.] Matthew B. Richmond; [ed.] B. of S. St. Clair College - Pt. Huron, Mich., B. of A. Toledo University - Toledo, Ohio, M. of A. - Defiance College - Defiance, OH; [occ.] Artist, Writer, Sculptor; [oth. writ.] "Winter World" (poems), "Time Passages" (poems), "Artistry of Ben Richmond" hard bound, "The Raven's Cry," a novel hard bound/mystery.; [pers.] Writing is another diversion used to cleanse my spirit and keeps my creative demons in balance. A verbal communication served from the sanctuary of my otherwise dormant chambers in my mind.; [a.] Marblehead, OH

RIESS, KENNETH
[b.] March 27, 1970, Brian, OH; [p.] Don and Beth Riess; [m.] Shawna Marie Riess, March 6, 1995; [ch.] Kimmberly, Christopher, Danielle; [ed.] High school; [occ.] Assistant Manager; [pers.] Life isn't always Rainbows and Roses. Dark skies and rain come before rainbows and roses have thorns. I was greatly influenced by Edgar Allen Poe.; [a.] Rogersville, MO

RIFFLE, LINDA
[b.] March 18, 1969; [p.] Margaret Moffat, Donald Moffat; [ed.] Duquesne University, Penn State University; [occ.] Speech-Language Pathologist, Monroeville, PA; [memb.] ASHA, PSHA, Sierra Club; [pers.] Speech—either in written word, spoken word, or gesture—is a cleansing of the soul.; [a.] Pittsburgh, PA

RIGGS, ANDREW D.
[pen.] Rahvin; [b.] May 8, 1980; SLC, UT; [p.] Debbie Jones and David Riggs; [ed.] Hunter High School (current); [occ.] Student; [hon.] District school competition in writing; [pers.] Love is like thin ice on a lake of hate.; [a.] WVC, UT

RILEY, MELROSE I.
[b.] February 13, 1912; [p.] Herbert Riley; [occ.] Retired Federal Employee; [pers.] I have been interest in poetry eversince I learned how to spell. Never sad any but wrote quite a few.

ROBERTS, JOHN
[pen.] John Roberts; [b.] April 27, 1951; USA; [p.] Mom and Dad; [ed.] Some College; [occ.] Poet; [memb.] Central Iowa Astronomers; [oth.writ.] Astronomy Newsletter Poems; [a.] Des Moines, IA

ROBERTS, STEVE
[pen.] Robert Wilson; [b.] November 29, 1978, Springfield, OR; [ed.] Thurston High, Lane Community College; [occ.] Student; [memb.] National Honor Society; [hon.] Twin Rivers Rotary Good Citizen of the Month for January 1997; [oth.writ.] Several short stories and a short novel yet to be published.; [pers.] "I did it!"; [a.] Springfield, OR

ROBLES, WILLIAM (ANTHONY)
[pen.] Scorpio ssc Mc International Inc; [b.] November 19, 1969; Los Angeles, CA; [p.] William and Priscilla Robles; [m.] Shawna Thompson (Fiancee); February 14, 1998; [ch.] Dashawn, Anthony and William A. Robles II; [ed.] General Ed, Computer Technician; [occ.] Sales Kirby and Shipping and Recieving; [oth.writ.] Valentine In Paradise (Book) From Here To Eternity, From My Heart, I Miss You, Woman Of Desire, Special Love, You Are My Destiny, Open Arms, Miles of Separation, Lay Beside You, Never Walk Alone, I Am Your Fortress, Angel, Valentine In Paradise; [pers.] Always follow your heart for true love is waiting for your speak from your heart and you'll never go wrong. Fear and love walk hand and hand for everyone fears love. Scorpio ssc Mac International Inc; [a.] San Jose, CA

ROCHLIN, LEONARD
[b.] October 20, 1919; Middlebourne, WV; [p.] Benjamin and Eva Rochlin; [ed.] Brown High School, Cambridge, OH, Art Center College of Design, Lost Angeles, CA, Special studies at University of Calif., Beverly Hills, CA; [hon.] Number of graphic design awards, Los Angeles, Beverly Hills, CA; [oth.writ.] World of Poetry, Sacramento, CA, Golden Poet 1990, 1991, Short Stories, unpublished; [pers.] My poems are personal expressions of feelings, viewpoints, observations and experiences, on life, nature, and the pursuit of understanding my own reason for being; [a.] Baltimore, MD

RODRIGUEZ JR., JULIO
[b.] January 30, 1976, Puerto Rico; [p.] Julio Rodriguez, Marisel Rodriguez; [ed.] Butter High, Harlem High, Paine College, Kerr Business College; [occ.] Assistant Manager, Sales; [hon.] Being selected for publication by The National Library of Poetry.; [pers.] I write in hopes of keeping dreams alive and to keep the emotions of happiness in the readers of my work.; [a.] Hephzibah, GA

ROSE, SHERRILL D.
[pen.] Sheri Rose; [b.] March 25, 1948; Bakersfield, CA; [m.] June 1, 1969, unmarried former spouse; [ch.] Curtis Dean Rose 25, Sherill Lynn Rose 22; [ed.] Presently a Sophomore at Olympic College, Bremerton, WA, Phi Theta Kappa (Recording Officer, 1996) National Dean's List; [occ.] Student Education (E.C.E.); [memb.] Phi Theta Kappa; [oth.writ.] I have written a few essays and poems. But "My Casso" is the first I have submitted for publication. Other writings have been shared with friends, family, and other Christians; [pers.] Life is amazing, but there's always a pathway to success if one truly seeks. I believe one should explore each twist and turn to find what works for him or her.; [a.] Bremerton, WA

ROSKOV, NICOLE
[pen.] Nicole; [b.] January 12, 1979; Jefferson County; [p.] Diana and Rick Roskov; [ed.] Currently a Senior in high school - Accepted to University of Monterallo, Fall 1997; [memb.] Senior Editor of high school newspaper. FHA, FBLA; [hon.] President's Award for Educational Improvement from McAdory High School; [oth. writ.] Poems, short stories, currently writing a novel titled, The Evil Within; [pers.] Dedication: "This is dedicated to Jerica Morris, Lena Townsend and Misty Hocutt; also my mom." [a.] Bessemer, AL

ROULEAU, JOSEPH E.
[b.] August 29, 1932, Woonsocket, RI; [p.] Joseph A. and Marie A. Rouleau; [m.] Delma A. Rouleau; [ed.] Degree in Music, degree in Literature, studies in Journalism; [occ.] President JER-JLM Enterprises, Inc.; [memb.] Local Historical Society, Ohio Composers Alliance; [hon.] Honored in Forbes for doing business in Russia and other foreign countries (Ref. Forbes A.S.A.P. Tech. Supplement, Apr. 1994); [oth. writ.] Contributing editor local newspapers, misc. essays published in MI, RI, MD, two books-(pending publication), "Hell Hath No Bounds" and "Paris Murders," short stories for children.; [pers.] Greatly influenced by T.S. Elliott, Gore Vidal and Jean Le Carre.; [a.] Chillicothe, OH

ROVEZZI, SHIRLEY M.
[pen.] Shirley M. Rovezzi; [b.] January 8, 1928, Worcester, MA; [m.] Henry A. Rovezzi (Deceased), September 21, 1957; [ch.] James Lee Rovezzi; [ed.] B.S. in Education, Worcester State College; [hon.] Kappa Delta Pi, Psi Chi, Dean's List; [oth. writ.] Several unpublished poems, articles published in local newspaper.; [pers.] "To thine own self be true" is my motto. I admire poets such as Poe, Kipling and Sylvia Plath.; [a.] Worcester, MA

RUDDLE, CAROL L. TOBEY
[b.] December 24, 1937; Chicago, IL; [p.] Lucille M. Tobey-Tuma, Robert Tobey; [m.] Divorced; [ed.] 8 Ph. D's (Phi Beta Kappa): 4 Northwestern Univ. W/1945 graduation Walso 2 Master's and several Bachelor's Degrees/ Ph.D EA Yale Harvard Johns Hopkins, Wm and Mary Medicine; 1944 and WW II[occ.] Writer; Mgmt. Consultant; Telemarketer Model; [memb.] Kingdom Hall of Jehovah's Witnesses; Methodist Church Of U.K. Missionary as well as Jehovah's Witness Missionary; [hon.] Up for Pulitzer prize 3 times, won 3rd time but disqualified as they said I lied and not true story, but this was untruth and I told truth; [oth.writ.] Many all stolen, except real writer, The winds of war as given to Herman Wouk for Doctor in publishing London. Psychiatry/Surgery (heart) on USA Gov't. Survey in 1949, votes by USA military doctor colleages as in top 10 best WW II Sergeons and to 25 Psychiatriest WW II; [pers.] I tried to write all in Christian contest as regarded my early Jehovah's witness bringing as wel as write for market for my life suport; [a.] Floin, IL

RUSSEL HARMON, SONIA L.
[pen.] Le Roia; [b.] November 8, 1959; New York City; [p.] Ernestine and LeRoit T. Russel; [m.] Joseph N. Harmon; November 3, 1991; [ed.] Malverns High School, New York Institute of Technology; [occ.] Mortgage processor, Chase Manhattan Bank; [pers.] I write because I dream. I dream because my imasination allows me to. I hope to share my dreams with the world through other writings in near future; [a.] Tobyhanna, PA

RUSSELL, ROSALINDA C.
[b.] December 19, 1913; E. Braintbee, MA; [p.] Margaret and James Green; [m.] John A. Russell-1913-1991 Dico; August 1, 1937; [ch.] Joanne, James, Thomas; [ed.] Elementary, Hingham, MA, Grad. Hingham High-1930 Vesper George School of Art-Comm. Design. Grad. 1933 Boston; [occ.] At Home Mem. Old so. Cong. So. Wey. Mass.; [memb.] 1st Cong. Church Claremont Assoc. Mem. Cong. Church Briston, R.I. Mem. Bible Study Group-Presbyterian Church-Rochester, NY; [oth.writ.] Several verses published in "Story A Day" children mag. poetry and verses in church publications. Interprative writings re-religious celebrations; [pers.] Advancing years may dim the vision,

dull the sense of hearing but the mind and heart inspired by God's love and beauty stay young forever!; [a.] E. Rochester, NY.

RUTHERFORD, RUTH A.
[b.] March 25, 1943; Axtell, KS; [p.] Harry R. and Nola M. Crowley; [m.] M. Allen Rutherford; November 16, 1963; [ch.] Kimberly Janee Augusto; [ed.] Axtell High School, Western College; [occ.] Secretary to Corporate Manager; [memb.] American Diabetes Association Business/Education Partnership; [hon.] To most, honors and awards depict being acknowledge by others for something they have achieved. At the risk of sounding simple in a complex world, I am honored to be granted each new day, my awards are my family. My rewards will be received when I close my eyes in death; [oth.writ.] A few other poems-unpublished; [pers.] My poetry has been influenced by drawing on life's experiences; [a.] Lawrence, KS

SALGADO, MYRNA M.
[b.] August 8, Arecibo, PR; [p.] Ramona Rodriguez-Zemen and Rafael Salgado; [ch.] Israel Rios, Marianne Rios-Valentin; [ed.] College; [occ.] Billing Specialist, AT&T; [memb.] Liberty Falls Collectors Club; [hon.] Quality Implementation, H.E.R.O. Awards 1990 and 1993, Performance Awards 1994 and 1995; [oth. writ.] Poems: "My Love For You" and "The Glowing Flame"; [pers.] I strive to touch the hearts of those who read my poetry and leave a legacy of my poetry to the loved ones that have inspired my writings.; [a.] Chicago, IL

SAMBLANET, DEBRA B.
[b.] February 13, 1957, Rensselaer, IN; [p.] Raymond W. Nagel, Norma J. Nagel; [m.] Kevin P. Samblanet, November 13, 1982; [ch.] Sarah Beth, Jeanna Lynn, Robert Paul; [ed.] Kankakee Valley High, St. Joseph's College, Rensselaer, IN; [occ.] Substitute Teacher, Hamilton City Public Schools; [memb.] St. Peter in Chains Catholic Church; [hon.] St. Joseph's College Dean's List; [pers.] I am inspired by my children.; [a.] Hamilton, OH

SANCHEZ, KATHRYN
[pen.] Kat Thompson; [b.] March 9, 1978; Ventura, CA; [p.] Sandra Sanchez, Adolfo Sanchez, Jr; [ed.] Glendora High School; [occ.] Student; [pers.] Do what you feel is right, not what others tell you is right.; [a.] Glendora, CA

SANDERS, ESTELLA
[b.] March 14, 1941; TangPahoe, Paris; [p.] Mrs. Pauline and Frank Sanders; [m.] John Robert French; April 3, 1976; [ch.] Donna and Dionne; [ed.] High School and Practical Nursing; [memb.] Baptist; [pers.] I give assisting to the disabled and handicap patients who grocery bags may be a little defect out to carry to their auto. I thank God for giving me every specific gift; [a.] Roseland, LA

SANDFORD, BLAKE
[b.] July 4, 1966, Carlsbad, NM; [p.] Ron and Mary Jane Sandford; [m.] Helen, August 28, 1995; [ed.] BS San Houston State University, high school—Westwood (Austin, TX); [occ.] Teacher - History, Baseball/Football Coach; [memb.] Association of Texas Professional Educators, Texas High School Coaches Assoc.; [hon.] Coach of the Year 1996; [a.] Bremond, TX

SCHIEGG, GENIE C.
[pen.] Orianna Oates, Elena Oates; [b.] June 15, 1932, Hagerstown, MD; [p.] Stewart Page and Elsie Oates Cline; [m.] Robert L. Schiegg, April 15, 1987; [ch.] Diane Kay Pike Allen, Pamela Sue Pike, Daniel Patrick Pike; [ed.] Hagerstown High

School, SMU, Adult Continuing Ed. (Graphic Arts); [occ.] Manager, Executive Suite for 6-1/2 years, graphic arts or related field for 30 years; [hon.] Nominated for Church Woman of Year in 1965 in Columbus, Ohio. Honorable mention for photo of Magi, our cat, taken at Bucks County, PA and judged in Columbus.; [oth. writ.] Some children's stories. Many chapters of a family history novel are transfixed in my brain, this year I shall begin word processing it. Editor of new (in 1973) weekly newspaper at Indian Lake, Ohio. Editor of company monthly newsletter for 7 years.; [pers.] I have a gift for communication with people, which gives me comforting insight about humanity. Nurture people and animals, hush prejudices, then watch the thread of life weave towards great happiness.; [a.] Dallas, TX

SCHMOE, TERI LYNN
[b.] August 7, 1980; Yakima; [p.] Pam and Steve Burch; [ed.] Harrah Elementary Davis High School Franklin Middle School; [occ.] Student; [oth.writ.] Lots of other poems, short stories, etc. poems hate-obstacles forever and always no one and tears; [pers.] To my beloved best friend, who helps me to do the best I can, and we are still together. I love you Page; [a.] Selah,WA

SCHNEPP, SHANNON
[b.] February 28, 1981; Pontiac, MI; [p.] Dale Schnepp, Peg Schnepp; [ed.] I am currently in my Sophomore year at Waterford Mott High School; [memb.] I am active in student council, church, basketball, softball, HAM Radio, Homecoming Committee, Prom Committee, and in the running for class president; [hon.] Molly Brennan Award (Most Well-rounded Female Student), Best Sportmanship, Most Team Spirited, Most Helpful Student, Honor Roll (4.0 GPA); [oth.writ.] I write many poems for my personal well being, but this is the first contest that I have entered, and I entered in honor of my Grandma.; [pers.] "The Greatest Lesson Ever Learned" and other poems of mine were written in honor and remembrance of my grandmother who passed away January 18, 1997. I love you, Grandma!; [a.] Waterford, MI

SCHNITZLER, DOUGLAS C.
[b.] August 10, 1955; Marshfield, Wis; [p.] Donald and Gloria T. Schnitzler; [m.] Lorena L. Schnitzler; April 12, 1986; [ch.] Jessica, Jason, Lesley, Kristopher, Sylvia; [ed.] High School, Creative writing and short story courses; [occ.] Custadian Laborer U.S. Postal Service, Wisconsin Radios, Wis; [hon.] Pershing Professional Certificates Letters of Commendation, letters of Appreciation, good conduct and army Commendation Medals; [oth.writ.] I want to be a writer published in a delicate balance my blessing published in carvings in stove. Apology to my son published best poems of the 90's; [pers.] Love to write, especially for children; [a.] Chili, WI

SCHROLL, FRANCES LUCILLE SNYDER
[pen.] Fran Schroll; [b.] January 31, 1910, Fairfield, PA; [p.] John Phillip Snyder and Emily Reiling; [m.] Clarence Edwin Schroll, June 9, 1934; [ch.] Edwin John Schroll, Yvonne Schroll; [ed.] Cape Vincent Central School, Cape Vincent, NY, Watertown School of Business, Watertown, NY; [occ.] Deceased; [memb.] Order of the Eastern Star, Women's Republican Club, United Church of Cape Vincent, NY; [oth. writ.] Various poetry and essays; [a.] Cape Vincent, NY

SCHWARTZ, MICHAEL
[pen.] Mike Schwartz; [b.] September 23, 1964; Newark, NJ; [p.] David, Rochell Schwartz; [ed.] BS Political Science/Minor Sociology NT Teaching

Certificate of Hondicapped; [occ.] Teacher of Handicapped, I teach emotionally disturbed students/blind and Multiply Handicapped; [memb.] Grassroots environmental organization, coalitier for the homeless; [oth.writ.] Nothing else published yet; [pers.] I write on the goodness at man, love and social issues. I feel its a gift from the Lord and have been influenced by the masters Whitman, Poe, Shelley, Dickinson; [a.] Cranford, NJ

SCHWENDT, BECKY
[pen.] Barbie Doll; [b.] March 7, 1983; San Diego, CA; [p.] Elizabeth Schwendt, Leroy Schwandt; [occ.] Assistant Religion Teacher, Saint Joan of Arc Church, Spring Hill, FL; [memb.] National Junior Beta Club, Advanced Band; [hon.] Superior Medal for a flute solo, Honors Band; [pers.] I've learned that the best way to deal with problems, no matter how scared you are, is to face them. I've also learned that you can't do anything alone. My mom is cool.; [a.] Spring Hill, FL

SCOTT, EVAN A.
[pen.] Evan A. Scott; [b.] July 1, 1978; Rock Hill, SC; [p.] Andy Scott, Nancy Scott; [ed.] High school, not yet completed (Senior); [occ.] Bagger at Grocery Store (Harris Teeter); [memb.] NJROTC (no literary organizations), St Paul's Episcopal Church, Traditional Karate Association; [hon.] No honors or awards, poetry written for myself, normally not for public display, though I have no objections; [oth.writ.] "The Fool," "Mr. Volk," "Unborn Time," "Behind the Rain," "What's In It?" "Robots of Delusion," "Sigh," "Let The Ropes Fall," "Humble Repent," "Crumbs Of Life," "Where Did She Go?" "Broken Wings," "When I Looked Down," "Burried Alive," "Talk About Nothing," "Explain This," etc.; [pers.] I try to base my work on life, such as God, society, government and personal experiences as well as inner battles of mind and emotions.; [a.] Wilmington, NC

SCOTT, JON S.
[pen.] Smitty; [b.] September 9, 1926; North Carolina, Fayetteville; [p.] John Bell and Eugenia Jacobs Scott; [m.] Elaine Claire Bradford Scott; August 1, 1953; [ch.] Angela La Morcita; [ed.] BS Degree, Math and Physics, Hampton Institute-Hampton, VA, class 1947; [occ.] Retired-last Job, "Correctional Office Manager" (15 yrs.), Fulton County Corrections, Atlanta, GA; [memb.] Omega Psi phi Fraternity Lambda Alpha Graduate Chapter Southern University, "Red Stick", LA, Brotherhood of St. Andrew; [hon.] Armed Forces Day activities Announcer, Keesler AFB, Biloki, Mississippi 1951 (an honor); [oth.writ.] None published; [pers.] Dedicated believer in God. Believe in each man's individual fulfillment in life, we all contribute somehow; [a.] Calumet City, IL

SEILER, BRANDY MARIE
[b.] January 25, 1979; Altona, PA; [p.] Bruce and Cheryl Seiler; [ed.] High school graduate, future 4 years at Juanita College in Hurtingdon, Pennsylvania to major in Chemistry; [memb.] National Honor Society, Central High School Chamber Singers, Central High School Drama Troupe; [hon.] Who's Who Among American High School Students; [oth.writ.] Nothing previously published; [pers.] While striving to achieve the complex, remember the simple. (Brandy Seile); [a.] Duncansville, PA

SENNETT, TONYA K.
[b.] April 5, 1982, Elkhorn, WI; [p.] Katherine and Donald Schultz; [ed.] Freshman at Marian Central Catholic High School; [occ.] Election Work (summer), Student; [memb.] Marian Soccer Team,

Marian International Club; [pers.] Tomorrow never comes so stop putting things off till tomorrow.; [a.] Woodstock, IL

SERINO SR., JOSEPH
[pen.] Grandpa; [b.] January 19, 1907, New York City; [m.] Anna, April, 1931; [ch.] Four; [ed.] Public school and school of hard knocks. Built my own auto racers.; [occ.] Retired - expert Automechanic; [memb.] Auto racing clubs way back when the "AAA" used to sanction most racing events; [hon.] Won many trophies for custom cars entered at different shows, etc.; [pers.] People who work hard - sleep well, and a clear conscience makes life worth living.; [a.] Woodside, NY

SETTLE, MICHELLE
[b.] November 28, 1972; Weirton, WV; [p.] Patrick Settle, Shirley Settle Adams; [ed.] Seneca Valley High School; [occ.] Account Rep./Corporate Admin. - Oakwood Apartments; [memb.] N.L.P. Distinguished Member, H.S.U.S., World Wildlife Foundation, Marine Mammal Conservatory, Int'l. Thespian Society, Dance Club; [hon.] Editor's Choice Awards, Best Dancer Award; [pers.] My love for theatre and the work of the late James Dean has inspired my interest in poetry. I hope that in reading my work, people will be able to reflect on their memories and reach for their dreams.; [a.] Alexandria, VA

SHARIEFF, ADILEH
[b.] June 12, Peshawar, Pakistan; [p.] Aamer Ali Sharieff, Shaista Sharieff; [m.] Jawad Nazir Paracha, January 1, 1997; [ed.] Electrical Engineering, from N.W.F.P. University of Engineering and Technology, Peshawar, Pakistan; [memb.] Pakistan Engineering Council; [oth. writ.] Several articles and poems were published in college/university magazines and in national newspapers.; [pers.] I want to thank my parents and family for all their support and love. Also, thanks to my husband for always believing in me. I love you all.; [a.] College Park, MD

SHEININ, KAROL
[b.] April 18, 1977, Russia; [p.] Arkady and Nina Sheinin; [ed.] Adelphi Academy—high school, Northeastern University—college; [occ.] Student, Professional Traveler; [memb.] Scottish National Party; [pers.] "The Untested Kosmos my abode, I pass a wilful stranger, my mistress still the open road and the bright eyes of danger" - Robert Louis Stevenson.; [a.] Brooklyn, NY

SHERWOOD, GEORGE
[b.] May 5, 1981; Manhasset, NY; [p.] Karyn Sherwood, James Sherwood III; [ed.] I am currently studying for my highschool diploma; [occ.] Student, Northwest Academy, Naples, ID; [hon.] I was recognized by the Kiwanis Club for most improved student; [oth.writ.] I have written over 100 poems most of which are untitled. Some of my poems have been published in the Cedu family of Services News letter; [pers.] I open with my interpretation of nature. This particular poem I wish to dedicate to my best friend; [a.] Plandome, NY.

SILVA, PAUL M.
[pen.] Paul MP Silva; [b.] July 19, 1951; San Francisco; [p.] Norman and Dolores Silva; [ed.] B/A English with the emphasis in creative writing, minor in Spanish, San Francisco State University 1979. Legal Assistant Certificate 1981, Loma 1991; [occ.] Ordinance Enforcement Specialist, Planning and Land Use City of Santa Fe; [memb.] Quinto Entanario (Spanish Toast Masters), St. Bedes Episcopal Church; [hon.] Several corporate, municipal and philanthropic awards; [oth.writ.]

Several novels in progress, as well as poems, songs and short stories; [pers.] I want to dramatize the tenacity of the human spirit. I strive to be mindful and in the moment. I'm curious as to how one sets boundaries and limits.; [a.] Santa Fe, NM

SIMMONS, DENA LEAH
[pen.] Leah Simmons; [b.] August 6, 1958, Detoit, MI; [p.] Marie Abraham; [ed.] I attended Cody High School in Detroit, after graduation I attended the American Travel School; [occ.] I am a former travel agaent, due to a back injury I obrained while attending college to obtain a degree in travel and tourism. While I was immobilized for several months I began writing poems abut a variety of life's situations about people and places which made an impression on me. In writing poety I feel these is a vast canvas open to create an expression of feelings and experiences which can be shared with others; [memb.] My other writings include poems I've written called the "Essence of my Being", "The Game" and "Thin Blue Line" also I'm writing a novel; [hon.] I wish to show in my writing the joys and sorrows of life to which we all are touched in our journey through life; [a.] Detroit, MI

SIMMONS, TRACY
[b.] March 23, 1966, La Mesa, CA; [p.] John and Colleen Simmons; [ed.] Granite Hills High School, Florida State University, California State University - Fullerton; [occ.] A.P.E./Mentor Teacher; [memb.] CSUF Alumni Association; [hon.] Golden Key National Honor Society, Dean's List, CSUF Hall of Fame; [oth. writ.] Articles published in high school and local newspapers.; [pers.] My poetry is a journal of thoughts that come from my heart. It is truly the window to my soul.; [a.] Long Beach, CA

SIMONS, ASHLEY L.
[b.] August 30, 1984, Atlanta, GA; [p.] Cathy Theodose and Jim Simons; [ed.] Student - Burley Middle School, Honor Roll Student; [hon.] Honor Roll, Gymnastics Awards, awards for math, science and spelling; [a.] Charlottesville, VA

SIMONS, LAURINE C.
[b.] December 14, 1931, Enfield, NC; [p.] James and Bertha Cotten; [m.] Samuel K. Simons (Decreased), September 11, 1925; [ch.] Kirkland L. Simons; [ed.] BS NCA&T State University, Institution Management 12 mo. Internship, Freedmen's Hospital (Howard Hospital now) in Nutrition, Registered; [occ.] Retired; [memb.] Vine Memorial Baptist Church, Philadelphia NCA&T Alumni Chapter, Haddington Lane Block Association, Philadelphia Neighborhood Housing Services, Ex. MEM. Delta Sigma Theta Sorority and National Dietetic Association; [hon.] Cum Laude and Who's Who Among 1995 Students by my University Certificates of Recognition: Phila. Literacy Program as a Reading Coach, Phila. Neighborhood Housing as a Volunteer, Certificates of Appreciation: Vine Memorial Church gave several for Christian service rendered; [oth. writ.] Diet & Nutrition Section in over 55 by Theodore G. Duncan, M.D., Diet In Diabetes Section in The Good Life With Diabetes by Theodore G. Duncan, M.D.; [pers.] Those who have should always share with those in need.; [a.] Philadelphia, PA

SINGLETON, JENNIFER L.
[pen.] Jazle Ess; [b.] June 6, 1955; Willows, CA; [p.] Francis and Dorothea Haznes; [m.] John C. Singleton; July 18, 1992; [ch.] Amanda, Amberly, Travis; [ch.] Fashion Design/Merchandising, Marketing/Sales, Business Admin. [occ.] Director of Operations Starlight Theatres, owner of Partners, a public relations firm; [oth.writ.] Poetry, moti-

vational works, educational materials; [pers.] I don't want silence as a rule. What I want is the alternative of a silent mind.; [a.] Redding, CA

SINHA, SANJAY
[b.] January 24, 1984; Prince Albert, Sask (Canada); [p.] Chandra P. Sinha, Maya Sinha; [ed.] Desert Springs Elementary, Desert Shadows Middle School; [memb.] AWA Arizona Wado Association; [hon.] National Junior Honor Society; 1st in District Poetry Contest, Honorable Mention of the district level Reflections Contest, poetry has been published in the newspaper; [pers.] I endeavor to change the tide of poetry from writing about nature and material subjects, into writing about real situational context of today's world.; [a.] Scottsdale, AZ

SLAY, DENISE
[pen.] Denise Bernard; [b.] February 22, 1953; New Jersey; [p.] Ralph and Dorothy Fair; [m.] Michael Saly; May 24, 1997; [ch.] Amber Hagen and Alicia Hagen; [ed.] Delsea Regional H.S; [oth.writ.] Several other poems that I hope to have published in a love poem collection; [pers.] My poetry is inspire by my life experiences; [a.] Homes Beach, FL

SMITH, CERDAN ADRIAN
[b.] August 21, 1952; Washington, DC; [p.] Leroy and Naomi Smith; [ed.] McKinley High School, Graduate Art Majoy Student and 1 Year of College at Maryland School of Art/Design; [occ.] Retired Designer/Actor, Model/Poet; [memb.] Volunteer for YMCA, Food Bank; [hon.] International Hall of Famer, National Editors Award, Cocoran School of Art/Maryland School of Art/Design Smithsonian School of Art/Hollywood Model Guild; [oth.writ.] "The Human Factor Tearfulality", "The Conniseur Of Life" and "DynoIcess"; [pers.] Problems aren't problems by priorities and attitude is themain thing but everything.

SMITH, KENNETH E.
[b.] October 30, 1970; Garden City, MI; [p.] Kenneth R. and Frances M. Smith; [m.] Shana L. Smith; June 21, 1997; [ch.] Jordan Tyler, Braden Drake Smith; [ed.] Attended Garden City High School, Cambridge Adult Education; [oth.writ.] Now; Life; (Several Poems in Personal Collection looking to be published); [pers.] "Anyone can write, it sthe person you are writing to that makes it feel right"; [a.] Garden City, MI

SMITH, MARION CARD
[b.] February 14, 1913, Stockport, NY; [p.] Susan and Clarence Card; [m.] Kenneth Ray Smith, April 30, 1938; [ch.] Linda, Kenneth and Timothy; [ed.] Grammar school, high school, Albany Business College; [occ.] Housewife; [memb.] (1) Columbia Memorial Hosp. Aux. - BD Press (1st Woman), Sec, (2) Columbia Co. Hist. Soc., (3) Fortnightly (local lit. 100 yrs. old); [oth. writ.] Many historical books and papers: "Hudson Valley Sketchboo,k, "Greenport, The Forgotten Town" and others (books and sections). Our area is very interesting historically. Poems for relatives and friends - "On Wings Of Song" book.

SMITH, ROWENA
[b.] June 27, 1938, Glen Elder, KS; [p.] Walter Smith, Gladys Smith; [m.] Divorced; [ch.] Michael Fanning, Alvin Fanning; [ed.] Glen Elder High; [occ.] Electronics Assembler; [pers.] In recent years I have learned that we should value true friendship and the beauty of people and things around us. Also to be thankful for them and for what we have.; [a.] Wichita, KS

SMITH, SHARON MCINTOSH
[pen.] Sharon Smith/SKS, Sharon McIntosh, Sharon McIntosh Smith; [b.] October 19, 1951; Houston, TX; [p.] Joan Vincent McKenzie, Ernest H. McIntosh; [m.] Roy P. Smith; September 7, 1996; [ch.] Chris Vacek; [ed.] Bay City High School; [occ.] Dental Assistant; [memb.] The National Library of Poetry; [hon.] Editor's Choice Award for Outstanding Achievement in Poetry by The National Library of Poetry; [oth.writ.] The Winking Hummingbird, published in Of Moonlight and Wishes; [pers.] My writings are from my inner thoughts at particular moments in my life. This poem was written on a stormy night in TX in February, 1997; [a.] Bay City, TX

SMITH, JR., JAMES A.
[pen.] Jamez; [b.] November 22, 1953; Atlanta, GA; [p.] Lorena Sudduth, James A. Smith, Sr; [m.] Jeanee Renee's Smith; October 21, 1979; [ch.] Lauren, Natalie, Kristen and Mikaela; [ed.] Forest College of Art and Atlanta Port Folio Center of Advertising; [occ.] Electrician and Freelance Artist and Writer; [oth.writ.] I am currently working on a rewrite of a chid's book and putting together a book of my own Poems. "Flower among the thorns" was written about my wife, the way I truly see her in her strengths and beauty; [pers.] I strive to write wonds of hope and encouragement for others that may be suffering from the disease known as depression. My words are from the soul and heart searching for "hope and a future"; [a.] Fayetteville, GA

SNOW, CATHERINE L.
[pen.] K.C. Cordell; [b.] April 5, 1947; Kingston, AR; Divorced; [ch.] Russ, Ruth, Caitlin Snow; [ed.] Ark Tech University, Russellville, Ark. Boise State University, Boise, ID; [occ.] Communication, Secondary Ed. Teacher Student; [memb.] United Methodist Church, Alliance for the Rights of Children; [oth.writ.] Studies in Reciprocity and Abuse, Famous Poets Society; [pers.] Giving hope to the hurting and joy to those around me; [a.] Middleton, ID

SNYDER, JOSEPH M.
[b.] December 16, 1977; Cumberland, MI; [p.] Ronald and Bonnie Snyder; [ed.] Fort Hill High School, Allegany College; [occ.] Federal Information Center, Information Specialist. Writer Copy Editor Weekend Adventures Magazine; [memb.] Planetary Society Member; [hon.] The Sentinel Award, for Leadership and Talent that was primarily responsible for the success of my high school newspaper, Honor Student, Allegany College; [oth.writ.] Numerous Columns for Weekend Adventures; [pers.] "Nothing creative is ever done in vain"; [a.] Cumberland, MD

SORRELL, CONNIE DARLENE
[b.] March 6, 1959; Guthrie, OK; [p.] Vernon And Bertha Miles; [m.] Thomas Dwane Sorrell; October 15, 1977; [ch.] Lyndall, Susan, Jennifer, Rodney, Kevin Gerald; [ed.] Graduate of Guthrie High School; [occ.] Staff member of Path of Life School; [memb.] Words wright Christian Writer's Organ, Church of God; [hon.] Certificate from the Institute of Children's Literature; [oth.writ.] Articles for the faith and victory, short stories for the Beautiful Way since 1982; puzzles for Shining Star, other articles and poems in different publications; [pers.] May my writings point the reader to higher ground; [a.] Guthrie, OK

SOUTHERN, MICHAEL G.
[pen.] Michael Southern; [b.] February 14, 1951, Spartanburg, SC; [p.] Frank and Shirley Southern; [m.] Mary L. Williams-Southern, April 19, 1997;

[ch.] Jennifer, Sherry, Eric, Shannon, Amy; [ed.] A.S. Thomas Nelson, B.A. Christopher Newport University; [occ.] Quality Technician - Manager; [memb.] Wythe Presbyterian Church Deacon and Stewardship Chair, CNU (Member) Masterworks Chorus; [hon.] Eagle Scout, Lifetime Member of VA Jaycees, 1980-81 Outstanding Young Men in America; [oth. writ.] Numerous poems and philosophical writings.; [pers.] I believe that each and every one of us can make a difference within the lives of families, friends and even strangers!; [a.] Newport News, VA

SPINNER, DAVID
[b.] October 11, 1950; Cincinnati, OH; [p.] Manuel and Margaret Spinner; Divorced; [ch.] 3; Joshua, Deborah, Esther; [ed.] U.S. Navy; [hon.] Air Medal with Clustes Vietnam; [oth.writ] Numerous Poems, none published; [pers.] I wrote this this poem among many written about futility of war written during service with the US Marine Corps in Vietnam; [a.] US Navy, USS Independence.

SPLETZER, RAMONA
[b.] January 5, 1970, Philadelphia; [p.] Joseph and Lucy Spletzer; [ed.] Phila. HS for girls, Temple University; [occ.] Software Engineer; [memb.] ICCA; [hon.] Dean's List, President's Award, Unisys Scholarship; [oth. writ.] Several poems published, currently finishing second novel.; [pers.] Happiness of the heart unclouds the mind and soothes the soul.; [a.] King of Prussia, PA

SPRIGG, STEVE
[b.] August 23, 1974; Kalamazoo, MI; [p.] Richard and Lois Sprigg; [m.] Megan; December 27, 1997; [ed.] Princeton High School College of Wooster; [occ.] Software Engineer at Ipat in Cincinnati, Ohio; [memb.] International Thespian Society; [hon.] National Honor Society; [oth.writ.] Write Poetry as a Hobby; [pers.] Words that feed the mind feed the emotions that feed the heart; [a.] Cincinnati, OH

STAFFORD, JENNY SUE
[b.] July 20, 1947, Carrollton, KY; [p.] Ruby and Ell Granger; [m.] Donald B. Stafford, May 3, 1982; [ch.] Mitchell and Michele Kindoll; [ed.] Graduate of Owen Co. High in Owenton, KY; [occ.] Quality Technician; [memb.] I started "The Mitchell W. Kindoll Memorial Fund" in memory of my beloved son. He was taken from me in a car accident. Proceeds go to needy children and scholarship awards.; [oth. writ.] "A Mother's Love," "Legacy of Love," "Once In A Lifetime," "My Children," "Time," "My Son And Me," "Our Boss," "God's Answer," "My Talk With God" and more.; [pers.] Most of my work is inspired by my great love for my two children. My poems show what a source of pride and joy they are to me. My more recent poems are inspired from the loss of my son.; [a.] Worthville, KY

STAGGS, BRANDON W.
[b.] March 7, 1981, Phoenix, AZ; [p.] Bob and Terri Staggs; [ed.] High School; [occ.] Poet and studies of martial arts; [memb.] Soccer Club for Northeast Raiders; [oth. writ.] I'm currently writing a book of my poetry. The name of this book is, A Lifetime of Darkness.; [pers.] This poem was one of many I wrote in dedication to my ex-girlfriend Tammy. It's included in my book I'm currently writing.; [a.] Saint Petersburg, FL

STANLEY, ELVINA ESTELLE
[b.] July 6, 1937; Arlington, CA; [p.] Mother Rella I. Pantenburg; [m.] Wayne A. Stanley; June 22, 1991; [ch.] 3 children - 3 step chi- 12 grandch., 1 great grandch; [occ.] Ordained Minister - through

Rock of Faith Fellowship of Ontario, CA; [memb.] Rock of Faith Fellowship; [pers.] I believe my writings to be inspired by God and my faith in His Word; [a.] Ontario, CA

STARY, ANN F.
[pen.] Ann Livingston Stary; [b.] September 13, 1908; [m.] Walter Edward Stary; 1936; [ch.] Paul Edward Stary; [ed.] College, Kansas State Teachers, Pitsburg, Kansas; [occ.] Taught first grade in public schools, midwest, east and west coast, total eleven years; [oth.writ.] Rhythmical stories for preschool and beginning reading; [pers.] Life time devotion to helping children build a firm foundation of successful reading skills.

STASHKO, DAVID
[pen.] L. Fulci; [b.] September 1, 1970, Michigan; [p.] Daniel and Yvonne Stashko; [m.] Kimberly Stashko, October 2, 1989; [ch.] One Daemon Stashko; [ed.] Holly High, Musicians Institute; [occ.] Bassit - P***s FlyTrap, Writer; [oth. writ.] Several short horror stories, several alternative children's stories, various scripts, screenplays and one novel (Siki City).; [pers.] Thoughts and dreams are but passing emotion until they are realized upon paper. There they become real and immortal.; [a.] Los Angeles, CA

STERLING, DEVON
[b.] September 12, 1997; Kirkwood, MD; [p.] Sandy and Jerry Sterling; [ed.] Stephen Mack Middle School 6th Grade; [memb.] Greater Swiss Mountain Dog Club (GSMDC) and Heartland Greater Swiss Mountain Dog Club; [pers.] Have fun and have no worries about life; [a.] Freeport, IL

STEWARD, ADRIENNE
[b.] January 16, 1973; Charleston, SC; [p.] Arnold Steward, Alma Steward; [ed.] St. George High, USC-Salkehatchie, USC-Columbia, USC-Aiken, Midlands; [occ.] Data Entry at UPS; [memb.] Pi Mu Epsilon; [hon.] Pi Mu Epsilon-National Mathematics Honorary, 1996 YWA Queen, Soil Conservation Contest Winner-Seventh Grade; [oth.writ.] Several poems in the local newspapers; [pers.] I strive to be the best I can be in everything with the help of God so I may recieve all "My Prizes". I have been influenced by hangston Hughes' poems in particular, "Mother To Son," because I'm continuing to climb for "life for me ain't been no crystal stair."; [a.] West Columbia, SC

STICKLE, CHARLES E.
[b.] January 1, 1941, Clinton, IN; [p.] Adolph Stickle, Myrtle Stickle; [m.] Marie Stickle, December 19, 1986; [ch.] Randy Dean, Troy Alan, Michelle Leigh; [ed.] Clinton High School, Clinton, IN, Bachelor's - U. of Nebraska at Omaha, NE, Master of Science - Troy State U., Troy, AL; [occ.] Freelance Poet; [memb.] AARP, The Retired Officer's Association, Consumers Union, The International Society of Poets; [hon.] Listed in Who's Who in U.S. Writers, Editors and Poets, The International Directory of Distinguished Leadership, Two Thousand Notable American Men, Five Thousand Personalities of the World, Community Leaders of America; [oth. writ.] Many poems published by the American Poetry Association and The National Library of Poetry; [pers.] To combat the constant negativity in today's world, I try to be positive and uplifting in my writings.; [a.] Montgomery, AL

ST. LAURENT, MARGIE WORRIX
[pen.] Margie Worrix St. Laurent; [b.] September 11, 1927; Catoosa, OK; [p.] Mina Marshall and John Ell Worrix; [m.] Arthur (Pete) St. Laurent; August 5, 1951; [ch.] Gary and Linda; [ed.] Verdi-

gris Ele, Catoosa High, (Oklahoma); [hon.] My poem, "The Boy That Time Forgot," Great poems of the Western World." I also won silver poet award for 1990; [oth.writ.] The Boy That Time Forgot, My Oklahoma, The Old House, Lance, Rose Of Sharon; [pers.] My writings are etched with memories of the places and people that have touched my life. My husband and my mom were probably my greatest inspiration; [a.] Morris, AL

STONE, RUTH
[pen.] Elizabeth Jones Stone; [b.] January 1, 1949, Sheffield, AL; [p.] R. W. and Clara B. Jones; [ch.] Ella Elizabeth Ann Stone (9); [ed.] B.S. Elementary Ed. FSU UNA, M.A. Reading Specialization, Ed.D. English/Psychology Vanderbilt UN; [occ.] College Professor of Psychology; [memb.] AEA, NEA, Phi Beta Kappa, Tuscumbia First United Methodist Church; [hon.] 1971 Egypt Abroad (overseas seminar to develop curriculum materials K-12), 1979 Who's Who Among Am. Women, 1996 Outstanding Educator; [oth. writ.] Books: Children's Moments with God, 5 easy steps to Good Cursive Writing, poems: "A Friend," "Why," "The Mirror" and "A Poem for Ella"; [pers.] A day without reading is like a day without sunshine. My love of poetry was greatly influenced by my mother who wrote poetry herself and read to me the great poems in literature.; [a.] Tuscumbia, AL

STRANDER, NANCY L.
[b.] February 9, 1950, Pottstown, PA; [m.] Knute A. Strander, December 30, 1977; [ch.] Casey Garrett; [ed.] Graduated Boyertown H.S. 1976, McCann Business College 1979; [occ.] Homemaker; [hon.] Editor's Choice Award 1997, "Daddy's Little Girl," in Tracing Shadows; [oth. writ.] Currently working on a book of contemporary poetry and prose.; [pers.] Through my writings, and with God's world as my inspiration, I attempt to delve into the light and darkness of the human condition with the overall belief in the strength and endurance of the "Spirit."; [a.] Folsom, LA

STROBEL, DEBBRA P.
[pen.] Debbi; [b.] August 30, 1957, Milford, DE; [p.] Herman and Greta Parsons; [m.] Robert Strobel, October 30, 1987; [ch.] Jeffry Rowe and Rebecca Rowe; [ed.] Sussex Central High, Delaware Tech., Wor-Wic Tech.; [occ.] Office Nurse - Peninsula Surgical Group, Salisbury, MD; [memb.] Active in American Cancer Society, P.T.A., AAON; [hon.] Honors Program Wor-Wic, Dean's List; [oth. writ.] Written other poems for family and friends. To date none have been published.; [pers.] "Sweet Lindsey" was written for Lindsey Brooke Cooper and her family. Although Lindsey's life was short (5 years), she touched the hearts of everyone around her.; [a.] Salisbury, MD

STRODE, MARLENE
[b.] September 8, 1959, New Zealand; [m.] Rick Strode, May 21, 1994; [ch.] Sam Strode; [ed.] Currently studying Human Development (tertiary level certificate); [occ.] Caring for my daughter full-time; [oth. writ.] This is my first published work.; [pers.] In order to see ourselves, that which we love and hate about ourselves, we only need to watch our children. That which we try to hide, they reveal to us. Children influence my poetry.; [a.] Cohasset, MA

STUART, RUTH
[b.] January 9, 1930; Lupton City, TN; [p.] Rev. Joseph and Sarah E. Ivey; [m.] Marvin T. Stuart; August 3, 1946; [ch.] Francie Howell, Suzanne Smith; [ed.] 8th Grade with further high school studies; [occ.] Housewife; [hon.] Honored by city

of Soddy Daisy for poem sent to Saudi Arabia. Poem written for Anheiser Busch Co. in St. Louis, MO. Poems published in 4 books for The National Library of Poetry. Poem broadcast on local radio station; [oth.writ.] U.S. 101. 2 short stories published. I have written poems and stories on any subject. Especially if they make someone happy. I thank God for the gift of ability to write what I feel for others. A. Soddy Daisy, TN; [a.] Soddy Daisy, TN

STUDLER, STEPHANIE
[b.] December 5, 1982, Lubbock, TX; [p.] Mary Anne Studler; [ed.] Cavazos Jr. High; [occ.] Student; [memb.] National Jr. Honor Society, Cavazos Recruiting Team; [hon.] Outstanding 8th Grade Female of Cavazos Jr. High, National Jr. Honor Society; [oth. writ.] Poems published in other NLP anthologies and other companies.; [pers.] This poem was for my father, and he means the world to me. I Love You!; [a.] Lubbock, TX

SUMMERS, KEVIN G.
[pers.] Do nothing that you would be ashamed to have announced over an intercom to a group of your closest friends and worst enemies.; [a.] Ashburn, VA

SUNDAY, MICHAEL WALTER
[pen.] I.M. Sunday, M.W. Sunday; [b.] August 2, 1955; Columbus, OH; [p.] Esther F. Alten and Walter L. Sunday; [m.] Sue Ann Fouse; March 30, 1989; [ch.] Teresa Michelle Sunday; [ed.] Grad' Whitehall High 1973, graduated US Army Computer School 1982, graduated Denver Technical College B.A. in S.B.A. w/Minor in I.S., graduated Longridge Writers Course 1996; [occ.] Freelance Amatuer Photography Writer, and Disabled Veteran; [memb.] D.A.V. Christ Community Church (RCA), I.F.P.O., N.P.C.A., N.A.R.A.L., Democratic Party; [hon.] Served with distinction at Ronald Regan's inauguration. Honorable Discharge after 9 and 3/4 years of service in the U.S. Army; [oth.writ.] "Heroin Addicts Prayed," in Best Poems of 1997 (NLP), "Passion," In Silence of Yesterday (1997 NLP); [pers.] "The more you let God, the more you let go. 'For God so loved the world...' " (see John 3:16 for more).; [a.] Denver, CO

SUNG, JEAN
[pen.] Kiwi, Sailor Mars; [b.] June 14, 1983, Seoul, South Korea; [p.] See Yong Sung and Kyung Ja Sung; [ed.] Still in school; [occ.] Student, entering high school in fall of 1997; [memb.] Beck Players Drama Group; [hon.] First Place, Courier Post Education Express Short Story Contest; [oth. writ.] Poetry in: Anthology of Poetry by Young Americans (1994, 1995, and 1993 ed.) Walk Through Paradise, and Best Poems of the '90s, stories in newspapers.; [pers.] "We're all in some kind of trouble, am I the only one that sees it?" — Lucas, "Empire Records"; [a.] Cherry Hill, NJ

SUNN, JEFFREY
[pen.] Jeffrey Sunn; [b.] February 1, 1973, Milwaukee, WI; [p.] Albert and Patricia Sunn; [ed.] Vincent High School, University of Wisc-Milwaukee; [occ.] Petroff's Bowling Center, Menomonee Falls, WI; [hon.] WIAA Scholar-Athlete, W.H. Brady Academic All-Star Scholarship Recipient, Swimming (athletic) Scholarship to VW Milwaukee; [oth. writ.] None published; [pers.] Poetry is the fire which burns in us eternally. Writing one's dreams may help them be realized.; [a.] Milwaukee, WI

SVETECZ, MICHAEL
[b.] January 14, 1960; Bethlehem, PA; [ch.] Michael Jr., Meghan; [ed.] Bethlehem Catholic H.S, Allentown College; [occ.] Operations Manager;

[oth.writ.] Several poems published in magazines and newspaper; [pers.] My poems are simple and positive. I hope they bring us much pleasure in reading them as I get from writing them; [a.] Lancaster, PA

SWEAT, DAVID
[b.] January 10, 1977, Spartanburg, SC; [p.] James Sweat, Lavonia Hill; [ed.] Dorman High School, Spartanburg Methodist College; [occ.] Student; [hon.] National Dean's List, National Junior College, Academic All American; [oth. writ.] Poems in school literary magazines, articles in school papers; [pers.] I enjoy looking at ordinary things and situations from different perspectives. Who knew bugs talked like that?; [a.] Moore, SC

SWEENEY, ROBERT TODD
[b.] September 19, 1978, KI Swayer AFB, MI; [p.] Rick Sweeney, Diana Sweeney; [ed.] Olympic Heights Community High School; [pers.] This is a poem from my life. God bless my family, friends, and the band U2. All are my inspiration. Peace.; [a.] Boca Raton, FL

SWIDERSKI, THERESA
[b.] May 15, 1973; Chicago, IL; [p.] Frank and Mae Crech; [m.] Keith William Swiderski; May 31, 1996; [ed.] ASStagg High, Morome Valley Community College; [occ.] Housewife; [hon.] 2nd place state Confernce in DECA 1989; [pers.] Without the love and support of my husband Keith, my grandmother Cathy., Radakovits and my good friend Pauline Stratton, I would not be who I am today; [a.] Worth, IL

SWISHER, JUDY
[b.] January 31, 1954, Perry, GA; [ed.] High school diploma; [occ.] Dental Assistant; [oth. writ.] I'd like to write a lot more.; [a.] Venice, FL

TAVITIAN, VEHIG S.
[pen.] Suzann Davidson; [b.] October 7; New York City; [b.] Karekin Tavitian and Lucy (Manoogan) Tavitian; [ed.] Washington Irving H.S., NYC Graduate (with Regents diploma); [occ.] Editor/ Writer (Retired) IBM Corp. Education Div.; [memb.] MENSA, Literacy Volunteers Tutor and Editor of "Literally Yours" of LVA-Dutchess County, Mid-Hudson American Club Co-Chair, IBM Quarter Century Club, Community Baptist Church-various comm. chairs; [hon.] IBM Suggestion Awards (2), IBM Cost Effectiveness Triple Reward, IBM Certificate of Honor, IBM Information Planning Workshop Award of Distinction, NAFE 100,000 Club Certificate. Mid-Hudson Writer's Workshop Certificate of Participation in One-Act Play Contest, Certificate of Appreciation from: 1) Creston and Baptist Church (Bronx), 2) Green Street Baptist Church (Melrose, MA), 3) Community Baptist Chruch (Wappingers Falls, NY), 4) Holy Cross American Church (Lawrence, MA), 5) St. Gregory American Church (NYC); [oth. writ.] Also have translated two lectures by the American Musicologist Gomidas titled "Music and the Child" and "American Folk Music and Dance" publication in the book "GOMIDAS" on the 100th Anniversary of his birth; [pers.] God has granted me many talents and I try to make use of them to the best of my ability.; [a.] Wappingers Falls, NY

TAYLOR, DONALD
[b.] October 10, 1976, Portland, OR; [p.] Catherine and Allen Taylor; [occ.] Second year student at South; [pers.] Gentiles should not condemn the Jews. We all put Jesus on the cross. If the Jews are condemned, we are condemned. The Jews will be redeemed.; [a.] Seattle, WA

TAYLOR, LULA
[p.] Lillian Beasley, Meadows; [m.] Divorced; [ch.] Tim, Jim, Duane; [ed.] Graduate Trap Hill High, Surveyor, Wiva; [occ.] SR. Lead Film Librarian in Radiology; [oth.writ.] Always love (The lasting mirage); [pers.] Inspired by family and friends that touch my life especially Stan M; [a.] Cleveland, OH

TEMPLE, KENNETH F.
[b.] September 28, 1941; Potsdam, NY; [p.] Deceased; [m.] Nancy C; August 26, 1961; [ch.] Beth Temple Doggett; [ed.] Masters Credits - 18 hrs; [occ.] Driver Trainer for Great Coastal Express; [memb.] Bass Club, Chess Federation, VA Power Boat Assoc.; [hon.] A bunch - not recent; [oth.writ.] My Mother; [pers.] Happiness is the institution of sanity; sadness the correlation; [a.] Chester, VA

TERRELL, JULIE
[b.] December 3, 1977; New Albany, IN; [p.] Walter and Joyce Terrell; [ed.] 1996 Graduate of Floyd Central High School. Now a student at Indiana University Southeast; [occ.] File Clerk for a doctor's office; [memb.] Christian Student Fellowship, Scottsville Christian Church; [hon.] Girl Scout Silver Award, Girl Scout 10 Year Pin; [pers.] "I can do all things through Christ who strengthens me." -Philippians 4:13.; [a.] Borden, IN

TETREAULT-DUCHARME, YVETTE EVE
[pen.] Yvette Ducharme; [b.] October 24, 1939; Granby (Que) Canada; [p.] Lindor Tetreault; [m.] Irene Laberge; [ed.] Baccalaureate Arts - Brebeuf College, Montreal Law Degree-University Montreal Security Teacher -Concordia University Public Relations Degree; [occ.] Security Officer and Trainer; [memb.] Canadian Olympic Academy -Canadian Bar Association -Academy of Security Reductors and Trainers -Unitarian Universalist Church; [hon.] Governor General of Canada for Participation in 1988 Olympic Games; [oth.] Law articles - security manual -magazine comments, local church paper articles on political events. Published in USA and in Canada; [pers.] "Higher, Stronger, Farther" too strong will not break.; [a.] Ft. Lauderdale, FL

THOMPSON, DENISE
[pen.] Deedee; [b.] March 11, 1956; Oakland, LA; [p.] Pete and Joanne Jackson; [m.] Dennis; April 29, 1979; [ch.] Raymond, Janelle and Aaron; [ed.] National University (Suma Cum Laude)-Teaching Credential, Chapman University CLAD Certification; [occ.] Teacher; [memb.] Sisters of Color Incorp.; [oth.writ.] Various poems-more than thirty. One poem published in a local newsletter; [pers.] My work strives to relate issues I've experienced or other have or may have experienced. It is extremely difficult for me to verbally express I write. Hopefully others will be able to relate to my poetry in a way that soothes, touches or encourages them; [a.] Newman, CA

THOMPSON, MUHAMMAD
[pen.] John Thompson; [b.] January 15, 1952, Portland, OR; [p.] Cecil Thompson and Helen Kent Thompson; [ch.] Fatih Jan Thompson (Son); [ed.] BA in Islamic Studies, Istanbul, Turkey, MA in Near Eastern Languages and Civilizations, University of Washington, Seattle; [occ.] Counselor working with people with developmental disabilities.; [memb.] Middle East Studies Association, University of Washington Alumni Association, Nature Conservancy, Vedanda Society of Washington; [oth. writ.] Poems have been published in The Community Review, Today's World, "Poets Against The War, Winter Blooms" and have an as yet unpublished anthology, "The Lord's Stallion."; [pers.] The present evolutionary changes

in human consciousness and our emergence into Divinity is my greatest interest. I am most influenced by Islamic Suji poets and mystic writers.; [a.] Everett, WA

THOMPSON, STEVEN B.
[b.] December 11, 1959, New York; [p.] Mary Ann and Ronald Thompson; [m.] Lori; [ed.] Christopher, Bryan, Kelly; [oth. writ.] Children's stories, Monsters Under My Bed, Wind, The Tomato Snatcher, Monster Land, Harry Returns, poems: My Bike, Being Little, I Will Be Me, To Bite Your Nails Isn't Very Nice; [pers.] This poem is dedicated in loving memory of my mother, Mary Ann Thompson.; [a.] Locust Valley, NY

THURMAN, TERESA K.
[pen.] Teresa Kathleen Thurman; [b.] March 31, 1975, Midwest City, OK; [p.] Terry and Kathy Thurman; [ed.] University of Oklahoma, currently senior majoring in Bio-Chemistry; [memb.] GSUSA Adult Volunteer and Council Program Consultant, Territory Tellers, Okla's Assn of Storytellers; [hon.] Golden Key National Honor Society, National Dean's List, Phi Theta Kappa; [oth. writ.] Short story contest winner, several stories written to be performed for various community and church organizations.; [a.] Del City, OK

TILLER, NADINE
[b.] October 22, 1951, Trenton, NJ; [p.] Rose and Willie Roberson, (The Late Jesse Logan); [m.] James Tiller; [ch.] Tiffany Brown and The Late Jonathan Richardson; [occ.] Nurse - Helene Fuld Hospital, Trenton, NJ; [memb.] Macedonia Baptist Church - Trenton, NJ, Friends of Friends Social Club, Compassionate Friends (Mercer County); [oth. writ.] All Things In Time published 1997 in Into The Unknown, many other poems for pleasure.; [pers.] This poem was written and dedicated to my late son Jonathan who I'll love forever (deceased, January 12, 1997).; [a.] Trenton, NJ

TOOLE, DEBORAH D.
[b.] November 6, 1964; Aiken, SC; [p.] M.D. Toole III, Bonnie Toole; [ed.] Associate of Science, Architectural Design and Construction Technology; [occ.] CAD Operator/Technical Writer Profold, Inc., Sebastian, FL; [hon.] Distinguished American High School Students, Beta Club, Honor Society; [oth.writ.] Several poems written for family and friends' birthdays or special occasions; [pers.] I believe life is an exprience that should be lived to the fullest; man was not put on the earth to waste time. I write from past and present experiences in my life.; [a.] Vero Beach, FL

TRAMMELL, EDDIE
[b.] January 26, 1944; Athens, TX; [p.] Madison Trammell, Opal Trammell; [ch.] Cody Lynn Trammell; [ed.] Henderson County Junior College North Texas State University Associate Arts Degree; [occ.] Texas Dept. Of Corrections Correctional Officer 3; [oth.writ.] 200 original songs; [pers.] Be kind to one another; [a.] Athens, TX

TURNER, KATRINA M. NEWMAN
[b.] September 20, 1965; Mascatine, IA; [p.] Helen and Rovert Newman; [m.] Scott E. Turner; April 11, 1997; [ed.] BS in Psychology from Coe College, Cedar Rapids, IA; [occ.] Bander/Loan Officer; [pers.] this poem is in memory of my "step father" who really was my father; [a.] Marion, IA

USHER GRANT, SHARON A. M.
[pen.] Samu, Samu G; [b.] March 23, 1961; Jamaica; [p.] Trevor and Cynthia Usher; [m.] Nigel H. St. P. Grant; August 29, 1987; [ch.] Taylor Monet, Morgan Ashleigh; [ed.] Titchfield High,

Jamaica, Howard University, Washington D.C; [occ.] Homemaker; [memb.] National Paralegal Assoc; [hon.] Headgirl of Titchfield High 1979-80, Lakeridge Elementary School Volunteer Award 1996-97 School year; [oth.writ.] Poem published in High School Magazine; [pers.] Whatever you do, do to the best of your ability; [a.] Riverdale, GA

VACANTI, DEBORAH M.
[b.] June 16, 1952; Buffalo, NY; [p.] Elizabeth and Thomas Mulkeen; [m.] Gary L. Vacanti; March 28, 1978; [a.] Hamburg, NY

VACCA, DAVID M.
[b.] January 25, 1964; Morris, IL; [p.] Wilburt and Marge Vacca; [m.] Gwen Vacca; September 22, 1990; [ed.] High school graduate; [occ.] Custodian—Morris Elementary; [oth.writ.] Doodling, Ode To My Love, My Lady's Love, Troubled Soul, A Birthday Gift, Lovers and Together, all unpublished poems; [pers.] The vast reaches of the unexplored mind are opened by the power of fantasy.; [a.] Coal City, IL

VAIL II, DAVID L.
[b.] June 25, 1973; Tampa, FL; [p.] Nancy and David Vail; [m.] Patricia V. Angello; January 17, 1997; [ed.] High School Diploma various college classes; [occ.] Emergency medical tech; [memb.] National Registry of Emergency Medical Technicians Instructor of adult and child CPR with the American Neant Association; [oth.writ.] Many other writings, however none other published as I have just begun to pursue my publication of my writings; [a.] Chesapeake, VA

VAN HOOK, LINDA B.
[pen.] Linda B. Van Hook; [b.] November 11, 1949; Taneytown, MD; [p.] Roy J. Bankert, Anna Mae Jones; [m.] Ray C. Van Hook; May 22, 1993; [ch.] Dwayne and Lori Reeves, Eric and Shane Van Hook; [ed.] West Minster, MD H.S., Ottawa University; [occ.] Special Events Specialist, Glendale, AZ; [memb.] Regional Toastmasters of the Year, MADD Award for Public Speaking; [pers.] It is your attitude that determines your altitude in life.; [a.] Phoenix, AZ

VANBLARICUM JR., GARY
[b.] November 9, 1970; Flint, MI; [p.] Gary and Carrie VanBlaricum; [occ.] Race Car Mechanic; [oth. writ.] Song writer by heart. Yet unpublished; [pers.] Often I stop to take a look at nature. I ponder about our existence with it.; [a.] Gladwin, MI

VANCE, ERIKA
[pen.] Wind Dancer and Stray Kat; [b.] September 2, 1975; [pers.] My only true wish in life is to travel the stars. I have most been influenced by my summer school English teachers, Mrs. Frambers and Mrs. Lister, and by the Vampire LaCroix. Long live the night.; [a.] Tucson, AZ

VARGAS, KETTY
[b.] March 16, 1953, Guayaquil, Ecuador; [p.] Pedro Molina, Gladys Molina; [m.] Efren Vargas, M.D., February 19, 1973; [ed.] Guayaquil State Univ., School of Medicine; [occ.] Physician (not working); [hon.] Dean's List; [oth. writ.] Several acrostics for my friends. A few unpublished poems and writings.; [pers.] My poems are the result of my personal struggle to understand life.; [a.] Town South Hill, VA

VELDHUIS, LINDSEY
[b.] July 19, 1959, Findlay, OH; [p.] Ruth Hempen and Charles Shull; [m.] Richard Veldhuis, February 11, 1995; [ch.] Keli and Adam; [ed.] Nurse with Associate of Arts Degree; [occ.] Program Services

Coordinator for Muscular Dystrophy Assn.; [memb.] National Nurses Association, St. Mark Lutheran Church; [hon.] Currently Dean's List - Grand Rapids Community College and Western Michigan University, Honoree at Student Involvement Committee, 1991; [oth. writ.] Nursing School - 1991, Sir Greely and Me - 1986; [pers.] Deep reflection whether finding humor, sadness, fear or anger evokes great feelings and these are shown in my poetry. My children's books are from the kid inside of me.; [a.] Kentwood, MI

VENTURIN, MARGARET ROSS
[b.] August 31, 1913, Newark, NY; [p.] Clara and Anthony Ross; [m.] Deceased, Thanksgiving Day; [ch.] Faye and Gail; [ed.] One and a half years of college; [occ.] Retired; [memb.] Salvation Army (entertain children, senior citizens) including nursing homes; [hon.] Can't recall. There were several. King of Thailand sent me letter of appreciation. A conversational English taught to Thais. (Volunteer) Private Audience with Pope Paul VI; [oth. writ.] Poetry, stories, essays, plays, songs; [pers.] "Do unto others," etc., etc.; [a.] Jacksonville, FL

VILLAREAL, VERONICA M.
[pen.] Ronnie; [b.] May 12, 1975; Norman, OK; [p.] Margaret and Anthony; [ed.] Sanford Browal College, Graduate - Certified office specialist 1994 - St Charles Country Community College - present English/Life at use; [occ.] Administrative Assistant; [memb.] SCCCC Singers; [oth.writ.] Published in 1995 and 1996 Editions of "Charlie" the SCCCC literary magazine; [pers.] "And when the Broken Hearted People, living in the world agree, there will be an answer - let it be..." - the beatless; [a.] St. Peters, MO

VILNER, LUCY M.
[b.] May 16, 1946, Zagorsk, USSR; [p.] Boris Stepanov, Margaret Stepanov; [m.] Bertold J. Vilner, December 24, 1974; [ch.] Alex B. Vilner; [ed.] Belorussian State University, USSR; [occ.] Biologist, American Type Culture Collection, Rockville, Maryland; [oth. writ.] Some poems to my friends (birthdays, anniversaries), but they were not published.; [pers.] I believe that poetry, music and fine arts help people to be more kind, open-hearted and humane.; [a.] Kensington, MD

VINCENT, MICHAEL S.
[b.] January 18, 1952, Burlington, KS; [ed.] B.S., M.B.A., San Diego State University; [occ.] Writer; [oth. writ.] 3 novels: 1) Family, 2) The Clown Man (Family Part II), 3) Family Part III (Their Ultimate Demise); [a.] Chino, CA

WALLACE, PHILIP
[pen.] Phil Wallace; [b.] October 5, 1978, Phoenixville; [p.] Mary Wallace; [pers.] I am very misanthropic, and I try to write about man's tendency to kill and destroy, and make the earth, his only home, uninhabitable for himself and all other life on it.; [a.] Phoenixville, PA

WALLACE, SONJA K.
[b.] November 11, 1965; Dallas, TX; [p.] Gary Cooper, Kay Cooper; [ch.] Andrea Nicole, Gary Michael; [ed.] Pine Grove High, McCann School of Business; [occ.] Occupancy Manager; [oth.writ.] Through the Eyes of a Child, published in local newspaper; [pers.] We should all believe in children. Listen close to their actions, through them we may find ourselves. Be there concrete, so they can build a tomorrow; [a.] Pottsville, PA

WALROD, CHAD
[b.] November 16, 1971, Ogallala, NE; [p.] Larry Walrod and Shary Walrod; [ed.] Gordon High, University of Nebraska, Lincoln; [occ.] Pfizer Animal Health; [memb.] National Honor Society; [a.] Lincoln, NE

WALTER, MASCHA NADINE
[b.] January 30, 1977, Offenbach, Germany; [p.] Ludwig Walter, Monika Walter; [ed.] Marienschule der Ursulinen, Wingate University; [occ.] Student, majoring in Sec. Education; [memb.] Photographer for The Gate; [hon.] Wingate University's Dean's List, recipient of the Philip Chan Scholarship, Marvin and LaVonne Little Scholarship, and the Poplin Scholarship; [oth. writ.] Children's book: The Purple Bottle, and several other poems; [pers.] Always lead—never follow. I seek to leave common boundaries. I have been inspired by travels that let me experience the diversity of our world.; [a.] Offenbach, Germany

WAMBAUGH, ANNA M.
[b.] August 30, 1942, Philadelphia, PA; [p.] Charles and Mary E. (McDade) Gindhart; [m.] Lawrence Daniel Wambaugh, September 8, 1962; [ch.] Carol Ann, Linda Ann; [ed.] St. Monica Grade School, St. Maria Goretti High School 2 1/2 yrs, 1 yr St. Monica Commercial, Phila., PA; [occ.] Homemaker; [oth. writ.] "Cast to the Wind" is my first piece of work to be published from a small number of other poems and writings.; [pers.] Seek to love God with your whole heart, mind, body and soul and He will give you treasures beyond measure. You will come to know and find that, like a well spring, you will be filled with a pouring out of wisdom, understanding and knowledge on the issues of life and that He will fill your heart with such an abundance of His love that it will feel as thought it will burst! With all this you will come to know and love yourself as He loves you and in turn to love one another in peace and serenity.; [a.] Cincinnati, OH

WATKINS, ANNE HOWELL
[pen.] Kai-Nicole DeLacey; [b.] February 6, 1961; Roanoke, VA; [P.] Virginia Fariss Powel; [m.] James N. Watkins; December 25, 1995; [ch.] Shae, Cheir, Adelia, Christi, Katie; [ed.] Northside High School, National Business College, National Real Estate School; [occ.] Real Estate/ Property Management; [oth.writ.] "No More Lies" short fiction, presently working on a novel called, "Joint Custody"; [pers.] My seventh grade science teacher (at Ruffner Junior in Roanoke, VA), Tom Shupe, encouraged me to follow my dreams.; [a.] Hermitage, AR

WATKINS, CURTIS D.
[pen.] Malcom D. Watson; [b.] September 09, 1928; Jackson, KY; [p.] Jasper Watkins and C. Smith; [ch.] Joan Watkins, Olga, Reginald C. Watkins; [hon.] several; [oth.writ.] prose, "A Prayer For Smokey", a dog story, "History was Made", story of an auction, "It's Fun to be Fine"; [pers.] I started late in writing, I am highly motivated, I write from life experiences; [a.] Dallas, WV.

WESSON, JACQUELINE A.
[pen.] Jacquie Wesson; [b.] October 4, 1958; Warwick, RI; [p.] John R. Mirandou and Marguerite T. Mirandou; [m.] Ricky D. Wesson; September 3, 1978; [ch.] Joshua David, Tiffany Jacqueline; [ed.] East Greenwich High, Katherine Gibbs, CCRI; [occ.] Business Consultant, Metropolitan Ins. Co; [oth. writ.] Collection of published and unpublished poems; [pers.] Writing poetry releases the spirit and frees the soul.; [a.] East Greenwhich, RI

WEST, CARLA
[b.] May 25, 1964; St. Louis, MO; [p.] Nello and Ruth West; [ch.] Jerime Alexander West; [ed.] McCluer North High., Central Missouri State University; [occ.] Administrative Assistant.; [pers.] This poem comes from the Heart. It stems from all the love I feel for my son Jerime.; [a.] St. Louis, MO

WHEELER, SHELLEY
[b.] September 2, 1983; [p.] Pam and Chuck Wheeler; [m.] Brandy Bailey; [ed.] 7th Grade, Henry County Middle School; [a.] McDonough, GA

WHELAN, ANN
[pen.] Anka; [b.] May 11, 1931, Johnstown, PA; [p.] Amelia Menor and Stofan Dudukovich; [m.] Clinton D. Whelan Jr., February 22, 1969; [ch.] Mary Ann Madigan (Deceased), Michael, Devin, James, Brian Madigan and Alice Ann Grommett; [ed.] Johnstown Central High School, Irvine Valley College, U.S. Air Force; [occ.] Vocal Teacher, Writer, Poet, Retired-Clerical Supervisor-Farmers Insurance; [memb.] Past President V.F.W. Post 2122, Irvine Valley Chorale, St. Stevens Cathedral Choir, Member L.A. Chapter, National Assoc. Teachers of Singing; [hon.] Won first place poetry contest with Farmers Insurance in 1996; [oth. writ.] Published in Serb World, Remembering Christmas Past, Memories of Johnstown Flood of 1936, poem Kosava Peonies - several articles and poems in newspaper American Suburban.; [pers.] "I believe that God gave us our talents to be cultivated and shared with our fellow man."; [a.] La Habra, CA

WHITE, GARY
[pen.] G P White; [b.] March 25, 1960; Urbana, OH; [p.] Donna and Richard Wite; [m.] Jill White; [ch.] Joey and Teah White.

WIESE, MELISA R.
[b.] September 5, 1975, Spencer, IA; [p.] Marlene Koopman; [pers.] If you become in touch with yourself, you set yourself free.; [a.] Martelle, IA

WIESNER, EUGENE F.
[b.] April 22, 1956; Hays, KS; [p.] Eugene and Helen Wiesner; [m.] Maria P. Wiesner; May 23, 1988; [ch.] Simon D. Wiesner; [ed.] Billings Senior High (1974), Billings Vo-Tech (1975), Eastern Montana College (1975, 1980); [memb.] St. Patricks Church; [oth.writ.] I have written many letters to newspapers throughout the northwest United States. I had two poems published in "A Muse to Follow" and "The Colors of Thought"; [pers.] Love your brother as yourself and God with your whole heart.; [a.] Laurel, MT

WILKINSON, LUCILLE
[b.] August 25, 1951; Bronx, NY; [p.] Vernon Stockes, Jane Stokes; [m.] Divoced; [ch.] Carmen, Heather, Kwajo; [ed.] Copigue High School, Copiague, NY; [a.] Boston, MA

WILLIAMS, DEANNA
[b.] May 25, 1978; Niles, MI; [p.] Dana Williams -Mother; [ed.] Student at Webster University, studying Literature and Creative Writing; [hon.] National Merit Award in English, Short Story Editor of "The Grape Vine"; [oth.writ.] The Magician, Pain As Pleasure, both published in Parkway North's literary magazine, "The Grape Vine"; [pers.] "A coven of freaks and physicians, we poets, that shock and heal" -me.; [a.] St. Louis, MO

WILLIAMS, JOHN
[pen.] Jack Williams; [b.] May 5, 1944; Brookline, MA; [ed.] Brookline High School; [occ.] Musician; [oth.writ.] 1st Book of Poetry (unpublished)

called "Between the Ears"; [a.] Encimtas, CA

WILLIAMS, REGINA
[b.] December 28, 1977; IL; [p.] Michael and Karen Jestis; [ed.] Thunderbird High School Phoenix, AZ; [occ.] Secretay Rudy's Auto Center Tucson, AZ; [pers.] Writing is my one true goal. I wish to share all my poems and insights with the world; [a.] Glendale, AZ

WILLIAMS II, PRESTON
[b.] December 27, 1958, Folkston, GA; [p.] Rev. and Mrs. Preston Williams Sr.; [m.] Jacqueline H. Williams, November 9, 1996; [ch.] Preston III, Portia, Keri; [ed.] Lee College, Ribault Sr. High; [occ.] Buyer/Credit Analyst National Auto Finance, Inc.; [memb.] Board of Advisors (Broward Community College), Distinguished Member of the International Society of Poets; [hon.] 1. Outstanding Young Men of America Award 1994 and 1996, 2. Phi Beta Lambda Fraternity, 3. Editor's Choice Award - Nat'l Lib. of Poetry, 4. Poet of Merit - Internat'l Society of Poets; [oth. writ.] 1. Published in "Echoes of Yesterday" anthology c/o The National Library of Poetry, 2. "Whispering Silhouette" manuscript unpublished (100 pg) recently completed; [pers.] "The only limits to my accomplishments in life . . . are self-imposed."; [a.] Boca Raton, FL

WILSON, EDWARD F.
[pen.] Cpl. Edward F. Wilson; [b.] April 9, 1917; Topeka, KS; [p.] Riley Wilson and Agnes (McCall) Wilson; [m.] Bertha Marie Booth; June 5, 1948; [ch.] Gayla (Wilson) McGuire, Jill (Wilson) Greenwexl, Rod Wilson, Tdunja (Wilson) Chadwick; [ed.] 7th Grade - Quincy, KS; [occ.] Deceased - December 31, 1996, Retired Oil Field Worker, WW II Veteran; [memb.] DAV (Disabled Veterans of Foreign Wars), VFW (Veterans of Foreign Wars), American Legion, Temple Baptist Church, El Dorado, KS; [hon.] WW II Decorations Silver Star for Conspicuous Gallantry, (4) Bronze Stars for Bravery, (2) Purple Hearts for wounds received in battles, the French Croix de Guerre, The Combat Infantry Badge Presidential Unit Citation, Distinguished Unit Citation. Was one of only 200 men who have received a personal recommendation from the President of the United States - given to him by Harry S. Truman; [pers.] This poem was written during or between heavy fighting battles in WW II. Written in Italy either while crossing Volturno River or at Monte-Cassino Battle. Dad was sad, lonely, and had the responsibility of soldiers' lives to care for. God inspired him to write this poem.; [a.] DeSoto, TX

WILSON, JUDY
[b.] October 12, 1954, Salt Lake City, UT; [p.] Ruel and Donette Unsworth; [m.] Norman Scott Wilson, August 1, 1993; [ch.] Four - two boys, two girls; [oth. writ.] I've written one short story that began as a nightmare and ended as a fictional horror story. Tons of poetry!; [pers.] I write poetry to release everything I feel inside. Sometimes that's the safest way.; [a.] Denver, CO

WILSON, NATALIE M.
[b.] May 5, 1987; Corbin, KY; [p.] James and Donna Wilson; [ed.] Cookson Elementary, Troy, Ohio; [memb.] I attend Troy Church of God Mt Assembly Church; [hon.] Honor Roll, Checker Champion Award (out of the 4th, 5th and 6th grade competition), Female Sportsmanship at Church of God Jr. Camp 1996; [oth.writ.] Poetry 1st place at Church of God Jr. Camp 1996, 8-10 years old; [a.] Troy, OH

WILSON, TUPUIVAO ROBERTO GIMENO
[pen.] Robert; [b.] February 26, 1979; Pforzheim-Germany; [p.] Dannie Lee, Joaguina Elisa Wilson; [ed.] Chula Vista High School, June 12, 1997; [oth.writ.] The World of poems 1996 at the age of 16; [pers.] I just want to thank my family and friends for all the support and love they give me. Thank you; [a.] Chula Vista, CA

WISEMAN III, WILLIAM J.
[pen.] William Wiseman; [b.] Mississippi; [p.] Bill and Nancy Wiseman; [ed.] C.D. Hylton High School; [occ.] Firefighter with the U.S. Air Force; [hon.] Being published by The National Library of Poetry.; [oth. writ.] Several poems (yet to be published, I hope), one called First Snow published in school paper.; [pers.] Always be yourself because when you stop, you're someone else.; [a.] LR AFB, AR

WOLAVER, SAM
[pen.] Sam Wolaver; [b.] June 5, 1936, Bynum, TX; [m.] Jan; [ch.] Stephen Wayne, Richard Alan; [ed.] Italy public schools, Navarro College, U.T. Arlington; [occ.] Police Officer and Dispatcher; [memb.] First United Methodist Church, Masonic Lodge, Texas Steele Guitar Assn.; [oth. writ.] Children's book, "The Littlest Christmas Tree," in process of being published for Christmas 1997; [pers.] I believe in the goodness of man and to seek it in all you meet.; [a.] Italy, TX

WOLFE, CASSANDRA
[pen.] Cassie Wolfe; [b.] July 16, 1984, Madras, OR; [p.] Cyril Wolfe and Rhonda Clements; [ed.] Jefferson County Middle School, Warm Springs Elementary; [occ.] Student; [memb.] JCMS Basketball, Major League Baseball Team member; [hon.] Student of the Month, sports recognition award (basketball, baseball); [oth. writ.] Other poems for school projects, gifts, personal; [pers.] I write about anything on my mind, my feelings, something I see, my family.; [a.] Warm Springs, OR

WOOD, NANCY JANE
[pen.] Mary Fairchild; [b.] May 3, 1950, Wheeling; [p.] Davis Wilison Wood; [m.] Gue Irene Fry, (Divorced); [ch.] Bryan L. and George K. Nagy; [ed.] I graduated from Wheeling High School in 1969 and attended Wheeling Beauty College and WUNC College where I studied computers; [occ.] Unemployed due to medical reason; [memb.] I am a member of St. Matthews Episcopal Church; [hon.] The only honor I have received was having my poem "It" published.; [oth. writ.] I have written around six other poems, and I'm in the middle of writing a book and hope someday to have it published as well.; [pers.] I would like to say never let your dreams die, for I believe if we never dream, then how can we live. For life begins with one little dream.; [a.] Wheeling, WV

WOOD, WILMA L.
[pen.] Wilma Spaur Wood; [b.] February 26, 1933, Braxton Co., WV; [p.] Perry H. and Gertrude Spaur (Deceased); [m.] Earl P. Wood (Deceased January 4, 1996), June 21, 1952; [ch.] Jeffrey L., Stephen P., Jayne Wood Harris; [ed.] Sutton High School, Mountain State Business College, Parkersburg, WV, additional - credits through Glenville State College; [occ.] Retired - WV Dept. of Health and Human Resources; [memb.] Gassaway Baptist Church Choir Member, Treasurer, Member of International Society of Poets; [hon.] Blue, Red and White Ribbons on poetry - Arts and Crafts Fair. Poem published in "A Moment to Reflect" - poem selected for "Best Poetry of 1997," poem selected for "The Other Side of Midnight."; [oth. writ.] Unpublished, unsubmitted book of poetry entitled, "Through The Looking Glass." Cur-

rently working on book on my grandmother and mother's life 1892-1990.; [pers.] Reflecting Christ and hope for mankind. To glorify God and encourage others through love, laughter and tears.; [a.] Gassaway, WV

WOODS, VICKI R.
[b.] February 6, 1962; Bloomington, IN; [p.] Gordon E. and Patricia I. Cole; [m.] Edward R. Woods; June 4, 1983; [ch.] Heather M. Woods; [ed.] Bedford N. Laurence, Bedford In, and Ivy Tech, Indianapolis, IN; [oth.writ.] I had a few short stories published in school book at Ivy Tech; [pers.] I believe my ability as a poet was inherited by my aunt Wilma, and I'd like to take this time to thank her for it; [a.] Mooresville, IN

WOOTEN, BRENDA L.
[pen.] "Bren"; [b.] October 12, 1951; Newport News, VA; [p.] Mr. and Mrs. Clyde Steward; [m.] Dennis Lee Wooten; December 29, 1981; [ch.] Belinda Steward, Lelia Steward, Ronnie Steward, Catine Steward, Gerald and Jerrell Allen (twins); [ed.] Ding Dong Kindergarten School Nen. Va, Newsame Park Elm N.N. VA, George Washington Carver High N.N., VA; [occ.] Housewife; [memb.] Gold Trust Inc. Religion AL-Islam; [hon.] Sewing, Cooking and Upholstering; [oth.writ.] "None", but I would like to give thanks to "Allah" and my family and friends for believing in me. Most of all to my husband "Dennim", I love you thank you; [pers.] A mother's love for her child is as deep as the depth of darkness and a boundless as time "no-matter what"; [a.] Raleigh, NC

WRIETH, LUC
[b.] Hastings, NB; [p.] Francis and Annabelle Leichleiter; [ch.] Kimberly Sue; [ed.] Harvard Public School, Harvard, NB, Metro College, Omaha, NB, U.N.O, Omaha, NB; [occ.] Nurse at Internal Medicine Associated - Cardiology Dept., Omaha, NB; [oth.writ.] While working at quality living, I wrote articles for the "Immanuel Newsletter"; [pers.] The real beauty in the world comes from the little things: a smile, a laugh, a hug and a kiss for luck. Also, I believe in the "Lucky Perry." [a.] Plattsmouth, NB

WRIGHT, DOUGLAS B.
[pen.] Doug Wright; [b.] June 20, 1934; [ed.] Brigham Young, University BA 1971; [occ.] Retired former school teacher, San Rafael Jr. High; [memb.] Utah Historical Society Foster Care Citizens Review Board Square Dance Club; [hon.] For Foundation Fellowship Award, Robeth L. Campbell Award, (given by the Utah Education Assoc. many Utah Press Association Awards); [oth.writ.] Several poems and stories published in local newspapers. One story published in magazine. Several unpublished manuscripts. Write all legal documets for our city; [a.] Clawson, UT

WRIGHT, HUGH D.
[b.] February 25, 1924; Omoa, Honduras; [p.] James and Maude Wright, deceased; [m.] Moira Wright; December 31, 1964; [ch.] Hugh, Jr; [ed.] Maheia's Private School, St. Michael's College, Both located in Belize City, Belize, Central America; [occ.] Retired clerk; [memb.] National Notary Association AARP, Distinguished Member of I.S.P; [hon.] Recipient of a 1997, Editor's Choice Award by N.L.P; [oth.writ.] Three poems published by the National Library of Poetry. Article in local bank newsletter of my mini Kaleidoscope vacation of Europe with my family in 1971; [pers;.] To paraphrase Robert Frost - courage to act on limited knowledge, courage to make the best of what is here and not whine for more; [a.] Brooklyn, NY

XIONG, AMMY
[pen.] Ammy Xiong/Ammy Cheyenne; [b.] January 11,1981; [p.] Christina Reynolds; [ed.] High School Student (sophomore); [pers.] Poetry is the language of profound individuality, self-concept and understanding. My language is poetry; [a.] Appleton, WI

YDRIS, KASSI
[b.] November 4, 1970; Micheacan, Mexico; [p.] Antonia Mendoza; [m.] Thomas Kristoffersen; May 24, 1995; [ed.] Monterey Institute of International Studies (Matesol); [occ.] Student; [memb.] Teachers of English to speakers of other Languages; [hon.] Eagle scout, editor of "Dreams; creative writing journal, 1988-'89, poem, 1st place poetry constest winner with "crystal hearts" saddleback community college; [oth.writ.] "Journal of A Sad Winter" a novel, "Winter Poems," Capanhagen Poems"; [pers.] I strive to reflect the beauty inheren't within my memories and life experiences; [a.] Monterey, CA

YEATTS, JAMES WILLIAM
[pen.] James William Yeatts; [b.] October 11, 1970, Danville, VA; [p.] Howard T. Yeatts Jr., Louise K. Yeatts; [ed.] Graduated from Gretna Senior High School, Gretna, VA; [occ.] Farming: Piney Fork Farms; [memb.] Piney Fork Baptist Church; [oth. writ.] Several more heart touching poems; [pers.] My words come from within my heart. I strive to touch other hearts with tender words and true feelings. That means so much to me.; [a.] Gretna, VA

YOUNG, EDITH HOLLAND RUSHING
[pen.] Holland Young; [b.] January 15, 1921; Rushing, AR; [p.] Mark H. and Lorah E. Rushing; [m.] Gordon L. Young; January 20, 1946; [ch.] Carolyn E. Marsh; [ed.] Centerville High School, State Teachers College, Draughon's School of Business; [occ.] Retired; [memb.] Lifetime member Parents and Teachers Association; [hon.] Class Valedictorian, Defense Award for War Bond Sales; [oth.writ.] Sports reporter high school newspaper, numerous poems, short stories and songs; [pers.] My life long interest in music, history and literature was encouraged and nurtured by my father and excellent high school teachers. I have spent many enjoyable hours reading, memorizing and reciting poetry.; [a.] Sherwood, AR

ZAIDE, LOREL DON
[pen.] L. Zaide; [b.] July 2, 1974; Chicago, IL; [p.] Rogelio and Eva Zaide; [ed.] Niles West High School University of Nevada, Las Vegas; [occ.] Hotel Administration Student; [memb.] PHI Delta Theta International Fraternity; [oth.writ.] Poems and writings in my own anthology called "Planet L. Zaide"; [pers.] My writings are an invitation into the depths of my soul, and everyone's invited. Welcome to my planet; [a.] Las Vegas, NV

ZAPPARELLI, JENEA D.
[pen.] "Dreamer"; [b.] September 18, 1974; Philadelphia, PA; [p.] Jacque Leone and Ernest J. Zapparelli; [ed.] St. Jude Grammer School, Chalfont, PA, Lansdale Catholic Graduating Class of 1992; [occ.] My current occupation, seems to be a bit different than mot others for I work only for one Leadership and society and government.; [memb.] As for memberships, yes, again, I am as everyone, a member of the most high heavenly Kingdom.; [hon.] As for Honors and Awards well, this here, opportunity I'm presently receiving, to express my feelings here, straight forward upon such an open forum, available to the masses is porbably the most distinct and honorable mention I could share.;

[oth.writ.] Hey! I have a million! Maybe more, and I wish to grace you with the ideas of pleasurable knowingness to the works done throuhg me, by the Spirit of course.; [pers.] I only have one: And that remains as is - Truth, is manifested here, in and through out each on e of us located in our perfect soul self that cordially invites us, every moment, through ups and downs to join Him in his well known abundance, freedom and joy, comfort, Love and wisdom - True! And untainted and yours everlasting. [a.] Philadelphia, PA

ZARATE, JANET K.
[pen.] Janet Kathleen; [b.] March 22, 1954; Inglewood, CA; [p.] Mr. and Mrs. Frank A. Zarate; [ed.] St Marys Academy High School, W.L.A. Jr Col, El Canino Sr. College, CSUN, Northridge; [occ.] Ha'rsts list unemployed; [oth.writ.] I written a few articles. Also I've written to President Clinton; [pers.] I believe everything is relative and if we just start relating from our hearts the world would be a much more comfortable; [a.] Bellflower, CA

ZAWITOSKI, JOHN P.
[pen.] Nightwing; [b.] March 23, 1962, Baltimore; [p.] Edward and Jean; [m.] Donna, May 26, 1986; [ed.] Allegany College, AA Forest Technology May 1982, University of Maryland BS Agriculture May 1986; [occ.] District Director USDA, Farm Service Agency; [hon.] One Line Honor - weekly poetry competition - 1st place Whispers in the Dark 8/96, 1st place Distance 10/96, 1st place The Love That Grows Inside 11/96, 1st place Shattered by the Wind 4/13/97, 1st place Try and Understand 4/20/97; [oth. writ.] Several poems published on the on-line magazine called, Delirium, Aug. 1996 Issue (Children of the Sun, Beautiful Dancers, Winds of December, Schooner Fare, Shattered by the Wind, Distance); [pers.] Inspiration comes from my interactions with humankind and the world around me. Some very special people helped me discover the gift of writing for which I will be forever grateful - thanks June Milley, Kathy Terry, Ladawnna, Dianne Charron.; [a.] Severn, MD

ZIELKE, DAVID
[b.] September 23, 1959, Baroda, MI; [p.] Arthur and Virginia; [ed.] "The Road Less Travelled"; [occ.] Songwriter/Musician; [pers.] God bless all whose travels pass here.; [a.] Fairhope, AL

ZIEMBA, LINDA
[p.] John and Mary Ziemba; [ed.] Hoosac Valley High School; [oth. writ.] Several other poems, currently writing short stories.; [pers.] I own draft horses and long for the good old days of covered wagons and simple ways.; [a.] Savoy, MA

ZIMA, PHILLIP A.
[b.] August 2, 1953, Cleveland, OH; [p.] Nicholas and Anna Zima; [m.] Jennifer (Hall) Zima, May 5, 1979; [ch.] Jason, Ashlee and Chianne; [ed.] University of Arizona, Rincon High; [occ.] Sales Manager with Circle K, a division of Toso Marketing; [memb.] Masons, Boy Scouts of America; [hon.] Eagle Scout with 3 palms; [pers.] My family is important to me. I now know that happiness lies in sharing my life, what's ahead? I don't know, but whatever it is, I'll work it out.; [a.] Mesa, AZ

ZIRK, LOIS L.
[pen.] Lois Zirk; [b.] January 6, 1925, Walnut, IA; [p.] Winfield and Mabel Smathers; [m.] Kenneth H. Zirk, May 10, 1974; [ch.] 1 plus 4 step-children; [ed.] Grade 1 through 8, in rural Iowa country school - 4 yrs high school in Iowa - Normal Training Cert.; [occ.] Homemaker - Gardener - Wild Life Advocate - Cat Lover; [memb.] Nat'l Wildlife Assoc., Audubon Society; [oth. writ.] Many verses and poems throughout the years - sent to friends and family.; [pers.] I have very simple values, which come from my parents, who were farm folks during the Depression years. I have a special feeling for animals and birds, and the beauty of our world.; [a.] Portland, OR

Index
of
Poets

Index

A

Abe, Mark 79
Abel, Chrissy 226
Abouzahr, Robin V. 192
Acosta, Ray 70
Adamitis, Carole A. 18
Adamo, Deborah Kaye 96
Adams, Brandi 120
Adams, Gloria N. 252
Adams, John 60
Adams, Rosalie 34
Adams, Sarah 205
Adams, Travis 135
Aderman, Daphne M. 89
Agnes, Sister Curran, PBVM 148
Agrawal, Roma 232
Aguirre, Geoffrey 216
Aitken, Andy 69
Ajah, Ofem I. 254
AKIBA 144
Albert, Nichole 20
Alcorn, Mike 118
Alexander, John 212
Alexander, Joy 214
Alexander, Lewis C. 178
Alexander, Louise J. 243
Alexander, Matthew Lane 87
Alexander, Tiffany 193
Allan, Willard 134
Allange, Stephen V. 131
Allen, Deann 58
Allen, Gary David 139
Allen, Joe W. 41
Allen, Kathleen A. 141
Allen, Tina 87
Alleyne, Lennox 152
Allison, Barbara 194
Allison, Lanna 92
Altman, Ashley 75
Alvarado, Esther L. 69
Amiga, Fiel 52
Ampadu, Akua 140
Andazola, Monica 145
Anderson, Amy 255
Anderson, Candice Beth 74
Anderson, Dynsdale 253
Anderson, Elise 6
Anderson, Tammy 222
Anderson, Tracy 249
Andrews, Leland Embert 60
Andrews, Nichole 140
Andrewsen, Todd 141
Andrusin, George 187
Anemone, Christopher 190
Angeles, S. F. 179
Angelopoulos, Stavroula 216
Ann, Betty Watters 98
Ann, Rose Dunlap 40
AnnEngle, Kimberly 186
Ansell, Lisa Marie 146
Argent, Janet 255
Argyros, Chris 122
Arnold, Christina 4
Arnold, Diane Elizabeth 20

Asin, Leslie 190
Atchison, Stefani 44
Augustine, Rebecca Howard 57
Ault, Daniel 212
Aurand, Rhonda J. 44
Ayala, Helen 223
Azoulay, Eliya 138

B

Babec, Maureen A. 98
Bailey, Alma 150
Bailey, B. 130
Bailey, Clara B. 18
Bailey, Dee 121
Bailey, Derek 68
Bailey, Jacquelyn H. 87
Bailey, Tara C. 55
Baker, Anna 160
Baker, Judith J. 201
Baker, Julie Melissa 215
Baldauf, H. Alexander 72
Baldwin, Grace Rosen 27
Bales, Cathryn 231
Ballard, Michelle 244
Balz, Timothy A. 136
Bandelow, Walter F. 35
Banks, Karen R. 125
Bansemer, Ryan 142
Barber, K. A. 40
Barlow, Fern 45
Barner, Tyrone 261
Barnett, Ronda 246
Barnhill, Terri 200
Barnwell, Shawn D. 113
Barron, Johnna 196
Barsch, Gayla Lynn 195
Barthlein, Domanick Angelaca 42
Bartlett, Alberta Lynn 61
Bass, Virginia L. 29
Bassett, C. Kay 27
Batchelor, Heather 154
Bates, Doug 234
Bates, Jan 104
Bauer, Sandra 41
Bauer, Saundra J. 100
Beam, Kathryn A. 165
Bean, Stephen 228
Beard, David 220
Beasley, Linda 123
Beck, Stephanie 61
Becker, Evelyn 63
Becker, Rachele 24
Beckford, Laurentz D. 40
Beckler, Jennifer 47
Bedard, Ellen Larson 55
Bedford, Kimberly A. 94
Beinke, Joshua 221
Belbutowski, Paul M. 188
Belcher, Carrol 30
Bell, Adrianne M. 218
Bell, Cherie L. 140
Bell, Daniel A. 42
Bell, Gregory 107
Bell, Leona 210
Bell, Madelyn J. 219
Bellville, Miriam 22
Belyski, Barbara Ann 216
Benfield, Roger M. 137
Benjamin, Anthony S. 40
Benjamin, Goldine 98

Benjamin, Lynette 173
Bennett, Christine Alison 59
Bennett, Marc 164
Bennett, Mildred J. 84
Berdeguez, Michael R. 45
Berg, Benjamin 104
Bergeron, Bobbi 219
Bergert, Kitty 97
Bergman, Douglas 186
Berkich, Krysta Marie 195
Berman, Tressa 7
Bernard, Denise 186
Bernard, Pearl 89
Bernatovich, Donna 129
Berridge, Connie 164
Berry, T. Victor 9
Bess, Carissa 13
Bevis, Ann 256
Bhakta, Maya 48
Bibee, Winston 50
Bingham, DeAnna 66
Bingham, Lila 64
Bishop, Elizabeth 192
Bishop, Julia 84
Blaies, Joan 196
Blair, Nicole 77
Blanche, Ian 207
Blank, Jessi 54
Bledsoe, Freda 84
Bliss, Cathy A. 83
Blitstein, Albert 140
Blocker, Snake 125
Bloom, William H. 27
Bloss, Natalie L. 112
Blubaugh, Glenn L. 97
Boccelli, Phillip 200
Bock, Jessica 249
Bodner, Kimberly N. 129
Bogner, Myles Brandon 195
Bohl, Mary 180
Boisvert, Tracy L. 245
Bolin, Brian 118
Bonarigo, David 67
Bonbright, C. W. 208
Booker, Jomero J. 244
Bookout, Jay Michaal 46
Borgen, Alex James 193
Bosch, Swanny Anita 213
Boston, Ruby L. 22
Boswell, Lisa 108
Boush, Charlene J. 198
Bousley, Marguerite Campbell 209
Bowen, Brian 258
Bowen, Doris A. 76
Bowen, Norval 116
Bowens, Alice Lucille 224
Bowers, Rita J. 197
Bowie, Dr. Joyce Guillory 72
Bowles, Lynda 213
Bowles, Stacey 86
Boyko, Alisa Dawn 53
Boynton, Seth 51
Bradley, George A. 21
Bradley, Jaclyn 170
Bragg, Heather 80
Branch-Clarke, Melicent 185
Braun, Eric 193
Breaux, Kathleen Ann 88
Breedon, Elizabeth H. 96
Brelsford, Robert 191
Brest, David 167

Brewer, Jeff 107
Bridges, Dorothy L. 159
Brigante, Derek 177
Briggs, Jacqueline 223
Britt, Emily 125
Brittsan, Yvonne 204
Brock, Lisa C. 78
Brody, Samantha 226
Brooke, Georgie 14
Bross, Kevin 168
Brown, Carmel Finnery 3
Brown, Christopher Michael 86
Brown, Edward L. 26
Brown, Gilberte 36
Brown, John 89
Brown, Johnnie 192
Brown, Kimberly S. 36
Brown, Linton 208
Brown, Pamela R. 113
Brown, Pat 187
Brown, Richard A. 114
Brown, Ronnie 159
Brown, Virgil 209
Bruce, Joyce Hoffman 225
Brunken, Rosemary 237
Bruns, Carolyn 42
Bruns, Sister Barbara, PHJC 9
Buatois, Edward 8
Buck, Janet Irene 3
Buckwalter, Jennifer May 185
Buehring, Brandon 231
Buggage, M. 249
Bullett, Audrey Kathryn 21
Bullock, Geraldine 25
Bunch, Gail M. 56
Bundschuh, Walter 61
Bunes, Margaret R. 141
Bunuan, Andy L. 16
Burcham, Margaret D. 196
Burford, Mary 68
Burgess, Donnie J. 256
Burgess, Krista 154
Burgoyne, Keith 107
Burke, Frances 110
Burke, Ruby 23
Burke, Shelley 89
Burley, Robert 167
Burnett, Betty A. 181
Burnett, Helen 253
Burnett, Tami 79
Burnett, Theda 200
Burow, Nicole 189
Burrows, Elizabeth MacDonald 18
Burton, Ruth A. 158, 6
Bustos, Jose A. Jr. 203
Butera, Marianne Lester 236
Butler, Ann Marie 8
Butler, Ashley 80
Butler, Dianne 93
Butler, Dorothy 66
Butler, Kayla 236
Buttino, Daniel T. 137
Buys, Jarrett 36
Bybee, Ben 234
Bye, Sheila 192
Byers, Kelly A. 156
Byers, Robert K. 59
Byun, Michael I. 25

C

Caeidhe, Ana W. 140
Calchera, Angela 175
Calderon, Candida E. 127
Caldevell, Charles 154
Caldwell, Phyllis Stanley 138
Califano, Lisa 101
Camacho, Stephen 96
Camp, Rebecca E. 132
Campbell, Justin 102
Campbell, Lindsay 51
Cantone, Jason 43
Capalby, Christina M. 217
Capie, Frances Kelley 65
Cappadona, Janet 97
Cardona, Dennise S. 109
Carlson, Becky 151
Carolan, Patty 95
Caron, Shirley Ruth 128
Carpenter, Nicole 246
Carr, Betty K. 245
Carr, Emily 165
Carr, Ian 41
Carr, Kristin Noelle 190
Carrara, Donna J. 259
Carreno, Corrie 8
Carreno, Patricio 260
Carroll, DE 244
Carso, Alana 190
Carter, Charles Jr. 182
Carter, Elizabeth Talbott 247
Carter, Kat 67
Carter, Maurice 88
Carusillo, Frances 147
Casavant, Carol A. 122
Case, E. R. 63
Casper, Janet E. 196
Castner, Lisa 118
Catanzaro, Barbara P. B. 20
Cater, Sir Dionysus 211
Cattrano, Kristin 48
Caudle, Tom 21
Cavil, Lillian M. 18
Chakoian, Mark 176
Chang, Janice M., J.D., Ph.D. 16
Chapman, Lorie M. 190
Chappell, Morgan 115
Charboneau, Rita 54
Charles, Hensworth Hensley 115
Charley, Matipa 88
Chase, Alice 28
Cheek, Lanell 142
Cheng, Jennifer 163
Cherico, Steve 62
Cherry, Mildred L. 141
Child Of God 45
Chippewa-Sapulpa, Della 99
Chism, Margie S. 149
Chlebanowski, Matt J. Sr. 31
Choukas, Malissa 139
Christensen, Heidi 235
Chu, Steven 190
Chumo, George Jr. 97
Cipolla, J. 123
Clark, Jewell 232
Clark, Kay Sturgeon 92
Clark, Sara Beth 168
Clark, Sarah A. 191
Clark-Brown, Annette, MD 44
Clarke, Thomas W. 61

Clayton, Elizabeth Teasley 205
Clem, Carol Ann 116
Clements, Kiersten 151
Close, Haley L. 195
Cochran, Annabelle 100
Cogburn, Beni 221
Cogdell, Daisy 117
Cohen, Naomi 183
Coker, Gaines M. Sr. 247
Colaneri, Marie E. 14
Coleman, Rebecca Jane 222
Coleman, Rhea M. 131
Colen, Jennifer D. 195
Collins, Ken 258
Collins, Xtian 66
Colontonio, Nicholas J. 250
Combs, Marie 7
Comis, Lori 71
Commissiong, Sue-Ann 251
Compton, Patricia J. 135
Connolly, Ann 128
Connolly, Shermy 25
Conrad, A.C. 67
Conrad, Amber Raeschel 165
Cooksey, James 13
Copeland, Jerry 33
Corkins, John 170
Corso, Lonna 199
Couch, Martha 62
Courtier, Elaine 70
Courtney, Barbara E. 97
Cox, Tim 191
Craig, Don C. 234
Craig, Nancy B. 225
Crawford, Brookie L. 177
Crawford, Lucille 38
Creaser, Irina 64
Creed, Amanda 135
Cronin, Robert 55
Crook, Marcelle Kerouac 199
Crosby, Dave 228
Crough, Kelly Michelle 7
Cruea, LaurieAnne 140
Culler, Margaret L. W. 106
Cullipher, Ricky 178
Culver, Ruth 60
Cumming, Jessica 130
Cummins, Amanda 150
Cunningham, Jennie 95
Curran, Robert J. 194
Curry, James G. 245
Curry, Karmen Marie 64
Curry, Meredith 155
Curtis, Wesley K. 158

D

Dabb, Chris 162
Dagen, Austin 101
Dahl, Melanie 111
Dahlem, Irene Brown 115
Dahne, Robert 138
D'Amico, Sarah Ann 175
Dana, Rachel 107
Dandron, Jeremy 259
D'Angelo, Francesca 34
Daniel, Kimberly 90
Daniels, Betty 232
Daniels, Joyce A. 21
Daniels, Pamela 53
Darrell, Lawrence 38

Daugherty, Ken 101
Davenport, Marie 76
Davidson, Aaron J. 194
Davidson, Charlotte Jean 236
Davin, Lawrence S. 137
Davis, DeLee 121
Davis, Eletha 253
Davis, Erica 95
Davis, Katie L. 236
Davis, Maria 156
Davis, Ryan 245
Davis, Viola I. 187
Day, Nicole 123
De Vita, Alexis Brooks 225
De Vries, Sharon 50
DeAnna, Marissa 169
deBarros, Mary H. 107
DeBerry, Shirley 192
Decker, Amy 66
Decker, Jenny 70
Decker, Lisa 63
Dedmond, Laura 132
Deemer, Jackie C. 18
Delafield, Corinne C. 76
DeLaughter, Jonathan 167
Delcourt, Dawn 244
Dellabella, Scott 68
Delp, Shalina 99
del Rio, Rosa 47
DeLuca, Julia 106
Demmons, O'Rita B. 218
Dentz, Howard R. 153
DeRose, Richard J. 202
Desaigoudar, Yeshaswini 4
D'Esposito, Gerard 237
Dey, Beth 138
Deyden, Renee C. 166
Dickens, Brenda F. 257
Dickman Allred, Amylyn 10
Dill, Barbara Myers 86
Dillon, Jackie 46
Dirks, Conor 233
Dixon, Anita M. 193
Dixon, Doris Wirtz 60
Do, Dexter P. 194
Dockery, Rachell 229
Doll-Ewertz, Audrie 139
Dombrowski, Rose A. 69
Domondon, Cornelia B. 17
Donnelly, Katie 70
Donnelly, Matthew A. 85
Dopwell, Arlene D. 111
Doran, Christine A. 144
Dorman, Lisa 227
Dorsey, J. E. 120
Dorsey, Jennifer 208
Dougherty, Christina 46
Dougherty, James 243
Douglas, Bonnie 248
Douglas, Suzanne 156
Doyle, Alice M 55
Dozier, C. N. 189
Drenberg, Dan 136
Drinnon, Janis B. 15
Drowley, Doug 42
Dubinsky, Norma M. 99
Dubrovsky, Yana 73
Duddy, JohnWall 61
Duerson, Lawrence W. 57
Duffy, Shirley 70
Dunham, Lani D. 17

Dunkin, Joe 19
Dunnells, Kristin Ann 93
Dunseith, Melissa Renee 103
Duntley, Liesl 72
Duperry, G. J. 124
Duquet, Don 87
Durham, Bonnie 16

E

Ealy, Darla Jill 59
Earls, Gwen 192
Eason, Karen 187
Eastwood, Paula Jane 243
Eberly, Daniel E. 83
Eckert, Belinda 234
Edens, Jeffery Frank Jr. 170
Edge, Linda 105
Edgeman, Emily Elisabeth 91
Edmonds, Betti 17
Edwards, Debbie 66
Eldridge, Jennifer Lee 116
Eldridge, Mary 147
Elissa 155
Ellis, Deloris W. 79
Ellison, Jonathan 260
Elschlager, Jason 173
Elwood, Gwen 81
Emershaw, Brian 206
Emerson, Shawn A. 178
Endris, Norma Jean 181
Engelhardt, Sarah 51
Enloe, Laura M. 75
Entena, Cathleah V. 48
Escalera, Hector P. 225
Ess, Jayle 32
Essig, Thomas 254
Estes, Candy A. 73
Estes, Edward 42
Estrada, Erwin 112
E. T. 87
Eudaly, Melissa Starr 161
Eury, Eric Patrick 242
Evans, Lori P. 27
Even-Nur, Ayelet 4
Evers, Holly Victoria 226
Ewersen, Virginia Pease 39

F

Fabian, Diana 120
Fable, Larry A. 66
Facey, Patrick C. 258
Fappas, Steve 28
Farly, William J. 152
Faustin, Widchard 11
Felder, Lauren 189
Feldman, Jack A. 60
Fell, Derek 26
Felter, Christina 93
Feltmann, Becky Ann 182
Ferenc, R. Shaun 170
Fernandez, J. S. 197
Fetters, Mark Steven 193
Fettman, Surie 189
Fickett, Michael 225
Field, Raymond W. 191
Fielder, Geddes 190
Fields, Margaret R. 25
Fields, Mary G. 169
Figone, Sharon 145

Finch, Evelyn 136
Fink, Brian 58
Finney, Shirley Lee 155
Finocchiaro, Gina M. 210
Fiore, Tony 249
Firmingham, Cynthia J. 210
Fisher, Gerald F. 200
Fisher, Mary 43
Fisher, Sharon 108
Fisher, Tina 66
Fister, Ralph 80
Fitzgerald, Lynn 106
Fitzwilliams, Timothy J. 39
Fleckenstein, Heather 244
Fleischer, Adeline 59
Fleming, Francesca D. 10
Flores, Frank G. 138
Flores, Rene 172
Flowers, J. C. 16
Fluger, Kathy 12
Fobert, Gloria 96
Fogell, Louise E. 36
Fondacaro, Anthony 249
Ford, Vanessa C. 214
Forster, Stefanie A. 141
Foster, B. 197
Foster-Lamoreaux, Mary 213
Foti, Bridget 168
Fox, Joan 90
Fox, Regis C. 203
Fraga, Helen 114
Francis, May R. 149
Francis, Wayne 143
Franey, Barbara M. 155
Frangia, Peter G. 24
Franklin, Anntonia 188
Franklin, Kista V. 129
Frater, Betty 172
Frazier, Tiffany Noel 161
Freed, David A. 148
Freeman, Cambri 75
Freeman, Nancy 56
Freemire, Amy J. 177
French, Carole 29
French, Tamara 116
Frey, Imelda 53
Froning, Jeffrey N. 65
Fucci, James 202
Fuller, Freddie J. Jr. 57
Fuller, William 111
Fulton, Phyllis Burchfield 133
Funderburk, Verna L. 235
Fuqua, Chris 157

G

Gagnon, Ashley 190
Gagnon, Kimberly J. 214
Gallagher, Beatrice Shepherd 64
Gallus, Felicia 105
Gambino, Christopher J. 177
Ganz, Dalia 133
Garay, Migdalia 246
Garay-Guerrero, Alma N. 184
Gardner, Margaret 84
Garfield, Susan Lynn 251
Garippa, Michael 184
Garlock, James 109
Garnett, Shree 208
Gartee, Beatrice M. 60
Garza, Ruth O. 38

Gaskins, Jerry 9
Gaynor, Valerie 8
Geer, Jeffery 49
Geiger, Randy D. 10
Gelvin, Ryan 245
Genchur, Phillip A. 221
Gentry, G. J. 178
Georgy, Catherine 109
Gholston, Katryna 252
Ghoston, Louise 126
Gibbs, Quinn T. 215
Gigante, Chrisi 179
Gilbert, Opal 83
Gillingham, Christine 98
Gillon, Rachel 193
Giovannelli, Anthony O. 37
Girouard, Richard 127
Gleason, Barbara Joy 143
Glover, Dennis A. 111
Goben, Mirella S. 259
Goetzinger, Janice 78
Goldstein, Jeremy B. G. 145
Gomez, Humberto A. M.D. 241
Gomez-Bracety, Miriam L. 63
Gonzalez, Maria Venicia 218
Gonzalez, Nicole 168
Gonzalez-Greeley, Alicia 231
Gooden, Chris 137
Goodin, Michael 211
Goodliegh, Orville 112
Goodwin, Adam 164
Gordon, Clanthie F. 221
Gordon, Ellen K. 115
Gordon, Lindsay 249
Gordon, Stacie J. 199
Goudreau, Jesseca 218
Grady, Meghan 146
Grant, Daniel L. 166
Granzow, Eve 142
Gratton, Jeremy Bruce 11
Graulau, Janice M. 118
Graves, Janet Duke 105
Graves, Shana 65
Graziaplena, Louis 38
Green, Bruce 258
Green, Mary Mechling 234
Greene, Alex 94
Greening, Virginia 15
Gregory, Bonita 13
Gremmel, Rebecca 254
Griffie, Susanna 239
Griffith, Lydia 225
Grohoski, Joseph E. 178
Gross-Culp, Sharon 179
Grove, Joann 114
Grover, Barbara 205
Guajardo, Violet 106
Guarda, Sonia 24
Guidry, Kathleen 4
Guidry, Stephanie C. 52
Gunn, Helen F. 12
Gustafson, Samuel 207
Gustave, Pierre-Marie 90
Guzmeli, Maria Delos Angeles 121

H

Hackett, Laura 180
Hadden, Paulene 132
Haith, Betty F. 227
Hall, Katy 52

Hall, Tami 68
Hamann, Mary 86
Hamilton, Carline Diana 81
Hammond, Julie 190
Hanrahan, Thomas DeZolt 150
Hansen, Claudine M. 106
Hansen, Kety Y. 185
Hanson, Heidi 208
Hanson, Richard A. 224
Hanson, Sandy 133
Harblin, Jennifer 162
Hardenburgh, Harry 260
Hardwick, William C. 39
Harman, Gerrie 30
Harmon, Colleen 15
Harper, J. D. 38
Harrell, Ronnie 80
Harrington, Judy 185
Harrington, Kevin J. 145
Harrington, Linda 223
Harris, Gladyse W. 257
Harris, Kenneth 65
Harrison, Elizabeth 161
Harrison, Jane D. 260
Harrison, Jennifer 8
Hart, April Michelle 67
Hartford, Muriel Lea 216
Harvell, Dolores 60
Hatker, Ashley Marie 142
Hauze, Jeanne 238
Havener, Roxann 68
Havrilesko, Shelley 108
Hawes, Ronda 38
Hayes, Edward F. 170
Hayes, Judy A. 60
Hayes, Thomas 89
Haynes, Adam 248
Hazelwood, John J. III 90
Heaney, Susan-Kate 173
Hearn, Maedel 195
Heaton, Kimberly Joyce 61
Hebert, Frannie 177
Hein, Connie 93
Heinke, Kathryn 23
Hemmer, Tonya 207
Henderson, Charity 12
Henderson, Lori 117
Henderson, Tonetta 187
Hendon, Robert L. 241
Hendricks, Scott H. 67
Henley, Shawn 139
Henningson, Josh 149
Henry, Rita 46
Henry, Y. L. 42
Henson, Melvin Levon Jr. 204
Hernandez, Kristin M. 172
Hernandez, Mike A. III 122
Hernandez, Peggy 110
Hernandez, Samantha D. 186
Herrera, Tomas D. 136
Herriott, Christina 139
Hesley, Justin T. 161
Hess, David S. 192
Hester, Gail 80
Heyen, Donna 32
Hibbs, Roy 121
Hickman, Tammy 261
Hicks, Jane L. 218
Higginbotham, C. 29
Higham, Erin 156
Hill, Margie 76

Hill, Sheryl 235
Hipp, C. M. 88
Hirahara, Kevin 47
Hirschenbaum, Monika 127
Hiscox, Stephanie M. 52
Hite, Terry 214
Hitz, Judy A. 248
Hizer, George H. 193
Hoag, Clara 246
Hoffman, Debra 41
Hoffpauir, Tracey 165
Hogan, Craig Gerard 134
Hogarth, Frank 58
Hollins, Kathleen 197
Holman, William B. 94
Holtgrefe, Paul 149
Holtz, Jeannie R. 111
Honablue, Bernice W. 242
Hood, Jason 222
Hoover, Janet D. 111
Hoover, Thelma V. 60
Hopkins, Doris 252
Hossain, Mohammed 195
Hotujec, Edward J. 24
Houk, Chris R. 24
House, Abbie 67
Howard, Sarah 68
Howard, William D. 133
Howe, Tom 50
Hrin, Theresa D. 12
Hrynyk, Dorothy 73
Hsu, Rita Syers 196
Hubbs, Cheri Ann 109
Hubler, David M. 177
Hudnell, Nina 204
Huff, Donna 136
Hughes, Billy 105
Hughes, John M. 96
Hughes, Misty K. 6
Hughes, Susan Lee 114
Hulsing, Kevin 237
Humble, Hermann J. 76
Hunt, Jodi R. 95
Hunter, Christopher R. 140
Hunter, Kent 110
Hurst, Tracy 49
Hurtado, Deborah 48
Hussain, Yasser 44
Hutchins, Audre G. 11
Hutchinson, Carol Lynn 34
Huthmacher, Mary-beth K. 92

I

Iacovangelo, Teresa 116
Idzi, Wendy 5
Igboaka, Primus Chuks 176
Ihlo, Monica 231
Ilich, Susan H. 75
Ingnam, Carole A. 256
Irish, Charles K. 114
Island, Jacques R. 137

J

Jacks, Deborah A. 181
Jackson, Benjamin F. 93
Jackson, Charles A. 11
Jackson, Leslie Ayn 187
Jackson, Rebecca Mardelle 249
Jaffe, L. 191

James, Joyce 112
Jameson, Nicholas 70
Jaquint, Holly 76
Jaryga, Olga 173
Jeff, Phyllis D. 14
Jenkins, Frank 169
Jenkins, Gwen 170
Jennie Barnes 98
Jennings, Arthur W. 233
Jennings, James W. 166
Jerome, Gary 162
Jesson, Elizabeth 19
Jetty, David Edward 179
Jiang, Jennifer 186
Jipson, Sharon M. 31
Jobe, Jennie 224
Joel, Shirley A. 131
Johannes, Jeffery 214
Johansen, Erik Jay 147
Johns, Bruce Robert 70
Johnson, Elaine M. 211
Johnson, Elizabeth 63
Johnson, Emerson 79
Johnson, Gerda M. 250
Johnson, Joy 139
Johnson, Mark 69
Johnson, Martha E. 83
Johnson, Steven D. 151
Johnston, Diane L. 167
Jones, Betty Jean 122
Jones, Christopher 159
Jones, Jacqueline 54
Jones, James E. Jr. 257
Jones, Jeffery P. 37
Jones, Lynn 33
Jones, Patricia Ann 107
Jones, Samora 157
Jones, Toni R. 216
Jorgensen, Libby Jo 259
Joyner, Bryant 247
Joynes, William T. 95
Judkins, Jennifer 218
Judnick, Rose 138
Judson, Ronald L. 144
Jump, Gladys J. 101
Juneau, Kellie 127
Juneja, Tika 204
Jury, Bryan L. 90
Justin, Tom 48

K

Kalinowska, Aga 80
Kallios, Ann 225
Kamber, Deirdre J. 10
Kamps, Marjorie 175
Kane, Erin 222
Kansaki, Onam 105
Kanter, Irene 19
Kasper, Charles J. 63
Katolick, Julia L. 162
Katz, Nettie 15
Kaynor, Wanda 230
Kazandjian, Vahe A. 22
Kealoha, Dennis P. 149
Keil, M. Jane 71
Keith, Marvin Kenneth 172
Kelley, Georgia P. 171
Kelley, Jeriann 86
Kelley-Leathers, Jodi 109
Kelly, Dot Hutchinson 26

Kelly, Ryan J. 221
Kenez, Maria T. 203
Kennedy, Brandon 219
Kenneman, Paula 140
Keyser, Melissa 73
Kiefer, Jean 215
Kielhofer, Lenore 7
Killinger, Francis 188
Kimm, Samuel 210
King, Bethany L. 202
King, Betsy 186
King, Diana 257
King, Dwayne A. 255
King, Gary W. 90
King, Katie 211
King, Linda 203
Kinloch, Valerie 125
Kinnaird, Charles L. 104
Kinziger, Nola 57
Kirby, Norma 245
Kirkpatrick, Charles M. 241
Kirschbaum, Tim 44
Kirschner, Bina 202
Kissam, Ann B. 153
Kittrell, Cheryl 233
Klick, Martha 174
Kline, Patricia 3
Klinger, Kara C. 193
Knapp, Mary Alice 145
Knoderer, Rhea 191
Kocel, Kourtney C. 213
Kochanski, Beverly W. 59
Kocher, Jeniffer 232
Kohn, Michael J. 166
Kokkoros, Panos 38
Koller, Margo 27
Korbus, Jason 211
Korecki, Charles J. 85
Koyl, Christina 206
Kramer, Jerry L. II 147
Krause, Cathy 250
Krazy, D. C. 100
Krebbs, Candy 55
Krim, Elizabeth 201
Kron, Crystal 192
Krosky, Dorothy Husar 41
Kubiak, Greg D. 127
Kuehnert, Lila G. 28
Kuhns, Sally 213
Kupcunas, Erin 207

L

Labrie, Joan 63
Lafevor, Mandy L. 75
LaHood, Julie Ann 39
Lake, Amberly J. 148
LaMagna, Michael A. 186
Lambert, Allan H. 20
Lambert, Doris 25
Lamberti, Anita 158
Lampkin, Eugene Jay 8
Landry, Pauline A. 157
Lane, Eldwin Kendall 138
Lanier, Michael 162
Larimore, Brenda Faye 28
Lars, Janalyn 219
Larson, Irene Mary 116
Larson, Krister 66
Lassley, Shandra 59
Latham, Jessie Meyers 245

Latorre, Andrea 122
Latzy, Bernard T. Jr. 104
Laurence, E. 71
Lavender, Linda 212
Law, Dorothy 121
Lawless, Diana 259
Laws, Phil 189
Lawson, Adolphus 165
Lawson, Christina 68
Lawson, James 120
Lawson, Lesa M. 183
Lazare, Daniel 117
Leather, Albert E. 183
LeClair, Caitlin Elizabeth 248
Lee, Betty 31
Lee, Linwood 200
Lee, Loretta M. 174
Lee, Michael R. 113
Lee, Samantha 253
Lehrman, Albert 227
Lemieux, Toni 121
Leonhard, Scott 167
Lerner, Donna G. 188
Lesley, Rosemary 172
Lewis, Jordan M. 230
Lewis, Joshua J. 219
Liccketto, Laura Tesoro 33
Liebel, Catherine 180
Liebel, Charlotte M. 23
Liedtke, Maria 251
Lietz, Heinz 34
Linder, Jen 235
Line, Ruby 218
Linford, Ronald 32
Lipinski, Serenity 250
Little, Kayla D. 82
Little, Matthew James 128
Loeb, Susan 153
Logan, Linda 212
Logrie, Robert A. Jr. 37
Loiseau, Amy 146
London, Quenten 7
Long, Ashley 201
Long, Dorothee 95
Lopez, Cheree Renee 81
Lopez, Luis A., Jr. 56
Lopez, Tiara 201
Lorengo, James M. 103
Lorenzen, Elizabeth 169
Louderbough, Tony 182
Louis, Marsha 168
Loving, Lisa 59
Lovold, Samuel 8
Lowell, Barbara J. 62
Lowery, Kerry 65
Lowrance, Thomas L. 137
Lowry, Crystal J. 175
Lubecke, Jan 153
Lunsford, K. D. 222
Luster, Diane K. 90
Luttig, Katy 49
Luttrell, Curtis W. 175
Luttrell, G. Milton 59
Lyles, Thurman Wardell 29
Lyman, Alice 61
Lyman, Chad 35
Lynch, Chimere 151
Lynch, Michael 186
Lynn, David 225
Lynnette, Chysawndra Petty 221

M

Mack, James L. 31
Mack, Leslie Claire 195
Mack, P. 159
Mafuta, Diasonama J. 152
Mair, Margaret 191
Maith, Vanessa 173
Majka, Marijean 142
Mallory, Scott M. 94
Malloy, Tina E. 244
Malmstrom, Natasha 91
Mancini, Melinda 258
Mangan, Anthony 239
Manning, Ed 22
Mansfield, Aimee 250
Mansfield, Marion Highsmith 126
Marchesiello, Greg 150
Marie, Diane 89
Marizan, Ayelet 215
Marks, Eugene 82
Marley, Chris J. 96
Marlowe, Brandon 50
Marlowe, Pamela 154
Marshall, Andy 40
Marshall, T. George 118
Martin, Andy 30
Martin, Bill 108
Martin, Christina 191
Martin, Jennifer 87
Martin, John C. 15
Martinez, Bob G. 20
Martinez, Deanna Jeanne 256
Martinez, Yolanda 62
Martino, Carla 228
Martins, Gabriela 188
Mary Crouch-Lantz 136
Mason, Trisa 257
Massey, Joe T. 254
Masters, Jack 119
Matesic, Deana 155
Matheney, Helen B. 177
Matheney, Katherine Smith 211
Mather, Gary 120
Mathias, Elmo Pinard 67
Mathis, Mona 73
Matisziw, Liana 124
Matteson, Joan E. 3
Matthews, Valerie L. 149
Mattison, Kim 67
Mattison, Merri J. 223
Mattix, Sam 64
Maturan, Eulalio G. 252
Maximous, Stephanie 173
Mayo, Alice 67
McAfee, Derek 139
McBride, Michael D. 122
McCammon, Tiffany 186
McCarter, Tricia 239
McCarthy, Lee 242
McCaskill, Stephanie 177
McCleary, Patrick II 237
McClellan, Cory P. 154
McClure, Doris E. 29
McCombie, Brian 224
McCord, Luciel 72
McCoy, Brenda 7
McCullough, Hollie 61
McDermott, Chantele B. 74
McDonald, Jennifer 52
McDuffie, Loretta 257

McEwen, Pater 260
McFarland, Caira 201
McGaughey, Katherine E. 41
McGeary, Frank L. 114
McGee, Glendon M. II 120
McGill, Victoria 171
McGowan, Jennifer 128
McGrath, Mary 231
McGuirt, Steven M. 115
McIntire, Muriel Jr. 39
McKelvey, Dana 219
McKenzie, C. Mark 227
McKeon, Erica 251
McKiney, Louis O. 53
McKnight, Deborah 132
McLaughlin, Annette 160
McLaurin, A. M. 216
McMahon, Erin Anne Oneisom 52
McMillan, Bobbydyne 151
McQuistom, Louise H. 58
McRoberts, Jay 37
Mechler, Teresa 246
Meck, Jessica 150
Medrano, Mamie 21
Meier, Robert J. 182
Meily, Prudence 33
Mell, Nancy 252
Melville-Bacon, Monica C. 217
Mendez, Helen 102
Mendez, Rosa 164
Menefee, Angie 180
Merenda, Ray 91
Merideth, Carolyn 118
Merriman, Malanna 115
Meyer, Ila 215
Miehl, James A. Jr. 220
Mike, Olga M. 232
Milbourne, Robert Allen Jr. 113
Milkoff, Shirley Hall 26
Miller, Hazel Gray 70
Miller, Janice 226
Miller, Lila V. 226
Miller, Mary Ann 83
Miller, Rocky 91
Milligan, Taunya A. 135
Mimms, Windell R. Jr. 148
Minardi, Mathew 167
Minehart, Randal R. 96
Minion, Rodney 89
Minor, Tonia 139
Mitchell, Angela 110
Mitchell, Bee 197
Mitchell, Debra J. 217
Mitchell, Jeffrey 230
Mitchell, Steve 255
Mitchell, Susan 204
Mizer, Kari 183
Mohammed, Nedra 35
Mole, Joseph L. 194
Mongan, Mary 208
Mongioi, Joseph 247
Monteforte, Merle 151
Montfort, Julie 69
Montgomery, Jean 39
Monthei, Debra 11
Moody, Will 6
Moon, Silver 189
Moore, Easter 151
Moore, Kay 50
Moore, Larry R. 250
Moore, Marvin Eric 88

Moore, Mary Lou 112
Moore, Stella 127
Morales, Nancy 198
Morales, Randy 85
Moravec, Andrea 34
Moressi, Amanda 92
Morgan, Oliver L. 43
Morley, Bryan 229
Morris, LaVera M. 187
Morris, Michael Lloyd 163
Morrissey, Megan E. 105
Morse, Jennifer 71
Morse, Jenny 229
Moses, Michael Peterson 57
Moses, Sam 8
Mosesova, Irina A. 238
Mosley, Ronald A. 113
Moss, Chakiris M. 183
Moyer, Erin Elizabeth 43
Mueller, Dan 233
Mullaly, Cynthia 63
Muller, Brittany 131
Mulloy, Megan 189
Mulready, Lori 198
Munich-Deger, Barbara 6
Murray, Lori 109
Murrell, J. Edward 103
Muus, Alice I. 76
Myhand, Rickey 230

N

Nairn, Thomas F. 34
Nandresy, Dorothy 41
Napolitano, Cristin A. 152
Nash, Shanika 196
Nash, Tina 150
Natal, Marycelis 49
Nave, Amanda 30
Naylor, Nick 205
Neave, Terrie 77
Nefzger, Elaine 185
Neitz, Laura 73
Nelson, C. M. 147
Nelson, Dennis L. 56
Nelson, Madge Haines 123
Neumann, Doris V. 63
Newbery, Mary Ellen 135
Newman, Harry 45
Newman, Thomas 15
Newman-Turner, Katrina 174
Nguyen, Diem 140
Nichols, David A. 68
Nicholson, Alys 81
Nicholson, Marie P. 252
Nicholson, Rachel 44
Nicolucci, Roseanne M. 223
Nicosia, Angelo Louis II 84
Nied, Lou 55
Nielson, Dean 18
Nitsche, J. Neal 100
Nixon, Shileen 163
Noble, Chas 13
Noennich, Robin L. Sr. 103
Nolfi, Kristen 132
Norcutt, O. L. Jr. 94
Nordberg, Anna 5
Nordlund, Lucille, SFO 171
Norris, Lorrie Ann 86
Norton, Nile B. 51
Nosker, Sue 192

Noud, Jill 137
Novak, Amber 138
Nowfar, Sheila 199
Nurenberg, David 65
Nwosu, Benjamin 248
Nyhoff, Stefanie 224

O

Oakes, Amy 117
Oakes, Christopher 181
O'Bannon, Karen 179
O'Brien, Edward J. 13
Oddo, Scott 194
O'Donnell, Erin Elizabeth 67
Ogden, Bryan 87
Ohman, Virginia Ann 172
Oiwa, Marc 171
Olechnowicz, Rebecca 238
Olin, Ashley 150
Olson, A. M. 196
Olson, Remy E. 255
O'Neill, Debbie 67
O'Neill, Kevin 171
Ortega, Rey 122
Ortiz, Diadel K. 179
Ortiz, Nicole 256
O'Shaughnessy, Agell 108
Ota, Carla Lee 64
Ott, Nancy M. 208
Overa, Kevin 212
Overfield, Krista L. 128
Owens, Jessie 81

P

Pabst, Pat 32
Padilla, Sophie 102
Palatnick, Amy 10
Palmer, Carolyn Y. 92
Palmer, Jennifer 176
Palmer, Patricia 176
Palomino, Barbara 49
Palser, Spring S. 74
Panagopoulos, Celia 181
Paparella, Cristina 5
Pape, Moritz E. 129
Parish, Gina 238
Park, Daniel 48
Parker, Gloria J. 243
Parker, Liz Cole 224
Parker, Natalie Elizabeth 193
Parker, Robin 61
Parker, Thomas Sean 115
Parks, Brenda G. 117
Parsley, Chad 64
Partyka, Cheryl 82
Pass, Joseph 226
Patch, Truman 137
Paterson, Meridith 160
Pather, Darshan 135
Pathipvanich, Parima 47
Patmore, Dominic 240
Patterson, Charlene 79
Patterson, Suzanne 185
Patton, Marilyn D. 85
Paul, Sophia 133
Pauletti, Pat 194
Pavelo, Maria 198
Payne, JC 157
Pearce, Richard 210

Peek, Jason D. 68
Pemberton, Lillian R. 108
Pendleton, Jerry 71
Perkins, Anthony E. 82
Perna, Lauren 206
Peters, Mark 193
Peters, Tricia 129
Petersen, Kelley E. 49
Peterson, Alan 260
Petrasek, Ruth 161
Petty, Nathan 223
Pevar, Maxwell 248
Pfankuchen, Carol 21
Phair, Patrick 5
Phelan, Thomas A. 251
Phillips, Marvella 187
Phillips, Sally 111
Phipps, Bradley Jay 147
Phipps, Steve 163
Pickett, Marge 188
Pierce, Mark A. 227
Pierson, Shawna 100
Pietruszewski, Peter 222
Pina, Sarah J. 179
Pine, Anita 210
Pinkerton, Rachel 209
Pinnegar, Stephanie 135
Piotrowski, Stephen 62
Piquette, Marice Ann 238
Pitts, Janice A. 188
Plume, Richard A. 141
Poe, Georgia 70
Poellnitz, Kim 104
Policastro, Vicki A. 184
Polk, Shirlene 99
Polka, Walter S. 185
Pollock, Noah 75
Polzin-Elsasser, Katalina 168
Porter, Karen 68
Porter, M. V. 119
Prahl, LaVon 17
Pratt, Elizabeth 230
Pratt, Jennifer 256
Preda, Lucia 28
Primack, Gretchen 6
Prince, Charles T. 160
Proctor, Jennifer 133
Puckett, Christa 46
Puicon, Glen 93
Pursley, Thomasine 191
Pusateri, John Thomas Jr. 259
Putney, Jason W. 153
Putney, Maxine A. 113

Q

Qi, Ningjun 154
Queen, Erika V. 88
Queen, Opal J. 84
Quinn, Becky J. 196

R

r. paul production, an 101
Rabatin, Miranda R. 152
Racey, Harry 255
Rachel Gladstone-Gelman 196
Rader, Alice 211
Radford, Travis 155
Radovic, Ljubica 171
Rae, Kristina 101

Raimondo, JoJo 244
Ramirez, Angela 238
Ramirez, Christine 146
Randolph, Bradford Earle 148
Rasmussen, Sadie 157
Rassi, Suzanne M. 165
Ratajack, Amy 224
Rathgeber, Abby Lynn 198
Ratnam, Diana 217
Ray, Carlotta C. 86
Ray, Consiwella R. 26
Raymo, Shirley 169
Reader, Mel 220
Rebeck, Betty 88
Reckart, Richard W. 188
Rector, Thomas J. 157
Redford, Breonna 206
Reding, Eunice Abby 17
Reecher, Frank 117
Reed, Eugenia S. 235
Reed, Marylin Matthews 24
Reeder, Beulah A. 200
Reeder, Bonita A. 104
Rees, Sarah 9
Register, Cetaya 127
Reid, Eleanor Pinnell 16
Reigel, Connie 196
Reiter, Aaron 99
Reitmeier, Aaron 47
Remillard, Jesse 223
Renales, Richard F. 145
Renne, Danelle 174
Renninger, Nicholas D. 224
Reven, Mary Lee 253
Reyes, Imelda 149
Reyes, Lisa 209
Reynard, Brenda L. 236
Reynolds, Inzie 160
Reynoso, Santiago De Jesus 78
Rhodarmer, Ashley 209
Rhodes, Betty J. 9
Richards, Jenny 242
Richardson, Charles L. 176
Richardson, Elizabeth 69
Richardson, Wilma 34
Richberg, Rosalyn Antoinette 106
Richeimer, Mary Jane 137
Richmond, Ben 120
Ricketts, Evelyn 23
Ricks, Sharon L. 215
Riddle, Belinda 32
Riedy, Lynne Adele 20
Rieke, Jodi A. 184
Riess, Kenneth 101
Riffe, Nancy 14
Riffle, Linda L. 85
Riggs, Andrew 92
Riley, Benjamin 56
Riley, Melrose I. 195
Rinderknecht, Kelly 171
Rischar, Roy 1
Robbins, Michael Wayne 103
Robert E. 198
Robert, George Newcomb 123
Roberts, Bonnie Jay 160
Roberts, John F. 59
Roberts, Steve 104
Robinson, Brenda 165
Robles, William A. 83
Rochlin, Leonard 199
Rodrigues, Naomi 209

Rodriguez, Julio Jr. 169
Rogenski, David 33
Rogers, David W. Jr. 240
Roma, Al 194
Rondette, Wendy 11
Rose, Genny 125
Rose, Sherill D. 28
Roskov, Nicole 37
Rossi, Gerard A. 156
Rotert, C. J. 164
Roth, Jane Butkin 50
Rouleau, Joseph E. 259
Rovezzi, Shirley M. 151
Rowe, Lynn 134
Royal, Deanna 196
Ruddle, Carol L. 82
Ruffin, Deborah 64
Rundle, Matthew 7
Russell, C. Rosalind 158
Russell, Sonia L. Harmon 141
Rutherford, Ruth A. 136
Ryan, Robert 189

S

Sadighi, Alexander 238
Sakkal, Aida 66
Salgado, Myrna M. 94
Samblanet, Debra B. 128
Samuel, Dwan 234
Sanchez, Frank R. 174
Sanchez, Kathryn 100
Sanders, Estella 96
Sanders, Melissa Kardos 207
Sandford, Blake A. 70
Sandifer, Kimberly J. 200
Sankaran, Ravi 247
San Pablo, Noel 70
Saucier, Nellie B. 172
Savala, Sylvia 69
Savine, Irene 224
Schackart, Laurie 45
Schade, F. Tucker Jr. 173
Schaefer, Sister M. Sharon 192
Scheurer, Janelle 237
Schiegg, Genie C. 125
Schlesinger, Adam 232
Schmidt, Carl 60
Schmidt, Jeneane 9
Schmoe, Teri L. 46
Schnepp, Shannon 228
Schnitzler, Douglas C. 16
Schreck, Mindy 189
Schroeder, Jeff 114
Schroll, Frances 157
Schultz, Irene 62
Schulz, Adam 162
Schwart, Michael 40
Schwartz, A. L. 192
Schwartz, Michael J. 163
Schwenk, Mary A. 261
Scott, Anna 110
Scott, Evan Andrew 188
Scott, James Cobb 12
Scott, JoAnn 198
Scott, Jon S. 68
Scott, Linda 139
Search, Anne M. 96
Sears, Bonnie M. 98
Segarnick, Lester 69
Seidel, Laralee 95

Seiler, Brandy Marie 43
Selvage, Patricia A. 134
Sennett, Tonya 55
Serino, Joseph Sr. 141
Serrano, Candice 50
Settle, Michelle L. 130
Shannon, Gerri 136
Sharieff, Adileh 225
Sharkey, Charlotte 220
Sharp, Mary F. 70
Shaut, Richard A. 14
Shawcroft, Richard G. Sr. 241
Shea, Helen 246
Sheinin, Karol 162
Shellenberger, Emily 33
Sherwood, George 129
Sherwood, Gertrude 166
Shields, Andrew 191
Shifrin, Robyn Lori 10
Shivers, Kathryn 75
Shlakman, Sally 141
Shoretz, Michael 119
Short, Stacey 53
Shuman, Terry Ann 183
Silagy, Louis S. 139
Siler, Kenda L. 225
Silva, Paul M. P. 220
Silvera, Laura E. 255
Simkin, Karen 83
Simmons, Leah 30
Simmons, Michele L. 124
Simmons, Tracy L. 68
Simons, Ashley L. 74
Simons, Laurine 152
Simpkins, Charlotte 61
Singh, Sabi 43
Singletary, Joseph 206
Singleton, Michael Patrick 156
Sinha, Sanjay 229
Sippel, Mark A. 51
Sloane, David H. 258
Sloniker, Jamie 190
Small, Lynne 79
Smart, Liz 130
Smith, Cerdan 26
Smith, Jamez 237
Smith, Jennifer C. 57
Smith, John L. 213
Smith, Kari E. 223
Smith, Kenneth E. 243
Smith, Marion C. 205
Smith, Rowena N. 174
Smith, Sharon McIntosh 239
Smith, Shelley 94
Smith, Tammy 194
Smith, Thomas Gideon Sr. 119
Smith-Nonini, Sandy 4
Snow, Frances E. 54
Snow, L. Catherine 182
Snyder, Cathy L. 178
Snyder, Joan D. 182
Snyder, Joseph M. 261
Snyder, Kevin 97
Snykers, Alfred Burton 187
Solis, Anica 52
Soliz, America 154
Sorrell, Connie 224
Sotelo, Gracie 157
Southard, Schaefer M. 188
Southards, Donald 43
Southern, Michael G. 146

Sparrow, Gloria E. 64
Spearman, Tom 253
Spencer, Steven Dwayne 222
Spier, Cathy L. 158
Spieth, Sarah 53
Spinner, David 213
Spletzer, Ramona 202
Spratley, Gymmie S. 244
Sprigg, Steve 205
Stafford, Jenny Sue 159
Staggs, Brandon 133
Stamper, Cheryl 241
Stanley, Elvina E. 136
Starlin, John R. 138
Starr, Fallen 239
Stary, Ann Livingston 126
Stashko, David 154
Stavis, Rachel 231
Stearns, Arthur Earl 131
Steele, Vincent Christopher 161
Stephens, Harland L. 62
Sterling, Devon 131
Stevens, Michael 137
Steward, Adrienne 78
Stewart, Jim Jr. 82
Stewart, Mattie M. 64
Stickle, Charles E. 22
Stillerman, Marci 5
Stilley, Janice M. 126
Stingle, Lorraine 210
St. Laurent, Margie Worrix 56
Stone, Fiona 58
Stone, Ruth Elizabeth Jones 73
Storms, Savannah Jean 50
Strande, Stephen 209
Strander, Nancy L. 39
Straub, Terry 65
Strebeck, Leland 74
Strobel, Debbra Parsons 184
Strode, Marlene 199
Strommen, John A. 19
Stroud, Natalie 3
Stuart, Ruth 30
Stubbs, Patricia L. 142
Studler, Stephanie 49
Stutman, Zachariah 12
Sudeikis, Jamie 235
Sullivan, Wayne John 211
Summerhill, Rachel 156
Summers, Kevin 189
Sunday, Michael Walter 35
Sung, Jean 15
Sunn, Jeffrey A. 78
Sutphin, Holly 90
Svetecz, Michael 61
Swan, Black 58
Swartz, Diane 135
Sweat, David 150
Sweeney, Amy 197
Sweeney, Robert 229
Swiderski, Theresa 196
Swisher, Judy 195
Szobodi, Donald 129
Szymczak, Dan 138

T

Tacchei, Nicole 254
Tafoya, Nicole 105
Talley, Laurie 80
Tavitian, Vehig S. 201

Taylor, Donald 71
Taylor, Lula 201
Taylor, Sharion 144
Teachout, Jenny 61
Temple, Kenneth F. 202
Terhune, Thomas Jr. 187
Terrell, Diane 166
Terrell, Julie 206
Teter, Verna L. 32
Tetreault-Ducharme, Yvette Eve 183
Thomas, Bobbie 243
Thomas, Lorie 4
Thompson, Deborah 134
Thompson, Denise 204
Thompson, John 162
Thompson, Juanita 228
Thompson, Larry 91
Thompson, Melinda 83
Thompson, Sandra 138
Thompson, Shawn 190
Thompson, Steven B. 163
Thompson, T. J. 35
Thorne, Christopher 160
Thornton, Lyndse 254
Thurman, Teresa Kathleen 158
Thurn, Jennell 176
Tieu, Eddie 197
Tiller, Jason 34
Tiller, Judith 27
Tiller, Nadine 32
Tillman, Ann Elizabeth 42
Timmons, Delphine 180
Tischer, Beverly 146
Tobin, Thomas J. 11
Todd, Joanna 66
Tolbert, Mildred 23
Tolley, Stephanie 126
Tomlinson, Sharon 192
Toole, Deborah D. 156
Torgerson, Robert 64
Torres, Yaneth 103
Townsend, Ashley 79
Tracey, Raymond S. 44
Trammell, Eddie L. 77
Trevino, Ed 261
Trevino, Julia Hernandez 102
Trigger, Loren 137
Troutman, Carol E. 86
Troutman, Penny A. 240
Tschopp, Charlene Faye 254
Tucker, Mary Elizabeth 21
Tuley, Ann Cashwell 254
Tullis, John F. 65
Turkheimer, Eve 44
Turner, Beth 37
Twymar, Rebecca Ann Martin 54
Tyink, Cheryl P. 77
Tyra Luckett-Robinson 184
Tyrakowski, Chet Sr. 70

U

Uhler, Chris 14
Unger, Robert 19
Unrein, Shane 230
Urban, Patrick 146
Usher-Grant, Sharon A. M. 89

V

Vacanti, Deborah M. 49

Vacca, David M. 74
Vail, David 94
Vaillancourt, Rita 93
Van, Linda B. Hook 179
Van Nostrand, Sarah 175
VanAntwerp, Risa 223
VanBlaricum, Gary 249
Vance, Erika 109
VanDeest, Jane E. 97
Vandergriff, Chad 58
Vanek, Kristen 31
VanVlerah, Sunshine 221
Vargas, Ketty Molina 65
Vasbinder, Melissa Marie 181
Vaughn, Sheena 240
Veeh, Sharon 106
Veldhuis, Lindsey 247
Venturin, Margaret Rose 55
Ver, Christopher Allen Strate 99
Vereen, Angela 148
Vernon, Robby 164
Vetter, Edith 161
Vickery, Loyce Craig 59
Victory, Ernestine 219
Villareal, Veronica M. 105
Vilner, Lucy 233
Vincent, Michael S. 106
Vincenzi, Julie 172
Vinson, Shirley McCallister 203
Viverette, Curtis C. 233
Vogelgesang, Barbara J. 241
Volkmann, Gordon H. 77
Volpe, Eileen R. 23
Voytek, Laura 102

W

Wadzinski, Mary B. 130
Wagley, Clifton M. 214
Wagner, Dieter 124
Wagner, Shellie 231
Waide, Lora R. 202
Walborn, Gail 5
Walker, A. 184
Walker, Barbara 103
Walker, Ruth L. 241
Wall, Edith Hotchkiss 136
Wall, Shirley H. 185
Wall, Wayne M. III 148
Wallace, Phil 66
Wallace, Sonja K. 126
Waller, Rebecca 236
Walling, Derald 159
Walney, Florentina M. 196
Walrod, Chad 47
Walter, Mascha N. 215
Wambaugh, Anna M. 110
Ware, Hattie 212
Wargo, Stephanie 51
Warner, Judith L. 234
Washington, Tina M. 129
Watkins, Anne Howell 227
Watkins, Curtis D. 27
Watkins, M. C. 85
Watson, Cletus, T.O.R, Franciscan 261
Watson, Edith M. 112
Watson, Sherri T. 204
Watters, Jeana C. 14
Way, Megan 231
Wayne, Virginia Tellez 224
Wearing, Carolyn 247

Weber, Jacob R. 52
Wehr, Eugenia 245
Weidner, Frances H. 178
Weigand, Jason 143
Weinstein, Martin 12
Weiser, Rachel 170
Weitz, Jeff 66
Welkey, Lauren P. 172
Welsh, Barbara A. 240
Wendel, Tiffany A. 139
Wendorf, Matthew G. 118
Wesson, Jacquie 63
West, Carla L. 40
Westaby, Eve 17
Weston, John S. Jr. 167
Wheeler, Shelley 193
Whelan, Ann 98
Wherritt, Lucilyn 147
White, G. P. 189
Whitehead, Diana L. 77
Whitesell, Dava 229
Whiteside, Paul 77
Whitesitt, Linda 132
Wiese, Melisa R. 137
Wiesner, Eugene F. 18
Wigboldus, Heather 132
Wilhelm, Frank L. 22
Wilkinson, Lucille 220
William, James Yeatts 180
Williams, Alison 242
Williams, Anthony J. 37
Williams, Carol T. 253
Williams, Deanna 67
Williams, John 46
Williams, Leigh Anne 78
Williams, Loretta H. 242
Williams, Marge 26
Williams, Nelson 240
Williams, Nikki 217
Williams, Preston II 205
Williams, Regina 190
Williams, Rita 186
Williams, Sharon 222
Williams, Tammara J. 215
Williamson, Amy 134
Williamson, Jodi 217
Willis, Melissa 62
Willis, Wendee 138
Wills, Amanda Dawn 45
Wilson, Cpl. Edward F. 102
Wilson, Erlene 119
Wilson, Judy 144
Wilson, Kraig 97
Wilson, Natalie 260
Wilson, Rebecca 63
Wilson, Tupuivao 142
Wimberly, Margaretreto 187
Winegar, Ruby R. 252
Wiseman, William 54
Wisnowski, Thomas 62
Witkowski, Dianna 124
Witmer, Jamie L. 124
Witten, Joann P. 91
Wofford, Daniel 239
Wojcik, Dorreen Lyn 198
Wolaver, Sam 159
Wolfe, Cassie 194
Wolfer, Margaret M. 103
Wolford, Peggy A. 25
Womack, Allen 117
Wonderly, Christopher 205

Wong, Norman Jr. 163
Wood, Nancy J. 174
Wood, Paula Marie 79
Wood, Wilma Spaur 35
Woodfin, Jeanette jj 225
Woods, Debra A. 72
Woods, Vicki R. 218
Woodyard, Crystal 119
Woolford, Pamela 51
Wooten, Brenda L. 258
Worlds, William J. 69
Wrieth, Sue 228
Wright, Amber 166
Wright, Doug 85
Wright, Hugh D. 29
Wright, Leianne 153
Wyatt, Robert H. Sr. 19

X

Xiong, Ammy 81

Y

Yasin, Ifra 239
Ydris, Kassi 212
Yelton, Amy Michelle 63
Yergen, Debi 130
Young, Alesia 113
Young, Cary 3
Young, E. H. 141
Young, Jason 58
Young, Mordecai 14

Z

Zaide, Lorel Don 45
Zapparelli, Jenea 175
Zarate, Janet 141
Zawislak, Jamie 98
Zawitoski, John 251
Zecca, Arlene 36
Zeller, Christine 237
Zeller, Melissa Sue 194
Zesati, Yolanda 206
Ziegler, Phyllis R. 228
Zielke, David D. 54
Ziemba, Linda 144
Zima, Phillip 188
Zimmerman, Connie E. 140
Zirk, Lois L. 69